THE COMPLETE PROJECT MANAGEMENT METHODOLOGY AND TOOLKIT

PROJECT MANAGEMENT TITLES FROM AUERBACH PUBLICATIONS AND CRC PRESS

Managing Web Projects
Edward B. Farkas
ISBN: 978-1-4398-0495-7

The Complete Project Management Methodology and Toolkit
Gerard M. Hill
ISBN: 978-1-4398-0154-3

Implementing Program Management: Templates and Forms Aligned with the *Standard for Program Management* — Second Edition (2008)
Ginger Levin and Allen M. Green
ISBN: 978-1-4398-1605-9

Project Management Recipes for Success
Guy L. De Furia
ISBN: 978-1-4200-7824-4

Project Management of Complex and Embedded Systems: Ensuring Product Integrity and Program Quality
Kim H. Pries and Jon Quigley
ISBN: 978-1-4200-7205-1

Leading IT Projects: The IT Manager's Guide
Jessica Keyes
ISBN: 978-1-4200-7082-8

Building a Project Work Breakdown Structure: Visualizing Objectives, Deliverables, Activities, and Schedules
Dennis P. Miller
ISBN: 978-1-4200-6969-3

A Standard for Enterprise Project Management
Michael S. Zambruski
ISBN: 978-1-4200-7245-7

Global Engineering Project Management
M. Kemal Atesmen
ISBN: 978-1-4200-7393-5

Effective Communications for Project Management
Ralph L. Kliem
ISBN: 978-1-4200-6246-5

Managing Global Development Risk
James M. Hussey and Steven E. Hall
ISBN: 978-1-4200-5520-7

The Strategic Project Leader: Mastering Service-Based Project Leadership
Jack Ferraro
ISBN: 978-0-8493-8794-4

Determining Project Requirements
Hans Jonasson
ISBN: 978-1-4200-4502-4

Practical Guide to Project Planning
Ricardo Viana Vargas
ISBN: 978-1-4200-4504-8

The Complete Project Management Office Handbook, Second Edition
Gerard M. Hill
ISBN: 978-1-4200-4680-9

Staffing the Project Office for Competitive Advantage
J. Kent Crawford
ISBN: 978-0-8247-5477-8

Project Management Maturity Model, Second Edition
J. Kent Crawford
ISBN: 978-0-8493-7945-1

Optimizing Human Capital with a Strategic Project Office: Select, Train, Measure, and Reward People for Organization Success
J. Kent Crawford and Jeannette Cabanis-Brewin
ISBN: 978-0-8493-5410-6

The Complete Project Management Methodology and Toolkit

GERARD M. HILL

CRC Press
Taylor & Francis Group
Boca Raton London New York

CRC Press is an imprint of the
Taylor & Francis Group, an **informa** business
AN AUERBACH BOOK

CRC Press
Taylor & Francis Group
6000 Broken Sound Parkway NW, Suite 300
Boca Raton, FL 33487-2742

Printed in the United States of America on acid-free paper
10 9 8 7 6 5 4 3 2 1

International Standard Book Number: 978-1-4398-0154-3 (Hardback)

Library of Congress Cataloging-in-Publication Data

Hill, Gerard M.
The complete project management methodology and toolkit / Gerard M. Hill.
p. cm.
Includes index.
ISBN 978-1-4398-0154-3 (hardcover : alk. paper)
1. Project management. I. Title.

HD69.P75H53 2009
658.4'04--dc22 2009015823

Visit the Taylor & Francis Web site at
http://www.taylorandfrancis.com

and the CRC Press Web site at
http://www.crcpress.com

Contents

SECTION II METHODOLOGY PRACTICE GUIDE

Acknowledgments

In my recent publication, *The Complete Project Management Office Handbook, Second Edition* (Auerbach Publications, 2007), I indicated the importance of methodology management as a key function of the project management office (PMO) at any stage in its development. As well, in my recent conference keynote addresses, webinar presentations, and even consulting engagements, I have prompted audiences to consider project management methodology development and deployment within the organization as possibly the most important and primary responsibility of both new and existing PMOs. In such venues, I have responded to inquiries about the "who, how, when, and where" of project management methodology development and deployment. These inquiries caused me to think more and more about the need for methodology implementation within the organization.

Therefore, it is the various professionals I have encountered in the field of project management who have influenced me to prepare the project management methodology guidance and toolkit contained in this publication. The need for such methodology guidance also appeared supported by a number of recent studies that I reviewed in which the use of an established organizational project management methodology process was presented as a recommended means to achieve not only project success but also business success. I believe most practitioners would agree that an effective methodology solution also contributes significantly to increased organizational maturity in project management.

It is with those thoughts that I am extremely pleased to present this published version of the ProjectPRISM™ Project Management Methodology that was created a few years ago based on my 15-plus years of methodology development experience with internationally recognized clients. It has been revised and refined to present a methodology solution that can be used by most individuals and virtually all organizations.

Finally, and once again, my third publication was made possible by the love, encouragement, and support of my wife, Rita, who continues to shine a persistent light on the paths I take to pursue my life's work and my professional interests.

Gerard M. Hill

Ghill@HillConsultingGroup.com

Introduction

PROJECT MANAGEMENT METHODOLOGY INTRODUCTION

Project management has been emerging as a professional discipline for some time now, and it is coming into the mainstream just when it appears to be most needed as a business solution. The author has been noted for saying in published works and presentations that "project management, in so many ways, is business management." To that end, it is appropriate that the processes of project management be aligned with business needs and interests. It is likewise important for business processes to be aligned with needs and interests in the project management environment. The introduction of an effective project management methodology within the organization will help to achieve that prescribed alignment.

The basis or foundation for project and business management alignment already exists in many organizations today, but too often resides in a latent state that is still awaiting management acknowledgment and active collaborative use. That foundation exists in organizational processes that are common to both project and business management, but which are sometimes still applied as separate and uncoordinated sets of activities. That foundation is also seen in organizations where standard and repeatable processes are established to compile or aggregate results at the project, program, and portfolio management levels as a means to provide relevant and timely information to strategic managers and business decision makers in the organization.

Basic business processes are often performed, knowingly or unknowingly, at the project level when project management practices are applied to achieve business results for each project. Organizations need to recognize the business contributions of project management, and ensure that they achieve the maximum business value and return on the project management investment. An effective project management process, introduced through methodology implementation across the organization, is an essential component for achieving the desired project and business management alignment.

Evolution from a Technical Background

In earlier years, an organization's technical methodologies were expected to fulfill project management process needs. They often fell short of applying what we know today as "professional project management" concepts and practices. This is because the technical methodologies that were used to achieve desired levels of excellence in technical products and services still had a technical focus and did not particularly address all of the essential activities of project management.

Some technical methodologies were subsequently "enhanced and improved" to serve broader project management interests by introducing key concepts and practices of modern project management. However, while such methodology adaptations gave the technical manager expanded insight into project management, the basic processes—the critical processes of the methodology—were still technical in nature. Still, some of the adaptations did serve to demonstrate a relationship between technical management and project management.

Many of today's technical methodologies have considerably improved project management content over earlier adaptations. However, to a large extent, they are still intended for primary use by technical managers rather than by project managers. They simply lack essential pieces and parts of a rigorous project management process.

It is important to note that there is and will continue to be an ongoing need for technical methodologies—each as a guide toward excellence in the technical effort for which it was created. But a distinction is still warranted. A good technical process will ensure product and service design, development, and delivery excellence. In contrast, a good project management process will ensure project success and, by extension, business success.

Over time, it has often been shown by many practitioners that project management fits well into the scheme of most technical methodologies and can be supportive of technical activities and objectives. Today, public and private sector organizations alike are coming to realize the benefits of having one standard and repeatable project management process that can be used across the enterprise. That implies use of the same, common project management practices across the different technical functions and business units in the organization. Implementing a project management methodology that provides a standard and consistent approach to project management across the enterprise should also inherently contribute to technical achievements.

Therefore, today's consideration of an enterprise-wide project management methodology reverses the earlier scheme of the technical methodology. Now, instead of integrating key project management activities into the preferred technical process, the enterprise approach examines the ways in which the various technical methodologies (used in the different organizational business units) can be integrated and aligned with the project management methodology that is prescribed for use across the enterprise. Thereby, each business unit that conducts projects will integrate its own technical activities and intricacies at relevant points in the prescribed project management process. (See how this integration works in a diagram presented in the *Methodology Practice Guide* Introduction section.)

Today, it is also being shown that project management processes can be viewed as an extension of business processes. This project and business management relationship is not usually addressed by technical processes. However, it is consistent with the concepts of modern project management, and it is usually endorsed in the specification of responsibilities of the professional project manager. This consideration prompts the need for the organization to implement a project management process that recognizes and responds to business needs and interests across the enterprise.

The ProjectPRISM™ Project Management Methodology

The *ProjectPRISM Project Management Methodology* is an innovative, matrix-based approach to conducting project management that introduces relevant concepts, practices, and tools in a project management solution that has a distinct purpose toward fulfillment of organizational business needs and interests. It was originally conceived and created by the author a few years ago, and has since been reviewed and revised several times to achieve consistency of content. A subsequent detailed review of concepts and content was performed, and refinements were made for purposes of this publication.

A detailed description of the *ProjectPRISM Project Management Methodology*, along with its structure and components, is presented in the *Methodology Process Guide* Introduction section, as contained in Section I of this publication.

This methodology is particularly intended for broad implementation within an organizational or enterprise setting. It can be examined and will serve as an exceptional basis for customization. But for organizations with limited time for methodology development and implementation, it also provides a ready-to-use project management solution. Its prescribed processes, practices, and tools will ensure that essential project management activities are being conducted consistent with widely accepted project management standards.

As well, individuals will gain benefits from using this methodology when they follow prescribed guidance to ensure that all essential project management activities are being accomplished on every project. For some users, the process and practice guidance contained in this publication may help expand individual skill and knowledge in applying concepts of project management. At a minimum, individual users will have a comprehensive reference document for conducting project management activities.

Implementation as a Business Solution

The concepts, practices, and tools of the *ProjectPRISM Project Management Methodology* provide a combined project and business management solution that will be valuable for most project managers and their organizations. It is a "business-ready" methodology that can be introduced across many different industries and business environments, and it provides relevant guidance for use by both novice and seasoned project managers.

That broad description means the *ProjectPRISM Project Management Methodology* is ready for use "off-the-shelf" or "out-of-the-book," as you care to reflect on it. It means that it is aligned with common business practices that already exist within many organizations. And, it means that it includes comprehensive guidance for completing all the essential activities of project management.

That broad description also means that it is not fine-tuned for any particular technical endeavor, business organization, or industry. It does not address either unique technical or business requirements within the organization, or any unique personal expectations of senior and executive managers. However, it does provide an exceptional basis for creating a fine-tuned project management practice and business solution in the organization.

Therefore, each user and using organization should examine the methodology concepts and content for customization to achieve greater consistency with organizational needs and interests. The individual user or small business organization may not require any methodology customization. However, medium- to larger-sized organizations will likely want to consider some customization to make the methodology more consistent (and complementary) to existing business practices.

Customization considered, the ultimate potential for finding success in the methodology as a project management solution lies in and is directly associated with its implementation. Such implementation, when properly performed, represents a significant change that must be managed within the organization. Please be sure to take a look at the next section, *Project Management Methodology Implementation*, for some additional insight into recommended methodology implementation activities. You may find it necessary to consider using professionals who are experienced in project management methodology deployment to assist in your methodology development, customization, and implementation efforts. It will save you time, and it will undoubtedly be cost effective for your organization.

PROJECT MANAGEMENT METHODOLOGY IMPLEMENTATION

Methodology implementation is the means by which a project management process is presented for use with other business processes in the organization. The individual who selects a methodology for personal use will normally already have some level of interest and intent to learn the content and proper use of the methodology process. However, these conditions may not necessarily be present for all potential methodology users across the entire organization. Therefore, organizations will need to consider planning and conducting a series of activities to implement the methodology to achieve maximum benefit from its use.

Benefits of Methodology Implementation

It is recommended that a structured and planned approach be used when implementing a project management methodology. When the methodology is properly implemented as an organization-wide solution, there is potential to achieve several if not most of the following benefits:

- *A standard approach to the practice of project management*
  - Consistent use of repeatable processes and documentation
  - Reduced need to "reinvent" project management tools and techniques
  - Access to shared project management history, experience, and best practices
  - Greater assurance that critical project management activities are accomplished
  - A common frame of reference for project team members and stakeholders
  - A common understanding of project responsibilities in the organization
- *An effective business communication and reporting mechanism*
  - Use of standard project management terminology in the organization
  - Consistent information and data processing across all projects and programs
  - Ability to roll-up (aggregate) project reports and information to the executive level
  - More effective project team interactions and customer relationships
- *A state-of-the-art project management practice*
  - Increased customer satisfaction
  - Conformance to customer requirements and project objectives
  - Ability to achieve planned project schedules
  - Effective project cost control
  - Shortened development and implementation cycles
  - More predictable project (and business) performance
  - Increased profitability and reduced project costs
  - Improved resource planning, allocation, and management
  - Use of tools that provide a competitive business edge
- *Enhanced business benefits*
  - Quicker realization of profit or payback on investment
  - Earlier availability of products to market (or for internal use)
  - Clearer business case evaluation and ongoing business case validation
  - More effective, more knowledgeable business decisions

The potential for achieving these benefits can be realized when methodology implementation is properly planned and conducted in the organization.

Methodology Implementation Activities

An organizational methodology package could be used erratically or even remain dormant until the prominent stakeholders in the organization in general and the end users in particular (1) understand how to use it, (2) recognize benefits from using it, and (3) develop motivation, through personal interest or organizational mandate, to actually use it.

Methodology implementation issues can affect the entire organization, even business areas not traditionally viewed as having involvement in or responsibility for project management. Therefore, the complexity of methodology implementation is often increased when it is conducted on a national or global basis, or when multiple organizations, each with its own basis for implementation, are involved.

The following list provides a broad outline of several areas of activity that should be considered to ensure an adequate and proper project management methodology implementation effort. Many of these activities represent early planning that is important for achieving successful methodology deployment in the organization.

Plan Methodology Implementation

- *Establish executive management support.* Identify (or assign) an executive sponsor at the highest reasonable level in the organization that will use the methodology; ideally this is the CEO for an enterprise-wide implementation. Conduct collaboration across senior management to achieve senior-level buy-in and to create personal understanding and support for the initiative at the highest levels in the organization. Plan and conduct executive-level announcements about the importance of the methodology deployment initiative, the progress being made toward implementation, and any anticipated mandate or requirements for methodology use within the organization.
- *Form the methodology implementation team.* Identify members of the team who will have responsibility for planning and conducting the methodology customization and implementation effort, usually from among senior managers and project managers already involved in project oversight. Ensure representation from all affected business areas. Identify any external resources (i.e., experienced project management methodology consultants) needed to guide or otherwise assist the implementation team in areas of implementation planning, customization, rollout, training, mentoring, etc. In some organizations, this responsibility will be assigned to the project management office (PMO) for staffing and fulfillment purposes; in others, the methodology implementation team represents the initial structure of a PMO-like business unit. In all cases, ensure selected team members are inherently available and allotted sufficient time to participate in the various activities of the methodology deployment initiative.
- *Specify methodology implementation scope.* Determine the extent to which the project management methodology will be needed and deployed within the organization to include the identification of business units as well as local, regional, national, and international rollout locations. Specify collaboration requirements for locations involved in the methodology deployment initiative. This may include the preliminary identification of business units or locations that can be used for any "pilot implementation" activities, with resulting details incorporated into the methodology implementation plan.
- *Determine methodology utilization policies.* In collaboration with the executive sponsor, and any other involved senior managers, begin developing the policies for methodology distribution and use. Specify who will use it (e.g., project managers, team members) and the extent to which it must be applied to project work: always, sometimes, occasionally, or at the discretion of the project manager. It is recommended that the methodology utilization policies mandate methodology use on every project conducted within the relevant organization or business unit conducting the implementation. Options for the depth of methodology process use can be developed for different types of projects found within the organization (i.e., project classification), and other variations from routine use can be incorporated during methodology customization.
- *Develop methodology promotions for user awareness and acceptance.* Plan, prepare, and issue announcements, newsletters, or other media to inform individuals within the organization of the new methodology implementation initiative. In particular, inform potential users of the methodology about progress, actions, and timelines that will directly affect them. When possible, use senior management and executive-level announcements to demonstrate support for the initiative, and to convey the importance of methodology implementation and use for the organization.
- *Develop a methodology training plan.* Determine the roles and positions within the organization that will represent the end users of the methodology, and thereby identify associated individuals who will require some level of methodology training. Normally, a complete methodology training program is needed for all project managers (including managers of project managers and program managers). Many organizations will also include and schedule project team members for the complete methodology training program. Such a program can usually be completed in two to three days, depending on the depth of coverage desired by the organization. Executives and senior managers, along with peripheral project stakeholders and part-time members of project teams, can be introduced to the project management methodology using a shorter methodology familiarization program—usually one-half to one day in duration. This planning might also warrant an examination of additional project management training needed for individuals within the project management environment, and extended training can be specified in this plan as well.
- *Plan user support during methodology implementation.* Consider the support activities that will be needed by methodology users during the methodology implementation period, and plan and assign resources to satisfy

those needs. Prominent among the support activities to consider is the need for project management mentors—experienced individuals who are qualified to answer user questions about project management concepts and methodology use, and who are available on site to respond to user problems and dilemmas during the implementation period. An alternative activity might include creating a "help center" that new users can contact when they have questions about project management or methodology use. Additionally, user support should include a methodology user feedback mechanism, whereby users can identify problems and issues that can be examined and resolved in advance of methodology implementation at subsequent locations. Another user support mechanism to consider is the formation of a methodology user group that can facilitate information sharing and problem resolution among key participants in the methodology implementation initiative.

- *Prepare the project management methodology implementation plan.* Prepare a plan that will be approved, distributed, and used to guide project management methodology implementation. This plan should present a timeline of activities to be pursued that includes incorporating most of the previous and subsequent items in this list. Like any project plan, this implementation plan becomes a central document for the methodology deployment initiative. This plan should also identify plans for collaborating activities of the methodology initiative with customers and vendors, as needed.

Customize the Project Management Methodology

Any methodology customization to be accomplished can be planned and begun in conjunction with methodology implementation planning—after the requisite executive or senior management support and endorsement have been obtained. Methodology customization can be used to adapt the foundation methodology processes for better alignment with current project management practices. It can also serve to integrate important existing technical and business processes of the organization.

Methodology customization usually entails a review of the foundation methodology within the organization, usually by members of the methodology implementation team (which may be called the methodology development team at this point in time). The next step involves one or more meetings to resolve differences of opinion and to specify how the content of the foundation methodology should be modified. This second step will often include facilitation by the methodology developer or a consultant experienced in methodology design, who can lead the development team in their design and modification deliberations. The final step is that of preparing the new methodology content that will be ultimately distributed and used within the organization.

Sometimes the customization effort includes identifying the use of an automated platform on which the project management methodology will reside and provide electronic access to users. This sometimes involves an examination of current automated systems to determine how the methodology can be incorporated or otherwise linked electronically. Otherwise, it may involve the review and selection of a new system in the marketplace that is compatible with the methodology and with anticipated use in the organization.

A final note regarding customization is one that prompts methodology implementation managers to recognize that actual transition to use of the new methodology cannot and should not occur until an approved project management methodology is (1) fully developed and finalized, (2) published (or otherwise accessible online), and (3) ready for use by project managers, project team members, and other designated stakeholders in the project management environment.

Plan Project Transition

The project transition plan is often considered a component of the methodology implementation plan, but it is separated here for purposes of discussing recommended transition plan content. Smaller organizations or those having fewer projects will usually be able to plan for project transition in a simplified manner—what is the project, when will it transition, and how will it transition to the new methodology (i.e., at what methodology point will it start). This same basic information is also used by larger organizations and those with a high volume of projects. However, the increased number of projects offers a plan with more complexity, and this complexity is increased further when there are multiple business units and implementation locations involved. It can be seen that transition plan preparation time will normally be longer for organizations with more complex conditions.

In general, the following elements are recommended for inclusion in the project transition plan.

- *Prepare the project transition strategy.* Specify the approach that will be taken for project transition. Identify broad criteria that will help determine how projects will be transitioned: (1) a new (or recently started) project that will commence using the new methodology at the beginning of the methodology, (2) a project in progress that will transition to some point in the new methodology, or (3) a project near completion that will not transition to the new methodology. The transition strategy may also account for when project transition will take place, which is particularly important for the methodology implementation that will take place across multiple regional, national, or international locations. Finally, the strategy could include conducting one or more pilot transition and implementation programs as a means to learn and improve upon plans for subsequent project transition and implementation activities.

- *Survey and review project status.* Identify and examine each and every project currently under way within the organization, and then add to the list those projects that are expected to start during the methodology implementation period. Review project status and progression, and make a preliminary determination about the transition strategy (criteria) that will be applied for each project.
- *Conduct project transition interviews.* In personal meetings with each affected project manager, review the planned transition strategy and transition schedule for his or her project. Consider that some projects will have unique conditions to be managed in association with methodology implementation, and be prepared to make adjustments to the transition plan in collaboration with each project manager. Complete individual project manager meetings by establishing mutual agreement regarding the project transition strategy and schedule.
- *Prepare the project transition plan.* Compile the results from all transition planning meetings and prepare the final project transition plan. Include the overall transition schedule, which should be consistent with other implementation activities such as user training and planned user support. The transition plan can be incorporated into the broader methodology implementation plan or used as a stand-alone document.

Conduct Methodology Implementation

Methodology implementation actually begins in advance of user training and methodology deployment, such as when preliminary executive and senior management support is pursued and established, and such activities can be included in the overall implementation plan. Nevertheless, there are several key activities to monitor and manage during methodology implementation, as highlighted in the following list:

- Execute the methodology implementation plan.
- Conduct methodology user training.
- Provide for methodology document distribution to users (or online access).
- Execute the project transition plan.
- Conduct user support and mentoring in association with methodology deployment.

Methodology implementation is the beginning of an investment for the organization. To gain the maximum return on that investment, the organization should ensure that all essential implementation activities are conducted in a timely manner. A decision to implement an organization-wide project management methodology may warrant consideration of an external consulting resource who can apply expert knowledge and experience to help guide the organization toward a successful project management methodology implementation effort. The support of a qualified project management consultant or consulting team can often reduce implementation time by months or, in some circumstances, by a year or more.

PROJECT MANAGEMENT METHODOLOGY MAINTENANCE

After the project management methodology is deployed in the workplace, a reasonable effort is needed to oversee its use and maintain its viability. The implementing organization's PMO, the methodology implementation team, and potentially an expert external consultant or consultant team can be used to perform several important methodology maintenance activities at appropriate intervals in time.

The following are highlights of three prescribed methodology maintenance activities.

Evaluate Methodology Deployment

Beginning with the initial or "pilot" methodology implementation, and continuing through any subsequent implementation periods, the organization should examine how well the introduction of new project management processes and practices is being accomplished and received by methodology users. This usually includes looking at

- Completion or progress of the methodology training schedule
- Completion or progress of methodology implementation activities
- Completion or progress of project transitions
- Achievement of initial methodology performance capability
- User acceptance of the new methodology
- Stakeholder acceptance of the new methodology
- Management support factors
- Implementation feedback results and trends

If there are multiple deployment actions such as a pilot implementation followed by successive location deployments, interim results from the initial evaluation can be examined to help improve successive methodology deployment activities.

Analyze Methodology Performance

Examine methodology performance to ascertain methodology utilization levels, methodology effectiveness, and the achievement of benefits from methodology implementation. The analysis can include an examination of the following indicators:

- Number of users—full or partial methodology use
- Type of users—project managers, team members, business managers, etc.
- Extent of nonuse—reasons for nonuse
- Project planning improvements—project work plan, management plans, support plans
- Project tracking and controlling improvements—variation identification and analysis
- Project performance results—cost, schedule, and resource utilization
- Project success factors—customer satisfaction, deliverable quality and acceptance, etc.

The implemented methodology should be reviewed for these elements on an annual or sometimes an 18-month basis. To that end, evaluators should analyze current conditions, performance results, and issues associated with indicators in the above list. Corrective actions should be taken to rectify weak analysis indicators. This recurring examination is normally the responsibility of the PMO or the methodology implementation team.

Manage Methodology Improvements

Simply stated, the originally implemented methodology will undoubtedly need some adjustment, correction, or other improvement action over the course of time. Processes can be adapted, or new processes can be added or changed for better integration with business operations. New tools, including project management software tools, can be introduced to support methodology use. In general, the methodology is updated to reflect the current organizational needs and the "best practices" available for conducting project management.

As well, the initial methodology implementation may have been simply a set of fundamental processes, and with time the initial methodology has been expanded to contain a full life-cycle solution for project management. This will require attention to ensure that all approved changes are being properly implemented within the prescribed user group.

Likewise, new project managers, project team members, and other project stakeholders may be introduced into the project management environment, and they will require methodology training or familiarization as a part of the continuous improvement effort within the organization.

Methodology Process Guide

I

INTRODUCTION—PROJECT MANAGEMENT PROCESS OVERVIEW

The *Process Guide* describes the essential activities of project management that should be performed for each project undertaken in an organization. It addresses four project management phases—Profile, Plan, Perform, and Post—and matches these phases against the following six project management performance areas: customer, project, staff, vendor, business, and management. Through this matrix approach, the essential activities of project management are accounted for, and each can be scaled to meet the needs of size and scope for the various types of projects encountered.

The phases and performance areas of this methodology are depicted in the **process matrix** shown in Figure I.1, with the phases described in the next section. The *process elements* shown with their *process steps* in this matrix are described in subsequent sections of this process guide.

The flow or sequence of process element performance is generally numerical, where process element 1.1 is followed by process element 1.2, and so on. To a large extent, multiple process steps will be performed concurrently. Also, the methodology uses a design feature whereby each process step offers single-location point-of-data collection ("repository") for relevant information related to that project process step. Therefore, when considering process flow or sequence, users will necessarily return to or go forward to use or update process elements in the matrix. Therefore, it is suggested that this process matrix be used as the basis for guiding and reviewing the project management effort.

The **process flowchart** can be referenced (Figure I.2) and may be helpful in showing the general sequence and flow across process elements at the process-step level. The depicted process flow is very generic and can be adapted by users for application in their organization.

THE FOUR PHASES OF THE PROJECT MANAGEMENT METHODOLOGY

The *ProjectPRISM™ Project Management Methodology* defines four phases of interrelated project management activities. This guidance is often distinct from any technical methodology that may also be used. Such a technical methodology, which sometimes can have five, six, seven, or more phases, can be embedded into the project management methodology phases to present a seamless interface. To a large extent, technical work will be associated in the *plan* and *perform* phases of this process guide. However, technical methodology alignment can be achieved throughout the project management life cycle.

The technical methodology will help ensure a quality technical product, including product design, development, implementation, and testing. The project management methodology will help ensure a successful project in terms of managing and fulfilling cost, schedule and resource utilization objectives, project deliverables, and relevant business interests. The following sections describe the nature and purpose of the four phases of this methodology.

Profile Phase

The Profile Phase encompasses the processes needed to translate an external or internal customer opportunity into a valid project effort. It specifies the relevant aspects of the project in terms of "profiles" for each of the six performance areas. The Profile Phase compiles the basis or reason for conducting the project, and several profiles should be examined at intervals during the project to ensure that the basis is still accurate and applicable—from the customer's perspective and from an internal business perspective.

The Profile Phase is designed to identify the opportunity and the customer. It will focus on selecting the project as a bona fide work effort within the organization, accomplished through detailed information collection, reviews,

	1–PROFILE	2–PLAN	3–PERFORM	4–POST
CUSTOMER	**1.1–CUSTOMER PROFILE** ■ Customer Directory ■ Customer Business ■ Customer Opportunity ■ Customer Record	**2.1–CUSTOMER PLAN** ■ Customer Requirements ■ Customer Technical Solution ■ Customer Change Control Plan ■ Customer Quality Management Plan	**3.1–CUSTOMER PERFORMANCE** ■ Customer Meeting ■ Customer Status Report ■ Customer Change Management ■ Customer Acceptance Management	**4.1–CUSTOMER POSTING** ■ Customer Lessons Learned ■ Customer Evaluation ■ Customer Satisfaction Survey ■ Customer Transition & Closeout
PROJECT	**1.2–PROJECT PROFILE** ■ Project Definition ■ Project Estimates ■ Project Classification ■ Project Record	**2.2–PROJECT PLAN** ■ Project Work Plan ■ Project Risk Management Plan ■ Project Communication Plan ■ Project Support Plans	**3.2–PROJECT PERFORMANCE** ■ Project Tracking & Control Report ■ Project Risk Management ■ Project Communication Management ■ Project Plan Management	**4.2–PROJECT POSTING** ■ Project Lessons Learned ■ Project Performance Evaluation ■ Project Administration Closeout ■ Project Plan Closeout
STAFF	**1.3–STAFF PROFILE** ■ Staff Directory ■ Staff Structure ■ Staff Qualification ■ Staff Record	**2.3–STAFF PLAN** ■ Staff Requirements ■ Staff Management Plan ■ Staff Acquisition (Request) ■ Staff Assignments	**3.3–STAFF PERFORMANCE** ■ Staff Meeting ■ Staff Status Report ■ Staff Performance Review ■ Staff Management Report	**4.3–STAFF POSTING** ■ Staff Lessons Learned ■ Staff Performance Evaluation ■ Staff Performance Recognition ■ Staff Reassignment & Closeout
VENDORS	**1.4–VENDOR PROFILE** ■ Vendor Directory ■ Vendor Business ■ Vendor Qualification ■ Vendor Record	**2.4–VENDOR PLAN** ■ Vendor Solicitation ■ Vendor Management Plan ■ Vendor Proposal Evaluation ■ Vendor Contract	**3.4–VENDOR PERFORMANCE** ■ Vendor Meeting ■ Vendor Status Report ■ Vendor Performance Review ■ Vendor Contract Administration	**4.4–VENDOR POSTING** ■ Vendor Lessons Learned ■ Vendor Performance Evaluation ■ Vendor Invoice Management ■ Vendor Contract Closeout
BUSINESS	**1.5–BUSINESS PROFILE** ■ Business Case ■ Business Risk Examination ■ Business Financial Analysis ■ Business Recommendation	**2.5–BUSINESS PLAN** ■ Business Requirements ■ Business Solution ■ Business Proposal ■ Business Contract	**3.5–BUSINESS PERFORMANCE** ■ Business Meeting ■ Business Status Report ■ Business Performance Review ■ Business Contract Administration	**4.5–BUSINESS POSTING** ■ Business Lessons Learned ■ Business Performance Evaluation ■ Business Invoice Management ■ Business Contract Closeout
MANAGEMENT	**1.6–MANAGEMENT PROFILE** ■ Management Directory ■ Management Portfolio ■ Management Charter ■ Management Record	**2.6–MANAGEMENT PLAN** ■ Management Oversight Plan ■ Management Audit & Review Plan ■ Management Facility Plan ■ Management Supply & Equipment Plan	**3.6–MANAGEMENT PERFORMANCE** ■ Management Meeting ■ Management Status Report ■ Management Performance Review ■ Management Audit & Review Report	**4.6–MANAGEMENT POSTING** ■ Management Lessons Learned ■ Management Evaluation ■ Management Satisfaction Survey ■ Management Closeout

Figure I.1 ProjectPRISM™ Methodology Process Matrix.

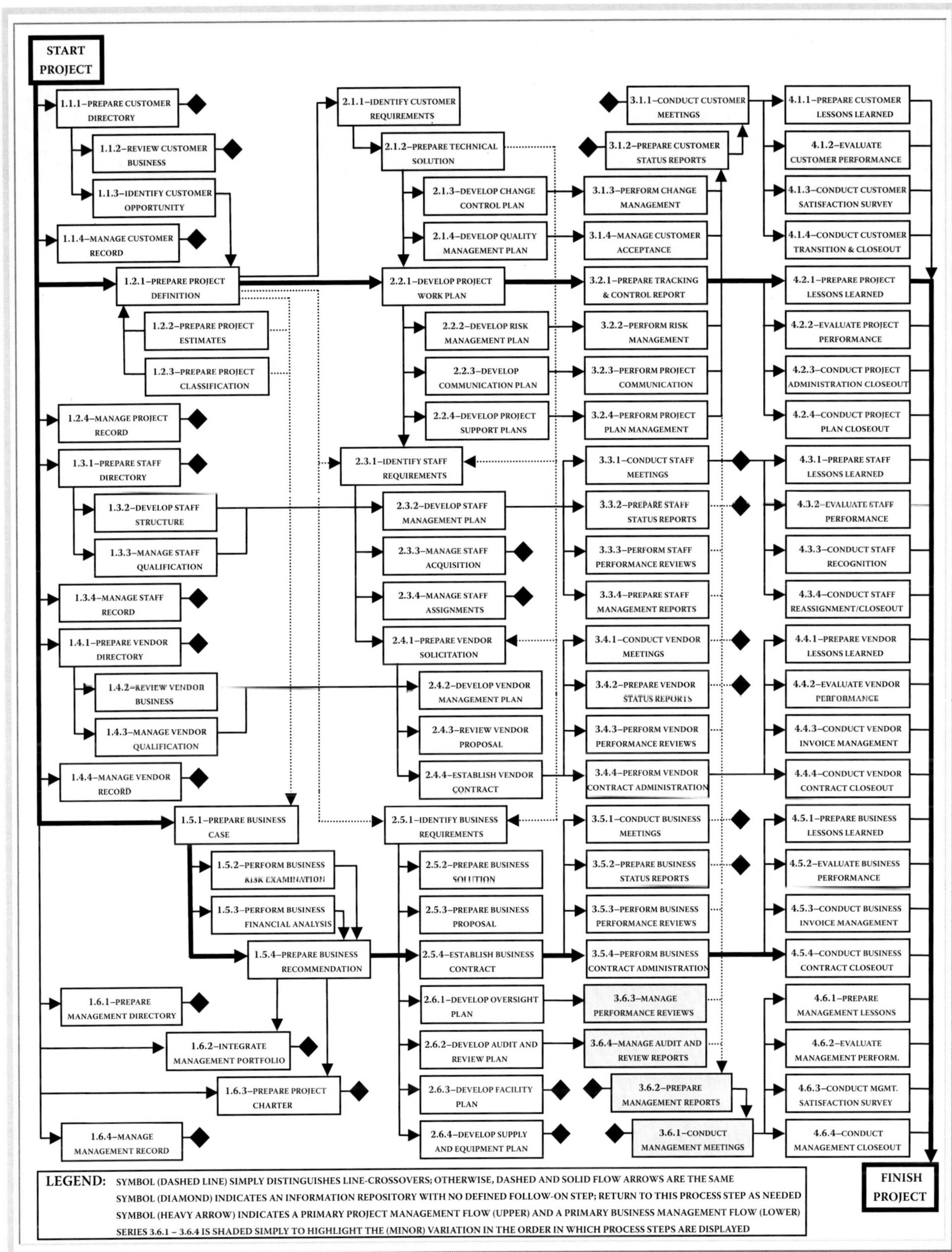

Figure I.2 ProjectPRISM™ Methodology Process Flowchart.

and analyses, including financial analyses. Project selection is a business commitment that reflects a more or less formal confirmation that the project will fulfill internal business needs, interests, and objectives; a sufficient number of qualified resources are available to staff the work effort; adequate and necessary project funding is available and will be applied as needed to the work effort; and the customer, internal or external, is similarly committed to a successful project outcome.

If projects are a means of revenue from external customers, the Profile Phase will facilitate the transition from business development (sales) to project management. It ensures that everything the business manager knows is conveyed to the project manager. In turn, the project manager will review information from a variety of sources on a recurring basis and expand or modify several profiles over the course of the project. When the opportunity is identified as internal, it will also help to initiate early interactions with the internal customer.

The Profile Phase of project management is used to define the project, that is, what the work effort or initiative to be undertaken is all about. It captures preliminary thoughts on project scope and project objectives, and allows for a preliminary high-level estimate of project cost, schedule, and resource utilization to be performed. It identifies the key players and stakeholders of the project, and provides for information collection across the several profiles that can be used to facilitate management of stakeholder requirements, interests, and participation in the project.

The Profile Phase prompts users to establish directories—customer, staff, vendors, and management—to enable identification and contact with key project participants, and to track and oversee relevant project stakeholder participation, as needed.

If the project management in your organization has executive and senior management-level interest, this phase will help integrate management participation for fulfillment of project management oversight responsibilities, including portfolio management. To that end, it identifies and assigns a project executive/sponsor or an executive control board that has the responsibility of fulfilling the project objectives—and, in turn, they will prepare the project management charter for use by the project manager and project team members.

Plan Phase

The Plan Phase encompasses the processes needed to establish requirements for customer, staff, business, and management. It also develops the required project management plans that all together comprise the *Project Plan*. This means that a *Project Plan* is not necessarily one single document, but rather a collection of several plan documents or components.

Organizations will normally specify the minimum content required for their *Project Plan*. This guide prescribes several project management plans as essential to every project.

First, many practitioners would likely agree that the Project Work Plan is the most critical of plans that are developed to support the project management effort. The Project Work Plan represents the preparation of the project work breakdown structure (WBS), and the incorporation of cost, schedule, and resource utilization estimates at the work package level.

There are six primary project management plans also prescribed as essential documents for project management, including

- Customer—Change Control Plan
- Customer—Quality Management Plan
- Project—Risk Management Plan
- Project—Communications Plan
- Staff—Management Plan
- Vendor—Management Plan

The selection and use of these plans can be determined by the project manager upon entry into the Plan Phase. While these plans are considered essential, there will be some projects (usually those smaller in scope and lower in overall value) that inherently do not require the full set of six plans. Conversely, larger projects (usually those of significant business interest and value) may require an expansion of prescribed plan content as well as the preparation of additional project management support plans.

There is a large number of optional project management support plans that can be developed to support the project management, business management, and technical management needs of the project. A partial list of support plans is presented for user consideration in the *Practice Guide*. The organization can examine this list to determine and specify if any support plan should routinely be prepared for every project conducted within the organization.

The Plan Phase is designed to guide users through the process of developing the planning documents needed for the project. It contains guidance that will assist users in the information and content collection process for each of the prescribed project plans, and it inherently provides for the reuse of standard content for recurring plan development. It also is a guide that enables users to construct and compile documents related to proposal submittals and contract acquisitions. When needed for projects that have outsourcing needs, the Plan Phase also includes process steps to plan and conduct the vendor acquisition process.

The Plan Phase begins by prompting users to thoroughly review customer requirements to ensure that they have a complete understanding of technical needs and a solid basis for creating the required project management plans. This leads to creating the Technical Solution, a process whereby users identify the technical approach and specify project milestones and deliverables.

Similarly, the Plan Phase also prompts users to review business requirements. It then helps users to create the Business Solution, including an examination of business issues and the development of solicitation fulfillment, customer pricing, and contracting strategies.

The Technical Solution and the Business Solution are then integrated for presentation to the customer in a consolidated proposal document. Users will be able to monitor and manage proposal preparation and submittal in the Plan Phase.

In specific process elements, users will be guided to establish staffing requirements in a resource requirements matrix and identify project documentation and reporting requirements for project and portfolio reviews and other oversight activities during the project. A highlight of the Plan Phase is the inclusion of a series of relevant project management logs. The Plan Phase elements provide users with the ability to track and manage project information resulting from project plan implementation, including the following 17 logs:

- Customer Requirements—Documentation Management Log
- Customer Technical Solution—Deliverables Log
- Customer Technical Solution—Milestones Log
- Customer Change Control Plan—Change Request and Approval Log
- Customer Quality Management Plan—Quality Testing and Acceptance Log
- Customer Quality Management Plan—Quality Technical Reviews Log
- Project Risk Management Plan—Risk Management Log
- Staff Management—Training and Development Activity Log
- Staff Assignments—Individual Assignment and Activity Tracking Log
- Vendor Management Plan—Training and Development Activity Log
- Vendor Contract—Modification Log
- Business Contract—Modification Log
- Business Contract—Contract and Negotiation Activity Log
- Management Oversight Plan—Oversight Activity Log
- Management Audit and Review Plan—Audit and Review Log
- Management Facility Plan—Facility Management Activity Log
- Management Supply and Equipment Plan—Supply and Equipment Log

To a limited extent, these logs can be used independently or in a manner that applies an abbreviated process to manage the project.

Perform Phase

The Perform Phase encompasses the processes needed to conduct the ongoing project execution effort and associated project management activities to oversee project progress, performance, and fulfillment. It enables the project manager to attend to the variety of actions and activities that are happening concurrently within the project, and to identify and respond to any issues and problems that may surface. In addition, it provides for general and specific communication among the key participants and stakeholders of the project.

The Perform Phase prompts and helps arrange the conduct of meetings and the preparation and distribution of reports that inherently facilitate necessary communication and collaboration on the project. Meetings and reports relevant to all key project participants are addressed, including

- Customer meetings and status reports
- Project tracking and control reports
- Staff meetings and status reports
- Vendor meetings and status reports
- Business meetings and status reports
- Management meetings and reports

The Perform Phase is highlighted by activities that will help manage project performance, and it prescribes relevant activities for project tracking and controlling. It facilitates the collection of information and project data that can be contrasted and compared to the established project plans to ascertain project earned value and variance. In turn, it will help document and manage project control actions that are applied to correct a veering project and get it back on track toward success. This includes activities to identify and respond to issues and problems across the project, as well as to influence or otherwise request customer and management attention to such matters.

The Perform Phase is designed to help the project manager oversee work performance, and provides the ability to monitor and document staff and vendor performance. It provides for reporting of work progress and assessment of associated project status and progress. As may be needed or required, it provides for the conduct of project, project management audits, and technical reviews, and oversees the achievement of prescribed project deliverables.

An important focus of the Perform Phase is in its facilitation of contract administration activities for the customer contract and any vendor contracts. This ensures proper management of billing and invoicing, oversight of the fulfillment of contractual obligations, and contributions to the oversight of other business aspects of the project.

Post Phase

The Post Phase presents the processes needed to close out the project and all associated business, technical, and project management activities. It includes obtaining project stakeholder acknowledgment and acceptance of project closure.

The Post Phase attends to the closeout of customer activities and associated discontinuation of further project-based affiliation with the customer. Although normally achieved in the Perform Phase, closeout activities will monitor completion of customer project deliverables acceptance actions. They will also prompt a postproject examination of customer participation, including an associated evaluation of customer satisfaction.

The Post Phase has a major focus on the collection and documentation of lessons learned as a means to improve and enhance future project and project management performance. Lessons learned are prescribed in all six methodology performance areas—customer, project, staff, vendor, business, and management. This phase provides the guidance for conducting and documenting project lessons learned from all relevant sources.

The Post Phase further prescribes steps for the evaluation of performance across most project stakeholders, particularly the evaluation of staff and vendor performance. It likewise provides capability for evaluation of PMO management, project manager, and customer performance.

The Post Phase also ensures closeout of contractual obligations and contract documents. This includes steps to monitor final invoice payments (incoming and outgoing) as important criteria for project closure.

PROCESS ROLES AND RESPONSIBILITIES

The *Process Guide* identifies individuals having roles and responsibilities within the various process steps. The following list provides a general description of those individuals and their associated roles and responsibilities. Position titles (roles) and responsibilities will vary from organization to organization and across industries. *Process Guide* users should examine these descriptions against existing titles and terminology in order to align and assign individual methodology responsibility in the organization.

The primary roles used in this process guide are presented in the following list.

- *Business Development Manager*—This individual has the responsibility for acquiring new business, maintaining revenue from current business, and often managing customer relationships. In many organizations, this role is represented by the sales staff; in others, it may be handled by a customer program manager or customer representative.
- *Business Operations Manager*—This individual has responsibility for managing a technical function, business operation, or business unit. Resources, including project managers, may be aligned with business managers. Business operations managers are project stakeholders to the extent that projects affect their business operations. They are generally concerned with project performance in terms of how well projects fulfill business interests and objectives.
- *Contract Manager*—This individual has responsibility for contract oversight, and this role might be represented by a team of contract managers. Similarly, this role could be a staff position within the more mature PMO. The contract manager oversees administration of customer and vendor contracts and advises the project manager on contract management matters that do not require professional legal intervention.
- *Executive Control Board*—The executive control board is the senior-level management group that is responsible for providing business guidance and direction for application in the project management environment. It is also normally responsible for deliberating business opportunities and selecting projects to be pursued. This executive-level body may exist within the organization under different naming conventions. It might be called the project control board, management oversight committee, project portfolio committee, or, in a technical organization, the systems control group. It may report to a higher-level executive or board of executives, or may itself be the group of senior executives in the organization. The project executive or sponsor should normally be a member of this group, and ideally the PMO head is also a member. In some instances in smaller organizations, a single executive may perform the deliberation and decision-making functions of this group.
- *Opportunity Manager*—The opportunity manager is the individual who has responsibility and relevant authority for examining new business opportunities and managing the associated project selection process. The opportunity manager combines technical expertise with business acumen to fulfill these responsibilities. In some organizations, this is a distinct and separate role or one aligned with the PMO. In others, this may be a part of the business development manager's responsibility. In some smaller organizations, the project manager may also serve as the opportunity manager.
- *Proposal Team*—This team is a group of individuals formed to develop and submit the combined technical and business proposal to the customer. The proposal team may include project team members, and, in

smaller organizations, the proposal team is the project team. However, a proposal team member could also be part of the PMO staff that regularly assists in or facilitates the proposal development process, or an individual assigned to just the business aspect of the proposal development effort (usually as a specialist in such areas as pricing strategy, contract negotiations, legal terms and conditions, etc.). The proposal team can be disbanded upon contract award (or upon proposal submittal to the customer).

- *Project Customer*—The project customer is the internal or external recipient of project deliverables based on the needs and requirements that have been established, and thereby the customer has a vested interest in project progress and project status. Customers warrant active involvement in all phases of the project, but customer participation levels may sometimes vary. Customer interaction and management is a prominent activity of project management, and customers should be encouraged to participate in collaboration, coordination, and acceptance or approval activities in a timely manner. External customers usually conduct projects as a business endeavor, using some type of formal contract or agreement that maintains accountability for both parties. Similarly, a contract or agreement should be established for internal customers and used in a manner so as to maintain mutual accountability and to guide outcomes for internal projects.
- *Project Executive (Sponsor)*—The project executive is the individual who has responsibility for achieving strategic business objectives through project selection and performance. This role usually has particular interest in four business areas: revenue generation, operational efficiency, customer satisfaction, and new product development. The project executive is the likely owner of a portfolio of projects that have been selected to achieve strategic business objectives. In addition, the project executive may sit on or possibly chair an aligned executive control board (or some other committee) that is used to review, select, and prioritize project work efforts. For purposes of this methodology, the terms *project executive* and *project sponsor* are used interchangeably. The project sponsor normally has authority to allocate resources, assign project managers, and terminate the project at any time. In some larger organizations, the project sponsor may be a distinct role from that of project executive. If distinct, the project sponsor works with the project executive to ensure strategic business alignment.
- *Project Management Office*—The PMO is the internal entity (possibly a business unit) that has responsibility for central project management oversight, control, and support. In this role, it represents project managers and project performance to executive management, and executive management policies and guidance to the project management environment. Its charter can include specific project management functionality or full authority to act in areas of business and technical process integration within the project management environment. It normally has central responsibility for developing, implementing, and maintaining the preferred project management methodology and associated practices.
- *Project Manager*—The project manager is the individual who is assigned responsibility and relevant authority for achieving the objectives of a specific project. The professional project manager should have combined technical and business expertise to fulfill this role. Under the concepts of modern project management, there is a wide range of activities to be performed and a number of diverse responsibilities to fulfill. Therefore, this should be a full-time position on most projects. The project manager should be designated by and work under an established project charter, issued by either the PMO or the project executive (sponsor), which identifies the roles and responsibilities to be fulfilled. On larger projects, project management assistants can be designated to reduce the burden on one person. Sometimes this assistance resides in the PMO, where it can be accessed simultaneously by multiple project managers.
- *Project Planning Team Member*—The project planning team member is a resource assigned to conduct planning activities for a specific project. This may be a full-time or part-time role. The project planning team member may also be a project team member, who will remain on the project after preliminary planning is completed. Where practical, the project planning team should be composed of project team members. However, the project planning team member could also be a member of the PMO staff who regularly assists in or facilitates the planning process, or an individual assigned just to the planning aspect of the project (usually as a specialist in such areas as quality control, project estimating, project scheduling, etc.). The project planning team can be disbanded upon completion of the initial planning effort, but team members usually remain on call (if not already assigned as project team members) for the duration of the project in order to refine or update project plan components as the need arises.
- *Project Team Member*—The project team member is an assigned resource for a specific project. This may be a full-time or part-time role. In general, anyone who works within one or more phases of the project can be considered a project team member. This means there are points in time at which the so-called "operational" personnel are participating as project team members.

However, for many organizations, the project team member is represented as an element of the technical, administrative, or labor staff who is specifically assigned to the project for a prescribed period and for the purpose of performing specific types of work.

- *Resource Manager*—The resource manager is the individual who has responsibility for providing the resources needed for assignment to specific projects. This person can be a supervisor or resource "owner" at various levels in the organization. In a matrix-based project management organization, the resource manager is normally external to the project but supplies the resources needed to accomplish the technical work upon requests from project managers, consistent with allocations made by the project executive (sponsor). In an integrated project management organization, the project manager or PMO may be the resource manager.
- *Vendor*—The vendor is an external individual or organization whose products, services, and capability are acquired for a specified performance period associated with the pending opportunity or project at hand. The term *vendor* is used to represent the outsourcing of work to resources that have demonstrated the staff qualification and capability to achieve required project deliverables. This term can be used interchangeably with related external product and service providers such as contractor, consultant, supplier, etc.

SCALING PROJECTS USING THE METHODOLOGY

The *Process Guide* prescribes guidance for accomplishing the essential elements of project management. It uses a process step format, in which each process step is supported by a process tool contained in the accompanying *Process Toolkit*. This allows users to know that when a tool is completed, the associated process step is similarly completed, or at least initially completed.

Project management is inherently a rigorous activity. However, rigor will increase or decrease based on the size, value, and complexity of the project. The *Process Guide* supports a rigorous approach to project management when it is needed. However, it can also be adapted for projects that do not require such rigor.

There are three ways that users can adapt the *Process Guide* to different types of projects: (1) scaling the methodology process, (2) creating a methodology "Lite" toolkit, and (3) using project management logs as the primary tool.

Scaling the Methodology Process

This methodology might be considered a rigorous process because of its comprehensive approach to project management. The focus, however, should be on how the methodology presents the several or, more precisely, the 24 "essential" elements of project management. These elements are the things that need to be done on each project to ensure that it is properly managed. The greater detail with which projects are managed will provide a higher level of confidence that a project will be successfully completed—on time and on budget.

Performing these essential elements of project management is recommended for every project undertaken by the organization. It is the depth to which they are performed and the time available (or needed) to perform each element that are variable and somewhat negotiable. For example, a high-value, multiyear project might warrant forming a team of several people to perform an extensive project risk assessment that takes several days, or even weeks, and then requires frequent tracking and follow-up action. Conversely, a smaller project that is barely a month long might simply require the project manager to follow fundamental aspects of the prescribed process, set aside some time, maybe an hour or less, and then consider and document some thoughts on project risks. The point made here is that a project risk assessment was performed for both the complex project and the simple project; the depth of performance was adjusted according to project needs. In a similar manner, all primary process elements should be performed for every project.

The example here shows adaptation or scaling of the process element for risk between two extremes. All process elements can (and probably should) be scaled for virtually all projects. Consider the following ways to scale the methodology for use on different projects:

- *Requirements Scaling*—The organization identifies the outputs that will be required for each process element, and then specifies how that output will vary for different types of projects. This is translated into specifying what information collection and analysis is conducted using the *Process Toolkit*, that is, which sections of each tool will be required and which will be designated as optional for different types of project work.
- *Process Step Scaling*—The organization determines which of the process elements require full attention and completion on every project, and then specifies which underlying process substeps may be adapted for limited or optional use.
- *Project Manager Scaling*—The individual project manager determines the depth and extent to which each methodology process element will be completed to ensure effective project management.

It is appropriate to mention at this juncture that some organizations may also wish to increase the rigor of the methodology (or selected process elements) by incorporating or integrating additional processes, by adding more information collection and reporting requirements, or by expanding the management-level reviews of project management processes accomplished.

Scaling Projects by Creating a Methodology "Lite" Toolkit

The organization or end user may wish to develop a set of downsized tools that will be designated as the Methodology "Lite" Toolkit. It can be used for smaller projects in place of the standard toolkit. It can also be used in combination with the standard toolkit to customize and conduct the process step scaling described earlier.

A recommended approach for doing this is to take key extracts from the standard toolkit. That is, take and use only the key content items of each standard tool. For example, the first section of each tool within each of the 24 process areas can be combined. This results in having 24 tools rather than 96 tools to manage, and reduces the number of tools necessary to perform a process element to one instead of four. The standard toolkit remains available for use, should one or more process elements require a more detailed management capability.

Scaling Projects Using Project Management Logs

Another feature of this methodology is the inclusion of a wide assortment of management logs in the various tools. If the methodology process has to be extremely limited, then the organization or end user may wish to extract a relevant series of logs for use as an alternative approach that will still provide a reasonable level of project management effectiveness, although not quite as good as when using the complete methodology toolkit.

When such a Logbook is created, it enables the end user to capture much of the critical project management information that transcends the project. Constant maintenance and frequent review of the Logbook will ensure that no major problems occur to hinder project progress.

STANDARD FEATURES OF THE PROCESS GUIDE

The *ProjectPRISM™ Process Guide* is constructed to provide the following information for each process element:

- Process Description
- Schedule or Timing
- Process Steps and Toolkit Reference
- Responsibility (for performing the process element)
- Process Input
- Process Output (project management deliverable)

This information can be used to guide project progress, as well as to monitor and manage the accomplishment of project management activities to ensure project success. The text following presents the process elements prescribed for each of the four project management life-cycle phases.

Chapter 1

Phase 1: Profile Processes

1.1 CUSTOMER PROFILE

This process element creates a *Customer Profile* that enables the project manager, project team, and other key project stakeholders to learn about the customer's organization relative to the work to be undertaken. This knowledge or awareness about the customer will allow stakeholders in the performing organization to manage customer contacts and expectations, and to gain insight into the nature of the customer's business. It will provide for the collection and review of preliminary information about the opportunity the customer has identified, and it will facilitate the transition from prospect to customer. Over time, the information compiled in this process element will assist the project manager and others in making and communicating decisions that are consistent with the customer's business interests and requirements for the project.

Schedule/Timing

The *Customer Profile* is created during the initial examination of the customer's needs, interests, and ability to fund the project. It can be started upon identification or notification of the customer opportunity. The resulting profile may be used and updated throughout the project's duration.

Process Steps and Toolkit Reference

The following four process steps will be accomplished to create the *Customer Profile*:

- **1.1.1 Customer Directory**—Identify the customer's organization as well as the key business and technical contacts in the customer's organization who will convey needs and requirements, establish the contract or agreement, collaborate on the project planning effort, and manage the performance and payment of project services and deliverables.
- **1.1.2 Customer Business**—Compile and review the customer's business information to gain reasonable insight into the customer's business operations. This information can be used to facilitate subsequent business activities, project solution planning, and future business opportunities through demonstrated awareness of the customer's business.
- **1.1.3 Customer Opportunity**—Obtain and examine relevant information to gain a reasonable understanding of the customer's business needs and interests as a basis for describing the customer opportunity. Use this information when preparing the project definition and in planning and collaborating the business and technical solutions with the customer.
- **1.1.4 Customer Record**—Compile any current or previous work performed for this customer to review the customer's business history. Use this to examine business risk, reasonableness of the customer's pursuit of the opportunity, and probability of selection by the customer. Monitor and manage issues associated with the customer.

Responsibility

Primary

- Business Development Manager
- Project Manager

Alternates and Adjuncts

- Opportunity Manager (Alternate)
- PMO (Alternate)
- Project Customer
- Project Executive (Sponsor)

The *Customer Profile* may be started by the business development manager if the customer is external and is acquired through business development or sales efforts. If there is no accompanying sales activity, the project manager (or alternatively, opportunity manager or PMO) will have responsibility for fulfilling the prescribed process element. An opportunity manager may be assigned to oversee organizational interests and control the opportunity prior to a project manager being assigned. The opportunity manager may reside within the PMO, or the PMO may have direct responsibility for this process element. The project customer may be contacted directly (or through the business development manager) to assist in completing this profile. The project manager then has responsibility for maintaining this profile for the duration of the project. The project executive (sponsor), as well as other project stakeholders, may conduct initial and interval examinations of the *Customer Profile*, usually as a part of subsequent business case reviews and project gateway reviews.

Process Input

The following information, actions, materials, and resources represent relevant inputs to this process:

- Customer business telephone directories
- Customer organizational charts
- Customer brochures and prospectus materials
- Business articles and information pertaining to the customer from Internet business Web sites
- Market information on publicly held companies from Internet business Web sites
- Technical information on previous customer project work from the internal project archives
- Business information on previous customer project work from the internal project archives
- Opportunity information from meetings and telephone calls with relevant customer contacts
- Issues and actions information related to the customer opportunity
- Solicitation documents (e.g., requests for proposals [RFPs], requests for information [RFIs], etc.), as released and provided by the customer

Process Output (Project Management Deliverable)

The primary output of this process is the *Customer Profile*. This profile contains information that facilitates project management, develops the customer relationship, and helps achieve the customer's expectations.

1.2 PROJECT PROFILE

This process element creates a *Project Profile* that enables the project manager, along with various adjunct participants, to prepare a complete description of the project effort. A *project definition* is created to ensure that project planners and project team members have a clear and common understanding of the purpose and boundaries of the pending work effort. Project estimates for cost, schedule, and resource utilization are prepared and aligned with the project definition. A *project classification* is established not only to align the effort with internal business interests but also to identify the extent and depth of project management required. Finally, a project record is created to examine stakeholders and manage project issues, and project archives are accessed to contrast the current opportunity with previously performed projects by review of any related lessons learned that should be applied to the pending effort.

Schedule/Timing

The *Project Profile* is created during the initial examination of the business opportunity concurrent with the identification or notification of the customer opportunity. It requires sufficient information and input from the customer to properly capture the purpose and boundaries of the project. The resulting profile is used and updated throughout the project's duration.

Process Steps and Toolkit Reference

The following four process steps will be accomplished to create the *Project Profile*.

- **1.2.1 Project Definition**—Compile relevant information to develop a complete and comprehensive description of the project work effort. Specify project objectives and scope. Prepare initial project estimates (use process step 1.2.2 for more detailed planning estimates). Identify and associate project deliverables. Examine project assumptions and constraints.
- **1.2.2 Project Estimates**—Initial project estimates are usually order-of-magnitude estimates associated with the Project Definition. Budget and definitive estimates are more detailed and aligned with the project work

plan and work breakdown structure (WBS). Use lessons learned reviews to help prepare project estimates.

- **1.2.3 Project Classification**—Determine project classification based on an examination of criteria that describes and evaluates project business interests, project performance characteristics, and project complexity. The initial determination of project classification may be adjusted following subsequent business and opportunity analyses.
- **1.2.4 Project Record**—Identify the key project stakeholders involved in project performance, deliverable acceptance, and resource assignments. Review and identify lessons learned from previous projects of similar nature to this project to guide project definition development. Monitor and manage issues associated with project performance.

Responsibility

Primary

- Project Manager

Alternates and Adjuncts

- Opportunity Manager (Alternate)
- PMO (Alternate)
- Business Development Manager
- Project Customer
- Project Executive (Sponsor)
- Project Team Members

The project manager (or alternatively, opportunity manager or PMO) applies project management skill, knowledge, and experience to construct the *Project Profile*. An opportunity manager may be assigned to oversee this process element prior to a project manager being assigned. The opportunity manager may reside within the PMO, or the PMO may have direct responsibility for this process element. If a business development manager is assigned, contributions from that source should be solicited. However, the *Project Profile* is largely a technical document for which the project manager (or alternately, the opportunity manager or PMO) should have the lead responsibility. Project team members qualified in areas of planning, project estimation, and scope management can also become contributors if so delegated. Similarly, the project customer should be solicited for content input and review. If the project customer has issued a solicitation document, one or more clarification meetings might also be arranged. The project manager then has responsibility for maintaining this profile for the duration of the project. The project executive (sponsor), as well as other project stakeholders, may conduct initial and interval examinations of the *Project Profile*, usually as a part of subsequent business case reviews and project gateway reviews.

Process Input

The following information, actions, materials, and resources represent relevant input to this process:

- *Customer Profile* (process element 1.1), as concurrently developed
- Technical lessons learned from previous projects from the internal project archives
- Business lessons learned from previous projects from the internal project archives
- Standards, metrics, and methods for estimating cost, schedule, and resource utilization
- Opportunity information from meetings and telephone calls with relevant customer contacts
- Opportunity information from discussions with the business development manager
- Issues and actions information related to the potential conduct of the project
- Solicitation documents (e.g., RFPs, RFIs, etc.), as released and provided by the customer

Process Output (Project Management Deliverable)

The primary output of this process is the *Project Profile*. This profile contains information that facilitates business case review and project selection, guides subsequent project planning, contributes to project gateway review decisions, and provides some limited influence for establishing project management oversight requirements.

1.3 STAFF PROFILE

This process element creates a *Staff Profile* that enables the project manager, along with adjunct participants, to influence the allocation of project resources during the Profile Phase, and to manage resource assignments and performance during the Plan Phase and the Perform Phase. The *Staff Profile* is a summary document that can be used in determining the need of and requesting resources for project assignments. It establishes the project structure that is preferred by the project manager, consistent with organizational guidance. It also identifies and tracks any project-specific qualifications required for project team members. The *Staff Profile* can be an integral part of the business case review conducted by executives and senior managers.

Schedule/Timing

The *Staff Profile* can be initiated in conjunction with creating the project definition, but it can be accomplished at any time during project initiation. Its preparation sometimes continues into the Plan Phase (where resource acquisition actually occurs). The resulting profile is used and updated throughout the project's duration.

Process Steps and Toolkit Reference

The following four process steps will be accomplished to create the *Staff Profile*:

- **1.3.1 Staff Directory**—Identify the staff organizations from which project staff can be acquired. Specify any notable technical leaders assigned to this project team. List the individual staff members of the project team who will be assigned for purposes of performing project work.
- **1.3.2 Staff Structure**—Identify and describe the staff organization that will be created to support the project effort. List relevant resource managers who will supply staff resources. Develop a formal or informal depiction of the project organization chart.
- **1.3.3 Staff Qualification**—Review and specify project staff qualification requirements—things that have to be accomplished for individuals to work on the project. This includes certifications and licenses, specification and management of security and access clearances, and general training (see process step 2.3.2 for preparing a detailed training and development log).
- **1.3.4 Staff Record**—Manage staff resources information relative to project team assignment requirements, individual qualifications, experience, and project history, and manage results of staff work performance and postproject activities.

Responsibility

Primary

- Project Manager
- Resource Manager

Alternates and Adjuncts

- Opportunity Manager (Alternate)
- PMO (Alternate)
- Business Development Manager
- Project Executive (Sponsor)

The project manager (or alternatively, opportunity manager or PMO) applies project management skill, knowledge, and experience to construct the *Staff Profile*. An opportunity manager may be assigned to oversee this process element prior to a project manager being assigned. The opportunity manager may reside within the PMO, or the PMO may have direct responsibility for this process element. If a business development manager is assigned, contributions from that source should be solicited relative to customer staff performance issues and expectations. However, the *Staff Profile* is largely a project management document for which the project manager (or alternately, the opportunity manager or PMO) should have the lead responsibility. Although resource acquisition is not formalized until the Plan Phase, the project manager can begin discussions with relevant resource managers in this step in anticipation of identifying specific resource needs. The project manager then has responsibility for maintaining this profile for the duration of the project. The project executive (sponsor), as well as other project stakeholders, may conduct initial and interval examinations of the *Staff Profile*, usually as a part of subsequent business case reviews.

Process Input

The following information, actions, materials, and resources represent relevant inputs to this process:

- *Customer Profile* (process element 1.1), as concurrently developed
- *Project Profile* (process element 1.2), as concurrently developed
- *Staff Plan* (process element 2.3), as concurrently or subsequently developed
- Technical staff information and performance records
- Staffing information from discussions with the business development manager
- Staffing information from discussions with individual project team members
- Staff training and certification records
- Issues and actions information related to staff selection and performance
- Solicitation documents (e.g., RFPs, RFIs, etc.), as released and provided by the customer

Process Output (Project Management Deliverable)

The primary output of this process is the *Staff Profile*. This profile contains information that facilitates team member acquisition and assignment, and team member performance management.

1.4 VENDOR PROFILE

This process element creates a *Vendor Profile* that enables the project manager, project team, and other project stakeholders to learn about and maintain information on each vendor's organization relative to the work to be undertaken. This information will provide for the collection and review of preliminary information about the vendors' offerings, and contribute to the identification and selection of qualified vendors for project work. Over time, the information compiled in this process element will assist the project manager and others in making and communicating decisions about vendor utilization and performance management.

Schedule/Timing

The *Vendor Profile* can be initiated in conjunction with constructing the Staff Profile, but it can be accomplished at any time vendor acquisition occurs during the project. The resulting profile is maintained and updated throughout the project's duration when vendors are assigned or affiliated.

Process Steps and Toolkit Reference

The following four process steps will be accomplished to create the *Vendor Profile*:

- **1.4.1 Vendor Directory**—Identify the vendor organization and vendor contacts that will establish and manage the vendor contract and agreement, collaborate on the vendor's work planning effort, and perform and manage the vendor's project work as well as invoicing of vendor products and services.
- **1.4.2 Vendor Business**—Obtain and examine relevant information about the vendor's business organization as a basis for vendor selection, vendor retention and assignment, vendor management, and for gaining insight into the vendor's business capability and business approach.
- **1.4.3 Vendor Qualification**—Track and manage the list of vendors qualified by the organization and eligible to perform work assignments on this project. If desired, maintain two lists: one for vendors who will serve primarily as staff members to provide products and services, and one for vendors who will serve primarily to provide goods and supplies.
- **1.4.4 Vendor Record**—Compile and review any previous project or services work conducted by each vendor (for the organization or for the customer) to check for vendor fit with this project. Use this when examining vendor business risk and vendor selection. Monitor and manage issues for this vendor.

Responsibility

Primary

- Project Manager
- Vendor

Alternates and Adjuncts

- Opportunity Manager (Alternate)
- PMO (Alternate)
- Project Executive (Sponsor)

The project manager (or alternatively, opportunity manager or PMO) applies project management skill, knowledge, and experience to construct and manage the *Vendor Profile*. An opportunity manager may be assigned to oversee this process element prior to a project manager being assigned. The opportunity manager may reside within the PMO, or the PMO may have direct responsibility for this process element. The project manager then has responsibility for maintaining this profile for the duration of the project, as vendors continue to be assigned or affiliated with the project. The vendor is often involved in this process element for purposes of collaborating and communicating vendor capability information and vendor project performance plans for consideration during the vendor selection process. The project executive (sponsor), as well as other project stakeholders, can conduct initial and interval examinations of the *Vendor Profile*, usually as a part of subsequent business case reviews.

Process Input

The following information, actions, materials, and resources represent relevant inputs to this process:

- *Project Profile* (process element 1.2), as concurrently developed
- *Staff Profile* (process element 1.3), as concurrently developed
- *Staff Plan* (process element 2.3), as concurrently or subsequently developed
- *Vendor Solicitation* (process step 2.4.1), as concurrently or subsequently developed
- *Vendor Proposal* (process step 2.4.3), as concurrently or subsequently developed
- Vendor capability brochures
- Vendor performance information and records
- Issues and actions information related to vendor selection and performance
- Solicitation documents (e.g., RFPs, RFIs, etc.), as released and provided by the customer

Process Output (Project Management Deliverable)

The primary output of this process is the *Vendor Profile*, and one is created and maintained for each vendor. This profile contains information that facilitates aspects of the vendor selection and acquisition process, and assists in vendor performance management.

1.5 BUSINESS PROFILE

This process element creates a *Business Profile* that is an essential part of the project selection process. It allows the project manager to document the business advantages to be achieved, and it enables senior and executive managers to examine the opportunity relative to its potential to fulfill business interests and achieve strategic business objectives. The project manager and business development manager, or key alternates, compile a significant amount of information about the opportunity, screen that information against established project selection criteria, conduct an examination of business risk, and prepare the business case along with project selection recommendations for review by decision makers in the organization.

Schedule/Timing

The *Business Profile* can be initiated in conjunction with constructing the Customer Profile and Project Profile, and normally should be reviewed for consistency with the Staff Profile. The resulting profile is maintained and updated at intervals in the project to ensure that the business case remains valid for the duration of the project.

Process Steps and Toolkit Reference

The following four process steps will be accomplished to create the *Business Profile*:

- **1.5.1 Business Case**—Obtain and examine relevant business information as a basis for making a project selection decision. Use this information in combination with other profile sheets to answer the fundamental question, "Why should this project be selected?"
- **1.5.2 Business Risk Examination**—Compile and review previous project work and associated business results for business risks that could be encountered with the selection and performance of this project. A general review of risk areas should be followed by a detailed analysis of business risks.
- **1.5.3 Business Financial Analysis**—Compile and review any previous project work and associated business results to ascertain the cost/benefits of performing this project. Select the financial analyses to be performed, conduct the analyses, and enter the results of each analysis.
- **1.5.4 Business Recommendation**—Review the business case, along with other profile information and project definition to develop a recommendation for project selection. Also, identify the prominent selection criteria used, and summarize the prepared pro-and-con arguments.

Responsibility

Primary

- Project Manager
- Business Development Manager

Alternates and Adjuncts

- Opportunity Manager (Alternate)
- PMO (Alternate)
- Project Executive (Sponsor)
- Executive Control Board

The project manager (or alternatively, opportunity manager or PMO), usually in collaboration with the business development manager, applies project and business skill and insight to prepare and manage the *Business Profile*. An opportunity manager may be assigned to oversee this process element prior to a project manager being assigned. The opportunity manager may reside within the PMO, or the PMO may have direct responsibility for this process element. The project manager then has responsibility for maintaining this profile for the duration of the project to ensure that the business case remains valid until project completion. The executive control board is usually responsible for determining and providing the project selection criteria applied in business case preparation. It is also responsible for conducting a review of the business case as a basis for project selection. The project executive (sponsor), as well as other project stakeholders, should conduct initial and interval examinations of the *Business Profile*, usually as a part of subsequent business case reviews and project gateway reviews.

Process Input

The following information, actions, materials, and resources represent relevant inputs to this process:

- *Customer Profile* (process element 1.1), as concurrently developed, and when finalized

- *Project Profile* (process element 1.2), as concurrently developed, and when finalized
- *Staff Profile* (process element 1.3), as concurrently developed
- *Vendor Profile* (process element 1.4), as concurrently developed
- Financial analysis worksheets, as completed
- Business information and performance records, from project management archives
- Solicitation documents (e.g., RFPs, RFIs, etc.), as released and provided by the customer

Process Output (Project Management Deliverable)

The primary output of this process is the *Business Profile*. This profile contains information that enables management to review key elements in the Business Recommendation process step to render a business decision regarding project selection. It also includes the specification and commitment of funding for projects that are selected.

1.6 MANAGEMENT PROFILE

This process element creates a *Management Profile* that enables the project manager, project executive (sponsor), and other key project stakeholders to establish the project as a viable work effort in the organization. It will provide information that enables the project manager to support senior manager and executive oversight requirements relative to the project just selected. It will provide for the collection and review of preliminary information about the portfolio into which the project is being integrated, and it will help manage the transition from opportunity to project. It provides for the project charter, with particular emphasis on specifying the authority of the project manager. Over time, the information compiled in this process element will assist the project manager and others in making and communicating project management decisions that are consistent with management's business interests, requirements, and expectations for the project.

Schedule/Timing

The *Management Profile* is created to start the project. It can be prepared upon notification of project selection from process element 1.5. The resulting profile is maintained and updated throughout the project's duration, as management participation and decisions occur.

Process Steps and Toolkit Reference

The following four process steps will be accomplished to create the *Management Profile*:

- **1.6.1 Management Directory**—Identify and record the internal management contacts that will oversee or otherwise influence project performance, establish the contract or agreement, collaborate work planning, allocate staff, facilitate customer and vendor relationships, and manage deliverables and associated invoicing and payments.
- **1.6.2 Management Portfolio**—Examine the project for integration to the applicable portfolio in the organization, and establish the project priority and schedule for project and portfolio reviews. Identify the executive (sponsor), executive team, or control board responsible for portfolio management, and for subsequent project and portfolio reviews.
- **1.6.3 Management Charter**—Identify the project manager and specify the range of the project manager's authority and responsibility. Identify the managers having various types of oversight responsibility for the project, and the persons to whom the project manager can turn when issues of authority need to be resolved or otherwise elevated.
- **1.6.4 Management Record**—Manage information relative to management team requirements and preparations for, and conduct of, portfolio and project performance reviews. Monitor and record other management activities and involvement in project management oversight and in pre- and postproject activities.

Responsibility

Primary

- Project Manager
- Project Executive (Sponsor)

Alternates and Adjuncts

- Opportunity Manager (Alternate)
- PMO (Alternate)
- Project Control Board

The project manager (or alternatively, opportunity manager or PMO) uses information about participating senior managers and executives, along with any relevant senior manager or executive guidance, to prepare and manage the *Management Profile*. An opportunity manager may be assigned to oversee this process element that results in a project manager being assigned. The opportunity manager may reside within the

PMO, or the PMO may have direct responsibility for this process element. The project manager then has responsibility for maintaining this profile for the duration of the project to ensure, in particular, that project executive (sponsor) involvement in the project is optimized. Executive control board actions and activities may also be monitored under this process element. The project executive (sponsor), as well as other project stakeholders, may request interval examinations of the *Management Profile*, usually as a part of subsequent business case or project performance reviews.

Process Input

The following information, actions, materials, and resources represent relevant inputs to this process:

- *Business Profile* (process element 1.5), when finalized or as updated
- Senior manager and executive meeting schedules
- Senior manager and executive business decisions relevant to the project
- Issues and actions elevated to the senior management and executive level
- Senior manager and executive project portfolio management decisions relevant to the project

Process Output (Project Management Deliverable)

The primary output of this process is the *Management Profile*. This profile contains information that enables the project manager to maintain senior manager and executive involvement and interest in the project, and to monitor their participation in project decisions and activities.

Chapter 2

Phase 2: Plan Processes

2.1 CUSTOMER PLAN

This process element creates the *Customer Plan* as a single point of reference for information on the customer's perspective on the technical aspects of project work. This information will help ensure that the customer's perspective and the project team's perspective are consistent. In maintaining that consistent perspective, the project will achieve the end results desired by the customer.

The process prompts users in gathering, documenting, analyzing, and validating the customer's requirements for the project. This leads to the development of the technical approach that is used to fulfill customer requirements, and includes specification of project milestones and deliverables. A Change Control Plan is prepared and implemented, and a Quality Management Plan is introduced to guide development of project deliverables in a manner that achieves the customer acceptance for each deliverable.

Schedule/Timing

The *Customer Plan* can be created immediately following project selection and is normally the first process element to be pursued in the Plan Phase. Sometimes, the *Customer Plan* (particularly, the Customer Requirements process step) may be started in the Profile Phase; however, it necessarily needs to be completed early in the Plan Phase as the basis for much of the remaining project planning effort.

Process Steps and Toolkit Reference

The following four process steps will be accomplished to create the *Customer Plan*:

- **2.1.1 Customer Requirements**—Identify and compile information pertaining to the business, technical, and functional requirements of the project. Review source materials, and examine sources to ensure consistent translation of needs and specifications to project requirements. List the requirements, and then validate them to create a baseline.
- **2.1.2 Customer Technical Solution**—Identify the technical solution (technical approach) to be used to fulfill customer requirements, noting the type of technical effort to be performed and examining associated technical requirements. Specify the deliverables and milestones to be monitored and achieved—this supersedes the initial list in the Project Definition.
- **2.1.3 Customer Change Control Plan**—Identify the means by which changes to project scope and customer requirements will be requested, reviewed, approved, and implemented. Maintain a central log of change requests, and monitor and manage their approval and implementation; monitor cost (value) associated with implementing approved changes.
- **2.1.4 Customer Quality Management Plan**—Identify the standards to be used and the means by which quality assurance and quality control activities will be performed. Specify quality testing requirements, procedures, and customer acceptance criteria for associated project deliverables. Identify, schedule, and conduct quality testing and project quality technical reviews.

Responsibility

Primary

- Project Manager
- Project Planning Team Members
- Project Customer

Alternates and Adjuncts

- Project Team Members
- PMO
- Project Executive (Sponsor)

The project manager performs or assigns planning team members (or adjunct project team members) to perform requirements review activities and to develop the change control plan and the quality management plan. The business development manager can provide follow-on collaboration and input during the requirements-gathering step. The project manager leads the project team members in constructing the technical solution. The project manager and project executive (sponsor), sometimes with PMO participation, meet with the project customer, collaborate and review documented requirements and establish a requirements baseline for the project. They also collaborate and review the quality management plan for concurrence by all participants.

Process Input

The following information, actions, materials, and resources represent relevant input to this process:

- *Customer Profile* (process element 1.1)
- *Project Profile* (process element 1.2), with focus on Project Definition content (process step 1.2.1)
- Results and outcomes from customer requirements meetings, interviews, and workshops
- Solicitation documents (e.g., RFPs, RFIs, etc.), as released and provided by the customer
- Other customer requirements documentation
- Quality standards and metrics
- Established procedures from prior related project plans

Process Output (Project Management Deliverable)

The primary output of this process element is the documentation and review of mutually agreed upon Customer Requirements. It also provides the Change Control Plan and the Quality Management Plan that will help monitor and control project requirements, as well as facilitate the customer's acceptance of project deliverables, as occurs during the Perform Phase of project management.

2.2 PROJECT PLAN

This process element creates several key components of the *Project Plan* that will be used to guide the project management effort. The Project Plan is generally considered to be the compilation of all primary and supporting plans used on the project. The creation of the project plan begins with the development of the Project Work Plan, which includes a work breakdown structure (WBS) with cost, schedule, and resource estimates aligned for each WBS "work package" element. The Project Work Plan (containing the WBS) is often considered to be the primary tool of project management. It also establishes thresholds for managing cost, schedule, and resource utilization variance during the project.

Then, a Project Risk Management Plan is created, and it provides a risk management log for monitoring identified project risks. This is followed by the creation of the Project Communication Plan, which guides information exchange and includes procedures for project reporting and project document control. The final activity in this process element is the examination of needs and associated development of any other Project Support Plans needed, as determined by the project manager or established guidance.

Schedule/Timing

The *Project Plan* can be created following project selection, but it is usually accomplished in conjunction with or immediately following the completion of the *Customer Plan* process element.

Process Steps and Toolkit Reference

The following four process steps will be accomplished to create the *Project Plan*:

- **2.2.1 Project Work Plan**—Apply prescribed procedures and prepare a WBS with cost, schedule, and resource estimates to guide project work. List the summary-level results of WBS construction, and identify variance thresholds to be monitored. Use automated tools or extension sheets to show further task decomposition.
- **2.2.2 Project Risk Management Plan**—Develop procedures to identify, analyze, and prioritize project risks that have a high probability of occurrence or a high impact on the project. Prepare and maintain a project risk management log to summarize and monitor major project risks. Specify procedures for performing ongoing project risk management activities.

- **2.2.3 Project Communication Plan**—Develop the approach for managing project communication. Identify requirements and protocols for project information exchange and collaboration with various project stakeholders. Specify issue and problem escalation procedures. Prepare project report and document management procedures and a distribution matrix.
- **2.2.4 Project Support Plans**—Review project management, technical and business planning requirements, and identify the individual project support plans that will be used in the project effort. Manage plan preparation activities.

Responsibility

Primary

- Project Manager
- Project Planning Team Members

Alternates and Adjuncts

- Project Team Members
- PMO
- Project Customer
- Project Executive (Sponsor)
- Business Development Manager

The project manager leads the project planning team (or adjunct project team) in developing the Project Work Plan. This planning effort can be facilitated by the PMO or other qualified facilitation resource. The business development manager can provide follow-on collaboration and input during the requirements-gathering step. The project manager leads the project planning team (or project team members selected for technical expertise) in constructing the technical solution. The PMO can contribute expert insight and review during technical solution development, and it may establish the capability to facilitate the work-planning effort. The project manager and project executive (sponsor) will normally collaborate and review the project work plan with the project customer. The project manager may also collaborate and review the Project Risk Management Plan, the Project Communication Plan, and any Project Support Plans with the project executive (sponsor), project customer, and other relevant project stakeholders, as appropriate. This series of plans is then distributed to the project team and other specified project stakeholders for implementation.

Process Input

The following information, actions, materials, and resources represent relevant input to this process:

- *Customer Profile* (process element 1.1)
- *Project Profile* (process element 1.2), with focus on *Project Definition* content (process step 1.2.1)
- *Customer Plan* (process element 2.1)
- Any project management plans and project support plans that require WBS action elements, as concurrently or subsequently prepared
- Standards and metrics for estimating project cost, schedule, and resource utilization
- Established procedures from prior related project plans

Process Output (Project Management Deliverable)

The primary output of this process element is the documentation and review of a mutually agreed upon *Project Work Plan*. It also provides for a *Project Risk Management Plan* and a *Project Communication Plan*, and well as additional *Project Support Plans* that are needed.

2.3 STAFF PLAN

This process element creates the *Staff Plan* that facilitates specifying, acquiring, and assigning the resources needed to conduct the project. It includes preparing a staff responsibility matrix and managing team formation to fulfill resource requirements. It also provides the mechanism, a resource request form, to expedite the resource acquisition process when resource managers external to the project are involved in contributing resources to the project effort. The *Staff Plan* also allows the project manager or other responsible individual to maintain relevant project team member information and to track individual assignments and performance.

Schedule/Timing

The *Staff Plan* can be created in conjunction with the Project Work Plan and finalized with the completed development of the project WBS. The *Staff Plan* in general may be prepared simultaneously with other project plan components.

Process Steps and Toolkit Reference

The following four process steps will be accomplished to create the *Staff Plan*:

- **2.3.1 Staff Requirements**—Review customer requirements and the technical solution to determine the project staff positions needed to perform this project. Specify the category and number of resources needed in the manpower matrix. List the staff roles (and code) by name or position title/technical discipline (e.g., engineer II) in the responsibility matrix.

- **2.3.2 Staff Management Plan**—Review project resource staffing requirements to prepare guidance for project team formation and management during the project. Include a sourcing analysis to identify how staff requirements will be filled. Maintain a log of group and individual training and development activities that make the team a cohesive, capable unit.
- **2.3.3 Staff Acquisition (Request)**—Compile, monitor, and manage information that is used to request project staff members and to oversee the staff acquisition and team formation process. Identify project staffing needs, prepare the acquisition request, and track the acquisition of staff resources.
- **2.3.4 Staff Assignments**—Compile, monitor, and manage information that is relevant to assigned project team members. Track individual project task assignments and associated work performance. Annotate leadership or task specialty assignments. A copy can be provided to the named staff member.

Responsibility

Primary

- Project Manager
- Project Planning Team Members
- Resource Managers

Alternates and Adjuncts

- Project Team Members
- PMO
- Project Executive (Sponsor)
- Executive Control Board

The project manager leads the project planning team (or adjunct project team members) in developing the resource requirements matrix to identify staffing needs and assigns project planning team members (or adjunct project team members) to prepare the associated Staff Management Plan. The project manager also oversees preparation of resource acquisition requests that are sent to and collaborated with internal resource managers. Resource managers' commitments of resources are tracked, and in some cases it will be necessary for the project manager to collaborate or even negotiate for resource time with individual resource managers. As resources are assigned to the project, the project manager and key assistants will work with the growing project team to develop its capability and cohesiveness. In turn, individual assignments and performance will be tracked and managed under this *Staff Plan*.

Process Input

The following information, actions, materials, and resources represent relevant input to this process:

- *Project Profile* (process element 1.2)
- *Customer Plan* (process element 2.1)
- *Project Plan* (process element 2.2), with focus on WBS and Work Plan content (process step 2.2.1)
- *Business Recommendation* (process step 1.5.4)
- *Management Charter* (process step 1.6.3)
- Any project plan elements and project support plans that prescribe project resource integration
- Standards and metrics for resource utilization
- Established procedures from prior related project plans

Process Output (Project Management Deliverable)

The primary output of this process element is the documentation and review of a *Staff Management Plan*. This plan includes a resource responsibility matrix, and the means to track and manage resource acquisition and project assignment performance.

2.4 VENDOR PLAN

This process element creates the *Vendor Plan* that facilitates acquiring and managing vendors needed to conduct designated parcels of project work. It includes preparing the vendor solicitation document (one for each set of unique work requirements that will be offered to vendors), specifying the approach to vendor management, and monitoring and evaluating vendor proposals for potential selection and contract award. The *Vendor Plan* also allows the project manager or other responsible individual to establish necessary vendor contracts (or subcontracts) that will be administered during vendor participation on the project.

Schedule/Timing

The *Vendor Plan* can be created in conjunction with the *Project Work Plan*, and finalized with the completed development of the project WBS. However, it can be initiated or updated at any time during the project, particularly at times when the need for vendor support is being addressed.

Process Steps and Toolkit Reference

The following four process steps will be accomplished to create the *Vendor Plan*:

- **2.4.1 Vendor Solicitation**—Identify the need for subcontracting or outsourcing, and describe the solutions needed in a statement of work. Indicate the WBS elements to which vendors will be assigned, and specify the vendor's deliverables.
- **2.4.2 Vendor Management Plan**—Review vendor subcontracting or outsourcing requirements that have bearing on the vendor's work effort. Prepare the plan that will guide vendor participation in the project, with focus on vendor integration and work performance.
- **2.4.3 Vendor Proposal Evaluation**—Monitor and manage information that is relevant to the vendor acquisition and selection process. Review vendor screening indicators, examine vendor interests and intent, and evaluate the vendor's proposal per the weighted factors specified in the associated solicitation.
- **2.4.4 Vendor Contract**—Compile the elements of the vendor contract (and modifications for each vendor contract), and execute the contract when a vendor agreement has been reached. Use this to guide and manage vendor work performance and project participation, and to track contract compliance matters.

Responsibility

Primary

- Project Manager
- Project Planning Team Members

Alternates and Adjuncts

- Vendor
- Contract Manager
- Project Team Members
- PMO

The project manager leads the project planning team (or adjunct project team members) in developing the Vendor Management Plan, which indicates where vendors are needed, when they will be acquired, and how they will be used and managed. Then the project manager leads the project planning team (or adjunct project team members), with contract manager collaboration, in developing the vendor solicitation, reviewing vendor proposals, selecting qualified vendors, and establishing the contracts needed to acquire vendor participation in the project. The PMO or a distinct internal contract management office might perform this activity on behalf of the organization and in lieu of the project manager. However, the project manager needs to be involved in all facets of vendor selection, as the responsibility then falls to the project manager to administer the vendor contract and manage vendor performance for the duration of the vendor's participation on the project. As well, relevant vendors may have varying degrees of involvement in this process element.

Process Input

The following information, actions, materials, and resources represent relevant input to this process:

- *Project Profile* (process element 1.2)
- *Vendor Profile* (process element 1.4)
- *Customer Plan* (process element 2.1), especially the Technical Solution (process step 2.1.2)
- *Project Plan* (process element 2.2), with focus on WBS and Work Plan content (process step 2.2.1)
- Any project plan elements and project support plans associated with vendor participation
- Standards and metrics for vendor proposal review and selection
- Established procedures from prior related project plans

Process Output (Project Management Deliverable)

The output of this process element is the *Vendor Plan*, with particular note of the Vendor Management Plan and the Vendor Contract (or subcontract). This plan and contract will guide oversight of vendor performance and management on the project.

2.5 BUSINESS PLAN

This process element creates the *Business Plan* as a single point of reference for information on the business aspects of project work. This information will help ensure that the customer's perspective and the project team's perspective are consistent with regard to the business being conducted. In maintaining that consistent perspective, the project will achieve the business interests and objectives associated with the project.

The process prompts users in gathering, documenting, analyzing, and validating the customer's business requirements for the project. This leads to the development of the business approach that will be applied to fulfill business requirements, and includes the specification of contract terms and conditions applicable to the project. It also includes the specification of pricing or cost for conducting the project. A business proposal is prepared (usually integrated with the technical proposal described in process step 2.1.2), and this is presented to the customer for review and acceptance. Upon acceptance of the proposal and award of the project, a business contract is prepared and executed to show the business relationship between the customer and the performing organization.

Schedule/Timing

The *Business Plan* can be created in conjunction with the *Project Work Plan* and finalized with the development of the project WBS. However, the *Business Plan* can be initiated or updated at any time during the project, particularly at times when business matters are being addressed in association with gateway reviews, or in association with contract administration.

Process Steps and Toolkit Reference

The following four process steps will be accomplished to create the *Business Plan*:

- **2.5.1 Business Requirements**—Obtain and review relevant internal and external business information as a basis for preparing the business solution and the business elements of the proposal for submittal to the customer. Ensure that customer-specified business factors and proposal evaluation factors are identified and addressed in the proposal.
- **2.5.2 Business Solution**—Identify the business solution (cost and pricing) that will be offered to fulfill customer requirements. Be sure to describe the type of management effort to be performed. Specify the pricing requirements and the desired contracting approach. Identify the preferred terms and conditions for the contract.
- **2.5.3 Business Proposal**—Identify proposal team members, and assign and track actions to develop and submit the combined technical and business proposal to the customer in a timely manner. Manage proposal preparation and submittal to the customer, and monitor customer proposal review and selection activities.
- **2.5.4 Business Contract**—Compile and review the elements of the customer contract or contract modification. Execute the contract when an agreement has been reached with the customer. Use this contract document to guide and manage project team work performance and to manage business aspects of the project.

Responsibility

Primary

- Project Manager
- Proposal Team
- Business Development Manager

Alternates and Adjuncts

- PMO (Alternate)
- Project Team Members
- Contract Manager
- Project Executive (Sponsor)

The project manager, usually in collaboration with the business development manager, leads the proposal team (or adjunct project team members) in developing the Customer Business Proposal. This responsibility may fall to the PMO if suitably equipped to perform this function. The technical solution component (created in process step 2.1.2) is combined with the business solution constructed in this process element. All designated participants conduct a review of internal and external business requirements to formulate a business solution that will be offered to the customer. A pricing strategy and a contracting strategy are developed to guide proposal preparation. The project manager (alternate: PMO) or designee performs administrative oversight of proposal writing and preparation activities, and then combines all proposal components for submittal to the customer. The project executive (sponsor) may review and approve the proposal at various stages of development and may be the signatory when the proposal is formalized as an offering to the customer. The project manager then monitors the customer's review and selection activities.

Process Input

The following information, actions, materials, and resources represent relevant input to this process:

- *Project Profile* (process element 1.2)
- *Vendor Profile* (process element 1.4), when vendors are key resources for the project effort
- *Business Profile* (process element 1.5), especially the Business Case (process step 1.5.1) and the Business Risk Examination (process step 1.5.2)
- *Customer Plan* (process element 2.1), especially the Technical Solution (process step 2.1.2)
- *Project Plan* (process element 2.2), with focus on WBS and Work Plan content (process step 2.2.1)
- Solicitation documents (e.g., RFPs, RFIs, etc.), as released and provided by the customer
- Any project plan elements and project support plans associated with contractual fulfillments
- Standards and metrics for business solution development

Process Output (Project Management Deliverable)

The output of this process element is the *Business Plan*, and includes key elements of the Business Proposal and the Business Contract. The *Business Plan* will guide the oversight of project management performance and fulfillment of business requirements on the project.

2.6 MANAGEMENT PLAN

This process element creates the *Management Plan* that specifies and facilitates the oversight, control, and support required for the project. This plan is developed from the perspective of the project manager but may be used by other managers as well. In particular, it identifies how PMO involvement and senior management guidance will be integrated into the project management effort. To a large extent, the Management Oversight Plan represents collaboration with the PMO to specify its oversight, control, and support responsibilities for the project (when a PMO exists). The *Management Plan* also identifies the project and portfolio reviews that will require PMO or senior management participation. Additionally, it provides guidance and serves as a repository for the project's Management Audit and Review Plan, the Management Facility Plan, and the Management Supply and Equipment Plan.

Schedule/Timing

The *Management Plan* can be created in conjunction with the technical solution and the business solution, or generally once customer requirements have been identified. Its content usually needs to be finalized prior to project execution (Perform Phase).

Process Steps and Toolkit Reference

The following four process steps will be accomplished to create the *Management Plan*:

- **2.6.1 Management Oversight Plan**—Review management requirements and prepare guidance for PMO and senior manager involvement during the project. Specify PMO and Executive Control Board responsibilities and support requirements, and maintain a log of management oversight activities.
- **2.6.2 Management Audit and Review Plan**—Identify requirements and specify procedures for conducting project, business, and technical performance audits and reviews. Examine and specify the types of audits and reviews to be conducted. Maintain a project audit and review log.
- **2.6.3 Management Facility Plan**—Identify and manage the requirements, acquisition, assignment, use, and disposition of one or more facilities (or work locations) required for the project. Maintain a facility management activity log.
- **2.6.4 Management Supply and Equipment Plan**—Identify the internal requisition and external (vendor) sources for project supplies, materials, and equipment; monitor and manage project supply requests, acquisition, and utilization. Maintain a supply and equipment log.

Responsibility

Primary

- Project Manager
- Project Planning Team Members
- PMO

Alternates and Adjuncts

- Project Team Members
- Project Executive (Sponsor)
- Executive Control Board

The project manager, usually in collaboration with the PMO, leads the planning team members (or adjunct project team members) in identifying PMO and management oversight, control, and support responsibilities. This responsibility may fall to the PMO, which could have a standard approach for these procedures. The project manager may also collaborate with the project executive (sponsor; alternate: executive control board) to discuss his or her desired level of participation and to arrange and schedule follow-on project and portfolio review meetings. The project manager then leads the planning team members (or adjunct project team members) in preparing the Management Audit and Review Plan, the Management Facility Plan, and the Management Supply and Equipment Plan associated with this process element.

Process Input

The following information, actions, materials, and resources represent relevant input to this process:

- *Project Profile* (process element 1.2), with focus on *Project Definition* content (process step 1.2.1)
- *Vendor Profile* (process element 1.4), when vendors are key suppliers for the project effort
- *Business Profile* (process element 1.5)
- *Customer Plan* (process element 2.1), especially the *Technical Solution* (process step 2.1.2)

- *Project Plan* (process element 2.2), with focus on WBS and *Work Plan* content (process step 2.2.1)
- *Business Plan* (process element 2.5), especially the *Business Solution* (process step 2.5.2)
- Any project plan elements and project support plans associated with management requirements
- Solicitation documents (e.g., RFPs, RFIs, etc.), as released and provided by the customer
- Senior manager and executive meeting schedules
- Senior manager and executive business decisions relevant to the project
- Senior manager and executive project portfolio management decisions relevant to the project

Process Output (Project Management Deliverable)

The output of this process element is the *Management Plan* that identifies and guides the oversight, control, and support activities of the PMO and other managers, as required for the project.

Chapter 3

Phase 3: Perform Processes

3.1 CUSTOMER PERFORMANCE

This process element monitors and manages customer project participation, collaboration, and interactions. It provides for requisite project and business meetings conducted with the customer, and it specifies the reports and report content for conveying relevant project information to the customer. These actions and communication, in turn, help the customer to be informed about project status and progress; to provide reactions, responses, and guidance back to the performing organization; and to examine and determine the level of need for customer participation in the business, technical, and project management aspects of the project.

The process also prompts oversight of project change control activities and the customer's acceptance of project deliverables. Project change control inherently involves customer approval, and this process element guides the performance of change control, including pre- and postcustomer change approval actions. Prescribed activities for customer acceptance monitoring and management are also presented.

Schedule/Timing

The *Customer Performance* process is usually introduced as a recurring set of activities when the project advances to the Perform Phase. Also, some process steps, such as the meetings process step, can be used in association with activities contained in earlier and later project management phases. This process element can be accessed at any time that customer communication and collaboration is needed.

Process Steps and Toolkit Reference

The following four process steps will be accomplished as part of *Customer Performance* activities.

- **3.1.1 Customer Meeting**—Specify the location and planned arrangements for the customer meeting to be conducted. Identify and notify the meeting participants. Prepare and include the meeting agenda for premeeting review and preparation by customer-meeting participants.
- **3.1.2 Customer Status Report**—Identify the general state of the project along with any pertinent problem areas for customer awareness. Specify general variance and project deliverable status for the period. Prepare a brief discussion of key project activities, and request customer assistance as needed.
- **3.1.3 Customer Change Management**—Identify the change requested and include a brief description of pre- and postchange conditions. Evaluate and recommend change request disposition—describe the implementation effort and project impacts. Obtain approvals, and implement the approved project change.
- **3.1.4 Customer Acceptance Management**—Specify the project deliverables and associated acceptance criteria under consideration. Monitor internal and external deliverables testing, and manage the customer's response to each interim and final test. Obtain formal customer review and acceptance for each deliverable.

Responsibility

Primary

- Project Manager
- Project Team Members
- Project Customer
- Project Executive (Sponsor)

Alternates and Adjuncts

- PMO
- Business Development Manager

The project manager performs or assigns project team members to conduct customer meetings and to prepare and submit recurring and special reports for customer review. The project manager will normally lead customer meeting activities or defer to the customer's representatives for such purposes. From time to time, the project manager should invite the project executive (sponsor) to selected meetings with the customer. Also, the project executive (sponsor) may opt to hold independent meetings with the customer, usually at higher management levels in the customer's organization. The project manager should review and sign all reports presented to the customer. In some organizations, the business development manager may be involved in customer meetings and could be "copied" on reports sent to the customer. The PMO may, from time to time, be involved in customer meetings and other customer interactions as deemed necessary.

Process Input

The following information, actions, materials, and resources, with general application to customer meetings and reporting, represent relevant input to this process:

- *Customer Profile* (process element 1.1)
- *Project Profile* (process element 1.2), with focus on *Project Definition* content (process step 1.2.1)
- *Customer Change Control Plan* (process step 2.1.3)
- *Customer Quality Management Plan* (process step 2.1.4)
- *Project Plan* (process element 2.2)
- Quality standards and metrics
- Established procedures from prior related project plans

Process Output (Project Management Deliverable)

The output of this process element includes the following items and actions:

- Documentation and review of customer meeting agendas and any meeting follow-on actions
- Customer review and response to Customer Status Reports
- Customer review and approval of change control actions (as required)
- Achievement of customer acceptance of one or more project deliverables

3.2 PROJECT PERFORMANCE

This process element monitors and manages project status and progress. It serves as the basis for collecting and compiling various types of project information and project data that are used in many of the reports prepared in the Perform Phase. It guides project tracking activities and facilitates the introduction of remedies and controls for poor project performance.

The *Project Performance* process element monitors project risks, including identifying any new project risks. It ensures that risk events are tracked and managed, and that risk response strategies are implemented when needed. It provides for oversight of project communication and implementation of the Project Communication Plan. It similarly monitors and manages "performance" of all relevant project plans as they compose the overall Project Plan.

Schedule/Timing

The *Project Performance* process is usually started as a recurring set of activities when the project enters the Perform Phase. Some process steps may linger for use in the Post Phase.

Process Steps and Toolkit Reference

The following four process steps will be accomplished as part of *Project Performance* activities:

- **3.2.1 Project Tracking and Control Report**—Review pertinent project management indicators on a routine, recurring basis. Examine and report project variance (cost, schedule, and resource utilization) and earned value, and apply project management controls or corrective actions as needed.
- **3.2.2 Project Risk Management**—Examine current project risks for control and abatement. Evaluate new risks to identify, analyze, and prioritize those that have a high probability of occurrence or a high impact on the project. Implement the risk response strategy for each priority project risk as needed.
- **3.2.3 Project Communication Management**—Compile and maintain logs and information related

to project management and oversight. Establish the Document Management Log, the Correspondence Management Log, and the Consolidated Project Issue Management Log, as needed.

- **3.2.4 Project Plan Management**—Compile and maintain a log and information related to project plan management and oversight. Perform and list all relevant actions related to project plan creation, review, update, distribution, and implementation.

Responsibility

Primary

- Project Manager
- Project Team Members

Alternates and Adjuncts

- PMO
- Executive Control Board
- Project Planning Team Members

The project manager leads the project team in collecting and analyzing project performance information. The analysis normally should include the calculation of earned value and related variance analysis constructs. In turn, the project manager prepares the recurring Tracking and Control Report as a basis for identifying project progress and status. The project manager maintains surveillance over project risk through implementation and constant updating of the Project Risk Management Plan. Project team members are assigned or otherwise guided in the preparation and use of communications and document control logs. The project manager, with likely project team assistance, will implement issue management procedures and introduce the use of an issue management log. Project performance is reliant upon guidance provided in the form of the Project Work Plan as well as accompanying primary and secondary project plans. This process allows the project manager and project team to keep track of plan effectiveness as well as to monitor and document plan revisions and updates. The PMO may be involved in recurring reviews and analyses of reports prepared by the project manager and the project team, as will the project executive (sponsor) and members of the executive control board.

Process Input

The following information, actions, materials, and resources represent relevant input to this process:

- *Project Profile* (process element 1.2)
- *Project Plan* (process element 2.2), with focus on the *Project Work Plan* (process step 2.2.1), along with attention to the *Project Risk Management Plan* (process step 2.2.2), *Project Communication Plan* (process step 2.2.3), and any primary and secondary project management plans that have been developed and implemented
- *Project Status Reports* from individual project team members and subteams (process step 3.3.2)
- Issues and communication logs

Process Output (Project Management Deliverable)

The primary output of this process element is the Project Tracking and Control Report. Other outputs include use, review, and possible revisions of the Project Work Plan, Project Risk Management Plan, and Project Communication Plan, as well as any additional Project Support Plans that have been developed.

3.3 STAFF PERFORMANCE

This process element is used to monitor and manage project staff performance and to guide project staff participation, collaboration, and interactions. It provides for requisite project and business meetings conducted with project team members, and it specifies the reports and report content for conveying relevant project team member work progress to the project manager. In turn, the project manager will be sufficiently informed about individual team member progress and performance to provide reactions, responses, and guidance back to each project team member and the project team as a whole.

The process incorporates activities to conduct project team member performance reviews. It also includes steps for reporting conditions of staff strength and management allocation fulfillment to organizational management (i.e., the project executive [sponsor] and the executive control board).

Schedule/Timing

The *Staff Performance* process is inherently a part of project management activities in the Perform Phase. Some process steps, such as staff meetings and reporting, may be used in earlier phases, and others may linger for use in the Post Phase.

Process Steps and Toolkit Reference

The following four process steps will be accomplished as part of *Staff Performance* activities:

- **3.3.1 Staff Meeting**—Specify the location and planned arrangements for the staff meeting to be conducted. Identify and notify the meeting participants. Prepare and include the meeting agenda for premeeting review and preparation by staff meeting participants.
- **3.3.2 Staff Status Report**—Identify the staff member and the general progress of project task assignments, along with any pertinent issues or problems for project manager attention. Prepare a brief discussion of key project activities and request project manager/supervisor assistance as needed.
- **3.3.3 Staff Performance Review**—Identify the staff member and relevant information pertaining to the member's project assignment. Specify general ratings for each performance category and overall. List staff member performance comments for discussion and conduct a performance review meeting.
- **3.3.4 Staff Management Report**—Identify the current status of project staff strength. Specify staff strength forecasts and identify status of critical positions to be filled. Prepare a brief discussion of pertinent project staff management actions and request PMO/management assistance as needed.

Responsibility

Primary

- Project Manager
- Project Team Members

Alternates and Adjuncts

- Resource Managers
- Project Team Members (Technical Leaders)
- PMO
- Project Executive (Sponsor)

The project manager performs or assigns project team members (usually designated technical leaders) to conduct project staff meetings and to prepare and submit recurring and special reports for project manager review. However, the project manager should normally lead staff meeting activities when possible. From time to time, the project manager should invite the project executive (sponsor) to selected meetings with the project staff.

The project manager has primary responsibility for performing project staff management on most projects. This includes preparing and conducting staff performance reviews. This responsibility may be shared with resource managers in some organizations. For some larger projects, certain activities such as staff management and staff performance reviews may be delegated to interim-level technical managers.

The project manager is usually the primary point of contact for preparation and submittal of staff management reports that are presented for management review.

Process Input

The following information, actions, materials, and resources represent relevant input to this process:

- *Staff Profile* (process element 1.3)
- *Management Charter* (process element 1.6.3)—also known as the *Project Charter*
- *Customer Plan* (process element 2.1), with focus on the *Customer Technical Solution* content (process step 2.1.2), and attention to the *Customer Change Control Plan* (process step 2.1.3) and the *Customer Quality Management Plan* (process step 2.1.4).
- *Project Plan* (process element 2.2), with focus on *WBS* and *Project Work Plan* content (process step 2.2.1)
- *Staff Plan* (process element 2.3), with focus on *Staff Management Plan* content (process step 2.3.2)
- Any project plan elements and project support plans that prescribe project staff management activities

Process Output (Project Management Deliverable)

The primary output of this process element is the development of a cohesive project staff that can accomplish planned project work in a timely and efficient manner, consistent with project objectives and customer expectations. Additional output includes project staff performance reviews and associated performance review meetings, and reports to management on project staff strength and performance.

3.4 VENDOR PERFORMANCE

This process element is used to monitor and manage vendor performance and to guide vendor participation, collaboration, and interactions. It provides for requisite project and business meetings conducted with project vendors, and it specifies the reports and report content for conveying relevant vendor work progress to the project manager. In turn, the project manager will be sufficiently informed about vendor progress and performance to provide reactions, responses, and guidance back to each project vendor. The process incorporates activities to conduct project vendor performance reviews. It also specifies guidance for conducting vendor contract administration.

Schedule/Timing

The *Vendor Performance* process is inherently part of project management activities in the Perform Phase. Some process steps, such as vendor meetings and reporting, may be used in earlier phases, and others may linger for use in the Post Phase. In particular, the Vendor Contract Administration process is used in the Perform Phase, with some residual vendor contract administrative activity in the Post Phase.

Process Steps and Toolkit Reference

The following four process steps will be accomplished as part of *Vendor Performance* activities:

- **3.4.1 Vendor Meeting**—Specify the location and planned arrangements for the vendor meeting to be conducted. Identify and notify the meeting participants. Prepare and include the meeting agenda for premeeting review and preparation by vendor meeting participants.
- **3.4.2 Vendor Status Report**—Identify the vendor's task leader and pertinent vendor information. List the general progress of vendor task assignments. Prepare a brief discussion of key vendor project activities and request project manager assistance as needed.
- **3.4.3 Vendor Performance Review**—Identify the vendor and relevant information pertaining to the vendor's project assignment. Specify general vendor ratings for each performance category and overall. List vendor performance comments for discussion and conduct a performance review meeting.
- **3.4.4 Vendor Contract Administration**—Identify each vendor and associated vendor contract information. Conduct vendor contract reviews as needed. Summarize vendor contract performance status. Identify any administrative or legal activity associated with a listed vendor's contract.

Responsibility

Primary

- Project Manager
- Project Team Members
- Vendors

Alternates and Adjuncts

- Project Team Members (Technical Managers)
- PMO
- Project Executive (Sponsor)
- Contract Manager

The project manager performs or assigns project team members (usually designated technical leaders) to conduct vendor meetings. In turn, the project vendors attend meetings and prepare and submit recurring and special vendor reports for project manager review. The project manager should normally attend vendor meetings and provide project leadership within such activities. From time to time, the project manager may invite the project executive (sponsor) or PMO representative to selected meetings with project vendors.

The project manager has primary responsibility for vendor management on most projects. This includes preparing and conducting vendor performance reviews and overseeing vendor contract administration. This responsibility may be delegated to those qualified technical leaders on the project team, particularly for some larger projects or for projects having multiple vendor participation. Vendor management and performance evaluation also may be conducted in collaboration with the PMO in some organizations.

The project manager also has responsibility for ensuring that the contractual obligations of each vendor, as well as those of the performing organization, are fulfilled. The project manager may call on or otherwise defer to the expertise of the internal contract manager to help accomplish vendor contract management.

The project manager is usually the primary point of contact for preparation of vendor management reports that are presented for management review. The project manager is also normally the primary recipient of status reports prepared and submitted by project vendors.

Process Input

The following information, actions, materials, and resources represent relevant input to this process:

- *Vendor Profile* (process element 1.4)
- *Customer Plan* (process element 2.1), with focus on the *Customer Technical Solution* content (process step 2.1.2), and attention to the *Customer Change Control Plan* (process step 2.1.3) and the *Customer Quality Management Plan* (process step 2.1.4)
- *Project Plan* (process element 2.2), with focus on *WBS* and *Project Work Plan* content (as prepared in process step 2.2.1)
- *Vendor Plan* (process element 2.4), with focus on *Vendor Management Plan* content (as prepared in process step 2.4.2)
- Any project plan elements and project support plans that prescribe vendor management activities

Process Output (Project Management Deliverable)

The primary output of this process element is the integration of one or more vendors to accomplish planned project work in a timely and efficient manner, consistent with project objectives and customer expectations. Additional output includes project vendor performance reviews and associated vendor performance review meetings, along with vendor status reports to the project manager and project manager reports to management on project vendor contracts and performance.

3.5 BUSINESS PERFORMANCE

This process element is used to monitor and manage business performance and to guide project managers toward the achievement of organizational business interests and objectives. It provides for project and business meetings conducted to discuss and deliberate business conditions, and it specifies the reports and report content for conveying relevant business status and progress within the performing organization. In turn, the project manager, project executive (sponsor), and other stakeholders in the organization will be sufficiently informed about the extent to which the project is influencing business outcomes.

The process incorporates activities to conduct business performance reviews. It also specifies guidance for conducting the business contract administration.

Schedule/Timing

The *Business Performance* process is incorporated as a part of project management activities in the Perform Phase. Some residual business contract administrative activity may occur in the Post Phase.

Process Steps and Toolkit Reference

The following four process steps will be accomplished as part of *Business Performance* activities:

- **3.5.1 Business Meeting**—Specify the location and planned arrangements for the business meeting to be conducted. Identify and notify the meeting participants. Prepare and include the meeting agenda for premeeting review and preparation by business-meeting participants.
- **3.5.2 Business Status Report**—Identify key business information and review preferred business indicators related to the project. Compile the expense (costs) summary for the report period and incorporate revenue numbers to complete the financial analysis portion of the report.
- **3.5.3 Business Performance Review**—Identify the project portfolio owner/manager and relevant portfolio information. Specify general ratings for each performance category and overall. List comments for discussion and provide recommendations for managing business aspects of the project.
- **3.5.4 Business Contract Administration**—Identify business contract information. Conduct customer contract reviews as may be needed. Summarize business contract performance status. Identify any administrative or legal activity associated with the customer's business contract.

Responsibility

Primary

- Project Manager
- Project Executive (Sponsor)

Alternates and Adjuncts

- Contract Manager
- PMO (Alternate)
- Executive Control Board
- Project Team Members
- Business Development Manager

The project manager leads the project team in collecting and analyzing project performance information having business relevance. In turn, the project manager prepares the recurring Business Status Report as a basis for identifying business outcomes associated with the project. The project manager, with likely executive-level guidance, will implement controls and actions resulting from management review of the Business Status Report. Business performance is evaluated relative to the project's Business Case and other business guidance. This process allows the project manager and project team to keep track of contributions of the project to business. To that end, the project manager is responsible for overseeing business contract administration and ensuring that qualified individuals have been delegated appropriate authority to work with the customer on contract administration matters.

The PMO, project executive (sponsor), and any relevant executive control board will also be involved in reviewing and responding to business reports and associated matter, giving guidance to the project manager as necessary to maintain the business perspectives of the project.

Process Input

The following information, actions, materials, and resources represent relevant input to this process:

- *Business Profile* (process element 1.5)
- *Customer Plan* (process element 2.1), with focus on the *Customer Technical Solution* content (process step 2.1.2), and attention to the *Customer Change Control Plan* (process step 2.1.3) and the *Customer Quality Management Plan* (process step 2.1.4)
- *Project Plan* (process element 2.2), with focus on WBS and *Work Plan* content (process step 2.2.1)
- *Business Plan* (process element 2.5), with focus on *Business Contract* content (as prepared in process step 2.5.4)
- Any project plan elements and project support plans that prescribe management activities

Process Output (Project Management Deliverable)

The primary output of this process element is the oversight to accomplish planned project work in a manner that contributes to business efficiency and business success, consistent with project objectives and customer expectations. Additional output includes project business performance reviews and associated business performance review meetings, along with business status reports to management on project business contracts and business performance.

3.6 MANAGEMENT PERFORMANCE

This process element is used to monitor and manage management performance and to facilitate management participation, collaboration, and interactions associated with the project effort. It provides for project and business meetings conducted with the PMO, project executive (sponsor), and executive control board, and it specifies the reports and report content for conveying relevant project management information. In turn, the executive-level managers of the organization will be sufficiently informed about their contributions and "performance" to provide reactions, responses, and guidance back to the project manager.

The process incorporates options to conduct management performance reviews. It also specifies guidance for conducting project management audits as an executive/PMO-directed effort.

Schedule/Timing

The *Management Performance* process is a part of project management activities in the Perform Phase. Some process steps, such as project and postproject audits, may be extended into the Post Phase.

Process Steps and Toolkit Reference

The following four process steps will be accomplished as part of *Management Performance* activities.

- **3.6.1 Management Meeting**—Specify the location and planned arrangements for the management meeting to be conducted. Identify and notify the meeting participants. Prepare and include the meeting agenda for premeeting review and preparation by management-meeting participants.
- **3.6.2 Management Report**—Identify the general state of the project, along with any pertinent problem areas for management awareness. Specify project variance and deliverable status for the period. Prepare a discussion of key project activities and request management assistance as needed.
- **3.6.3 Management Performance Review**—Identify the project portfolio owner/manager and relevant portfolio information. Specify review results relative to checklist items. List comments for discussion and provide recommendations for managing performance aspects of the project.
- **3.6.4 Management Audit and Review Report**—Outline key planning elements, identify documents reviewed and interviews conducted, specify pertinent audit/review findings, and determine corrective and follow-on actions that need to be performed, including the identification of responsible individuals.

Responsibility

Primary

- Project Manager
- Project Executive (Sponsor)

Alternates and Adjuncts

- PMO (Alternate)
- Executive Control Board (Alternate)
- Project Team Members

The project manager, usually in collaboration with the PMO, leads the project team members in identifying PMO and management oversight, control, and support performance outcomes. This responsibility may be retained by the PMO, which could have an advantageous position for collaborating with management relative to its performance and contributions. The project manager may also collaborate with the project executive (sponsor; alternate: executive control board) to review its level of involvement and to schedule its participation in project and portfolio review meetings. The project manager applies established guidance or current management directives to arrange and conduct any required project management audits on behalf of management.

Process Input

The following information, actions, materials, and resources represent relevant input to this process:

- *Business Profile* (process element 1.5)
- *Customer Plan* (process element 2.1), with focus on the *Customer Technical Solution* content (process step 2.1.2), and attention to the *Customer Change Control Plan* (process step 2.1.3) and the *Customer Quality Management Plan* (process step 2.1.4)
- *Project Plan* (process element 2.2), with focus on *WBS* and *Project Work Plan* content (process step 2.2.1)
- *Business Plan* (process element 2.5), with focus on *Business Contract* content (as prepared in process step 2.5.4)
- *Management Oversight Plan* (process step 2.6.1)
- *Management Audit and Review Plan* (process step 2.6.2)
- Any project plan elements and project support plans associated with management requirements
- Senior manager and executive meeting schedules
- Senior manager and executive business decisions relevant to the project
- Senior manager and executive project portfolio management decisions relevant to the project

Process Output (Project Management Deliverable)

The output of this process element includes deliberations, resolutions, and action items from meetings between the project manager and the PMO or senior managers of the organization, as well as Management Reports and management responses to them. The management performance reviews and associated business performance review meetings are also outcomes, along with any project management audit activity reports.

Chapter 4

Phase 4: Post Processes

4.1 CUSTOMER POSTING

This process element provides for project closeout activities associated with the customer. It prompts a meeting or other means of collaboration for discussion and identification of lessons learned relevant to the customer's participation in the project. It likewise facilitates an internal examination and evaluation of the customer's project participation by the project manager and project team members.

This process contains a customer satisfaction survey that enables the customer to provide independent feedback to the project manager on contentment with project performance and outcome.

This process includes activities that formally transition any resulting deliverables to the customer, ensure all required work is completed, track final invoicing and payment, and close out the customer's participation in the project relative to overall project closure. *Customer Posting* is completed when the customer signs off to acknowledge project closure.

Schedule/Timing

The *Customer Posting* process is primarily conducted during the Post Phase of the project. However, should any customer closeout activities be required earlier, perhaps due to early project termination, then this process could be applied in earlier phases of the project management life cycle. Similarly, for longer projects, some organizations prescribe surveys of customer satisfaction at mid-project or other intervals in the project. This would be another example of using this process earlier in the project.

Process Steps and Toolkit Reference

The following four process steps will be accomplished as part of *Customer Posting* activities:

- **4.1.1 Customer Lessons Learned**—Review the project from the perspective of customer activity and interactions, with a focus on what went well and what did not. Reference the short checklist and attempt an unbiased review. Identify conditions (lessons), but do not evaluate yet, as that is done in a separate activity. A facilitated group session is recommended.
- **4.1.2 Customer Evaluation**—Conduct an internal evaluation of the project experience with the customer to rate indicators of customer performance. Identify key and notable customer contacts and provide comments about working with this customer.
- **4.1.3 Customer Satisfaction Survey**—This customer satisfaction survey is to be completed by the customer at the end of the project (or other designated interim evaluation period). The overview section can be filled in prior to distribution.
- **4.1.4 Customer Transition and Closeout**—Review customer transition and closeout activities with the customer and track their status toward completion. When completed, obtain the customer's sign-off for final deliverable acceptance and termination of the project. This generally concludes the customer business relationship portion of the project.

Responsibility

Primary

- Project Manager
- Project Team Members
- Project Customer
- Business Operations Manager (per any transition requirements)

Alternates and Adjuncts

- PMO
- Contract Manager
- Project Executive (Sponsor)
- Business Development Manager

The project manager performs or assigns project team members to conduct customer closeout activities. To the extent possible, the project manager should be directly involved with the customer at this juncture in the project to elicit customer feedback for lessons learned and to administer the customer satisfaction survey. Many of these activities can be performed by the PMO, but should at least be done with PMO collaboration. The project manager should also collaborate with the contract manager or other designated contract oversight person to review and issue a final invoice to the customer. In turn, customer payments need to be reviewed, and immediate acknowledgment is needed upon receipt of the customer's final payment. If not already done, the project manager needs to secure the customer's sign-off for deliverables acceptance and project closure. The business operations manager may be involved if there is a significant transition effort. The project executive (sponsor) and business development manager should meet or contact the customer in association with project closure activities.

Process Input

The following information, actions, materials, and resources are relevant input to the customer closeout prescribed by this process:

- *Customer Profile* (process element 1.1)
- *Project Profile* (process element 1.2)
- *Customer Change Control Plan* (process step 2.1.3)
- *Customer Quality Management Plan* (process step 2.1.4)
- *Project Work Plan* (process element 2.2)
- Any project plan elements and project support plans that prescribe project customer management activities
- Project deliverables and customer acceptance logs

Process Output (Project Management Deliverable)

The primary output of this process element is the documented sign-off by the customer to acknowledge that the project has been fulfilled and hereby closed. Other output includes the customer lessons learned, the customer satisfaction survey, and the completed customer closeout checklist.

4.2 PROJECT POSTING

This process element provides for project closeout activities associated with the project work effort and associated documentation. It prompts a meeting or other means of collaboration for discussion and identification of lessons learned relevant to the project performance and outcomes achieved. It likewise facilitates an internal examination and evaluation of the primary project management activities conducted by the project manager and project team members. This process also contains an administrative activity that enables the project team to review, close out, and store project materials and documentation for possible future use on similar projects.

This process prescribes a final activity that enables the project team to review and archive all relevant project planning documents for possible future use on similar projects—an effort focused on plans that complements the preceding administrative closeout actions. *Project Posting* is completed when all project materials, documents, and plans have been archived or otherwise stored for possible future use.

Schedule/Timing

The *Project Posting* process is primarily conducted during the Post Phase of the project. In some circumstances, materials and documents that have fulfilled their purpose can be administratively closed and stored or archived in earlier phases.

Process Steps and Toolkit Reference

The following four process steps will be accomplished as part of *Project Posting* activities:

- **4.2.1 Project Lessons Learned**—Review the project from the perspective of planned and actual work performance, with a focus on what went well and what did not. Reference the short checklist and attempt an unbiased review. Identify conditions (lessons), but do not evaluate yet, as that is done in a separate activity. A facilitated group session is recommended.
- **4.2.2 Project Performance Evaluation**—Conduct an internal examination of project planning and

management activities to rate indicators of project performance. Identify key and notable project contacts. Provide comments on managing this project's performance. Obtain management-level review.

- **4.2.3 Project Administration Closeout**—Compile project materials, work products, and documents as a reference list, and prepare them for archiving. When completed, obtain archive manager and project manager sign-off for this aspect of the project. This is normally the last closeout performed, and it concludes the communication and correspondence of the project.
- **4.2.4 Project Plan Closeout**—Compile project planning documents, including materials used for project estimating and any proposal documentation. List and prepare them for archiving. When completed, obtain plan manager and project manager sign-off. This concludes the plan documentation and change control portions of the project.

Responsibility

Primary

- Project Manager
- Project Team Members

Alternates and Adjuncts

- PMO
- Project Executive (Sponsor)

The project manager performs or assigns project team members to conduct project closeout activities. To the extent possible, the project manager should be directly involved with the project team at this juncture in the project to elicit project team member feedback for lessons learned and to conduct the project performance evaluation. Some of these activities can be performed by the PMO, but should at least be done with PMO collaboration. The project executive (sponsor) can be involved as deemed necessary in the examination of project performance.

Process Input

The following information, actions, materials, and resources represent relevant input to this process:

- *Project Profile* (process element 1.2)
- *Customer Change Control Plan* (process step 2.1.3)
- *Customer Quality Management Plan* (process step 2.1.4)
- *Project Work Plan* (process element 2.2)
- *Customer Performance documents* (process element 3.1)
- *Project Performance documents* (process element 3.2)

Process Output (Project Management Deliverable)

The output of this process element includes documentation of lessons learned relative to project performance, an evaluation of project performance, and the storage or archiving of project materials, documentation, and plans.

4.3 STAFF POSTING

This process element provides for project closeout activities associated with the project staff. It prompts a meeting or other means of collaboration for discussion and identification of lessons learned relevant to project team members' participation in the project. It likewise facilitates an internal examination and evaluation of the project team performance by the project manager and project team members themselves.

This process contains a team-level evaluation that enables the project manager to provide feedback to the project executive (sponsor) on project team performance and outcomes. It also provides a process step for recognizing the contributions of project team members, particularly those who have excelled in their work.

This process includes activities that enable project team members to be released from the project for reassignment to another project, return to their Resource Manager, or other staff disposition options. *Staff Posting* is completed when all project team members have been released from the project and are no longer charging time or expenses to the project.

Schedule/Timing

The *Staff Posting* process is primarily conducted during the Post Phase. However, should any project team member depart the project in an earlier phase for any reason, this process can also be applied in managing that individual's release and closeout from the project.

Process Steps and Toolkit Reference

The following four process steps will be accomplished as part of *Staff Posting* activities:

- **4.3.1 Staff Lessons Learned**—Review the project from the perspective of planned and actual project staffing, with a focus on what went well and what did not. Reference the short checklist and attempt an unbiased review. Identify conditions (lessons), but do not evaluate yet, as that is done in a separate activity. A facilitated group session is recommended.
- **4.3.2 Staff Performance Evaluation**—This internal evaluation is prepared by the project manager or any

supervisor of a distinct group within the project team to evaluate collective team performance. Identify key and notable project contacts. Obtain management-level review.

- **4.3.3 Staff Performance Recognition**—Specify the location and planned activities for the event. Prepare citations for staff members who have excelled in project work performance. Be sure to include staff members who left the project team prior to its official closure. Identify and notify the event participants.
- **4.3.4 Staff Reassignment and Closeout**—Monitor staff departures from the project upon completion of assignments and time commitments. Use the departure checklist for individual disposition and fill in the checklist for en masse team departures at the end of the project. List actual staff departures from the project team.

Responsibility

Primary

- Project Manager
- Project Team Members

Alternates and Adjuncts

- Resource Managers
- PMO
- Project Executive (Sponsor)
- Project Vendor

The project manager performs or assigns project team members to conduct staff closeout activities. To the extent possible, the project manager should be directly involved with the project team members at this juncture in the project to elicit project team member feedback for lessons learned and to conduct the project team performance evaluation. Some of these activities can be performed by the PMO, but should at least be done with PMO collaboration. The project executive (sponsor) should be involved, particularly in performance recognition activities, and possibly in the review and endorsement of project staff performance evaluations. As may be desired, project vendors can be included in performance recognition activities.

Process Input

The following information, actions, materials, and resources represent relevant input to this process:

- *Staff Profile* (process element 1.3)
- *Management Charter* (process step 1.6.3)—also known as the *Project Charter*
- *Customer Plan* (process element 2.1), with focus on the *Customer Technical Solution* content (process step 2.1.2), and attention to the *Customer Change Control Plan* (process step 2.1.3) and the *Customer Quality Management Plan* (process step 2.1.4)
- *Project Plan* (process element 2.2), with focus on *WBS* and *Project Work Plan* content (process step 2.2.1)
- *Staff Plan* (process element 2.3), with focus on *Staff Management Plan* content (process step 2.3.2)
- Any project plan elements and project support plans that prescribe project staff management activities

Process Output (Project Management Deliverable)

The output of this process element includes documentation of lessons learned relative to staff performance, an evaluation of staff performance, activities and actions used to recognize staff performance, and project team member release and reassignment from the project.

4.4 VENDOR POSTING

This process element provides for project closeout activities associated with project vendors. It prompts a meeting or other means of collaboration for discussion and identification of lessons learned relevant to vendor participation in the project. It likewise facilitates an internal examination and evaluation of vendor performance by the project manager and project team members.

This process includes activities to manage final vendor invoice submittal and payment. It also includes a process step for formal closeout of each vendor contract.

Schedule/Timing

The *Vendor Posting* process is primarily conducted during the Post Phase. However, when any project vendor departs the project in an earlier phase for any reason, then this process could be applied in managing that vendor's release and closeout from the project.

Process Steps and Toolkit Reference

The following four process steps will be accomplished as part of *Vendor Posting* activities:

- **4.4.1 Vendor Lessons Learned**—Review the project from the perspective of vendor activity and interactions, with a focus on what went well and what did not. Reference the short checklist and attempt an unbiased review. Identify conditions (lessons), but do not evaluate yet, as that is done in a separate activity. A facilitated group session is recommended.

- **4.4.2 Vendor Performance Evaluation**—Conduct an internal evaluation of the project experience with the selected vendors to rate indicators of vendor performance. Identify key and notable vendor contacts and provide comments on working with each vendor.
- **4.4.3 Vendor Invoice Management**—Post and manage vendor invoices for accuracy and timely submittal, as received throughout the project. Track vendor invoice receipts and payments, and perform invoice actions as necessary. Perform closeout of vendor invoices in association with the final payment to each vendor.
- **4.4.4 Vendor Contract Closeout**—Review vendor closeout activities with the vendor and track their status toward completion. When completed, obtain the vendor's sign-off for termination of vendor participation in the project. This generally concludes the vendor's business relationship portion of the project.

Responsibility

Primary

- Project Manager
- Project Team Members
- Project Vendor

Alternates and Adjuncts

- Contract Manager
- PMO
- Project Executive (Sponsor)

The project manager performs or assigns project team members to conduct vendor closeout activities. To the extent possible, the project manager should be directly involved with the project vendor at this juncture in the project to elicit vendor feedback for lessons learned and to conduct the vendor performance evaluation. Some of these activities can be performed by the PMO, but should at least be done with PMO collaboration. The project executive (sponsor) may be involved in final meetings with each vendor, particularly for any vendor recognition activities, and for reviewing the evaluation of vendor performance. As may be desired, project vendors can be included in performance recognition activities conducted for project team members.

Process Input

The following information, actions, materials, and resources represent relevant input to this process:

- *Vendor Profile* (process element 1.4)
- *Customer Plan* (process element 2.1), with focus on the *Customer Technical Solution* content (process step 2.1.2), and attention to the *Customer Change Control Plan* (process step 2.1.3) and the *Customer Quality Management Plan* (process step 2.1.4)
- *Project Plan* (process element 2.2), with focus on *WBS* and *Project Work Plan* content (process step 2.2.1)
- *Vendor Plan* (process element 2.4), with focus on *Vendor Management Plan* content (process step 2.4.2)
- *Vendor Performance* documents (process element 3.4), with focus on vendor invoice management
- Any project plan elements and project support plans that prescribe vendor management activities

Process Output (Project Management Deliverable)

The output of this process element includes documentation of lessons learned relative to vendor performance, an evaluation of vendor performance, activities and actions used to recognize vendor performance, and the vendor's final payment and release from the project.

4.5 BUSINESS POSTING

This process element provides for project closeout activities associated with the project's business elements. It prompts a meeting or other means of collaboration for discussion and identification of lessons learned relevant to the project's business contributions. It likewise facilitates an internal examination and evaluation of business performance by the project manager and project team members.

This process includes activities to manage final customer invoice submittal and payment. It also includes a process step for formal closeout of the business contract with the customer.

Schedule/Timing

The *Business Posting* process is primarily conducted during the Post Phase. However, when any project is terminated in an earlier phase, for any reason, then this process could be applied in managing contract closeout and associated closeout of the project.

Process Steps and Toolkit Reference

The following four process steps will be accomplished as part of *Business Posting* activities:

- **4.5.1 Business Lessons Learned**—Review the project from the perspective of business activity and interactions, with a focus on what went well and what did not. Reference the short checklist and attempt an unbiased review. Identify conditions (lessons), but do not evaluate yet, as that is done in a separate activity. A facilitated group session is recommended.
- **4.5.2 Business Performance Evaluation**—Conduct an internal examination of project business activities to rate indicators of business performance. Identify key and notable business contacts. Provide comments on managing this project's business performance. Obtain management-level review.
- **4.5.3 Business Invoice Management**—Post and manage business invoices for accuracy and timely submittal, as submitted throughout the project. Track customer invoice submittals and payments, and perform invoice actions as necessary. Perform closeout of business invoices in association with the final payment from the customer.
- **4.5.4 Business Contract Closeout**—Review business closeout activities and track their status toward completion. When completed, obtain the PMO or portfolio manager's sign-off for termination of project business activities. This generally concludes the formal activities of the project.

Responsibility

Primary

- Project Manager
- Project Executive (Sponsor)

Alternates and Adjuncts

- Contract Manager
- PMO (Alternate)
- Executive Control Board
- Project Team Members
- Business Development Manager

The project manager performs or assigns project team members to conduct business closeout activities. To the extent possible, the project manager should be directly involved in business closeout at this juncture in the project and in preparing business lessons learned and conducting the business performance evaluation. Many of these activities can be performed by the PMO, but should at least be done with PMO collaboration. The project executive (sponsor) and executive control board should be involved in final business-related meetings, particularly those reviewing the evaluation of business performance.

Process Input

The following information, actions, materials, and resources represent relevant input to this process:

- *Business Profile* (process element 1.5)
- *Customer Plan* (process element 2.1), with focus on the *Customer Technical Solution* content (process step 2.1.2), and attention to the *Customer Change Control Plan* (process step 2.1.3) and the *Customer Quality Management Plan* (process step 2.1.4)
- *Project Plan* (process element 2.2), with focus on *WBS* and *Project Work Plan* content (process step 2.2.1)
- *Business Plan* (process element 2.5), with focus on *Vendor Management Plan* content (process step 2.4.2)
- Any project plan elements and project support plans that prescribe management activities

Process Output (Project Management Deliverable)

The output of this process element includes documentation of lessons learned relative to business performance, an evaluation of business performance, the organization's final invoicing and receipt of payment, and contract closure to end the project.

4.6 MANAGEMENT POSTING

This process element provides for project closeout activities associated with the PMO and management. It prompts a meeting or other means of collaboration for discussion and identification of lessons learned relevant to PMO and management participation in the project. It likewise facilitates an internal examination and evaluation of PMO and management project participation by the project manager and project team members.

This process contains a management satisfaction survey that enables the PMO and other management to provide feedback to the project manager on contentment with project performance and outcome.

This process includes activities that formally close out PMO and management participation in the project relative to overall project closure. *Management Posting* is completed when the PMO or project executive (sponsor) signs off to acknowledge project closure.

Schedule/Timing

The *Management Posting* process is conducted during the Post Phase. Occasionally, some management satisfaction surveys may be conducted at interim points earlier in the project.

Process Steps and Toolkit Reference

The following four process steps will be accomplished as part of *Management Posting* activities:

- **4.6.1 Management Lessons Learned**—Review the project from the perspective of management activity and interactions, with a focus on what went well and what did not. Reference the short checklist and attempt an unbiased review. Identify conditions (lessons), but do not evaluate yet, as that is done in a separate activity. A facilitated group session is recommended.
- **4.6.2 Management Evaluation**—Conduct an internal examination of PMO/senior manager activities to rate indicators of management performance. Identify key and notable management contacts. Provide comments on managing this project's management performance. Obtain management-level review.
- **4.6.3 Management Satisfaction Survey**—This management satisfaction survey is to be completed by senior managers in the PMO and business units at the end of the project (or other designated interim evaluation period). The overview section can be filled in prior to distribution.
- **4.6.4 Management Closeout**—Review management closeout activities and track their status toward completion. When completed, obtain the PMO or project sponsor's sign-off for termination of project management oversight activities. This concludes any involvement of the PMO, business unit managers, and control boards, and represents project closure.

Responsibility

Primary

- Project Manager
- Project Executive (Sponsor)

Alternates and Adjuncts

- PMO (Alternate)
- Executive Control Board (Alternate)
- Project Team Members

The project manager performs or assigns project team members to conduct management closeout activities. To the extent possible, the project manager should be directly involved in management closeout at this juncture in the project, and in preparing management lessons learned and conducting the management satisfaction survey. Many of these activities can be performed by the PMO, but should at least be done with PMO collaboration. The project executive (sponsor; alternate: executive control board) should be involved in final management-related meetings, particularly in completing the management satisfaction survey.

Process Input

The following information, actions, materials, and resources represent relevant input to this process:

- *Business Profile* (process element 1.5)
- *Customer Plan* (process element 2.1), with focus on the *Customer Technical Solution* content (process step 2.1.2), and attention to the *Customer Change Control Plan* (process step 2.1.3) and the *Customer Quality and Acceptance Plan* (process step 2.1.4)
- *Project Plan* (process element 2.2), with focus on *WBS* and *Project Work Plan* content (process step 2.2.1)
- *Business Plan* (process element 2.5), with focus on *Vendor Management Plan* content (process step 2.4.2)
- Any project plan elements and project support plans associated with management requirements
- Senior manager and executive meeting schedules
- Senior manager and executive business decisions relevant to the project
- Senior manager and executive project portfolio management decisions relevant to the project

Process Output (Project Management Deliverable)

The output of this process element includes documentation of lessons learned relative to management participation, a survey of management satisfaction, and management participation closure to formally end the project.

Methodology Practice Guide II

INTRODUCTION—PROJECT MANAGEMENT PRACTICE OVERVIEW

This introductory section of the *Practice Guide* presents an overview of the fundamental concepts and terminology used in the performance of professional project management. It includes foundation information in the following topic areas:

- Project Management in the Organization
- Project Management Life Cycle
- The Professional Project Manager
- The Project Management Executive
- The Project Management Office (PMO)

PROJECT MANAGEMENT IN THE ORGANIZATION

There are three prominent types of activities found in the project management environment: *project management*, *program management*, and *portfolio management*. In some organizations and industries, the terms *project* and *program management* are sometimes used interchangeably. In others, there are efforts made to distinguish between the two. Similarly, *program management* is sometimes used to imply *portfolio management*, which is not an accurate characterization. The following subsections examine these terms and their use in the project management environment.

Project Management

Organizations undertake projects as a means to implement technical solutions and to achieve desired business results. The *project* is a work effort of limited duration and defined scope, performed for the purpose of producing required deliverables and achieving specified objectives. The Project Management Institute's *A Guide to the Project Management Body of Knowledge* (PMBOK®)* provides the following widely accepted definition:

> **Project**—a temporary endeavor undertaken to create a unique product, service, or result.

It follows that *project management* is an effort that applies knowledge and skill to achieve project objectives; produce project deliverables for a customer; and manage the people, processes, and tools in the most effective and efficient manner possible within a given project management environment.

To that purpose, the following are primary activities that highlight what project managers do when concepts of modern project management are applied:

- Manage project initiation activities.
- Form and manage the project team (staff members).
- Plan and manage the project effort (cost, schedule, and resource utilization).
- Manage project stakeholder interests and participation in the project.
- Establish and manage customer and vendor contracts.
- Manage technical and business risks and rewards on the project.
- Manage project deliverable quality and acceptance by the customer.
- Compile and report project performance results (i.e., status and progress).
- Manage project closeout activities.

This broad scope of responsibilities for the project manager is brought into perspective by the project management methodology that is implemented within the organization.

---

* PMBOK® is a registered trademark of the Project Management Institute.

Program Management

When there is a myriad of project activity in the organization, some intermediate level of oversight and management of similar or related projects may be desired. This is often the responsibility of the project management office (PMO), or it may be a responsibility assigned to program managers who look after high-level aspects of projects under their purview. This is not distinctly project management; however, many aspects of traditional project management may be used or adapted for this role. The program manager generally oversees a collection of projects for the purpose of managing their combined performance, and usually the performance of each project manager as well. To that end, a *program* is a collection of related work efforts (projects) that are brought together and managed for contrast, comparison, and combined success within the relevant organization. Along this line, the Project Management Institute's *A Guide to the Project Management Body of Knowledge* provides this definition:

> **Program**—a group of related projects managed in a coordinated way to obtain benefits and control not available from managing them individually. Programs may include elements of related work outside of the scope of the discrete projects in the program.

Thereby, *program management* is the coordinated management of a more-or-less related collection of projects that are grouped by having the same customer, the same central authority (e.g., PMO or business unit), or an alignment with the same purpose, product line, or type of work performed. Programs are sometimes represented by ongoing, lengthy efforts, but in their own right, programs are not merely larger projects.

In contrast to project management, here is a list of key activities that represent what *program managers* do:

- Manage (supervise) project managers.
- Develop and set standards and metrics for project performance.
- Develop and implement processes for project management.
- Assist in or facilitate the accomplishment of project management activities (e.g., project planning, issue and problem resolution, and team acquisition and development).
- Monitor project performance and identify "troubled" projects.
- Compile, analyze, and report program performance based on aggregate project results.
- Participate in project audits and reviews, and "troubled" project recovery efforts.
- Apply a business perspective to oversight, control, and support of project performance.
- Represent management interests in the project management environment.

See the discussion later in this introduction section about the PMO for a more detailed examination of centralized program management concepts.

Portfolio Management

Project portfolio management monitors and uses results from project management and program management, but distinguishes itself because of the business nature of the effort and inherent requirement for executive and senior manager-level involvement in the management process. More precisely, the Project Management Institute's *A Guide to the Project Management Body of Knowledge* provides this definition:

> **Portfolio**—a collection of projects or programs and other work that are grouped together to facilitate effective management of that work to meet strategic business objectives. The projects or programs of the portfolio may not necessarily be interdependent or directly related.

Therefore, *portfolio management* is the oversight of a collection of projects or programs selected and owned by an executive or executive control board and grouped for purposes of monitoring and managing their contribution to business performance. When it exists, the PMO normally will be involved, perhaps even leading the portfolio management effort. However, project portfolio management decisions should be made by those executives having responsibility for achieving business objectives within the organization.

Since executives have responsibility for achieving business objectives, and to the extent that projects are a means toward business fulfillment, project portfolio management represents executive involvement in project management with emphasis on oversight of business performance. See more guidance in the *Portfolio Management* practice.

Project portfolio management generally includes the following activities that can be performed by executives with the support of others in the project management environment:

- Business strategy determination—an executive-level responsibility usually conducted by the board of directors or other senior manager group within the relevant organization
- Project selection criteria development—normally prepared by the PMO, with executive review and approval

- Project business case—normally prepared by the project manager, program manager, or PMO (with business manager input), with executive-level review and approval
- Project selection—per fulfillment of established criteria and with executive concurrence
- Project prioritization and portfolio integration—a decision made by the executive (or executive control board), with administrative actions managed by the PMO
- Project resource allocation—a decision or approval made by the relevant executive (or executive control board) about the number of resources to be allocated to the project; specific resource assignments normally managed by the PMO, program manager, and project manager in conjunction with project managers' requests for resources
- Project portfolio reviews—executive review for project continuation, termination, or placement on hold, per established review points in the portfolio management process
- Project portfolio closeout—per individual project closeout activities reported to the executive or executive control board, with administrative actions managed by the PMO

Project portfolio management relies on input from project managers in the form of status and progress reports. To that end, some elements of portfolio management could be a part of the project management methodology that is used—primarily to ensure that the project manager (and for that matter the project team) has awareness of strategic business interests and objectives.

PROJECT MANAGEMENT LIFE CYCLE

The project management life cycle specifies the sequence and flow of progressive project management activities that are usually aligned within distinctive phases of the project. *Process phases* provide a high-level perspective of advancement through the life cycle and a general indication of project management progress and accomplishments. Within each process phase, project management *process activities* specify the actions to be accomplished, and they are prescribed to provide for consistent and repeatable application by all users. Defined *process steps* for project management are incorporated into each activity to provide more detailed guidance (i.e., what to do and what not to do) regarding the accomplishment of project management activities.

The project management life cycle provides step-by-step guidance for performing project management activities. As a *process*, the project management life cycle is essentially the *methodology* used to manage projects, and the two terms are often used interchangeably.

Life Cycle Phases

Table II.1 presents a generic four-phase project management life cycle. It depicts the four phases of the life cycle—Profile, Plan, Perform, and Post, which are the names of the phases in the ProjectPRISM™ methodology. The table also lists some high-level activities that are commonly associated with each project management phase.

The complete list of ProjectPRISM™ life cycle activities is located in the *Process Guide*. However, you can refer to the foregoing table to see the nature of activities that are normally associated with each successive project management phase.

Using this generic perspective, the phase names can and do vary across organizations, industries, and technical or professional specialties that use a project management life cycle model. Here are a few examples of alternate life cycle phase names that are commonly used:

- Profile Phase—aka Concept, Initiation, Opportunity, Business Development
- Plan Phase—aka Solution Development, Research, Survey, Requirements, Design
- Perform Phase—aka Implementation, Execution, Control, Development, Installation, Testing, Validation, Delivery
- Post Phase—aka Transition, Closeout, Acceptance, Maintenance, Warranty

Life Cycle Models

A life cycle model is a way to depict the process flow and general relationships of the prescribed project management process steps. Descriptions of the *waterfall diagram* and the *matrix diagram* life cycle models follow.

Waterfall Diagram

The *waterfall diagram* is a common life cycle model that is used, in concept, in many organizations that have formal and even informal project management practices. It depicts a progression of project management activities from the start of a project through project completion. Using the four-phase life cycle described earlier, the waterfall diagram (Figure II.1) shows how the activities of these phases normally relate to each other.

In this depiction, the four key life cycle phases are noticeably overlapping. The project begins in the Profile Phase, and project management work products and output from the activities of that phase "fall" into the Plan Phase for additional use and refinement or for informational purposes. Similarly, project management work products and output from the Plan Phase "fall" into the Perform Phase,

Table II.1 Generic Project Management Activities by Phase

Profile	Plan	Perform	Post
• Identify the customer • Identify the opportunity • Examine business interest • Select the project • Prepare the project charter	• Form the project team • Identify customer requirements • Specify the technical solution • Prepare the project work plan • Prepare project support plans • Prepare proposal • Establish contract	• Manage customer • Manage variance • Manage change • Manage delivery and acceptance • Manage staff • Manage vendors • Manage contracts • Prepare project & business reports	• Prepare lessons learned • Prepare project evaluations • Prepare project archive material • Manage invoices and payments • Close contracts

where documents such as project plans are used to guide project work performance. This "falling" is depicted by the heavy arrows.

A few thin arrows are also depicted to indicate that there can be selective flow of information or developed material backward (upward) to a previous phase when conditions warrant it. For example, when changes occur during project performance, this might necessitate some replanning. The diagram shows that this requirement would be returned to the Plan Phase, where project planning guidance is presumably available for any further project planning that is conducted. In turn, the updated plan then "falls" again to the Perform Phase, where it is used to manage the revised approach to work performance. On rare occasions, it might occur that information or material in the Perform Phase is sent all the way back to the Profile Phase, where mostly preplanning activities take place. Then again, it is sometimes necessary to revisit such things as the project definition, business case, or project charter.

The Post Phase is also depicted in a manner that shows final actions that will complete the project. As a matter of routine, it is not really common for information or materials to be returned to an earlier project phase in the midst of project closeout. However, it could occur, and this model acknowledges that possibility with a dashed arrow. One notable exception would be when the Post Phase includes "customer acceptance" activities. Then, it would be more likely for materials in the Post Phase to be returned to the previous phase as a matter of fine-tuning a deliverable or adjusting it to conform to last-minute customer requests.

The waterfall diagram is a high-level, phase depiction of project activity flow. It is advantageous when the project management methodology also contains a process flow at lower activity levels. Such a depiction shows how specific methodology process steps relate to others, and this also usually provides some indication of precedent project management actions within each project management phase.

An activity-level flowchart for the ProjectPRISM™ life cycle is located in the *Process Guide*. However, it is the matrix life cycle model that served as the primary basis for constructing the ProjectPRISM™ project management methodology.

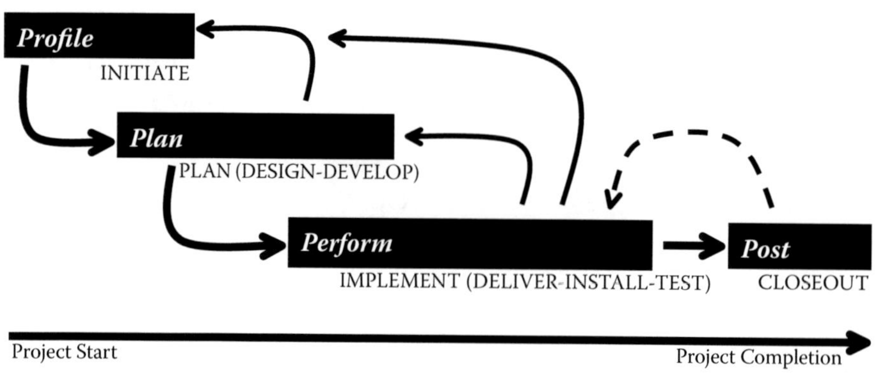

Figure II.1 Waterfall diagram life cycle model.

Matrix Diagram

The *matrix diagram* is an alternative life cycle model that can be considered for contrast and the potential benefits it can provide within the project management environment. It applies the concept that there is one process for each primary project management activity, and users can initially use and then return to each process, as needed, to accomplish prescribed project management activities. A simple depiction of the matrix diagram life cycle model is presented in Figure II.2.

As with references to "matrix" concepts, the matrix diagram life cycle model provides for bringing a project management activity or process step into play when it is prescribed by the methodology flow, or as otherwise needed to achieve project management objectives. That is, the matrix diagram promotes a prescribed sequence of activities to be performed, but each activity is performed only in its process step. Therefore, if an activity needs to be repeated or recurs during the project, you simply return to that process step for guidance and tools needed to complete that step.

Another feature of the matrix diagram is that it associates project management activities with key performance areas of project management—in the foregoing diagram, these elements are located in the left-hand column. This aligns each of the project management process steps with the project performance element to which it is normally most closely associated. The diagram also shows that there are "numbered" project management activities in each phase, and while the depiction shows only one number (e.g., C-2) as an example, there are in fact several numbers—one for each of the process steps in the phase.

Here are a few brief examples of how the matrix diagram guides project management. First, if you have to conduct planning in association with acquiring staff for the project, you would go to the S-2 process step. If you need to prepare a business report associated with project performance, you would reference the B-3 process step. And, if there is a need to conduct an end-of-project customer satisfaction survey, you would use guidance in the C-4 process step.

The *Process Guide* does provide a flow or sequence of activities such as that associated with the waterfall diagram, but it also offers the characteristics of the matrix diagram life cycle model. The six project performance areas presented in the diagram are described in the *Process Guide*.

Technical Process Integration

Many professionals recognize that the primary purpose of technical processes is to ensure that a quality technical product or solution is developed and conveyed to the customer. In contrast, project management processes are used to ensure that the project is successful in terms of achieving its business objectives (usually objectives dealing with cost, schedule, and resource utilization). Therefore, organizations that have existing technical methodologies will need to find a balance in process content to achieve both technical and project management objectives.

Technical methodologies such as software development life cycles (SDLCs) are sometimes introduced and used for project management purposes. This is generally accepted as long as the essential activities of project management are adequately included in the technical process. However, closer examination may reveal that technical methodologies do not always provide for comprehensive project management coverage.

A solution to this dilemma lies in creating an alignment or integration of the technical process with the pending or established project management methodology used in the organization. An organization may have a range of business units in which different types of projects are conducted using different technical processes, usually along department lines. Each department, then, would select and use their preferred "technical methodology," but for organizational consistency, each technical effort should also be aligned with the prescribed processes and activities presented in the standard project management methodology.

Ideally, the project management methodology is implemented as primary guidance for the project management effort, and technical processes and tools are introduced, as needed, to perform technical elements of work. In some cases, however, the technical processes are so well established in the organization that a more direct type of process alignment is

PERFORMANCE AREA	PROFILE	PLAN	PERFORM	POST
CUSTOMER	ACTIVITY C-1	ACTIVITY C-2	ACTIVITY C-3	ACTIVITY C-4
PROJECT	ACTIVITY P-1	ACTIVITY P-2	ACTIVITY P-3	ACTIVITY P-4
STAFF	ACTIVITY S-1	ACTIVITY S-2	ACTIVITY S-3	ACTIVITY S-4
VENDOR	ACTIVITY V-1	ACTIVITY V-2	ACTIVITY V-3	ACTIVITY V-4
BUSINESS	ACTIVITY B-1	ACTIVITY B-2	ACTIVITY B-3	ACTIVITY B-4
MANAGEMENT	ACTIVITY M-1	ACTIVITY M-2	ACTIVITY M-3	ACTIVITY M-4

Figure II.2 Matrix diagram life cycle model.

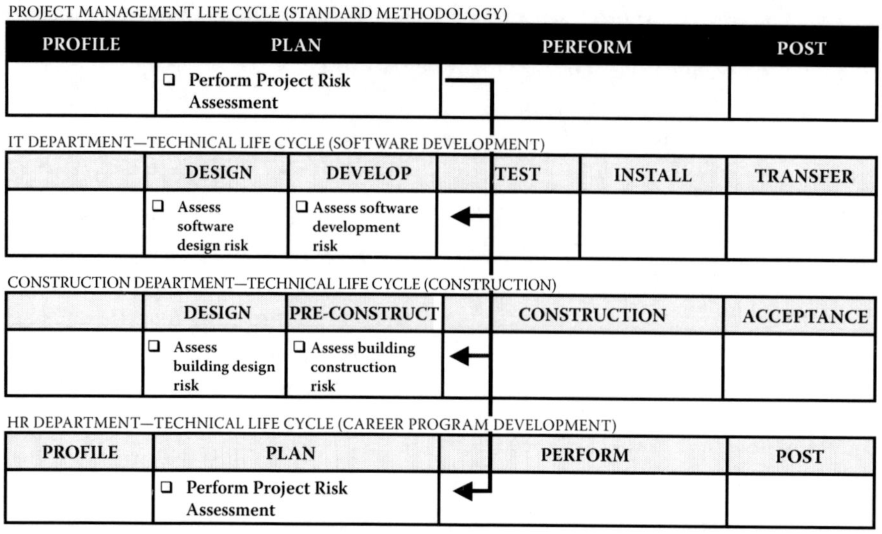

Figure II.3 Technical life cycle "hooking" or "linking."

needed. To create a more direct process alignment, it is not uncommon for an organization to construct a six-, seven-, or eight-phase life cycle as a means of delineating technical activities and integrating the technical process with project management methodology content.

Diagram (Figure II.3) presents a depiction of "hooking" or "linking" technical processes with the project management methodology, and illustrates a few examples for different "technical" departments.

The top lines of the diagram show how the organization's project management methodology serves as a standard, umbrella-type approach to project management, with "hooks" or "links" to preferred technical methods integrated into the life cycle process.

In this simple example, the methodology calls for a project risk assessment in the plan phase. Each department (technical discipline) then performs that project risk assessment using project management methodology guidance, plus any technical risk assessment guidance called for by the technical methods that are used in the respective department. You can see that the plan phase of the standard methodology is further delineated for use within departments having technical specialties.

You may also notice that the foregoing sample shows the HR department to essentially use the standard project management process; a department such as HR would not necessarily have a distinct "technical" methodology of its own to follow. This allows the methodology to be applied to all aspects of the business—even business units that have no particular technical focus. The standard methodology provides for the default process guidance in the absence of any technical-specific process guidance.

Business Process Integration

It is sometimes said that project management is business management to the extent that projects are the means to achieve organizational interests and strategic business objectives. To that end, project management processes are inherently aligned with business processes. It is a matter of discernment whether or not the business processes that are used also adequately support project management interests and purposes. However, that is an aspect of business that should be examined from time to time.

Fundamentally, business management processes should be the same ones used for project management as a matter of business efficiency. This includes such processes as those used for contract management, quality assurance, vendor and contractor management, internal reporting, and an additional array of related processes to be found within the organization. Ideally, the methodology implemented for project management will be a major influence on the associated business processes that are used in the project management environment and elsewhere in the organization.

The integration of project and business management processes is a desired condition in the organization.

THE PROFESSIONAL PROJECT MANAGER

Simply stated, projects require project management. Project management, in turn, requires individuals with sufficient skill, knowledge, and experience to oversee the project effort.

In today's challenging business environment, project management is no longer a secondary skill or a secondary work effort.

This section examines the preparation and credentials needed for leaders in today's project management environment.

Project Manager Qualifications

The achievement of project manager qualifications helps the organization to align the skill and capability of individuals with the management requirements of each project. The entry-level project manager will normally take on smaller projects or be assigned a role under a more seasoned project manager or mentor. Conversely, individuals with broader experience and advanced skill are normally assigned to manage larger, higher business-value projects.

To this end, project managers and their organizations should consider professional qualification in three particular areas: education and training, experience, and certification.

Project Manager Education and Training

Individuals, for the most part, pursue education and training credentials to achieve qualification in a technical or professional discipline of their interest. When deemed appropriate to certain curricula, practical elements of project management may be included in those courses of study. In other programs, however, project management topics may not be specifically covered. As well, some project managers may not have completed a formal degree program as a basis for their work in project management. Therefore, as an organization establishes a professional approach to project management, it may be appropriate to consider providing formal training for all individuals involved in project management as a means to

- Supplement current experience and any underlying technical or professional training
- Improve upon current routine project management practices and reduce use of ineffective practices
- Establish minimum skill and knowledge requirements in the application of professional project management practices within the organization
- Demonstrate support for a common approach to project management as is achieved through use of an effective project management methodology process

As a matter of project manager qualification, the organization should evaluate its needs and specify preferred education and training requirements for its project managers. It is generally accepted that a project manager should have at least a basic degree in science, technology, or business as a prerequisite credential for leading a project. Some organizations may even want to consider individuals with basic or advanced degrees in project management, as are currently offered by many colleges and universities. At the same time, organizations should not dismiss those individuals who bring a combination of less formal technical training and project management experience as valuable credentials for project manager qualification. See more guidance on this topic in the *Project Staff Training and Development* practice.

Project Manager Experience

The experience credential is closely aligned with individual skill development and competency in project management. In general, as an individual advances through a career associated with project management, experience increases from simple, lower-value projects to more complex, high-value projects and even programs.

Experience is achieved when individuals apply skill and knowledge, and then receive personal confirmation or indications of the accomplishments achieved—learning what works well and what needs improvement. Experience also results as skill and knowledge are gained from the variety of work that is performed when advancing from small to large project management efforts. It also represents the individual's attitude toward the pursuit of higher levels of project management responsibility and the personal effort needed to qualify for the broader project management assignments that provide that experience.

As a matter of project manager qualification, the organization should prescribe or align any desired levels of project manager experience with the prominent types or classifications of projects that are pursued within the organization. This qualification factor may be combined with education and training when considering individual project managers for assignment or for career advancement.

Project Manager Certification

The certification credential is further recognition and acknowledgment of project manager professional qualifications. Certification of professionals in the project management environment is an excellent way to promote a consistent level of project management performance within the organization. It is usually based on standards selected to guide the development and implementation of project management concepts and practices. Those same standards can be used to measure and manage individual professional growth and capability in project management. A certification program, at a minimum, provides a snapshot at a point in time of individual qualification to perform all or portions of the job at hand. If the certification requires follow-on updates, or recertification at intervals, that snapshot is extended across time to add even more validity to individual skill, knowledge, and competency. A certification program, when using aggregated results of all project managers, may also provide an indication of overall organizational capability in project management.

As a matter of project manager qualification, project management certification programs come in two primary forms—external certification and internal certification. The organization can consider the benefits of each as a basis for defining the type of certification that will be used. In some organizations, both forms of certification are used. External certification serves to obtain a third-party validation of professional competency, usually based on examination against widely accepted standards. An internal certification program allows the organization to consider industry-specific issues and requirements, as well as applicable organizational and business interests, in the certification of its project managers.

Certification is normally the final credential and indicator of qualification level of a project manager. It is awarded upon examination of individual skill, knowledge, and competency associated with experience, education, and training, and some certifications will also consider the individual's current professional involvement in advancing project management as a professional discipline and potential for future advancement.

Project Manager Responsibility

The fully qualified project manager can have a broad range of responsibilities on a complex or otherwise mainstream project in the organization. Four primary areas of project manager responsibility are summarized in the following text. In particular, these responsibility areas are also indicators of the types of skill and knowledge that individuals should pursue and develop through training and education, or through other means such as mentoring, in order to demonstrate project management competency using modern project management practices.

- Project Oversight Responsibility
  - Planner and plan manager
  - Scheduler and schedule manager
  - Estimator and budget manager
  - Tracking and controlling manager
  - Analysis and reporting manager
- Technical Oversight Responsibility
  - Technical expert
  - Procedure developer
  - Trainer
  - Performance evaluator
  - Quality manager
- Business Oversight Responsibility
  - Customer relationship manager
  - Vendor relationship manager
  - Logistics manager
  - Proposal manager
  - Contract manager
  - Procurement (supply) manager
  - Auditor
  - Labor relations manager
  - Accounting specialist
  - Computer applications expert
  - Business manager
- Interpersonal Skill/Staff Management Responsibility
  - Staff supervision
  - Stakeholder management
  - Time management
  - Facilitation management
  - Conflict management
  - Negotiations management
  - Team building
  - Communications management—oral and written
  - Decision maker
  - Problem solver

The extent to which an individual project manager has and uses all of the aforementioned capabilities is essentially a factor of organizational culture—usually determined by the extent to which the organization has integrated business and project management.

Project Management Advancement Model (Career Path)

The professional project management advancement model defines who's who in the project management environment. The most fundamental model is one that designates individuals as *project managers* within the organization. If no other position is recognized in the organization, the project manager designation must be examined for use and assigned to those individuals deemed qualified to lead project efforts. This title or designation can differentiate levels of qualification based on responsibility, seniority, or experience, but the designation implies one thing: qualified to manage projects in this organization!

Another fundamental consideration of the project management advancement model is that it can specify the progression of advancement for individuals in the project management environment. The model suggests that there is a variety of individuals who work on professional project management activities, and they should have designations aligned with their responsibilities.

This concept of designating individuals according to the progression specified by a project management advancement model can be examined with reference to the following brief list of considerations. The list examines how project team members and other project stakeholders may be gaining professional project management experience and, therefore, will have some professional career path alignment if they

- *Participate in project planning activities.* They need to convey technical expertise, and they also need to identify technical solution cost, schedule, and resource utilization.
- *Prepare or compile project status or progress reports.* They need to understand project status and correctly interpret conditions to properly structure project report content.
- *Lead or perform technical or business activities associated with projects.* They need to recognize how their activities are integrated and affect project performance outcomes, and be able to apply specified project performance tracking and control procedures.
- *Manage resources used in the project environment.* They need to know how resources are identified, assigned, and used on projects, and they need to understand their own responsibilities for resource commitments to the project effort.
- *Report to a project manager.* They need to have at least a basic understanding of their reporting official's professional project management role and responsibilities.
- *Hold designated responsibility in the project management methodology.* They need to recognize how their contributions are integrated into the overall project management effort, and know how to apply the preferred project management practices.
- *Contribute professional business expertise to project management.* They need to know how and when to provide timely and meaningful input on such topics as legal advice, finance and accounting guidance, customer service management, and contract management.
- *Hold business responsibility for project success.* They need to understand fundamental concepts of modern project management as a means for evaluating project and project manager performance, and for applying performance results to business decisions.

The organization should develop a project management career advancement model (career path) as a means to align roles and responsibilities in the project management environment. This model should represent the various preferred position designations that will be used in the organization to define individual participation in association with project efforts.

The following are suggested project management advancement levels for consideration by the organization when defining roles and responsibility designations in the project management environment.

Support-Level Positions

Every project manager has to start somewhere. The organization can use *support-level* career positions to identify professional potential in individuals and to provide for further skill and knowledge development. Activities at this level will prepare individuals for expanded responsibilities in project management and for progression along the project management career path.

Participants at this career level could include those with recently completed formal education who are just beginning their professional careers in a business environment. It also could include individuals with varying levels of business experience who are transitioning into a professional project management environment or who find the project management environment growing around them. The focus of activities at this career level is on supporting project management efforts.

The following are representative support-level positions that the organization can consider for inclusion in its project management career advancement model:

- *Project Assistant*—Performs traditional administrative duties to include graphics design and document preparation and reproduction; schedules and arranges meeting facilities and participant attendance; maintains telephone and visitor logs; prepares and manages project correspondence and shipping of project deliverables.
- *Project Coordinator*—Facilitates collaboration among project team members and across project teams, business units, and other project stakeholders; manages project team information and knowledge exchange, including the project team online knowledge space; manages project facilities, equipment, and supplies (acquisition and assignment).
- *Project Administrator*—Monitors, receives, and compiles reports from project team members to the project manager; manages change control, project plan updates, project document storage and control, and project issues and action logs; monitors and manages project deliverable due dates, risk mitigation actions, and contractual obligations; manages customer and vendor/contractor invoices and payments.
- *Project Business Analyst*—Performs specialized project management activities such as schedule development and management, budget preparation and oversight, and resource workload management; provides project estimating and planning support and expertise; analyzes cost, schedule, and resource utilization performance and variations; contributes expertise to project management planning in areas of specialty, for example, risk, quality, procurement, etc.

The positions just highlighted are appropriate entry-level positions in many organizations because they provide a starting role for individuals with only fundamental project management skills. Conversely, a support position designation may sometimes warrant a fully qualified individual on larger- or higher-value projects. In some cases, even *qualified-level* professionals may need to be assigned in support roles on larger projects. The organization should recognize that a support-level position is not necessarily a junior or entry-level role on the project, and it should consider that in its development of a project management career advancement model.

Qualified-Level Positions

The capabilities identified in the foregoing text for positions at the support level are presumed for *qualified-level* project managers who will likely perform many of those duties themselves, as needed, on small- to medium-size projects. Therefore, they do not have to be repeated for this level in career progression.

However, there can be several distinct roles at the qualified level. The following are representative qualified-level positions that the organization can consider for inclusion in its project management career advancement model:

- *Project Technical Staff Member*—Performs technical or skilled work to achieve project objectives. Includes such roles as engineer, scientist, analyst, researcher, developer, etc.
- *Technical Task Leader*—Leads technical task efforts; supervises work of other project technical staff members and ensures quality in the timely development of project deliverables.
- *Project Leader*—Performs in a manner similar to the technical task leader but with an emphasis on completion of essential project management actions in addition to technical performance management. This position may be assigned to lead smaller project efforts.
- *Assistant Project Manager*—Monitors and guides project and team performance; represents the project manager in meetings and communication with internal and customer managers; performs other project management activities as assigned by the project manager. An individual in this position may be a qualified project manager but is assigned an assistant capacity because of the size, value, or complexity of the project.
- *Project Manager*—Conducts project management activities using preferred organizational practices and established processes as contained in the project management methodology; demonstrates leadership in the project management environment; holds accountability for project cost, schedule, and resource utilization performance and the achievement of project and business objectives.
- *Senior Project Manager*—Performs in the same manner as the project manager but is recognized for achievement of advanced training and education credentials, extended project management experience, or demonstrated success on previous projects. Also, this professional level represents competency to oversee the larger project efforts conducted by the organization.

Project team members and task leaders may be assigned to roles on multiple projects, requiring them to be effective task and time managers. Project managers and senior project managers are also likely to have multiple project responsibilities in small- to medium-size organizations. The capability to handle this type of responsibility should be considered by the organization when defining position designations for the project management career advancement model.

Business-Level Positions

Ideally, the capabilities described for the previous two levels of the project management career path are readily demonstrated by individuals serving in positions at the business level. *Business-level* roles in project management represent a wider management perspective, usually including responsibility for oversight of multiple projects or management of large and extended project engagements. Therefore, some capability and comprehension of modern project management concepts and practices is distinctly needed. However, in some organizations, the perceived need to assign relatively senior managers to these roles sometimes precludes the completion of formal project management education and training, and the associated experience gained at the qualified level.

To that end, business experience or identified individual business management potential is a prime qualifier. To be successful at the business level, qualification must include some hands-on capability and experience in understanding modern project management concepts, applying project management methods, using common project management tools and terminology, and leading project teams. Also, the organization should recognize that technical expertise and advancement does not necessarily imply advanced project management capability.

The following are business-level positions that the organization can consider for inclusion in the project management career advancement model:

- *Program Manager*—Manages the performance of multiple project managers, oversees multiple project performance, and lends business guidance to collections of related projects. Alternatively, a program manager may be assigned to oversee a long-term program characterized by multiple-discipline technical task performance requirements, large and evolving program/project team compositions, and usually a single customer with participation of the customer's several and diverse business units.
- *Program Director*—Manages the performance of program managers and possibly some project

managers, usually on a regional, national, or global basis. Responsibility may focus on a product line or market segment. The director position ensures that business interests are appropriately addressed in project and program technical solution deliveries and in associated customer relationships.

- *PMO Director*—Holds responsibilities that may include those of a program director, but also includes responsibility for establishing a centralized project oversight, control, and support capability within the relevant organization. The PMO director should also demonstrate capability to manage the PMO as a separate business unit if PMO maturity and business needs warrant such an entity within the relevant organization.

The positions aligned with the business level of the project management career path are focused on (a) identifying, developing, and implementing processes and practices that enhance and expand project management effectiveness and capability within the organization, and (b) guiding and managing project performance to achieve strategic business objectives.

Executive-Level Opportunities

Executive roles in project management—involving vice presidents, CEOs, CFOs, CIOs, and others at the strategic decision level—are catching on. It would be nice to have the discipline represented by a prevalent cross-industry need for chief project officers (CPOs). They do exist in some organizations, particularly those having global reach, but the term "CPO" is rarely used. Nevertheless, there is now a precedent for elevating the professional project manager to the *executive level* in an organization, and the organizations that do so appear to be those generally at the higher levels of project management maturity.

Executives distinctly need business competencies, but they also need to understand and apply project management competencies. A home-grown vice president who emerges from the project management career path is desirable, but not essential. More important is that executives associate their professional background and experience to the project management environment they are joining, and perhaps leading.

The following are executive-level positions that the organization can consider for inclusion in the project management career advancement model:

- *Vice President of Project Management*—Heads the relevant organization's project management center of competence (i.e., an advanced-stage PMO) that serves business interests on a regional, national, or global scale; lends leadership and guidance to PMO development initiatives and to the infusion of modern project management tools and practices; and often holds associated responsibility for achieving strategic business objectives.
- *Director of Project Management*—Holds responsibilities and authority similar to that of vice president of project management but is so named when an executive-level position cannot be established.
- *Vice President of Business Unit Operations*—The project management career advancement model should provide for cross-functional professional position opportunities. Project managers at senior levels gain tremendous business experience that, along with relevant education and training, prepares them to lead business unit operations. The organization should examine how opportunities outside the project management environment can be incorporated into the project management career advancement model.

Executives will be introduced from within the organization and from external sources. The organization should facilitate collaboration with current executives to develop future roles and responsibilities of executives aligned with the project management career advancement model.

THE PROJECT MANAGEMENT EXECUTIVE

Project management practices can account for a large part of business performance. In particular, if projects are the means by which the organization's products and services are delivered to the marketplace, the contribution of project management to business performance is significantly increased. It would seem appropriate then for executives and senior managers in the organization to be well informed regarding project performance and associated project accomplishments, as that represents the pursuit of business for which they have responsibility.

As projects enable the delivery of the organization's products and services, they also represent a business activity that should be controlled at the highest management levels in the organization. Executives have ultimate responsibility for the achievement of strategic business objectives and interests, and that suggests they should have significant interest and participation in key project decisions—that is, project selection, continuation, and termination—that are the primary activities of project portfolio management. To that end, executives and senior managers need to monitor project performance as a key indicator of business performance. If they are responsible for revenue, and projects are the means to that revenue, then they should be involved in "managing" projects from a strategic perspective.

The following are a few areas the organization can examine to create executive-level awareness and support for project management. To a large extent, most of these recommendations imply or prescribe the establishment and use of a PMO that serves executive-level business interests.

- *Business Decisions*—Executives need access to fundamental project information in a timely manner in order to make accurate business decisions. This type of information is not generated solely from business manager advice and guidance; in some instances, that is just speculation and conjecture, and business units that are part-time or inactive project stakeholders cannot be expected to generate this information about projects. Rather, this type of information is generated at the project team level, tracked at the project management level, compiled across all projects and analyzed at the PMO level, and then presented for executive review and deliberation. Project information used at the executive level has business relevance. Executives need to support, endorse, and fund the development and implementation of processes, procedures, and tools needed to provide this type of business solution.
- *Strategy Implementation*—Executives need to convey business strategies and decisions to the project management environment for implementation. This is readily achieved when the PMO's role and responsibilities extend into the business environment, where strategy is initially communicated. In turn, the PMO can focus on the people and processes affected by executive decisions, recognize business performance impacts, and serve as a single point of strategy implementation rather than having the project management environment bombarded from all sides by multiple business-unit managers attempting to introduce executive guidance from a variety of perspectives. Executives need to recognize the benefits of the PMO not only serving as a representative of the project management environment but also as an entity serving as a business performance leader conveying executive decisions to the project management environment.
- *Resource Acquisition and Allocation*—Executives need to have an ongoing awareness of project resource requirements. Possibly the largest expense in the project management environment, project resources need to be managed at mid-levels according to the decisions made at the executive level. Therefore, executives need to understand the implications of their resource allocation decisions as a function of business performance. Fundamentally, this means ensuring that necessary resources are available to conduct each project that is pursued in conjunction with the prescribed business strategy. It also means attending to peripheral considerations such as resource training, qualification, assignment selection, performance management, professional development, recognition, and termination. The processes created for resource management on projects can well serve the business needs of executives. The PMO, serving as a project resource clearinghouse, can compile resource information that is needed to make resource acquisition and allocation decisions at the executive level. It can identify current resource strength and utilization, and prepare resource requirement forecasts—information the executive needs to ensure that business pursuits are not impaired by gaps in resource availability or resource management issues. Executives should use PMO expertise and established capability in the project management environment to examine resource requirements relative to business performance.
- *Technical Performance*—Executives need to review and recognize the effectiveness and value associated with technical performance from a perspective of customer satisfaction and from a perspective of business advantage or industry competitiveness. The alignment of technical processes and project management practices can provide for such business performance insight. The PMO can establish functionality to capture and analyze technical performance results across all projects internally and to compare them to industry-wide results. In turn, analysis results can be conveyed to executives for examination relative to business interests that include
  - State of core technical competencies
  - Perceived value of technical capability in the marketplace
  - Quality–cost comparisons of products and services
  - Technical resource competency
  - Technical management capability
  - Reliance on vendor/contractor technical resources

  Again, this is business information that has its origins in the project management environment. Executives need to recognize that the PMO, at an interim management level, can establish functionality to evaluate technical performance conditions and provide routine and exception reports that will bring value to executive business deliberations and decision making.
- *Centralized Oversight, Control, and Support*—Executives need to understand the formal and informal boundaries of the project management environment and then maximize the effectiveness of that condition on business performance. The formal project management environment that conducts project management under PMO guidance is normally an efficient and effective means for conducting business. In contrast, the informal project management environment, usually represented by business unit oversight and intervention, is not always aligned with central PMO guidance or

preferred practices. Therefore, such part-time interventions in project management could introduce opposing business perspectives and possibly target business objectives that are different from planned. In a sense, project management processes can be used to manage business performance, but business processes cannot necessarily be used to manage projects, particularly when there are variations for each business unit having influence. The PMO can be instrumental in coordinating a common approach to managing project contributions to business performance, integrating multiple business unit processes and procedures into a standard approach, and leading collaboration among business unit participants in their ongoing contributions to the formal project management environment. Executives should establish the PMO as a single point of reference that enables their decisions on oversight, control, and support to be implemented not only in the project management environment but also across the business units within the organization.

THE PROJECT MANAGEMENT OFFICE

During the past few decades or so, modern project management precepts have emerged to instill a vitalized, professional approach to project management across countless organizations and industries. Individual capabilities in project management have been strengthened and enlarged through a combination of project management process and technique development, training program implementation, and automated tools that use advanced design concepts and technology. As a result, project managers who practice these principles will find themselves in the dual roles of technical expert and business leader for the project.

Organizations are extending these modern project management concepts and considerations into the scope of project management *oversight*, *control*, and *support*. They recognize the need for an organizational entity—the PMO—to perform in a capacity that achieves one or more of these three operational objectives. They often position the PMO as a business integrator—whether in a role that is limited to managing multiple projects as a program or expanded to serve as a business unit representing the organization's project management environment—to encompass all the people (project stakeholders), processes (methodologies and practices), and tools (automated systems and work aids) that manage or influence project performance. In any logical role assigned, the PMO helps both the project manager and the organization to understand and apply professional practices of project management and to adapt and integrate business interests into the project management efforts with which they are associated.

The PMO concepts presented here are based on content from the publication *The Complete Project Management Office Handbook* by Gerard M. Hill (Auerbach Publications, Second Edition, Taylor & Francis, Boca Raton, FL, 2007).

Project Management Office Roles

The following are the three primary roles of the PMO:

- *Oversight*—Knowing and reporting what is going on in the project management environment in order for collaborative decisions to be made
- *Control*—Intervening to ensure that
  - Established standards and preferred practices are followed
  - Problems are identified and corrective actions are taken
  - Business objectives are achieved
- *Support*—Helping project managers and their teams to succeed in achieving project and project management objectives

These roles can be described in appropriate ways that are consistent with the organization's business culture in order to achieve necessary acceptance in the organization. However, the purpose and essence of the PMO's roles should be maintained as best can be done.

The PMO Competency Continuum

The PMO competency continuum provides a vehicle that defines a series of PMO stages that can be examined for application in an organization. The naming convention is relatively simple and somewhat consistent with PMO implementation efforts across most industries. However, these names provide only a frame of reference; other names can be applied as appropriate to the nature of PMO responsibilities and the business environment in which it operates.

Five general stages of PMO competency are prescribed. Table II.2 presents an overview of the PMO competency continuum and a description of each of its stages.

These five PMO stages represent a progressive competency and advancement of functionality that can be attained to meet project management environment needs and associated relevant organizational business objectives. It is presumed that a higher-stage PMO will have achieved the competencies prescribed for any lower-stage PMOs. That is, if an organization wants to establish a Stage 3 Standard PMO, it will also have to ensure it has first realized the competencies prescribed for Stage 1 and Stage 2 PMOs. It is also suggested that a PMO at any stage can pursue activities at any level to address the needs within the relevant organization, which is far more important than stepping through

Table II.2 Overview of PMO Capabilities Across the PMO Competency Continuum

Project Oversight	*Process Control*	*Process Support*	*Business Maturity*	*Strategic Alignment*
Stage 1 PROJECT OFFICE Achieve project deliverables and objectives for cost, schedule, and resource utilization • 1 or more projects • 1 Project Manager	Stage 2 BASIC PMO Provide a standard and repeatable PM methodology for use across all projects • Multiple projects • Multiple PMs • Program Manager • Part-time PMO support staff	Stage 3 STANDARD PMO Establish capability and infrastructure to support and govern a cohesive project environment • Multiple projects • Multiple PMs • Program Managers • Director or Senior Program Manager • Full-time and part-time PMO staff	Stage 4 ADVANCED PMO Apply an integrated and comprehensive project management capability to achieve business objectives • Multiple projects • Multiple PMs • Program Managers • PMO Director or Vice President • Dedicated PMO support staff	Stage 5 CENTER OF EXCELLENCE Manage continuous improvement and cross-department collaboration to achieve strategic business goals • Multiple programs • Vice President or Director of Project Management • Dedicated PMO support staff • Enterprise-wide support staff

levels of competency in sequence. Moreover, discerning the approximate level of PMO competency that the relevant organization needs is critical. Not every organization needs to have a PMO at Stage 5. In fact, for most organizations, some adaptation of the Stage 3 Standard PMO is probably more than adequate.

The PMO Functions

A PMO can be viewed as having 20 functions for the practical application of oversight, control, and support solutions in the project management environment. These functions have a combined influence on the business environment and on the project management environment, and there are interrelationships among many of the PMO functions: some functional processes or procedures overlap, and some cross-function references will be apparent.

The 20 PMO functions are aligned with five function areas, and are summarized as follows.

- *Practice Management*—Provides a common approach and frame of reference for conducting project management activities within an organization. This function area establishes project management processes, tools, and practices; specifies project performance standards and metrics; and creates a collaborative project management environment that includes project archives and a reference library. It concentrates on developing effective organizational project management capability at the project level.
- *Infrastructure Management*—Facilitates establishing a professional project management environment. This function area examines the current state of project management, prompts collaboration of plans for the future state, and introduces the policies and oversight mechanisms needed to achieve organizational competency and maturity goals. It helps to define the project structure and stakeholder involvement necessary to support successful project performance and provides for administration of facilities and equipment needed to accomplish project objectives.
- *Resource Integration*—Manages the competency, availability, and performance of project resources. This function area enables the PMO to collaborate with resource managers to acquire, assign, and manage project managers and project team members, and it allows the PMO to administer training in the project management environment. It also enables the PMO to influence project manager career progression and support aspects of project team development.
- *Technical Support*—Provides project management advice, counsel, and support to project managers and project teams. This function area leverages the skill, knowledge, and experience of available project management experts to provide mentoring in the project management environment, and it provides a range of

project planning, facilitation, and support activities. It plans and conducts routine and special project audits and project management reviews, and provides appropriate project recovery support as needed.

- *Business Alignment*—Introduces the organization's business perspective into the project environment. This function area oversees project portfolio management and facilitates executive involvement in project management to include overseeing project management contributions to business performance. It also conducts customer and vendor/contractor relationship management and facilitates their project roles.

These function areas are in turn further divided into specific PMO functions prescribed for comprehensive and complete coverage of PMO responsibilities in the organization. It is reasonable to acknowledge that each PMO will not likely have designed and deployed all 20 PMO functions. Rather, each organization must ascertain which PMO functions are needed to fulfill the requirements that are present in the project management and business environments.

Table II.3 presents a snapshot of the diverse activities of each function.

These PMO functions and associated activities are presented for due examination and consideration by individuals and organizations looking to establish a PMO capability that will enhance project performance and project management maturity, and integrate business interests and objectives. They suggest or prescribe what can be. Undoubtedly, PMO function model adaptations and adjustments will be the rule rather than the exception.

Table II.3 Overview of PMO Functions

Practice Management	*Infrastructure Management*	*Resource Integration*	*Technical Support*	*Business Alignment*
PROJECT MANAGEMENT METHODOLOGY • Establish basis for project management methodology • Develop methodology solution • Conduct methodology implementation • Manage methodology maturity	**PROJECT GOVERNANCE** • Prepare and maintain PMO charter • Develop project management policies • Develop project classification guidance • Establish project manager authority • Establish executive control board • Align business and technical committees	**RESOURCE MANAGEMENT** • Acquire project resources • Assign project resources • Deploy project resources • Manage resource performance • Close project resource assignments	**MENTORING** • Establish project management mentoring program • Engage project management mentors • Conduct project management mentoring • Evaluate mentoring program	**PORTFOLIO MANAGEMENT** • Set up project portfolio management • Perform project selection • Integrate projects in the portfolio • Conduct project and portfolio reviews • Manage portfolio attrition
PROJECT TOOLS • Select project management tools • Implement project management tools • Evaluate tool performance	**ASSESSMENT** • Conduct competency assessments • Conduct capability assessments • Conduct maturity assessments	**TRAINING AND EDUCATION** • Establish training program • Manage training program • Evaluate training program	**PLANNING SUPPORT** • Establish project planning capability • Facilitate project planning workshop • Administer project planning	**CUSTOMER RELATIONSHIP MANAGEMENT** • Manage customer relationships • Manage customer contracts • Manage customer satisfaction
STANDARDS AND METRICS • Implement project management standards • Determine project metrics requirements • Introduce and use project metrics	**ORGANIZATION AND STRUCTURE** • Set up the PMO structure • Establish project structure • Develop stakeholder participation	**CAREER DEVELOPMENT** • Develop project management career path • Support project management career planning • Establish professional certification	**PROJECT AUDITING** • Set up project auditing capability • Conduct project auditing • Manage project auditing results	**VENDOR RELATIONSHIP MANAGEMENT** • Manage vendor/ contractor relationships • Manage vendor/ contractor acquisition • Manage vendor/ contractor performance
PROJECT KNOWLEDGE MANAGEMENT • Establish knowledge management framework • Introduce knowledge management system • Implement knowledge management system	**FACILITIES AND EQUIPMENT** • Establish project team requirements • Manage project facilities • Management project equipment	**TEAM DEVELOPMENT** • Facilitate cohesive team formation • Facilitate virtual team management • Enable project team development • Monitor project team performance	**PROJECT RECOVERY** • Develop recovery assessment process • Plan and conduct project recovery • Capture recovery lessons learned	**BUSINESS PERFORMANCE MANAGEMENT** • Develop integrated business solutions • Manage business collaboration • Manage PMO business fulfillment

Chapter 1

Project Initiation

A new project begins when it is identified as a bona fide opportunity within the performing organization. For purposes of this methodology, an opportunity can be named as a project at the onset of the project initiation process and then simply be discontinued (i.e., terminated) if it does not subsequently gain required internal or external customer selection and approval.

In a sense, Project Initiation is a series of preselection practices that recognizes a potential work opportunity, aligns it with a specific customer (either internal or external), and defines it in terms of the project management effort to be pursued. All opportunities are required to undergo a more or less formal internal project selection process. Some selected projects must also undergo an external customer's acquisition and selection process that involves proposal preparation and a formal bidding process. These project initiation practices, in conjunction with project selection practices, will assist the project manager (or other designated project "initiation" manager) in preparing the opportunity for either of those encounters.

To that end, *Customer Identification* and *Opportunity Identification* practices are applied. As more information about the customer and the opportunity becomes known and evaluated, the necessary indications will emerge regarding whether the opportunity warrants internal selection and external pursuit of the customer's work. Also, the information compiled by project initiation practices will often prove invaluable to communication and collaboration activities that are conducted throughout the subsequent Plan and Perform Phases.

This practice area is highlighted by the need to define the project—that is, specify its objectives and scope, nature of work, preliminary estimates, and several other details that enable the project effort to be envisioned before it begins, and before time, resources, and costs are allocated. *Project Definition Development* provides an overview of the project to help managers deliberate project selection within the organization. In turn, *Project Classification Development* is sort of an extension of the project definition; it describes the project against an established classification scheme that prompts recognition of the project size, type, complexity, etc., without having to describe all characteristics in detail to all concerned project stakeholders.

Ideally, the project manager, the project management office (PMO), or some other representative of the project management environment is involved at the project initiation stage. However, it is not uncommon for this practice area to be largely associated with business development, particularly in organizations where projects represent revenue-generating opportunities that are uncovered in the marketplace. In the context of project management, project initiation practices are necessary steps that will facilitate the transition of an opportunity into a project. Project Initiation precedes actual Project Selection (a separate practice area), but the information and output of project initiation distinctly contributes to project selection.

There are four primary practices associated with Project Initiation:

- Customer Identification
- Opportunity Identification
- Project Definition Development
- Project Classification Development

Methodology users should note that, while these prescribed practices specify primary activities and steps for initiating a project, other project management practice areas could also contribute in some degree to the accomplishment of project initiation, as may be determined within a particular organization.

1.1 CUSTOMER IDENTIFICATION

The customer is the person or organization for whom the project is being undertaken. This could be an internal customer in the business environment or an external customer in the marketplace. In either case, knowing about the customer and the customer's business interests is a prerequisite to project success.

The project manager should examine sufficient customer information during project initiation to ensure that any proposed business and technical solution will be appropriate to the customer's organization. Many of the more common customer information elements are associated with technical needs, but good project management suggests that other information related to the customer's business is valuable as well. This practice discusses customer information that can be compiled to assist not only in learning about the customer for project initiation purposes but also in managing the ongoing customer relationship during the project.

Concept of This Practice

This practice provides the project manager, the project team, the business development manager, and the organization with relevant information about each project customer.

The underlying purpose of this practice is quite simple: know the customer! Know who the customer is, know what the customer wants, and know who represents the customer's interests in business transactions. In knowing the customer, the project manager will gain insight into the customer's business interests and sensitivities. Also, the project manager will identify the personalities within the customer environment that will influence matters such as contract award, customer participation, deliverable acceptance, deliverable payments, and the general demeanor of key and prominent customer representatives.

Customer Identification is normally conducted in the Profile Phase in association with project initiation, but it can be accomplished or updated at any time during the project.

Customer Contact Information

Every project has a customer. Therefore, there is at least one primary customer point of contact for every project. That person needs to be identified as a means of establishing the necessary communication with the customer. On smaller projects, that individual will be the source of and will control customer information; he or she may even represent the sole interested stakeholder in the customer's business environment. On larger, more complex projects, there could be multiple customer points of contact that need to be identified for their roles and responsibilities in coordinating and collaborating with the project manager on relevant project and business information.

Therefore, it is sometimes necessary to look for at least two prominent customer points of contact for larger projects—the customer's *business manager* and the customer's *technical manager*, as discussed in the following text.

Customer Business Manager

This individual in the customer's business environment will usually hold responsibility for and interest in areas of contract administration and compliance—managing issued contracts and associated extensions or amendments, managing invoices and payments, and overseeing acceptance of project deliverables specified by the contract. This role is not necessarily the customer's "contracting officer" who would prepare, negotiate, and sign any relevant contract for project work; but this person could fill that role. The business manager could also have interest in monitoring project staff strength, qualification, and availability. Also, this role could hold responsibility for project fund distribution, including review and approval of any expenses incurred and reported by project staff members, and analysis of overall expenditure trends.

Customer Technical Manager

This individual in the customer's business environment will usually hold responsibility for and interest in areas of technical performance and technical deliverable development. This person often serves as the point of contact for the specification of technical needs and requirements, and sometimes conducts or participates in technical feasibility studies and analyses, technical design and plan reviews, and deliverable testing and acceptance activities. On occasions when the customer fields a project team, this individual could serve as the customer's project manager.

The customer is the most prominent external stakeholder in the project management environment, and arguably the most important. Therefore, it is essential that appropriate points of contact with the customer be established early in the project so as to facilitate two-way communication with the project manager and the performing organization. This can be facilitated by preparing a directory of customer points of contact. Also, customer points of contact should as well be considered for inclusion in any stakeholder analysis that is conducted as a means to discern and manage their participation in and influence on project performance.

Customer Business Information

The project manager or other responsible manager (e.g., business development manager) in the performing organization should acquire and manage customer business information as a means to becoming more effective in customer communication and collaboration, fulfilling business needs (associated with project execution), and understanding the current status of the customer relationship. This includes three types of customer business information:

- *Customer Business Profile*—The customer's business profile contains any relevant information the performing organization deems necessary to gain an adequate understanding of the nature of the customer's business. Fundamental information elements in the customer business profile can include:
  - Customer business description (e.g., product, service, industry, etc.)
  - Customer business size (e.g., number of employees)
  - Customer business locations (e.g., local, regional, national, global, etc.)
  - Customer business status (e.g., sales, revenue, stock position, outlook trends, etc.)
  - Customer business management (e.g., executives, directors, private owners, etc.)
  - Customer business affiliations (e.g., partnerships, industry memberships, etc.)
- *Customer Relationship History*—Information on customer relationship history should be kept on record in order to examine past business dealings with the customer. Its focus is on being able to review past business with the customer, but it can also look at the customer's other dealings in the industry and in the marketplace. Fundamental information elements in the customer relationship history package can include:
  - Major business transaction history with the customer, and the outcomes
  - Project work history with the customer, and the outcomes
  - Partnership or business affiliation history with the customer, and the outcomes
  - Key customer participants in projects and business transactions
  - Sales and revenue history with the customer
  - Customer invoice payment history
  - Prominent types of products and services outsourced by customer
- *Customer Business Approach*—Information about the customer's business approach may well be included in the customer relationship history but is separated here to distinguish the nature of information compiled. The primary information elements collected can sometimes be based on the discernment and judgment of managers in the performing organization in contrast to absolute factual data. This information helps to examine the customer and associated opportunities from a business interest perspective of the organization. Fundamental information elements in the customer business approach package can include management perspectives on
  - Alignment of customer business objectives and interests
  - Customer's business decisions and outcomes
  - Impacts of customer's business values
  - Demonstrated customer loyalty
  - Importance of particular customer retention

These perspectives can be developed by the project manager on smaller projects. Larger, high-value projects may require polling additional internal project stakeholders, to include the project executive/sponsor, the business development manager, and the PMO manager.

These three areas of customer business information can be comprehensive or basic according to established business needs and the capacity to manage a formal customer identification process. To the extent that a project knowledge management system is established, that system would be a primary means for introducing customer information for use by the PMO, by project managers, and by others in the project management environment.

1.2 OPPORTUNITY IDENTIFICATION

In conjunction with compiling customer business information, the project manager will also have to learn about the customer's unique needs, requirements, and expectations for the pending project. This will allow the project manager, business development managers, and any other participating managers in the performing organization to develop the preliminary business and technical solutions that will help achieve the customer's desired objectives.

The opportunity is specified with sufficient detail to enable the project manager to gain an understanding of the project work that needs to be accomplished. In turn, this "specification" is used to collaborate and confirm an accurate understanding with the customer and to further convey that understanding to additional project team members who will participate in business and technical solution development, proposal preparation, and project planning.

Concept of This Practice

This practice provides the project manager, the project team, the business development manager, and the organization with relevant information about what the customer needs and what the customer wants.

The purpose of this practice is to ensure that the project opportunity has been specified in some way and examined to some reasonable extent in order to ascertain the customer's perspective of the needs, requirements, and desired outcomes of the pending project. Furthermore, the project opportunity is analyzed to determine the customer's readiness to pursue the project, the customer's intended means of selecting the performing organization (and likelihood of selection), and the availability of project funding at the onset of the project.

Upon completion of opportunity identification, the performing organization should have a preliminary indication of whether or not to pursue the project based on an examination of customer need and interest indicators.

Opportunity Identification is always done in the Profile Phase during project initiation. It would be unlikely to revisit this activity once the project has started. However, on rare occasions, new information may surface, the customer's needs and requirements may be modified, or the customer's perspective on spending may change to warrant revisiting opportunity identification.

Initial Project Requirements and Specifications Review

Requirements and specifications represent the customer's perspective of what needs to be achieved by the project, and these items should be collected and reviewed as a part of opportunity identification. In some cases, it may be necessary for the project manager, project team, or business development manager to assist the customer in preparing this information. If so, it is important that such information always reflect the customer's interests and point of view of what is to be achieved.

A few sample information elements collected and used in opportunity identification include:

- Request for Proposal (RFP)
- Statement of Work (SOW)
- Business/Technical Needs Analysis
- Technical Specifications Document
- Technical Survey Document
- Technical Design Document

Project requirements and specifications documents are used and examined more closely at the onset of project planning (see *Project Requirements Examination* under the Project Planning practice area for additional guidance on establishing and managing project requirements).

Customer Readiness Assessment

Whether the opportunity is a competitive one in the marketplace or one in response to an internal request or mandate, it is still necessary to consider the customer's perspective on "offering" the opportunity. A customer readiness assessment allows the preproject customer relationship to be examined, if only briefly. In turn, it also gives the performing organization preliminary insight about whether or not to pursue the opportunity.

The assessment can be an exhaustive, numerical-based calculation or a simple review of factors that will contribute to the customer's decision for awarding the project to the performing organization. The performing organization, in turn, should consider the following indicators:

- Customer awareness of previous work (by the performing organization)
- Customer value of previous work (by the performing organization)
- Customer interest in using the performing organization
- Customer intent to actually pursue the opportunity
- Customer selection outlook (probability for selecting the performing organization)

These items should provide insight into the preproject relationship with the customer and an indication of the potential to win the opportunity. For an internal, noncompetitive customer opportunity, it can provide an indication of the nature of the interaction to be expected during project planning and execution.

Customer Opportunity Analysis

The initial examination of opportunity documentation, combined with any direct contact and communication with the customer, provides the information needed for the opportunity analysis. This considers not only the requirements for the project but also the requirements for obtaining the project.

The most common method for obtaining a project in the marketplace is through the submittal of technical and business proposals to the prospective customer. This is prevalent in a competitive marketplace. However, even when the opportunity is an internal, noncompetitive one, it is still good practice to prepare and submit a proposal to the end customer to identify the technical approach (e.g., work plan) and any associated funding requirements that may be incurred through cross-department accounting methods.

The opportunity analysis considers the following information:

- Type of opportunity
- Customer estimates of opportunity cost, schedule, and resources
- Customer needs analysis (including any relevant feasibility studies and analyses)
- Customer proposal activities and schedule
- Customer selection or award requirements and criteria

- Customer funding availability

This information will help the project manager to conduct further project initiation activities, proposal development and management activities, and subsequent project planning activities.

1.3 PROJECT DEFINITION DEVELOPMENT

Each business opportunity or internal mandate is examined in sufficient detail to ascertain if it is within the current capabilities and business interests of the performing organization to conduct such a project. The project definition is a primary contributor to that determination because it provides the first preliminary description of the project from both business and project management perspectives. In a sense, albeit somewhat abbreviated, it is the essence of the first "project plan" that is developed, and it is subsequently used to guide the more detailed project planning that is conducted following project selection.

Project definition development is a critical prerequisite to project work plan development. In some organizations, project definition is sometimes considered a part of the *Project Charter Development* effort. While it is treated separately within this methodology, project definition can be easily integrated along with other Profile Phase materials into a project charter package, as may be desired within the organization.

Concept of This Practice

This practice provides the project manager, the project team, and the organization with relevant information about the project so as to distinguish it from other projects and to place logical and rational boundaries on the work to be performed.

The purpose of this practice is to specify known-to-date customer requirements in project management terms—project objectives, project scope, a preliminary list of project deliverables, and any project assumptions and constraints. Most project definition documents also include initial estimates of cost, schedule, and resource utilization requirements, and this is included in the following discussion. However, in this methodology, project estimating is treated separately (see the project estimating practice area), but those estimating practices can be used to prepare initial estimates in conjunction with project definition development. Upon completing the project definition, the project manager and the performing organization should have a reasonable understanding of what the project will entail in terms of cost, schedule, and resource utilization. The project manager should be the lead developer of project definition.

Project Definition Development is always performed in the Profile Phase during project initiation. It is used again in conjunction with project selection activities, and during project planning, when it serves as the basis for many project planning documents. Project definition should be used and maintained as a project management tool throughout the duration of the project.

Project Objectives

The project's objectives may already be stated in customer requirements documents, or they may have to be developed by the project manager and project team based on a general understanding of the customer's requirements. If not otherwise provided by the customer, project objectives that are developed need to be reviewed and confirmed by the customer.

Simply stated, project objectives are those matters that need to be achieved as a result of project performance. They are the reason the project is being conducted. The project is successful when its primary objectives are achieved. Therefore, all project management plans, decisions, and work efforts should be aligned with and directed toward achievement of project objectives. Conversely, if an action or work effort on the project does not contribute to achieving specified objectives, then doing that work is a misdirection of valuable time and effort and should not be included in the planned project effort.

This necessitates that project objectives are clear, concise, and reasonable to pursue. The concept of "S-M-A-R-T objectives" is often used in preparing project objectives. This process is recommended, and the term *S-M-A-R-T* is represented in the following way:

- *Specific*—Project objectives need to have specific rather than broad statements of what is to be accomplished. *Specific* can also mean unambiguous to the extent that all project stakeholders should have a similar understanding of the objectives.
- *Measurable*—Project objectives need to be measured in order to know when they have been achieved. It is not uncommon for such measurements to be numerical, but they can also be of binary nature, for example, true/false, yes/no, or on/off. They can likewise be related to thresholds, for example, monetary value ($), time values (hours), and volume (work effort/hour), and the achievement of such thresholds as completion of project deliverables.
- *Agreed To*—Project objectives ultimately become mandates for the project, and therefore it is necessary to achieve reasonable consensus when developing them. Inasmuch as they will guide all subsequent project and project management activities, key project stakeholders

need to share their buy-in or agreement with stated project objectives.

- *Realistic*—Project objectives need to have a rational basis and a reasonable opportunity for success. This means that project objectives should not aim for unreasonable time constraints, unreasonable work efforts that cannot be completed with the anticipated project staffing, or results that have not been achieved before because of technology limitations.
- *Time-Based*—Project objectives need to guide the project's time frame, which will have a discernable finish point. Therefore, the stated objectives should reflect the time-based conditions in which they will be completed or otherwise achieved.

When project objectives need to be developed, this is normally a team-based activity. Ideally, the customer is a participating member of this team. However, sometimes project objectives can be prepared by a qualified individual for subsequent project manager, project team, executive sponsor, and customer review and acceptance.

It is better to have fewer objectives than more objectives, and three to five objectives for a project are usually manageable. You should rarely have more than seven stated project objectives, and if such a need does occur, that may signal a need to reconsider two or more separate projects in lieu of the original project.

Project objectives need to be precise, as indicated by the S-M-A-R-T objectives process described earlier. They will be aligned with and used (directly and indirectly) to guide virtually all subsequent project management activities and project planning document preparation. Therefore, having viable project objectives is essential to overall project success.

Project Scope Statement

The project scope statement is prepared to describe the nature and extent of the work effort that will be performed to achieve project objectives. The scope statement is a broader characterization of how the project objectives will be achieved.

Essentially, the scope statement indicates what is to be accomplished, when and where it will be accomplished, by which individuals or groups, and at what cost, schedule, and resource utilization thresholds. It can likewise be a statement of what will not be achieved. That is, the scope statement places boundaries on the work effort. The challenge for the scope statement developer (again, ideally a team effort) is to neither understate the scope in a way that does not sufficiently guide the project nor overstate the scope so as to inundate readers, reviewers, and project team users with unnecessary detail and complexities that are better placed elsewhere, perhaps in accompanying project plans.

A simple project scope statement can be developed and is recommended for most projects. The simple scope statement identifies the high-level work effort (e.g., design and develop) using required or designated specifications and standards (e.g., Customer Spec #1) and producing the required deliverable (e.g., a blue widget).

A more comprehensive project scope statement can be prepared to better discern the boundaries of the project work effort. To that end, it would have additional detail to address what is *in scope* and what is *out of scope*:

- What work will be done, and what work will not be done
- What specifications will be used or achieved, and what will not be used or achieved
- What level of design and development detail will be used, and what will not be used
- What technical tools and processes will be used, and what will not be used
- What deliverable functionality will be achieved, and what will not be achieved

The level of simplicity or complexity applied in creating the project scope statement is a factor the performing organization needs to consider and specify in a policy or addendum to this practice guidance. Inasmuch as a simple scope statement is desired, it is sometimes necessary to develop a more comprehensive scope statement relative to the complexity of the project, the expectations of the customer, or the nature of the business. Remember, however, that the project scope statement should be consistent with and indicative of how project objectives will be achieved.

Project Initial Estimates

Estimates prepared at this juncture in the project are referred to as *Order of Magnitude* estimates. That means they are generally within plus or minus 75% of the expected actual values. While this could represent the cost of almost two similar projects, this is widely accepted as a reasonable estimate because complete information about the project is not yet available, and the technical solution is not yet fully defined. Also remember, at this juncture, that we have not yet selected the project but are still trying to determine if it is to be pursued. There will be more detailed planning and estimating after the project is selected.

Project initial estimates can be prepared to include the following three primary elements:

- *Initial Time Estimate*—This represents the first "guess" of what the project timeline will look like to achieve project work that is associated with specified high-level phases and activities. This estimate can be prepared in conjunction with the resource utilization estimate that follows, as the resource allocations made will influence the project work schedule.

A basic approach to this estimate is to simply identify the major phases of the project as the basis for a timeline. If more detail is desired, this initial estimate could be prepared at the activity level, where more detail about the project effort is specified.

Be sure to consider and include time estimates for the following types of activities:

- Project planning activities
- Technical performance activities (i.e., the "project")
- Project management activities
- Research and review periods
- Travel, shipping, and waiting periods
- Administrative support activities
- Project delivery, acceptance, and closeout or maintenance activities

■ *Initial Resource Utilization Estimate*—This represents the first "guess" of what the project staffing requirements will be. Its focus is on identifying the types of resources needed, perhaps key resources as well as vendors and contractors that will be identified to conduct the project. Such resource utilization information will assist decision makers in their examination of resource availability, and which available resources will be allocated to the project.

A basic approach to this estimate is to simply specify the number of resources that will be needed within the major phases of the project. If more detail is desired for this initial estimate, specific resources can be identified according to the timeline elements (phases and activities) established earlier, to include consideration of the following types of resources:

- Project manager and project management resources
- Technical experts and activity leader resources
- Technical staff resources
- Administrative staff resources
- Labor group resources
- Business unit resources
- External resources

■ *Initial Cost Estimate*—This represents the first "guess" of what the project will cost the performing organization, and represents a project investment that is expected to ultimately show financial returns to the organization. This effort should be performed by a team or an individual who is familiar with project cost elements. It is also wise and highly recommended that a review of the project archives, particularly lessons learned, be conducted to examine prior project estimates on similar projects to see how well those estimates supported actual project performance.

A basic approach to this estimate is to simply specify the overall costs that will be needed to conduct the major phases of the project. If more detail is desired for this initial estimate, major cost items can be identified according to the timeline elements (phases and activities) established earlier, to include consideration of the following types of costs:

- Resource costs
- Materials costs
- Vendor costs
- Supplies and equipment costs
- Contingency fund costs

See the separate project management practice area, *Project Estimating*, for more information and guidance on preparing project estimates.

Project Deliverables

Project deliverables are those products and services presented to the customer as a result of project work accomplished, and, to a large extent, they represent the achievement of specified project objectives.

For project definition purposes, project deliverables are described at a high level and represent only those items that will be transferred to the customer. Therefore, internal or interim deliverables are not usually a part of the project definition, but they may be specified in accompanying plans when they are developed.

Project deliverables are normally aligned with the completion of certain project activities, as may be specified in the *Work Breakdown Structure*, which is normally constructed during project planning. However, at this early juncture, usually only a general description of the deliverables can be identified. The project manager and other project definition preparers can then specify anticipated project deliverables within project phases. This list of project deliverables will need to be reviewed and refined as more detailed requirements and information from the customer are applied to the project planning effort.

The specification and management of project deliverables are presented in greater detail in the separate project management practice area, *Project Planning*, under the Project Requirements Examination practice.

Project Assumptions and Constraints

Project definition provides an early description of what has to be accomplished in order to have a successful project outcome. Many of the project activities, events, and conditions that are initially considered are based on items such as "status quo," "common knowledge," "routine responses," and "reasonable expectations." These may be "common and reasonable," but since they are not necessarily factual, there could be alternate perspectives, and they need to be stated as the project's assumptions and constraints.

Project Assumptions are factors considered to be true, real, or certain for the purposes of making project decisions. Assumptions involve a degree of risk. Examples of assumptions to be considered include specifications or statements related to

- Dates when a key person is available
- Budget and resource availability
- Time requirements
- Organizational structure and culture
- Staff availability, training requirements, and experience
- Number and identity of stakeholders
- Level of project complexity
- Size and duration of the project
- External needs
- Extent of risks
- Level of technical capabilities

Assumptions made are not inherently project risks. However, the basis of each assumption must be checked to validate it. At the same time, if assumption validity is weak, it could become a project risk, and should be included for consideration in the project risk assessment that is performed.

Notwithstanding, project assumptions are identified for the very fact that they are not factual but assumed conditions. Once identified, the validity of assumptions should be monitored during planning activities and throughout the project to ensure a reasonably sound basis for project decisions and direction.

Project Constraints are generally known factors that will limit project management options. Specifically, constraints may restrict the planning of project cost, schedule, and resources needed to achieve the project scope; affect when or how an activity can be scheduled; or lead to team pressure to complete the project on time, within budget, and according to specification. Examples of constraints to be considered include

- Cost
- Schedule
- Staffing requirements or availability
- Funding availability
- Available technology
- Contractual factors
- Government regulations
- Risk factors
- Scope expectations and feasibility
- Market or economic factors
- Organizational structure
- Organizational culture
- Collective bargaining agreements
- Preferences of the project management team

Similarly, constraints in and of themselves are not project risks. However, they could become risks if the constraining condition unexpectedly changes to affect project performance.

Constraints should be monitored and validated on an ongoing basis.

1.4 PROJECT CLASSIFICATION DEVELOPMENT

It is important for project management stakeholders to have a common frame of reference regarding the types of projects being performed. The establishment of a project classification scheme addresses this need. This determination is usually a part of the project governance function because it has distinct business implications. However, in the absence of a formal project classification system, this methodology will assist users in classifying their project using generic criteria.

Concept of This Practice

The purpose of this practice is to specify the classification for every project in order to assist in describing the important characteristics of each project (i.e., an adjunct to *Project Definition Development*) and to allow stakeholders to immediately associate the importance of each project to the business. Project classification, when constructed with consideration for the business interests of the relevant organization, will be an aid in the following areas:

- Selecting, prioritizing, and managing projects in portfolio management
- Aligning projects with business objectives
- Identifying business and technical risks that may be encountered
- Calculating levels of project work performed in different technical areas
- Providing general indications of duration, resource requirements, and complexity
- Identifying and assigning project managers with appropriate skill and experience
- Qualifying team members for participation in the project effort
- Selecting vendors and contractors for participation in the project effort

The use of a project classification scheme will convey a significant amount of information about each project in just a few words.

Project Classification is normally conducted during project initiation (in the Profile Phase) but can be reviewed or updated at any time during the project.

Project Classification Criteria

The PMO or other governing body is normally responsible for creating and implementing an organization-wide project classification scheme. This is done when project classification criteria are developed to describe projects in the organization in terms of the business interests and the project work effort. This methodology prescribes a relatively simple yet fairly complete project classification scheme as a default, generic solution. The prescribed classification criteria can be modified to suit specific organizational needs.

The project classification criteria presented will consider the four factors of business interest, project management level, project performance indicators, and project complexity indicators to classify projects. Each of these is discussed here.

- *Business Interest*—This criteria area refers to the importance of the project to the organization and prescribes five classification options:
  - Operational Project—Work is conducted to fulfill operational needs, usually to develop or maintain internal operating capability.
  - Innovation Project—Work is conducted to design or develop new products, services, or technology for subsequent internal use or external sale.
  - Mandate Project—Work is conducted to satisfy the requirements of an internal (business) or external (industry or government) mandate.
  - Customer Project—Work is conducted to provide product or service deliverables and to fulfill objectives specified by internal/external customers.
  - Strategic Project—Work is conducted to achieve a marketplace position, or to achieve business expansion or another strategic objective.
- *Project Management Level*—This criteria area refers to the extent and complexity of project management needed to ensure project success and prescribes five levels of project management that could be associated with a given project:
  - Level 1—Simple (routine) technical specialty requirements, and/or no business complexity
  - Level 2—Advanced technical specialty requirements, and/or minimal to no business complexity
  - Level 3—Multiple technical specialty requirements, and/or low business complexity
  - Level 4—Unique or advanced technical specialty requirements, and/or moderate business complexity
  - Level 5—Multiple advanced technical specialty requirements, and/or high business complexity
- *Project Performance Indicators*—This criteria area refers to project features that can help delineate project performance requirements, to include
  - Project duration—How long will the project take to complete?
  - Project team size—How many resources will be assigned?
  - Project value (cost)—How much will the project cost? How much will it earn?

  Project performance criteria are evaluated and rated in relative terms of very low, low, moderate, high, and very high. Weights are then assigned to each criteria level, and an overall value for project performance is calculated.
- *Project Complexity Indicators*—This criteria area refers to a combination of project and business factors that can help delineate project complexity requirements, to include
  - Strategic Value—A project becomes more complex when it becomes more important to business success. This element examines the alignment of the project with strategic business objectives, the level of importance associated with marketing efforts, and business factors such as net present value and cost–benefit analysis results.
  - Business Risk—This factor considers the business risk produced primarily by external business influences, along with any technical risk associated with new product development, recurring project work, and development of state-of-the-art technology.
  - Technology—The amount of technology that is introduced into the project will have an effect on the capability to provide the intended technical solution. This includes consideration of new technology, current technology, the likelihood of technology changes, and technology training requirements.
  - Organization Scope—The number of business units participating in the project—including cross-functional participation and external vendors and contractors, their locations considered—will affect project performance and project management requirements.
  - Technical Scope—The depth or extent of technical expertise or specialization needed by assigned resources to properly conduct the project will affect project complexity.

  Project complexity criteria are similarly evaluated and rated in relative terms of very low, low, moderate, high, and very high. Weights are then assigned to each criteria level, and an overall value for project complexity is calculated.

These four project classification areas should sufficiently identify projects in most organizations. Although there are various options, the intent is to provide a classification "code" that is generally recognized throughout the organization. A few examples using the default criteria in this methodology include:

- Project A Classification: Customer-3. The classification uses only the business interest and project management level of indicators. It tells users that this project is for an external customer that requires a small variety of technical services.
- Project B Classification: Operational-1. The classification again uses only the business interest and project management level of indicators. It tells users that this project is for an internal customer that requires only basic or limited technical capability.
- Project C Classification: Mandate-4/5. The classification uses the business interest and project management level of indicators, along with a summary value of the project performance and complexity indicators. It tells users that this project is mandated and it requires some advanced technical capability to perform. The additional indicator shows that this project has "above average" complexity.

Project Classification Development can then be used to identify the type of projects being undertaken within the organization. It provides the common frame of reference that allows all key project participants (and project stakeholders) to recognize the type and nature of each project, and it facilitates decisions along the way.

Chapter 2

Project Selection

A project should not be pursued unless it can be shown to have a business basis and is approved by senior management as confirmation that it is aligned with the strategic business direction of the organization. Once approved, a project manager needs to be assigned sufficient authority and organizational backing to fulfill the business aspects of the project. Once approved, the project also needs to receive the ongoing attention and support of senior management, which participates in the project's progress at the portfolio management level.

A project does not have to be a revenue-producing effort, but it does require alignment with the business direction. Conversely, a project should not be a whim or a mandate that does not serve any direct or indirect business purpose. To that end, project selection is presented to specify or "select" the projects that will be pursued within the organization. The components of this practice area prescribe activities that inherently include senior managers as key participants over time. Each organization and each senior manager should examine the ways in which this participation can be optimized to avoid unnecessary involvement but ensure sufficient involvement by senior managers or an executive board that has ultimate responsibility for successful business outcomes.

There are four practices associated with Project Selection:

- Project Screening
- Business Case Development
- Resource Allocation
- Final Project Selection

Each of these practices has direct influence on project management and direct alignment with executives and senior managers involved in the portfolio management process.

Project Selection will take initial information that describes the opportunity identified earlier in the life cycle process and translate it into a project that becomes a business investment for the organization. Project Selection activities will provide the means for initial project selection, and they will provide the means to validate the project for continuation through completion.

2.1 PROJECT SCREENING

Once the project opportunity has been adequately identified, it can undergo project screening, which is a quick, first look at available information to determine if the opportunity is a viable business investment.

Concept of This Practice

This practice provides the project manager, the executives and senior management team, and the organization with preliminary indications about pursuing the project opportunity as a basis for continuing subsequent, more cumbersome project selection activities.

The purpose of this practice is to complete a preliminary examination of the project opportunity in order to provide an indication of whether or not the more time-consuming and costly effort of business case development should be undertaken. Therefore, only fundamental indicators are examined as a matter of process efficiency.

Project Screening is always done during project initiation (in the Profile Phase). However, elements of project screening can also be applied, as needed, during later project stages as part of the project business validation process and ongoing *Portfolio Management*.

Conducting Project Screening

Project opportunities are screened to determine their fit and contribution to the organization's business objectives. Screening is conducted using relatively simple criteria that can be applied by project managers and business managers alike to determine the next steps, if any.

The screening criteria should provide sufficient indication whether to accept or reject the project opportunity. If the opportunity is accepted, it will proceed to more detailed project selection activities, starting with business case development. If it is rejected, it simply is reported to any oversight authority for acknowledgment and is then removed from the organization's "project opportunities list."

The application of the same project screening criteria to all project opportunities lets managers in the organization know what is important for a project to be considered for selection. It also ensures that consistent decision making is applied when all projects are measured by evaluators using the same criteria for each opportunity.

The default project screening criteria for this methodology includes an examination of several criteria.

First are the primary screening elements:

- Strategic Interest—Does this project opportunity make a positive contribution to the overall portfolio?
- Nature of Project Work—Does this project opportunity represent the application of a core competency?
- Resource Capacity—Is sufficiently skilled staff available for assignment to this project opportunity?
- Competitive Position—Is this project opportunity competitive, or perhaps aligned for competitor selection?
- Customer Readiness—Has the customer validated the need, made funding available, and established the project opportunity as a priority effort?

Additionally, here are some secondary screening elements that can be considered:

- Break-Even Time—Does this project opportunity provide a business payback in reasonable time?
- Internal Impacts—Does this project opportunity contribute to business lines and organizational interests?
- Market Position and Market Share—Does this project opportunity contribute to market position and market share expansion?
- Business Risk—Does this project opportunity provide more business benefit than business threat impacts?
- Cost of Ownership—Are the costs of owning associated deliverables acceptable on this project opportunity?

Project screening can be as basic as determining "Yes–No" answers to simple criteria. However, more specific criteria can be developed by the PMO or other project management leadership group to indicate "Yes–No" thresholds or even graduated responses to criteria examination. Criteria should be reviewed and approved by executives and senior managers who can also identify how they are to be applied to the project screening process. Thereby, the organization determines what criteria evaluation results will allow the project opportunity to go forward.

Screening provides a preliminary examination of the project opportunity and enables the organization to determine if the opportunity warrants further consideration. The premise that a project must be aligned with business strategy is a focus of project screening. In particular, the criteria established to examine strategic fit is applied in this methodology. Opportunities that satisfy the criteria will go forward to final project selection and further detailed planning.

In the event that an organization may want only a single step and consider this activity to be their primary project selection step, it will need to conduct project screening as a more rigorous process. That rigor should emphasize the importance of business strategy alignment as the prominent criteria for project selection. As well, this approach also warrants a subsequent go/no-go decision gateway activity to confirm the initial selection decision.

2.2 BUSINESS CASE DEVELOPMENT

Project business case development represents the integration of preliminary project opportunity information and associated business information to facilitate project selection. The business case is sometimes referred to as the *project business plan* and can be used throughout the project to guide the organization's business interests for a given project.

Concept of This Practice

This practice provides the project manager, the executives and senior management team, and the organization with the business basis for selecting and continuing each project.

The purpose of this practice is to compile the requisite business and project information and perform the necessary analyses to determine if the project opportunity warrants pursuit by the organization. It introduces the project's strategic alignment information and integrates other pertinent information elements compiled in the Profile Phase.

Also, information related to allocating resources is often considered to be a critical part of the business case, and that concept is endorsed in this methodology. However, that effort is also presented as a separate practice (see the *Resource Allocation* practice) because of its importance to project and business success. Therefore, it is only referenced in this practice. The project business case is also the governing document in the portfolio management process by which ongoing executive involvement and project continuation decisions are facilitated.

Business Case Development is first performed during project initiation (Profile Phase), when it is used for project selection. The business case is then reviewed and updated (as necessary) throughout the project, and is used to confirm project continuation at junctures in the project.

Project Information Element Integration

The project business case is constructed to contain certain business-relevant project information, which is updated continuously through the project management life cycle. Initial and interim reviews of this plan facilitate validation of business purpose (per selection criteria), recurring determination of consistency with the organization's business strategy, and executive and senior management decisions about project continuation.

The following are information elements that are frequently considered to be a part of the business case and can be integrated from other project management practice areas:

- Customer Information—as covered in the *Customer Identification* practice
- Project Opportunity—as covered in the *Opportunity Identification* practice
- Project Definition—as covered in the *Project Definition* practice
- Project Classification—as covered in the *Project Classification* practice
- Business Risk (Preliminary)—as covered in the *Project Risk Management* practice area
- Resource Allocation—as covered in the *Resource Allocation* practice
- Portfolio Management—as covered in the *Portfolio Management* practice

The specific content and format of the project business plan is a matter of the organization's established practices or preferences. The practical consideration of this component is to provide all necessary information to enable a detailed opportunity evaluation for project selection to be accomplished.

These project opportunity information elements can be prepared separately or in conjunction with the business case development effort. When analyzed together, they present an overall picture of the project opportunity. That information is then combined or integrated with strategic opportunity information that is the focus of the business case development practice.

Strategic Alignment Review

The project business case is constructed to contain certain business-relevant project information, which is updated continuously through the project management life cycle. The criteria used in the business case facilitate validation of business purpose, confirm ongoing consistency with the organization's business strategy, and enable executive and senior management decisions concerning project continuation.

This section examines four prominent strategic perspectives that should be examined in developing the project business case. This includes revisiting more detailed aspects of the project performance perspective than were considered during project screening.

Business Perspective

The organization's business strategy is supported by particular business objectives that consider sales and revenue objectives, market position, and competitive strategies. Therefore, criteria for this business perspective should be considered during business case development:

- *Project costs*—Projects are selected based on criteria for achievement of
  - Project cost reduction initiatives
  - Product/service pricing strategies that cover specific incurred project costs
  - Product/service pricing strategies that attract new, expanded, or specialized business
  - Cost management objectives associated with resource use and optimization
- *Product and service quality*—Projects are selected based on criteria for achievement of
  - Product/service quality measures and objectives
  - Entry of high-quality products/services in the marketplace
  - Delivery of the highest-quality products/services in the industry
- *Customer satisfaction*—Projects are selected based on criteria for achievement of
  - Customer needs and requirements fulfillment
  - Customer business relationship development
  - Customer product and service deliverable acceptance
  - Customer reorders and retention
- *Business advantage*—Projects are selected based on criteria for achievement of
  - Increased revenue objectives
  - Enlarged customer base objectives
  - Expanded market share objectives
  - Increased marketplace recognition objectives
  - Global business expansion objectives

- *New products/technology*—Projects are selected based on criteria for achievement of
  - New product/service development opportunities and objectives
  - New technology introduction objectives

The criteria developed for project selection using business perspective factors will show how well a project fulfills or otherwise supports the organization's business objectives.

Financial Perspective

Each organization and industry has different requirements for the financial returns that are necessary for a project to be considered or approved. These requirements normally are based on the perceived risk and rewards inherent to that industry. Executives must examine the financial parameters of their business and determine what financial factors weigh into the criteria for selecting projects. Therefore, criteria for this strategy alignment perspective can be developed relative to such factors as

- *Investment commitment*—Projects are selected based on criteria for achievement of the specified initial or progressive limit of the investment amount allowed by type of project.
- *Investment returns*—Projects are selected based on criteria for achievement of the specific acceptable range of investment return or objectives for increased investor value. For example, one type of project may require a minimum 12% return, while another high-risk effort can be started only if the return falls into the 15–20% range.
- *Investment period*—Projects are selected based on criteria for achievement of specific acceptable time frames for achieving the desired returns per organization standards or general industry constraints. For example, a short capital project may be expected to pay back in three to five years, while a new product launch will be given as long as five to seven years.
- *Investment allocation*—Projects are selected based on criteria for achievement of specific financial funding pools that are established and available for allocation to project work. For example, specified funding pools may be used to allocate available investment funds to only certain classification of projects.

The criteria developed for project selection using financial perspective factors will show that a project has the capability to achieve the specified financial aspects of the business strategy.

Performance Perspective

Projects are selected when general project performance indicators reflect the likelihood of successful outcomes. Executives specify or otherwise influence these criteria against which all projects are evaluated, and they emphasize these criteria at every decision gateway. These criteria inherently expand on the business and financial perspectives criteria discussed previously and provide more detail to the project selection effort. Therefore, criteria for this strategy alignment perspective can be developed relative to such factors as

- *Nature of work (competency)*—Projects are selected based on criteria that confirm the application of existing competencies within the organization to achieve project objectives. Such criteria could specify competency within one or more technical or professional disciplines. It also could specify competency in conducting a particular business process, developing a particular product, or providing a particular service. For example, a checklist could be developed to identify which of the organization's core competencies are being applied to the project under consideration.
- *Extent of work (capability)*—Projects are selected based on criteria that confirm the organization's capability to fulfill project performance requirements. While an organization has fundamental competency in a technical or professional discipline, it must ascertain its capability (and its limitations) to accomplish projects at various and necessarily advanced or higher levels of monetary value, duration, risk, technical or professional discipline, diversity, and complexity—all within the constraints of a particular type of client or industry. For example, an organization may develop criteria that specify selecting a highly complex project of six-month duration but not one of two-year duration.
- *Extent of risk (or opportunity)*—Projects are selected based on the type and amount of technical work performance and business risk the organization is prepared to accept. Therefore, criteria should be created to specify the thresholds of risk that could be encountered as a result of project selection. For example, criteria could be specified for prominent categories of project risk and include the thresholds for project selection.
- *Resource availability*—Projects are selected based on the organization's ability to perform the specified work through the assignment of qualified resources. Criteria are formulated to ensure that resource availability—primarily in terms of numbers and necessary skills—is addressed and confirmed prior to project selection.

Nonnumeric Perspective

Projects are selected when business needs warrant them. Executives and senior managers need to identify criteria that will introduce projects for purposes generally outside the first three project selection perspectives. Also, these criteria are often characterized not only by using numerical thresholds but also by applying business decisions. Therefore, criteria for this strategy alignment perspective could include such considerations as

- *Executive mandate or directive*—Projects are selected based on the executives' determination to require them. In such cases, the project is selected and performed because the executive perceives some business value or benefit to be gained by the effort. Often, the executive applies some unspecified "numeric criteria" to such a mandate, and normally such criteria can be found to be an expansion or extension of one or more of the criteria listed earlier. When applied to the project selection process, these criteria specify that when an executive project decision is received, just do it.
- *Operating need/infrastructure*—Projects are selected to maintain or achieve certain levels of operational efficiency or effectiveness. These types of projects are selected, sometimes as part of a larger organizational program or initiative, but often because of the inherent operational improvement benefits to be received from a range of project activities that include such items as process development and implementation; infrastructure upgrades; software and computer network system upgrades and implementation; and facility construction, maintenance and refurbishment. Criteria for this project selection perspective are usually aligned with the need to achieve operating capability objectives that are specified elsewhere in an organizational business plan.
- *Competitive necessity*—Projects are selected based on the need to maintain business advantage, if not business parity. Project criteria are usually prescribed per specific business, market, or industry indicators, to include such items as the introduction of new technology, emergence of new industry or technical practice standards, and, sometimes, in response to competitor actions and activities in the marketplace. For example, an organization may select a project to fulfill the achievement of "facility certification" that many of its customers want as a basis for ongoing association.
- *Regulatory requirement*—Projects are selected based on the need to fulfill external mandates that facilitate business performance or otherwise enable the organization to continue as a viable business entity. Often, government agencies are the source of the regulatory requirements that must be addressed for such purposes as receiving government-sponsored contracts and business considerations, obtaining business licenses and authorizations, and complying with new or revised laws and regulations. However, self-regulation in industry could also be a source of regulatory requirement. The criteria in this area are simply that of weighing the business impact of not doing such a project versus the benefit of doing the project for compliance with the mandate.

Business Case Preparation

The project business case presents the results and analyses conducted relative to a given project opportunity. Before business case preparation, it is still in a period in time when a project can be declined following a review that is more rigorous than initial project screening. There is sometimes a tendency for criteria evaluators to lean toward achievement of criteria to enable the opportunity to be accepted as a bona fide project. The implementation of realistic criteria thresholds and the specification of required levels of analysis will moderate that tendency.

This section provides an overview of project business case preparation activities using the following recommended and stepped procedures.

Establish Business Case Development Team

Specify the members of the team responsible for developing the business case. This team should be led by the project manager or business development manager in the organization. Other team members can be obtained from the project team, business unit, or project management office (PMO). Members of the team should be proficient in tasks required for business case preparation. In some cases, particularly smaller projects, business case development is performed by just one person, ideally the project manager. To the extent possible, the project manager should be involved in business case preparation.

Review and Integrate Project Information Elements

Incorporate the information compiled during project initiation activities to examine it in conjunction with project selection criteria and in accordance with any separate analyses performed. During project information review and integration, consider potential impacts relative to the following particular potentially adverse findings or indicators:

- The customer is not yet ready or otherwise not yet committed to begin the project.

- The customer does not have a final statement of work for the technical effort.
- The customer's points of contact are not at the decision-making level.
- The customer is experiencing organizational or personnel changes.
- The project definition is incomplete.
- The project classification is inconsistent with accompanying information.
- Vendors appear to be needed to perform in core competency areas.
- The project manager (or an alternate skilled project leader) was not involved in the preparation of preliminary project information.
- The project manager is not involved in business case development.
- The project already appears to be selected (questioning need for a business case).

The identification of these or any similar findings or indicators should be reported to the project sponsor, project executive, or other project oversight authority while continuing to prepare the business case. Likewise, they can be mentioned in the project business case recommendation for due consideration by the reviewers who are responsible for project selection.

Also, the business case development team should have competency to prepare any and all of the project information elements, and can correct any of the incomplete items.

The review of project information elements should establish a frame of reference for those involved in business case preparation. A "package" of these elements can be prepared and included as part of the project business case.

Incorporate the Resource Allocation

Review project information to determine the number and type of staff required to complete the project so that sufficient resources can be allocated to the project. This represents a request for resource allocation, which is approved by the project executive in conjunction with project selection. Details on how to proceed with this effort are presented in the *Resource Allocation* practice. This activity addresses resource allocation—how many people and what types and levels of skills will be authorized to work on this project. It does not address resource acquisition, resource assignment, or other resource management activities, which are presented separately in the project staffing management practice area.

Prepare Financial Analysis

Examine all available information to prepare the requisite financial analysis for the project. Use the established methodology guidance or other internal methods to determine if the project under consideration is financially viable.

Financial analysis considers financial aspects of the project investment and uses quantifiable metrics and mathematical formulas to distinguish and determine project selection (and retention) appropriateness. Ongoing and candidate projects are scrutinized, and forecasts of competing projects in the portfolio are examined. Either a specified number of top project contenders or all projects meeting specified criteria are selected.

The following list presents several representative financial calculation mechanisms that could be applied to an organization's project selection and retention process.

- *Benefit–Cost Ratio Analysis*—financial evaluation that contrasts the benefits to be realized per the varying levels of cost investment
- *Economic Analysis*—the process of establishing project value in relation to other corporate standards, project profitability, benchmarks, financing, interest rates, and acceptance criteria
- *Feasibility Study*—a method used to examine technical and cost data to determine the economic potential or practicality of the project, such as time-value of money
- *Financial Source Analysis*—the techniques and methods related to providing the sources of monies and methods to raise funds for the project
- *Prospectus Review*—the evaluation of profitability studies and all pertinent technical data in a report prepared for review by the project's sponsor and funding manager
- *Project Investment Analysis*—the evaluation of all the cost elements (capital and operating) of a project as defined by an agreed-upon scope of work, to include costs incurred during the period from the completion of the project to the beginning of normal revenue earnings on operations
- *Inflation/Escalation Allowance Analysis*—an examination of the factors in cost evaluation that must be predicted to account for price changes with time
- *Cash Flow Analysis*—an evaluation of monthly in/out and accumulated project cash flow data to measure actual versus budget, allow for funding at lowest carrying charges, and measure spending; includes techniques providing the measure and means to assess total income relative to expended monies (e.g., present value, return on investment, discounted cash flow, internal rate of return, etc.)

The organization will likely already have robust financial analysis models in place as a fundamental aspect of business management. Executives and senior managers need to identify financial analysis models that can be applied to project portfolio management, and specifically to project selection and retention.

Assess Preliminary Business Risk

Examine the business risk that is associated with the project at hand. This addresses such factors as business competition, marketplace demands, customer demeanor, etc. Its focus is on "business" risk because a project work plan has not yet been constructed to assess potential risks on the project. Details about this effort are presented in the *Project Risk Management* practice area.

Analyze Business Perspective Information Elements

Examine the information presented by the business perspective in sufficient detail and as per the available time. Consider potential impacts relative to the following particular findings or indicators:

- The customer does not have a final statement of work for the technical effort.
- The customer has terminated other similar projects prematurely.
- The project effort is primarily one that involves a new technical product or service.
- Another (competitive) project provider is an on-site incumbent for the project effort.
- The project effort is one in which previous project providers have failed.

Include these and any other related findings when deliberating the business case recommendation.

Analyze Financial Perspective Information Elements

Examine the information presented by the financial perspective information in sufficient detail and as per the available time. Consider potential impacts relative to the following particular findings or indicators:

- The preliminary project cost estimates are larger than any project done previously.
- The project investment period is significantly longer or shorter than normal.
- The project return on investment is significantly larger or smaller than normal.
- The project investment break-even point is uncertain or very late in the project.
- The project shows no financial return on investment.

Include these and any other related findings when deliberating the business case recommendation.

Analyze Performance Perspective Information Elements

Examine the information presented by the performance perspective information in sufficient detail and as per the available time. Consider potential impacts relative to the following particular findings or indicators:

- The project effort is primarily one that involves a noncore technical competency.
- Resource allocation recommendations are unrealistic for the proposed work effort.
- Resource allocation recommendations cannot be achieved with current staffing levels and staff commitments to other projects.
- One or more significant business risk factors could affect project performance.

Include these and any other related findings when deliberating the business case recommendation.

Analyze Nonnumeric Perspective Information Elements

Examine the information presented by the nonnumeric perspective information in sufficient detail and as per the available time. Consider potential impacts relative to the following particular findings or indicators:

- The total number of pending projects characterized as "mandated"
- The total number of pending projects characterized as "mandated" by one manager
- An external regulatory mandate that is unclear or questionable
- An external regulatory mandate that is imposed solely on this organization

Include these and other findings when deliberating the business case recommendation.

Each organization will need to review these progressive steps and then define its own process for business case preparation.

Business Recommendation

The project business case development effort concludes with the delivery of a project selection/nonselection recommendation to executives and senior management reviewers in the organization. The business recommendation essentially summarizes the contents of the business case and the findings of the business case development team.

To that end, the business recommendation is prepared as a written document that serves as a "cover" for the business case and all other integrated information and materials. This package then provides a comprehensive collection of business and project information that substantiates the business recommendation. The package is published or otherwise reproduced in sufficient quantities for distribution to designated reviewers. For projects that are selected, this package is used also by the project manager to manage business aspects of the project, along with any guidance or adjustments made by the reviewing authority.

The arrangements for executive and senior management participation in the business case review are an integral part of this effort. This effort necessitates developing a schedule for a few key business case review activities:

- Publication and distribution of the business case package and business recommendation
- Time for business case examination and selection determination by reviewers
- Time for any points of clarification required by reviewers
- Meeting of reviewers for final discussion of the business case and final project selection decision

The intensity of this effort is reduced when there is a single reviewer who has ultimate authority for project selection. The effort is similarly reduced when there is a project control board or other similar group designated to conduct project selection review and deliberation activities.

2.3 RESOURCE ALLOCATION

Projects can go forward only with adequate resources to support them. Ordinarily, an organization has limits on resources and must make choices about which projects to support. Project selection, nonselection, termination, or adjustment is dependent, ultimately, on the availability of resources—personnel and financial—to support projects. Consequently, considerations for allocation of the organization's resources are an integral part of the Project Selection practice area.

Concept of This Practice

The *Resource Allocation Practice* provides the project manager, the executives and senior management team, and the organization with the means to specify and examine staff requirements as a basis for allocating resources to each project.

The purpose of this practice is simply to ensure that the organization's finite resources and their availability to perform project work are considered as an aspect of business case preparation and as part of the ultimate project selection decision. Tools used for developing staff requirements and a staff management plan, which are prepared during the Plan Phase, will also be used to provide the necessary examination for early and recurring resource allocations. Therefore such tools can be incorporated into the business case as information for review by executives and senior managers who must decide the specific allocation of resources for the project at hand and across all projects.

Resource Allocation is first performed during project initiation (Profile Phase), when used in preparing the business case and for project selection. Along with the business case, staff requirements and the staff management plan are also reviewed and updated (as necessary) throughout the project.

Review Project Resource Financial Impacts

Each project opportunity must be examined for anticipated resource needs and related financial impacts. This warrants a review of the following items.

- *Resource Requirements*—Initial resource estimates may be available to provide a preliminary list of resource requirements. However, the more detailed examination of staff requirements prepared in the Plan Phase will be a primary source of information that can be used to facilitate early resource allocation decisions. Decision makers should review that information for confirmation or adjustment, and to examine
  - What resources are currently required? What is projected for the future?
  - What personnel can be assigned to this project? What is the cumulative impact of all personnel requirements?
  - Is resource availability within our current capability? Are external resources needed? Are financing and partnering capabilities needed and available?
  - Are resources available to achieve the current project scope? Are scope adjustments needed to better utilize resources?
  - How will project schedules impact workload? Are adjustments needed?
  - Are personnel overutilized or underutilized? Are certain resource skill types overburdened? Do current personnel need additional training to meet anticipated project requirements?

  Again, the development of project staff requirements may be done in conjunction with resource allocation examination activities, using tools prescribed for process steps in the Plan Phase. The results of this examination will also provide some insight into financial impacts resulting from the resources required for the project.

- *Project Cost and Schedule Impacts*—Costs for specific skills, unique specialties, or turnovers during the project—all of which raise the costs of projects over time—should be evaluated. Information to be examined includes
  - Are all necessary skills available within the company, or is external resource acquisition necessary?
  - Are the skills necessary to complete the project part of the core competency, or is this a new business area?
  - What is the time dimension for the project under evaluation and for all projects using the same resources? Will the deadline or the cumulative impact of all affected projects require funding of outside assistance?
- *Quality Management*—Both anticipated and unexpected changes in the quality factors of the project and in the people required to ensure quality may incur cost adjustments as the project goes forward. This warrants examination of
  - What quality specifications in the project might generate staffing costs?
  - Will a different level of product or service quality expectation require a new level of effort that will affect resource allocations and costs?
  - Does the required resource level for quality expectations exist within the organization?
- *Vendor, Supplier, Contractor, or Subcontractor Agreements*—External agreements and arrangements may affect pricing over time. Identifying and accessing external resources can save costs in some instances:
  - What agreements have been made with external organizations?
  - Are firm external organization commitments needed early in this project?
  - What external vendor, supplier, contractor, or subcontractor costs for products and services stay the same or increase over the life of the project?
- *Costing Methods*—The use of different costing methods can produce different results, and must be normalized or must use standard methods across all projects. A review of methods helps to ensure costing method accuracy:
  - What cost methods have been used? Hours versus dollars? Are the methods consistent across the period of project work?
  - Will the skill mix required on the project change over time? Will that change affect costs and internal or external personnel utilization?
  - Have all costs been accounted for in each project? (For example, have administrative and support costs, as well as costs to perform project management activities, been included in all projects?)
  - Have previous projects' cost data been used to estimate costs here?

The financial and staffing requirements deliberated and developed in this step should be considered when preparing the listing of staff requirements.

Review Organizational Resource Availability Impacts

Resource requirements for the current project opportunity should be evaluated against the total portfolio of projects. This examination can be presented using a spreadsheet or other tool contained in this methodology. It includes an examination of other projects' resource allocations (or extracted summaries) and provides for a review of the total resource commitments and staffing requirements tallied across all projects. The following considerations can be deliberated to assess resource availability impacts.

- Are the required resource projections within the capability of the organization if this project is added to the portfolio?
- Are changes to project scope or outside financing needed to do this project?
- Is the pending resource utilization commitment financially sound? Is there flexibility to handle unanticipated changes?
- What is the total impact on personnel relative to the number and types of particular skills available?
- Do interests in applying resources to this project make any other projects stand out to be adjusted or eliminated?
- Relative to resource skill and availability, is this project too big? Too risky? Too unknown? Of marginal benefit?
- Can project schedules be adjusted or the scope scaled to have a different impact on financial resources or on resource utilization?
- Can personnel be grouped or clustered so that several projects can be supported simultaneously?

The results from this examination of the impact on organizational resource availability should be considered as a part of the business case recommendation.

Specify Resource Allocations for the Project

Using either information attached to the business case or the selection recommendation document itself, it is prescribed that a written statement or indication of the approved resource allocations be included in the business recommendation for the project that has been selected.

A document that can be used for this purpose is the Resource Allocation Plan, which is one of the optional project support plans that can be prepared during the Profile Phase. This plan can be used to provide a more detailed examination of resource requirements and availability, and to specify and record executive and senior management resource allocation decisions and the associated approvals for the allocations made. If prepared, this plan should be monitored by the project manager throughout the project and reviewed by executives and senior managers at decision gateway points.

2.4 FINAL PROJECT SELECTION

The transition from a project opportunity to a bona fide project is performed in this final project selection activity. It is a relatively straightforward process that involves the participation of executive and senior management-level decision makers. It is inherently a part of the portfolio management process but is presented here because it is an integral part of project selection activities that should include the project manager (see the *Project Portfolio* practice in the Project Business Management practice area).

Concept of This Practice

The *Final Project Selection* practice provides the project manager, executives and senior management team, and the organization with the means to select projects that will be undertaken within the organization. This activity is highlighted by a senior management-level decision that connotes project alignment with the organization's business strategy and interests, and an assertion that adequate staffing resources and financial capability (funding) will be provided to conduct the project and ensure its success.

The purpose of this practice is to provide the means to identify, review, and select those projects that executives and senior management deem consistent with the business purposes of the organization. It includes the considerations of project opportunity, project business case, and project resource requirements. It is essentially the first step in the project portfolio management process (see the *Portfolio Management* practice).

Final Project Selection is always done during project initiation (Profile Phase). However, elements of final project selection can also be applied, as needed, during later project stages or upon reaching project gateways as part of the project business validation and resource allocation review process. It should be noted that, if the project opportunity is a competitive one that requires a proposal for customer review and award, then this selection activity simply confirms the organization's interest and intent to pursue that course.

Project Selection Principles

The *Final Project Selection* process begins with consideration of several principles that should be applied to the decision-making process to support better project choices:

- Principle 1—Be explicit about the selection criteria and ensure that all projects are held to the same standard, no matter how many interesting options may be available.
- Principle 2—Be clear about the procedure for choosing projects and ensure that all projects are selected by the same method.
- Principle 3—Be prepared to challenge (and defend) all assertions in a project business case, since overly rosy or incomplete predictions do not promote success.
- Principle 4—Convene a review group (e.g., project control board) of diverse stakeholders to examine candidate project opportunities, since the impact of selecting each project will transcend the organization and possibly even have impacts outside it.
- Principle 5—Include the project management staff, as is consistent with organizational business practices and procedures, in the project selection process.

These principles are not established at or during each final project selection activity, but rather they are implemented as part of governance established relative to business needs identified in a supportive project management environment.

The remaining subsections of this practice present the prescribed steps for conducting the final project selection.

Determine Final Project Selection Methods

Over time, organizations have typically emphasized financial goals as indicators of performance, almost to the exclusion of other values in the organization. Benefit–cost ratios, return-on-investment, and stockholder value have been typical quantitative measures employed. Increasingly, organizations are realizing that they need a broader decision framework than just financial performance for the organization to continue to survive and thrive in a more holistic but fast-paced business environment.

In general, project selection methods range from simple paper-and-pencil calculations to highly analytical and mathematical models, to value-driven and performance-based methods, to decision software packages. A thorough review of selection framework models should be conducted before a particular framework is adopted to ensure that a method is chosen that matches the strategic intention and business needs of the organization. Again, this framework is something that is established as a capability within the project management environment, not something that is done for each project.

The financial analysis discussed in the business case development practice covers several financial-based mechanisms for project selection. The project selection mechanisms presented in the following text illustrate a range of additional project selection mechanisms available to the organization. The organization may choose one of these fundamental mechanisms, develop a combined mechanism, develop its own approach, or seek a more comprehensive project selection mechanism from among a variety of advanced tools and techniques available today.

- *New Project Classification Mechanism*—This mechanism is a framework for project selection and evaluation that considers projects in four strategic classifications:
  - Breakthrough—projects that move the organization to new markets, new competitive position, or new competencies
  - Evolutionary/Extension—projects that support the internal operational needs of the organization, such as human resource management systems, financial systems, information management, and decision support
  - Infrastructure—projects that are an iteration of what the organization is currently doing, capitalizing on a core competency, or extending current product lines
  - Customer Service and Support—projects that focus on customer expectations, requirements, and improvements to better competitive advantage

  An organization can use these classifications to delineate the nature of work associated with each project and to determine what efforts are being pursued against specific strategic business objectives. Each ongoing and candidate project is listed by its focus and alignment within one of the four classification areas. Then, each project is ranked by importance relative to the achievement of strategic objectives within each of the classifications. This ranking can be supported or adjusted by further examination of subcriteria within each classification (e.g., risk, resource utilization, and investment returns).
- *Balanced Scorecard Mechanism*—This mechanism is a framework for project selection based on the balanced scorecard evaluation approach developed by Robert Kaplan and David Norton,* and presented initially in the *Harvard Business Review*. It presents a "whole organization" perspective in four evaluation areas:
  - Financial Perspective—Links financial objectives to organizational strategy for improvement of financial performance, and addresses timely and accurate reporting and management of organizational expenses and assets in the project management environment. It includes project management metrics that deal with increasing revenues, lowering costs, improving productivity, upgrading asset utilization, and reducing risk.
  - Business Process Perspective—Entails specification of internal business processes and activities necessary to support product and service value for customers and shareholders. Measures associated with project management can include such elements as project management and technical performance process time; process quality and process cost; and vendor and supplier selection, performance, and management processes.
  - Customer Perspective—Considers the customer and market segments that will deliver the revenue to meet the organization's financial objectives, and specifies the value proposition that will be applied to target customers and segments. Measures associated with project management that help an organization retain and expand its business with targeted customers include such elements as product and service quality, timeliness of project deliverables, degree of satisfaction in customer business relationships, and image and reputation in the marketplace and industry.
  - Learning and Growth Perspective—Provides the infrastructure and capability that enables the other three perspectives to be achieved. This includes a particular focus on capability to implement change for business advantage. For project management, this perspective considers such metrics and measures as tool implementation and utilization, training, quality elements of planning and performance, and application of lessons learned.

  This mechanism for project selection focuses on project value relative to these four dimensions of business. Organizational goals are listed for each of the four dimension categories, and measures for attaining the specified goals are added to the matrix. The projects under consideration or under way are listed according to the business goals they will achieve. The measures of the projects should match or be related to the measures of the business goals.
- *Rank Order Matrix Mechanism*—This mechanism is a framework for project selection based on a method

* Kaplan, R. and Norton, D., "The balanced scorecard—measures that drive performance," *Harvard Business Review*, Jan/Feb 1992, pp. 71–79.

developed by Martin Buss,* as initially presented in the *Harvard Business Review*. It provides a benefit–cost approach that does not rely on quantitative data but examines and ranks project benefits in four areas that could be interpreted as follows:

- Financial Benefits—cost versus such metrics as revenue returned and cash flow impacts resulting from the project effort, expense reduction (or increase) resulting from the project management approach, and further business opportunities resulting from project success (or failure)
- Technical Benefits—cost versus such metrics as opportunity for the introduction of new products and the potential for technical innovation or breakthrough
- Core Competency Enhancement—cost versus such metrics as demonstration of new or enlarged performance capability, expansion of project manager and project team member skill and experience
- Harmony with Corporate Culture—cost versus such metrics as achievement of business objectives that endorse or enhance organizational customs, traditions and values, fit and impact on the cultural aspects of the organization, and validation of individual affiliation with the organization

While metrics have been suggested for the rank order matrix, the value of this project selection mechanism is found in the more intuitive nature of evaluating the project cost versus the discernable benefits to be gained.

- *Poor Man's Hierarchy Mechanism*—Many executives have difficulty making choices when a whole list of options are offered but have less difficulty making a selection when pairs of choices are presented. The Poor Man's Hierarchy is a pairwise comparison method that reduces the need to make a choice from a long list of projects. This mechanism will facilitate review and prioritization of projects under consideration.

  In a grid pattern, list all the projects on the left side of the page and copy the same list in the same order across the top. Cross out or place Xs or stars in the top left square and all the squares in the diagonal to the bottom right corner, since there is no point in comparing a project against itself. The project at the top left is compared for preference (or other criteria) to the second project named across the top row. If the project on the left is preferable to the project listed across the top, a '1' is placed in the cell. If the project listed across the top is preferable, a '0' is placed in the cell. Note, too, that comparisons need to be made only above the diagonal. Then add the total scores across the row to determine the ranking of the projects. Tie scores may occur but can be assigned a priority.
- *Peer/Oversight Committee Review Mechanism*—Whether an individual or group has made project selections and regardless of the selection method, selected projects should be examined rigorously before they are ultimately entered into the portfolio. A peer/oversight committee review is a means used to challenge each project. The reviewers, comprising either a peer group or a cadre of stakeholders, should convene to confront all assertions and claims of progress, resources, and schedules and to address the alignment with strategic objectives. They should look for gaps, overreaching, and unclear detail in each project. Each project sponsor and project manager who has put the project forward should be ready to defend the project.

  The peer/oversight committee review has two important additional benefits beyond evaluating and clarifying projects. First, each reviewed project is challenged by a fresh perspective and a broad array of expertise; and second, the sponsor, project managers, and reviewers all become more committed to the projects evaluated as a result of delving into the details of each project. Ultimately, key personnel gain knowledge of and commitment to all of the projects in the relevant organization.

Conduct Candidate Project Review

The executive authority or project control board should conduct project selection reviews, beginning with an individual and independent review of the project information (perhaps even some preliminary plans) that is available to date. The board then convenes to apply the selection mechanism of preference. It will deliberate and discuss the merits of the business case and the resource allocations needed, making any adjustments deemed appropriate through consensus.

The selection authority review should focus on several key areas during the examination of project opportunity:

- Consistency with strategic objectives
- Project opportunity business evaluation
- Business and project risk indicators
- Points of executive participation in business case review
- Subsequent decision points or project gateways for further project examination
- Recommended project portfolio position
- Decision appeal options (for the project sponsor or project manager)

* Buss, M., "How to rank computer projects," *Harvard Business Review*, Jan/Feb 1983, pp. 118–124.

Conduct Final Project Selection

Following review and deliberation, this activity should lead to a decision for one of the following actions:

- *Select project and proceed.* Begin project start-up administrative actions and proceed to convene the project team (or proposal team) for detailed project (or technical) planning.
- *Select project on contingency.* Indicate that the project has been selected but is pending a project start date to be determined.
- *Defer selection.* Indicate that a selection decision has not been made or otherwise finalized and is pending a request for more information and further review.
- *Nonselect project.* Indicate that the project was not selected and discontinue project opportunity evaluation.

This activity determines whether or not a project is selected for inclusion in the relevant project portfolio. The results of this deliberation could be either a mandate for the project manager to proceed, or it could be a recommendation of project selection to a higher approval authority. A project that is not selected is normally not reported to the higher approval authority.

The approved project selection decision should be conveyed to the relevant project manager and project sponsor, and communicated to key project stakeholders in the organization.

The final project selection represents the formal start of business and project management for the project. This is generally characterized by the start of the following activities:

- Integration of the project into the relevant project portfolio represents executive and senior management involvement in the project (see the *Project Portfolio* practice).
- Preparation of the project charter represents project manager, project sponsor, and other project leaders' involvement in the project (see the *Project Charter Development* practice).
- Ongoing monitoring and attention to business issues and the start of project oversight, control, and support by the PMO, as well as general management oversight (see the *Project Governance and Oversight* practice).

Chapter 3

Project Planning

A project is organized and structured to satisfy requirements and to achieve specified work in a specified period of time, and within a specified budget. Translating requirements into solutions necessitates project planning that will provide direction for skilled people to accomplish the work that produces the desired project outcome. Project planning is also needed to enable responsible and capable individuals to subsequently manage the progress of that project work.

Preceding the actual planning effort, it is necessary to gain a comprehensive understanding of what is needed and what should be attained or achieved through the project work effort. This represents the identification and examination of *Project Requirements* that are used to guide project planning activities. Then, a *Technical Solution* is developed as a high-level description of how project requirements will be fulfilled. Work elements are then defined, and a project *Work Breakdown Structure* (WBS) is constructed.

There are three practices associated with project planning:

- Project Requirements Examination
- Technical Solution Development
- Work Breakdown Structure Construction

Estimates of project cost, schedule, and resource utilization are normally prepared in a concurrent manner (see the separate Project Estimating practice area). When these estimates are incorporated into the work elements of the WBS, a project work plan is created, and that plan provides the capability to implement and manage the preferred technical solution. The project planning practices provide the primary input in the creation of the project work plan—the fundamental document required to perform project management (see the separate *Project Work Plan Development* practice section under the Project Management Plans practice area).

3.1 PROJECT REQUIREMENTS EXAMINATION

The identification of requirements is a necessary beginning to the project planning process for every project. It specifies the project outcomes to be achieved, usually in terms of system, product, or service deliverables. Project requirements provide the specification of the desired project outcome—what is it, along with the specification of its business purpose, functional capability, and technical dimensions and description.

This information provides the basis for project planning, assists in project management, and guides project technical work. It provides a common frame of reference for all stakeholders relative to the customer's expectations about the project's deliverables. This frame of reference warrants the communication, collaboration, and validation activities that are prescribed when identifying project requirements.

Concept of This Practice

This practice provides the project manager, the executives and senior management team, the project team, the vendors, the customer, and the organization with a specification of what is required for a successful project outcome. Project requirements will particularly become the guiding reference for managing the quality aspects of the project.

The purpose of this practice is to guide the performance of activities that are used to compile, analyze, and validate the requirements for each project.

Project Requirements Examination prominent activities are normally done in conjunction with the early activities of Project Planning (Plan Phase). However, preliminary work with requirements actually begins when requirements information is first gathered and compiled during Project Initiation (Profile Phase). This practice prescribes four primary activities associated with the examination of project requirements:

- Requirements Gathering
- Requirements Documentation and Analysis
- Requirements Validation and Approval
- Requirements Baseline Setting

These activities are described in the following text.

Requirements Gathering

The process of gathering requirements represents the identification of one or more information sources, the methods or approach that will be used to obtain requirements from each source, and the specification of the type of information that is needed from each source.

Project requirements gathering can be conducted using the following methods and sources.

- *Statement of Work*—Project requirements may be directly or indirectly specified in the statement of work issued by the customer. The statement of work may be included as a part of solicitation materials or be a stand-alone document. It may also be found, in some cases, included with a customer's work order or purchase order, or it may be inherently represented by the work order or purchase order itself. The statement of work can be a source of requirements information for less technical and less complex project work, or it could represent a higher-level specification of requirements for such technical and complex project work. The statement of work should be reviewed with sufficient examination to identify any specified project deliverables or other requirements.
- *Request for Proposal* (RFP)—The RFP document, as well as similar matter such as the Request for Information (RFI) and Request for Quote (RFQ), should be reviewed for content that describes project requirements. This type of document issued by the customer could include sections that present a statement of work, listing of project deliverables, or reference to technical standards and specifications. The RFP needs to be adequately reviewed to identify direct or indirect references to project requirements.
- *Technical Specifications*—Technical specifications usually provide a more detailed description of the product or deliverable that should result from project performance. The "technical" nature of the specification usually implies a reference to a level of detail or descriptive that can be used to create the technical aspects of the end product or deliverable. The technical specification, however, can sometimes include information that is used across business, technical, and functional types of requirements. The technical specification can also include direct or indirect references to standards that are applicable to the nature of work to be pursued. Any technical specifications for the project need to be used as the "blueprint" for creating the end product or deliverable, to include addressing requirements for their technical composition, operating features, functional capability, and business application.
- *Business Specifications*—Business specifications provide guidance for conducting the project relative to business-type requirements. This could represent a wide range of business-related requirements and include such elements as
  - Proposal/response due dates
  - Fulfillment of required proposal/response content
  - Fulfillment of required administrative actions
  - Specification of cost and schedule thresholds
  - Specification of required staffing skills and competencies for the project team
  - Specification of required customer and end-user involvement
  - Specification of required or acceptable contract types
  - Specification for required contract terms and conditions
  - Specification for fit of the end product or deliverable in the business environment
  - Guidance or requirements for the use of contractors, vendors, and suppliers

  Business requirements are used prominently in constructing the business solution but may also surface as elements of the project work plan, which should include such business-related project management activities.
- *Surveys and Analyses*—Surveys and analyses are sources of requirements information that deal primarily with technical-type requirements. They provide a means to fine-tune or otherwise create specifications for the technical solution, and could include
  - Site surveys (e.g., engineering, construction, etc.)
  - Business process engineering
  - JAD sessions
  - Prototype development
  - Structured design and analysis
  - Benchmarking analysis

  Surveys and analyses are used to decompose and clarify high-level technical requirements or to construct the technical solution based primarily on referenced industry or technical standards.
- *Workshops*—Workshops provide a structured and facilitated approach to the specification of business, technical, and functional requirements. They bring together relevant participants who discuss and deliberate the requirements for a project, and who jointly decide on

the needed requirements set. Workshop participants can be a homogeneous group or include representation from both internal and external organizations having diverse interests in the project's outcome. Workshop participants should be chosen for their expertise in the technical nature of the project. Workshops can be used to conduct many of the group-based surveys and analyses activities that were mentioned in the previous paragraph, or they may be conducted as self-structured requirement development meetings.

- *Interviews*—Interviews provide for requirements collection based primarily on one-on-one conversations with relevant project stakeholders, which are very often the end users. The interview process begins with the development of a standard questionnaire that will be used by the interviewer, includes the scheduling and conduct of interview meetings with selected individuals, and concludes with an examination and analysis of interview results and outcomes. While one-on-one contact is the normal interview approach, team or group interviews can also be conducted to generate early consensus in the determination of requirements. Some may consider such a group interview to be more aligned with the workshop method for gathering requirements.

Requirements Documentation and Analysis

The process of documenting and analyzing requirements is simply one that lists all of the requirements associated with a project and examines them regarding how, when, and where they will be applied to project work. This "specification" of requirements enables the project manager to align and plan project work toward the accomplishment of each project requirement. As may be needed, this process enables requirements to be decomposed into discrete statements that are then tracked and monitored for fulfillment. It also enables requirements to be aligned with specific WBS work elements.

Requirements analysis includes the following actions:

- *Requirements Statement Examination*—Each decomposed requirements statement is reviewed for clarity and completeness—does it describe a requirement that is understood? Each statement is also examined for stability—will the requirement remain the same through fulfillment, or will it become subject to change during project execution? To that end, this examination may prompt an assessment of project risks associated with the stability of requirements.
- *Cross-Requirement Examination*—The collection of requirements statements is compared to determine if there is any repetition or potential redundancy that could cause incorrect references to be made. This step also examines the collection to identify any conflicts or inconsistencies across specified requirements.
- *Requirements Identification*—Each requirement is assigned a unique identifier for tracking and monitoring purposes.
- *Requirements Type Designation*—Each requirement is aligned with one of the types of requirements that are distinguished in the organization. The following are the default requirement types used in this methodology:
  - Business
  - Technical
  - Functional
  - Other

  The organization can use these, modify or expand them for better fit in the organization, or create its own requirements types that best serve its management needs. In turn, each requirement can be managed relative to the "type category" in which it is placed. Each requirements statement can have specified actions or characteristics that are associated with a certain requirements type. For example, the following characteristics could be aligned with requirements types:
  - Area of Responsibility—requires business, technical, or project management oversight
  - Source of Requirement—indicates the individual or organization that prescribed the requirement and that will serve as a point of contact for clarification or change
  - Requirement Specification Document—indicates the requirement's reference document that contains the requirements description or complete requirements statement
  - Testability—indicates that requirement testability can be used to determine fulfillment
  - Standard or Regulation—indicates association with a particular industry standard or government mandate

  The specification of requirement designations and the alignment of these or other requirements-type characteristics is an organizational action taken in conjunction with methodology deployment.
- *WBS Alignment*—Each WBS work element, at least at high levels of work decomposition, are aligned with the requirement to be fulfilled.

Requirements Validation and Approval

The process of validating project requirements is one of review and feedback to the project manager (or other requirements managers). It is a process of communicating defined requirements and receiving feedback information regarding how well the requirements are perceived to satisfy needs and fulfill expectations.

In general, project requirements validation is an effort to examine and confirm three things:

- *Specified requirements are verifiable.* There is consistent understanding among key stakeholders of what is to be accomplished, recognition that it can be realistically accomplished, and agreement regarding what will indicate that the requirement has been fulfilled, as supported by the following:
  - The project manager and customer have the same perspectives on requirements.
  - The project manager and customer both agree that the requirements are realistic.
  - The project manager and customer have established completion criteria.
- *Specified requirements are discernable.* Prepared requirements statements provide adequate indications of boundaries to reduce or eliminate scope creep.
- *Specified requirements are independent.* Prepared requirements statements can be examined independently, do not present conflict or opposition to other specified requirements, and independently and sufficiently describe the result to be achieved.

Some of the methods just prescribed for identifying project requirements can also be used to validate project requirements. Also, other methods and objectives can be implemented.

In turn, prominent managers in the performing organization and in the customer's organization should establish for themselves sufficient understanding of the project requirements to enable them to sign off and approve the requirements baseline.

Requirements Baseline Setting

The process of requirements baseline setting provides an initial and ongoing reference to approved project requirements. It includes the following general activity elements:

- *Project Stakeholder Review*—Project requirements are examined by primary project stakeholders (e.g., the project manager and project executive) to gain appreciation for the project effort, but also to review the project requirements validation that has been conducted. In this review, stakeholders can view and understand the bases for specific project deliverables, and, when uncertainty arises, they can elevate their concerns for additional consideration by the customer and the project approval authority. In essence, this is a final project requirements validation step.
- *Project Authority Review and Approval*—Project requirements come to the project approval authority following their validation. At such time, the requirements should be clear and specific, and they provide a quick understanding for the level of project authority used. Each organization may designate approval authority in the project business plan, project charter, or other document, according to established organizational business practices or as per the classification of the project. This could include authority granted to or retained by the
  - Project Control Board
  - Project Executive (Sponsor)
  - Project Manager
  - Business Manager
  - Project Management Office

  An approved set of project requirements enables detailed project planning to begin.
- *Project Requirements Baseline Establishment*—The approved set of project requirements represents a baseline that is referenced when creating the project solution and associated work plan. The baseline is subject to somewhat rigorous change control procedures, as may be implemented for the project at hand. As well, all work conducted on the project is directly or indirectly related to the project requirements baseline, and project plans are monitored and managed to ensure that they address all elements of the project requirements baseline.

3.2 TECHNICAL SOLUTION DEVELOPMENT

The project technical solution presents a description of the project work to be accomplished, and specifies the milestones and deliverables associated with that work. It is used to guide the technical work effort but is also valuable for use by nontechnical managers as a means to ascertain the level of effort and progress.

Concept of This Practice

This *Technical Solution Development* practice provides the project manager and customer with a general specification of work to be performed by the project team, as dictated by project requirements. It presents the organization's approach to achieving the statement of work provided by the customer. It often contains a description of the major project phases but may also contain more detailed descriptions of work elements as well as the steps needed to fulfill project requirements. The level of detail is usually determined by the project manager, consistent with customer needs and organizational practices.

The purpose of this practice is to provide a basis for constructing the project WBS, which is the key component of the *Project Work Plan*. To that end, the technical solution is often included as the "technical approach" in the technical portion of any proposal submitted to the customer for consideration.

The technical solution is normally done during Project Planning (Plan Phase). However, it should be reviewed and updated as necessary throughout the project.

Preparing the Technical Solution

The technical solution is the descriptive element of the project. It can be a broad and general written statement or a very detailed written description of the work to be performed.

The technical solution will frequently describe the work to be accomplished at the phase level of a project, and thereby it helps to define or otherwise identify those phases. To that end, the technical solution carries much of the related information contained in the project definition to the next level of detail. Sometimes, as per local practices or project manager determination, the technical solution will also describe project activities and tasks within each project phase. When this greater level of detail is achieved, the information is then ready for entry into the WBS.

Preparing the technical solution prompts the use of action verbs, which is similar to the content of the WBS. It is the first attempt to specify project work actions, particularly at the activity and task levels. The technical solution will be used to guide the construction of the WBS, and is an intermediate step between specifying requirements and developing the WBS. In-as-much as the technical solution represents a high-level or abbreviated view of work to be performed, it can be used to illustrate the project to project stakeholders and other individuals who do not require the details of a WBS examination.

Specifying Project Milestones

Project milestones are the technical solution elements that provide a means to monitor and track critical activities associated with the technical solution. By definition, milestones are zero-time events; they have no duration. Rather, they serve as indicators of such matters as

- Completion of specific work actions
- Progress of specific work assignments
- Passage of increments of time
- Measurement of increments of cost
- Achievement of resource utilization objectives
- Transfer of project deliverables

Project milestones are used to indicate project progress at a high level. They are often imbedded in the work breakdown structure to show progress without showing each and every work element. When the work breakdown structure is filtered to display only milestones, this provides a means for senior managers and executives to peruse project progress without examining all of the details contained in the WBS.

In some organizations, milestones are used to represent deliverables and show the timely (or delayed) transfer of project deliverables to the client. However, such "deliverable milestones" can be incorporated on their own merit, as described in the following section.

The organization should identify the type of milestones it wants to monitor, and the project manager can also identify and include personal preferences for milestones during development of the technical solution.

Specifying Project Deliverables

Project deliverables are the technical solution elements that identify what the client will receive as a result of the project effort. Deliverables will likely be a product, a service, or an automated system (or hardware or software component). More precisely, a deliverable is any measurable, tangible, verifiable outcome, result, or item that must be produced to complete a project or part of a project. Project deliverables are the output of the project work packages defined in the WBS and are normally linked directly to the work packages they fulfill. The project manager, in collaboration with the customer, can use the following concepts when specifying project deliverables:

- Begin the specification of deliverables based on any preliminary deliverables listed in the project definition (scope statement).
- Consider the following when specifying project deliverables:
  - What should be delivered?
  - When should it be delivered?
  - Where should it be delivered?
  - How should it be delivered?

  Answers to these simple questions will contribute to better planning of work efforts that will produce each deliverable.
- Address the following conditions when specifying deliverables:
  - Determine whether adequate cost, duration, and resource utilization estimates can be developed for the identified deliverable at the work package level.
  - Determine if the complete deliverable can be defined in tangible, verifiable terms at the work package level, or if only deliverable components can reside there.
  - Determine if the deliverable can be appropriately scheduled and budgeted at the work package level.
  - Determine whether the deliverable can be assigned to an individual, an organizational unit, or an

external vendor, or otherwise can remain within the immediate purview of the project manager.
- Address the need for specifying deliverables other than customer deliverables:
  - Is there a need to specify any internal deliverables resulting from project management activities (e.g., project plans, reports, etc.)?
  - Is there a need to specify any internal deliverables resulting from organizational mandates (e.g., reviews, audits, performance reports, etc.)?
  - Is there a need to specify any interim deliverables resulting from partial work on or component development of customer deliverables (e.g., system component-A to the overall customer system deliverable)?

The project manager should carefully plan the inclusion of each project deliverable following these considerations. The project's customer and stakeholders will judge the performance of the project by the quality and timeliness of the deliverables. Above all, the project manager must ensure that each deliverable meets the needs and requirements of the project.

Project deliverables can then be imbedded as "deliverables" or as "deliverable milestones" in the WBS. This can be done in a way that allows the progress of deliverables to be tracked and reported (in a filtered view) for review by senior managers, executives, customers, and other project stakeholders.

3.3 WORK BREAKDOWN STRUCTURE CONSTRUCTION

The WBS represents the specification and decomposition of project work, normally to the *work package* level—the lowest level of work at which cost, duration, and resource utilization are assigned. The WBS is normally a deliverable-oriented group of project work elements that organizes and defines the total scope of the project. Any work that is not contained in the WBS is considered to be outside the scope of the project.

Concept of This Practice

This practice enables project planners to translate the project definition elements, particularly the project objectives and scope statement, into discrete work steps to be performed. It provides the project manager, project team, and customer with a breakdown of all work to be accomplished by the project, and a means to monitor those accomplishments. It facilitates coordination and collaboration of work between project team members and across project stakeholders, and establishes a common frame of reference for those communicative processes.

The project manager and project team can use the WBS to accomplish

- Budget estimating (cost management)
- Work duration estimating (schedule management)
- Staffing allocations (resource utilization management)
- Project tracking and control (project variation management)
- Risk assessment and response management
- Communication planning and implementation
- Quality planning and implementation
- Procurement and contract planning and implementation
- Project performance measurement
- Milestones monitoring
- Deliverables tracking

The WBS is widely considered to be the most essential tool needed for effective project management. Developing a realistic project work plan is not possible without first developing a WBS that identifies each project work element that will be used to achieve project objectives.

The WBS is normally developed during Project Planning (Plan Phase). However, it should be reviewed and updated as necessary throughout the project.

Preparing for WBS Development

The first step in preparing the project's WBS is a review of the project definition. This review should provide high-level insight and guidance for developing the WBS. Project planners should conduct this review to include an examination of

- Project objectives
- Project scope statement
- Sponsor and stakeholders
- Assumptions and constraints
- Preliminary cost estimates
- Preliminary schedule estimates
- Key resources and preliminary resource utilization estimates
- Preliminary project and business risks

Ideally, the interim steps of preparing a more detailed project requirements document and a technical solution (as discussed in previous sections) are accomplished for each project. When available, these documents do represent a translation of the project definition contents for use in planning the project work effort. Project planners should use these items along with a review of project definition elements when preparing for construction of the WBS.

Developing the WBS Structure

The WBS breaks down a project's activities and tasks into the lowest achievable level that can be budgeted, scheduled, assigned to resources, and ultimately evaluated. Each descending level represents an increasingly detailed description of the project's work elements. Project work is often decomposed according to the following structure:

- *Project*—The highest level at which the work effort to be performed is identified and distinguished from other work efforts in the organization.
- *Phase*—The specification of a very high-level component of project work; where there are usually about four–seven phases specified for each project (e.g., plan, design, develop, test, transfer, accept, etc.), according to the technical nature of work to be performed. The technical nature of work is then contrasted with the phases of the project management methodology to ensure that all essential project management activities are also included in the project WBS. Phases can overlap, and their combined timeline duration represents the duration of the entire project.
- *Activity*—The specification of a higher-level component of project work; where it represents a collection of subordinate work elements that usually have some similarity in the nature of work performed, a common product, system component, or service result to be derived, or other work-based relationship. The activity level represents the roll-up or aggregation of all work elements below it in the structure. Therefore, every activity will have at least two subelements of work. One subelement of work would merely be the activity itself, as per the concept of work roll-up or aggregation.
- *Task*—The specification of a more detailed component of project work; where it represents either a discrete work effort or a roll-up or aggregation of two or more lower-level work efforts that have some common skill, knowledge, or labor effort applied. Again, a sole subelement of work would only be the task itself, as per the concept of work roll-up or aggregation.
- *Subtask*—The specification of a very low-level component of project work; where there is usually a significantly homogeneous work effort performed.

This structure can be used across most small, mid-size, and even some larger projects. Very large projects and so-called "mega projects" could require additional work element levels to be defined, and this structure can be decomposed further by using additional subtask levels. Also, any naming convention can be applied to these structure elements as long as such terminology is communicated widely and used uniformly across the organization.

There are two additional concepts to consider when structuring project work. The first is the concept of "work package," and the second is the concept of "cost account."

- *Work Package*—The work package is the level at which all cost, schedule, and resource utilization estimates are created. The project work package is a discrete element of work that represents the lowest level where work is assigned and project progress is tracked.

  Project management tradition has evolved to show (and some standards promote) that a work package should be performed in no more than 80 hours to be fully manageable. This "80-hour rule" applies to most medium-size projects. However, for larger, more complex projects costing several millions of dollars, defining the lowest WBS level at 80 hours can be unrealistic in some circumstances. Sometimes a work package becomes several weeks or even several months in duration for "mega projects." For smaller projects, an 80-hour work effort may actually be too much time, when only one day or a few hours are needed to complete the work effort. Project planners should use the "80-hour rule" when possible but reconcile use of a smaller or larger work package duration when necessary.

  Each work package should produce some discernable output or "deliverable" for the project, which is not necessarily the deliverable for the customer. Sometimes a work package is created to represent distribution of project work to an individual or to a specific team, giving them an assignment for achieving a desired work package outcome or "deliverable." It can also be used to show development of a component of the customer's deliverable. Also, the work package can be used to specify work needed to accomplish internal project management and planning "deliverables" associated with the project.
- *Cost Account*—The cost account is the level in the project work structure that is used to provide guidance and information to the functional areas in the organization that will account for the costs associated with the project work effort. It will normally reside in the structure at one level above the work package level. For a medium-size project, this would be the activity level. The cost account provides a means to estimate budgets and to track, monitor, and control the work being conducted within each cost account. Therefore, in contrast to the use of work packages cited earlier, the cost account would normally be used to show work elements that are distributed or outsourced to external vendors and contractors, and it could also show work elements distributed to other teams within the organization.

Project planners should use the concepts presented here to construct the WBS, which can be created in a variety of formats. This methodology suggests consideration of two prominent format options:

- *Outline Format*—An outline format is a detailed task list incorporating numbers corresponding to each WBS activity, task, and subtask work element. This format is the most common one for developing and building a WBS, where each level of indent indicates a lower level of work effort. The outline format organizes the project work by defining all the tasks that must be performed for each activity and at each phase of the project life cycle. As the levels become more distinct, all the activities and tasks, along with any subtask or lower efforts to be accomplished, are identified. Figure II.3.1 depicts a simple WBS outline format.
- *Gantt Chart Format*—The Gantt chart format transposes the WBS from outline form to a horizontal bar chart with a time dimension, which is useful for developing and monitoring the project schedule. Figure II.3.2 depicts a simple WBS Gantt chart format. Please note how lower-level work efforts aggregate or roll up to comprise the next higher work element.

Sometimes it is useful to combine these two format options, as is done when using any of today's project management software applications. These applications present the WBS outline and Gantt chart formats side by side. They also present a variety of other WBS and project schedule formats that can be selected by the user.

Also, most automated applications will help the user to create the WBS. This is done effectively when work is entered at the lowest, work package level. Then, the user identifies related or similar work packages for aggregation or roll-up, and uses the application to combine them. As this is done, the application will also automatically calculate the duration for all successively higher work element levels, which is the "combined duration" of lower-level work elements. The convenience and accuracy of this calculation will rely on ensuring that all work element relationships (e.g., predecessors) are properly defined at the work package level.

Constructing the WBS

The actual construction of the WBS is generally accomplished using one of two prominent approaches: the top-down (analogy) approach or the bottom-up approach.

- Top-Down WBS Construction Approach—In the top-down approach, project activities and tasks are sequentially decomposed into related work package work elements. Using this approach, all major project phases are first broken down according to the primary activities to be performed. Then, those activities are further decomposed to the task and subtask levels, as needed, until the work package level is developed as a work element that can be reasonably monitored and managed. It is at the work package level that planners should incorporate cost, schedule, and resource utilization estimates. Continue the decomposition until the capability to introduce that information is reasonably achieved. A rule of thumb is to create work packages at a level where work accountability can be assigned and managed.
- Bottom-Up WBS Construction Approach—The bottom-up approach begins with the identification of all the work elements needed to fulfill project objectives and manage the project to completion. These tasks (and subtasks) are then combined into related groupings, which are then rolled up or aggregated to the higher-activity level. In turn, related activities are aggregated to the phase level, and so on, to the project level. This approach is best accomplished by a planning team or

WBS Outline Format

WBS Element #	Activity and Task Level
1.0	Plan Project (Phase)
1.1	Develop Work Plan (Activity)
1.1.1	Prepare Project Work Plan (Task)–Cost Account
1.1.1.1	Construct WBS (Sub-Task)–Work Package
1.1.1.2	Incorporate Estimates (Sub-Task)–Work Package
1.1.2	Prepare Support Plans (Task)–Cost Account
1.1.2.1	Prepare Risk Plan (Sub-Task)–Work Package
1.1.2.2	Prepare Quality Plan (Sub-Task)–Work Package

Figure II.3.1 WBS outline format.

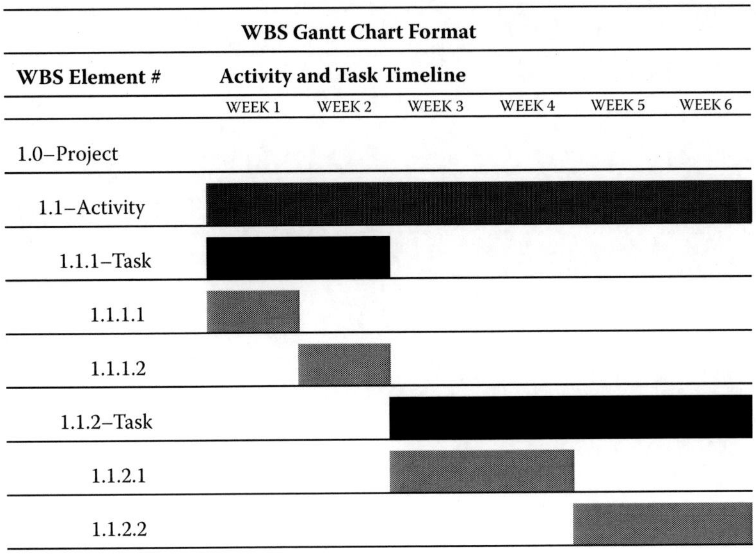

Figure II.3.2 WBS Gantt chart format.

members of the project team who will actually perform the work. It often begins by using group brainstorming techniques to identify as many of the required project work elements as possible. Then, as the team proceeds to aggregate related work elements, any gaps or missing work elements can be identified and incorporated into the structure. Again, it is at the lowest levels of work, the work package, that cost, schedule, and resource utilization estimates are introduced.

When constructing the WBS by either approach, project planners should ensure that it accurately defines the entire project effort. Essentially, if a work effort is not included in the WBS, you should not expect that it will be accomplished. Conversely, only work that is considered within the scope of work should be included in the WBS.

Project management involves the planning of work to be performed and then managing that plan for work accomplishment within the allotted cost, time, and resource availability. To that end, the project WBS is the fundamental tool of project management. Whatever format the WBS ultimately takes, a project simply cannot be effectively managed without it.

As the WBS is constructed, it is worth noting a few tools that are similar to the WBS in format but that are used to manage additional project information:

- *Contractual Work Breakdown Structure* (CWBS)—A decomposition of work that describes a total product and the associated work to be accomplished on a specific contract; it often includes identifying the level of reporting and delivery provided to the customer.
- *Organizational Breakdown Structure* (OBS)—A decomposition of work elements as per assignments to specific organizational units, vendors, and sometimes individuals.
- *Resource Breakdown Structure* (RBS)—A decomposition list of project work as per assignments to the specific resources; a variation of the OBS.
- *Bill of Materials* (BOM)—Describes and quantifies, in hierarchical pattern, the list of physical materials, parts, and components required to manufacture a product at the assembly or subassembly level.
- *Project Breakdown Structure* (PBS)—Serves the same purpose as the WBS, and this term is often applied when the BOM is incorrectly identified and used as a WBS.

Once created, the WBS can be refined at points where estimates are incorporated, and thereby the WBS is translated into the *Project Work Plan*. See more information regarding how this translation or transition is accomplished in the project estimating and project planning practice areas.

Chapter 4

Project Estimating

Project estimating is the practice of assessing the probable values of cost, duration, and resource efforts needed to produce the required product, service, or system deliverables. Project estimates are aligned with work elements contained in the project's work breakdown structure (WBS), normally at the work package level.

Many organizations continue to rely on the estimating skills of project managers and their teams to derive the project cost, schedule, and resource utilization estimates. In some organizations, senior managers (including business managers and project managers) are called upon to participate in project planning teams, where they bring business acumen along with industry-based estimating skill and experience to the project planning effort. In a few organizations, skilled estimators are employed and join the project planning team to provide a more accurate and reliable set of project estimates than would otherwise be provided by planners with less experience.

Project estimating is primarily a matter of knowing what to estimate and how to estimate it. To that end, this practice area prescribes some estimating concepts and techniques for

- Project Cost Estimating
- Project Schedule Estimating
- Project Resource Utilization Estimating

The *Project Work Plan* is created when these estimates are appended to the project's work breakdown structure (WBS). The project work plan then becomes the primary project management tool that allows the project to begin and continue through the fulfillment of its objectives and deliverables.

Project Estimating is normally conducted during project planning (Plan Phase). However, estimates should be continuously reviewed and updated as necessary throughout the project. There are several key events or indicators that should automatically trigger follow-on reviews (and possible updates) of project estimates. These include

- Changes in project scope or in the scope of any WBS work element
- Changes in any project risk event or the addition of any new risk event
- Project replanning, to include changes to any project plan component
- Examination and approval of project change requests
- Failure to achieve customer quality acceptance
- Failure to achieve timeliness of customer deliverables
- Changes in project resource assignments or availability
- Conduct of management gateway reviews in the project management life cycle

The organization or project manager should note these triggers and develop any additional ones needed to prompt a review of project estimates for other specific events or at critical points in the project management life cycle.

4.1 PROJECT COST ESTIMATING

Project Cost Estimating entails establishing the expected cost that will be needed for the organization to conduct the project or otherwise provide the product, service, or system deliverables. This practice presents the fundamental concepts and technique guidance for estimating project costs.

Concept of This Practice

This practice enables the project manager and project planners to assign estimated values for cost to project work elements. In turn, project cost (i.e., the project budget) can be tracked and controlled against those estimates.

Project Cost Estimating is normally conducted during project planning (Plan Phase). However, cost estimates should be continuously reviewed and updated as necessary throughout the project. Please refer to the key events or indicators (listed earlier on the project estimating practice area introduction page) that should automatically trigger follow-on reviews (and possible updates) of project cost estimates.

Identify Types of Cost Estimates

Across organizations and industries, estimates are defined to indicate a range of accuracy for the estimate prepared. The range of accuracy is normally related to the extent and reliability of information that is available and is used to create the estimate; it is also related to the experience of the individual or team preparing the estimate. The following are common types of estimates used in the project management environment. These estimate types normally refer to cost estimates but could be used in a broad sense with schedule and resource utilization estimates.

- *Order-of-Magnitude Estimate*—This high-level estimate provides only low accuracy in the range of –25 to +75%. Therefore, if an order-of-magnitude estimate is $100, this suggests the actual cost could range from $75 up to $175. This type of estimate is usually prepared without very much supporting information, and it represents the type of estimate normally used for project initiation activities. It provides a "rough" indicator for decisions regarding whether or not a project opportunity should be pursued. This type of estimate may also be known as a conceptual, preliminary, or feasibility estimate.
- *Budget Estimate*—This mid-level estimate provides for moderate accuracy in the range of –10 to +25%. Therefore, if a budget estimate is $100, this suggests the actual cost could range from $90 to $125. This type of estimate is prepared when more information about the project becomes available, and includes such items as scope of work, technical specifications, and requirements documents. It is often used to obtain internal project funding approval and to allocate resources in association with obtaining approval to proceed with the project. A budget estimate is usually the preferred level of accuracy in *Business Case Development*.
- *Definitive Estimate*—This detailed-level estimate provides significant accuracy in the range of –5 to +10%. Therefore, if a definitive estimate is $100, it suggests that the actual cost could range from $95 to $110. A definitive estimate is prepared from well-defined data and is used for establishing the project budget (cost baseline), submitting cost proposals, and managing change orders, legal claims, and government approval requests. Definitive estimates generally fit well with the bottom-up approach used to create work packages for the project WBS.

Apply Cost Estimating Techniques

The following list includes some of the more common models and techniques that can be considered for estimating project cost:

- *Analogous Estimating*—This model is also known as "top-down" estimating. It focuses on the use of actual costs of previous similar projects as the basis for estimating the current project cost. It is created through the application of expert or professional judgment and is frequently used when there is a limited amount of information about the project. This technique requires estimators who have the ability to combine perspectives on organizational and industry history to apply the organization's standards and utilize personal skill. While this method is less costly than other techniques, in most cases it is also less accurate.
- *Delphi Technique*—This is used by several experts working as a team to derive independent cost estimates and then act to resolve any discrepancies to provide for estimates that can be used for the project. The results depend on the experts' experience as well as their ability to work together as a team. This can be a cumbersome method, but when project team members are the estimators, the process will provide for a group commitment.
- *Parametric Modeling*—This estimating method uses project characteristics (parameters) in a mathematical model to ascertain project costs. Parametric models are usually aligned with an industry or type of work effort (e.g., construction costs per square foot). The models for this estimating method are usually obtained either through internal development or through industry-based organizations and vendors. Both the cost and accuracy of commercially available parametric models vary. They are more likely to be accurate when the historical information used to develop the model is accurate and when parameters used in the model are readily quantifiable.
- *Constructive Cost Model* (COCOMO)—This estimating model is used in software development. There are three versions of COCOMO, which differ in detail and accuracy—basic, intermediate, and detailed models.
  - Basic—Useful for quick order-of-magnitude estimates of software development cost, but has limited accuracy
  - Intermediate—Includes personnel quality and experience, and use of modern tools and techniques

as factors in terms of their aggregate impact on overall project cost
  - Detailed—Accounts for the influence of the factors in the intermediate model during individual project phases
- *Function Point Analysis* (FPA)—The function point analysis technique is used to determine software development cost. It creates estimates based on the premise that application development time is proportional to weighted counts for the number of
  - External inputs
  - External outputs
  - Logic master files
  - Interfaces to other systems
  - External inquiries

  A variation of the FPA technique uses feature points, rather than function points, and considers algorithms in addition to input and output files.
- *Bottom-up Estimating*—Using this method, cost estimates are determined for each work package in the WBS. This model produces thorough estimates and minimizes omissions. It does, however, require a comprehensive WBS, and it can yield a false sense of security by equating detail with precision. The cost and accuracy of this technique are driven by the size of the individual work packages—smaller work packages increase both cost and accuracy. The project management team must balance the need for additional accuracy against the additional cost of the time needed to produce that accuracy.

Estimators should examine business and project management processes to determine which models and techniques will be used when preparing project cost estimates. Persons having responsibility for cost estimating should be familiar with the methods and techniques they use. Relevant experience with the nature of work to be performed is also a key factor in preparing project cost estimates.

Determine Types of Project Costs

The project manager does not have to be a certified accountant to manage cost, but reasonable familiarity with cost elements is essential to successful cost accounting and budget management. Also, in today's world of technology-based software applications, it is generally recommended that a good software application package be selected and used to assist the project manager (and the organization) in the management of various project costs.

The following types of project costs should be considered for inclusion in the estimates created at the work package level and ultimately presented as the budget in the *Project Work Plan.*

- *Labor Costs*—Project resource utilization requirements are usually incorporated into the WBS at the work package level. Associated labor cost estimates are also entered at the work package level and then aggregated at successively higher WBS levels to provide the total project labor cost. The loaded labor rate for each resource, by person or by job code, is entered into the work package, and when using an automated application, it will then calculate the labor cost according to the number of hours allotted for the work element. If the project has a long duration, salary increases and other factors affecting future hourly rates should be considered. Note that the number of hours per resource is an estimate of time that is created and illustrates the collaboration needed between the cost and schedule estimating processes. Similarly, the number and type of resource utilization needed also has bearing on the cost, and those data are likewise considered and prepared concurrently with cost and schedule estimates. Labor cost estimates should be prepared for
  - Project management (project managers, project sponsors, project executives)
  - Professional and technical team members
  - Labor and skilled workers
  - Administrative aides and assistants

  Some of the resources in this list may be inadvertently excluded in project planning. Sometimes that exclusion is intentional. Unless these resources are part of a central project management office (PMO) or the organization has an "integrated" workforce structure (i.e., assigned resources already report directly to the project manager or PMO), there should be cost accountability for resources working on the project. In the absence of such accountability, data relating to total project labor costs will be inaccurate. Alternately, the cost of project management and administrative personnel may be aligned with indirect costs described in the following text.
- *Direct Costs*—Project direct costs should be entered at the work package level for most items acquired by direct purchases. Certain cost items might be more manageable at a higher level in the WBS, but caution should be used when making such an assignment at mid-levels in the WBS to ensure that the cost is properly aggregated upward. Direct costs are accounted for by entering the unit cost for each item in the work element in which it is used. If an item is used in association with multiple work elements, this warrants consideration for entering the cost at a higher level of the WBS. When the project has a long duration, inflation and other cost escalation factors should be factored into the cost estimates. Direct costs are those costs that will be

attributed directly to the project and usually include the following types of cost items:
  - Materials (raw or piece materials used to create or construct the customer deliverable)
  - Equipment and equipment part replacements
  - Contract workers' (subcontractors'), vendors', and consultants' labor fees
- *Indirect Costs*—Project indirect costs are usually not directly attributable to specific work packages. On certain larger projects, the cost associated with planning and managing the project may become an indirect cost. Therefore, it is important to include these costs in the project budget. The following are examples of project indirect costs:
  - Overhead allocation (administrative resources, facilities, office equipment, etc.)
  - Computer hardware and peripherals (including LAN and connectivity items)
  - Software applications
  - Communications (telephone, fax, e-mail)
  - Travel
  - Training and education
  - Administrative supplies
  - Office space (facility allocation)
- *Contingency Funds*—These funds are project costs that have been approved and set aside as a means to deal with *uncertain* future circumstances (e.g., labor extensions, modified requirements, or responses to project and business risk events).
- *Management Reserve*—These funds are project costs that have been approved and set aside as a means to deal with *unknown* future circumstances impacting project cost, schedule, or performance objectives.

Prepare the Project Cost Estimate

Project cost estimating is the process of establishing an approximation of the total cost of the resources (human and material) and other miscellaneous expenses needed to complete the project. To that end, cost estimating should be done in conjunction with schedule estimating and resource utilization estimating. Project costs also include the expense for conducting project planning and management. Additionally, project cost estimating should include identification and consideration of various costing alternatives.

The project planning team is convened (sometimes as a component of the project team) along with others having skills and experience in estimating project costs, and they meet to conduct the estimating portion of the project planning effort. The following cost estimating steps are prescribed for this process:

- *Conduct the estimating team kickoff meeting.* The project manager reviews the approach to cost estimating with the planning team and assigns responsibilities based on individual skills and experience.
- *Gather the required data.* The planning team gathers all the information about the cost elements that need to be estimated and determines the type of estimating method, model, or technique to be used.
- *Obtain the required estimating tools.* The necessary software application, parametric models, or other cost estimating tools must be made available to the estimating team.
- *Prepare the project cost estimate.* The planning team prepares the estimate using appropriate and available tools.

For external projects—those projects performed under contract—cost estimating must be distinguished from pricing. Pricing is a business decision about how much the organization will charge for the product or service provided. The cost estimates produced here only provide an indication of organizational cost commitments that are needed before any business return on investment is specified or realized.

Establish the Project Cost Baseline

Upon completion of project cost estimates, the results are usually forwarded to the project executive (sponsor) and perhaps other management entities (e.g., PMO) for review and approval. Otherwise, the project manager may have the authority to approve the project cost estimates (project budget) as per standard procedures within the organization or as specified in the *Project Charter*. In some situations, the customer may also be a reviewer of early cost estimates.

A cost baseline is established when the ultimate review authority within the organization has approved the cost estimates. The cost baseline is normally set by the project manager, and any changes to this baseline must go through a change management process. The cost baseline is normally established in conjunction with setting the schedule and resource utilization baselines.

When using project management software, there is normally an automated feature or function available to establish and save the approved cost estimates as a part of the project baseline.

4.2 PROJECT SCHEDULE ESTIMATING

Project Schedule Estimating entails developing the work activity schedule and associated activity relationships and dependencies that will be needed for the organization to conduct the project or otherwise provide the product, service, or system deliverables. This practice presents the fundamental concepts and technique guidance for estimating the project schedule.

Concept of This Practice

This practice enables the project manager and project planners to assign estimated values for work effort duration to project work elements. In turn, the duration (i.e., the project schedule) can be tracked and controlled against those estimates.

Project Schedule Estimating is normally conducted during project planning (Plan Phase). However, schedule estimates should be continuously reviewed and updated as necessary throughout the project. Please refer to the key events or indicators (listed on the Project Estimating practice area introduction page) that should automatically trigger follow-on reviews (and possible updates) of project schedule estimates.

Schedule Development Overview

To a large extent, "schedule development" and "schedule estimating" mean the same thing and are interchangeable terms. However, we should recognize that some authorities would use the term "schedule estimating" to indicate a focus on the determination of work activity duration. In this methodology, "schedule estimating" refers to all aspects of schedule development.

The project schedule guides the expected duration of the project work effort, helps identify the number and types of required resources, and establishes a baseline for project tracking and controlling. The primary objective of project schedule development is to ensure that the project is completed on time. Project schedule development is linked to the processes for developing the project scope, WBS, cost estimates, and resource utilization estimates. Changes in any of these areas are likely to affect the schedule.

Scheduling terminology is used to give planning team members a common frame of reference for developing the project schedule. The following scheduling terms are frequently used:

- *Activity*—A work effort performed in a specified period of time that corresponds to a work element (normally a work package) contained in the project WBS.
- *Activity Duration Estimate*—A quantitative assessment of the duration of work periods or the amount of time needed to complete an activity.
- *Activity Relationship*—The relationship that exists between one or more project activities, as illustrated in Figure II.4.1 for the six numbered activities:
  - Finish-to-Start—Activity 1 must be totally finished before activity 2 can start. This is the most common activity relationship, with lag or lead time added as needed.
  - Start-to-Start—Activity 3 cannot start until activity 2 begins, or they can actually begin at the same time. If needed, a lag or lead period can be specified.
  - Finish-to-Finish—Activity 4 cannot finish until activity 3 finishes, or they can actually finish at the same time. If needed, a lag or lead period can be specified.
  - Start-to-Finish—Activity 5 must start before activity 6 can finish. This is a much less common relationship than the other three. Lag or lead time adds more complexity.
- *Dependency*—A logical relationship among activities in a project's WBS; an external dependency is a logical relationship to work activities of another project or program.
- *Lag Time*—An adjustment to a logical relationship in the project schedule such that there is a delay in the start time of a subsequent activity.
- *Lead Time*—An adjustment to a logical relationship in the project schedule such that there is acceleration in the start time of a subsequent activity.
- *Slack Time (or Float)*—The amount of time during which no activity is performed, as determined by the logical relationships of work activities; this is also the difference between when an activity *can* start (its earliest start time) and when it *must* start (its latest start time before causing a project delay).
  - Float greater than zero means that time is available along a particular activity path.
  - Float equal to zero means the activities along that path are critical.
  - Float less than zero means that the project is behind schedule, critically late, and replanning may be necessary.
- *Milestone*—An activity having duration of zero time.

Determine Activity Sequencing

Activity sequencing identifies and documents dependencies among project activities. It represents not only activity dependencies but also task constraints. Activities must be sequenced accurately to support development of a realistic and achievable schedule.

The project planning team performs activity sequencing to determine the predecessor and successor activities as well

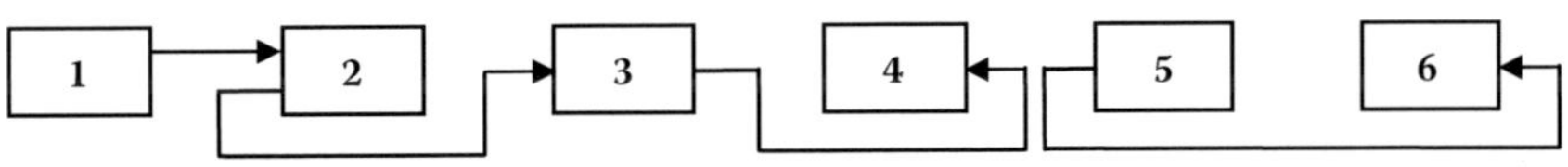

Figure II.4.1 Activity relationships.

as to specify the types of relationships (start-to-finish, start-to-start, finish-to-start, and finish-to-finish, along with any required lag or lead time). The following are general steps for accomplishing activity sequencing:

- The project planning team members review the work elements of the WBS (i.e., activities, tasks, subtasks, etc.) to examine the required flow of work activity.
- The team then establishes the activity relationship dependencies for each work element at the lowest, work package level, as a means to achieve the desired work activity flow.
- Display activity sequencing by creating a network diagram, either manually or through use of an available project management software application package.

In association with activity sequencing, the project planning team may find it necessary to make adjustments to the elements of the WBS, which is done by adding, deleting, or modifying project work elements in the WBS. The following are common methods for displaying activity sequencing:

- *Precedence Diagramming Method* (PDM)—This method of constructing a project network diagram uses nodes to represent the activities and arrows connecting the nodes to show the dependencies. This is sometimes called the activity-on-node (AON) diagram, and this method is found in many project management software packages.
- *Arrow Diagramming Method* (ADM)—This method of constructing a project network diagram uses arrows to represent the activities and connections at nodes to show the dependencies. This is sometimes called the activity-on-arrow (AOA) diagram. It is a technique that is less common than PDM but may still be used in some application areas. ADM uses only finish-to-start dependencies and may require the use of "dummy activities" (e.g., "start" and "finish" activities) to properly present all logical relationships.
- *Conditional Diagramming Method* (CDM)—This method of constructing a project network diagram enables nonsequential activities such as loops or conditional branches to be created. A prime example of this technique is the Graphical Evaluation and Review Technique (GERT).
- *Project Activity Templates*—Standard activity templates can be used to expedite the preparation of project network diagrams. These templates can include an entire project or just a component of it. They are useful when projects include some recurring identical or nearly identical work efforts that are repeated on each project.

Estimate Activity Duration

Activity duration estimating involves determining the working time that will be needed to complete each specified project activity. If the work effort is resource driven, then the duration will depend on the number of people assigned to do the work. Therefore, it is critical that this process be conducted concurrently with resource utilization estimating. In some cases, the duration of a task can be shortened by adding resources to it, but not in all cases.

Estimating duration usually considers *elapsed time*, which represents the calendar days, weeks, or months that pass from the project start date to the project finish date. Estimating duration also considers *working time*, where weekends and holidays are considered, as well as vacation, other nonworkdays, and general availability of the resources needed for the work effort.

Estimating activity durations requires that each project activity be examined to determine how much time is needed to complete it. Planners must discern between elapsed time and working time, and sometimes must resolve issues created by each type of duration estimate:

- If you are estimating based on elapsed time, then the work activity inherently requires the passage of time to enable an activity to start or be completed. Some examples of using elapsed-time estimating considerations could include
  - Awaiting shipment or delivery of required items on a specified date
  - Awaiting resource availability (e.g., vacation, hiring, not yet assigned)
  - Awaiting paint to dry (it requires some minimum period of elapsed time)
  - Awaiting action or document review and approval responses over a specified period of time (or over the period of time the review process actually takes)
  - Awaiting product development over a specified period of time (or over the period of time the development process actually takes)
  - Awaiting a specified activity or process (of known duration) to be fulfilled

  It can be seen that items estimated using elapsed time generally require their block of time for completion to be specified. This is not a situation where you can complete the activity sooner by using additional resources. Elapsed time activities will take just as long whether there are 3 or 10 resources available or assigned to the effort.
- If you are estimating based on working time, then work estimates are considered relative to the level of effort. Some examples of using working time estimating considerations could include

- Loading and unloading materials on the delivery truck
- Moving furniture; painting the walls
- Developing lines of software code
- Conducting product or system testing
- System, subsystem, and equipment installations
- Writing a technical or business document

It can be seen that items estimated using working time generally represent the level of effort of one or more individuals and that they are presumably qualified to perform the assigned project activity. To that end, working time activities can be completed sooner by increasing the level of effort of the individual or by increasing the number of resources assigned to accomplish the particular project activity.

Some common methods used for estimating activity durations include

- *Historical Information*—Durations that resulted when performing similar work efforts in the past can be reviewed and applied to activities in the current project work effort.
- *Expert Judgment*—Durations are often difficult to estimate because of the number of factors that can influence them (for example, resource levels and resource productivity). Expert judgment (guided by historical information) can be used to sort out the complexities and determine duration estimates. Such expertise may be provided by any group or individual with specialized knowledge or training in the type of work that is planned. This expertise is available from a variety of sources, including other units within the performing organization, consultants, professional and technical associations, and industry groups. Sometimes this expertise is conveyed by means of written materials rather than by individuals.
- *Analogous Estimating*—This method is often referred to as "top-down estimating." Analogous estimating uses the estimated duration of a larger, broader scope activity as the basis for estimating the durations of any of its component activities. This method can also be used when higher-level activity duration is "mandated," and durations of one or more subordinate activities must contribute to achieving that "mandate."
- *Simulation*—Simulation involves calculating multiple durations with different sets of assumptions. A common simulation method is Monte Carlo analysis, in which a distribution of probable results is defined for each activity and used to calculate a distribution of probable results for the total project.

Develop the Project Schedule and Critical Path

The project schedule is developed when each project work activity has a specified duration estimate for completion, the necessary relationship alignment with predecessor and successor activities has been created, and the project critical path has been identified.

The *Critical Path* is defined as the longest logical path through the project network diagram. It is the path with zero float (slack), and also the path that provides the shortest time to complete the project.

Most project management scheduling software will calculate and display the critical path for a project. The following steps can be used to manually calculate the critical path:

- Establish a project "Start" activity and align all successive project activities relative to their predecessors and successors (i.e., create and examine the network diagram).
- Establish a project "End" activity (i.e., the final activity).
- Conduct a forward pass through the network to determine the *early start* time for each activity. The early start is the earliest an activity can start based on the defined logic.
- Determine the natural end date based on the results of the forward pass through the network.
- Conduct a backward pass through the network to determine the *late start* for each activity. The late start is the latest an activity can start without delaying the project completion date.
- Calculate float (slack).
- Identify the critical path along the path from project start to project finish that has zero float (slack); also examine any other paths having low levels of float.
- Use project network management techniques to eliminate any negative float.
- Insert hard constraints to override normal critical path calculations and remove naturally occurring float. Hard constraints can also be used to create project milestones and position project activities to eliminate excessive float.

It should be noted that calculations could result in a project having more than one critical path. This is not unusual for large, complex projects. However, a final examination should be performed to determine if the schedule can be reduced to one single critical path.

Make Subsequent Schedule Adjustments

There are a few actions that can be taken to improve project schedule efficiency, as follows:

- *"Crashing" the Project Network—Crashing* means accelerating the completion of tasks on the critical path to complete the project earlier or, in the event of a delay, to resume the original schedule. This is an intensive, iterative process having the following steps:
  - Determine the desired total project duration.
  - Examine and prioritize the project activities along the critical path.
  - Specify the crash (duration reduction) time desired or needed for each high-priority project activity along the critical path.
  - Select a high-priority activity and determine ways in which a time reduction can be achieved.
  - Apply changes to reduce the selected activity's duration; then examine how much the total project duration has been brought closer to the desired time.
  - Verify the critical path as remaining the same; examine consequences if the critical path is changed; and, if changed, restart the "crashing" effort at step 2 in this list.
  - Continue reduction of the selected priority activity until the desired activity "crash" time is attained.
  - Proceed to the next priority activity and repeat this process to continue "crashing" (duration reduction) until the desired total project duration is achieved.
- *Optimizing Resource Utilization*—Activity duration can be reduced in the following ways:
  - Assigning resources to work overtime to complete the activity sooner
  - Using more resources to increase the level of work effort
  - Increasing productivity by using improved technology, or improving the process involved in accomplishing the work effort
  - Increasing productivity by using resources with higher skill and qualifications
- *"Fast Tracking"*—The project schedule can be adjusted (reduced) by performing some of the project activities in parallel (fast tracking) instead of one after the other (in sequence). The schedule can also be adjusted by changing the relationship among activities until the critical path is shorter.

Establish the Project Schedule Baseline

Upon completion of project schedule (duration) estimates, the results are usually forwarded to the project executive (sponsor) and perhaps other management entities (e.g., PMO) for review and approval. Otherwise, the project manager may have the authority to approve the project activity durations (project schedule) as per standard procedures within the organization or as specified in the *Project Charter.* In some situations, the customer may also be a reviewer of early schedule estimates.

A schedule baseline is established when the review authority has approved the schedule estimates. The schedule baseline is normally set by the project manager, and any changes to this baseline must go through a change management process. The schedule baseline is normally established in conjunction with setting the cost and resource utilization baselines.

When using project management software, there is normally an automated feature or function available to establish and save the approved schedule estimates as a part of the project baseline.

4.3 PROJECT RESOURCE UTILIZATION ESTIMATING

Project Resource Utilization Estimating entails specifying the human skills, competencies, and talent levels needed to conduct the project work effort and provide the required product, service, or system deliverables. This section presents the fundamental concepts and technique guidance for estimating project resource utilization.

Concept of This Practice

This practice enables the project manager and project planners to assign estimated values for types and numbers of project resources needed to conduct project work efforts. In turn, actual project resource utilization can be tracked and controlled against those estimates.

Project Resource Utilization Estimating is normally conducted during project planning (Plan Phase). However, resource utilization estimates should be continuously reviewed and updated as necessary throughout the project. Please refer to the key events or indicators (listed on the Project Estimating introduction page) that should automatically trigger follow-on reviews (and possible updates) of project resource utilization estimates.

Resource Utilization Estimating Overview

In many organizations, resource utilization estimating is a niche within the project cost estimating effort and is accomplished in direct alignment with cost estimating. Resource utilization estimating can also involve consideration of "material" resources—supplies, materials, and equipment. The focus of this practice will be on estimating the human resources needed to staff the project, but with due consideration for "material" resources, which users should apply as necessary. *Project Resource Utilization Estimating* deals with

- Identifying the resource skills and competencies needed to complete the project
- Specifying the number and types of resources required for each project work element
- Examining resource utilization constraints for each project work element
- Establishing the resource allocations needed for the total project effort

Each of these resource utilization estimating facets is discussed here.

Identify Resource Skills

The project manager, with planning team assistance, will specify the types of resources that are needed to successfully accomplish project objectives. In general, this means looking at the several types of skill sets the project may require:

- *Professionals and Technicians*—Identify skills needed to perform the stated professional or technical aspects of the project—the primary disciplines needed to produce and deliver the product, service, or system specified in the scope of work. This includes identifying skills needed for
  - Reviewing and comprehending technical and business requirements
  - Developing technical solutions to fulfill project requirements
  - Preparing and implementing project technical plans and documentation
  - Performing design, development, testing, and installation of deliverables
  - Conducting quality control and assurance, application of standards, on-the-job training, risk assessments, and management
  - Managing and supervising the people applying technical disciplines and specialties used by the project
- *Skilled Workers and Laborers*—Identify skilled and unskilled labor required by the project, to include identifying skills needed for
  - Packaging, shipping, and freight activities
  - Facility custodial, maintenance, and cleanup activities
  - Transportation
  - Manual labor (e.g., rubbish removal, grounds work, materials moving and handling)
  - Skilled labor (e.g., masonry, plumbing, carpentry, electrical)

  The manual and skilled labor items generally refer to individuals involved with major construction or product development projects. On other, smaller projects, nearly everyone on the project team contributes to accomplish any necessary "labor" efforts.
- *Administrative Aides and Assistants*—Identify skills needed to perform necessary administrative duties associated with the project. These may be either "assistant" positions or primary roles in their own right, and this includes identifying skills needed for
  - Correspondence, report, and document preparation
  - Communications management (e.g., phone, fax, courier receipt, and distribution)
  - Project operations, business, and staff collaboration
  - Meeting management (e.g., facility schedules and arrangements, participant notifications, and meeting minutes collection)
  - Project recordkeeping and archiving
- *Project Management*—Identify skills needed to perform prescribed project management actions. This resource may include one or more individuals who are needed to support or complement the skills of the assigned project manager (particularly for larger, more complex projects). Conversely, the project manager working alone on smaller, simpler projects may have to bring skills in this area as well as skills in the other areas just mentioned. This includes identifying skills needed to
  - Provide project leadership
  - Manage business aspects of the project
  - Manage and supervise the technical work of the project
  - Manage project documentation and project plans
  - Manage project performance (e.g., planning, tracking, and controlling—cost, schedule, and resource utilization oversight)
  - Manage project reporting and analysis
  - Manage customer and stakeholder participation and expectations
  - Manage and supervise project team members

This initial step in resource utilization estimating is completed when the general types of resources and the "first guess" for the number of people needed in each resource category are identified. In some organizations, this might be done in alignment with established resource codes for each specialty. Otherwise, it is simply an initial step in estimating that allows the planning team to focus on identifying the different types of skills needed and a preliminary examination of their sourcing. This resource utilization estimating step is often performed in conjunction with the following step on specifying resource requirements for many types of projects, particularly smaller, less complex ones.

Specify Project Resources

Resource utilization estimating takes form with an examination of each work element in the project WBS. These work elements, usually at the work package level, are reviewed to determine the type of resource and the level of effort needed to accomplish specified project work. Here, planners often begin to attach names to project work packages, or at least specify a resource type and level of resource qualification needed.

The following steps present the primary activities prescribed for specifying project resource requirements:

- *Review each WBS work element.* This is done to ascertain the type of work to be accomplished and to align a competent resource (or resource type) with the effort. This is normally done at the project work package level, where work efforts are usually separate and distinct. If the work package is a "task," then tasks will aggregate or roll up into activities, and activities into project phases. Therefore, any resources specified at work package levels will be accounted for upward and throughout the project. In some cases, resources may be aligned at a higher level in the project WBS—say, the "cost account" level. This would be appropriate if the resource is involved in all or most of the tasks below it. This step produces a preliminary resource requirements matrix.
- *Refine resource qualification requirements.* Examine the resources assigned to each work element to ensure that the qualifications of each identified resource are appropriate—both for the nature of work to be performed and the level of effort. If not already done, incorporate resource qualification levels, perhaps using internal resource or position codes, into the resource requirements matrix.
- *Identify proposed resources.* When possible, name the individual resource that will be requested for participation on the project. This resource should be consistent with the specified position qualifications. This identification also contributes to the separate effort of acquiring and assigning project team members (see the Project Staffing Management practice area).

Examine Resource Utilization Constraints

This is an effort that provides further refinement of the resource responsibility matrix and contributes to realistic considerations of the availability of preferred or specified resources. This action examines conditions associated with several types of constraints that could affect estimating resource utilization.

- *Logic-Driven Conditions*—Examine project activity relationships to identify areas in which activity dependencies will drive resource requirements. This helps determine when resources will start and end a work effort, and affects resources available for assignment.
- *Resource-Driven Conditions*—Examine how project activities will drive resource requirements, that is, the number and qualification of resources to be used for each work activity.
- *Resource Evaluation*—Examine resource availability against that resource's current activity assignment commitments to ascertain any assignment conflicts.
- *Resource Allocation*—Examine factors that could limit the allocation of project resources; plan the project work around established resource pools, and request allocation of that pool to the project.
- *Qualification Factors*—Examine resources to determine if appropriate and necessary qualifications will be fulfilled. Look at opportunities for outsourcing if current resources are not available or are otherwise not qualified. Examine what is needed and what can be done to achieve qualification for currently available resources.
- *External Factors*—Examine any business or technical performance areas where external factors or conditions could affect resource availability and assignment to the project.

It is suggested that issues resulting from identified resource utilization constraints be considered as a part of the estimating effort, with adjustments made to the resource responsibility matrix when such issues adversely impact the project staffing effort.

Establish the Project Resource Utilization Baseline

Upon completion of project resource utilization estimates on the resource responsibility matrix, resources are then entered into the WBS normally at the work package level. This compilation will enable total project staff strength to be specified for all project activities. In turn, this represents the number of resources that will be requested for the staffing allocation.

The resource utilization estimate is forwarded to the project executive (sponsor) and perhaps other management entities (e.g., PMO) for review and approval. Otherwise, the project manager may have the authority to approve the project resource utilization estimates as per standard procedures within the organization or as specified in the *Project Charter*. In some situations, the customer may also be a reviewer of early resource utilization estimates.

A resource utilization baseline is established when the review authority has approved the resource utilization estimates. The resource utilization baseline is normally set by the project manager, and any changes to this baseline must go through a change management process. The resource utilization baseline is normally established in conjunction with setting the cost and schedule baselines.

When using project management software, there is normally an automated feature or function available to establish and save the approved resource estimates (as assigned to project activities) as a part of the project baseline.

Chapter 5

Project Management Plans

Project management plans are created to guide the performance of all activities associated with the project. To that extent, the organization can prescribe standard plans—those required for every project conducted by the organization, and optional plans—those developed at the discretion of the project manager.

Project management essentially entails developing and executing a viable *Project Work Plan*, tracking and managing the progress of that plan's execution, and implementing remedies to redirect efforts back to the specifications of that plan. In that context, the project work plan is usually considered the most vital document of project management. Therefore, the project work plan should be developed with adequate and reasonable rigor for the type of project being pursued, and with sufficient knowledge of the project management process.

Similarly, other project planning documents can be created to offer detailed guidance to additional project management, business, and technical efforts associated with the project. This section describes a variety of such plans for consideration and use by the project manager.

There are three practices associated with Project Management Plans:

- Project Work Plan Development
- Primary Project Management Plans Development
- Project Support Plans Development

Project Management Plans provide the means to plan and conduct all aspects of a project. For the most part, they contain procedures, instructions, information, guidance, and specifications that are often derived from separately prepared estimates, analyses, assessments, methods, and standards. To that end, some plans will merely contain references to some type of source material. Other plans are created to meet the unique requirements of the projects they serve.

A Special Note on "Project Plan" Content

It is important to distinguish the *Project Work Plan* as an element or component of the overall Project Plan, and not as being the Project Plan itself. The *Project Work Plan* is used to guide the project work that is performed, and it is an essential tool for the project manager. However, it is just one of the several documents that are components of the larger collection of project management documents known as the Project Plan.

The content and makeup of the Project Plan varies from organization to organization, and across industries. This methodology prescribes the overall Project Plan as one that includes any or all of the following components:

- *Project Requirements Documents*—Documents that identify the customer's needs and describe the requirements for project performance, to include such items as
  - Statements of work (including detailed work orders)
  - Requests for proposal (RFPs)
  - Technical specifications
  - Business specifications
  - Surveys and analyses
  - Workshops
  - Interviews

  Concepts dealing with development and use of *Project Requirements* documentation are addressed in the *Project Requirements* practice.
- *Project Business Plan*—The document that defines the project and guides the business aspects of project management, to include such items as

  - Project Definition—Presentation of the project scope, objectives, high-level preliminary schedule and cost, and resources; project assumptions and constraints.
  - Technical Solution—Specifies steps and detailed description of how project objectives will be achieved, including identification of techniques and technologies used; it is characterized by the *Project Work Plan*.
  - Project Business Case—Customer information, customer needs and expectations, technical capability to perform the project, strategic business interest, business risk, feasibility, and financial and cost–benefit analyses.
  - Business Solution—Costs, fees and expenses, vendor costs, contract terms and conditions, and payment strategy applied to the work effort.
  - Project Charter—Identification of the project manager, project sponsor and any key resources, and specification of project manager authority and initial and subsequent project funding.

  The Project Business Plan is addressed in the *Business Case Development* practice.
- *Project Work Plan*—The project Work Breakdown Structure (WBS), with cost, schedule, and resource utilization estimates identified and appended for each work package. The concepts for compiling this plan are presented in the *Project Work Plan Development* practice.
- *Project Management Plans*—Documents that are prepared to expand on concepts and provide routine (and often standardized) project management guidance. The concepts for identifying and compiling these plans are presented in the Project Management Plans practice, as well as in relevant "management" practices.
- *Project Support Plans*—Documents that are prepared to expand project management guidance, as needed, with regard to organizational policies, achievement of business objectives, industry practices, project complexity and risk factors, and the experience level of the project team. The concepts for developing and using project support plans are presented in the *Project Support Plans Development* practice.
- *Technical Plans and Documentation*—Documents that provide technical specifications, and that are used to guide technical design, development, and deployment activities; these items can be closely related and, in some cases, may even be the same elements contained in the project requirements documentation. The concepts for developing and using technical plans and documentation are addressed in the *Project Support Plans Development* practice.

An organization can use these documents or establish its own preferred content for the collection of documents it calls the Project Plan, as per the many documents discussed in the three sections of this practice area.

It should also be noted that, while project plans and documentation are created in many organizations as written text documents, many of these plans and documentation can also be compiled electronically and could reside on project management software applications in text, spreadsheet, and database formats.

5.1 PROJECT WORK PLAN DEVELOPMENT

Project Work Plan Development is an essential activity of project management that specifies all project work, and aligns factors of cost, schedule, and resource utilization to each planned work element. The following items are generally accepted as key components of the project work plan:

- *Work Breakdown Structure* (WBS)—A specification and decomposition of project work activities, normally to the work package level, where work element cost, work duration, and resources required to accomplish the work are assigned. (See *Work Breakdown Structure Construction* practice.)
- *Cost*—A specification of the estimated cost to be incurred for each work package or other work element in the WBS. (See *Project Cost Estimating* practice.)
- *Schedule*—A specification of the estimated time duration to be expected, per work element relationships that are established, to complete each work package or other work element in the WBS. (See *Project Schedule Estimating* practice.)
- *Resource Utilization*—A specification of resources, usually by name or type, that are needed to accomplish each work package or other work element in the WBS. (See *Project Resource Utilization Estimating* practice.)

The project work plan is fundamentally the project WBS with project cost, schedule, and resource utilization information appended at the work package level. Project work plan preparation is a collaborated and coordinated effort that brings these planning elements together. This added information is sometimes referred to as the *WBS Dictionary*, which expands on and clarifies the description and requirements for each project work element in the WBS. Also, project deliverables and milestones information can be appended as desired or as needed.

Concept of This Practice

This practice provides the project manager, project team, and customer with a detailed specification of work that will be performed by the project team. It provides the basis for assigning and managing project work, measuring project work progress, and reporting project work status and progress.

The purpose of this practice is to provide a common reference document for all project stakeholders who have responsibility for planning, performing, and evaluating work associated with the project. To that end, the project work plan may also be included in the technical portion of any proposal submitted to the customer for consideration.

The project work plan is normally prepared during Project Planning (Plan Phase). However, the project work plan should be reviewed and updated as necessary throughout the project.

Prepare the Project Work Plan

The project work plan represents the course of actions that will be taken to achieve project objectives and to complete project deliverables. Ideally, it specifies the actions and activities for all persons and organizations having responsibility for project work. It identifies what work needs be performed, and then enables the project manager to measure and track work efforts to ensure that planned work is actually performed—on time, on budget, and with adequate types and strength of qualified resources. The project work plan is essentially completed when the WBS and associated cost, schedule, and resource utilization estimates are completed. Therefore, this practice for developing the project work plan is focused on a final examination of the WBS and associated estimates for cost, schedule, and resource utilization.

It is presumed (and recommended) that an automated project management software package will be used as a "database" to capture and store the detailed information of project cost, schedule, and resource utilization, in alignment with some format of the WBS. Alternately, these data can also be maintained using a standard database program or spreadsheet application. Thereby, estimates prepared for the project can be incorporated relative to each WBS work element in the "database" for relative ease in developing an automated project work plan.

Examine and Finalize the WBS

Details of how to construct the project WBS are presented in the *Work Breakdown Structure Construction* practice. Here we prescribe the examination needed to finalize the WBS work elements as a component of the project work plan.

The project manager or other project planners should examine the WBS relative to its capability to drive project performance. Does it appear that the project will be properly and adequately completed using the specified WBS work elements? Consider the following general checklist in this examination:

- Does the WBS adequately reflect the scope of the project?
- Do the project work elements fulfill project requirements (and deliverables)?
- Are the project work elements realistic given the qualification of available resources?
- Are all critical work activities adequately addressed in the WBS?
- Are there any major (or minor) gaps in the work prescribed by the WBS (e.g., does the work effort flow without any missing activity steps; does it account for shipments, deliveries, and other "waiting" periods; and does it account for *all* activities that require project team or other stakeholder time commitments)?
- Are project management activities that incur time commitments included in the WBS (e.g., staff, vendor and customer meetings, resource acquisition activities, project plan preparation, performance tracking and analyses, and report preparation)?
- Are relevant risk management and mitigation activities incorporated as distinct work elements in the WBS, where practical?

Finalization of the WBS is achieved concurrently with the introduction of cost, schedule, and resource utilization information into the project work plan, as described in the following text. The WBS will be finalized as these elements become finalized.

Examine and Incorporate Project Cost Estimates

Procedures for estimating project costs are presented in the *Project Cost Estimating* practice. Here we prescribe the examination needed to introduce that cost information into the WBS work elements as a component of the project work plan.

Project cost is usually affected by what work is done (complexity), who does it (qualification), and how long it takes to get done (time constraint). This roughly translates into the concept of "triple constraints," which describes a relationship between cost, schedule, and scope of work (quality). The concept suggests that, when one of the triple constraints changes, at least one other constraint must also change. This concept has a basis in the cost estimate examination that is presented in the following text, as *Project Work Plan Development* prompts planners and the project manager to consider cost, schedule, and resource utilization trade-offs.

The project manager or other project planners should examine cost estimates relative to the nature and extent of project work. Consider the following checklist items in this examination:

- Do project cost estimates appear reasonable?
- Do project cost estimates show consistency with project work effort durations?
- Do project cost estimates show consistency with the quality, experience, and availability of the project resources expected to be utilized?
- Do project cost estimates vary across any of the same type and duration of work efforts? If so, why are they different?
- Do project cost estimates provide for contingency and management reserve funding?
- Do project cost estimates account for all anticipated project expenses?
- Are the aggregated project cost estimates within the thresholds or limits of funding specified by management and by the customer?

When all cost estimate questions are resolved, enter the costs into the WBS work elements in the "database," or into the WBS dictionary, ideally at the project work package level.

Examine and Incorporate Project Schedule Estimates

The procedures for estimating project work durations (i.e., project schedule) are presented in the *Project Schedule Estimating* practice. Here we prescribe the examination needed to introduce that schedule information into the WBS work elements as a component of the project work plan.

Project schedule estimates should be reviewed relative to the concept of triple constraints. In particular, every project manager must recognize that expediting project work, or otherwise compressing the schedule for a project work element, will have direct effects on cost and quality. Therefore, schedule estimates should be reviewed for realistic attainment and desired outcomes as they are integrated into the WBS. It is usually better to improve the accuracy of front-end work planning (e.g., schedule estimating) than to risk repeating a work element that requires extended project time to ultimately get it right.

The project manager or other project planners should examine schedule estimates relative to the nature and extent of project work. Consider the following checklist items in this examination:

- Do project work duration estimates appear reasonable?
- Do project work duration estimates show consistency with the quality, experience, and availability of the project resources expected to be utilized?
- Do project work duration estimates account for all required work intended (or implied) by the work element? (e.g., does a work element entitled *Paint Walls* account for paint acquisition, setup, painting, cleanup, and drying of the paint?)
- Do project work duration estimates vary across the same type of work efforts? If so, why are they different?
- Do the aggregated project duration estimates create a critical path that provides the desired schedule?
- Does the critical path represent an unrealistic schedule or a schedule that requires further coordination with management, the customer, or other project stakeholders?

When all schedule estimate questions are resolved, enter the work durations into the WBS work elements in the "database," or into the WBS dictionary, ideally at the project work package level.

Examine and Incorporate Project Resource Utilization Estimates

The procedures for estimating project resource utilization (i.e., staffing) are presented in the *Project Resource Utilization Estimating* practice. Here we prescribe the examination needed to introduce that resource information into the WBS work elements as a component of the project work plan.

Project resource utilization estimates should be reviewed relative to the concept of triple constraints, but particularly relative to the schedule and the individual's ability to commit to that schedule. Resource qualifications, capability, and availability to perform specified work according to the schedule should also be examined.

The project manager or other project planners should examine resource utilization estimates relative to the nature and extent of project work. Consider the following checklist items in this examination:

- Do project resource utilization estimates for all work elements appear reasonable?
- Do the aggregated resource utilization estimates maintain individual utilization at or below 100% time commitment? (i.e., is there any unreasonable overloading of work assignments that produces more than 100% time commitments for any individual?)
- Do project resource utilization estimates vary across the same type of work efforts? If so, why are they different?
- Do adjustments made in resource utilization require any changes in the project cost or project schedule estimates?

- Number of resources assigned to a specific work package
- Qualification of resources assigned to a specific work package
- Available "start time" of resources assigned to a specific work package

■ Are project resource utilization estimates consistent with the resource commitments that can be achieved?

■ Are project resource utilization estimates consistent with the staff allocations that have been made and approved?

When all resource utilization estimate questions are resolved, enter the resources and their work commitment levels into the WBS work elements in the "database," or into the WBS dictionary, ideally at the project work package level.

5.2 PRIMARY PROJECT MANAGEMENT PLANS DEVELOPMENT

Primary project management plans are the core documents that provide essential concepts and guidance for managing the project. These primary plans should contain more detail as the projects they support become more complex. However, they are essential components of project management, and therefore they should be developed for use on every project conducted by the organization.

It is important for the organization to recognize a standard set of component documents that are used to guide project management activities, as prescribed by the set of primary project management plans that are presented in this practice. However, the organization should also review its need for these plans and then either confirm their use or adjust and specify another set of primary project management plans that are used for every project. The content and level of detail of primary project management plans may vary according to project size, value, and duration, but their purpose is generally applicable to all projects conducted by the organization.

Concept of This Practice

This practice provides the project manager, project team, and various stakeholders with a basis for conducting project management. It specifies the documents that will be used to guide the essential project management activities that are to be performed for all projects.

The purpose of this practice is to provide some consistency in project planning and a common frame of reference for all project managers, and for all managers above project managers. It also provides, as may be included in each plan, for common report elements, a common tracking and controlling approach, and a common set of measurements of project performance—so that such information from each project in the organization has a common basis and therefore can be aggregated for compiled use.

Primary Project Management Plans Development is accomplished during project planning (Plan Phase). However, resulting plans should be reviewed and updated as necessary throughout the project.

Using Primary Project Management Plans

The following list presents six *Primary Project Management Plans* that are prescribed for use by all project managers across all projects conducted in the organization. More details about preparing these plans are contained within other relevant practices related to their purpose.

■ *Risk Management Plan*—This plan specifies the activities for managing risk throughout the project management life cycle. It identifies the project team members and other stakeholders responsible for managing various types of project risk, and it compiles the identified project risk events and response strategies established through a project risk assessment and other ongoing efforts to identify and manage risks. See the *Risk Management Plan Development* practice for more plan content considerations.

■ *Communications Management Plan*—This plan describes the methods for gathering, distributing, and storing various types of project information. In particular, it specifies the content, format, and frequency of required and optional project reports. It can also specify project document requirements and control procedures.

  This plan also identifies project stakeholders and, to the extent possible, specifies their roles and responsibilities. Also, this plan indicates the protocol for project communication—what are the preferred and authorized interactions for communications among project team members, senior management, the customer, vendors and contractors, and other project stakeholders. Finally, this plan can include instructions for identifying problems and escalating project issues to the project manager, the project management office (PMO), and senior management. See the *Project Communication Implementation* practice for more plan content considerations.

■ *Change Control Plan*—This plan describes the management and control of project scope. It particularly includes specification of the preferred change management process as an integral component of scope management. It also specifies individual responsibility for managing scope, and it specifies "dos and don'ts" for project team members as guidance for avoiding unintentional modifications to the work effort that represent scope changes. This plan can contain a checklist of indicators of drifting scope. See the *Project Change Control* practice for more plan content considerations. Note that in some organizations, a *scope management plan* may be used in lieu of, or is regarded to be the same as, the change management plan.

- *Quality Management Plan*—This plan describes how the project team will implement its quality policy and practices on the current project. It includes the identification of quality requirements for direct and indirect project deliverables, specifies the technical reviews and threshold values of quality control, and identifies the quality assurance activities to be accomplished as a matter of ensuring successful technical performance.

  It also can identify scheduled and ad hoc technical and project management audits that may be conducted as a part of the project oversight effort. It can reference applicable technical standards and specification documents, and adjunct technical plans having greater quality process and procedural details. When possible, it can identify individuals and organizations responsible for quality management. Finally, the quality management plan should specify the procedures and criteria for customer acceptance of project deliverables. See the *Project Quality Planning* practice for more plan content considerations.
- *Vendor Management Plan*—This plan describes how external resources will be integrated into the project effort. This includes specification of their primary point of contact, and key roles and responsibilities that will be fulfilled. If not otherwise provided in a separate support plan, the procurement process for vendor and contractor acquisition can be incorporated in this plan.

  This plan also will specify the deliverables to be accomplished by the vendor/contractor, the methods that will be used to accept vendor and contractor deliverables, and the process for receiving and approving invoices associated with vendor/contractor deliverables. This plan should also prescribe the management activities that will be accomplished to ensure effective and timely vendor performance on the project. See the *Vendor Performance Management* practice for more plan content considerations.
- *Staffing Management Plan*—This plan describes the project resources needed, allocated, and assigned to the project effort. The plan is constructed to help the project manager and technical team leaders identify the number and type of resources needed to accomplish the project effort; when, how, and from where they will be sourced; and what steps will be taken to manage their timely acquisition and assignment. It frequently contains a project resource responsibility matrix to show alignment of individuals with project work responsibilities.

  A portion of the plan should specify how the project team and individual team members will be dispersed following completion of their assigned duties. Finally, this plan should prescribe the management activities that will be accomplished to ensure effective and timely staff performance on the project. See the *Project Staff Management* practice for more plan content considerations.

5.3 PROJECT SUPPORT PLANS DEVELOPMENT

Project support plans are the adjunct documents of project management. They provide many essential concepts and guidance for managing various aspects of the project. These "adjunct" plans should be used to satisfy the technical and business aspects of project management, and they, too, will become more detailed as the projects they support become more complex. Also, larger, more complex projects may warrant the use of additional project support plans than may be required by smaller projects. In some organizations, the support plans listed in this practice may even be cited as primary project management plans because of their inherent need in each and every project.

To that end, the organization should examine its needs and prescribe any standard or recurring project support plans that it requires for use in every project conducted by the organization.

Concept of This Practice

This practice provides the project manager, project team, and various stakeholders with a basis for managing the technical and business aspects of each project, in addition to providing increased or expanded guidance for project management. For example, a primary plan may specify the need for project management audits, providing some basic details about the audits to be conducted. In turn, an Audit Management Plan might be created (as a support plan) to provide more information about how, when, and where to conduct any required project management audits.

The purpose of this practice is to provide sufficient guidance within the organization and options for project managers when planning their approach to project management for a given project. There are possibly as many different project support plans as the mind can conceive that address all aspects of project business and technical management. The project support plans in this practice highlight some of the more prevalent planning documents that can be considered for use by project managers.

Project support plans are normally prepared during Project Planning (Plan Phase). However, they should be reviewed and updated as necessary throughout the project.

Using Project Support Plans

The following list presents a variety of project support plans that can be prescribed or otherwise considered for use at the discretion of the project manager, or as per the nature of technical work, business requirements, or skill and experience of the project team on each project.

- *Auditing Plan*—Specifies the scheduled and unscheduled technical, business, and project management reviews to be conducted; may be an extension of or included in the quality management plan.
- *Budget Plan*—Presents the company, division, or relevant organizational unit annual budget for consideration relative to the current project and project planning effort.
- *Business Case Plan*—Specifies the preparation, analysis, and presentation of business assessments that provide the justification to pursue the project opportunity.
- *Configuration Management Plan*—Describes the procedures used to apply technical and administrative direction and oversight to identify, document, and control specification of the functional and physical characteristics of any deliverable item or system.
- *Cost Management Plan*—Presents the procedures for tracking and managing cost variance and provides guidance for general oversight of the project budget, including management of cost changes.
- *Construction Plan*—Provides information for coordinating, communicating, and directing the construction of a capital facility in terms of scope, quality, time, and cost.
- *Project Contingency Plan*—Identifies alternative strategies to be used if any specified risk events occur; this plan may be an extension of, or included as a part of, the project's risk management plan.
- *Customer Relationship Management Plan*—Specifies the steps to be taken to manage customer expectations and involvement in the project effort.
- *Customer Support Plan*—Describes the activities designed to assist the customer with a product or service after acceptance. (Sometimes called a *Maintenance Plan*)
- *Documentation Plan*—Specifies the design, development, storage, and disposal of reports, correspondence, information, records, logs, references, and other project data and technical documents; this plan may be an extension of, or included as a part of, the project *Communication Management Plan*.
- *Engineering Design Plan*—Describes the project deliverables in the form of specifications, drawings, data flow diagrams, or any other methods that can be used to provide detailed information on how to build the product.
- *Equipment Management Plan*—Prescribes how any major equipment and material used on a project will be acquired, managed for efficient use, and disposed of at the conclusion of the project.
- *Estimating Plan*—Specifies the information required and the steps necessary for conducting an effective estimate of cost, schedule, and resource utilization. This can be an extension of, or included with, the project work plan.
- *Facilities Management Plan*—Designates the facilities that will be used to support project work, provide staffing locations, and serve related project facility needs. It will prescribe the actions and responsibilities associated with acquiring, managing, and maintaining project facilities. It will provide guidance for vacating, returning, transferring ownership or use, or otherwise disposing of facilities at the conclusion of the project.
- *Financial Performance Plan*—Stipulates business unit performance goals for a given financial period (or a given project).
- *Health and Safety Plan*—Outlines the performance standards and requirements designed to promote healthy and safe practices to protect project team members' health and safety in the work environment.
- *Inspection Plan*—Presents the design for the examination or measurement of work to verify whether an item or activity conforms to specific requirements. This may be a separate plan or incorporated into the *Project Quality Management Plan*.
- *Inventory Management Plan*—Presents the design, approach, and procedures for the use and control of materials required to execute the project.
- *Logistics Support Plan*—Presents the design, approach, and procedures for the acquisition and movement of materials and personnel required to conduct the project.
- *Make-or-Buy Plan*—Explains the procedures for analyzing whether a particular product or service can be produced or performed in a cost-effective manner by the performing organization or if it should be contracted out to another organization.
- *Manufacturing Plan*—Provides the scheme for building the product or deliverable required by the project effort.
- *Materials Procurement Plan*—Describes sourcing of raw or prefabricated materials to support execution of the project.

- *Operations Plan*—Defines interface roles and responsibilities between the project team and the relevant organization's business units.
- *Peer Review Plan*—Structures the content and method of peer technical reviews of the deliverable product.
- *Portfolio Management Plan*—Identifies pending and approved products of the relevant organization; defines the prioritization of approved products and projects, and the current project.
- *Procurement Management Plan*—Describes management of the procurement processes from solicitation planning through contract closeout.
- *Product Life Cycle Plan*—Defines how the technical product will be created and will evolve into a new offering, and how it will be maintained during its "life."
- *Project Organization Plan*—Defines the management structure for the project and how it interfaces with the relevant organization; this may be an extension of, or included in, either the project charter or the project *Staff Management Plan.*
- *Regulatory Compliance Plan*—Explains how the work of the project will be managed to conform to applicable government regulations or industry standards.
- *Resource Allocation Plan*—Specifies resources, at least in terms of type and numbers, that are deemed necessary and are approved by executives and senior management for assignment to the project, usually as a part of the project selection process.
- *Resource Utilization Management Plan*—Presents the procedures for tracking and managing resource utilization variance, and provides guidance regarding how to measure and manage project team member assignments and performance.
- *Schedule Management Plan*—Presents the procedures for tracking and managing schedule variance and provides guidance for general oversight of the project schedule, including management of schedule changes.
- *Staff Training Plan*—Specifies training to be undertaken by designated or potential project team members so that they may qualify in project skill, knowledge, and competency requirements.
- *Staff Transition Plan*—Addresses staff replacement issues and migration from the project to other assignments in the organization; this may be a part of, or an extension of, the project *Staff Management Plan.*
- *Strategic Business Plan*—Sets the organizational business direction and context for decision making in the development and execution of the project.
- *Systems Integration Test Plan*—Defines operating requirements and standards for combined elements of a system or the system as a whole.
- *Technical Plan*—Describes how the scope and deliverables of the project will be achieved from the perspective of the technical or professional work to be performed.
- *Testing Plan*—Defines the method and criteria for checking the conformance to requirements of the deliverable product or its components.
- *Tooling Plan*—Provides the design for manufacturing equipment used to produce product components.
- *Transportation Plan*—Defines how the product will be transported through distribution channels to reach the customer's points of product acceptance.
- *Verification Plan*—Provides for the evaluation of the correctness of the project output (deliverable) for various stages of product development based on the criteria for that stage.
- *Warranty and Field Support Plan*—Provides for replacement and repair of parts and extended services associated with product delivery.

An attempt was made to present items in the preceding list with generic titles as a means to offer the organization a perspective in what can be accomplished relative to project planning. Undoubtedly, there are numerous technical and business planning components that are unique to industries and organizations that are not listed here. The organization should identify those requirements and create the preferred format and content guidance for inclusion in the project planning process.

Chapter 6

Project Risk Management

Project Risk Management helps project managers to achieve specified project goals by avoiding, reducing, or eliminating problems that can delay the project or otherwise cause unexpected and unplanned project losses. Some industries and organizations also align *project opportunity* assessments with the project risk management effort. That is not specifically prescribed by this practice area, simply because we will focus on discovery and management of potential adverse impacts. Project opportunities certainly can be addressed in the preparation of adjunct plans for each project if that is an activity desired by the relevant organization.

The *Project Work Plan* is often not considered finalized until it undergoes a risk assessment and until risk response strategies have been developed for each risk event identified in the work plan. To that end, any other project guiding plans and documents might warrant a similar risk examination. In addition, business risk is also examined and managed throughout the project, particularly during the Profile Phase, and that type of risk management will be briefly covered in this practice area. The extent and frequency of risk management throughout the project is normally addressed in a project risk management plan.

There are three practices associated with *Project Risk Management*:

- Risk Assessment
- Risk Response Strategy Preparation
- Risk Management Plan Development

Each of these practices is presented in the following sections of this chapter.

6.1 RISK ASSESSMENT

The risk assessment activity involves looking at business activities and project work elements to identify any conditions or potential events that could hinder or otherwise adversely impact project performance and the successful outcome of the project. Project risk assessment should be performed initially during planning and then at relevant intervals throughout the project to ascertain potential project risk impacts, with the intent to either remove the risk threat or to plan actions that reduce the impact in the event of risk event occurrence.

Concept of This Practice

This practice provides the project manager, project team, and various stakeholders with a method to identify and analyze potential adverse impacts on the project effort. The purpose of this practice is to provide the project manager and risk managers associated with the project team with guidance for conducting an adequate examination of project and business risk within the organization to enable the project to be successfully completed.

Risk Assessment activities are normally accomplished during Project Planning (Plan Phase). However, risk is also examined in conjunction with *Business Plan Development* during Project Initiation (Profile Phase) and throughout the project as risk indicators and triggers are encountered.

Risk assessment is characterized by three primary activities:

- Risk Identification
- Risk Analysis
- Risk Prioritization

These activities are described in this practice immediately following the presentation of a few fundamental concepts that are important to the risk assessment process.

Risk Components

Risk is characterized by the identification of three fundamental components:

- *Event*—The specification of what could happen, called the *risk event*, that would be detrimental to some aspect of project performance and ultimately to project success.
- *Probability*—The degree of chance or likelihood that the specified *risk event* will actually occur, called *risk probability*, is usually expressed as a percentage for the chance of occurrence.
- *Impact*—The extent of adverse consequences or "amount at stake" to the project (and the organization) if the risk event occurs. *Project impact* is often expressed in monetary terms—what will be lost if the risk event occurs.

Understanding these components is important for effective risk assessment. In particular, it should be noted that a risk event is a future potential event that has not yet happened and may or may not happen in the future. It is an uncertain event that warrants the examination of probability of occurrence. If a risk event has a probability of 100% that it will occur, then that event or condition is a certainty, and therefore not a risk. It should likely be treated as a project constraint would, or as some other means available to the project manager.

During risk assessment, project team members must also be careful to differentiate between describing a risk event and describing the cause of a risk event. The risk event indicates what will happen to adversely impact the project; the risk cause is the aspect to be managed to reduce or eliminate the occurrence of the risk event.

Risk Assessment Perspectives

Risk management is often performed by the project team, some risk specialists, or another set of project stakeholders. All participants bring their own perspectives on risk to the examination of project risk. The following risk management perspectives, as may be held by individuals and relevant groups, will influence the project risk assessment:

- *Risks are situational.* Similar risk events may show some variation in their probability and impact as they are observed across different projects. A seemingly similar risk event may have significantly different causes and impacts on different projects. The experience each team member brings to the table will have influence on his or her perspective of the cause and impact of a risk event.
- *Risks are interdependent.* Risk events can be related, particularly when the cause of one risk event contributes to creating another on the project. Similarly, action taken in response to a risk event could subsequently create a new one or modify the impact or probability of an existing risk event.
- *Risks are magnitude dependent.* Project, technical, and business risks can be accepted or rejected based on the consideration of what might be achieved or gained. Therefore, higher levels of risk become more acceptable when a greater benefit can be achieved. This perspective is normally a factor of individual and organizational value systems.
- *Risks are value based.* Risk assessments are influenced by the organizational culture and the perspectives of individual executives and managers. The risk acceptance level varies from person to person. Both personal values and organizational culture will affect the level of risk that will be accepted.
- *Risks are time based.* Risk is a future event created by actions that are occurring today. The perception of the risk event, its importance, its probability, and its impact depend on how long into the future the risk event is expected to occur.

Risk Assessment Techniques

The team responsible can select from among several methods that will facilitate risk assessment. The following are some techniques that can be used for conducting risk assessments:

- *Checklists*—A checklist of prescribed risk examination areas can be created to facilitate risk identification. A simple checklist is contained in the accompanying methodology toolkit for both business and project risk examination, and checklist items are further described later in this practice. Users may wish to expand on these checklists or create their own for greater alignment with business or industry interests. The checklist should prompt examination and discussion of the source by participating team members and thereby allow them to identify the cause of potential risk on the project.
- *Delphi Technique*—This technique facilitates information gathering as a group process. The effort begins with the preparation of individual input by expert or experienced participants, with limited or no interaction with other members of the group. It then evolves into a finalization of results as follows:
  - A group of people having expertise or experience in risk identification is identified.
  - Individuals are surveyed, and they prepare personal comments (opinions) on specific areas of concern, along with relevant reasons for those opinions.

- All individuals are shown the aggregated opinions of all the participants surveyed as subsequently reduced to standard or common statements.
- Participants then reevaluate the aggregated opinions and further substantiate them or change those opinions that cannot be substantiated.
- This process of participant feedback is iterative and continues until there are no further changes in the aggregate opinion.
- The participants' final opinions are used to compute a set of median values to represent the expert group opinion.

- *Brainstorming*—This technique is an interactive group process as per the following steps:
  - A group (e.g., the project team) is convened to examine risks.
  - Each participant provides a personal perspective on and input into potential risks for the project at hand.
  - Participants are encouraged to generate new ideas or to expand on those of other team members.
  - A member of the team is designated to record all ideas. All ideas are captured; no ideas are evaluated or discarded at this time.
  - When all participant input has been received, the group examines each item on the list and discusses the merits of each idea. Some ideas concerning risks may be eliminated, while the remaining ideas are consolidated and categorized.
  - The resulting categorized risk list represents the group's risk identification list.
- *Nominal Group Technique*—This technique is a group risk identification process with the following steps:
  - A group (e.g., the project team) is convened to examine risks.
  - All team members write down what they see as major risks, and this is done without verbal communication among team members.
  - All team members successively read one risk they have identified on their list, and each item is recorded on a board or chart in front for everyone in the group to see.
  - Risk item identification continues until all the individual lists are exhausted.
  - All team members then individually rate and categorize the risks.
  - The individual results are then tabulated as the group's output.
- *Analogy Technique*—This technique is based on the assumption that no project represents a totally new system. The project work elements (work packages) that have been done before provide historical data for the current examination. The technique is performed as follows:
  - The type of project activity (e.g., risk assessment) to be accomplished is reviewed.
  - Similar projects or similar work from previous projects are identified.
  - Information from previous projects that the team deems relevant is then collected.
  - The work elements of the current project are examined relative to results and outcomes from similar previous projects, and any potential risks are identified.

While the aforementioned methods are specified as risk assessment techniques, it can be seen that these techniques can be used in other areas of group discussion and deliberation as well. The key is to set the frame of reference for participants toward their deliberation objectives.

Risk Identification

Risk identification is a project team activity that should occur throughout the project management life cycle, but particularly during

- Creation of the project definition, business case, and scope of work
- Development of a detailed *Work Breakdown Structure* (WBS)
- Preparation of resource, schedule, and cost estimates
- Establishment of terms and conditions in contracts and subcontracts
- Selection of subcontractors, vendors, and suppliers
- Evaluation and execution of contract or technical change requests

During the project, individual team members also hold inherent responsibility for identifying new risks within their project areas.

Business Risk Examinations

The risk management process actually begins with an initial risk assessment performed during the project Profile Phase in conjunction with new project opportunity identification. This higher-level risk examination is performed as the project is qualified, and in association with business plan preparation. Often, only limited information is known about specific project work during this initial project management phase, so the assessment is inherently focused on contractual and business risks in addition to a preliminary look at project work performance risks. The results of this assessment contribute to *Business Case Development*, which is used in the project selection process. To that end, this is called the *business risk assessment*.

Business risk assessment is used to identify and eliminate questionable or marginally valued projects based on risk before incurring extensive proposal, planning, and performance costs. It includes an examination of the following potential areas of risk associated with the project under consideration:

- *Marketplace Risk*—Examine the status of the organization in the competitive marketplace, determine how well it is responding to the pressures and demands of the marketplace, and identify areas of the business that are susceptible to marketplace risk.
  - Industry standards
  - Government mandates
  - Consumer interests
  - Social conditions
  - Environmental impacts
  - Acts of nature
  - Competition moves
- *Financial Risk*—Examine financial indicators relative to the nature of the business and the influence of the project on that business; determine any financial areas that could be affected and that could create a business risk during project performance.
  - Inflation/taxation
  - Currency values
  - Stock market changes
  - Cash flow
  - Project estimates
  - Funding commitment
- *Legal Risk*—Examine project requirements and planned project performance for any legal issues that could create some level of business risk.
  - License requirements
  - Contract ambiguity
  - Bankruptcies
  - Lawsuits
  - Copyrights
  - Partnership impacts
  - Union agreements
- *Technology-Based Risk*—Examine the nature of pending project work for areas in which the use (or lack of use) of certain types of technology or technical capability will present the potential for risk.
  - Qualified technicians
  - User qualification
  - New technology
  - Unique technology
  - Old technology
- *Customer-Based Risk*—Examine the customer's profile and previous work history, the current state of customer business operations, and the indications of intent to fulfill the project to identify any areas of business risk that could emanate from the customer.
  - Satisfaction factors
  - Change requests
  - Decisions and no decisions
  - Funding commitment
  - Strategy adjustments
  - Management personnel changes

Once these elements have been examined, employ the following procedures for conducting the risk analysis and prioritization, as well as subsequent guidance for developing risk response strategies for identified business risks.

Project Risk Examinations

Project risk identification relies prominently on an examination of the project's WBS, which ensures that risk events associated with project performance are considered. The process requires an examination of each WBS work element to identify associated risks. If a large number of work packages are found to prohibit such a detailed examination, then the project manager may opt to perform risk identification at a higher level in the WBS.

In addition to the WBS, other facets of the project and project management can also be examined. This would include various internal and external risk factors, which can be addressed using the following checklist.

During risk examination, as per use of any of the techniques described earlier in this practice, project risks should simply be listed, and no immediate judgments should be made regarding their validity. Risk identification is intended only to compile a preliminary list of project risks.

Project risk assessment is used to identify and eliminate potential adverse impacts on project performance. It requires an examination of the following potential areas of risk associated with the project under consideration:

- *Customer*—Examine the customer-related factors that can influence project outcomes or affect project performance.
  - Expectations
  - Responsiveness
  - Decision making
  - Scope management
  - Funding
- *Project Team*—Examine the project-team-related factors (forming, developing, and managing the project team) that can affect project work.
  - Staff availability
  - Technical expertise
  - Work performance
  - Work quality
  - Leadership

- *Project Management*—Examine the project management factors that will influence project performance.
  - Plan adequacy
  - Plan estimations
  - Schedule
  - New technology
  - Communication
- *Vendor Management*—Examine the vendor- or contractor-related factors that will contribute to project performance.
  - Contract
  - Technical expertise
  - Work fulfillment
  - Work quality
  - Leadership
- *Internal Influences*—Examine the internal factors that will affect project performance.
  - Corporate culture
  - Manager decisions
  - Leadership changes
  - Portfolio priority
  - Business strategy
- *External Influences*—Examine the external factors that will affect project performance.
  - Regulatory issues
  - Legal issues
  - Natural hazards
  - Public interest
  - Market variations

Compile Project Risks

Once the project team identifies all risks, then it can examine the validity of each. Risk conditions are confirmed, risk redundancies are removed, and insignificant risks are eliminated. This review and compilation should help the team construct a risk list of manageable size. Furthermore, risk categorization may be advisable, as it will be helpful later in the assessment process when risk response strategies are developed.

Risk Analysis

Risk analysis involves examining previously identified risks to determine indicators of possible effects on project performance or project outcome, so this effort is primarily concerned with determining which risk events warrant a response. Specifically, each risk is analyzed to determine the probability of its occurrence, the impact expected if it occurs, and the overall or combined risk of those two factors.

Simply stated, the steps for performing a detailed project risk analysis include the following:

- Establish a risk analysis method.
- Determine project risk probability.
- Determine project risk impact.
- Calculate overall project risk impact.

These steps are described further in the following subsections.

Establish a Risk Analysis Method

A standard method for analyzing risk should be established for use by all project team members. The following are three common, albeit simpler, approaches that can be used:

- *Quantitative Method*—Quantitative methods are used when each risk event can be assigned a numerical indication of value. For example, probability would be expressed as a percentage (e.g., a 50% chance of occurrence). Impact is often expressed in monetary or financial terms (e.g., an added cost of $20K, or in terms of days, weeks, or months for schedule impacts). In some cases, organizations or industries will acquire or develop and apply other metrics to such a quantitative analysis.
- *Qualitative Method*—Qualitative methods are used when risks become too difficult or too time consuming to quantify. For qualitative analysis, criteria is established for the analysis, and this is often simplified by using terms such as "high," "moderate," and "low" to describe either probability or impact. In qualitative analysis, the specific metrics and measurements needed to make a quantitative determination are not available; therefore, a more subjective scale is used (e.g., a moderate probability that this risk event will happen, and, if it happens, it will have a high impact). This method also provides for easy comprehension by most analysis team members who may have uncertain risk analysis skills.
- *Narrative Method*—Narrative methods are more descriptive than analytical. In general, this method is used to simply describe events that may preclude project activities from being fulfilled, or it identifies the risk source or the cause of risk.

Quantitative values should be assigned only when there is a reasonable degree of certainty or confidence in the validity of those metrics. Assigning quantitative values to risk events whose probability and impact are largely unpredictable could convey a false sense of accuracy and reliability, and that would be misleading. If quantitative analysis is not possible, qualitative or narrative methods should be used.

Determine Project Risk Probability

Risk probability provides an indication of the likelihood of the occurrence of a risk event. The project team should examine each risk independently to determine the probability of risk occurrence. This step can be performed separately, or concurrently with determining the impact. Whenever possible, the team should try to quantify the probability.

Risk events can be examined and their probabilities determined using methods prescribed by the organization or the project manager. This effort can be advanced through a variety of means:

- Risk analysis/assessment software applications
- Risk models that provide quantitative output
- Risk experts who lend knowledge and experience to the analysis
- Risk metrics that are developed internally or are industry based
- Risk management experience of the project manager and project team

Risk probability is preferably expressed in quantitative terms, and that would provide for it to be expressed as a percentage value. When there is insufficient information or insufficient means to produce a numeric probability, qualitative methods can be used. Simple qualitative methods provide indications of risk probability in terms of high, moderate, or low likelihood of occurrence, which is based on the subjective assessment of the participating team.

Determine Project Risk Impact

The impact of a risk event is a value that indicates the gain or loss that will be encountered if the risk event occurs. The project team should review each risk independently to determine its impact value. The risk impact could involve cost, schedule, and resource utilization as well as factors affecting project performance and outcomes.

Again, the accuracy of quantitative impact analysis methods is preferred if a sufficient means to do so is available. For example, if a risk event that occurs causes an additional cost of $40K, then $40,000 is the impact of that risk. Similarly, if the risk event causes a schedule delay of one week, then a one-week project delay is the impact of that risk. However, qualitative methods can also be used to simply assess risk impact in terms of high, moderate, or low values, based on a subjective assessment of the participating team.

Calculate Overall Project Risk Impact

Overall project risk impact is calculated by combining the risk probability and the risk impact of a risk event. The overall risk rating is generally represented by the following formula:

$$\text{Probability} \times \text{Impact} = \text{Overall Risk Impact}$$

This calculation is fairly straightforward if the quantitative method is used to determine the risk probability and risk impact. The impact (in dollars or duration) is multiplied by the probability factor (i.e., 1–99%). In addition, the organization may wish to introduce a risk weight factor to show the degree of importance that can be applied for additional quantification of the risk event. This added risk weight factor (e.g., normally a value from 1 to 10) is represented in the following formula:

$$\text{Probability} \times \text{Impact} \times \text{Weight Factor} = \text{Overall Risk Impact}$$

Using this formula, the analysis can include special consideration for types or categories of risk by assigning certain weighted values to the risk event. If the qualitative method of analysis is used, then an additional layer of subjective evaluation is added to the process. However, that still provides value if care is taken when combining the probability and impact values. Here, evaluators will combine risk probability values such as high, moderate, and low with risk impact values of high, moderate, and low to arrive at a relevant overall project risk impact value. Values of "high" and "high" would obviously give an overall impact value of "high," as "low" and "low" combinations would provide an overall impact of "low." Analysts will need to examine each risk event carefully when calculating the overall risk impact for other combinations of high, moderate, and low.

Risk Prioritization

Project risk identification can result in a long list of risk events even for so-called smaller or medium-size projects. It is not always possible to track and manage every risk event at the relative expense that could be incurred in terms of cost and time. Therefore, risk prioritization is applied to identify the most significant project and business risks. These would include risks having the potential for the greatest or most severe impact on the project if the risk events were to occur.

Risk prioritization means determining which risks should be managed immediately through preparation of a response strategy and inclusion in a formal tracking process. This ensures that risks having the greatest potential impacts are monitored and managed. While most risks should be monitored, those with higher probabilities and impacts will usually require the most concerted attention of the project manager and project team. Also, lower probability and impact risk events should still be tracked and monitored because their probability and impact could change as the project progresses. An initially low probability and impact risk event could ultimately become one with high impact.

The result of risk prioritization is a list of identified risk events that can be examined at regular intervals during the project according to the assigned priority.

6.2 RISK RESPONSE STRATEGY PREPARATION

Risk response strategies are created with regard for the specific results of the risk assessment conducted, and they provide a means to reduce or eliminate the potential occurrence and impact of a project risk event. That is to say, having identified the potential for project risks, this activity provides for consideration of actions that can be subsequently applied in response to those risk events. Leaving identified high-value or otherwise significant risk events unattended is simply an indication of questionable management.

Project risk assessment should be performed initially during planning and then at relevant intervals throughout the project to ascertain potential project risk impacts, with the intent to either remove the risk threat or to plan actions in the case of risk event occurrence.

Concept of This Practice

This practice provides the project manager, project team, and other stakeholders with a means to respond to risk events having potential adverse impacts on the project effort.

The purpose of this practice is to provide the project manager and risk managers participating in the project team with guidance for developing viable responses to identified project risks. *Risk Response Strategy Preparation* is normally done during Project Planning (Plan Phase). However, this practice should be applied throughout the project as a part of the ongoing risk assessment effort.

Risk response strategy preparation is characterized by three primary activities:

- Identify risk response strategies.
- Implement risk response strategies.
- Assess risk response strategies.

These activities are described here.

Identify Risk Response Strategies

Risk Response Strategies are developed and applied to reduce or eliminate the probability of occurrence of a risk event or risk impact. There are four basic types of risk response strategies that are generally accepted across most industries. The project manager and project team should examine these strategies to determine which can be used to address identified project risks.

- *Risk Avoidance*—This response strategy provides for moving the potential risk away from the project, usually by removing the catalyst or perceived cause of the risk event. It changes the conditions of occurrence and impact so that the risk event does not affect the project. Some risk avoidance maneuvers include the following:
  - Reorganize facets of the project to eliminate the risk, for example, adjust the project team structure, realign the project team schedule and assignments, and realign or reschedule project work elements and associated task relationships.
  - Negotiate or otherwise collaborate with the customer or vendor/contractor/supplier to remove any significant risk-bearing project requirements.
  - Decline bidding on the project opportunity or on a portion of the project opportunity when the assessed risk exceeds acceptable levels, and other risk response strategies will not adequately contain such risk.

  Applying this type of strategy should result in the removal of the potential occurrence of an identified risk event from the project.
- *Risk Transfer*—This response strategy provides for transferring all or part of the risk impact to another participant outside the organization. The probability of occurrence is not necessarily reduced or eliminated, but the risk consequences or impacts within the organization are minimized. Some risk transfer strategies include the following:
  - Determine which project work elements can be outsourced, and contract that work to qualified vendors and contractors or to professionals and specialists who have relevant expertise (and associated low-risk outcomes) in performing such work.
  - Examine and transfer areas of project work that the customer can perform at a lower risk potential than can be done by the performing organization.
  - Obtain insurance that provides financial cost coverage for an occurrence of the risk event to recoup funds that enable repeating an "incomplete" work effort, to bear loss of revenue due to an "impacted" project work effort, or to fund a project recovery effort.

  Applying this type of strategy should result in the transfer of impact of an identified risk event to an entity outside the performing organization.
- *Risk Mitigation*—This response strategy is used to minimize the impact of a risk event by taking action to reduce the risk probability or the risk impact, or both. Some risk mitigation strategies include the following:
  - Closely track and control the project cost, schedule, and resource utilization for work elements associated with the identified risk event.
  - Prepare and communicate relevant risk response plans that specify the actions to be taken in situations of actual risk event occurrence, usually with response

actions directed at specific risk events—that is, if this risk event happens, we will take this action.
  - Closely manage the technical work performance of project work elements associated with potentially high-value risk events.
  - Develop realistic staffing plans and establish firm and reliable resource utilization commitments, particularly for project work elements shown to be at risk.
  - Be proactive in negotiating and implementing project changes to minimize impact or probability of risk events, which is best done immediately following risk identification.
  - Introduce a management reserve or contingency fund that can be accessed in response to risk events that cause cost overruns.

  Applying this type of strategy should result in the reduced probability of risk event occurrence or in a reduction of the adverse impact on the project in the event of risk occurrence.
- *Risk Acceptance*—This response strategy represents management's awareness of the identified risk event and further indicates a willingness by management to accept the consequences of impact in the event of risk occurrence. Some risk acceptance response strategies include the following:
  - Examine the conditions (usually low-probability, low-impact conditions) of an identified project risk event, and formalize and convey to relevant participants the decision to take no risk response actions.
  - Accept a risk event by preparing a contingency plan to specify required actions to be taken in the event of risk occurrence—that is, a response is provided after occurrence, not before.

  Applying this type of strategy will normally result in delaying any risk response until after the risk event actually occurs. It represents taking a chance on nonoccurrence, but this gamble may be acceptable when either the probability of risk occurrence or the risk event impact is minimal.

These risk response strategies should be reviewed as a part of risk management and applied in a timely manner to risks having a high likelihood of occurrence or a significant adverse impact on the project. In particular, it should be noted that risk acceptance becomes the default strategy for all potential risk events on the project when prescribed project risk assessments are deferred or otherwise not performed.

Implement Risk Response Strategies

This practice prescribes that response strategies be provided for all risk events that are considered to be high on the project risk prioritization list. Also, moderate and lower risk events should be addressed whenever possible and usually as time permits.

The project manager and project team members conducting the risk assessment will have to determine the appropriate response strategy for each identified risk event. This means reviewing each identified risk to ascertain assignment of a viable response strategy. In some cases, more than one risk response strategy can be considered for use. Also, response strategy selection decisions should include sufficient detail about how the strategy will be implemented, when it will be implemented, and who will be responsible for the implementation.

This warrants the consideration of two prominent types of risk response strategies that can be implemented consistently with preferred risk management practices.

Preventive Risk Response Strategies

Preventive strategies are those selected and positioned to be proactive in reducing or eliminating the probability or impact of a risk event. These strategies prescribe actions that are to be taken in advance of any risk event occurrence.

Preventive strategies are characterized by the fact that risk response actions can and should be entered into the work breakdown structure (WBS) as specific work elements. That is to say, the risk response action is included as a work element in the project work plan specifically for the purpose of reducing or eliminating the probability or impact of a specifically identified risk event. As a work element, it also includes the specification of the resources needed to implement the response strategy along with the assignment of responsible individuals to perform the action.

Preventive risk response strategy implementation is a preferred approach for resolving known risk events when it can be applied.

Reactive Risk Response Strategies

Reactive strategies are those selected and positioned in the event of risk occurrence. These strategies prescribe actions that are to be taken after a risk event occurs.

Reactive strategies are characterized by the specification of response activities that are held in abeyance until a risk event occurs. Associated risk response actions necessarily have to be planned and prepared in advance of risk event occurrence, but they are not implemented until the occurrence of the particular risk event.

Reactive risk response strategies are normally documented in the risk management plan for future reference and implementation if the risk occurs. Reactive strategies can also be tied to milestones that are included in the project work plan as a means to trigger strategy review and implementation if a particular risk event occurs.

Assess Risk Response Strategies

The final step in implementing risk response strategies is to assess the strategies put forth as part of project risk management. There are two aspects of assessment to consider. One occurs when a risk response strategy is formulated. The second occurs when the strategy is implemented.

Assess Strategy Formulation

The solutions that result when responding to some risks can sometimes create new risks, so each new strategy should be examined for that potential. The project team should examine the selected strategies to determine whether they have created additional risk. In some cases, this can be an intuitive effort; in others, a further detailed analysis (assessment) of risk is necessary.

Additional risk caused by strategy formulation can be minimized by considering the following examination of each new risk response strategy:

- What will this risk response strategy accomplish if implemented?
- What is the scope of influence across project work plan work elements if this response is implemented?
  - Cost influence
  - Schedule influence
  - Resource utilization influence
- As per the scope of influence identified, does any new risk event emerge relative to work plan work elements?
- Does this risk response strategy change or influence any guidance or procedures contained in project-planning documents?

The selected risk response strategies should be introduced when there is high certainty that the result of implementation will not only lower the probability of occurrence or the impact of any identified risk event but will also not result in creating any additional risk events of significance. This examination can also aid in deliberation when there is a need to select a risk response strategy from among two or more response alternatives.

Assess Strategy Implementation

From time to time, a risk event will occur to prompt the implementation of a reactive risk response strategy as may be contained in the project risk management plan. Similarly, the incorporation of preventive risk response strategies in the project work plan will provide for "scheduled" implementation of response strategies. The results produced from such strategy implementations should be examined and documented for both near-term and future use.

Implemented risk strategies should be immediately examined for effectiveness in reducing the probability or impact of the risk events with which they are associated. If necessary, strategy adjustments or new strategies can be applied for those found to be weak or ineffective.

Implemented risk strategies should also be examined for effectiveness relative to further use or use on other projects in the organization. This examination is often a part of risk management plan closeout activities and provides a recorded description of strategy use for future reference across future projects.

6.3 RISK MANAGEMENT PLAN DEVELOPMENT

The risk management plan provides documented guidance for the project risk management process, including conducting risk assessments and other project risk management activities.

Concept of This Practice

The purpose of this practice is to provide the project manager, project team, and other relevant stakeholders with an approach for developing the planning document needed to conduct project risk management.

The risk management plan is prepared to document the risk management process. It should address who is responsible for managing various areas of project risk; how the initial risk identification, analysis, and prioritization output will be maintained; what the specific response strategies are, including any contingency plans to be implemented; and whether a management reserve will be allocated.

Risk Management Plan Development is normally accomplished during Project Planning (Plan Phase). However, risk planning and plan content can be reviewed and updated throughout the project as risk management is performed. The development of the risk management plan is highlighted by three primary activities:

- Preparing the Risk Management Plan
- Conducting Risk Management
- Evaluating Risk Management

Each of these plan components is described in the following sections.

Preparing the Risk Management Plan

The risk management plan is a primary project plan component. It may be very detailed or broadly framed, depending on the needs of the project and the specifications of the organization. The elements prescribed for inclusion in the risk management plan are explained in the following subsections:

Risk Management Policy and Standards

Incorporate the organization's policy for managing project risk, or paraphrase important parts of the policy. This could include excerpts from organization or industry standards for risk management, along with references to specific practices or publications related to project risk management. In particular, policies related to allocating management reserves and establishing project contingency funds should be incorporated.

This section of the plan could also identify policy area exemptions that are applicable to the project being planned.

Risk Management Responsibilities

Use this section to identify and assign responsibilities to key risk management participants. The organization may wish to prepare a standard list of prescribed participants in risk management—from project team members to cross-business unit staff members. The following list identifies some of the more prominent participants normally associated with project risk management, and outlines their responsibilities:

- Sales and Marketing Team
  - Conducts preliminary business risk assessments during the Profile Phase, with or without the project team, as a contribution to the *Business Plan Development* process used in determining a go/no-go decision for the project opportunity
  - Collaborates on project and business risks and risk reduction with the project manager, project team, and project sponsor, as well as the customer (when appropriate), during the sales and marketing effort
  - Examines and discusses project and business risks and their potential impacts on business with the project manager and with other executives and managers responsible for making project go/no-go decisions
- Project Manager
  - Ensures that adequate business and project risk assessments are performed at appropriate times during the Plan Phase and at other critical junctures in the project
  - Leads development of risk response strategies and contingencies associated with identified risk events, and conveys these response strategies to
    - Pricing strategy development
    - Proposal development
    - Work elements in the WBS
    - Requirements for vendors, contractors, and suppliers
  - Prepares the risk management plan to guide all project team members and stakeholders in the performance of project risk management
  - Conducts ongoing risk examinations at appropriate intervals and maintains the risk management plan during the project's Perform Phase
  - Reports project risk status to project executives and sponsors
- Project Team Members and Selected Stakeholders (i.e., Project and Business Risk Experts)
  - Participate in project risk assessments and in subsequent examination and development of risk response strategies
  - Implement guidance for identifying and reporting new risk events as prescribed by the risk management plan
  - Implement risk response strategies and evaluate their effectiveness, as assigned
- Project Executive (Sponsor)
  - Establishes organizational policies for conducting project risk management
  - Reviews and approves project risk management plans to ensure alignment with business interests and objectives
  - Develops or acquires metrics for risk impact thresholds to guide risk identification, analysis, and prioritization activities
  - Prepares guidance for elevating risk coordination and collaboration for the project sponsor, project executive, and other managers as needed

Risk Assessment Approach

Provide a summary description of the approach to be used for project and business risk assessments. Include a reference or referral to the complete details of the assessment process that will be used.

Identify any standards associated with project risk management that will be applied to this project's risk management effort. Include in this section any scheduled meetings and venues to be used for project risk assessment activities. Identify meeting participants and specify requested assessment preparation actions that are needed. Identify any advance materials that will be available for review prior to the assessment activity.

Risk Management Guidance

Specify guidance for conducting risk management activities. This includes guidance for project risk assessments, project risk management, and project risk management evaluation.

The specific guidance elements will be related to the organization's culture, and particularly to established business practices surrounding risk management.

This plan section can also be used to incorporate guidance for implementing contingency plans; allocating money reserves; and managing cost, schedule, and resource utilization thresholds during risk strategy implementation.

Risk Event and Strategy Response List

The focus of project risk management is the assessment of potential project risk and the specification of strategies to eliminate or reduce the impact of significant risk events.

This section of the risk management plan provides a list of identified project risk events and associated response strategies for each risk event. This content is a direct output from *Risk Assessment* and *Risk Response Strategy* preparation activities performed by the project team. The content is populated following the completion of those activities.

The risk event list is adjusted or updated as an ongoing management effort to ensure that the current status of project risk is accurately represented in the risk management plan.

Conducting Risk Management

Risk management activities are conducted through every phase in the project management life cycle. A number of project management activities are directly or indirectly related to the project risk management effort as outlined here:

- Project Profile Phase
  - Evaluate customer profile.
  - Evaluate project opportunity.
  - Evaluate project management complexity (Project Classification).
  - Assess business risk (for inclusion in Business Plan Development).
  - Assign qualified managers capable of addressing risk issues.
  - Collaborate on business plan development.
  - Obtain authorization for contingency funding and management reserves.
- Project Plan Phase
  - Evaluate customer requirements.
  - Prepare the risk management plan.
  - Collaborate on technical proposal development.
  - Collaborate on business contract development.
  - Obtain review and approval of the risk management plan by management.
- Project Perform Phase
  - Track and monitor identified project risk events (see the subsection "Track and Monitor Identified Project Risk Events").
  - Implement risk response strategies (see the subsection "Implement Risk Response Strategies").
  - Identify new risk events (as per established indicators and triggers).
  - Evaluate risk response strategy implementation results (see the subsection "Evaluate Risk Response Strategy Implementation Results").
  - Maintain the risk management plan.
- Project Post Phase
  - Evaluate and document risk management effectiveness (see the subsection "Evaluate and Document Risk Management Effectiveness").
  - Close out the risk management plan.

A few of these activities warrant further breakout, as described here and in the next subsection.

Track and Monitor Identified Project Risk Events

A primary responsibility of the project manager is to monitor and track risk events during solution implementation in the Perform Phase. The risk management plan provides guidance on the frequency of risk event and response strategy tracking, and the project team should accomplish these tasks as planned.

In particular, three tracking activities should be pursued as a part of the risk management effort:

- Review the risk management plan at intervals to determine whether specified risk event analyses are still current, and proactive or reactive strategies are still appropriate.
- Review the WBS, contract changes, project plan changes, and significant project events to determine whether there are any new risks to be assessed, and if any additional response strategies need to be developed.
- Monitor triggering milestones on the project schedule that are set up to alert the project manager to implement or activate a series of tasks or contingency plans should an identified risk event occur.

Implement Risk Response Strategies

This step is primarily performed to implement reactive strategies. These are activated when a previously identified risk event occurs. After such a strategy is implemented, the project manager must revise the project plan to reflect the cost of implementing the action (e.g., time, resources, and money). This revision, which is necessary because the cost was not included in the original estimate, should also be noted in the strategy description in the risk management plan.

To ensure that the strategy is implemented as planned, the project risk manager or the project team member responsible for the WBS element associated with the risk event should monitor the status of the risk event to closure. In the case of preventive or proactive strategies, results must be monitored to ensure that the strategy is working as planned. Preventive risk response strategies are activated as part of the project plan, as specified in the project WBS. They are carried out as scheduled and periodically evaluated to assess their success in controlling risk or the need for further actions.

Evaluating Risk Management

There are two primary activities associated with evaluating the risk management capability as described in the following subsections:

Evaluate Risk Response Strategy Implementation Results

The ability to manage and control project risk depends on the effectiveness of the risk management plan. This plan requires continuous monitoring to ensure that it is current and valid. As needed, the plan must be updated to reflect the current status of the project relative to potential risk. The risk management plan and its effectiveness should be evaluated at regular intervals as follows:

- Periodically, at specified and scheduled intervals, throughout the project
- At major project milestones
- As part of the project change control process

Risk events, their probability, and their impact are constantly changing. New risks emerge, and old ones may even disappear. Risk mitigation actions may create new risks that were not predicted, or change the effects of existing ones. Therefore, evaluating the plan periodically is critical, and periodic reviews should be specified in the project schedule.

Major milestones are also logical points in the project management life cycle to evaluate how the project is doing and to assess changes in the project work environment. Every time a major project change is proposed and approved, the project team should look at how change affects the project and determine whether any new risks have been introduced. New response strategies must be developed to address any new risks.

Evaluating the effectiveness of the project risk management plan entails the following steps:

- Review the risk response actions implemented to date for effectiveness and the need for further action.
- Evaluate the major risk events for WBS elements currently being implemented and those to be implemented in the near future to see whether anything has changed or strategies should be modified.
- Identify any new risks, analyze them, incorporate them into the overall risk management process, and develop corresponding risk response strategies.
- Develop new response strategies or modify old ones if the current strategy works poorly or further mitigation is necessary.
- Escalate management of the risk if known risk thresholds are increased.
- Update the project plan, WBS, and pertinent supporting plans as appropriate to reflect changes in the project risk management plan.

Evaluate and Document Risk Management Effectiveness

Documentation of risk management efforts provides a historical trail of the project team's actions and results. By means of this effort, project managers can learn from experience. Similar to lessons learned, this documentation provides new project managers with valuable information on which strategies and actions have worked and which have not. It also provides experienced project managers with insight about potential risk during their project planning efforts.

Risk management documentation should be kept as simple as possible, but it should be current, complete, and accurate. The documentation of results can be incorporated into the risk management plan, which is subsequently archived for future use.

Chapter 7

Project Tracking and Controlling

Project tracking and controlling is a project manager responsibility as well as a project team effort. This practice area prescribes activities related to examining and reporting project performance. Such attention to project performance is a primary method for ensuring that the project is progressing satisfactorily and that it will fulfill objectives and expectations when completed on time and within budget. Also, it enables the project manager to prepare reports for review by others—for example, the project management office (PMO), the project executive (sponsor), and the customer—so that they too are informed about project performance progress and status.

There are three practices associated with project tracking and controlling:

- Project Performance Analysis
- Project Performance Control
- Project Change Control

This practice area will focus on conveying concepts and techniques designed for project performance tracking and controlling. While there is a significant amount of report preparation and transmittal occurring in conjunction with this practice area, guidance for project reporting is addressed within the separate Project Communication Management practice area.

7.1 PROJECT PERFORMANCE ANALYSIS

Project management is focused on planning the project work effort, monitoring work progress to determine if the plan is being followed, and then, as needed, taking corrective action to force the project back onto the planned track. Project performance analysis is that aspect of project management that examines planned project events and outcomes relative to actual project events and outcomes—primarily in terms of cost, schedule, and resource utilization.

Concept of This Practice

Project performance analysis provides the project manager and project team with analytical indications of project progress and status. *Project progress* is the specification of the advancements made in achieving planned project activities and objectives, that is, cost, schedule, and resource utilization objectives. *Project status* is the determination of what project progress indicators mean relative to the accomplishment (to date) of project management effectiveness, contractual obligations, customer satisfaction, and business interests.

The purpose of this practice is to provide the project manager and project team with guidance for collecting and analyzing project performance information. In turn, analysis results can be conveyed to other project stakeholders to inform them about project progress and status.

Project Performance Analysis is normally accomplished during the Perform Phase in association with project tracking and controlling activities. There are four primary activities prescribed for project performance analysis:

- Project Performance Tracking
- Earned Value Analysis
- Variance Analysis
- Other Related Analyses

Each of these activities will have bearing on or otherwise use *earned value analysis* concepts. With that, it should be noted that earned value analysis is a term that can be used to describe the overall analytical (and mathematical) approach that is applied to examine aspects of project performance. The term *earned value* can also be used as a singular descriptor of one formula or calculation within the entire set of earned value analysis concepts.

The three key elements of project planning (cost, schedule, and resource utilization) remain at the forefront of project management when conducting project tracking and controlling activities. The fundamental premise here is that "what is planned must be performed." Project management is the effort to oversee and manage how well that performance of planned activities is being achieved. To that end, you need to have a plan in order to conduct project management. In other words, you cannot really manage a project that is not planned.

The construction of a *Project Work Plan* and associated work breakdown structure (WBS) was prescribed in a separate practice as the basic planning document for each project, and it will be used here to track and analyze project performance.

Project Performance Tracking

Performance tracking begins with the collection of information needed to accomplish the prescribed analyses. Data collection can be specified to occur at some recurring point in time when data is needed for analysis purposes, or it may be accomplished as an ongoing activity over a period of time where data is collected regardless of when analyses are performed. The ongoing data collection approach is recommended, particularly if performance analyses are conducted infrequently, for example, only monthly or quarterly. This removes the burden of trying to capture or recreate past data that may have been replaced by current data. Also, ongoing data collection (even without formal analysis) can sometimes provide indicators of potential project performance issues or problems that would not otherwise surface in a timely manner.

The following three subsections provide some suggestions for information and data handling relative to the conduct of performance tracking.

Cost Tracking

Cost tracking is a critical project management activity. The cost-tracking effort considers the baseline cost estimates that were created in the Plan Phase (and that are currently aligned with work elements in the project work plan) and examines them relative to actual costs and expenditures that have been incurred by the project. The following are cost-tracking data sets that should be gathered for examination in this tracking process:

- *Labor Costs*—The costs incurred through use of internal staff resources to perform work associated with the project, for example, salaries, benefits, and overhead. Most projects will benefit from access to "loaded" labor rates for purposes of cost accounting. This cost data may be obtained from individuals who provide a timesheet or other time report, or from the organization's payroll or accounting and finance system.
- *Material Costs*—The costs of materials and supplies needed to conduct the project and produce the project deliverables, as may be obtained from vendors or suppliers. This cost data is usually obtained from purchase orders and invoices.
- *Capital Costs*—The costs associated with required capital expenditures, for example, buildings (construction or acquisition), equipment (computers, office furniture, etc.), and renovations and improvements. This information is usually obtained through the accounting and finance department.
- *Vendor and Contractor*—The costs of selecting, procuring, and assigning vendors and contractors to the project work effort. This cost data is usually obtained from purchase orders and invoices, as well as from vendor contracts and work plans.
- *Project Support Costs*—The costs of general administrative items associated with the project effort, for example, travel, computer software, specialist and consultant fees, permits and licenses, project team training, freight and courier services, and project documents and documentation materials.

Cost information is typically compiled weekly for shorter projects and at least monthly for larger projects. To ensure proper cost control, the project manager (or a qualified designee) should review and approve all invoices for external expenses incurred by the project. Such approval should not be "rubber stamped." Rather, the invoice approval process should prompt a detailed examination of planned project expense versus acquired value, in conjunction with verifying authorization for the expenditures.

Schedule Tracking

Schedule tracking is another critical project management activity. The schedule-tracking effort considers the baseline schedule estimates that were created in the Plan Phase (and that are currently aligned with work elements in the project work plan) and examines them relative to the actual occurrence of scheduled project events. The following are schedule-tracking data sets that should be gathered for examination in this tracking process:

- Scheduled start and finish dates for each relevant work package
- Actual start and finish dates for each relevant work package
- Percent complete or estimated completion date for the project

- Identification of pertinent milestones reached
- Identification of project deliverables achieved

Schedule information collection refers to the use of "relevant" work packages. This is a reference to those work elements that fall within the current time frame of the project and that have relevance for tracking purposes. It is not intended to prompt examination of every work package in the WBS unless the project is of considerably short duration.

Similar to cost information, this data collection is typically compiled weekly for shorter projects and at least monthly for larger projects. Weekly collection is preferred, as that is often the frequency at which staff time sheets are prepared and submitted, and the individual time sheet can be a source for identifying the time used on each work package. In lieu of time sheets, project team leaders or team members themselves can include hours expended in a progress report that is routinely submitted to the project manager. The compilation of all such reports should provide the project manager with sufficient information for schedule analysis.

Resource Utilization Tracking

Resource utilization tracking is another critical project management activity. The resource utilization tracking effort considers the baseline resource utilization estimates that were created in the Plan Phase (and that are currently aligned with work elements in the project work plan) and examines them relative to the assignment and performance of project work. The following are resource utilization tracking data sets that should be gathered for examination in this tracking process:

- Resource time planned versus actual for each relevant project work package
- Resource allocations versus actual assignments for relevant project work packages
- Resource qualification levels required versus actual for relevant project work packages
- Project management and project support resource levels for the period (e.g., project manager, project administrator, project management office [PMO] staff, and other staff members involved but not working on specific work packages)

Resource utilization reference to "relevant" work packages is the same as described earlier for schedule tracking; it does not necessarily refer to the entire project. Here, project work represents an expenditure of human resource time. Therefore, the tracking effort examines the number and types of project resources actually working on the project versus the number and types that were allocated to work on the project. Information collection is usually associated with recurring individual or team reports that come to the project manager, ideally on a weekly basis. Otherwise, the allocation and assignment of resources can be examined from relevant project staffing plans and staff management documents.

Earned Value Analysis

Earned value is the amount of planned work that has been accomplished to date and represents the value that has been achieved or earned by the project to date as a result of that work accomplishment.

Earned value analysis can be applied to a project work package, a series of work packages in the same period of time, or the entire project. However, it is normally used to examine project cost and schedule data for all work packages through the current date or the current period of examination. In turn, the analysis results provide a reliable indication of project performance. Earned value analysis is based on calculations of the following three earned value elements:

- *Budgeted Cost of Work Performed* (BCWP)—The value, in dollars, of the work accomplished to date. It is also known as *earned value* because the value associated with a particular work package is earned when the task is completed. BCWP is the planned value for the work completed.
  Example: For a work package that has a budget of $8,000 and 50% of that work package has been completed, the BCWP to date is $4,000.
- *Budgeted Cost of Work Scheduled* (BCWS)—The value, in dollars, of the work scheduled (planned) to be completed to date, that is, the project budget. BCWS is the planned value for the planned work.
  Example: If a work package has a budget of $10,000, and 80% of the scheduled time to perform that work has elapsed, the BCWS for that work package is $8,000.
- *Actual Cost of Work Performed* (ACWP)—The value, in dollars, of the actual cost expended for project work performed to date.
  Example: The actual use of $5,000 to accomplish work represents an ACWP of $5,000.

These elements of earned value provide the basis for further examination of variance and other earned value concepts that will enlarge the examiner's perspective on project performance.

Variance Analysis

Project variance analysis is an examination of the differences between what was planned and what actually happened for project cost and project schedule.

Critical cost and schedule variances can be calculated and evaluated using earned value concepts as follows:

- *Cost Variance* (CV)—The difference between the budgeted value of the work actually performed and the actual value of the work performed. CV is calculated as follows:

  $$CV = BCWP - ACWP$$

  CV represents the difference between what was expected to be spent for the work performed and what was actually spent. It avoids the common problem of assuming that the project is on target simply because the resources consumed in a given period match the resources planned for that period.
  Example: If BCWP is $9,000 and ACWP is $8,500, CV is $500. Here, $9,000 worth of work (BCWP) was done, and it only cost $8,500 (ACWP) to accomplish that work. The work effort cost $500 less than originally budgeted.
- *Schedule Variance* (SV)—The difference between the value of the work actually performed and the value of the work scheduled to be performed for a specified period. SV is calculated as follows:

  $$SV = BCWP - BCWS$$

  SV provides an indication of whether the work is being accomplished on schedule. Although an excellent indicator of the status of work in progress, SV is not a time measurement tool. Rather, it provides a measurement of the degree of schedule variation from the plan in terms of monetary units.
  Example: If the BCWP is $9,000 and the BCWS is $8,500, the SV is $500. In other words, for the evaluation period, $8,500 worth of work (BCWS) was supposed to have been done, but $9,000 worth of work (BCWP) was accomplished. Therefore, the effort is ahead of schedule by $500 worth of work.

Project variance, in terms of cost or schedule variance, is a key project performance indicator that shows how closely the project is following plans and particularly planned expenditures. However, it is the extent of variation that must be monitored as an ongoing project management activity.

The performing organization may have established variance standards or thresholds, or the customer may influence variance levels required for reporting purposes. Such standards or thresholds are normally identified early in the project during the Profile Phase, and no later than the Plan Phase. At that time, the tolerance levels for project variance are specified, and the project manager uses that guidance to manage and control project performance. For example, a cost variance may have a threshold of 7%. At such time when that level of cost variance is reached or exceeded, the project manager is obligated to take some control action to return project performance to within the required variance threshold. Of course, project managers should take note before the threshold is reached and consider actions to begin controlling variance as soon as it is identified.

Every project should be expected to have some level of cost and schedule variance; it is a very natural occurrence. It would be unrealistic to expect zero variance. Attempts to achieve zero variance may be unwise due to the potential for cutting corners, affecting quality, or creating undue overwork requirements. It is best to simply establish the variance threshold and mange project performance to stay within that threshold.

Other Related Analyses

Earned value analysis provides several additional measurements that the project manager and project team can use to track and control schedule and budget:

- *Budget at Completion* (BAC)—The estimated total cost of the project or a work package when completed; when combined with project contingency or management reserve funds, BAC equals the total project budget.
- *Estimate to Complete* (ETC)—An estimate of how much more money the project will require to be completed.
- *Estimate at Completion* (EAC)—The current measured (actual) cost plus the estimated cost for the remaining work. The formulas for calculating EAC are

  $$EAC = ACWP + ETC$$

  or

  $$EAC = \frac{BAC}{CPI}$$

- *Cost Performance Index* (CPI)—A numeric representation of how effective the project has been to date in terms of cost. CPI is calculated as follows:

  $$CPI = \frac{BCWP}{ACWP}$$

- *Schedule Performance Index* (SPI)—A numeric representation of project schedule performance at a given point in the project. SPI is calculated as follows:

  $$SPI = \frac{BCWP}{BCWS}$$

- *Variance at Completion* (VAC)—The difference between BAC and EAC. VAC is an indicator of the project variance that can be expected at the end of the project. When compared to CV, VAC will show whether conditions will improve or get worse. It is calculated as follows:

$$VAC = BAC - EAC$$

- *Percent Complete* (PC)—An estimate expressed as a percentage of the amount of work that has been completed on a work package, a group of work packages, or the project, notwithstanding the cost incurred to achieve that much work. PC is calculated as follows:

$$PC = \frac{BCWP}{BAC}$$

- *Percent Spent* (PS)—A percentage of the amount of work completed in terms of cost. This value will be identical to PC when the project is on time and on budget. Values different from PC will indicate potential for problems as that difference grows larger. PS is calculated as follows:

$$PS = \frac{ACWP}{BAC}$$

EAC, CPI, SPI, and VAC are more accurate and, therefore, more useful as the project progresses through the Perform Phase. PC and PS are generally useful throughout the project.

7.2 PROJECT PERFORMANCE CONTROL

Project Performance Control is the practice of applying control actions in response to project performance indicators that exceed established standards or variance thresholds or otherwise threaten the success of the project.

Concept of This Practice

The purpose of this practice is to provide the project manager, project team, and other relevant stakeholders with referential control actions that might be applied to remove variations or resolve problems that are affecting project performance. These can only serve as examples inasmuch as the relevant corporate experience of the organization and the professional experience of the individual will take precedence in identifying and applying particular controls to improve performance on a specific project.

Project Performance Control is normally accomplished during the Perform Phase in association with project tracking and controlling activities. There are three activities associated with project performance control:

- Control Project Cost
- Control Project Schedule
- Control Project Resource Utilization

These are noticeably the same key project management indicators that have been monitored and analyzed throughout the project planning, project estimating, and project tracking and controlling efforts.

Control Project Cost

The following actions can be considered for application to reduce project cost variation or otherwise to correct project cost performance:

- High Labor Costs
  - Ensure accuracy on staff time sheets, review earlier staff time sheets or reports, and correct them as necessary.
  - Review resource utilization levels for underutilized resources that can either leave the project or be applied to broader work efforts.
  - Examine the schedule and use resource leveling to optimize resource utilization.
  - Examine labor cost estimates for accuracy; reestimate work elements as needed.
  - Review the schedule for too much or too little level of work effort; examine use of overtime or multiple work shifts; ensure that only authorized work is being performed.
  - Examine time sheets and reports for indications of "too much, too frequent" overtime.
  - Conduct routine meetings with staff leaders and individual project team members to review their perspectives on labor costs, and examine ways to reduce such costs.
- High Material and Supply Costs
  - Examine material and supply quantity use for their being more or less than originally estimated; either condition could reflect a higher-than-expected cost, so reexamine quantity estimates.
  - Review the unit cost for materials and supplies; if higher than expected, consider alternate sources and suppliers, and, if as expected, find ways to reduce cost.
  - Examine material consumption to determine if any materials are being used prematurely in the schedule; place controls on materials use and make schedule adjustments as needed.
  - Examine material and supply cost estimates for accuracy; reestimate materials and supplies as needed.

- High Vendor Costs
  - Examine vendor invoices for comparison to the established vendor milestones and deliverables schedule and confirm that payments are due; if not, return or hold vendor invoices until payment is due.
  - Review the invoice schedule to determine whether the subcontractor is requesting payments prematurely; adjust the vendor's invoice and payment schedule as needed.
  - Review the vendor's scope of work in contrast to work performed to see if there are any indications of "scope creep"; if so, use project change control procedures to correct the incident—change the vendor's scope, or disallow the added and unauthorized work.
  - Identify any vendor billing patterns (e.g., frequency, timing, amounts, etc.) that might affect the perception or confirm the reality of higher vendor costs.
  - Conduct routine meetings with vendors to review their fees and expenses, and examine ways to reduce vendor costs.
- High General Costs
  - Examine individual and group expense reports to identify and rectify any unauthorized expenditures.
  - Review the scope of work in contrast to work performed to see if there are any indications of "scope creep"; if so, use project change control procedures to rectify the cause of higher costs.
  - Review travel expense reports in an active and timely manner to approve all travel-related expenses.
  - Apply rigorous examination and approval processes for project-related requisitions.
  - Identify any risk events that have occurred to influence higher-than-expected project expenditures; revisit the project risk management plan to determine if there are any additional, lingering threats to the project cost.
- Project Out-of-Control Costs
  - Revise the project scope—review cost, schedule, and resource utilization estimates, and revise the project budget as necessary in collaboration with the customer.
  - For cost overruns, identify any costs that can be passed to or otherwise shared with the customer; escalate cost issues to the PMO or project executive.
  - Consider performing "project recovery" actions, including an examination of current project conditions, identification of causes for those conditions, and review of potential reassignment of the project manager and project team members, and conduct a major project replanning effort.

Document any cost control actions taken. Examine areas where proactive controls can be used to prevent cost overruns. Revisit these control actions and their results when project lessons learned are being identified during project closeout in the Post Phase.

Control Project Schedule

The following actions can be considered for application to reduce project schedule variation or otherwise to correct project schedule performance—all actions apply to a project that is found to be behind schedule:

- *Work Delay Impacts*—Examine the project's critical paths to identify work elements that are delayed, causing schedule delays for subsequent work activities; remove the blockage and complete any delayed work; determine if schedule issues can be resolved by adding resources; acquire or escalate the need for additional project resources.
- *Project Scope Change Impacts*—Identify schedule delays that are the result of any inadvertent or perhaps even intentional changes in the scope of work; ensure that only authorized work is being performed by the project team and vendors, and rectify any conditions where "scope creep" has occurred.
- *Project Resource Availability Impacts*—Examine work elements to ensure that all scheduled work has been assigned to the project as planned; examine resource utilization and shift resources from noncritical work packages to work packages that reside on the project's critical path to fulfill the work requirements there.
- *Fast-Tracking*—Correct behind/late conditions by examining ways to accomplish project work packages in parallel rather than in sequence; fast-tracking can result in project rework, and usually increases the likelihood of project risk.
- *Concurrent Engineering*—Use this form of fast-tracking to conduct parallel completion of major product design and development work, a perspective higher than work packages.
- *Network Crashing*—Control the project schedule by analyzing cost and schedule trade-offs to identify ways to compress the schedule; network crashing usually includes the following activity steps:
  - Specify a new total duration for the remainder of the project.
  - Compute the project's network critical path.
  - Prioritize the work elements that fall along the project's critical path.
  - Identify the crash time for the highest priority work element.

- Shorten the highest priority work element by the specified crash time and examine the now adjusted total duration for the remainder of the project.
- Recompute the critical path, observing if it has changed dramatically.
- Repeat these work element duration reduction steps until the desired crash time (specified in the first step) is achieved.

It should be mentioned at this point that, as corrective actions are applied to the project schedule, most of them will incur additional cost for the project. Also, many of the solutions will increase the potential for additional project risk. These factors need to be considered and managed when applying controls to the project schedule.

Document any schedule control actions taken. Examine areas where proactive controls can be used to prevent schedule delays. Revisit these control actions and their results when project lessons learned are being identified during project closeout in the Post Phase.

Control Project Resource Utilization

The following actions can be considered for application to reduce project resource utilization variation or otherwise correct project resource utilization performance:

- Work Effort Control
  - Identify any "present-for-work" issues based on individual actions; review personal commitments with the member; rectify the cause of absences and their occurrence.
  - Identify any present-for-work issues based on organizational actions; review resource commitments from resource and functional managers; renew commitments.
  - Identify any areas of work assignment confusion, and routinely review the resource responsibility matrix to ensure that each team member is performing assigned work.
  - Monitor the work effort to ensure that it is being done within the scope of the project and according to the established project work plan and other related plans.
  - Examine customer actions, statements, or decisions that could have an impact on the completion of work elements; collaborate with the customer on any resulting work slowdown or delay effects, and attempt to rectify the condition with the customer.
  - Examine customer-based work delays (e.g., delays in completing review and approval activities that are specified in the WBS) that could have an impact on the completion of subsequent project work elements; collaborate with the customer on any resulting work slowdown or delay effects and attempt to rectify the condition with the customer.
- Work Performance Control
  - Identify any "quality-of-work" issues for individual team members; examine their personal approach to work, and provide any technical or business guidance needed to help them achieve work performance standards; consider the need for applying team member "reward and recognition" options where motivation is a factor.
  - Identify any technical skill and competency issues for individual team members; examine their education and training accomplishments along with professional experience, and provide any technical or business training needed to help them achieve technical competency standards; if training is not deemed reliable to enable the member to perform the required work, member replacement may be warranted (*Note:* this is not necessarily a team member problem; the member may have been assigned above his or her qualification and experience level).
  - Identify any quality-of-work issues for the project team as a whole; examine team members' approach to teamwork and provide any guidance or team-building activities needed to help them achieve team performance standards.
  - Identify any work specialization issues, and assign only resources with advanced skills and competencies to fulfill those work requirements.
  - Review supplier and subcontractor work quality and performance for possible deviations from contract-specified performance; correct variations as needed.
  - Identify work elements where individuals are overtasked or undertasked; consider areas where resource leveling actions can be taken to correct such conditions.

Document any resource utilization control actions taken. Examine areas where proactive controls can be used to prevent problems. Revisit these control actions and their results when project lessons learned are being identified during project closeout in the Post Phase.

7.3 PROJECT CHANGE CONTROL

Project Change Control is a practice used to manage modification of planned or contractually obligated project activities or specifications. Any adjustment in the time, cost, or technical requirements of a project is deemed to be a modification that requires project change control. Change also results when an associated customer contract is altered, expanded, or terminated prematurely. Also, any change to the project scope almost always necessitates a controlled adjustment to project cost, schedule, or resource utilization estimates and associated plans.

Project changes can occur inadvertently, and sometimes they can go unnoticed for a period of time. When discovered, such changes need to be recaptured and managed according to the project change control process, although in a reactive manner. Most changes should be deliberated, and purposeful adjustments should be made to the project that are managed through the established project change control process. The project manager as well as the project team must be alert to inadvertent changes and must provide due consideration to planned changes. They should expect that most projects will encounter change and therefore will need project change control.

Concept of This Practice

The purpose of this practice is to provide the project manager, project team, and other relevant stakeholders with an approach for conducting and managing project change control. Such a process would also be used to handle proposed changes as well as to recapture control for any changes that have occurred inadvertently.

Project Change Control is normally accomplished during the Perform Phase. However, it can be applied at any time in the project when a baseline document or contract is modified. The preparation of the *Change Control Plan* is usually accomplished in association with *Primary Project Management Plans* Development (Plan Phase).

The four primary activities associated with *Project Change Control* are

- Prepare the Change Control Plan.
- Manage Project Change Requests.
- Conduct Project Change Evaluations.
- Implement Approved Project Changes.

The project manager has ultimate responsibility for ensuring that project changes are properly managed and that they do not adversely impact project progress or the project's outcome.

Prepare the Change Control Plan

The change control plan provides team-based guidance for the change control process that will be used on the project, including specifying the implementation of the other activities cited in this practice. To a large extent, the activity descriptions for project change control presented in the subsequent sections offer fundamental content for the change control plan.

The primary purpose of the change control plan is to ensure that no inadvertent or otherwise unauthorized changes are made to the project scope (which inherently influences some change in planned cost, schedule, or resource utilization), and that any changes that are wanted or needed will undergo a somewhat formal examination and approval process—including appropriate levels of internal and customer collaboration—before any changes are implemented.

In addition to specifying the change control process, the change control plan can also include the following features:

- *Change control responsibilities*—Specification of each team member's responsibility to manage project scope, including guidance for project team members to use reasonable judgment before adjusting work that could be considered "out of scope," and related guidance for managing customer requests or directions for work adjustments that could present scope issues or otherwise be contrary to the established work assignment.
- *Change control authority*—Specification of who is authorized to approve changes in project scope—usually the project manager, but sometimes the project executive (sponsor) or other senior manager (or control board) retains this responsibility.
- *Control plan management*—Designation of a change control manager (for assignment on larger projects) who will maintain the change control log, manage incoming change requests, monitor change evaluations, and oversee approved change implementations; this may include authorization to collaborate on changes with the customer, in addition to negotiation of change requests with the customer.

Manage Project Change Requests

Throughout the project, requests for adjustments to the baseline scope of project work will likely be introduced by project stakeholders. To that end, it is essential that the project manager, the change control manager (if assigned) and, for that matter, most if not all project team members have knowledge of the scope baseline in order to identify whether a change request is required. Therefore, as resources are introduced into the project, individually or as a team, their orientation should include awareness of the change control process and the need to stay within the established project scope baseline. They also should understand the need to "do necessary research" to determine if a work effort to be performed, technical documents and specifications to be referenced, or practices to be used are consistent with the established project baseline elements and do not effect any change in project scope.

A change request is a formal, written statement asking to make a modification to the terms of the contract, to the description (specification) of the product or service to be provided, or to the scope of the project. Unless modified by local policy, a change request can usually be accepted from any stakeholder associated with the project, including the customer, the project manager, and any project team member. This broad group represents those having a vested interest in the project and presumably having a vested interest in a manageable approach to change control for those changes that will inevitably occur.

Reasons for Preparing a Project Change Request

Nearly every project undertaken will encounter a need or reason for change. This is probably because there are such a variety of circumstances or reasons for preparing a project change request, as indicated by the following examples:

- A new or modified government or industry regulation is implemented and is applicable to the project work being accomplished.
- The customer identifies an error or omission in the approved project scope or in the technical specifications of the product or service.
- The project manager or project team identifies an error or omission in the approved project scope or in the technical specifications of the product or service.
- An idea emerges for a different, more efficient or value-added approach to the project work effort or deliverable construct, perhaps associated with
  - An individual's previous technical or professional work experience
  - An advantage provided by the use of newer technology that was not available when the scope of the project was originally established
  - The availability of an added resource with new applicable skill and competency
- A risk event or other condition that adversely impacts the project occurs, and project rescoping or replanning becomes a necessity.
- An inadvertent change to a key aspect of the project was implemented and now needs to be examined for continuance or removal.

The organization, PMO, or project manager may wish to specify criteria or conditions for preparing project change requests as an addendum to this process.

Submitting the Project Change Request

All changes should be submitted on a standard change request form as provided in this methodology. This form becomes a record of the requested change that can be tracked and managed, and it can be used through subsequent change evaluation and change implementation processes.

There are fundamentally three elements of information used in the initial preparation of the change request form. The first element identifies the requester—knowing the individual requesting the change will provide some insight into the nature of the change. The second element is that of identifying the current condition, standard, or baseline related to what is requested to be changed—a logical starting place that also includes an implicit inquiry that asks, "Is it broke?" The third element is a description or specification of the new condition, standard, or baseline that would exist if the requested change were to be approved and implemented.

On smaller projects, change request forms can be submitted directly to the project manager. For larger, more complex projects (or at least projects with a larger number of team members), an individual could be appointed to serve as the project change control manager and as the point of contact for project change request submittals.

The submittal process for change requests should include actions similar to the following:

- Conveyance of the project change request form
- Acknowledgment of project change request form receipt (if not done in person)
- Entry of the new project change request form submittal into a change control log
- Prompt transfer of the project change request form to the individual or group that will conduct the change request evaluation
- Routine tracking of project change requests forwarded for evaluation, and follow-up with evaluators regarding when the evaluation will be completed
- Collaboration with the customer as dictated by the nature of the change requested and as per the project manager's guidance or direct involvement in contacting the customer
- Recurring communication and coordination of the change control log entries and status of change request evaluations under way with the project manager (if not already directly involved in the process)
- Receipt of completed change request evaluations, entry of evaluation recommendations in the change control log, coordination of recommendations with the project manager (or designated approval manager), and reply to the originator of the change request

Conduct Project Change Evaluations

The project manager needs to be involved in the change control process and could play an early and immediate role in change request evaluations and decisions. For example, if a requested change is distinctly minor and can be seen to have minimal or no impact on project cost, schedule, and resource utilization elements, the project manager could personally approve or reject the change request after brief consideration. Otherwise, closer examination is needed, as is provided by a more formal project change request evaluation process.

This evaluation process is sometimes considered to be internal to the performing organization, whereby an internal "understanding and approval" of the change request is sought before presenting it for consideration to a broader audience, including the customer. As suggested earlier, some change requests may not warrant customer involvement at early stages, but that is a determination made by the performing organization.

The following activities are prescribed as part of the project change request evaluation process:

- *Identify and assign an evaluator/evaluation team.* When a project change request is received by the project manager (or change control manager), the request is assigned to a qualified individual or team for evaluation. The project manager should be involved in identifying qualified individuals and teams for this purpose. Preidentification of evaluators enables a quick referral upon receipt of a project change request. Note that on smaller projects the project manager will likely be the sole evaluator, and a formal evaluation assignment is not needed under that circumstance.
- *Determine the need for customer involvement.* All project changes will ultimately be coordinated or otherwise negotiated with the customer, and the organization needs to establish whether such coordination begins at the time when the project change request is submitted for evaluation or after it has been "internally approved" for implementation. In some cases, the customer will be the originator of the change request and will likely already be aware of change impacts on the project. However, the customer should be an evaluation participant for all change request evaluations that have potential impacts on the project cost, schedule, or resource utilization, as well as on project scope, project technical specifications, or project contract. A general rule of thumb might be—if the change request evaluation requires a team effort, then the customer should probably be included on that evaluation team.
- *Conduct the change request evaluation.* The assigned evaluator or team will apply relevant skill and experience in conducting an evaluation of the project change request. This evaluation should include consideration of
  - The originator's need and intent in submitting the project change request
  - The value of the change as compared to the cost of implementation
  - The impact of the change on project cost, schedule, and resource utilization, as well as impact on project scope, project technical specifications, and project contract
  - Any effect on the WBS and other project planning documents
  - Alternative solutions to that indicated on the project change request

  The organization, PMO, or project manager may wish to complement this list with other focus points. Also, the evaluators may wish to contact the originator, the customer, or other project team members to obtain additional information for their evaluation.

  The evaluators should be purposeful and prompt in their examination and deliberation and not take undue time to complete the evaluation. This presents a somewhat profound consideration: is the time used for this evaluation included or otherwise accounted for in the project plan? The simple answer is that such resource time used is normally associated with either project management activities or administrative support activities that are presumably already incorporated into the work plan. The result of this evaluation should be a recommendation to accept or reject the project change request.
- *Provide recommendation to the project manager.* The project manager is given relevant evaluation materials and findings along with the recommendations for approval or rejection of the project change request. It is the project manager's responsibility to make the final approval or rejection decision on behalf of the performing organization. This step may be moot if the project manager personally evaluates the project change request. It should be noted that customer approval of accepted changes may still be required, as addressed in a subsequent step.
- *Obtain customer approval.* The project manager (or change control manager) provides the customer with relevant evaluation materials and the "internally approved" change request for further review and approval. In some cases, the customer may have submitted the change request or even been a participant in the evaluation, whereby the customer has tacitly approved the recommendation. Otherwise, the customer should be requested to conduct a prompt review and approval of the project change request.

- *Conduct necessary renegotiation.* This step may be performed concurrently with the preceding customer approval step. The approved change is thoroughly scrutinized by the project manager (or change control manager with relevant project team support) and the customer. Together they will identify what changes will require updates or modifications to contract or project documentation. This examination should identify any areas of the contract dealing with cost, schedule, and resource utilization that require adjustments or modifications. This also warrants an examination of any vendor or contractor plans and contracts. As needed, renegotiation of those contract elements and associated project deliverables should be conducted.
- *Return evaluation results.* The project manager or project change control manager will notify the originator of the change request (if that person has not already been involved in the evaluation process) about the outcome of the evaluated change request.

Implement Approved Project Changes

The project manager must ensure that all changes are properly implemented and that changes do not exceed their designated and intended scope. Each change should be described in the context of changes to the current contract document or to project documents. This provides a reasonable audit trail that tracks both the original contract and the changes.

For changes that do not require contract modification, a change order can be prepared to initiate implementation of approved changes in project plans and other documentation.

The following activities are prescribed as parts of the project change implementation process:

- *Execute any required contract or agreement modification.* As per results from the change request evaluation, initiate all of the specific changes by making appropriate changes or modifications to the customer contract.
- *Execute any required technical document changes.* As per results from the change request evaluation, initiate all of the specific technical changes by making appropriate changes or modifications to relevant project plans and other documentation.
- *Modify project baselines to reflect new work.* The WBS must be updated to add or modify any affected tasks or activities. The cost, schedule, and resource utilization estimate baselines must be updated to reflect the addition or deletion of tasks. The project work plan and supporting project plans must also be revised as needed.
- *Notify the project team and all relevant stakeholders.* All project team members and all other affected stakeholders should be notified of the change being implemented. Provide revised project documents for use and implementation by project team members and other stakeholders. Also, notify the customer when change implementation activities begin and when the process is completed.

Upon start and completion of the change implementation effort, enter appropriate remarks to identify implementation status in the project change control log.

Chapter 8

Project Quality and Acceptance Management

Project Quality and Acceptance Management is a process for ensuring that customer needs and expectations are achieved, as described in relevant contract and technical specifications documents. Quality is achieved by conformance to requirements, and quality and acceptance management is accomplished by (1) managing activities needed to achieve conformance to requirements, and (2) demonstrating to the customer that such conformance to requirements has been achieved.

There are three practices associated with Project Quality and Acceptance Management:

- Project Quality Planning
- Project Quality Management
- Project Customer Acceptance

To a large extent, quality management is a function of the industry and the product or service delivered. Therefore, the quality and acceptance management practices contained in this methodology could be influenced and should be adapted according to the prominent quality practices and standards already established within the organization.

8.1 PROJECT QUALITY PLANNING

Project Quality Planning is the practice used to identify quality management actions that will be applied to ensure conformance to requirements. It includes providing the project manager and project team members with fundamental quality management concepts that are used as a basis for conducting the project quality management practice described in the next section.

Concept of This Practice

The purpose of this practice is to provide a means for the project manager and project team to examine quality issues and plan the quality management approach in advance of the technical work that will be performed to achieve customer deliverables.

Project Quality Planning is normally accomplished in the Plan Phase. However, subsequent implementation and monitoring of the quality management plan is accomplished in the Perform Phase and closed in the Post Phase.

There are four elements considered as a part of project quality planning:

- Cost of Quality
- Quality Standards
- Quality Responsibilities
- Quality Management Plan

These elements are inherently included in the quality management plan.

Cost of Quality

It is better for quality to be "planned in" than for it to be "inspected in" the project effort. This means the project manager should be proactive in planning the approach to project quality management rather than reactive. The benefits of a planned quality program are realized when quality is considered as an integral part of the project management effort rather than as a separate effort that is positioned as an add-on function or performed by "someone else" later in the project.

In either case, there is a cost to be incurred in implementing a quality management program. As highlighted by the items in the following list, it can be seen that the cost to plan for (ensure) conformance provides a greater return on investment than does the cost of nonconformance.

The following are the types of costs that can be incurred to ensure quality on a project:

- Costs usually required to effectively plan and manage conformance with requirements
  - Planning for quality management
  - Training in quality management practices and procedures
  - Process control oversight or management
  - Product design validation
  - Test and acceptance
  - Quality audits and inspections
  - Maintenance and calibration
  - Field testing
  - Project quality manager role fulfillment, as required for major projects
- Costs often resulting from nonconformance with requirements
  - Scrapped materials and scrap disposal
  - Rework and repair efforts
  - Need for additional raw materials
  - Warranty repairs and service
  - Customer complaint handling
  - Legal liability judgments
  - Need for recalling products and deliverables
  - Field service extensions
  - Expediting subsequent deliveries
- Costs associated with *gold plating*, which represents giving the customer more than what the project's technical specifications require. This incurs the expenditure of additional time and money to achieve a higher technical specification, but with no particular value to be gained from that expenditure.

Most of the costs of quality are the direct responsibility of management—the project manager, the quality manager, and the project executive or sponsor. Management must inform the project team and other project stakeholders of the organization's quality philosophy. Management must also participate in conducting quality assurance, overseeing quality control, and implementing quality control systems to maximize deliverable quality while minimizing the occurrence of defects.

The brunt of the cost of quality is directly associated with management actions and efforts, and therefore requires certain levels of upfront funding for conducting quality assurance programs.

Quality Standards

Quality standards provide a basis for determining achievement and acceptability of project work and project deliverables. That is to say, quality standards can be applied to processes, or they can be applied to characteristics and features of the delivered product or service. The quality standards used can originate from within an industry, a governing body, an organization, or an individual. In all cases, any standards applied in the project management (and business) environments need to be documented for use across all projects in the performing organization. Such documentation then makes a given standard available across the organization and to all of its locations: locally, regionally, or around the world. Also, it provides a reference to external parties, who may also be required to use such standards when specified by a relevant contract or project management plan.

The project manager is responsible for identifying all quality standards that are applicable to the project at hand and specifying them in the quality management plan. There are a multitude of standards that could be considered for project use. The following are some of the common International Standards Organization (ISO) standards used in project management:

- *ISO 9000 Series of Standards*—Used to ensure that organizations are doing what they say they are doing, and to help organizations determine if their standards will satisfy requirements
- *ISO 10002 Standard*—Quality Management: Customer Satisfaction, Guidelines for Complaints Handling in Organizations
- *ISO 10005 Standard*—Quality Management Systems: Guidelines for Quality Plans
- *ISO 10006 Standard*—Quality Management Systems: Guidelines for Quality Management in Projects
- *ISO 10007 Standard*—Quality Management Systems: Guidelines for Quality Management in Complex Projects
- *ISO/TR 10013 Standard*—Guidelines for Quality Management System Documentation
- *ISO/IEC 90003*—Software Engineering: Guidelines for the Application of ISO 9001 to Computer Software

In addition to ISO standards, there are other quality standards and processes that can be applied in the project management environment. A representative sample includes the following:

- *Baldrige Award*—Provides criteria that serve as standards, with criteria accomplishment leading to the fulfillment of requirements for the Baldrige Award

- *Six Sigma Process*—Provides standards for business performance by meeting precise customer requirements and eliminating defects from existing processes
- *Lean Enterprise*—Provides standards for improving operational metrics
- *TL 9000*—Provides guidance for meeting quality management challenges faced in the telecommunications industry
- *QS 9000*—Provides guidance for meeting quality management challenges faced in the automotive industry

The aforementioned lists are by no means complete, and project managers and PMOs, along with their organizations, will have to identify those standards that are applicable to their businesses and associated with their product/service delivery models. The project manager should identify any applicable standards in the quality management plan.

Quality Responsibilities

Project quality management inherently includes project manager and project team member participation, but it also requires input and involvement from other key organizational and functional managers and stakeholders in the performing organization and from the customer. The following are the common quality management roles and responsibilities of various project stakeholders, which should be considered for inclusion in the quality management plan:

- *Senior Managers*—Executives in the organization are responsible for setting and implementing the strategic direction of the enterprise. To that end, they can participate in quality management in the following ways:
  - Develop the organization's policies for quality and quality management.
  - Develop the organization's policies for project management processes.
  - Establish metrics (goals) associated with implementing quality policies.
  - Conduct project performance and management reviews with an eye on quality.
- *The PMO and Mid-Level Managers*—Business unit managers have responsibility for implementing business strategies and associated policies, and can participate in quality management in the following ways:
  - Develop and implement quality management procedures.
  - Communicate quality management policies and procedures.
  - Implement and monitor performance of the quality management system.
  - Identify skills and competencies needed to achieve the quality objectives.
  - Provide workforce training for quality management and quality process implementation.
- *Project Managers*—Project managers are directly responsible for conducting project quality assurance activities and for ensuring the performance of quality control and testing and acceptance for each project. This responsibility includes achieving customer acceptance for all project deliverables. Project managers should then participate in quality management in the following ways:
  - Form and develop an empowered project team that "owns" project quality.
  - Ensure that all customer requirements are incorporated into the project plan.
  - Develop and implement a viable quality management plan.
  - Apply relevant project management practices to ensure that a proper *Project Work Plan* is constructed, with measurements and tracking of cost, schedule, and resources.
  - Implement a knowledge management system with reporting that enables frequent and accurate monitoring of project status and progress.
  - Perform project quality assurance activities, as required by the project.
  - Conduct periodic project quality management reviews and audits.
  - Monitor customer reactions to ensure that contract requirements and project expectations are consistent with the established project scope.
- *Project Team Members*—Project team members are responsible for performing project work using quality standards. They should participate in quality management in the following ways:
  - Contribute to the development of the project work breakdown structure (WBS), *Project Work Plan*, and other project planning activities.
  - Conduct project work according to the approved *Project Work Plan*, with attention to cost, schedule, and resource utilization guidance.
  - Perform project quality control activities, as required by the nature of project work.
  - Report work status and progress in an accurate and timely manner.
  - Report quality process achievements, issues, and problems as prescribed.
  - Serve as project quality manager, when assigned that responsibility on a given project.
- *Business Unit Members*—Business unit members in some organizations are inherently recognized as project team members, while in others they are viewed as adjunct project participants, entering and leaving the project at predefined points. They should participate in

quality management, according to their expertise, in the following ways:
  - Contribute business and technical specialization expertise to the development of the *Project Work Plan* and other project planning activities (e.g., estimating, risk assessment, contract administration, quality assurance and control activities, etc.).
  - Advise the project manager in business and technical specialization areas.
  - Perform project work associated with business or technical specialties, as necessary.
  - Conduct internal or arrange external project management and technical training in a timely manner, including project quality management policy and practice training.
  - Lead and manage project quality assurance and control activities, as designated by the organization, serving as the project's quality manager.
  - Conduct project quality management reviews and audits, as scheduled.
- *Customer Representatives*—Customer representatives may have varying levels of active participation, but they can participate in quality management in the following ways:
  - Conduct specified and requested project performance reviews in a timely manner.
  - Provide responses to issue and problem inquiries in a timely manner.
  - Attend project meetings and technical site planning visits, as required.
  - Facilitate interim and final project testing and acceptance activities, as required.
  - Partner with the project manager on arranging unique project needs such as special equipment, test participants, or test conditions.
  - Provide project deliverables' feedback and acceptance in a timely manner.

This list represents quality management as an activity that requires the attention and possible participation of a variety of project stakeholders. The project manager should identify required stakeholder participation, and specify that participation in the quality management plan for the project. In some organizations, this specification of roles and responsibilities is provided by a "template" that is used across most projects.

Quality Management Plan

The quality management plan is used to guide the implementation of quality management for each project. The following are the prescribed steps and the content for preparation of the quality management plan:

- *Determine quality management plan responsibilities and use.* The project manager or designated quality management plan manager, with the support of the quality department, develops the quality management plan using the scope statement, employing project and product requirements as guidance. The plan must be developed at the beginning of the project to ensure alignment with the work plan documents. The quality management plan can be managed by the quality department representative who will participate, as appropriate, in project status meetings throughout the course of the project. The project manager and the quality management plan manager should ensure that the plan remains aligned with customer and internal quality requirements, and that other supporting plans reflect such requirements.
- *Identify standards and regulations.* The project manager is responsible for leading project team members and appropriate project stakeholders in identifying and reviewing any ISO standards or regulations that may apply to the project.
- *Review the organization's quality management policy.* The quality management policy establishes the approach to quality management within the organization, as prescribed by senior management. If the organization does not yet have a formal quality management policy, the project team can develop an interim policy for the project. The policy should specify the use of quality management and control practices, and be distributed or otherwise made available for review by all stakeholders participating in quality management.
- *Identify quality management tools and techniques.* Identify the tools and techniques to be used in quality assurance and control:
  - Define the tools and techniques that will be used as part of project quality management for team-building activities, brainstorming, and developing cause-and-effect diagrams.
  - Define the tools and techniques that will be used with the customer and stakeholders (process control charts, types and number of reviews or audits, etc.).
  - Document the control measures. If necessary, revisit the WBS, adding tasks and identifying additional resources to implement and manage the quality processes.
- *Specify quality management procedures.* The quality management plan typically includes procedures for product delivery and customer acceptance. Also, include procedures for conducting quality assurance.
- *Specify quality audits and procedures.* Identify any audits associated with quality management that are scheduled or may be performed during the project. Specify

the procedures to be used for each type of quality management audit.

- *Specify quality control requirements and procedures.* The quality management plan typically includes guidance for performing quality control, including:
  - Project-specific information on quality requirements and quality objectives
  - Identification of customer requirements and methods for ensuring that quality goals are being achieved
  - Requirements for product's particular purpose and functional design
  - Information on what to control and when, what thresholds criteria to use for corrective action, and what measurement methods to use
- *Specify procedures for conducting and logging quality testing.* Specify the interim and final testing requirements for project deliverables and associated procedures for conducting required quality testing. Prepare and maintain a Quality Testing and Traceability Log.

8.2 PROJECT QUALITY MANAGEMENT

Project Quality Management is a project management practice that will guide the project manager and project team members to perform critical oversight activities necessary to avoid rework, concentrate on improvements, and reduce costs by enhancing or avoiding schedule delays.

Concept of This Practice

The purpose of this practice is to provide a means for the project manager and project team to oversee and manage quality associated with deliverable design and development. It ensures that requirements are properly translated into results that will be accepted by the customer. It illustrates that quality is a multitiered management effort: project staff members perform quality control, project managers perform quality assurance, and senior management performs (or influences the performance of) quality audits.

Project Quality Management transcends the phases of project management, from initial requirements gathering and planning to testing, acceptance, and closeout. The prominent project quality management effort is achieved in the Perform Phase.

There are three activities associated with *Project Quality Management*:

- Manage Quality Assurance
- Manage Quality Control
- Manage Quality Test and Acceptance

Each of these activities is discussed in the following subsections.

Manage Quality Assurance

Quality assurance represents management's oversight of project quality, and particularly quality concepts applied during the project's Perform Phase. Quality assurance is a prominent responsibility of the project manager, and any designated quality management plan manager. Quality management ensures that planned project activities conform to requirements and demonstrate confidence that the project will achieve specified quality standards and objectives. Quality assurance activities should be identified in the quality management plan. Quality assurance management is highlighted by the following activities:

- Identify project management documents (plans, etc.) to be used in conjunction with quality assurance activities. These items will have to be closely monitored and managed as a part of the quality assurance process, including:
  - *Customer Quality Management Plan*—Identify the quality assurance process, along with project assurance standards, tools, and techniques to be applied. This is the primary project management document used in the quality assurance effort.
  - *Project Work Plan*—Review and modify the project work plan to ensure that processes supporting quality management are properly incorporated.
  - *Requirements and Functional Design Documents*—Identify the requirements and specifications for each project deliverable so as to track their incorporation in project design and development efforts, and to assess the outcome of their use in constructing the project deliverables. Quality requirements and specifications may sometimes be included or prepared in separate project supporting plans.
  - *Project Business and Contract Documents*—The customer contract specifies the scope of work to be performed and thereby serves as a guide to applying quality assurance activities, particularly those used to retain the accepted project scope.
  - *Other Project Documents*—Identify any other documents having relevance to the quality assurance management function, and use them in the course of performing quality management and oversight.
- Schedule and use quality assurance tools and techniques, including the following analytical methods:
  - *Cost–benefit analysis*—This is used to identify the cost of quality and its projected benefits.
  - *Benchmarking*—This is used to compare similar activities or projects to the current project. This activity should generate ideas for deliverable improvement and new or alternate standards against which to measure deliverable construction.

- *Cause-and-effect diagrams and process flowcharts*—These are used to identify how pieces and parts of the total project deliverable (system) relate to one another, and provide general indicators of how they interact or otherwise work together.
- *Design of experiments*—This is used to provide an analytical approach to compile variables and identify those having major influence on deliverable construction.
- *Quality audits and reviews*—This is used to evaluate quality achievements, and to confirm that project deliverables are on track or to identify and make any necessary interim deliverable adjustments.

- Monitor and manage all project areas that could provide for additional quality and quality management improvement. This includes identifying and sharing all quality management practices from across the organization that have demonstrated success toward customer acceptance.
- Identify and use "expert" works, deliberation, and facilitation (authors and third-party consultants) to help define and design quality management methods that best fit within the performing organization; join and participate in quality-management-based professional organizations; and attend quality management programs offered by project management-based organizations.

Manage Quality Control

Quality control management involves measuring project quality expectations against project quality results to date. Every project team member has quality control responsibility. In turn, the project manager must ensure that team members have sufficient knowledge and skill to properly apply quality control methods to evaluate project results (deliverables). In some organizations, this activity is assigned to a dedicated quality control team that contributes quality control expertise across all projects. Nevertheless, each project manager still retains responsibility for making adjustments based on quality control indicators and results.

A few activities commonly associated with quality control management are presented in the following two areas: (1) applying quality control methods, and (2) managing quality control results.

Apply Quality Control Methods

The purpose of quality control is to identify quality weaknesses and indicators of poor quality (nonconformance) in project deliverables or processes. The following methods are a few prominent examples of such methods:

- *Quality Control Inspection*—This method is used to measure, examine, and test deliverables for conformance to requirements. Such inspections are planned for key points in deliverable construction. Common types of quality control inspections include process reviews, product reviews, audits, and technical walkthroughs.
- *Quality Control Charts*—This method is used to display quality results over time, when such results are foreseeable, as is often seen in association with recurring project deliverable construction. Quality control charts are used to track costs; monitor schedule variances; or identify common, special, or assignable causes of variations. Control charts also track planned versus actual results. The chart presents results over time, with the depiction of variation "spikes" that can appear above or below acceptable control limits. The project manager will use an interpretation of these spikes to determine the need and extent of any work or process adjustments to be made.
- *Pareto Diagrams*—This method is used to identify how many quality indicator results were generated by a type or category of identified cause, and is presented in histogram format. The Pareto theory suggests that a large percentage of quality results can be traced to a small number of causes. This provides a quick indication of which action is causing the greatest number of quality problems. The Pareto diagram will assist the project manager in determining areas that are causing the greatest number of quality defects (or nonconformance). For example, the diagram may reveal that 80% of the defects can be corrected by addressing only two of the five causes of poor quality. It would be ideal to address all five causes of poor quality, but time spent on correcting or adjusting processes or tasks to reduce or remove the two major causes will produce significant quality improvements.
- *Statistical Sampling*—This method is used to conduct an inspection on a sample portion of the project deliverables. A representative sample of the product is examined to give an indication of quality for all deliverables or the "total" deliverable. In general, this provides a level of confidence that total deliverable will have the same quality results as that of the sample.
- *Cause-and-Effect Diagrams and Process Flowcharts*—This method is used to identify the cause of defects by diagramming the relationships of processes (causes) to the end results (effects) they produce. A process flowchart is used to depict that relationship. The process depicted can be the flow of work or any other process that is conducted sequentially over time.
  - Trend Analyses—This method is used to apply mathematical techniques and historical data to

forecast future outcomes. Quality control charts can be used to provide data for trend analyses.

Manage Quality Control Actions

Quality control methods will provide indicators for quality management actions. The following actions can be applied, as needed, following a thorough examination of project quality control indicators:

- *Quality Improvements*—Quality control results will provide an indication of need for quality improvement. Improvement areas (e.g., process, materials, skill, etc.) can be identified for the current project and for all projects, and quality improvement solutions can be implemented.
- *Acceptance Decisions*—Quality control results will indicate how well project deliverables have achieved specifications and project quality objective. There may be multiple levels of deliverable acceptance, starting within the performing organization and moving into the arena of customer acceptance. Quality control results will indicate if the deliverable (product or service) is ready for acceptance.
- *Rework Decisions*—In contrast to the previously mentioned acceptance decisions, quality control results may also indicate the need for deliverable rework, that is, the additional work needed to enable a defective or nonconforming product (or service) to become compliant with quality specifications.
- *Process Adjustments*—Quality control results may indicate a process that is hindering the achievement of project quality objectives. The questionable process is examined and activity steps are adjusted to make the process more aligned with the project or quality of deliverable needs.
- *Quality Examination Point-in-Time Adjustments*—Quality control results may indicate a missed or late quality examination point and prompt consideration of specifying new or additional quality examination points-in-time for quality control purposes.
- *Quality Examination Level-of-Detail Adjustments*—Quality control results may indicate a missed specification due to a limited quality examination and prompt consideration of specifying an increased quality examination level-of-detail for quality control purposes.
- *Quality Control Personnel Skill and Training*—Quality control results may indicate one or more individuals with possible limited or inappropriate quality control skills or deliverable construction skills. In either case, the individual needs to be withdrawn from such activities until competencies are achieved.

Quality control is the responsibility of all project team members. However, the project manager is ultimately responsible for achieving project quality objectives and should make sure that project team members know required technical and quality control processes and support the project's quality control effort.

Manage Quality Test and Acceptance

Quality test and acceptance is usually performed internally by the project team (or dedicated quality control team) for interim and final deliverables or components. The customer, with support provided by the project team, may perform additional testing to achieve customer acceptance. See the next practice for particulars on *Project Customer Acceptance.*

Test procedures and acceptance criteria are developed by the customer with significant customer input and involvement. Logistics must be planned, and the test procedure must be drafted, reviewed, and approved by the appropriate parties.

The following activities are prescribed relative to quality test and acceptance management:

- *Identify quality test and acceptance criteria.* These can be developed independently for customer approval, derived from customer deliverable requirements, or conveyed separately by the customer.
- *Prepare a test and acceptance plan.* The project manager leads the preparation of plans and coordinates all activities surrounding test and acceptance activities. The test and acceptance plan should be sufficiently detailed to enable independent tests to be conducted by a qualified technical team (or qualified members of the project team). The test and acceptance plan may be incorporated as a component of the broader-in-scope quality management plan. The test and acceptance plan generally includes the following information:
  - Identification of number and types of tests to be performed
  - Identification of the test locations and dates
  - Description of the products or deliverable components to be tested
  - Specification of the testing procedures for each type of test
  - Identification of persons responsible for conducting and participating in each type of test
  - Description of the test design and anticipated test outcomes, per established quality testing criteria
  - Requirements for test and test outcome documentation, and associated distribution
  - Testing—Describes how the product meets each requirement, details how the tests are designed,

and identifies who will be conducting the tests and under what conditions
  - Acceptance—Specifies the methods for documenting customer acceptance, explains the measurable objectives developed for the tests, and describes the acceptance process and conditions for acceptance
- *Conduct quality testing.* Apply the guidance contained in the test and acceptance plan to perform the specified quality tests. Include ample time to arrange for customer and relevant stakeholder participation in testing, as required or necessary, for each test conducted.
- *Obtain customer acceptance of test results.* This activity is focused on the customer's acceptance for each interim and final test. It represents the customer's acceptance of particular test results specifically, and test progress and results to date in general. Quality testing outcomes should produce customer sign-offs for each test. Conversely, they also could prompt rework that requires retesting actions. To that end, all customer participation and acceptance or nonacceptance actions should be documented for each test and acceptance activity conducted. The broader scope of customer acceptance actions is presented in the next practice.

8.3 PROJECT CUSTOMER ACCEPTANCE

Project Customer Acceptance is the project management practice that is used to obtain and document customer acceptance of project deliverables, acknowledgment of the achievement of project objectives (progress), and, ultimately, agreement on the completion of all project requirements.

Concept of This Practice

The primary purpose of this practice is to provide a means for the project manager and customer to jointly acknowledge and document customer receipt and acceptance of project deliverables. This is discussed in the test and acceptance activities described in the previous practice, where interim and final deliverables are tested and presented to the customer for acceptance.

However, in a broader sense, this practice can also be an ongoing activity that is performed throughout the project, at various junctures, to examine and document such things as follows:

- Customer review and acceptance of project progress (per reports and meetings)
- Customer review and acceptance of product or service design (per design documents)
- Customer review and acceptance of testing approach and procedures (per plans)
- Customer review and acceptance of testing results (per test participation or test results)
- Customer review and acceptance of project goal achievements (per closeout activities)
- Customer acknowledgment of project closeout (per closeout activities)

Both primary and expanded project customer acceptance activities are conducted to provide formal monitoring and acknowledgment of the fulfillment of contractual obligations. They will also provide direct and indirect indications of the customer's attitude, expectations, and satisfaction with regard to project progress and outcomes.

Project Customer Acceptance is the prominent project quality management effort that is achieved in the Perform Phase, but it may also extend to the Post Phase. The primary and expanded considerations of *Project Customer Acceptance* are discussed in the following two sections.

Primary Customer Acceptance Activities

Managing customer acceptance of project deliverables is a fundamental, but essential, activity of project management that warrants sufficient attention by the project manager or designated technical leader. In the absence of adequate attention, the fundamental aspects of this activity can sometimes be transformed into a more complex and unwieldy effort.

Project customer acceptance is the process of conveying the project deliverables to the customer, and then having the customer acknowledge receipt of each delivered product or service as one that achieves specifications and requirements and fulfills contractual obligations. A further breakdown of this activity highlights how this process should be documented and identifies some critical attention points for the project manager and project team.

For more complex or piecemeal project deliverables, the process usually begins as follows:

- Conduct and document deliverable component testing.
- Arrange and document customer participation/involvement in component testing.
- Obtain and document (interim) component acceptance by customer.

Repeat these steps for each deliverable component, then

- Conduct and document deliverable unit/final testing.
- Arrange and document customer participation/involvement in unit/final testing.
- Obtain and document (interim) unit acceptance by customer.

Repeat these steps for each deliverable unit, then

- Conduct and document deliverable integration testing.
- Arrange and document customer participation/involvement in integration testing.
- Obtain and document (interim) integration acceptance by customer.

Repeat these steps for each deliverable integration activity. Then, the following steps provide for the finalization of more complex or piecemeal project deliverables and serve as the basic steps needed for simpler product and service deliverables:

- Conduct and document deliverable transfer/handover to customer.
- Monitor and document customer transfer/handover final review.
- Obtain and document customer deliverable final acceptance.

In addition to these essential test and acceptance activities, expanded activities can be used to monitor early project customer acceptance activities, as presented in the next section.

Expanded Customer Acceptance Activities

Per their brief mention earlier, this section further describes some of the expanded customer acceptance activities that can be used in the course of project execution.

- *Customer Review and Acceptance of Project Progress*—Monitor customer participation in routine and critical project meetings. Examine frequency and level of participation to ascertain if the desired (or required) level of customer involvement in the project has been achieved. Observe and document customer attitudes across progressive meetings. Note meeting discussions and presentations, and record and act to resolve issues and problems raised by the customer. Identify customer reactions to project report frequency and content. Monitor customer responses to the identification of project issues and problems. As needed, assist the customer in issue/problem resolution, and help clarify and resolve any points of contention. Obtain oral and written indicators of the customer's acceptance of project progress to date.
- *Customer Review and Acceptance of Product/Service Design*—Include the customer in deliverable design activities, particularly in a walkthrough or review of the final design or specifications for the deliverables. Monitor customer-initiated changes to designs, and ensure that any design changes remain within the established project scope. Obtain written customer sign-off for the final design document as representative of customer design acceptance.
- *Customer Review and Acceptance of Testing Approach and Procedures*—Provide an opportunity for the customer to review and approve (accept) how deliverable testing, if performed, will be conducted. Document the customer's review effort (i.e., include this activity in the project work plan or in a project journal). Obtain oral and written indicators of the customer's acceptance of the testing procedures to be used.
- *Customer Review and Acceptance of Testing Results*—Examine options for the presentation and deliberation of deliverable test results with customers. Generally, provide test result reports for preliminary review, followed by a meeting with the customer to deliberate results and achieve acceptance. Be prepared to address customer reactions to any of three likely test outcomes:
  - Test passes—Customer acknowledges and "accepts" passing results.
  - Test passes, with issues—Customer acknowledges "passing" results, but takes issue with some aspect of those results or the test itself, and prompts consideration for adjustments to the deliverable, or to current or future testing procedures or test result thresholds. This may also suggest the need for retesting after mutually accepted adjustments have been applied.
  - Test fails—Customer acknowledges and "accepts" failing results and prompts the requirements for reworking and retesting the deliverable.

  Ideally, the "pass" outcome will be prevalent on most projects. To that end, the objective is to obtain and document customer acceptance of test results. This represents a more detailed description of the primary customer acceptance activity.
- *Customer Review and Acceptance of Project Goal Achievements*—Provide for customer acknowledgment of satisfaction with project performance. This examines customer acceptance of the overall achievement of project goals, and allows the customer to consider how well they were achieved and how effective were the processes used to achieve project outcomes. While highlighted under the activities of customer acceptance, this is a form of customer evaluation, but one that warrants obtaining and documenting the customer's "acceptance" of the project.
- *Customer Acknowledgment of Project Closeout*—Provide for acknowledgment and "acceptance" of project closeout by the customer. This final area of customer acceptance provides for formal confirmation by the customer that the project has been completed (or otherwise terminated). It generally indicates that all project

objectives (through time of closure) have been achieved. Conversely, an unattained project objective could be the reason for early project termination, and closeout may not necessarily indicate successful achievement of project objectives in that instance. Under conditions of normal project closeout, the customer's written acceptance of project closure is desired.

Chapter 9

Project Contract Management

Contract management is performed to oversee the formal business relationship between a buyer and a seller, in this case the performing organization and the customer. Therefore, in terms of project management, the project manager is ideally situated to be the "contract manager" relative to the established customer business relationship for each project. This does not preclude using a more formal contract management position within the organization. It just means that the project manager should be positioned to oversee or influence contract management activities relative to project interests and objectives.

A related definition indicates a contract to be "an agreement about rights and responsibilities," and this leads to the consideration of contract administration and the management of activities performed to ensure compliance with the terms and conditions of each business relationship and each contract. The project manager usually has responsibility for this function relative to the project at hand.

Before establishing any contract, some form of communication takes place to convey an offer by the performing organization for acceptance by the customer. This could be as simple as a purchase order with appropriate terms and conditions appended. However, a common method for obtaining a customer's business is generally referred to as a *proposal*, a method that requires oversight and management in its own right.

There are three practices associated with Project Contract Management:

- Proposal Management
- Contract Execution
- Contract Administration

It is sometimes said that, while every contract is not a project, every project is a contract. Therefore, there will be a general need for some type of contract on every project as a basis for establishing the commitments and responsibilities between the involved parties.

It is also wise to establish some type of contract document for internal projects that are conducted within the organization. Often such contracts are referred to as internal memoranda of agreement, or simply internal agreements, as can be established between business units of the organization. While internal agreements may not have significant legal implications, they nevertheless have obligations that a professional project management organization should properly manage and fulfill. Therefore, while this practice is focused on contract management normally associated with external customer projects, a version of this practice should be adapted for use on projects delivered to internal customers.

9.1 PROPOSAL MANAGEMENT

Proposal Management is a practice used to develop the technical solution that specifies what work will be done (technical proposal), the management solution that specifies how work performance and quality will be guaranteed or assured (management proposal), and the associated pricing and business offering that is presented to the customer (business proposal). In many cases, one or all of these proposal components will become part of the subsequent contract that is executed to conduct the project. Therefore, proposal intentions and content should be clear and accurate since they often become contractual obligations that require attention and fulfillment.

Concept of This Practice

The purpose of this practice is to provide a means for the project manager and proposal team (project team members selected to assist in proposal development) to prepare and manage the customer proposal. In some organizations, sales or business development managers perform or lead this customer-facing activity. However, it is recommended that a project manager (ideally the one that would be assigned to the project) be a part of that proposal team to ensure proper representation of project management interests. Any existing project manaagement office (PMO) can also lend support to the business development effort to ensure that an adequate and effective business and technical solution will be presented to the customer.

Proposal Management is normally accomplished in the Plan Phase. However, preliminary proposal development work is also done in the Profile Phase, and subsequent monitoring of the proposal (as a part of the contract) is done in the Perform Phase and Post Phase.

These considerations are addressed by the following four progressive activities:

- Opportunity Qualification
- Proposal Preparation
- Proposal Submittal
- Contract Negotiation

Opportunity Qualification

Opportunity qualification applies expertise to evaluate the customer and the work effort for suitability within the performing organization. This activity is already specified in earlier practice areas, largely in the Profile Phase, and particularly with the *Business Case Development* effort. Practice highlights are reviewed here to show relation to early proposal preparation actions.

Opportunity qualification includes the following general activities:

- Identify the customer. Conduct a customer business information review.
- Identify the opportunity. Conduct a customer project information review.
- Develop the project definition and the project business case, in part to determine
  - Is there business interest to do this project?
  - Is there technical capability to do this project?
  - Is there a business reason to do this project?
- Assess business risk and opportunity.

See the *Business Case Development* practice and other Profile Phase practices for more specific descriptions of activities associated with opportunity qualification.

Proposal Preparation

The following are the prescribed components and general content for a proposal that is prepared as a business offer for conducting a customer project.

- *Technical Solution*—This proposal component presents the technical approach that the project manager will use to achieve project objectives and fulfill customer deliverables. It normally includes a work breakdown structure (WBS) and project task schedule, a description of each task, and the project resources that will be assigned to perform each task. It represents the performing organization's response to the customer's Request for Proposal (RFP) or statement of work, and shows how those and other customer requirements and specifications will be fulfilled.
- *Management Solution*—This proposal component is generally needed for any proposal, but it is primarily included on larger project proposals. It represents the organization and structure to be used to manage the project effort, and usually demonstrates the scope of resource control afforded the project manager for each important customer project. It allows the customer to identify the different project management and technical team leaders and to gain confidence and comfort that project management and technical leadership is appropriately aligned to ensure project success. Also, the management solution will demonstrate how project work performance will be managed to ensure achievement of specifications and quality standards. Finally, the management solution may also contain references to previous similar work for customer evaluation and consideration.
- *Business Solution*—This proposal component presents the business pricing offered for the accomplishment of the technical solution. For smaller project efforts, the business solution component may be combined with the technical solution component. This component is often separated to allow the customer to review the technical solution independent of the cost to be incurred. This component contains such elements as the list of contract terms and conditions, assumptions and constraints, costs associated with each project deliverable, and the proposed customer payment schedule. Also, it can refer to the contract type to be issued and address how terms and condition of the contract will be fulfilled. Sometimes, the management solution is incorporated with the business solution.

When appropriate to organizational procedures, a proposal can also be used to introduce internal project work. This allows the project manager and the internal customer to establish a common understanding and agreement of what is to be accomplished by the project effort. Usually, an internal project proposal will be fairly simple and focus only on the technical solution component, unless there is an interdepartmental cost transfer requirement that the internal customer must consider. In turn, an internal proposal can easily become the project agreement or "contract" under which the project is conducted.

The following proposal preparation steps can be considered for use in the organization. The accompanying methodology toolkit provides a basis for compiling prescribed content and constructing these three components of the customer proposal.

The Technical Proposal

- Compile and review project guidance documents.
  - Customer RFP/Request for Quote (RFQ)/Request for Information (RFI) documents
  - Other requirements documents (e.g., site surveys, needs analyses, etc.)
  - Deliverables specifications and standards
- Conduct preproposal technical collaboration meetings.
  - Requirements-gathering workshops
  - Customer technical meetings (e.g., preproposal meeting)
  - Project/proposal team requirements and document review meetings
  - Customer representative interviews
- Review and update the project definition.
- Prepare the technical solution.
  - Identify milestones and deliverables.
  - Specify the technical approach.
  - Develop the WBS and high-level work plan.
  - Incorporate staffing requirements (to validate workload and performance capability).
  - Identify vendor/contractor participants.
  - Examine project risk.
- Conduct technical proposal reviews.
  - Project/proposal team—walkthrough and refinement by proposal content preparers
  - Red team—critical examination by technical experts not involved in preparation
  - Management team—strategic-level examination for approval to submit

The Management Proposal

- Identify project management team (i.e., project manager, technical leads, executive).
- Develop staffing management plan—to demonstrate fulfillment of staffing requirements.
- Prepare the project organization chart—to show the project team structure.
- Incorporate vendor management plan (as necessary).
- Specify scheduled customer contact (e.g., reports and meetings from communication plan).
- Highlight the approach to quality management (from quality management plan).
- Highlight the approach to issue management and problem resolution.
- Introduce summaries of previous similar work for customer evaluation of experience.
- Conduct management proposal reviews.
  - Project/proposal team—walkthrough and refinement by project team leaders
  - Red team—critical examination by business experts not involved in preparation
  - Management team—strategic-level examination for approval to submit

The Business Proposal

- Compile and review business guidance documents.
  - Project business case
  - Customer profile
  - Business requirements (from RFP/RFQ/RFI documents)
- Examine business evaluation factors (contributing to selection and contract award).
  - Technical factors—fulfillment of technical work performance
  - Management factors—fulfillment of management performance
  - Business factors—fulfillment of prescribed terms and conditions
  - Administrative factors—fulfillment of proposal format and delivery requirements
- Prepare the business solution.
  - Solicitation fulfillment strategy
  - Pricing strategy
  - Contracting strategy
- Conduct business proposal reviews.
  - Project review—walkthrough and refinement by the project manager and sponsor
  - Red team—critical examination by business development experts/management
  - Management team—strategic-level examination for approval to submit

Every proposal preparation effort draws upon administrative support actions to prepare initial and final proposal documents for submission to the customer. As a part of project management, it is necessary to account for the time and workload associated with the proposal development and submission effort. Many of the requisite administrative actions that need to be accomplished are listed in association with the next activity.

Proposal Submittal

The following are the prescribed activities to be accomplished in conjunction with the proposal submittal to the customer:

- *Monitoring the Proposal Submittal Schedule*—The project manager or other designated individual (e.g., proposal manager) should review the schedule for critical proposal-related activities and ensure that this information is conveyed to proposal developers and managers.
  - Bidders' conference dates—including sign-up cutoff dates
  - Customer technical meeting dates—including sign-up cutoff dates
  - Proposal draft preparation due dates—internally determined and imposed
  - Proposal draft review dates—internally determined and imposed
  - Proposal final preparation due dates—internally determined and imposed
  - Proposal final review dates—internally determined and imposed
  - Proposal submittal time and date—deadline usually specified by the customer
- *Attending Proposal Presubmission Meetings*—Prior to the proposal being finalized and presented to the customer, there could be opportunities to meet with the customer to clarify requirements and specifications. Attendance at such "formal" events is important to the proposal development process and should be included in the development effort. In some cases, one-on-one meetings with the customer are also allowed and provide the best opportunity for clarification of needs and requirements. In other cases, particularly for sole-source procurements or other noncompetitive proposals, meeting with the customer can be accomplished as a matter of mutual schedule availability.
- *Proposal Preparation*—This is an administrative activity that begins with developing preliminary proposal content used for review and refinement within the organization. It then addresses the preparation of the final proposal document for submission to the customer. The project manager should ensure that qualified individuals are assigned responsibility for this activity and that sufficient time is allotted for preparation of the final proposal document. This effort represents the preparation of a final and combined technical, management, and business proposal document in prescribed content, format, and quantities for presentation to the customer before any specified deadline.
- *Proposal Submittal and Presentation*—The proposal document is delivered to the customer at the prescribed business location no later than the specified deadline. This represents the submittal of the written (printed) proposal document, and sometimes also includes preparation and delivery of the proposal in electronic format. In some circumstances, the customer may also request an accompanying oral presentation of the proposal. However, this is normally done subsequent to actual proposal submittal, and at a mutually agreeable time and location that is arranged with the customer.
- *Proposal Clarification*—The project manager (and sometimes the proposal team) may be called on to answer questions or to clarify points of technical, business, or management expertise being offered during the customer's proposal review period. This could include responding to written inquiries (e.g., e-mails), or even participating in face-to-face postsubmittal meetings with the customer.
- *Proposal Modification*—The project manager could be requested to meet with the customer to address changes to the proposed technical or business approach to accommodate the customer's needs and interests. Also, sometimes proposal modification requests are initiated by the performing organization when subsequent proposal changes are needed and as allowed by the customer's procurement process. Of course, any changes to the proposal by either party warrant an examination of the need for adjustments in the business (pricing) proposal.

In some industries and selected business environments, the proposal management process will be much less elaborate than that outlined here. Rather, the process may simply require the project manager to submit a business price quote and a general description of the work to be performed as a "work order" for consideration by the customer. The signed work order then becomes a basis for contract obligations or the agreement with the customer.

Also, any proposal development efforts for internal customers will not likely be as intense or comprehensive as those performed for external customers. In any case, the organization will have the option to establish a simpler internal proposal process, if one is needed.

Contract Negotiation

Each proposal should always be submitted on its own merit without expectations that customer negotiations will occur to rectify any questionable proposal content. This negotiation step almost always occurs at the request of the customer, but in some industries and business venues, that rarely happens. Therefore, unless the customer's solicitation specifies a negotiation period after proposal submittal, do not expect it to happen.

That said, the need for contract negotiation usually represents customer acceptance of the technical solution, but also usually indicates the customer's desire to achieve an adjusted price or modified work effort from that presented in the original proposal. Contract negotiations can be simple or complex, as is appropriate to the nature of the proposed work effort and the business importance to both the customer and the performing organization.

Some basic steps for conducting contract negotiations from the performing organization's (seller's) perspective are prescribed here.

- *Plan the contract negotiation.* Informal and simple contract negotiations, usually one-on-one discussions with the customer, generally require less preparation, but the authorized latitude to make proposal adjustments must be known by the negotiator. Conversely, more formal and more complex contract negotiations warrant additional preparation, usually by a small team of experienced negotiators, ideally including the project manager and the business development manager. The following are a few points of consideration in planning for contract negotiations, with consideration for the fact that the customer usually has control over the negotiation agenda.
  - Form a qualified team of individuals who have experience in contract negotiations to plan and conduct the negotiations; ensure that capability to discuss technical concepts and considerations are included in the team makeup, usually represented by the PMO, project manager, or technical leader.
  - Review any known points of customer contention, and review customer project and business information. Confirm the strategic business importance of this customer and this project. Examine leeway in proposed cost, schedule, and resource utilization, based on estimates presented in the customer proposal.
  - Prepare the negotiation strategy. Specify and prioritize negotiation objectives, identify fair pricing standards, examine alternatives to be encountered during negotiation (best case, most likely, worst case). Determine negotiation tactics and countertactics to be used.
  - Prepare a negotiation authorization plan that specifies the negotiation bottom-line price and other factors authorized for contract agreement.
- *Conduct the negotiation.* Meet with the customer to identify negotiation points and to deliberate, debate, and discuss negotiable options for the proposed project effort. This usually includes learning about the customer's negotiation objectives and sharing the resolution objectives of the performing organization. It also includes examining the customer's initial offers and presenting any counteroffers. In particular, it requires the determination and discussion of differences as perceived by each party. Ideally, this effort results in a settlement and agreement that enables the contract and associated project effort to be conducted.
- *Document the negotiated agreement.* A memorandum of agreement (MOA) should be prepared and signed by both parties, which will serve to identify the changes and adjustments that will be incorporated into the final contract. The MOA should include
  - Date of the agreement
  - Customer RFP/Statement of Work (SOW) reference and contract title
  - Identification of the negotiators
  - Adjusted work effort details (e.g., project scope, schedule, and resource utilization)
  - Adjusted financial details (e.g., contract price, type, and payment terms)
  - Discussion summary—other changes to the initial proposal or anticipated contract

In some cases, there could be multiple meetings required for negotiation of large-value contracts or complex technical project efforts. The negotiation team should remain intact to manage such an extended negotiation effort, revisiting the negotiation preparation steps prior to each contract negotiation session.

9.2 CONTRACT EXECUTION

Contract Execution is the practice used to create the formal business relationship between the performing organization and the customer. It establishes the contract that will be used as the guiding document for managing business aspects of the project effort.

The contract or agreement is the essential document that enables a project to be initiated and conducted. It confirms the customer's request for the project and represents the performing organization's intent to achieve project deliverables and objectives. In the commercial environment, the contract or agreement further stipulates the monetary considerations of payment by the customer for the products delivered or services rendered. Therefore, it is particularly important to have a valid, executed contract if customer payments for project performance are expected.

Concept of This Practice

The purpose of this practice is to provide an indication for the project manager, project team, customer, and all relevant stakeholders that a bona fide and authorized project is about to begin. It further establishes the business and legal bases for conducting the project, which incur commitments and obligations from the customer and the performing organization.

Many organizations will have a group or department that will initiate and administer such contracts, and they should do so in close collaboration with the project manager.

Contract Execution is accomplished almost entirely in the Plan Phase. This is simply the actions taken to have a valid contract in place in order to perform project work for the customer. The contract administration practice will pick up and address any subsequent contract management and closure activities in later project management phases.

The following sole section of this practice describes the steps prescribed for contract execution.

Executing the Project Contract

There are just a few key steps the organization should apply to execute or otherwise establish the customer contract for each project:

- *Verify contract documents*. This step provides verification that all contract documents are complete and accurate and properly reflect the results of any ensuing contract negotiations. It particularly includes a review and incorporation of project plans and technical documents that were adjusted as a result of contract negotiations.

  For internal projects, an SOW or similar document is usually the primary document that is reviewed and agreed to at this step.
- *Obtain contract approvals*. The project manager, PMO, or business development representative leading the negotiation team or contracting effort will present the contract or agreement for management review, to include a review by the legal department. Then, a final review within the performing organization is completed, and an authorized signature is placed on the contract document.

  For internal projects, management review and approval above the business units involved is not usually required, as per established procedures within the performing organization.
- *Book the contract*. Contract booking is merely the process of accepting a contract or purchase order into the business system, accounting system, and project repository. An account number is established for the project (contract), and the baselines for scope, schedule, and costs are validated in the accounting or project management information system. This process allows work orders to be issued, project work to begin, and invoices to be submitted to the customer.

  For internal projects, this step can be accomplished with any documentation or procedure used to show the transfer of funds from the requesting business unit (customer) to the performing business unit (project manager).
- *Transfer contract responsibility to the project manager*. It is really important that a project manager (or project manager designee) be involved during project initiation in the Profile Phase. It is absolutely essential that a project manager be assigned and in place to lead the project planning effort (to include leading, or being a key participant in, the proposal development effort) in the Plan Phase. However, if for some reason that role has not yet been established, a project manager must be identified to take ownership and control of the project at the point of contract execution.

  The project Perform Phase can begin when the contract is passed to the project manager for execution. However, in some instances, detailed project planning by the performing organization is deferred until a valid contract is received from the customer. In that case, the contract could be passed and in place when the project manager leads the detailed project planning effort that is conducted in the Plan Phase.

Many business environments have a dedicated contract management business unit that serves as the repository for all contracts and agreements. Otherwise, the project manager should establish rapport with the relevant PMO or procurement office for subsequent collaboration and oversight of contracts associated with the project.

9.3 CONTRACT ADMINISTRATION

Contract Administration is the practice used to ensure the fulfillment of contractual obligations by all parties to the contract. A key aspect of contract administration is managing the actions or interfaces among the various project stakeholders to ensure contract compliance and, in some cases, to avoid noncompliance. In particular, all project team members must be aware of the legal implications of their actions relative to the relevant contract.

Contract administration also accounts for conducting and managing project invoicing and payment activities as associated with project deliverables that are "accepted" by the customer.

Concept of This Practice

The purpose of this practice is to provide guidance to the project manager, project team members, and other relevant stakeholders for conducting contract administration. It begins with several prescribed activities that will help individuals to prepare for contract administration as a part of the project management effort. It includes options for stakeholder communication related to the contract—meetings and reports. It also provides some recommended activities that can be used to manage issues and problems that could arise in contract administration.

Contract Administration is conducted primarily in the Perform Phase, with associated contract closeout activity occurring in the Post Phase.

There are three primary activities associated with contract administration:

- Contract Administration Planning
- Contract Performance Management
- Contract Closeout

The organization should examine these activities for applicability and implementation in the business and project management environments.

Contract Administration Planning

The project manager needs to ensure that contractual obligations associated with the project effort are identified and appropriately addressed in project planning that is conducted (or refined) following contract award. The organization may have a dedicated contract manager to facilitate this, or the PMO could establish a staff position to perform contract administration planning and support. Alternately, the PMO could also assist the project manager in performing this activity by incorporating guidance into the project management methodology for reference by the project manager and project team members.

The following are a few of the more prominent contract administration planning activities that can be considered for implementation in the project management environment.

- *Establish a meetings schedule.* The meetings schedule required by the contract should be established and communicated to all project stakeholders. The schedule should include preliminary meetings, such as the customer's kickoff or initial planning meetings, along with recurring status meetings. It is important that project team members demonstrate awareness of and preparation for all customer meetings.
- *Establish deliverables, reports, and reporting schedules.* All contractually required deliverables, reports, and reporting schedules should be identified and communicated so that project team members and other stakeholders know when and how to provide project deliverables and project reports to the customer (and to internal management) in a timely manner.
- *Establish contract documentation oversight.* The PMO or other specified business unit may be the primary repository for contract documentation, but a project team member could be assigned to manage such documentation. The project manager and some project team members will need access to critical contract documents throughout the project. Also, the project manager and project team members may need to document ongoing interactions with the customer as per contract guidance.

  Documentation related to contractual obligations is also essential to provide proof of performance, management of changes, justification for claims, and evidence in the unlikely event of litigation. The purpose of documentation is to record facts and reduce reliance on human memory. Efforts to maintain documentation must be thorough and consistent. Contract documentation should include
  - The official copy of the contract
  - Contract modifications
  - Conformed working copies of the contract
  - External and internal correspondence
  - Invoices
  - Change orders
  - Meeting minutes
  - Project plans
  - Progress reports
  - Project diaries
  - Telephone logs
  - Photographs and videotapes

  These documents can be made accessible to a variety of stakeholders through access via the project knowledge management system implemented by the organization for use in the project management environment.
- *Establish a contract communication control system.* Communication is an essential part of contract administration. Compliance with contract terms and conditions requires effective communication about contract performance. The project manager must establish not only the communication procedures needed to ensure that project team members and all stakeholders know what to do but also the controls to ensure that the procedures are used in compliance with the contract. In addition to developing an internal communications system, the project manager must ensure that effective communication with the customer is practiced (to include communication about the customer's contractual obligations).

- *Establish procedures to solve contract issues and problems.* The means for project team members to use an issues log to identify, handle, report, and track project (contract) issues and problems should be implemented, as is presented in the accompanying methodology toolkit.
- *Establish contract change control procedures.* The project manager must ensure that acceptable change control procedures are established for each project effort having contractual obligations, and that all project team members know how to use it. Change control procedures normally provide guidance to
  - Ensure that only authorized people negotiate or agree to contract changes.
  - Estimate the effect of a change on cost and schedule, and gain approval for any additional expense and time before proceeding with a change.
  - Notify project team members that they must promptly report any action or inaction by the customer that does not conform to the contract terms and conditions.
  - Notify the customer in writing of any action or inaction that is inconsistent with the established contract terms and conditions.
  - Instruct team members to document and report in writing both the actions taken to comply with authorized changes and the cost and time required to comply.
  - Promptly seek compensation for increases in cost or time required to perform, and negotiate claims for such compensation from the customer in good faith.
  - Document all changes in writing and ensure that both parties have signed the contract or contract change; such written documentation should be completed before work under the change begins, if practical.

  See the *Project Change Control* practice prescribed within this methodology.
- *Set up procedures for claim and dispute resolution.* Project managers, some project team leaders, and other relevant stakeholders are responsible for achieving contract obligations, and therefore must be well versed in contract claim and dispute resolution procedures. Disagreements are inevitable and should be expected as a normal part of contract management. However, all contract parties must commit themselves to resolving disputes amicably. Although claims and disputes cannot be avoided, they can be resolved effectively, fairly, and without rancor and litigation. To that end, only professionally trained contract managers or legal counsel should initiate and conduct formal contract conflict and dispute resolution actions. However, the organization should ensure that each project manager and key project team member is familiar with the range of common resolution issues that can be encountered and the techniques that can be used to avoid escalation of contractual conflicts and disputes. Prominent techniques include
  - Negotiation—Similar to the negotiation conducted for award of the contract, this interaction between the involved parties seeks to compromise on issues leading to resolution of a conflict.
  - Mediation—Legal counsel is involved in this effort led by an impartial third-party participant who facilitates a compromise on issues leading to resolution from an unbiased perspective.
  - Arbitration—The disputed issues are submitted to a disinterested third party for a final decision. This approach is usually considered to be more expedient, less expensive, and a less formal resolution method that is often preferred over litigation.
  - Litigation—A highly formal and potentially lengthy process for resolving contractual disputes through the courts and applicable legal system. Litigation always involves lawyers.

The PMO's primary responsibility in dispute resolution is to work with each project manager to identify and attempt to resolve disputes when they are minor and showing only the earliest signs of disagreement. The project manager must seek the advice of the PMO, senior management, and legal counsel at the first indication that a customer dispute is emerging or escalating.

All of these planning actions and determinations can be compiled into a contract administration plan for use by the project manager and project team members. In some cases, depending on content, elements of a contract administration plan can also be shared with the customer for the purpose of enhancing contract management communication.

Contract Performance Management

The performing organization, through the PMO and project managers, should ensure that the achievement of contractual obligations is a pertinent theme within the project management environment. The following steps are prescribed for consideration in establishing a contract performance management capability that advances the customer business relationship and project success.

- *Manage commitments to the customer.* Ensuring that commitments made to the customer are accomplished within the approved scope of work is critical. The project manager is responsible for all such commitments. The project manager (or designated contract manager) will need to document and monitor all authorized commitments to the customer.

- *Monitor the contract for compliance.* Contracting parties should know and understand the terms of their contracts and keep their promises to comply with them in good faith. To ensure that this premise is achieved, active management of contract compliance must be pursued to include compliance with the terms and conditions, contractual dates, costs, schedule, and deliverables in the contract. Often, those individuals who have negotiated or otherwise established the terms and conditions of the customer contract are not those who subsequently perform the work that achieves the contract's objectives. Therefore, the project manager must ensure that all key personnel involved in managing technical performance are also advised and become familiar with contractual obligations associated with project performance. One means to accomplish this is to use the contract administration plan created in contract administration planning to familiarize all project team members and other relevant project stakeholders, as appropriate.
- *Manage customer acceptance of deliverables.* Many contracts have specified acceptance procedures. However, if that is not the case on a particular project, controversies can still be avoided by using a formalized acceptance procedure. The project manager should implement the prescribed steps for presentation of deliverables to the customer. The following are particularly important steps to include in the customer delivery and acceptance process:
  - Notifications to the customer
  - Acceptance meetings
  - Customer sign-off for acceptance

  See the *Customer Acceptance* practice for additional discussion of acceptance procedures.
- *Manage project cash.* The project manager must ensure that management practices are implemented to ensure proper oversight of the cash flow and to facilitate reduction in the cash-to-cash cycle, thus improving cash flow. Ideally, the PMO or financial managers are involved in early proposal preparation and any negotiations to evaluate project cash flow issues. However, the organization also must institute proper cash management procedures for use by the project manager in conjunction with project performance. Some considerations for the performing organization/PMO include
  - *Obtain partial customer funding.* If a contract is funded in phases, ensure that the customer is aware of funding requirements with sufficient time for the customer to accomplish funding approval actions.
  - *Monitor billing and receipt of payments.* Take actions to provide timely delivery of goods and services that enable early customer payments, examine ways in which the project schedule can be renegotiated to improve cash flow, remove blocks to the customer's payment approval process, track customer invoice receipt, hand-carry large-value invoices, and facilitate review meetings for incentive payments.
  - *Monitor payments to subcontractors.* Where possible, establish subcontractor payment schedules that match the customer's billing cycle.
  - *Perform effective change management.* Provide prompt attention to customer-directed changes and early identification of constructive changes, particularly those that require additional funding to accomplish.
  - *Expedite shipments.* Conduct shipping on schedule, complete conversion of inventory into receivables and cash as quickly as possible, and seek authority for accelerated delivery and early payment where possible.
  - *Maximize use of project equipment and residual material.* Manage and dispose of project equipment and used materials promptly to avoid costs resulting from extended equipment and material retention. Transfer customer-owned property back to the customer or to follow-on and related contracts, when possible, to avoid the need for equitable adjustment of costs specified in the contract.
  - *Reduce impact of liquidated and consequential damages clauses.* Continuously monitor the circumstances that cause payment of liquidated or consequential damages, and eliminate these clauses or obtain incentive clauses to offset the risk of penalties.
  - *Protect proprietary data.* Ensure protection of all proprietary data, including those of the third parties, monitor data submissions to ensure proper markings, and use appropriate nondisclosure agreements. Proper attention and care will ensure that contingency funds for potential litigation are not needed.
  - *Manage stop work orders and termination.* Attend to customer orders to stop work in a timely manner. Likewise, discontinue contractor and subcontractor work at the direction of the customer. Following the stop work response, ensure that the customer addresses valid partial payments and cost recovery actions. As per the conditions encountered, consider if legal counsel is needed to respond to customer work stop or termination actions.

Contract Closeout

Contract closeout is an integral part of *Contract Administration* and represents project completion. Closeout includes the last important project tasks for which the project manager is responsible, and it requires the same level of attention as tasks encountered earlier in the project management life cycle. The following are key steps in the contract closeout process:

- *Obtain customer acceptance sign-off.* Obtain official signatures for sign-off from the customer indicating final acceptance of the products and services of the project.
  - Ensure that all project deliverables have been fulfilled and accepted by the customer.
  - Resolve any performance issues or problems that develop in association with warranty or guarantee provisions of the contract being closed.
  - Resolve any remaining open questions or issues.
- *Conduct contract closeout actions.* Contract closeout is performed during the Post Phase of the project management life cycle. To formally close out the contract with the customer,
  - Ensure that contract terms and conditions have been fulfilled and that any final project reports have been prepared and submitted.
  - Prepare and distribute written instructions to all project team members and project stakeholders that the contract is completed and no further charges should be incurred for that project account.
  - Manage the disposition or return of the customer's property.
  - Provide notice to the responsible business unit, advising that action be taken to close out any associated subcontracts that remain open.
  - Ensure that final invoices have been sent to the customer and that the customer's final payment has been received; do not close the project or dismiss the project manager before this action is achieved.
  - Forward formal notification of contract completion to the customer.
- *Prepare contract closeout documentation.* At the completion of the contract, the project manager, contract manager, and project team should develop the required closeout documents. As per the associated methodology toolkit, this closeout documentation can include the following items:
  - Lessons learned—customer, project, staff, vendor, and business
  - Evaluations—customer, project, staff, vendor, and business
  - Evaluation—the effectiveness of the processes and tools used to achieve contract compliance
  - Evaluation—the effectiveness of the project planning documents used to achieve contract compliance
  - Recommendations for improvements to processes and tools

The completion of contract closeout activities should be monitored by the project manager and the PMO. In turn, contract closeout leads to project closeout activities, which have bearing on the utilization of resources in the project management environment and the achievement of business objectives in the performing organization.

Chapter 10

Project Staffing Management

Project Staffing Management in the project environment takes on as many different configurations and approaches as there are performing organizations. Across industries, most project resources are introduced to projects through matrix management—a resource manager in the relevant organization "lends" individual resources to project managers for specific project efforts. In some organizations, resources may be assigned directly to the project manager, who then serves as the resource manager and takes resources from project to project. In a few others, usually smaller ones, project resources may be assigned or affiliated with the project management Office (PMO), which serves as the sole or primary resource manager for the organization.

More precisely, project staffing management is the practice of establishing a viable team structure for the project and then acquiring, assigning, and managing resources aligned with that structure. In some organizations, it also involves managing team member development, individually and collectively.

There are three practices associated with Project Staffing Management:

- Project Staff Structure
- Project Staff Management
- Project Staff Training and Development

The PMO, if available, should facilitate the further development of this practice area within the organization, particularly relative to staff management actions associated with one or more resource managers.

10.1 PROJECT STAFF STRUCTURE

Project Staff Structure is a practice used to identify and implement the project staffing configuration used in the organization. This activity may be an organizational or PMO effort, or it could reside with the project manager for each project. It particularly contributes to creating the project team organization chart for each project.

Concept of This Practice

The purpose of this practice is to provide the project manager with guidance for organizing resources aligned with the project. Also, it helps project team members and other relevant stakeholders to understand their alignment within the project management environment and the performing organization. Fundamentally, project staff structure is examined to consider the working relationship between the project manager and project team members, the integration of external participants into that team, and the relationship each of those participants has with the PMO.

Project Staff Structure guidance is normally reviewed and implemented by the project manager as a part of Project Initiation (Profile Phase). It would be rare should any significant project staff structure changes surface in later phases of the project management life cycle. However, this practice warrants separate consideration and deliberation within the organization that usually occurs outside the methodology practices utilized by the project manager. See the *Project Governance and Oversight* practice for more about this organizational responsibility.

The following staff structure considerations are addressed in the following three sections:

- Project Team and PMO Relationship
- Standard Project Team Structure
- Extended Project Team Alignment

The project manager has ultimate responsibility for structuring project resources to optimize the benefits of their work performance. In turn, the PMO and the organization should give due consideration to the impacts of any project team structures they have mandated for use in the project management environment.

Project Team and PMO Relationship

This section considers the extent to which there will be formal affiliation of project managers and project resources with the PMO. It has long been a topic of discussion, and, for the most part, it appears in many organizations that project managers and project team members are not aligned with the PMO. However, at least some professionals in the project management discipline would agree that greater project effectiveness is achieved when all project resources are aligned to some degree under the PMO, and this methodology recommends that at least project managers be aligned in some way and to some extent with the PMO.

The concept of project resource alignment presented here suggests some range of PMO control or influence over project resource assignments, activity schedules, and performance. The following are four progressive configurations that the organization can consider for the PMO's relationship with project managers and project team members. The organization can also identify variations of these configurations to better describe resource alignment in its project management environment. This specification is valuable because it can be associated with impacts on project performance, and, also, it can indicate conditions that limit or facilitate advancements in project management capability and maturity.

No Alignment of Project Resources

This configuration is one in which the PMO has no apparent influence or control over resources assigned to perform work in the project management environment. This is normally associated with the smaller PMO operating at the basic stage of development, although it is not unusual for a standard PMO to also encounter this condition. A few of the prominent impacts of this condition on the PMO and the project management environment include

- Strong communication and collaboration extending into business units will be needed to develop and implement project management governance and guidance, project management standards, and common project management tools and systems.
- Recurring executive and senior manager involvement may be needed to direct and monitor timely project resource input for cross-project reporting and adherence to standards of report content for PMO review, analysis, and aggregation.
- The ability to implement preferred practices can be limited by individual professional interests and conflicting business unit priorities encountered outside the project management environment.
- Project manager and project team member training arranged through business units or individuals could be inconsistent with preferred project management practices.
- Capability to identify cross-project needs and reassign project resources on short notice to priority projects may be limited.
- Resource utilization across multiple project assignments may not be effectively planned and tracked when there is no central oversight, resulting in resource overcommitments and undercommitments to project efforts and project task work that is based on personal schedules and availability, not business priorities.
- Project resource performance evaluations can be inconsistent across the various reporting officials serving as performance evaluators.

Indirect Alignment of Project Managers

This configuration is one in which the PMO develops active working relationships with project managers who are still directly aligned with business units. In turn, those project managers will usually accept and apply PMO governance and guidance when an advantage is identified. Also, at least some of these project managers will likely demonstrate a willingness to participate with the PMO in developing and implementing standards and practices in the project management environment. This provides a reasonable level of PMO influence, albeit very limited in terms of project resource assignment and performance control. A few of the prominent impacts of this condition on the PMO and the project management environment include

- Project management practices may vary across different project efforts, and project team members will need to differentiate the approach and preferences used by the project manager on each project to which they are assigned.
- The PMO will likely need to compete for project manager time and influence with the project manager's reporting official in the business unit.
- Capability to develop a cadre of professional project managers within the relevant organization may be limited by an inherent focus on technical aspects of project performance rather than on effective implementation of modern project management practices.

- Modest levels of affiliation with the PMO will facilitate communication and an exchange of ideas and concepts among project managers who share the PMO as a central point of coordination and collaboration on project management practices.
- Project managers will gain a better understanding of the PMO's support capability in the project management environment, particularly identifying PMO support available for use on their projects, ideally achieving improved project management efficiency and effectiveness as a result of the PMO relationship.

Direct Alignment of Project Managers

This configuration is one in which project managers work for the PMO when assigned to lead efforts in the project management environment. For the most part, they will receive their assignment from the PMO, and they will be responsible to the PMO for successful project completion and the associated achievement of project objectives. In turn, the PMO will monitor project progress and project manager performance. Of particular note, direct alignment does not necessarily require direct assignment to the PMO, although that would be the preferred condition. Also, this alignment of project managers does not infer alignment of project team members, which is discussed in the next section on project team structure. A few of the prominent impacts of this condition on the PMO and the project management environment include

- This influential position of the PMO can be used to ensure that business interests and objectives of the relevant organization are integrated and managed across all projects.
- The PMO will be able to prepare performance reports that are consistent across all designated project managers, but it will likely have to coordinate and manage the incorporation of its individual performance evaluations with those of the business unit if project managers are not directly assigned to the PMO.
- The PMO will have greater ability and a more effective means of introducing a viable and repeatable project management methodology process that is mandated for use by all project managers; similarly, common project management practices and tools will be more likely to achieve widespread use.
- The PMO will need to establish the capability and infrastructure to properly manage aligned project managers, whether that is a small or large group, and that need is increased if project managers are assigned directly to the PMO.
- The PMO can qualify and assign project managers to projects consistent with their skill and knowledge, not just because they are available; it can also prescribe technical and professional competency improvement activities for individual project managers to broaden their availability for more types of projects.

Direct Alignment of All Project Resources

This configuration is one in which all project managers are assigned to the PMO as a component of the PMO staff. Other project resources are also aligned to a greater extent with the PMO, and many are directly assigned to the PMO, possibly under the purview of a project manager. There is a distinction to be made between general project resources and members of the PMO staff. However, once assigned to the PMO, that distinction may be reduced as per the nature of work assigned on projects or in the PMO as a part of optimizing staff utilization. A few of the prominent impacts of this condition on the PMO and the project management environment include

- The PMO can hold central accountability for the assignment and performance of all resources in the project management environment.
- The PMO can contribute to project initiation and planning activities by identifying and committing specific project resources to approved project efforts.
- The PMO can analyze skill and competency requirements, prescribe professional development activities, and forecast project resource strength in specific technical and professional competency areas in advance of needs.
- The PMO can monitor and manage resource utilization across all projects and redirect resources to critical tasks as warranted by project needs and business priorities.
- The PMO can effectively assess project management capability and organizational maturity, introduce and conduct improvement activities using available resources, and convey project management capability and maturity status and advancement to executives and senior managers in the relevant organization.

Standard Project Team Structure

The project team structure is primarily a representation of project resource ownership and project manager authority as defined by most project management standards applied in industry today. Project manager responsibility for achieving project performance objectives must be supported by an appropriate level of authority to control project resource utilization, assign and manage project task performance, and enforce accountability of project team members. Otherwise, the designated project leader is merely serving as a project coordinator or administrator and cannot reasonably be held responsible for project outcomes. This methodology examines project team structure in a manner that is generally consistent with most prominent standards, and it presents three project team structure models for the PMO and the organization to consider in defining and establishing a standard project team structure.

Functional Project Team Structure

This represents a project team structure in which the project manager has little or no authority over project resources. Instead, project resources are aligned with the resource provider, usually a functional manager in a business unit, who has primary authority over assignments and management of project resource contributions to the project effort. Other likely conditions resulting from this project team structure include

- A project manager may be designated; however, that individual probably fulfills only a portion of the responsibilities normally associated with professional project management. Decisions affecting project performance often are made outside the purview of the designated project manager by one or more functional managers, business managers, and technical managers.
- Project team direction, guidance, and the ability to apply effective project management practices can come from various sources. The oversight of resources by multiple functional managers could result in an inconsistent approach to project management and the uncertainty of project outcome. This condition of authority shared across functional managers also may indicate that there is no central project management authority below the executive or senior management level.
- Functional manager position and business experience may serve in lieu of formal project management skill and competency to guide project management activities and affect project progress and outcome.
- Project resources serve under the direction and conditions of a functional manager who will evaluate their performance and influence their career progression, and not the designated project manager. At best, a designated project manager will coordinate the efforts of assigned resources and achieve resource performance results primarily through personal attributes of influence and persuasion.
- Technical managers may be called to perform as project managers solely because of their demonstrated technical skill and competency rather than on capability and experience to manage the full range of project management activities.

Matrix Project Team Structure

This represents a project team structure in which the project manager has limited authority over project resources, which are now aligned with the project manager for purposes of project work. Some project management standards distinguish between a *strong matrix* structure and a *weak matrix* structure. In a strong matrix structure, the project manager has significant authority and control over project resources during their project assignment. In a weak matrix structure, the resource provider (i.e., functional manager) retains primary authority and control of the resource but fulfills resource commitments to the project manager. Other conditions that are often associated with this project team structure include

- The role of the project manager is distinct and presumably associated with individual qualification of skill and experience in applying project management concepts and practices. It is a role that is generally recognized and appropriately regarded by all project resources and functional managers within the relevant organization.
- The project manager will normally evaluate project resource performance as an element of project management. If the resource's project assignment is an extended one, the project manager may be solely responsible for conducting the annual performance review. If the assignment is shorter, the project manager is usually requested to provide an interim resource performance review for the assignment period, and that review is entered into the individual's personnel records as contributing input to performance reward and career progression decisions.
- The qualification and designation of project managers as the central point of project management responsibility facilitates the introduction of common and repeatable project management processes and practices. In turn, this capability is readily conveyed to those project resources in the matrix team structure, and they become more and more effective in their accomplishment of project responsibilities across all project assignments.
- The assigned project resource normally cannot be assigned to other project tasks or other projects without the concurrence and commitment of the resource provider. Similarly, if there is a precise period of performance specified for a particular project matrix team resource, untimely completion of preceding project tasks could affect project resource availability.
- The resource provider or functional manager who "owns" the resource can assert control or influence to remove or replace the resource assigned to the project. In turn, project managers will need to collaborate with

resource providers at regular intervals to ensure that current resource commitments and planned resource assignments are fulfilled in a timely manner—a small administrative burden that is encountered primarily when a weak matrix team structure is applied.

Integrated Project Team Structure

This represents a project team structure in which the project manager has primary authority over project resources, which are usually aligned through a direct and full-time assignment to a project manager or the PMO. Certain project management standards refer to this as a "projectized" project team structure. Here the term *integrated* is used to represent the full-time, ongoing alignment of project team members, project managers, and the PMO in the project management environment. Other prominent conditions for this project team structure include

- A distinct central point of authority and responsibility for project management and project performance is established at the project level and at the PMO level.
- Accountability and actions for integration of strategic business objectives into project management efforts become less cumbersome. Executives and senior managers can influence project management direction toward achievement of business objectives without having to personally manage projects.
- Project management needs of all business units can be served. Professional project management processes and practices can now be applied to all applicable business and technical interests within the various business units of the relevant organization.
- Project management resources can be developed and grown within the culture of the relevant organization as much as they are acquired. This structure promotes measurement of project management skill and knowledge alongside technical capability as a qualifier for professional advancement.
- Project resources have reduced task performance and scheduling conflicts resulting at least from their full-time alignment with a central project management authority, and possibly by having one supervising project manager.
- Project resource utilization planning and management should be more effective. Project resources can be assigned within the project management environment to respond to projects having business priority, fill in temporary resource vacancies, apply specialized skills, and contribute to PMO function area development and implementation. Any nonproject time can be accounted for in developing capabilities in the project management environment.
- Project resources have common performance standards across all projects to which they are assigned. Project managers contribute to establishing these standards and are instrumental in applying them to all project efforts.

These structures represent a progressive state of project team cohesion that could exist or be established within the performing organization. On examination of these different structures, many professionals in project management would likely agree that the most effective project team structure is probably represented by a combination of a prominent integrated project team structure with a matrix project team structure applied for some elements of project participation when needed. In reality, most organizations will probably implement structures that have characteristics from one or more of the structures presented.

Extended Project Team Alignment

The organization, with PMO assistance, will need to examine its culture and business environment in making decisions regarding extended project team alignment. This means determining how closely project stakeholders who are not project team members are aligned with the project and with the project manager. Specifically considered are four project stakeholder groups—customers, vendors/contractors, regulatory agents, and other stakeholders. It is beneficial to project performance for representatives from these groups as well as traditional project team members to know and recognize who comprises the group known as the "project team."

The organization can create a default approach for the inclusion of extended project team members, which can be adapted by the project manager on a project-by-project basis. Unless the nature of project work is so homogenous and the same project stakeholders tend to be present on recurrent projects, it is likely that each new project will warrant independent examination by the project manager regarding the need for extended project team alignment.

Customer Project Team Alignment

Some customers will collaborate on the project's technical solution and the plans to achieve it and then essentially remain uninvolved outside of routine status meetings and progress report reviews. This condition is probably not characteristic of a project effort that warrants significant customer inclusion or alignment as part of the project team.

Conversely, some project work inherently requires ongoing customer involvement in the development and delivery of the project's technical solution. This warrants consideration for having one or more customer representatives on the project team. In some cases, the customer may even have its own intact project team to be integrated. Presumably, there will be a customer contact or customer project manager who will serve as the point of integration.

The PMO or project manager should establish the protocol for this relationship early in the project effort, at or before the project kickoff meeting. In particular, the parties will need to decide how project team members will be assigned responsibilities and perform work together. A common approach is for the two project managers to coordinate their plans and then collaborate on the nature and extent of participation by necessary project resources. A related protocol point is establishing how technical or other subteams having combined participation will be managed, including specifying who will be the subteam leader. Finally, an important point of protocol is made when the customer distinguishes between being a project team participant and being a representative for acceptance of project deliverables obligated under a contract or agreement. Ideally, this will be distinguished by having two different customer groups.

Many project managers find it useful to have key customer activities included in their work plan. Even subtle customer activities associated with the project take time—a few days for a document review, allocation of time for meeting preparation and attendance, a period for customer deliberation and decision, etc. The project work plan should account for these types of customer "deadlines" and activities. In many cases, the project work plan can become the customer's work plan, and the inclusion of assigned tasks for the customer will allow everyone to see the sequence of activities for which he or she is responsible. Besides, if it is not specified in the work plan, how will everyone know that it is an important and timely project activity, or even one on the project's critical path?

Vendor/Contractor Project Team Alignment

Vendor/contractor alignment needs to be determined for each vendor and each project. If not specifically aligned as part of the extended project team, the vendor/contractor must have some other type of association with the project manager. Alignment and association may have a subtle difference in some cases, but it is one that should be examined to determine whether the vendor/contractor project manager works solely with the project manager, or if vendor/contractor participants are integrated with the project team.

The prescribed protocols for this project relationship are very similar to those indicated for the customer project team—only now with reversed roles. Here the project manager can determine the level of vendor/contractor integration, the preferred approach to technical leadership and resource management, and the point of contact for vendor/contractor deliverables. Of course, it is reasonable to expect the vendor/contractor to have direct control of the resources it brings to the project.

The PMO should prescribe conditions and standards, but the project manager will need to make the final decision regarding the integration of any vendor/contractor work plan with the primary project work plan. The conditions that normally warrant full integration of project work plans are associated with technical activities where vendor/contractor participants work side by side with primary project team members, serving as technical leads, technical experts, or technical assistants. In other project situations, the vendor/contractor may have responsibility for one or more deliverables that it prepares independent of any participation with the primary project team. That condition probably just requires that a single line item be included in the project work plan to represent the vendor/contractor effort relative to other project activities. Of course, the project manager or a designated technical leader on the project team must actively manage that work plan line item.

Regulatory Agent Project Team Alignment

The introduction of a regulatory agent as an extended participant on the project team may initially seem awkward. However, the purpose of identifying the extended project team in the first place is to ensure that the project manager is able to account for and manage all prominent project activities, with appropriate alignment of key participants. In some project management environments, a regulatory agent can be a prominent participant at least at critical junctures in the project management life cycle.

A regulatory agent is often thought of as an external government representative. However, as described in the next section on project stakeholders, the regulatory agent role could originate within the relevant organization also. Some industries may even have an external or internal regulatory agent participate over the entire duration of the project. Usually, a regulatory agent will be introduced into the project at points of product development or delivery. The decision to formally recognize regulatory agents as extended members of the project team will be determined by the protocol required and by mutual agreement between the regulatory agent and the project manager.

The points of protocol for regulatory agents may be preestablished by the regulatory agency or office and by the nature of their oversight role and the type of project. The PMO should understand these protocols for all regulatory agents and convey associated requirements for use by project managers and project team members.

Like any key project participant, it is wise to include regulatory agent activities associated with the project as elements of the project work plan. This enables the regulatory agent to identify preferred points of activity and, if necessary, coordinate adjustments as a matter of protocol or convenience. Equally important, the representation of regulatory agent participation on the project work plan serves as guidance and a reminder to the project manager and project team members regarding the probable need for timely completion of preceding project activities.

Other Stakeholder Project Team Alignment

All in all, the alignment of extended project team participants is a factor for PMO consideration based on relevant organizational culture and business needs. It helps the PMO and others in the project management environment to specify and recognize the standard composition of an active project team in the relevant organization.

In that regard, this practice does distinguish between members of the active project team, including primary and extended members and other project stakeholders. As per reference to the listing in the following section, the PMO can add or exclude any project stakeholder roles as active participants in the project team. In some cases, certain stakeholder roles will inherently be recognized as project team members by virtue of traditional team composition in the project management environment.

10.2 PROJECT STAFF MANAGEMENT

Project Staff Management is the practice applied to accomplish work through the efforts of project team members. It takes on as many different configurations and approaches as there are organizations and PMOs.

For the most part, project resources are introduced to projects through matrix management—a resource manager in the relevant organization "lends" individual resources to project managers for specific project efforts. In some organizations, resources are assigned directly to the project manager, who then serves as their resource manager. To a lesser extent, a few organizations have all project resources assigned or aligned with the PMO.

Regardless of the approach used across industries and organizations, there are two fairly common and generally accepted views about project resource management. First, the human resources (HR) department serving the performing organization has ultimate responsibility and overriding authority for resource management, and it directs, guides, or otherwise facilitates the resource manager in managing and supervising organizational resources. Second, if a PMO exists, it should be able to influence the quality and availability of resources used on projects, and it should be able to oversee or at least monitor resource assignments and performance in the project management environment.

Concept of This Practice

The purpose of this practice is to provide the project manager with guidance for introducing, using, and then closing staffing assignments on the project. Also, this guidance should help project team members and other relevant stakeholders (e.g., resource managers) to understand their responsibilities within the project management environment and within the performing organization.

Project Staff Management activities are performed in all phases of the project management life cycle, with prominent activities occurring in the Plan Phase and in the Perform Phase. The primary activities of project staff management are addressed in the following five sections.

- Acquire Project Resources
- Assign Project Resources
- Deploy Project Resources
- Manage Resource Performance
- Closeout Resource Assignments

The project manager has ultimate responsibility for performing project staff management, but delegation of that authority is a common practice, particularly on larger projects. Therefore, project team leaders and project supervisors will also benefit from using this guidance on project staff management.

Acquire Project Resources

The PMO can play a vital role in resource acquisition, facilitating the effort and ensuring that qualified people are available for project assignments. Specific project resource acquisition can be performed by the PMO or delegated to project managers according to acceptable practices in the organization. Resource acquisition requires close collaboration and coordination with affected resource managers so that they gain insight into and find acceptance of the process. The acquisition process also warrants input or review from the HR department to ensure that it adheres to all regulated or required personnel management actions and practices. The following three activities can be conducted in association with project resource acquisition.

Identify Resource Providers

The organization should ensure that providers of project resources are identified, and that these resource providers understand the nature of their responsibilities to provide resources to project efforts. Four primary providers of project resources are described here.

- *Human Resources Department*—The HR department is the primary source for new personnel. It performs recruiting and hiring of qualified personnel in response to resource needs and requests from resource managers in the relevant organization. It is also positioned to recognize staffing needs through attrition planning and can hire or transfer resources to fill authorized allocations. The PMO can work with the HR department to confirm resource needs for the project management environment.

- *Resource Managers*—The resource manager, by whatever reference name is used in the organization, is the primary provider of project resources in most organizations that use a matrix management structure for project staffing. Personnel assigned to resource managers may have a split and concurrent responsibility toward both their resource manager and the project manager associated with their project assignments. This "conflict" is compounded when the individual has full-time responsibilities for work assigned by the resource manager and only part-time work responsibilities assigned by the project manager. Close collaboration can resolve or minimize many of the issues and implications that could be encountered in this situation. Such collaboration includes using project resource requests (from the PMO or project manager) and managing resources and resource commitments according to the larger needs of the organization.
- *Project Management Office*—The PMO's role as a resource provider is a concept that is just beginning to emerge in some organizations that have a more mature project management environment. This centralized oversight capability optimizes the assignments of available resources and significantly reduces disarray and disjoint responsibilities for individuals. This concept also prompts consideration of full-time resource assignments that are directly aligned with individual project managers.
- *Vendors and Contractors*—Vendors and contractors are external resource providers. They are called upon, routinely in some organizations and less frequently in others, to perform work using skills and knowledge that are not available or not a core competency in the performing organization. Such acquisition is addressed in the Project Vendor Relationship Management practice area. It is mentioned here simply to recognize that this resource provider is available in the project management environment. It is not necessarily a direct part of the project resource acquisition request process.

A final point to make is that project managers are also project staff resources and need to be "acquired" for each project effort. It is prescribed that the PMO be a participant in this special effort. Ideally, project managers will be assigned or otherwise aligned with the PMO and therefore be available for assignment to projects through the PMO. However, it is the unique requirements of each organization that will determine how project managers are "acquired."

Establish Resource Requirements

At a minimum, the PMO should be included in coordination of project staffing requests and resulting actions to fulfill staffing requirements. Ideally, the PMO will review project resource requirements for accuracy and fulfillment capability within the performing organization and make decisions regarding the need to seek external project resources. However, the project manager will prepare resource requirements as a part of routine project staffing activities.

There are five prominent types of project resource requirements that can be identified and considered for acquisition in the project management environment:

- *Project Management Staffing Requirements*—A project manager will be needed for every project conducted in the relevant organization. In some organizations, an individual project manager will be assigned to lead more than one project. This should prompt oversight by the PMO to ensure that qualified project manager assignments adequately cover all projects, and that unreasonable project loads are not imposed on individual project managers.
- *Technical Discipline Staffing Requirements*—A variety of technical resources may be needed for different projects conducted by the organization. The PMO or project manager can work with technical leaders to identify qualified personnel and identify their availability for particular types of project work. The project manager should normally prepare more detailed staffing requirements (e.g., Resource Responsibility Matrix) for the types of technical positions required on the project at hand.
- *Skilled Laborer Staffing Requirements*—Some projects will require team members with nontechnical skills. These include skilled trade and craftsman types as well as manual laborers. The project manager should include these team members in the resource listings. Skilled laborers could include, for example, plumbers, electricians, carpenters, and custodians. Also, in certain industries, this workforce could be considered the primary "technical discipline" needed for the project. Although not unique, this staffing element may have labor union alignment and require management of requirements associated with that aspect of work.
- *Adjunct Discipline Staffing Requirements*—The introduction of nontechnical staff, those personnel who do not perform work directly related to achieving project objectives, is too often based on an assumed capability and presumed availability. The project manager

should identify these adjunct project team members and enable them to be specified in project requirements. This includes such participants as representatives from HR (the project may require a large influx of new recruits), Legal (the project may have regulatory components that require specialized attention), Procurement (the project may have large product or contractor purchasing needs), R&D (the project may necessitate the introduction of new technology), etc. Also, adjunct disciplines include any support personnel that assist the project manager and technical leaders in project coordination and administration activities. Rather than calling on these disciplines as needed, the project manager should include them in the resource requirements list.

- *PMO Staffing Requirements*—The PMO is a central participant in the project environment and can be a resource for staffing needed to accomplish certain aspects of project management, if not other technical work elements as well. Such requirements are not normally aligned with projects but rather with routine PMO oversight and support activities. However, the project manager should include any significant or nonroutine PMO resource utilization as resource requirements on the project.

Fulfill Resource Requests

The acquisition process culminates in obtaining the required resources from resource managers and other resource providers. It represents a series of actions to be performed by the project manager (or by the PMO in collaboration with the project manager when such capability has been established). The following fundamental steps can be used to fulfill internal resource requests within the performing organization.

- *Submit project resource request.* The project manager will prepare and forward the project resource request to the PMO for the record and to the resource manager having the appropriate resources required for the project effort. Also, the PMO could serve as a clearinghouse for such resource requests and identify the resource manager who will be given the resource request. In turn, the project manager should track all requests submitted, particularly if that involves multiple resource managers.
- *Conduct project resource request review.* The resource manager may independently review the request for content—type and number of personnel needed, period of project assignment, and any other relevant information needed to understand project resource requirements. If desired, the resource manager can also meet with the project manager and/or the PMO to clarify project resource requirements and to negotiate the conditions of the pending commitment of resources.
- *Obtain resource manager commitment.* Project resource fulfillment is achieved at the point when the resource manager signs off on the project resource request, indicating a commitment to provide the specified resources as described in the request (or subsequent modifications to the request). This step should be performed even when the PMO is the resource manager. It allows all involved parties to track and manage resource commitments.

The PMO may have direct or indirect involvement in performing this process. It should be included in (copied on) distribution of the resource responsibility matrix and any other resource commitment documents.

The result of staff acquisition is the commitment of required project resources, as per authorized allocations, that are now identified as available and committed to work on a specified project at times agreed to by the resource manager and the project manager. This resource commitment is the basis for the project manager to advance with planning resource utilization.

Assign Project Resources

The resource assignment process contains the prescribed steps for performing notification and introduction of the staff member to the project. There are three fundamental steps used to fulfill the staff assignment requirements of the project:

- *Prepare resource assignment notifications.* This provides for the formal notification of a project assignment that is conveyed to the selected resources. It is done as a written document that specifies as much information about the project and the individual's associated responsibilities as is available at the time of preparation. In particular, it provides the assignment period and identifies key dates for resource participation, with a focus on initial meetings and activities. This notification enables the individual to schedule and plan for participation, which is particularly important if the resource has concurrent commitments to other project work or business activities. This action can be performed by either the project manager or the resource manager. The project manager and PMO should receive or retain a copy of each staff notification document.
- *Obtain individual resource commitments.* The staff assignment notification document should provide a means for the individual to acknowledge receipt and essentially accept the project assignment. This step may often warrant a personal meeting between the individual selected and the project manager to clarify the level of participation needed, establish performance

expectations, and elicit the personal commitment of the staff member to the project effort. The selected individual will then sign off on the notification to indicate his or her commitment to the project.

- *Introduce resources to the project team.* The resource assignment process is finished when the staff member is first introduced to the project at a project kickoff meeting or other project team event. The project kickoff meeting serves as an initial introduction for all (or at least most) project team members. If the resource is being introduced to the project at an advanced project stage, then an individual introduction is warranted. Resource introductions should include identifying the individual's role and responsibilities on the project to other team members. In conducting group introductions, team-building exercises may be appropriate to enable participants to become a more cohesive team. All in all, the resource introduction step validates individual participation on the project team and reinforces individual commitment to the project effort.

The project manager can use assignment notification documents to allow the staff member to plan and prepare for participation in initial project team meetings.

Deploy Project Resources

Project resource deployment means getting the project team member to the work location fully prepared to begin the work effort. It is important to distinguish between simple deployment and global deployment. The smaller, internal project does not normally require much effort to deploy resources. If an assigned resource on an internal project "moves" from a permanent workstation, it is probably just to attend a meeting down the hall. Conversely, if a resource is assigned to a project effort that requires frequent travel or semipermanent relocation, perhaps to global locations, there will be considerably more logistical preparation activities to consider.

It is important to recognize that project resource deployment is more than just making travel arrangements. It means ensuring the individual is personally and professionally prepared to take on the project assignment, and the project is ready to accommodate the resource through adequate setup of required facilities and equipment—down the hall or across the globe.

The PMO can develop procedures to facilitate needs for both simple and global deployment activities. However, the project manager must still ensure that resource deployment is properly accomplished. To that end, simple deployments are covered by a relatively quick examination of needs and a brief check to ensure that required actions are being accomplished. More complex, global deployments will be addressed for those organizations that have a broader deployment perspective, and could require tracking and management to properly accomplish that staffing effort. Of course, there are project staff deployments that fall in between these two extremes, and the PMO should develop project resource deployment practices that facilitate the standard types of project deployment encountered in the organization.

There are three recommended project resource deployment activities for the PMO to consider.

Perform Deployment Administration

There are considerations that should be addressed on every project to ensure that the individual is ready to perform project assignments at the specified project work location. The organization or PMO may need to refine these for use in the organization. The project manager should conduct an examination of the following deployment items and issues in conjunction with resource planning and staff acquisition activities.

- *Project Workspace*—If the assigned individual is not working from a permanent location, a project workspace should be assigned. This may be a workspace belonging to the performing organization or one arranged at or near customer facilities. If the assigned individual can perform project assignments from an established permanent office workstation, then there are no particular requirements for this deployment element.
- *Standard and Special Equipment*—The assigned individual may require certain equipment in order to perform required project or project management tasks or to complete technical tasks. This element ensures that all necessary equipment is provided. Such activity ensures that individuals have the equipment they need—either through advance issuance or by having it on site for use at the specified project location.
- *Project and Customer Special Requirements*—This element of deployment deals with conveying information about the project and the customer's environment that is unique or warrants reminders as a matter of good business practice. Normally, project resources will obtain all the information they need to have about the work they are about to perform in project kickoff meetings, planning sessions, and technical requirements reviews. This element of deployment extends into the consideration and dissemination of special information or awareness needed by project team members. This may deal with such matters as
  - Customs, cultures, and conditions associated with travel to foreign locations
  - Customer facility and equipment utilization guidance
  - Project and customer communication protocols

- Time zone differential impacts at different customer facilities and project locations
- Special time accounting and reporting practices for project work
- Special vendor/contractor sourcing requirements for the project
- Medical and immunization requirements for customer and project locations
- Handling and protection of technology and business confidential information
- Project deliverable review and authorization authorities
- Group travel arrangements

The PMO should survey managers in the project environment to help identify what items will be examined and accomplished to address project and customer special requirements for each project. If smaller projects are the norm, this review may not be needed, but rather the standard setup becomes the norm.

- *Regulatory Requirements*—The concept of regulatory requirements in the context of this process refers to the influence or guidance asserted by governmental authority on a particular project. This process should ensure that project team members are aware of regulatory requirements applicable to the project and their work performance. The presence of regulatory requirements could prompt a review of relevant "regulations" at junctures in the project effort. It may also warrant the introduction of special team members such as legal advisors or specialty-area examiners to ensure that regulatory requirements are being properly addressed. However, this activity is primarily used to inform project participants of any applicable regulatory conditions or requirements.
- *Security Requirements*—As may be required by the nature of project work, deployment activities can include considerations related to handling and use of government or business-classified information and material. It could provide for the acquisition or confirmation of individual security clearances as well as review of security practices and procedures applicable to the project effort.

This listing of deployment administration activities should prompt consideration of how these actions are currently performed in the organization and help identify areas where they can be made more efficient.

Identify and Arrange Relevant Training

This second element of project resource deployment is focused on ensuring that each project member accomplishes any required training prior to beginning the assignment or as needed during the project effort. The project manager will need to identify any individual requirements for training and then develop the means to arrange and complete the training within the schedule of project activities. As necessary, required staff training can be incorporated as a work element in the project's work breakdown structure (WBS).

The introduction of a standard training curriculum for project participants is discussed in a subsequent section of this practice area. That training is pursued as a matter of routine individual qualification. The training required for deployment is that which is immediately needed to perform the work at hand. It very well may include programs from the established curriculum, or may include special internal or external training programs associated with achieving project objectives and meeting project requirements.

The project manager should consider the following types of training for possible inclusion in deployment preparation activities.

- *Project Management Training*—Identifies training associated with project management activities. This type of training could be needed by individuals who are taking on new project management responsibilities such as serving as a task leader, or by experienced project managers who need training in new project management practices or processes required by the customer or the performing organization for the current project.
- *Technical Skill Training*—Identifies training needed by project team members to expand their technical skill and knowledge for the current project effort. This could include the need to attend a training program offered by the customer in order to gain relevant information that will be applied to project work. This type of training could also be used to provide or enhance critical skills of project staff members who are assigned to the project on short notice. Also, unique project activities may warrant special project team training that provides the ability to understand new technical concepts, use special equipment, or otherwise qualify for project assignment.
- *New Technology Training*—Identifies training associated with use or implementation of new technology concepts, tools, and equipment. This may be a standard preproject training event in some organizations where new products are routinely manufactured. In particular, the project teams associated with new product implementation require ongoing training to ensure their knowledge and understanding of the product and its capabilities or application in the customer environment. In a related sense, this type of training also could apply to tools and equipment the project team uses in conjunction with normal project work efforts and addresses technology updates or replacements that

individuals will require training to use on the current project. It also could include upgraded version training for certain software applications.

In conjunction with facilitating the "just-in-time" training described here, the PMO may also be able to assist in forecasting training needs based on anticipated project work. Also, the PMO could be instrumental in arranging and providing large-scale training programs in which a large portion of the population in the project management environment is expected to be trained.

Monitor Travel Arrangements

A project management environment that deals with extensive travel requirements may warrant some oversight of travel associated with project work by the project manager or the PMO. This means that issues and matters of project-related travel are monitored to determine efficiency and to ensure that project resources are where they should be in a timely manner. In particular, the project manager or PMO can monitor staff travel in the following ways:

- Confirm individual travel plans associated with acceptance of project assignments.
- Coordinate group travel arrangements.
- Monitor vendor/contractor travel plans and expenses.

This project resource deployment element should not overburden the project manager, which is why PMO support is suggested. However, it should be applied to some extent as a contribution to the overall effort of ensuring efficient operations within the project management environment.

Manage Resource Performance

The PMO should play a lead role in developing a standard approach to managing project resource performance. It should be instrumental in ensuring collaboration among the approaches that project managers will take in managing project resources assigned to their projects. The PMO should work with project and resource managers to identify performance management responsibilities.

The following are resource performance management activities that are prescribed for the project manager, unless otherwise retained by or delegated to the resource manager or PMO.

Project Resource Management Planning

This activity begins as the project manager develops the first thoughts on forming the project team. It prompts consideration of the size and composition of the project team, including reflection on management styles needed for specific team members and the team as a whole. The following are some relevant resource management planning activities for project manager consideration:

- Identify (or estimate) the project team size to determine the need for the assignment of interim managers.
- Determine any unique technical specialties where the project manager may require "specialty" assistance to monitor and evaluate work performance.
- Identify any "weak" performers that will be assigned to the project team; this is done as a matter of planning how to optimize the work performance of such individuals.
- Identify any "strong" performers that will be assigned to the project team; this is done as a matter of planning possible leadership roles for such individuals, but also to "monitor and control" any potential for overbearing or scope-creeping performance.
- Establish the project team organization structure chart as a means to specify and distribute it for use by the project team and by other project stakeholders.
- Review resource utilization allocations to determine if the project is fully staffed; if not, determine methods to overcome deficiencies in the staffing plan and request or otherwise negotiate additional resources as needed.
- Establish the management approach that will be used in guiding the project team to the successful completion of the project effort, including the preparation of scheduled staff member performance reviews (evaluations).

Project Resource Performance Monitoring

This activity helps the project manager to plan and conduct staff performance observations of varying frequency and type. This may include a range of activities from very general observations to stricter monitoring required to ensure quality, achieve standards, or comply with contractual or regulatory obligations. The following are some relevant resource performance monitoring activities for project manager consideration:

- Staff Member Performance Reviews—Regular reviews of project performance are conducted to identify individual performance strengths and weaknesses, and individual contributions to the project effort. They can be accomplished through examination of specified elements in project reports; discussions with project team members, the PMO, and other project stakeholders who are privy to a staff member's project work results; and the project manager's personal observations of individuals' project work activities.

- Team Performance Reviews—Regular reviews of project performance are conducted to identify team performance strengths and weaknesses and the overall contributions of the team to the project effort. This activity examines project team cooperation and cohesiveness and can provide some indicators associated with individual staff member performance. These reviews can be accomplished through methods similar to staff member performance reviews, but with a focus on the team's effort.
- Staff and Team Performance Analyses—Performance indicators are prepared and examined to identify individual and project team trends. Trend analyses can be examined for individual performance across projects as a general indicator of demonstrated competency. Analyses also can be done to compare individual performance within a project team. Similarly, team analyses can be prepared particularly for project teams that have consistent team membership across projects. Performance analysis should be conducted within the norms of the organization and in conjunction with any HR department guidelines for monitoring and managing individual performance. This may be an appropriate activity for the PMO, if one exists.
- Performance Improvement Remedy Development—The project manager, ideally with PMO and resource manager collaboration, should identify and apply remedies for improving individual and team performance. This provides the capability to respond to the results of performance monitoring.

Performance Improvement Mentoring

This activity suggests methods for the project manager (or other project team leader) to use in influencing project team member work performance. It includes such activities as listening, facilitating, guiding, illustrating, etc., and results in the formulation of ideas and concepts the staff member can do to optimize personal performance on the project team. It could also include action that calls upon PMO-based project team mentors as available within the organization.

Performance Evaluation

This activity represents the standard approach to evaluating and conveying evaluation results to project team members. A prescribed staff member evaluation form should be used for consistency across team members. If such an evaluation is the primary performance evaluation in the organization, the form used should be approved by the HR department. The following are prescribed key elements of the staff member performance evaluation process:

- Establish the periods and frequency of reviews for project staff member performance evaluations early in the project management life cycle so that staff members can set their expectations relative to that information.
- Identify the impact of in-project evaluations—whether they represent corporate-level reviews (usually having high career impacts) or just reviews of project work (usually having minimal career impacts).
- Identify reporting officials who will conduct staff performance reviews for each team member.
- Solicit additional individual performance information from other sources (e.g., other project managers, resource managers, PMO managers) as needed for evaluation period coverage.
- Prepare staff member performance reports using established and approved evaluation forms; obtain any necessary higher-level reviews and concurrence or approval for each staff member evaluation.
- Conduct a performance review meeting with each staff member undergoing a performance review associated with the project and normally obtain the staff member's signature of acknowledgement of the evaluation; if preparing the evaluation only as a contributor, pass on the evaluation information to the relevant project manager or resource manager.

Performance Recognition and Rewards

An important aspect of resource performance management is to ensure that individuals and teams receive relevant and timely recognition and rewards for their contributions to the project effort. This, of course, should be consistent with organizational practices and policies in this area. However, some means should exist to recognize and reward individuals who have contributed to project success through innovation, demonstrated commitment, and performance excellence. The following are a few examples of recognition and reward actions that can be conducted for and on behalf of project team members:

- Conduct a team party to celebrate "success" at the conclusion of the project. Do not forget to invite past project team members, as appropriate, including those who departed the project at earlier stages or those who had only brief involvement.
- Provide gifts or souvenirs of the project at the conclusion of the project or as team members depart their assignments on the project (in good standing).
- Provide gifts or souvenirs as project team members come onto project assignments, as a means to confirm their affiliation with the new or established project team.

- Provide performance excellence recognition and rewards when individual achievements exceed standard performance levels.
- Announce performance excellence in broadcast emails or newsletters—both internal and external—as a means to recognizing and publicizing individual achievements.
- Provide promotions that are due relative to work performance results or tenure; provide internal project "promotions" by assigning new leadership responsibilities.
- Provide pay raises that are due in association with promotions or tenure.
- Provide on-the-spot monetary bonuses for performance excellence or innovation.

The PMO can be a valuable source for setting performance standards across projects and to otherwise assist project managers in their resource performance management activities.

Closeout Resource Assignments

The project manager ensures that necessary and appropriate actions are taken to close out individual assignments to projects. This is important because it specifies a point in time when the assigned staff member is no longer responsible for project work and no longer assigned to the project. This importance is compounded for individuals who must manage staff member participation on multiple projects. Closing out the staffing assignment not only relieves individuals of project responsibility but also makes them available for possible reassignment to a subsequent project assignment.

There are three primary project resource closeout activities that the project manager should address:

- *Coordinate Resource Extensions*—This action is a response used when it becomes necessary to extend the individual staff member's continuing participation in the project beyond the scheduled performance end-date. This action could be expedited by developing a process for coordinating the extension with any involved resource manager, and possibly with another project manager who might be affected by delays in the individual's follow-on assignment. This is a process that must be used sparingly and controlled to address only the most extenuating circumstances, particularly when a specified team member is needed for immediate assignment to a subsequent project effort. The organization may want develop the authorization criteria for this action and incorporate it into this practice.
- *Facilitate Transfers and Reassignments*—This action represents the routine response to project staff member departures from the project team. The project manager (or qualified designee) should conduct the following activities in association with project staff member departures:
  - Review the staff member's project work package responsibilities for completion (and possible reassignment).
  - Conduct an end-of-project or end-of-assignment staff member performance evaluation.
  - Prepare and conduct interim or final performance evaluations for team members who report to the departing staff member.
  - Solicit staff member lessons learned (in areas of responsibility).
  - Provide appropriate recognition and rewards for the project achievements of the staff member.
  - Arrange for a new assignment for the staff member as appropriate.

  This process addresses both individuals leaving a project at various junctures in the life cycle as well as those groups of individuals who close out and leave the project as a cohesive project team upon completion of project objectives.

  The project manager will have particular responsibility to identify, confirm, and announce subsequent project team member assignments as a matter of reducing individual concerns about their next role in the relevant organization. Such concerns need to be managed because they can arise prematurely to impact individual and group work performance before all project objectives have been achieved. This concern may not be as much of a factor for individuals who simultaneously hold operational positions in the organization. However, it can be a primary concern for individuals who rely on project assignments to maintain their tenure with the organization.
- *Manage Terminations*—This action represents the release of a project team member from the project and from the performing organization. There are three primary reasons for project resource terminations:
  - A business decision has been made to discontinue the individual's position.
  - There is no follow-on project assignment currently available for the individual.
  - A decision has been made in conjunction with HR department guidance to release the individual based on inability to achieve performance standards or other personnel-based action.

The organization should define the process needed by project managers to handle project team member terminations, including the involvement of resource managers, the HR department, and specification of PMO responsibilities in such matters. In the absence of a formal process, close collaboration with the HR department is strongly recommended.

10.3 PROJECT STAFF TRAINING AND DEVELOPMENT

Project Staff Training and Development is a practice used to help individuals and teams to increase competencies in the discipline of project management and in their selected technical profession. Development efforts also help individuals to become better project team members, and they help project teams to become more cohesive and effective in their work efforts.

An organization that conducts projects will inherently need project managers and project team members who are qualified to participate in the project management effort. An organization would not think of assigning an untrained or otherwise unqualified person to perform technical work on a project—the individual probably would not produce very much. Yet, organizations sometimes fail to recognize the fundamental need for training and development of project managers and their teams, and they assign partially qualified individuals to oversee critical aspects of their business—the management of projects. Professional discipline studies will often introduce aspects of project management in conjunction with technical or academic training. However, focused training in project management is needed to prepare individuals for the broad range of roles, responsibilities, and uses of practices that effectively address the project management aspect of business.

Concept of This Practice

The purpose of this practice is to provide the project manager (and the organization) with recommendations for identifying and using training and development activities in the project management environment. To a large extent, any established PMO would have a lead role in establishing that training and development capability in the organization. In the absence of a PMO or other formal project management training, the project manager needs to examine training opportunities offered by the organization as well as any available commercial programs that can be used to satisfy staff development needs in the project management environment.

Project Staff Training and Development can be performed at any time during the project management life cycle, as addressed in the following two sections.

- Project Stakeholder Training and Education
- Project Management Training
- Project Team Development

The organization should use the PMO, its cadre of project managers, and other qualified resources, some of which can be found in the HR department, to apply or otherwise build upon the staff training and development activities prescribed in this practice.

Project Stakeholder Training and Education

Project training and education is the underpinning of an effective project management environment. It provides individuals with the skill, knowledge, and competencies needed to implement project management as well as technical and business concepts and practices.

Project managers, with PMO training program setup support, can use the following list to examine training needs for project team members and other stakeholders in the project management environment.

- *Project Manager Training*—This represents training afforded project managers and emerging project leaders. The organization should consider defining training requirements for entry, standard, and advanced project manager levels. Also, project managers should be considered for selected types of technical training, particularly advanced technical or technology training, and relevant business training.
- *Project Manager Certification*—In addition to routine project manager training, the organization may also consider training that facilitates or otherwise supports internal and external project manager certification. This consideration represents identification of special training programs that focus on helping project managers to achieve skill, knowledge, and competency that qualify them for professional certification.
- *Professional Training*—Technical and business training should be integrated into the project management training program where possible. In some cases, separate training programs or courses will be needed to enable the individual to advance within a particular professional discipline or career pursuit. The organization should address these additional training requirements relative to the needs of individuals and the business interests of the organization.
- *Team Member Training*—Project team members are too often neglected in the delivery of project management training. It is through the combination of training and experience on the job that project team members gain the skill and knowledge to advance to become project managers. Additionally, the organization will benefit from project team members who readily understand the concepts and practices of project management in which they participate. The project manager should identify training requirements for

project team members, which could include some or all of the basic training courses available to project managers. The more the project team members know about project management, the more projects will have successful outcomes.

- *Executive Familiarization*—Too often, executives and senior managers are excluded from consideration for project management training. It is acknowledged that they do not require the details of project management competency that are needed by project managers. It also is recognized that members of senior management inherently do not have available time for extended training. However, an organization would be remiss in excluding executives and senior managers from gaining insight into and understanding of modern project management concepts and practices. The organization should identify training requirements normally in the form of shorter, one-half to one-day familiarization training or orientation programs for executives and senior managers in the organization. If possible, participation in longer training programs is recommended.
- *Stakeholder Familiarization and Training*—The PMO staff, adjunct project staff, and business unit participants are key stakeholders who would benefit from training conducted in the project management environment. The PMO staff will likely require participation in both standard and advanced project management training as a means to ensure a common frame of reference for the oversight, control, and support that they will provide. They also may require specialized training associated with PMO functions of process development, tools selection, etc. Individuals who serve in adjunct project roles may also benefit from project management training. This includes people in the HR department, legal department, procurement department, and others that participate in project activities on less than a full-time basis. The organization should define training requirements for such stakeholders.
- *Vendor/Contractor Integration*—Small vendor/contractor organizations (i.e., individual or one- to two-person operations) can be included in training requirements defined for the project management environment. This is particularly appropriate when vendors/contractors play a recurring role in the organization's project efforts over time. Also, larger vendor/contractor organizations can be influenced to consider training relevant to their participation in projects. The organization/PMO should design and convey vendor/contractor training requirements that are consistent with the training requirements specified for its own project managers and project team members.

In addition to these "standard" training and development activities, each project may have needs for special training related to such matters as new technology, new procedures, new software applications, etc. The project manager will need to identify any special training requirements and arrange for project team and stakeholder training to satisfy those project-unique requirements.

Project Management Training

The organization should examine options for training conducted in the project management environment, which is normally a responsibility of the PMO. In turn, each project manager will be able to identify the different training programs available as project team training needs for the project at hand are determined. This includes consideration of the following standard training program categories:

- *Core Project Management Courses*—Identify the several essential project management courses that are recommended or required for all project managers and, possibly, for project team members. Specify any preferred presentation order for course attendance and indicate any certificate associated with completion of each course and the overall curriculum.
- *Advanced and Optional Project Management Courses*—Identify the several project management courses that will be available to those individuals who have completed the core curriculum and who need advanced or specialized training otherwise not covered by the core curriculum. This may also include training in use of project management tools and project management methodology user training.
- *Technical Courses*—Identify training courses designed to support technical work activities associated with project efforts. This may also include any just-in-time training that satisfies business interests or provides for technical qualification.
- *Professional Development Courses*—The nature of individual assignments in the project management environment may prompt consideration for team member participation in professional development courses. These courses should include training that helps develop individual business skill and knowledge.
- *Executive Courses and Workshops*—Identify those project management training courses, workshops, seminars, and forums that are applicable to senior management involvement in and understanding of the project management environment. This category of training should include at least one course or workshop that enables executives and senior managers to quickly gain familiarization with the modern project management concepts and practices being implemented by the PMO.

The PMO can collaborate with the internal or external training resources to arrange training and make the training course schedule available to project managers. Some training programs or courses of instruction could be made available to project managers and their project teams as "on demand" programs.

Project Team Development

The project team is the fundamental staffing unit in the project management environment. When there is more than one person assigned to a project effort, a project team is formed—formally or informally. An effective project management environment necessitates that project teams be productive as early as possible on each project effort, and it usually falls on the project manager to facilitate the required team cohesion in a short time period.

Project team development activities can be formal or informal. Ideally, the organization recognizes the need for team development, and the PMO is assigned to oversee that effort. The following subsections provide some guidance for developing project teams.

Stages of Project Team Development

A standard model for examining project team development was prepared by Bruce Tuckman.* His model specifies the progressive stages of group development (project team or otherwise) and defines the characteristics of team evolution as highlighted here.

- *Forming*—There is high dependency on the project leader for guidance, including a need to respond to many team member questions. Project team member roles and responsibilities are unclear, and there is no discernable agreement about goals and objectives among team members.
- *Storming*—Uncertainties persist as project team members vie for position and the project leader's attention, and some power struggles may occur. The team still lacks focus on common objectives, and consensus decisions are difficult. Compromises may be needed to enable progress in the team's work.
- *Norming*—Roles and responsibilities become clear and accepted as commitment builds and the group finds consensus and begins work toward common goals and objectives. Big decisions are made by group agreement, and smaller decisions may be delegated to individuals. The project leader is generally respected in this stage, and team member socializing may become more prevalent as a demonstration of cohesiveness.
- *Performing*—Project team members act on a shared vision to achieve objectives with a high degree of autonomy, and they now tend to look out for one another; conflict may still occur, but is more easily resolved. The team does not require the project leader's guidance for work efforts.
- *Adjourning*—The purpose of the group has been fulfilled, and the time to break apart the project team has come. Project team members may become vulnerable to feelings of "loss" associated with team breakup or insecurities related to the next work assignment. Team and individual recognition and reward are appropriate at this stage in the team's development, showing them that, in becoming a mature and cohesive team, they have brought value to the project effort.

The project manager should maintain an awareness of the development stage at which the project team is operating. Also, the project manager should consider any team development activities that can facilitate early team advancements toward greater team cohesion.

Assessment of Project Team Development

It is in the project manager's best interest to have an efficient, highly cohesive team working on each project. In conjunction with established practices, the project manager can examine aspects of team dynamics as a basis for planning and accomplishing project team development.

The PMO should establish a formal or informal means for project managers to examine project team member activities and interactions in order to determine strengths and weaknesses encountered by the particular project team composition. Aspects of team dynamics to examine could include

- Observed or measured project team "stage of development"
- Frequency and types of discernable favorable behavior (e.g., collaboration, effective communication and listening)
- Frequency and types of discernable ineffective behavior (e.g., personality conflicts, disagreements, disgruntlement, and adverse emotional reaction)
- Situations of demonstrated leadership by individual team members (e.g., consensus building, encouraging and facilitating others' achievements, and volunteering for special or additional duties that contribute to project success)
- Situations of demonstrated indifference by individual team members (e.g., withdrawal from team activities, frustration, limited active participation, and missed deadlines)

* Tuckman, B. W., and Jensen, M. A., 1977, Stages of Small Group Development Revisited, *Group and Organizational Studies*, Vol. 2, pp. 419–427.

- Variations of project team member responses to project manager leadership and management styles
- Variations of project team member personality traits demonstrated in the project management environment

This type of assessment should be pursued from a positive perspective—a focus on making the project team more effective rather than a practice to identify poor performance. To that end, such an assessment should normally be transparent to project team members.

Project Team Development Activities

As project size and complexity grows, so does, normally, team size and complexity. A smaller two- or three-person project team could benefit from certain types of team development activities. A larger, more diverse, and possibly geographically separated project team distinctly requires team development activities to ensure project success.

The following is a partial list of some recommended project team development activities that can be introduced into the organization for use by the project manager, and that can serve to facilitate the progression to a cohesive project team.

- *Team Assessments*—There is a variety of methods that can be used to examine current team cohesiveness and provide a "road map" for achieving any further team development that is needed. The 360-degree assessment is prevalent means for personal discovery, in which each member contributes to a self-assessment as well as providing personal perceptions of other team members. This method is usually led by a trained facilitator or examiner, and compiled results are shared with all participating team members. Other assessment methods can also be used to provide valuable insight into the group's disposition, including such matters as (technical) competency assessments, performance reviews, qualification training evaluations, and individual leadership assessments. Also, an examination of pending team membership can be conducted prior to team formation as a means to identify those team members who will likely contribute most to early team cohesiveness.
- *Team Meetings*—This type of activity provides a forum for communication and collaboration between and among project team members, which is an essential element for developing team cohesiveness. The better individuals communicate, the stronger the team becomes in terms of its maturity. Team meetings earlier in the project can be used to introduce preferred or prescribed meeting formats and can test methods of communication and interaction that will maximize team effectiveness. Also, the team meeting can be used to examine and discuss group dynamics on the project team and facilitate resolutions to problems and conflicts that occur during earlier team development stages. However, this requires that the project manager (or other qualified person in a leadership role) be fairly well versed in facilitating such group discussions and activities at project team meetings.
- *Team-Building Activities*—Perhaps all of the items in this list can be considered to be team-building activities, but the intended focus of this one is on learning and practicing effective techniques for individual actions and interactions based on group dynamics. The organization's internal training unit, the HR department, or even an external consultant can provide relevant project team facilitation to advance individual understanding of group dynamics concepts and to demonstrate the benefits to be derived from applying effective techniques through practice scenarios with the project team.
- *Team Member Training*—Training and, in particular, learning contribute to increased personal competency in the subject matter covered. Technical training is always an option for personal development, and it often serves to elevate esteem if that is desired or needed in the context of team development. However, there are other areas of training that can be used as more direct influences on project team development. For instance, training in group dynamics itself should enhance awareness of individual contributions to the team and help individuals to create or renew their personal commitment as team members. Likewise, any training in areas of leadership or interpersonal skills will also have a direct impact on individual contributions to team development. Such topics include
  - Problem Solving
  - Decision Making
  - Conflict Resolution
  - Interpersonal Communication
  - Professionalism
  - Time Management
  - Negotiation

Consider these topics when examining team member training that will be applied for team development purposes.

- *Team-Based Incentives*—Work incentives can be defined simply in terms of monetary reward or time off from work. When such incentives are established and aligned with team performance, and not just individual performance, there is reason then for individuals to contribute favorably to team interactions and team work efforts that achieve the preferred level of team development. Such incentives could be prepared for work teams or for the entire project team. They could be time based as well as achievement based. The difficulty in this method lies in determining the discrete criteria that will be used to measure achievement of the incentive rewards. The HR department can usually contribute some good ideas here consistent with the existing culture of the organization.

- *Team Member "Spot Promotions"*—This is a special form of incentive that elevates an individual team member to a higher-level role and responsibility than initially assigned. Such a "promotion" might only apply to the project at hand, but it can be designed to examine the individual for a more permanent promotion in the organization. This incentive can be applied for purposes of motivating the individual toward a better understanding of team dynamics, or it can be done because the project manager anticipates value from the individual's influence with other team members as a result of the newly assigned position and responsibilities.
- *Team Member Social Events*—This is a special form of the team meeting but has a focus on interpersonal interactions rather than solely on business. It can be used at early stages in the project to help individuals get to know, and become comfortable with, one another, or it can be used later in the project to reinforce the team development level that has been achieved. It normally provides for a casual environment, perhaps at an off-site location, where project team members can hold conversations and build more personal relationships.

Chapter 11

Project Communication Management

Project Communication Management represents the activities associated with the creation, collection, distribution, storage, and end disposition of project information, and the identification of responsibilities for project team members and other project stakeholders who participate in project communication management. It provides the critical links among people, ideas, and information that are necessary for project management success.

The organization's knowledge management function is addressed under this practice area and prescribes a capability to communicate and collaborate within the project management environment. As well, stakeholders in the business environment of the performing organization are identified and managed. A project management office (PMO) needs to be involved in the creation of any viable project communication and knowledge management capability.

The project manager has responsibility for implementing and managing the project communication process at the project level. There are three practices associated with the *Project Communication Management* practice area:

- Project Knowledge Management
- Project Stakeholder Management
- Project Communication Implementation

The PMO, if available, should be highly involved in setting up a major portion of this project knowledge management and project information management capability within the project management environment.

11.1 PROJECT KNOWLEDGE MANAGEMENT

The emerging concepts of knowledge management are a prominent topic of debate: what it is, what it does, and who should use it. For purposes of this methodology, project knowledge management will be examined as a function of collaboration and coordination used to enable increased project management capability and to achieve business value.

This concept elevates fundamental communications in the project management environment from mere data transfer to conveyance of ideas, perceptions, experiences, and interpretations that transcend the simple exchange of information. When using knowledge management concepts, the traditional aspects of project management reporting and project information management are properly retained but are generally adapted to be more timely, comprehensive and widespread among stakeholders, and relevant to business interests.

Project Knowledge Management capability is not created for each project but is a capability established to support all projects. Therefore, management direction and support along with PMO involvement are inherently required to create a *Project Knowledge Management* function that could include any of the following features:

- Develop a preferred approach to project performance reporting.
- Construct an effective project management information system (PMIS).
- Facilitate project manager, project team, and project stakeholder collaboration.
- Manage activities of virtual and geographically dispersed project teams.
- Implement a project management knowledge reference library.
- Capture and utilize individuals' wisdom, perspective, intuitions, and experiences.
- Promote a learning organization among project managers.

The organization's knowledge management efforts should create a well-informed project management environment that operates efficiently, communicates effectively, and responds knowledgeably in providing customer and business solutions.

In turn, that capability will be accessed and used by project managers, project team members, project executives, and other stakeholders across the performing organization.

Concept of This Practice

This practice provides the project manager, the project team, and the organization with a means to access and use relevant information and knowledge about project and project management. This includes both real-time project information and archived, library-based project information.

Project Knowledge Management requirements for each project are usually determined by the project manager in the Plan Phase. The activities associated with managing project knowledge continue through the project's Post Phase.

This practice deals with using the following capabilities of project knowledge management that are preestablished for use within the organization:

- Project Management Information System (PMIS)
- Executive Dashboard
- Project Management Library
- Online Project Collaboration
- Other Knowledge Management Tools

Project Management Information System

The PMIS represents the fundamental capabilities of information capture and exchange within the project management environment. It is the traditional term and approach applied to project data and information handling. Also, it retains high importance within the context of *Project Knowledge Management*. The organization should strive to maximize its capability in project information management.

Traditionally, the PMIS has been a printed document, often characterized by the name "project binder." Today, information management has become an automated process that can be readily applied in the project management environment. Therefore, an examination of information components should consider printed tools and documents as well as automated or electronic tools and documents. If an automated PMIS capability has been established, the project manager and the PMO will need to identify software application features that help manage needed project management information. The following are prominent information components that could be selected by project managers and other stakeholders for use on individual projects.

Project Plans

The organization should design and implement the means to prepare and access the various plans used for project management:

- *Project Work Plan*—The project work breakdown structure (WBS) with cost, schedule, and resources identified and appended for each work element. See the *Project Work Plan Development* practice for more information about this plan.
- *Primary Project Management Plans*—Documents that are normally prepared on every project to expand on concepts and provide routine guidance in six important project management areas:
  - Risk management plan
  - Quality management plan
  - Change management plan
  - Communication management plan
  - Staff management plan
  - Vendor management plan

  See the *Primary Project Management Plan Development* practice for more information.
- *Project Management Support Plans*—Documents that are prepared to expand project management guidance, as needed, with regard to organizational policies, achievement of business objectives, industry practices, project complexity and risk factors, and the experience level of the project team; these plans may be prepared on an as-needed basis and used independently or appended to the project management support plan. See the *Project Support Plans Development* practice for a partial list of support plans.

Project Reports

The organization should design and implement the means to prepare and access project management reports, which can be used, as needed, for each project:

- *Project Progress Reports*—Normally prepared by project team members to indicate progress toward accomplishing assigned project tasks, with primary distribution to the project manager.
- *Project Status Reports*—Commonly prepared by project managers to indicate the current project status relative to planned cost, schedule, and resource utilization; identify problems, issues, and their resolution; specify deliverables and achievement of project objectives; confirm contract compliance or note contract modifications; and address the accomplishment of business objectives, with distribution to the project sponsor, executive control board, and the PMO.

- *Project Portfolio Reports*—Customarily prepared by the PMO and containing aggregate results or indicators of project performance, business case fulfillment, and recommendations for project continuation or alternative actions (such as project audits, temporary hold, termination, etc.), with primary distribution to the executive control board.
- *Project Audit Reports*—Usually prepared by the lead auditor (which is sometimes the project manager) to present the findings and recommendations of a project or technical audit or review, with distribution to the project sponsor and the PMO, as well as to other project stakeholders as deemed appropriate.

Project Management Documents

The organization should design and implement the means to prepare and access project management documents, which include the following common types for project manager use:

- *Project Directories*—Fundamental listing of project stakeholders, to include contact information for each person listed, that usually includes directories for customers, project staff, vendors, and management.
- *Project Initiation Documents*—A collection of documents (sometimes presented as "tools" in this methodology) that are prepared to assist in project selection and project initiation but usually still monitored throughout the project, including
  - Project Definition
  - Project Estimates
  - Project Classification
  - Project Financial Analyses
  - Project Business Case

  See relevant practices in the Project Initiation practice area for more content details.
- *Project Charter*—Specification of project management authority, funding allowance, and authorization to start project management and technical life-cycle activities. This document is sometimes incorporated as an element of the project definition document.
- *Change Request Log*—Management of project scope change requests, change request reviews and analyses, scope change approval, and change implementation actions.
- *Project Issues Log*—Identification and resolution management of project customer, project sponsor, and project team issues, along with issues in other project areas.
- *Actions Log*—Identification and management of critical project or technical responses to inquiries and for rectification of conditions (including postmeeting actions), which are not otherwise covered in the project work plan—usually applies to actions arising from the moment and resolved or completed in a short period of time.

Technical Plans and Documentation

The organization should design and implement the means to prepare and access project technical documents, which include the following that the project manager may use:

- Technical requirements document
- Technical specifications document
- Engineering and technical site survey
- Technical standards and procedures
- Technical design document
- Technical review document
- Technical testing and validation plan
- Product quality control plan
- Configuration management plan
- Construction and engineering plan
- Health and safety plan
- Inspection plan
- Logistics support plan
- Make-or-buy plan
- Manufacturing plan
- Field support plan
- Product life cycle plan
- Regulatory compliance plan
- Systems integration plan
- Tooling plan

See the *Project Support Plans Development* practice for a partial list of technical plans.

Contract Documentation

The organization should design and implement the means to prepare and access project contract documents, which include the following that can be used by the project manager:

- Customer technical and business proposal
- Customer contract
- Customer contract modifications
- Customer deliverable acceptance documents
- Customer invoice management
- Vendor/contractor proposal
- Vendor/contractor contracts
- Vendor/contractor contract modifications
- Vendor contractor document submittals and reports
- Vendor/contractor deliverable acceptance documents
- Vendor/contractor invoice management

See the Project Contract Management practice area for more guidance on using contract documents.

Meetings and Collaborative Events

The organization should design and implement the means to prepare and access information and documents related to project meetings and similar collaborative events (e.g., technical reviews, performance reviews, technical solution discussions, and so on), which include managing information related to

- Meeting agenda preparation
- Meeting scheduling (date, time, location, and method, such as in-person, online, via phone, etc.)
- Notification of meeting participants
- Meeting actions and follow-up responsibilities

Also, information should be managed for meetings and collaborative events that are conducted online, if that becomes a meeting method within the organization.

Executive Dashboard

The *executive dashboard* is normally an automated, online extension of the PMIS whereby project information can be viewed as a condensed and often graphical representation of the project status—in real time. Its name corresponds to instruments on an automobile's dashboard panel, which may vary from graduated dials to displays of specific values. Despite the naming convention, executives are not the only project stakeholders who can benefit from this type of information access. However, executive project information needs will usually be the primary influences in the design and development of the executive dashboard.

The project manager should review the requirements for contributing to the current executive dashboard database and specify project data collection that will fulfill those requirements. The organization can consider the following information elements when specifying content for the executive dashboard that serves the key project stakeholders of the organization.

Primary Dashboard Indicators

- Project Status
  - Green indicator—Project is proceeding according to plans.
  - Yellow indicator—Project has some variation, but it falls within allowable tolerances.
  - Red indicator—Project has some critical variations from plans.

  These indicators can be presented for the overall project or for each of the three critical work plan elements: cost, schedule, and resource utilization.
- Project Milestones
  - Project milestones
  - Milestone dates
  - Milestone achievement status (completed/not completed)
- Project Deliverables
  - Project deliverables
  - Deliverable dates
  - Deliverable achievement status (delivered/not delivered)

Secondary Dashboard Indicators

- Project Risk Management Performance
  - Risk events (for past project periods to date, perhaps by life cycle phase)
  - Risk response implementation (yes/no)
  - Risk control effectiveness (percentage of impact reduction)
- Project Issues Management
  - Issue date
  - Issue type (per categories such as customer, project team, vendor/contractor, etc.)
  - Issue description statement
  - Issue resolution statement
  - Issue status (open/closed)
- Customer Invoice Status
  - Invoices submitted (invoice ID, date, amount)
  - Invoice amounts paid (invoice ID, date, amount)
- Vendor/Contractor Invoice Status
  - Invoices submitted (invoice ID, date, amount)
  - Invoice amounts paid (invoice ID, date, amount)

This sample listing represents a few common executive dashboard content elements. The organization and PMO can decide which of these or other information elements are needed for dashboards implemented in the organization.

In that regard, the dashboard should contain sufficient information to give users an adequate high-level perspective of project status and performance. It should also provide links to more detailed project information according to individual user needs.

Project Management Library

The project management library is a reference capability (normally online) that virtually all stakeholders in the project management environment can use. Although selected content may warrant access control, a large part of this project knowledge management component should be accessible to project managers, project sponsors, and project team members.

The PMO can use the inherent automated capabilities of the project management information system and supplement them as necessary with other knowledge management system components to provide a complete and comprehensive project management library facility that contains the information elements described in the following text.

The project manager should determine the project team's responsibility for contributing to any project management library elements.

- *Project Lessons Learned*—Information and recommendations from previously completed projects that can be applied to current project planning efforts. For quick reference, lessons learned can be captured and organized into the following categories:
  - Customer feedback
  - Project manager feedback
  - Project team feedback
  - Project estimating results
  - Technical and technology feedback
  - Executive manager feedback and guidance
- *Project Archives*—A repository for project management plans and technical documents that can support post-project analyses and studies, provide reusable technical and project management solutions, and contribute to the examination of project management and technical process effectiveness. Project archives also may be aligned with the project team knowledge spaces described in the next section.
- *Policy Guidance*—A reference to applicable policy and governance information that has application in the project management environment. This may comprise such policies that direct use of project management and technical methodologies, tools and practices, standard business objectives for every project, and industry and government regulatory guidance and mandates.
- *Industry News*—A reference to current news articles and publication content that deal with pertinent business, technical, and project management topics. This can be managed as a collection of industry-relevant news and information that is captured and stored for later access by users, or it can be represented by links to specified Web pages that are compiled and categorized for subsequent user access via the Internet. This information collection effort can include automated and manual information searches based on relevant key words, as well as monitoring and participating in online business, technical and project management forums, chat rooms, and relevant news sources.
- *Papers and Presentations*—An online repository for relevant internal and external technical papers and presentations dealing with business, technical, and project management topics. Information that is submitted at professional conferences and conventions or obtained from those sources or individuals can be categorized and stored for access by individuals in the project management environment.
- *Project Audits Database*—An online repository of the different project and project management audits that the organization, PMO, or project manager conducts. In general, this is essentially a document repository, but some organizations may want to construct a more rigorous audit quantification system that provides a more detailed automated analysis capability. The project audits database will necessarily have restricted user access, and associated data can be used for subsequent internal studies in the project management environment.

Online Project Collaboration

The organization can maximize collaboration in the project management environment by implementing knowledge management tools. In the context of this methodology, collaboration means enabling project team members and other stakeholders to communicate and exchange information that helps to achieve project objectives.

The organization and PMO should consider three prominent tools for use by the project manager as a means to facilitate project team collaboration:

Project Team Knowledge Spaces

This is an online information center—often represented in Web-page format—that is established for every major project; however, other configurations may also be used. For example, the project manager, cohesive project teams working multiple projects, and even business units can set up team spaces. Possible content for such knowledge spaces includes

- Project charter
- Project definition and other descriptive information
- Project status information
- Project logbooks
- Project reports
- Project stakeholder directories (telephone, location, e-mail address, and so on)
- Customer information, including links to customer Web sites
- Vendor/contractor information, including links to vendor/contractor Web sites
- Links to relevant industry news and information Web sites
- Links to project plans and technical documentation (see *Handover Spaces* later in list)
- Links to relevant project management information portals
- Links for project management methodology access (such as process and practice guidance, as well as forms, checklists and templates, and so forth)

- A dedicated project team chat room to chronicle project management and technical discussions pertaining to the project (see also *General Discussion Rooms*, later in list)
  The project team knowledge space is an online location that provides quick and easy access to project information that the project team and other stakeholders require. This tool's Web-based nature makes its accessible to geographically dispersed project team members, and it will often be subject to access controls.

Product Review and Handover Spaces

This is an online repository of project and technical documentation for access by authorized project team members. This online workspace is where project and project management deliverables are created and stored, and it can be used to

- Store and access project plans, including retrieval for review and approval
- Store and access technical documents, with particular emphasis on retrieval and use of documents by different project team members (possibly at different geographical locations) for iterative design and development of project deliverables
- Store and access project deliverable electronic files and documents for quality review and approval, both internally and by customers
- Store and access vendor/contractor electronic file and document deliverables
- Provide simple or extensive feedback from technical and management reviews, as well as next-step guidance for iterative design and development activities
- Facilitate access to iterative deliverables for use in the concurrent engineering of other project deliverables (and sometimes access to deliverables on other projects)
  The product review and handover space can be used to convey any deliverable design and development documentation that project team members need, including access to actual project deliverables that are constructed in electronic formats.

General Discussion Rooms

This is an online collaboration feature that traverses the project management environment. It can be developed for a wide audience, such as all stakeholders in the project management environment, or for a specified user group, such as all project managers. It presents a capability for ongoing knowledge and information exchange about project management, which can be conveyed in formats such as live online chats and threaded project management topic forums. One or more online discussion rooms can be developed to provide such capabilities as

- Project manager knowledge and information exchange forum
- Online project management mentoring through an "ask the expert" forum
- New techniques and emerging technologies discussion forum
- Real-time distribution (and acknowledgment of receipt) of lessons learned
- Organizational news and announcements about current and new projects forum

The introduction of general discussion rooms emphasizes a cross-project and cross-business unit collaboration capability within the relevant organization.

Other Knowledge Management Tools

The concepts of *Project Knowledge Management* generally retain the traditional considerations of strong project communication while presenting a relatively new focus on intensive collaboration or interaction within the project management environment. To that end, this methodology does not presume to provide a comprehensive examination of emerging knowledge management concepts and practices. However, there are other project knowledge management tools and considerations that an advanced organization and its PMO may want to consider. The following list briefly describes a few.

- *Project Management Methodology System Access*—Provides interconnectivity between knowledge sources and the processes and practices of the preferred project management methodology.
- *Customer Information Knowledge Spaces*—Provides capability for customers to have their own Web page on the relevant organization's knowledge management system as a means to access information (such as project status, reports, and deliverables) relative to the customer project being conducted and possibly including an interactive communication capability, together with contract and invoice information.
- *Vendor/Contractor Knowledge Spaces*—Provides capability for preferred vendors and contractors to have their own Web page on the relevant organization's knowledge management system as a means to access relevant project information, as well as to provide information about their participation and progress, and their contract and invoice information.
- *Project Portfolio Management System Access*—Provides interconnectivity between knowledge sources and the

processes and practices of the preferred project portfolio management system.

11.2 PROJECT STAKEHOLDER MANAGEMENT

Project stakeholders are the individuals who have some type of vested interest in achieving a successful project outcome. These individuals can be internal or external to the performing organization, and it is essential that their responsibilities, affiliations, and participation be identified as a means to understanding the nature of their project or business interests.

While stakeholders normally have a common interest in achieving a successful project outcome, it should be noted that various stakeholders could also have different views or perspectives with regard to how project success is achieved. In other words, their desire to see the project succeed is relative to the associated business success that can be achieved within their areas of responsibility. This does not necessarily place stakeholders in competitive or opposing positions, but it will influence their judgment and decisions relative to project participation and project performance support. The project manager needs to know that a variety of stakeholder influences do exist in the project management environment and that early identification of project stakeholders will help to assess and manage the impact of that influence.

Concept of This Practice

This practice provides the project manager, project team, and the organization with a means to identify the project stakeholders for purposes of defining participating roles and responsibilities, managing project stakeholder participation, and determining project stakeholder needs and interests.

Project Stakeholder Management usually begins with a project stakeholder analysis that is performed by the project manager for each project. This is normally done in the Profile Phase, and this practice may be revisited as any new stakeholders are identified during the course of the project. The following categories of stakeholder involvement are considered in this practice as a basis for conducting project stakeholder analysis activities:

- Internal Project Performance Stakeholders
- Internal Business Performance Stakeholders
- Internal Support and Part-Time Performance Stakeholders
- Customer Stakeholders
- Vendor/Contractor Stakeholders
- Other Project Stakeholders

Stakeholders can be identified, listed, and analyzed, as needed, in the profile records of each relevant stakeholder group—customers, staff, vendors, and management.

Project stakeholder analysis begins with a brief look at a model of the *project management environment*, and then follows to examine a brief description of each of the potential stakeholders in the project management environment according the categories listed earlier.

The Project Management Environment

For purposes of establishing a common frame of reference, we define the *project management environment* as that portion of the *relevant organization* that accomplishes technical product and service delivery through direct or indirect involvement and influence on projects, including the people, practices, and tools (and sometimes facilities and equipment) used to achieve project outcomes, including extensions to customers, vendors, and other external agencies that have direct or indirect involvement and influence on any project. Figure II.11.1 presents a high-level model of the stakeholders that are commonly found in the project management environment.

The diagram notably depicts the intersection of the *project environment* (vertical oval) and the *business environment* (horizontal oval). It shows the prominent presence of the project executive, PMO, and project manager at a central point in the depiction. This helps to illustrate the integration of business and project management operations that intersect in the project management environment.

The diagram also shows a general delineation of internal and external stakeholders, where business units highlight the cast of internal stakeholders and the customer normally represents the most prominent external stakeholder.

Internal Business Performance Stakeholders

This stakeholder category represents those project participants that provide senior-level direction and decisions to guide project management toward the achievement of business interests and objectives. The following are prominent stakeholders in this category:

- *Project Executive (Sponsor)*—This senior manager has responsibility for project performance, including decision authority for project selection, continuation, and termination, and associated authorization of project funding. In some organizations, these responsibilities are deferred to a committee of executives or senior managers. However, this role still retains sponsorship and responsibility for the alignment of projects with strategic business objectives, as may be performed using a project portfolio management system, if implemented in the relevant organization. Related position

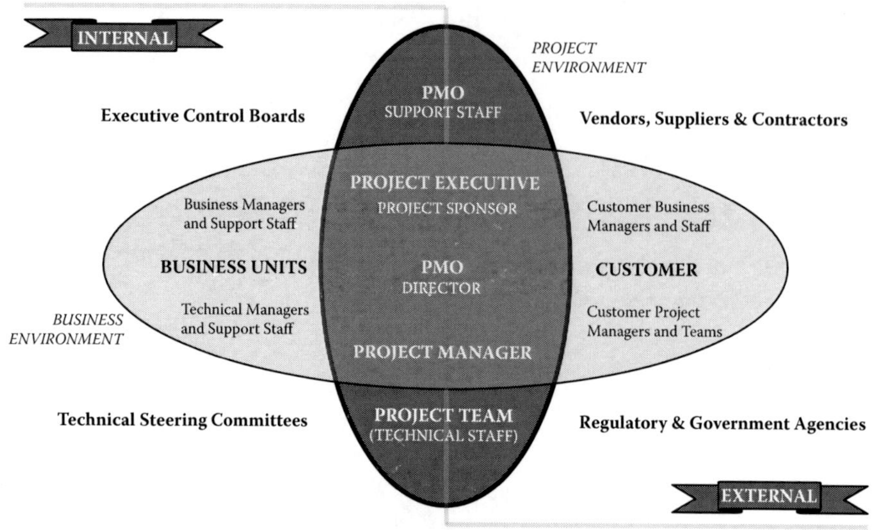

Figure II.11.1 Stakeholders in the project management environment.

titles include Project Sponsor and executive head of a business unit; in some smaller organizations, this role could be assigned at the C-level.

- *PMO Director*—The head of the project management office has responsibility for establishing and conducting project management oversight, control, and support across all projects in the relevant organization. The PMO Director advises and collaborates with the Project Executive, Executive Control Board, and other executives and senior management teams regarding overall project management capability and maturity within the organization. This role also provides for aggregate reports on individual and collective project activities and status. Program and Project Managers may report to or otherwise be aligned with the PMO Director, as per the established organizational structure. Related position titles may vary to include PMO Manager, Chief Project Officer (CPO), Chief Technical Officer (CTO), and Vice President for Project Management.
- *Executive Control Board*—This group of executives or senior managers resides within the relevant organization, and deliberates and decides on the capability instituted in the project management environment. It also may have responsibility for project selection, continuation, termination, and funding (when deferred by the Project Executive or by business mandate), and thereby it has vested interest in individual project performance. Related titles for this board include Project Management Oversight Committee, Project Control Board, and Executive Management Team.
- *Technical Steering Committee*—This group, usually having some executive-level representation, convenes to deliberate and decide technical processes and practices applied in the project management environment and in association with technical elements of project performance. Such committees could have special technical purposes, and there could be a committee aligned with each major technical discipline within the relevant organization. These groups usually collaborate with the PMO to achieve integration of technical processes with project management practices and thereby would have a vested interest in technical aspects of project performance. A variety of groups by different titles can be established to represent technical discipline interests, including the following examples:
  - Product Development Control Board
  - Technical Process Control Board
  - Configuration Management Team
  - Engineering Design Committee
  - Scientific Analysis Committee
  - Test and Acceptance Procedures Committee
  - Construction Management Board
  - Manufacturing Process Control Board
  - Technical Advisory Council

An additional stakeholder group (not depicted in the diagram) may sometimes emerge to influence the project management environment—the Board of Directors. This stakeholder group represents the highest level of executive management in the relevant organization and can include the CEO, CIO, CFO, and other C-level positions. This stakeholder group also represents stockholder and owner interests in business performance. It would be rare for these stakeholders to be visible in the project management environment, unless the enterprise is a relatively small business. However, the absence of visibility does not mean lack of interest. These stakeholders undoubtedly have some measure of regard and support for project contributions to business performance and therefore will have interest and influence in the methods used to achieve business results in the project management environment.

Internal Project Performance Stakeholders

This stakeholder category represents those project participants that are directly involved in conducting and managing the project effort. This group is normally responsible for producing required project deliverables and for achieving specified project objectives. The following are common stakeholders in this category:

- *Program Manager*—This position is responsible for oversight and success of multiple projects—usually a collection of projects that are interrelated by similar business interests, technical solutions, or customer base. This position (not specifically depicted in the diagram) will normally be aligned with the PMO when it exists, or it may serve in lieu of the PMO when that entity does not exist. Otherwise, it may be aligned with technical or business management oversight groups. Related position titles include Manager of Project Managers, Program Director, and Project Director.
- *Project Manager*—This position is responsible for conducting project management activities through all phases of the project management life cycle, managing project resource utilization and performance, and fulfilling project deliverables and objectives. Related position titles include Project Leader, Project Coordinator, and Project Administrator.
- *Project Team Member*—This is an individual who is responsible for planning, managing, and performing work efforts to accomplish project objectives and deliverables, and selected project management activities, as delegated by the project manager. This position reports to the project manager, either directly or through another project team member serving in an interim management or technical leadership position. A variety of technical and managerial roles can compose the project team. Some of the common roles include
  - Assistant Project Manager
  - Technical Leader
  - Technical Staff Member
  - Technical Specialist
  - Professional Scientist/Engineering Staff Member
  - Task Leader/Supervisor
  - Craft Specialist/Laborer

In some project management environments, the project team also may be augmented by full-time or part-time participation of PMO staff members.

Internal Support and Part-Time Performance Stakeholders

This stakeholder category represents those project participants within the relevant organization that serve as adjunct or part-time project team members. Their particular business, technical, or project management skill and expertise may warrant concurrent short-term assignments on several small-to-medium projects, or they could be assigned as full-time project team members on longer projects. The following are common stakeholders in this category:

- *PMO Support Staff*—This stakeholder group reports to the PMO Director to establish and implement PMO functionality, develop project management capability in the relevant organization, and support project managers and project teams to achieve fulfillment of project deliverables and accomplishment of project objectives. Support is provided relative to the established functional capability of the PMO.
- *Business Unit Resource Manager*—This stakeholder is responsible for collaborating with the PMO and project managers to identify requirements and fulfill commitments for qualified project resources. In turn, resource managers should solicit and incorporate project manager evaluations of project team member performance into the official performance reports for each assigned individual. In some cases, the resource manager will also participate in resource acquisition—the examination of qualified candidates and hiring of selected candidates to fill project staff positions. Related titles to this position will vary by organization and industry but usually refer to any functional manager or other internal source of project team members.
- *Business Managers*—These stakeholders are the individuals who head the business units or department in the relevant organization, including their staff and designees who routinely provide business support and collaboration to project managers and the PMO. Because of their interest in business outcomes on each project, they are viable project stakeholders. On larger projects, individuals with particular business expertise could be assigned as members of the project team on a full-time or part-time basis. Some examples of business unit stakeholders include
  - Business Development Manager
  - Customer Sales Representative/Manager
  - New Product Development Manager
  - Marketing and Advertising Manager
  - Human Resources Manager
  - Legal Advisor/Legal Counselor
  - Procurement/Contracts Manager

- *Technical Managers and Support Staff*—These stakeholders are the individuals who lead the technical effort within the relevant organization, including their staff and designees who routinely provide technical support and collaboration to project managers and the PMO. Because of their interest in technical outcomes on each project, they are viable project stakeholders. On larger projects, individuals with particular technical expertise could be assigned as members of the project team on a full-time or part-time basis. Some examples of technical support stakeholders include
  - Quality Assurance Manager
  - Quality Control Manager
  - Risk Assessment Manager
  - Technical Tools Manager
  - Technical Configuration Manager
  - Technical Training Manager

Customer Stakeholders

This stakeholder category represents those project participants that have the responsibility for ensuring that project outcomes fulfill the intended business purpose or need of the customer's organization. These stakeholders are members of the customer organization, and they conduct activities to ensure that customer needs and requirements are fulfilled by the project. The stakeholders listed in this category are not always active participants on every project. However, at least one of the roles listed here is normally identified as a primary point of contact for each project effort. Stakeholders in this category could include the following:

- *Customer Executive*—This stakeholder is the senior manager in the customer environment who authorized project selection and funding, and who holds strategic-level responsibility for project success. Although not always visible in the customer's project management environment, this stakeholder is undoubtedly present and working behind the scenes. This is also the point of contact for executive level discussions, if needed.
- *Customer Project Manager*—This stakeholder is responsible for providing project oversight and control on behalf of the customer's interests and perspectives for project success. This individual also may be called the Technical Manager, who, along with any customer project team members, will be involved in developing technical requirements and specifications, participating in preparing and approving project plans, and tracking project progress, including acceptance of project deliverables. When used, this customer stakeholder can serve as a point of contact to collaborate with the performing organization's project manager on technical and sometimes business matters as well.
- *Customer Project Team Members*—These stakeholders are responsible for performing technical, business, and project management activities on customer-initiated projects. In some cases, joint project management plans are prepared, and customer project team members join the performing organization's project team in its task performance efforts. In other cases, customer project team members simply represent the customer project manager to establish an oversight presence. On many projects, there is no customer project team in the project management environment.
- *Customer End Users*—These stakeholders are responsible for helping to implement the project's technical solution in the customer's business environment. They will ultimately use the solution that is delivered by the project. They may act in lieu of or in deference to any established customer project team to implement, test, approve, and accept project deliverables. They also may be designated as the customer's project team.
- *Customer Business Manager*—This stakeholder is the default customer representative and point of contact for project efforts. This role has responsibility for initiating the project request, managing the associated project contract or agreement, and overseeing receipt and approval of project deliverables and associated invoice payments. This role is the one usually encountered on a majority of customer projects across industries and is used in lieu of a customer project manager on projects where deliverables do not require intense technical oversight, scrutiny, and test and acceptance activities.

Vendor/Contractor Stakeholders

This stakeholder category represents those project participants that have the responsibility for ensuring that project outcomes fulfill the offering of the vendor/contractor. These stakeholders are members of the vendor/contractor organization and conduct activities according to established contracts or agreements. The stakeholders listed in this category are not always active participants on every project. However, when vendors and contractors are involved in the project, at least one of the roles listed in the following is normally identified as a primary point of contact for each project effort. Stakeholders in this category could include the following:

- *Vendor/Contractor Executive*—This stakeholder is the senior manager in the vendor/contractor organization who holds business responsibility for the offering. It is this individual who normally warrants the quality of products and performance, and the fulfillment of any associated contract or agreement. This stakeholder is also the point of contact for executive-level discussions, if needed.

- *Vendor/Contractor Project Manager*—This stakeholder is responsible for leading the vendor/contractor project team in conducting assigned project tasks and achieving the prescribed technical solution to fulfill the vendor/contractor's offer. When present, this stakeholder will serve as the vendor/contractor point of contact and will coordinate and collaborate directly with the performing organization's project manager to ensure successful completion of the vendor/contractor effort.
- *Vendor/Contractor Project Team Members*—These stakeholders have the responsibility for performing technical, business, and project management activities on assigned projects. In some cases, joint project management plans are prepared, and the vendor/contractor project team members join the performing organization's project team in task efforts. In other cases, vendor/contractor project team members will work independently to accomplish assigned project tasks. A vendor/contractor project team may not be established for each vendor/contractor offering.
- *Vendor/Contractor Business Manager*—This stakeholder is the default vendor/contractor representative and point of contact for project efforts. This role is prevalent when there is a particular product or service acquired, in lieu of technical services and development work. It is the position usually encountered in business or sales transactions with a vendor/contractor organization.

Other Project Stakeholders

This stakeholder category represents an additional set of project participants that have interests in the fulfillment of all or part of the project objectives. These stakeholders can be associated with the relevant organization or be introduced from an external organization. The stakeholders in this category are not always active participants on every project. The nature of each project will determine the need for their participation. Stakeholders in this category could include

- *Regulatory and Government Agency Stakeholder*—This stakeholder group normally performs inspections or examinations within the project management environment to ascertain quality or compliance. It could include external representatives who focus on compliance issues such as those from industry or technical standards organizations, or government regulatory agencies that have mandates to ensure compliance with government contracts or laws.
- *Business Partners*—These stakeholders have interest in achieving desired investment outcomes associated with project efforts. They are not normally visible in the project management environment but may be encountered through integrated activities within business units.
- *Industry Partners*—These stakeholders have interest in achieving technical and technology solutions that advance industry standards, enlarge markets, or promote associated professional disciplines. They could be visible in the project management environment when one or more projects are involved in developing or implementing a solution of interest to the partnership. In general, industry partners may be business partners, but business partners are not inherently industry partners.

11.3 PROJECT COMMUNICATION IMPLEMENTATION

Project Communication Implementation prescribes concepts and activities for planning, developing, and using effective communication skills and procedures as an inherent part of project management.

Concept of This Practice

This practice provides the project manager, the project team, and the organization with guidance for exchanging, coordinating, and collaborating on project and project management information. The project communication actions performed will use the manual processes and automated capabilities implemented by the *Project Knowledge Management* practice.

The purpose of this practice is to identify and plan for communication on the project through various means but particularly to identify the most crucial and business-significant communication that is required (by the organization) in the course of managing the project and its associated business interests.

Project Communication Implementation begins at the onset of the Profile Phase and continues through and including the information collected and distributed in the Post Phase. This practice addresses the following project communication elements:

- Project Communication Requirements
- Project Communication Responsibility
- Project Communication Plan Preparation

Each is described in the following sections.

Project Communication Requirements

Project communication requirements generally represent the information needed by the project manager, project team members, project executive/sponsor, affiliated business managers, and project customer, as well as other project stakeholders. Project communication requirements are identified and examined relative to

- Project organization structure and stakeholder responsibility relationships
- Nature of disciplines, departments, and specialists involved in the project
- Number of project participants and their locations
- Information needs of external parties such as the media or contractors

The information needs of the project manager, team members, executive/sponsor, and customer must be analyzed. In addition to determining the information needs, this analysis should consider the methods of communicating the information (including a review of supporting technologies that can be applied) and identification of the methods that can be used to meet the communication needs of the project. The following list identifies primary project stakeholders and the associated types of project information, documentation, and collaborative interaction that they could require:

- Project Manager
  - Project policy and procedure guidance documents
  - Documents associated with project initiation (e.g., project definition, etc.)
  - Analyses associated with project selection activities (e.g., financial and risk analyses)
  - Project business case
  - Project charter and funding authorization document
  - Human resource information (e.g., employment record, performance reviews, resource manager alignment, qualifications, availability, etc.)
  - Material resource information (e.g., sourcing, cost, and delivery information)
  - Project issues and action management information (i.e., identification, action steps, and resolution)
  - Project work plan, along with primary project plans and supporting plans
  - Project schedule information and related estimations, analyses, and working papers
  - Project budget information and related estimations, analyses, and working papers
  - Project staffing information and related estimations, analyses, and working papers
  - Project team member progress reports (individuals and subgroups)
  - Project manager status report to management
  - Project manager reports to customers and stakeholders
  - Cost, schedule, and resource utilization variance data
  - Customer contract documentation and modification control log
  - Vendor contract documentation and modification control log
  - Project requirements and technical specifications and analyses documents
  - Project change control log
  - General project correspondence
  - Project tracking and control documents
  - Project meeting minutes
  - Project supply log
  - Project logistics log
  - Project newsletters and press releases
  - Special project studies and analyses
  - Project audits and technical review reports
  - Project invoices and payments

  Also, the project manager may require access to any or all of the additional information specified in subsequent categories and in some cases becomes the source for its distribution. Most items listed earlier can be delegated to a qualified team leader for routine review and handling, but the project manager must ensure the personal review (and in some cases approval) of the most critical documents.
- Project Team Members
  - Project policy and procedure guidance documents
  - Project requirements and technical specifications and analyses documents
  - Project work plan, along with primary project plans and supporting plans
  - Project team member progress reports (individuals and subgroups)
  - Project manager status report to management
  - Project change control log
  - Project issues and action management information (i.e., identification, action steps, and resolution), as appropriate
- Project Executive/Sponsor/Business Managers
  - Analyses associated with project selection activities (e.g., financial and risk analyses)
  - Project business case
  - Project charter and funding authorization document
  - Project tracking and control documents
  - Project manager status report to management
  - Project manager reports to customers and stakeholders
  - Customer contract documentation and modification control log
  - Project audits and technical review reports
- Project Customer
  - Project requirements and technical specifications and analyses documents

- Project work plan, along with primary project plans and supporting plans
- Customer contract documentation and modification control log
- Project manager reports to customers and stakeholders
- Project change control log
- Project issues and action management information (i.e., identification, action steps, and resolution), as appropriate

During the Plan Phase, this list can be used to identify the various documents and the different types of communication required by project stakeholders for incorporation in the project communication plan. This list is by no means inclusive. The organization, PMO, and individual project managers will need to define standard, preferred, and special information requirements that are applied to each project.

Project Communication Responsibility

During the Profile Phase, the project manager begins to identify communication requirements associated with the project. Requirements are usually aligned with project responsibilities:

- The first area of responsibility to be addressed is that of project management, along with associated oversight of relevant business issues and interests. This responsibility area falls primarily on the project manager, but certain responsibilities can be assigned or delegated to other qualified members of the project team, as well as involvement from the project executive/sponsor and any relevant management control board.
- The second area of responsibility deals with technical work performance and oversight. This responsibility area falls primarily to members of the project team, with project manager and technical team leader oversight. It may also extend to any aligned vendors/contractors, as well as involvement from any relevant technical advisory committee.
- A third area of responsibility, which is sometimes less obvious, is that of "readiness-to-perform," which is characterized by the availability of staff, including their personal commitment to participate and qualification to perform the project work effort. This responsibility falls on virtually all project team members, as well as other full-time and part-time project stakeholders, particularly resource managers.

It may seem difficult at times to convey responsibilities to so-called "other" stakeholders, particularly if they are not fully integrated with the project team. However, effective project management skills, supported by management's focus on achieving business results in the project management environment, can be used to influence and induce stakeholder's acceptance of most responsibilities. Other mechanisms may also be used to define and assign responsibilities, such as relevant project plans, and prominently the project communication plan (described later in this section). The following lists provide a few examples of the types of responsibilities that can be considered and assigned according to the three responsibility areas mentioned earlier.

Project Management and Business Responsibilities

- Conduct Project Management Activities
  - Initiating the project (Profile Phase)
  - Planning the project (Plan Phase)
  - Conducting the project (Perform Phase)
  - Closing out the project (Post Phase)
- Prepare/Approve Project Management Documents
  - Project plans—the project work plan, along with primary and support plans
  - Project scope management—cost, schedule, and resource utilization
  - Performance evaluations—customer, project, project team, vendor/contractor
  - Project reports—status reports, management reports, and customer reports
- Prepare/Approve Resource Management Documents
  - Resource allocations
  - Resource acquisitions and commitments
  - Resource performance evaluations
  - Resource assignments and terminations
- Prepare/Approve Contract Documents
  - Proposal and bid documents
  - Customer contract documents
  - Vendor/contractor solicitation documents
  - Vendor/contractor contract documents
  - Contract negotiations
  - Contract changes and modifications
- Prepare and Approve Funding, Fund Dispersal, and Financial Documents
  - Project charter—with initial and subsequent project funding authorizations
  - Invoices to customer
  - Invoices from vendors and contractors
  - Project expense reports
- Review/Resolve Business Issues
  - Elevate or respond to elevated issues—decisions and determinations
  - Implement project control actions
  - Conduct customer relationship management

- Conduct vendor/contractor relationship management

Technical Management Responsibilities

- Prepare/Approve Technical Plans and Documentation
  - Project supporting plans—technical guidance
  - Technical standards
  - Drawings and specifications
  - Site surveys
  - Studies and analyses
- Monitor and Guide Technical Work Performance
  - Develop technical solutions
  - Review technical quality of deliverables
  - Prepare technical performance evaluations
- Introduce New Techniques and Technology
- Collaborate with the Customer and Vendor/Contractor on Technical Matters

Readiness-to-Perform Responsibilities

- Manage Project Team Member Prerequisites
  - Qualification training—required for project participation
  - Other training—desired for skill and competency enhancement
  - Project orientation participation—customer- or organization-based
  - Resource manager commitments
  - Individual team member commitments
- Address Project Team Member Preparedness
  - Removal of conflicting team member commitments
  - Travel and lodging arrangements
  - Travel-related issues—for example, inoculations, passports, visas

In addition to establishing individual responsibility areas, signature authority should be designated where needed. Any delegated authority and the limits of that authority should be specific and concise, and conveyed to all key stakeholders on the project.

Project Communication Plan Preparation

The project communication plan provides guidance for information gathering, report preparation and distribution, and document management. Also, it specifies the means by which information is exchanged or otherwise conveyed for use by the project team and other project stakeholders.

Project communication can be fairly simple for smaller project teams—it tends to be informal, individuals are generally aware of information sources, and conveyance is relatively quick. Add a new project team member who is not familiar with routine team communication practices, and the complexity of project communication intensifies, not just for the new member but for the entire project team. Enlarge that project team to more than a handful of people, then the complexity of project communication skyrockets. Now, add all other participating stakeholders.

The number of project team members and stakeholders involved in project communication can be represented by communication channels. The following formula is often used to calculate the number of communication channels within the project management environment. In this formula, N is the number of people (project team members, management, customers, and other stakeholders) having potential participation in project communication.

$$\frac{N(N-1)}{2}$$

Project communication requirements can become quite complex when a large number of project participants are involved, and that condition provides the requirement and prompts the need for preparing a communication plan.

The communication plan should present information and procedural guidance in the following areas of project communication:

- *Primary Communication Channels*—Identify who can communicate with whom on the project and in the organization, and for what reasons. These specify not only a "communication link" but also the authorization to communicate certain types of information across that link. Some examples of communication channels include
  - Team-member-to-team-member links provide for the exchange and collaboration of technical information associated with work performance and work progress.
  - Team-member-to-project-manager (team leader) links enable the submission and review of individual work progress reports.
  - Project-manager-to-management-links provide for the submission and review of status reports, and the elevation and collaboration of problems and issues.
  - Project manager-to-customer links provide for the conveyance of customer status reports and the discussion of issues, problems, and next steps with the customer.
  - Management-to-customer management links provide for discussions and the exchange of information at the executive levels of the participating organizations.

  Communication channels can be specified for virtually every project stakeholder using a "communication matrix." A standard communication matrix can be prepared (by the organization or the PMO) for routine use across all projects, with adjustments made to the matrix as necessary on particular projects.

- *Escalation Management Procedures*—Specify the prescribed escalation levels for internal project issue management and problem resolution. These could simply represent the flow of information from the project team member, through technical team leaders, to the project manager and onward to the PMO and the project executive/sponsor, and these are documented in the plan. Also, escalation management procedures identify the conditions or criteria that are used to trigger mandatory escalation of issues or problems. Some examples of conditions include
  - Project cost variance exceeds 9.5% for the reporting period.
  - A customer satisfaction issue at the mid-management level has surfaced.
  - A unilateral contract modification was issued by the customer.
  - A vendor/contractor has conveyed a "stop work" order.

  A multitude of conditions and criteria could be identified to warrant escalation. The organization should hold escalation requirements to only the most critical conditions, recognizing that the use of routine communication (reports, meetings, etc.) will present both routine and critical matters for review at elevated management levels in due time.

  Again, a standard set of issue and problem elevation conditions or criteria can be prepared (by the organization or the PMO) for routine use across all projects, with adjustments made to this list as necessary on particular projects.
- *Project Reporting Procedures*—Identify the various types of reports that will be required in the course of conducting the project, and specify the individuals responsible for report preparation and the range of recipients required for each project report. Again, restraint should be used to limit reports to primary users. However, that said, the organization and the project manager should identify all eligible report recipients who have a fundamental need for the information associated with each report that is distributed.
- *Project Documentation*—Identify the various types of project documents that will be required in the course of conducting the project, and specifies the individuals responsible for document preparation and the range of recipients required for each project document. The project manager should identify all eligible document recipients, with regard for any established document distribution practices in the organization.

The project communication plan can be used to include any other relevant information and guidance that are deemed necessary by the project manager or the organization. Some optional content might include the following:

- Format and content guidance to be used in preparing primary and supporting project management plans
- Format and content guidance to be used in preparing and conducting project-related meetings
- Format and content guidance to be used in preparing project-related reports
- Specification of *Project Knowledge Management* tools and capability to be implemented for use on the project (if not specified elsewhere)
- Identification of manager responsibilities and delegations of authority (as discussed earlier in this section)
- Listing of primary project stakeholders (as discussed in the previous section)
- Listing of recurring and special team, customer, and management meetings and conference calls associated with the project, including identification of participants
- Procedures for updating the project communication plan
- Listing of industry and technical standards applicable to project communication (including specified use of this project management methodology)

Chapter 12

Project Vendor Relationship Management

The management of external resources working on projects or otherwise influencing project performance is the focus of Project Vendor Relationship Management. These resources represent valuable contributions to a wide range of projects across many industries. Vendors bring specialized skill, knowledge, and capability to the technical nature of project work. They also fill temporary professional resource and skilled laborer gaps; serve as advisors to the project manager and project team members; and provide supplies, equipment, and materials needed to accomplish the project effort.

There are as many combinations of names for these resources as there are industries. Therefore, the term *vendor* often includes such descriptive names as supplier and provider; consultant and advisor; distributor and manufacturer representative, and contractor, subcontractor, and partner. This practice area captures the essence of all such resources under the term *vendor/contractor,* indicating they provide a product or service in support of the project effort, as per an established contract or agreement, undoubtedly for some remuneration. There are three practices associated with Project Vendor Relationship Management:

- Vendor Information Management
- Vendor Acquisition Management
- Vendor Performance Management

The project management office (PMO), if available, should be highly involved in setting up capability and support for project vendor relationship management. First, it can develop standard guidance for management of vendors and contractors in the project management environment. This precludes the need for project managers to figure out a different system for each vendor/contractor. In turn, preferred vendors and contractors will become familiar with the contract and performance management practices applied to their participation on projects in the relevant organization.

The PMO can also be proactive in identifying general and specific project needs for external vendor/contractor participation. It can be instrumental in prequalifying vendors and contractors for various types of project work, making them available for selection by project managers who are no longer burdened with finding the right resource in a short period of time.

As well, the PMO can collaborate with business units that facilitate the introduction of vendors and contractors into the performing organization—contracts, procurement, etc. In particular, the PMO brings the necessary expertise in project management and technical capability to assist business units in accurately preparing requirements documents, requests for proposals (RFPs), and qualifications to expedite the vendor/contractor identification and acquisition process. The project manager in most organizations, however, will retain responsibility for the direct oversight of project vendors and contractors, including the acquisition of vendors needed to support the project, the management of their performance, and the administration of vendor contracts.

12.1 VENDOR INFORMATION MANAGEMENT

Vendor Information Management provides facts and insight for achieving maximum benefits from vendor and contractor relationships. Sufficient information should be collected, compiled, and managed to properly accomplish vendor management and to ensure the achievement of vendor contractual obligations for the project.

Concept of This Practice

This practice provides the project manager, the project team, and the organization with relevant information about project vendors. Sometimes, there is more than one vendor participating in a given project, and organized information helps to improve the efficiency of managing each vendor.

The purpose of this practice is to compile and analyze vendor information as a basis for making project management decisions about vendor selection and for managing vendor participation on the project.

Vendor Information Management routinely begins in the Profile Phase when preliminary vendor information is collected, but vendor information management continues throughout the project up to and including the management of vendor performance, preparation of vendor evaluations, and closeout of vendor contracts conducted in the Post Phase. This practice deals with managing vendor information, as prescribed in the following two sections.

Vendor Information Collection

Vendor/contractor information collection can be quite exhaustive or a simple process, depending on the nature of project needs and the nature and extent of the business relationship. The performing organization will need to determine the specific information needed for managing its interests in the vendor/contractor relationship. The vendor/contractor information that is normally collected can be very similar to that which composes customer business information, and includes consideration of the following elements:

- *Vendor/Contractor Business Profile*—The vendor/contractor business profile contains any relevant information the project manager deems necessary to gain an adequate understanding of the nature of the vendor/contractor business. Fundamental information elements in the vendor/contractor business profile can include
  - Vendor/contractor business description (e.g., product, service, industry, etc.)
  - Vendor/contractor business size (e.g., number of employees)
  - Vendor/contractor business locations (e.g., local, regional, national, global, etc.)
  - Vendor/contractor business status (e.g., sales, revenue, stock position, outlook, etc.)
  - Vendor/contractor business management (e.g., executives, directors, private owners, etc.)
  - Vendor/contractor business affiliations (e.g., partnerships, industry affiliations, etc.)
- *Vendor/Contractor Relationship History*—Information on vendor/contractor relationship history examines past business dealings with each vendor/contractor. Its focus is on being able to review business given to each vendor/contractor and the resulting performance achievements. It can also include an examination of vendor/contractor dealings with other organizations in the industry and in the marketplace. Fundamental information elements in the vendor/contractor relationship history package can include
  - Major business transaction history with the vendor/contractor, and the outcomes
  - Project work history with the vendor/contractor, and the outcomes
  - Partnership or business affiliation history with the vendor/contractor, and the outcomes
  - Key vendor/contractor participants in projects and business transactions
  - Contract award history with the vendor/contractor
  - Vendor/contractor invoice management history
  - Prominent types of products and services provided by the vendor/contractor
- *Vendor/Contractor Business Fit*—Information about the vendor/contractor business fit warrants review from time to time. The primary information elements collected are based on the discernment and judgment of managers in the relevant organization versus absolute factual data. This information set helps to examine the vendor/contractor and associated business opportunities from the business interest perspectives of the relevant organization. Fundamental information elements associated with vendor/contractor business fit can include the following:
  - Management perspective on alignment of vendor/contractor business objectives and interests
  - Management perspective on vendor/contractor business decisions and outcomes
  - Management perspective on impacts of vendor/contractor business values
  - Management perspective on demonstrated vendor/contractor loyalty
  - Management perspective on importance of particular vendor/contractor retention

These three areas of vendor/contractor information can be comprehensive or basic, per established business needs and the capacity to manage them. To the extent that features and capability have been established, the project knowledge management system would be an excellent mechanism for storing and accessing vendor/contractor information for use by the PMO and project managers.

Vendor Information Utilization

Vendor/contractor information utilization is inherently discussed in subsequent practices related to vendor relationship management. This section offers an overview of vendor/contractor information to use as a basis for organizing and planning the information collection effort, and to provide the PMO, project manager, and other project team members with insight into the variety of vendor/contractor management activities that must be addressed. The following list presents some common (and perhaps some uncommon) concepts and suggestions for using vendor/contractor information on projects:

- *Vendor/Contractor Comparisons*—It is in the performing organization's best interest to select and use qualified vendors, and particularly to consider the most qualified of available vendors for the project work at hand. Information can be collected and used to compare and cross-reference vendor/contractor credentials and qualifications. This may be done in a prescreening or prequalifying activity; it can again be done to facilitate the vendor/contractor final selection and assignment process.
- *Vendor/Contractor Acquisition and Contract Management*—The performing organization will need to establish a formal business relationship with vendors and contractors during the acquisition process. This involves collecting and using contract documents and contractual information that will include the specification of terms and conditions for vendor/contractor participation in the project. It also includes obtaining the vendor's written concurrence and demonstrated understanding about the work to be accomplished, and establishing an invoice and payment process and schedule. The latter needs to be conveyed to the participating vendor/contractor, as well as other internal business units that have a role in vendor/contractor contract administration.
- *Vendor/Contractor Performance Management*—The project manager will normally have a prominent role in overseeing vendor/contractor performance on the project. There is an adage that asks the project manager, "The project is underway; do you know where your vendors are?" While this adage parodies older, similar sayings that many have heard, there is some validity in the implied need to ensure that vendor/contractor performance is monitored and managed at an appropriate level of detail to ensure their successful participation from the perspective of the customer and the perspective of the performing organization. Therefore, information needs to flow regularly between the vendor/contractor and the project manager (or designee) to enable collaboration on plans associated with vendor/contractor participation, to measure progress and accomplishments, and to rectify any faulty performance or areas of concern. This information should be collected throughout the project to facilitate ongoing performance evaluation of vendor/contractor performance. Such ongoing information collection becomes more valuable at the end of the project, when vendor/contractor performance evaluations can be prepared without relying on individual recollection from the extended period of project performance, and without limiting vendor/contractor evaluations to an indicator of just recent performance results.
- *Vendor/Contractor Closeout Management*—The need for accurate information is no more prevalent than in areas of financial management, and that includes the reconciliation of vendor/contractor deliverables with invoicing and payments due. Note that this is a three-step process that includes
  - A provision for vendor/contractor deliverables—Information needs to be collected and managed relative to the submittal of vendor/contractor deliverables, including aspects of quality, timeliness, and acceptance.
  - The reconciliation of vendor/contractor deliverables against invoices—Depending on the type of contract used, information needs to be collected to enable invoices presented by each vendor/contractor to be associated with completed deliverables. Information should be anticipated and collected to validate receipt of deliverables in conjunction with invoice reconciliation.
  - The payment of vendor/contractor invoices—Information needs to be collected regarding the progressive payments made to invoices issued by vendor/contractors. This simply represents good business practices that are applied to ensure that no double payments are made and that invoices are consistent (to date) with work accomplished by each vendor/contractor.

  Vendor/contractor closeout (conducted in the Post Phase, or as vendor/contractors leave the project) is focused on the financial payments due on deliverables received, and early collection of any information needed to support this process will ease the burden of this process when it comes to bear on the project manager and participating project team members.

12.2 VENDOR ACQUISITION MANAGEMENT

Vendor Acquisition Management provides the means by which vendors and contractors are introduced into the project management environment. Ideally, the PMO plays a major role in establishing and implementing this process as a support feature for each project. However, it is the project manager's responsibility to ensure that proper vendor/contractor acquisition is achieved, with or without PMO support.

Concept of This Practice

This practice provides the project manager, the project team, and the organization with fundamental guidance for conducting the sometimes intricate activities required for vendor/contractor acquisition. This practice should be examined for incorporation of any current organizational activities and processes related to vendor acquisition management.

Vendor Acquisition Management is normally conducted in the Plan Phase, but early indications of the need for vendors usually surface, and vendor prequalification can begin during the Profile Phase. Follow-on vendor/contractor selection and acquisition activities needed to fulfill subsequent project work requirements can be performed at later points in the project management life cycle as well.

There are three primary activities associated with vendor acquisition management:

- Identify and qualify vendors.
- Solicit vendor proposals.
- Prepare vendor contracts.

Each of these activities is described in the following sections.

Identify and Qualify Vendors

The identification and qualification of vendors and contractors should be accomplished according to the business relationship to be established. The process for vendor/contractor introduction is generally the same for all contract types, but it is usually the urgency of need that dictates the depth and schedule of the acquisition process.

The following vendor identification and qualification activities are prescribed:

- *Identify vendor requirements.* Customer requirements are evaluated to determine whether accomplishing the work using vendor/contractor support is needed, cost effective, and in the performing organization's best interest. The value of using vendor/contractor services may lie in the expertise to be gained, the need for resources, or the cost to be saved. Vendor/contractor requirements can be identified with reference to a specific project or for broader support that is anticipated in the project management environment. This activity is usually accomplished in collaboration with the project manager's development of resource requirements and associated staffing plans. Sometimes, this activity can be performed independently by the PMO when preparing a prequalified list of vendors that is subsequently used by project managers.
- *Perform make-or-buy analysis.* A make-or-buy analysis is a general management concept and technique that is used to determine whether it is more cost effective for a particular product or service to be produced internally by the performing organization, or if the product or service should be obtained from external vendor/contractor sourcing. Established organizational practices should be used to make this determination. In their absence, any viable comparison technique can be used.
- *Qualify vendors.* If a vendor/contractor information database has been created, it can be accessed to identify any prequalified vendors and contractors. Otherwise, a fresh examination of vendors and contractors sourcing in the marketplace will be needed.

  Once vendors and contractors have been identified, a review of their capabilities and expertise is used to create a short list of qualified candidates. Factors for vendor/contractor qualification can include
  - Technical capability, including certifications and licenses
  - Staff experience, including resume review
  - Familiarity with the vendor/contractor's products and services
  - Vendor/contractor familiarity with the organization
  - Geographic location and coverage
  - Previous similar jobs completed, including references
  - Financial stability, including bonding capacity

  The resulting vendor/contractor candidates on the short list for a particular project effort are then included in the distribution of the relevant project solicitation.
- *Determine pricing arrangements.* The objective of vendor/contractor pricing arrangements is to determine the contract type and price that will offer an acceptable level of vendor/contractor risk while providing the vendor/contractor with the greatest incentive for efficient and economical performance.

  Different types of contracts provide various ways to share risk between the buyer and the seller, particularly cost risk. The contract-type continuum shows the risk for fixed-price contracts is placed directly on the vendor/contractor (seller), whereas cost-reimbursement contracts place the risk on the performing organization (buyer).

- *Develop the independent cost estimate.* An independent cost estimate should be developed for all major vendor/contractor acquisition efforts. This represents the relevant organization's estimate of the cost of the effort to be undertaken. It is used in the acquisition planning process and is generally required when examining vendor/contractor proposals. The pricing for vendor/contractor solutions should fall within an acceptable range of the costs presented in the independent cost estimate. In some cases, the PMO may be adequately staffed to offer this as a support activity to project managers.
- *Prepare the vendor acquisition plan.* A vendor acquisition plan contains a compilation of the previously prepared elements plus guidance for conducting vendor/contractor acquisition activities. This plan is sometimes developed as a component of the broader *Vendor Management Plan* (see that plan in the section *Vendor Performance Management*). The vendor acquisition plan describes key acquisition events, including
  - Independent cost estimate preparation
  - Vendor/contractor candidate identification
  - Vendor/contractor solicitation preparation and distribution
  - Vendor/contractor proposal review and evaluation
  - Vendor/contractor contract discussion and negotiation period
  - Contract award date

This combined vendor identification and qualification process extends into proposal review activities. It essentially examines and qualifies vendor candidates who are believed to have capability to achieve desired vendor/contractor work performance objectives.

Solicit Vendor Proposals

The following activities are prescribed for preparing vendor/contractor solicitations, managing solicitation distribution, and reviewing responses (proposals) toward selecting one or more qualified vendors or contractors:

- *Prepare internal requisition document.* The needed requisition (purchase) requests are prepared in accordance with the policies and procedures established for vendor/contractor outsourcing. The requirements in the vendor acquisition plan are reviewed for internal approval. The approved requisition then authorizes the solicitation of vendor/contractor support and may include specification of basic information such as
  - Description of the item or service (statement of work) to be acquired
  - Quantity of materials to be ordered (for purchase orders)
  - Vendor/contractor performance period
  - Deliverables to be achieved and any key delivery dates
  - Funding required with identification of the internal funding source (account)
  - Applicable terms and conditions
  - Points of contact for requisition management and the ensuing solicitation

  The intended outcome of this activity, regardless of actual information content, is an approved requisition document that allows the project manager to prepare a solicitation or otherwise make a sole-source offer to acquire vendor/contractor support.
- *Determine type of solicitation.* The type of solicitation to be used by the potential bidders (vendor/contractor) must be determined and specified with sufficient detail to enable an adequate vendor/contractor response. The choices are normally either sole-source or competitive bid. Additionally, any other solicitation categories already established within the performing organization may be used.
- *Prepare vendor/contractor solicitation.* Identified or prequalified vendor/contractor candidates are informed about the work opportunity through the distribution of a solicitation that usually takes the form of an RFP or a request for quotes (RFQ). Such documents typically contain the following information:
  - Scope of work
  - Technical requirements
  - Performance schedule
  - Proposal format requirements
  - Terms and conditions
  - Subcontract type
  - Evaluation criteria

  This information must be compiled for distribution to vendors and contractors and is usually readily transferable from the internal requisition document.
- *Specify optional proposal actions.* In conjunction with the preparation of the solicitation package, the following actions, although optional, are sometimes performed to ensure a successful vendor/contractor proposal response for major projects:
  - Prepare a draft solicitation. A draft document can be used for unusual or complex bid packages to obtain feedback from potential vendors and contractors before issuing the final solicitation; this document can be of tremendous help in clarifying vendor/contractor requirements.
  - Conduct preproposal conferences and a site survey. Meetings can be conducted for potential vendor/contractors in cases of unusual or complex bid packages. This can include vendor/contractor candidate visits to the actual performance site for

services, construction, or installation work. These meetings can be used to ensure that all vendor/contractor candidates have a clear and common understanding of both the technical and contract requirements of the solicitation.
  - Respond to bidder inquiries and questions. A time period is established in which potential bidders may submit questions in writing. All identified bidders receive a list of all questions and the respective answers from the relevant organization. In some cases, responses to questions may be incorporated into solicitation documents as amendments.
- *Distribute the solicitation and manage vendor/contractor responses.* The solicitation package is distributed to vendor/contractor candidates on the qualified source list. Vendor/contractor responses should be tracked and managed. Deadlines for receipt should be adhered to or extended as a distinct proposal management action. The project manager, in conjunction with established practices, may provide notice of the approaching deadline to all vendor/contractor participants. Similarly, the project manager may request the courtesy of receiving replies of "no bid" from those vendor/contractor candidates who choose not to submit a proposal, and these replies too should be tracked for current and future reference.
- *Evaluate vendor/contractor response.* Vendor/contractor selection may be as simple as reviewing the proposal business elements and determining which competing set of prices is the lowest. On the other hand, response examinations may involve weeks or even months of proposal analysis, on-site visits, prototype development, and testing. Sometimes, one person can accomplish vendor/contractor proposal review and selection, and, at other times, it may require an extended effort by a panel of evaluators to complete this effort. The industry trend appears to lean toward more comprehensive screening and selection of fewer vendors and contractors for longer duration contracts. The vendor/contractor evaluation process typically includes the following actions:
  - Receive and evaluate proposals. Oral vendor/contractor presentations of their proposals tend to improve and expedite the vendor/contractor selection process. However, proposal document review is still a necessary means of examining the vendor/contractor candidates under consideration. Either way, proposals must be evaluated using the evaluation criteria stated in the solicitation regarding management, technical expertise, and price. Also, a weighting system should be used to determine which evaluation criteria are most important. Past vendor/contractor performance information should also be used to evaluate and verify the accuracy of information presented in the vendor/contractor proposal. Use of independent cost estimates, price realism, and competitive price analyses are part of the evaluation process. Use of qualified consultants to assist in this proposal review is also a method for project manager consideration.
  - Hold vendor/contractor discussions. Interactions with vendor/contractor candidates provide the opportunity to clarify ambiguities in proposals that are received. The project manager must also determine if conditions warrant an opportunity for candidates to revise their proposals and submit a best and final offer.
  - Receive and evaluate best and final offers. The receipt of revised, best, and final offers from vendor/contractor candidates should be monitored, and a final evaluation of their revised proposed solutions should be accomplished. Normally, the focus of a best and final offer is on pricing. However, inasmuch as pricing affects performance, there also could be changes in the technical solution to be considered. Each vendor/contractor should highlight the revisions contained in its best and final offer presented to the relevant organization. Also, it should be noted that the best and final offer does not necessarily represent the outcome of negotiations.
- *Conduct vendor/contractor negotiations.* The contract negotiation process comprises planning, conducting, and documenting the negotiations that are conducted. It involves clarification and mutual agreement on the structure and requirements of the contract prior to the award. To the extent possible, final contract language should reflect all agreements reached. Generally, vendor/contractor negotiations may include, but are not limited to, the following subjects:
  - Responsibilities and authorities
  - Staff qualifications and proposed assignments
  - Applicable terms and law
  - Technical and business management approaches
  - Contract financing and price
- *Select vendor/contractor.* This step represents the selection and notification of the successful vendor/contractor and is characterized by the following activities:
  - Vendor/contractor selection—A formal vendor/contractor selection decision is made. If the associated customer contract is a major one, the final decision may require some coordination with the customer and possibly customer approval. The customer can be included in the vendor/contractor selection and decision process to preclude the need for postselection vendor/contractor confirmation.

- Award of vendor/contractor contract or agreement—A final contract document, incorporating any negotiated modifications to the proposed offer and any customer required directives, is prepared. Obtain appropriate approvals, sign the contract, and provide a copy to the vendor/contractor.
- Debriefing—Notify unsuccessful vendors and contractors, and debrief them on the selection outcome for them. Hold discussions appropriate to the proposal effort with each unsuccessful bidder to present at least general vendor/contractor selection results as a means to promote and refine future proposals. The courtesy extended by offering this discussion also refines or builds any future business relationship opportunities with unsuccessful vendors and contractors.
- Vendor/contractor orientation—As is appropriate to the contract awarded, it is sometimes desirable to bring the core team of the winning vendor onsite for an orientation meeting. This also provides an opportunity (particularly on major, publicized project efforts) to conduct a joint presentation with the employee force or even with the media to announce the award and to demonstrate readiness to begin the project.

Prepare Vendor Contracts

The following are several basic activities prescribed for preparing vendor/contractor contracts. Some of these activities will be performed prior to or in conjunction with the contract award activities described in the previous section.

- *Verify contract documents.* This activity represents verification that vendor/contractor contract documents are complete, accurate, and reflect the results of any contract negotiations. It particularly includes incorporation of vendor/contractor project plans and technical documents that were adjusted as a result of contract negotiations.
- *Obtain vendor/contractor contract internal approvals.* The project manager, PMO, or business unit representative leading the vendor/contractor solicitation effort will present the contract or agreement for internal reviews by
  - Project Manager (if not already participating)
  - Project Executive/Sponsor
  - Corporate Legal Department
  - Contract Management Department (as appropriate)

  Then, an authorized signature is obtained prior to sending the contract document to the vendor/contractor.
- *Obtain contract approval from vendor.* Deliver the prepared vendor/contractor contract to the vendor for review and approval (i.e., signature); arrange for timely return of the original contract document for processing in the performing organization.
- *Book the contract.* Booking the vendor/contractor contract is the process of accepting a vendor/contractor contract or work order into the business system and the project repository. An account number is established for the vendor/contractor contract, and the baselines for scope, schedule, and costs are validated in the accounting or project management information system. This process allows work orders to be issued, project work to begin, and invoices to be accepted from the vendor/contractor.
- *Transfer vendor/contractor contract oversight to the project manager.* The work to be performed under the vendor/contractor contract officially begins when the contract is passed to the project manager for execution. This is done in the event the project manager has not already been directly involved in the vendor acquisition process.
- *Distribute vendor contract to project stakeholders.* As per an earlier project stakeholder analysis and the preparation of the *Project Communication Plan,* distribute a copy of executed vendor contracts to relevant project stakeholders, which could include the following individuals/business units:
  - Project Executive/Project Sponsor
  - Project Team Technical Leaders (particularly those individuals with vendor oversight responsibility)
  - Accounting and Finance (in conjunction with invoice processing)
  - Corporate Contracts Manager
  - Legal Department

  The project manager, the PMO, and the organization should examine this distribution list and adjust it to satisfy its business interests and needs.

12.3 VENDOR PERFORMANCE MANAGEMENT

Vendor Performance Management provides the means to oversee and manage the vendor contract and associated vendor participation in the project. Vendors should not be brought onto a project and then left to their own devices to accomplish assigned project work, prompting a condition of "rarely seen and rarely heard." Of course, the vendor's project role is different than that assigned for internal resources, and vendors normally do have to manage their own team's efforts. Nevertheless, to the extent possible, vendors should be integrated with the primary project team, and vendors should recognize that being monitored for contract fulfillment is not a project management option; it is a business necessity.

This practice recognizes that there will be varying levels of vendor monitoring and performance oversight per the different types of vendors and the different types of projects encountered. Good professional sense is needed to determine the level of oversight provided on a particular project. Oversight should be applied to confirm the vendor's performance of work, but not impede the vendor's work performance or otherwise be overbearing without due cause or concern.

Concept of This Practice

This practice provides the project manager, the project team, and the organization with the means to ensure that vendor/contractor contractual obligations are fulfilled, their roles and responsibilities associated with the project are outlined and understood, and their technical work is assigned and completed consistent with project interests and objectives.

Vendor Performance Management is primarily conducted in the Perform Phase, with some vendor contract closeout activities conducted in the Post Phase. However, it is inherently a part of the Plan Phase, when the approach to vendor management is established for each project. There are three activities associated with *Vendor Performance Management*:

- Prepare Vendor Management Plan.
- Administer Vendor Contracts.
- Monitor Vendor Performance.

Each of these activities is described in the following sections.

Prepare Vendor Management Plan

A key component in establishing effective vendor/contractor relationships is to identify how they will be introduced and used on projects and in the project management environment. As is common in most situations where there is direct project manager oversight and involvement, processes and procedures applicable to vendor/contractor participation that are managed by the project manager can be incorporated into the project management methodology.

The preparation of an effective vendor management plan is a prescribed way to organize and manage a wide range of vendor/contractor participation activities and issues. In some cases, a vendor acquisition plan is developed, and content from that plan can be incorporated into or serve as the initial content of the broader vendor management plan.

Examine the following points for possible inclusion in the vendor management plan:

- *Vendor/Contractor Acquisition Responsibility*—The project manager is responsible for acquiring necessary vendor/contractor resources to achieve project objectives; however, a qualified manager can be designated to lead or otherwise perform vendor/contractor acquisition actions for larger projects.

  The organization will also need to determine if the PMO will serve as a clearinghouse for vendor/contractor acquisitions or just serve as a resource for vendor/contractor information. The PMO's role in the vendor/contractor acquisition process should be stipulated in the vendor management plan.
- *Vendor/Contractor Acquisition Management*—This plan can specify the process or approach that will be used for vendor/contractor acquisition (consistent with established business practices). This includes content related to the make-or-buy decision, the preparation of a solicitation (e.g., RFP, RFQ, etc.), the review of proposals, and the selection of one or more qualified vendors. See the description for the vendor acquisition plan in the previous section for more information on prescribed content.
- *Vendor/Contractor Oversight Responsibility*—The project manager is responsible for managing vendor/contractor task assignments and performance. In collaboration with project managers, the organization will need to determine any PMO involvement in managing vendor/contractor participation. The project manager should identify the PMO's role in the vendor management plan.
- *Vendor/Contractor Project Affiliation*—The project manager should specify in this plan if the vendor/contractor is a member of the project team, or if the vendor/contractor will be performing its assigned role and tasks independent of the project team. The PMO in collaboration with relevant project managers should determine the preferred approach to vendor/contractor management in advance of this planning effort, and provide general guidance for use by all project managers.
- *Vendor/Contractor Project Management Responsibility*—The PMO should establish common activities and general guidance for vendor/contractor participation in project management activities and performance of their own project management efforts, per each vendor/contractor type. In turn, the project manager should use the vendor management plan to specify each vendor's responsibilities for project management:
  - Vendor/contractor collaboration: needs, requirements, and technical specifications
  - Vendor/contractor project planning and technical solution development
  - Vendor/contractor project management methodology deployment and use

- Vendor/contractor tracking and reporting requirements

This deliberation also results in establishing the project manager's role in overseeing vendor/contractor project participation and performance from a project management perspective.

- *Vendor/Contractor Technical Performance Responsibility*—If not otherwise specified by the customer contract or stipulated by the customer, the PMO should establish general guidance for vendor/contractor use of acceptable technical performance standards and technical competency requirements that will be used in measuring vendor/contractor performance. In turn, the project manager should use the vendor management plan to specify each vendor's responsibilities for ensuring technical performance:
  - Fulfillment of qualifications for vendor/contractor technical team members
  - Presentation of required technical plans, designs, and solutions for timely review
  - Demonstration of a viable configuration management process, as needed
  - Implementation of project deliverable quality control and assurance measures
  - Development of an acceptable product and service delivery timetable

  This deliberation also results in establishing the project manager's role in overseeing vendor/contractor project participation and performance from a technical perspective.
- *Vendor/Contractor Business Management Responsibility*—The PMO should establish general guidance for vendor/contractor business activity management, which is generally translated to mean putting mechanisms in place to ensure that the vendor/contractor has the capability to manage its contractual obligations. In turn, the project manager should use the vendor management plan to specify each vendor's responsibilities for demonstrating effective business management:
  - Capability to lead and control vendor/contractor technical team work efforts
  - Acceptance of the prescribed contract modification process
  - Receptiveness to executive and senior management collaboration, as needed
  - Presentation of preferred project progress and associated business reports
  - Adherence to invoice submittal practices

The nature and type of vendor/contractor involvement, combined with established PMO or organizational guidance, will influence the particular type of role and responsibility guidance that the project manager needs to specify in the vendor management plan.

Administer Vendor Contracts

The principal objective of vendor/contractor contract administration is to ensure the fulfillment of contractual obligations by all parties to the contract. The required level of effort for vendor/contractor contract administration depends on the magnitude and importance of the contract. On larger projects with multiple product and service vendors and contractors, a key aspect of contract administration is managing the interactions among the various participants along with all other contract administrative activities.

It is critical that all project team members be aware of the legal implications of actions taken when administering the contract. For vendors and contractors, the effort needs to focus on vendor/contractor delivery management rather than on personal interactions.

The following are several prescribed actions normally associated with vendor/contractor contract administration:

- *Establish vendor/contractor contract booking.* After the vendor/contractor contract has been awarded, the project manager must ensure that the vendor/contractor contract information is entered into the project and business databases; critical information includes anything impacting cost, schedule, meetings, and deliverables. There may be guidance for this action to be accomplished when the contract is established, but a good rule is for the project manager to verify the "booking" action through a notification to and an acknowledgment from the accounting department.
- *Organize vendor/contractor contract files.* The project manager must retain critical vendor/contractor contracting documents in a file created for each vendor/contractor. This process should be an integral part of the project management information system, a component of the *Project Knowledge Management* system. Vendor/contractor contract files typically contain the following information:
  - RFP/RFQ package
  - Vendor/contractor proposal (including related inquiries, preproposal meeting notes, and negotiation notes)
  - Vendor/contractor planning documents and modifications
  - Vendor/contractor performance management evaluations
  - Vendor/contractor correspondence
  - Vendor/contractor meeting minutes
  - Vendor/contractor reports
  - Vendor/contractor invoices

- Vendor/contractor change orders
- Vendor/contractor deliverable tracking and management logs

- *Establish procedures for contract claims and dispute resolution.* The project manager should work closely with the PMO and procurement personnel on this highly legalistic area and ensure that project team members (although not usually directly involved) are aware of the procedures to be followed.
- *Establish procedures to resolve issues and problems.* The PMO should establish guidance for use by project managers in identifying, managing, and reporting vendor/contractor issues and problems. The goal is to achieve early and effective resolution of any detriment to project success. The use of established procedures should be confirmed by the project manager.
- *Establish communication guidance.* The project manager should clearly specify to all project team members their responsibilities relative to vendor/contractor management, and convey authorization for their communication with the vendor/contractor. This is normally included in the project communication plan.
- *Monitor vendor/contractor performance.* Vendor/contractor performance should be monitored; this includes observing actual performance, conducting regular meetings and discussions, and reviewing written reports. Also, deliverables presented by vendors and contractors should be examined for quality, achievement of specifications, and fulfillment of requirements.
- *Manage vendor/contractor relations.* The participation of each vendor/contractor should be examined and management styles be leveraged to maximize vendor/contractor strengths and minimize weaknesses. The vendor/contractor should be held responsible for compliance with technical and contractual matters. The use of vendors and contractors who demonstrate loyalty and indicate a potential for long-term relationships should be encouraged.
- *Conduct meetings with vendor/contractor representatives.* An initial meeting should be conducted with vendor/contractor managers and representatives for purposes of introduction and to establish protocols associated with the project effort. Ongoing progress and status meetings should be held with the key members of the vendor/contractor project team as necessitated by the project effort.
- *Manage vendor/contractor contract changes.* The organization must establish a vendor/contractor contract change control process by which any vendor/contractor contract can be modified. The project manager will implement this process to ensure that only authorized changes are made. This will include assessing the business and technical value of requested changes, examining the impacts of requested changes on the project, accounting for any additional costs incurred by implementing the change, and conducting implementation of approved changes with timely notification to all involved parties.
- *Monitor vendor/contractor contract compliance.* The project manager has responsibility for vendor/contractor contract compliance to ensure that the vendor/contractor is authorized to perform work at the appropriate time and that work performed complies with any applicable terms and conditions. Project engineers or technical personnel usually manage the technical portion of the vendor/contractor contract, whereas procurement or financial personnel, who may or may not be assigned as project team members, manage the business portion. The project manager must ensure that an effective vendor/contractor contract administration is performed for major vendor/contractor contracts to ensure internal collaboration on vendor/contractor contract compliance.
- *Manage acceptance of vendor/contractor deliverables.* The project manager must ensure the management of vendor/contractor deliverables by project team members. It is critical that an effective quality control program be established and implemented to inspect and verify the adequacy of the vendor/contractor product. Acceptance of deliverables (goods, services, progress reports, documents, etc.) must be performed in accordance with both the prime contract and the vendor/contractor contract, and validation must be accomplished before invoices are authorized to be paid.
- *Manage vendor/contractor payments.* The vendor/contractor contract should contain provisions on invoicing and payment schedules. Payment terms should be defined within the contract and should involve a specific linkage between progress made and compensation paid. The project manager should also specify who is authorized to approve the invoices that are submitted in accordance with the relevant contracts. Frequently, invoices are tied to deliverables, and acceptance must be achieved before payment can be made. Following are several types of payments:
  - Progress payments tied to measurable progress in work, or based on cost incurred, with some determination of actual work. Progress payments should be used only if the costs can be recovered by the project.
  - Payments aligned with the achievement of specific milestones or deliverables.
  - Payments based on the "pay when paid" concept. That is, the vendor/contractor gets paid when the relevant organization receives payment from the customer.

- Payments can also be made at recurring intervals in association with ongoing vendor/contractor services that may or may not have specific deliverables.

  Vendors and contractors should be required to submit an invoice to receive payment. This ensures an ability to track and trace invoices, which is particularly important if there are multiple vendor/contractor participants. The vendor/contractor invoice should contain the following information: contract identification number, payment amount requested, and listing of the work performance associated with the requested payment.
- *Review and close out vendor/contractor contract.* Vendor/contractor contract closeout may occur at any time during the project, but it should be performed at least during the project's Post Phase. The following steps are normally performed to close out a subcontract:
  - Verify that all requirements are completed and accepted. Resolve any open or pending questions and issues.
  - Confirm that all vendor/contractor submittals and deliveries have been received. Ensure that deliverables have been accepted in accordance with any prescribed test and inspection procedures and that the customer has accepted the deliverables.
  - Ensure that the vendor/contractor issues a final invoice accompanied by any other required documentation, including final lien waivers, warranty documents, or certificates of completion.
  - Approve the final invoice, and monitor and verify the subcontractor's receipt of the final payment.
- *Manage vendor/contractor resource departures.* Ensure that vendor/contractor staff departures are managed and material resources are disposed of appropriately if no longer needed on the project. This includes managing turn-in of project equipment provided to vendor/contractor staff for use during the project, reallocation of workspace, and removal of vendor/contractor staff access to facilities and documents, as needed.
- *Prepare a postproject vendor/contractor performance evaluation.* Review vendor/contractor performance, contributions, and contract compliance, and prepare and archive a final report that includes the following suggested content:
  - Evaluation of the effectiveness of vendor/contractor staff and managers
  - Evaluation of the effectiveness of vendor/contractor processes and tools
  - Preparation of lessons learned from the vendor/contractor business relationship
  - Recommendations for appropriate vendor/contractor staff and manager recognition

  This evaluation can include collaboration with the vendor/contractor, or a copy of the postproject vendor/contractor performance report can be conveyed upon completion.

The PMO should refine these activities for use in the performing organization, which may or may not already have a basis for vendor/contractor contract administration. If one does exist, the PMO can simply incorporate existing practices for use in the project management environment. If one does not exist, a vendor/contractor contract administration process development effort is needed. Also, if one does not exist, the PMO may need to facilitate buy-in of managers who are unaccustomed to such scrutiny of vendor/contractor participation. That can be accomplished with relative ease by demonstrating the benefits to be achieved by effective vendor/contractor management, such as receipt of quality vendor/contractor work products and services, reduction of rework, proper payment of invoices and release of project funds based on validation and acceptance of vendor/contractor work products and services, and fulfillment of the primary customer contract through oversight and management of timely delivery of vendor/contractor work products and services.

Monitor Vendor Performance

It has been reiterated that the project manager is responsible for vendor/contractor performance management and oversight. This activity examines ways in which the project manager can fulfill that responsibility. Also, vendor/contractor oversight is an activity in which the PMO can support the project manager. In particular, there are vendor/contractor reviews and assessment activities the PMO can perform across all vendor/contractor participants to ascertain the individual and collective value and effectiveness brought into the project management environment by these external resources.

In some cases, centralized PMO reviews of vendor/contractor performance will serve business decisions regarding the current or proposed business relationship with a particular vendor/contractor. In other cases, PMO review and assessment findings can be conveyed to project managers for their consideration in selecting the next vendor/contractor needed for a particular project effort.

The following are a few examples of the activities the project manager can conduct to monitor vendor/contractor performance and ensure that value is being achieved by the introduction of vendor/contractor products and services into the organization's project management environment. Some of these activities will necessarily require either PMO or organizational business unit support.

- *Price Variation Analysis*—This review looks at how vendor/contractor pricing varies across projects, for the same vendor/contractor and for different vendors and contractors, particularly those performing the same or similar work. It will help determine if there are pricing inconsistencies among the vendor/contractor resources used or inconsistencies in pricing for a particular vendor/contractor. Significant variations should be identified, challenged, and rectified.

- *Deliverable Performance Analysis*—This review examines the trends in technical quality of vendor/contractor work products and services. It should ascertain any adverse trends in vendor/contractor deliverables, where the product or service routinely does not meet objectives, specifications, or expectations. This includes an examination of rework frequency, timeliness of product and service delivery, vendor/contractor responsiveness to requests for fixes, and ultimate endurance and usability of the delivered product or service. Conversely, this analysis also could identify positive trends in vendor/contractor deliverable performance. The organization can use these analyses results to identify preferred vendor/contractor relationships for future project work and business use.
- *Contract Add-On/Extension Analysis*—This review is used to identify any particular vendor/contractor having a recurring need to request or negotiate work extensions, with or without additional costs incurred. This could be an indication of weak estimating practices either within the performing organization or by the vendor/contractor, or possibly vendor/contractor underpricing in their proposals in anticipation of obtaining subsequent increases after work has begun. It could also be an indicator of vendor/contractor staff competency or vendor/contractor management attention and capability. Once indicators are identified, the project manager or PMO can determine the cause and implement rectifying actions.
- *Billing Practices Analysis*—This review can be applied to examine the accuracy of individual and collective vendor/contractor invoices and to ensure that prescribed billing practices are adhered to by each vendor/contractor, that is, timely submittal, appropriate description of work performed, etc. Also, this examination looks at internal handling of vendor/contractor invoices, particularly project manager approval, which serves as verification of product receipt and work performed. The project manager or PMO can then act to correct any discrepancies identified.
- *Management Retention Analysis*—This review addresses vendor/contractor manager assignments and associated effectiveness. It examines preferred vendor/contractor manager retention for subsequent or recurring efforts as a matter of developing their familiarity and experience within the performing organization. It also identifies the frequency of vendor/contractor manager turnovers on individual projects and across multiple projects in which the vendor/contractor is involved. The project manager or PMO can review vendor and contractor manager retention and turnover issues in terms of any project effectiveness issues that require attention and resolution.
- *Customer Satisfaction Analysis*—The project manager should review any indicators of customer satisfaction or dissatisfaction with any vendor/contractor. This is usually associated with vendor/contractor work that is visible to the customer. This examination should be distinguished from finding vendor/contractor blame, because the performing organization is responsible for selecting only qualified vendor/contractor participants and is doing itself a disservice in suggesting vendor/contractor blame to any customer. Rather, the project manager or PMO needs to obtain customer perspectives, if not approval, regarding the vendor/contractor products and services used, and this is a measure of customer feedback in that regard.
- *Project Manager Oversight Analysis*—This review solicits project manager input to vendor/contractor performance, and may be accomplished in conjunction with the preparation of a vendor/contractor evaluation report. However, here the PMO may be able to examine the input of multiple project managers, or multiple reports, to ascertain project manager perspectives on the vendor/contractor. In particular, this review focuses on the level of vendor/contractor management attention required and the identification of any undue burdens placed on the project manager resulting from vendor/contractor oversight requirements. The project manager or PMO will need to identify any vendor/contractor that presents an unacceptable burden on project manager time and effort.
- *Business and Investment Posture*—This review is conducted relative to the nature of the relationship with each vendor/contractor type. Closer business relationships—that is, partnerships—will have a different focus than will simple vendor/contractor relationships established for project-specific work. Some of the points that can be examined to ascertain business and investment posture in vendor/contractor relationships include
  - Financial contributions to partnering initiatives
  - Resource investments in the relationship
  - Demonstrated actions to introduce and use prescribed technical practices
  - Investments in new technology
  - Investments in communication and information-sharing tools
  - Information sharing

The results from each of these examinations should be entered into the appropriate vendor/contractor information file and made available through the *Project Knowledge Management* system used in the project management environment. Analysis results also should be considered in mid- and long-term planning for vendor/contractor support, as well as in the vendor/contractor acquisition process when obtaining new or renewed vendor/contractor contracts. The primary objective of this monitoring effort is to maximize business value from vendor/contractor participation in the project management environment.

Chapter 13

Project Customer Relationship Management

Every project has an internal or external customer who relies on the fulfillment of project objectives. Most external customers will have a financial stake in the project effort. Internal customers often seek more operational effectiveness and efficiency as a result of the product or service delivered by the project effort. Along with these considerations of revenue and efficiency, the third common element of the project–business equation is customer satisfaction. These three elements need to be managed from both business and project management perspectives.

Most customers will have some level of participation in the project and in project management activities. At a minimum, they will normally initiate a request for the project effort and execute the associated project contract or agreement. Some customers will be more involved than others in project performance and project management oversight. Any level of customer involvement in the project effort warrants managing those customer relationships.

There are three practices associated with Project Customer Relationship Management:

- Customer Information Management
- Customer Participation Management
- Customer Satisfaction Management

The project manager has inherent responsibility for managing the customer relationship for the duration of the project. Managing the customer relationship relative to project effort presents a range of interactions that can be adequately conducted only by those directly involved in the project management effort. As well, the customer's project and business experience can be enhanced when the customer has ongoing access to qualified professionals in project management who can both answer technical questions and resolve business issues solely from within the venue of the project management environment.

The business units of the organization that have customer relationship responsibilities will normally find an increase in efficiency and sometimes a reduction in workload when project managers have assigned customer relationship management capability. This includes such departments as business development, finance and accounting, legal/contracts management, etc. Professionals in these business areas can focus on more prominent duties or possibly problem areas associated with customer projects when project managers are able to contribute to developing and managing effective customer relationships as a natural part of the project management effort.

This project management methodology is ideally suited for incorporating business practices for critical customer relationship management beyond the scope of this practice area. This includes such matters as initial customer requirements examination, technical solution and proposal development, contract and agreement management, project deliverable acceptance and associated invoice management, and customer satisfaction evaluations at interim project points and at project closeout. See the relevant practice areas for more information about these practices.

This practice area supports customer-relevant activities and interactions, particularly customer information collection, throughout the project management life cycle. Performance of this customer relationship activity warrants a special side note. The project manager should ensure that internal customers and end users receive equal value from a professional project management capability within the relevant organization, as do customers and end users in the external, commercial marketplace.

13.1 CUSTOMER INFORMATION MANAGEMENT

Customer Information Management provides facts about and insight into the customer relationship. Sufficient information should be collected, compiled, and managed to enable desired levels of customer participation and to achieve customer satisfaction with project results.

Concept of This Practice

This practice provides the project manager, the project team, and the organization with relevant information about the project's customer. Significantly, more information is usually needed and gathered for external customers, but some relevant information is needed for internal customers as well.

The purpose of this practice is to compile and analyze customer information as a basis for making project management decisions about the customer and for including the customer as participant in various project and project management activities. Some customers will want more involvement, and some will want less. It is the project manager's job to ensure that an adequate amount of customer participation is achieved to enable the project objectives to be fulfilled.

Customer Information Management begins in the Profile Phase, and continues throughout the project, up to and including the information collected for customer evaluations, satisfaction surveys, and other customer closeout activities conducted in the Post Phase. This practice deals with managing customer project information and customer business information, as prescribed in the following subsections.

Manage Customer Project Information

Information needed to initiate and conduct projects and project management activities should be examined and compiled for each customer. These project information elements are primarily associated with technical needs and are addressed in other practice areas, but they may include other types of information as well. The following are a few primary areas of customer project information that will assist not only in project delivery but also in customer relationship management:

- *Project Requirements and Specifications*—This comprises a set of information representing the customer's perspective of what needs to be achieved by the project. Presumably, associated information items are prepared and presented by the customer as a part of the request for project assistance. A few sample information elements include
  - Request for Proposal (RFP)
  - Statement of Work (SOW)
  - Business/Technical Needs Analysis
  - Technical Specifications Document
  - Technical Survey Document
  - Technical Design Document

  Project requirements and specifications information elements are described in further detail in separate practice areas of this guide.
- *Project Definition*—This is a set of information representing the translation of customer requirements into a description of the project effort. The information is aligned with the customer's needs but represents the perspective of the performing organization regarding what needs to be achieved by the project. It is of course shared with the customer. In some cases, the project definition is contained as an element of the project business case document. A few sample information elements include
  - Project objectives
  - Project scope statement
  - Project deliverables and milestones
  - Project assumptions and constraints

  Again, project definition information elements are also described in the *Project Definition Development* practice, in a separate practice area of this guide.
- *Customer Contract*—This is a set of information that establishes the formal business relationship between the customer and the performing organization. It sets forth the agreement between the two parties, specifies their obligations to each other, and presents the terms and conditions under which the agreement and obligations are upheld. Often, the customer contract will append or reference the project information materials mentioned in the previous two items in the list.
- *Customer Management Plan*—This set of information is used by the project manager and project team members to guide their interactions with the customer. It is sometimes incorporated into the project communications plan, which presents the communication practices and protocols to be used in the project. This information specifies points of contact for business and technical collaboration, coordination, and decision making. In particular, it will identify the individuals and preferred interactions with any customer project manager or customer project team.

The project manager can consider these and other information elements when managing customer project information.

Manage Customer Business Information

Project information elements will not necessarily present a comprehensive depiction of the customer, but rather they will focus on customer technical needs for the project effort at hand. Therefore, it is recommended that the project manager also acquire and manage customer business information as a means to better understand the customer relationship. This includes the following three types of customer business information:

- *Customer Business Profile*—The customer's business profile contains any information needed to gain an adequate understanding of the nature of the customer's business. Fundamental information elements in the customer business profile can include
  - Customer business description (e.g., product, service, industry, etc.)
  - Customer business size (e.g., number of employees)
  - Customer business locations (e.g., local, regional, national, global, etc.)
  - Customer business status (e.g., sales, revenue, stock position and outlook, etc.)
  - Customer business management (e.g., executives, directors, private owners, etc.)
  - Customer business affiliations (e.g., partnerships, industry memberships, etc.)
- *Customer Relationship History*—Information about the history of the customer relationship allows an examination of past business dealings with the customer. Its focus is on reviewing past business, but it can also look at the customer's other dealings in the industry and in the marketplace. Fundamental information elements in the customer relationship history package can include
  - Major business transaction history with the customer, and the outcomes
  - Project work history with the customer, and the outcomes
  - Partnership or business affiliation history with the customer, and the outcomes
  - Key customer participants in projects and business transactions
  - Sales and revenue history with the customer
  - Customer invoice payment history
  - Prominent types of products and services outsourced by the customer
- *Customer Business Approach*—Information about the customer's business approach may well be included in the customer relationship history, but it is separated here to distinguish the nature of information compiled. The information elements collected are based primarily on the discernment and judgment of managers in the performing organization versus absolute factual data. This information set helps to examine the customer and associated business opportunities from a business interest perspective of the relevant organization. Fundamental information elements in the customer business approach package can include
  - Management perspective on alignment of customer business objectives and interests
  - Management perspective on customer's business decisions and outcomes
  - Management perspective on impacts of customer's business values
  - Management perspective on demonstrated customer loyalty
  - Management perspective on importance of particular customer retention

These three areas of customer business information can be comprehensive or basic, as per established business practices and the capacity to manage these items. To the extent a knowledge management system is established, it would be a primary mechanism for introducing customer information for use by project managers.

13.2 CUSTOMER PARTICIPATION MANAGEMENT

Customer Participation Management helps to guide the extent and frequency of customer involvement in the project and in project management. This can be as simple as brief introductions and limited coordination between the customer and the performing organization, or as elaborate as collaborative work efforts that include an integrated project team with customer participants.

Concept of This Practice

This practice provides the project manager, the project team, and the organization with an examination of relevant information about how the customer desires to participate in the project, as it also prompts consideration of ways to promote the desired level of customer participation.

The purpose of this practice is to identify points of opportunity and necessity for customer involvement in projects and project management. It is used by project managers to optimize customer involvement for purposes of business interest (i.e., achievement of relevant organization business objectives and obligations), technical performance (i.e., achievement of quality technical solution delivery), and project management interest (i.e., achievement of customer satisfaction).

Customer participation arrangements are generally made in the Plan Phase, but indications of participation desired by the customer often surface during the Profile Phase. Once identified, the prescribed customer participation is managed throughout the project's duration.

Managing Customer Participation

The following are prescribed areas of examination for incorporating customer participation as a basis for achieving the desired customer relationship and for fulfilling project objectives:

- *Project Management Activities*—The customer can participate in projects in association with activities that are aligned with phases of the project management life cycle.
  - Business needs collaboration
  - Technical requirements specification/statement of work development
  - Project planning and technical solution development
  - Project tracking and controlling
  - Project progress and status reporting
  - Project review and audit performance
  - Project change management review and approval actions
  - Project closeout actions
- *Project Technical Activities*—The customer can be a part of the progressive development of the project's technical deliverables at appropriate junctures in the technical effort.
  - Technical solution design
  - Configuration management reviews
  - Interim test and acceptance (quality control and assurance) activities
  - Product and service delivery and acceptance activities
- *Project Business Activities*—The customer should participate in several business-related activities associated with the project effort.
  - Contract or agreement negotiation
  - Contract modification actions
  - Executive and senior management collaboration
  - Project business reporting
  - Invoice receipt and payment

The nature and extent of customer involvement that is needed will also depend on the particular type of project work, industry and marketplace influences, and associated norms for customer involvement under those conditions or specifications.

13.3 CUSTOMER SATISFACTION MANAGEMENT

The achievement of customer satisfaction is a genuine contribution to ongoing opportunities associated with the customer business relationship. However, customer satisfaction issues and information also tend to surface in the marketplace to reflect on and communicate the project management capability of the performing organization. Therefore, the organization has to ensure that the customer's experience with project performance is one that meets the customer's business needs and expectations. The performing organization can do this by monitoring and responding to customer satisfaction issues on a near-continuous basis.

Concept of This Practice

This practice provides the project manager, the project team, and the organization with the information and guidance needed to gauge customer satisfaction throughout the project management life cycle and to respond to any indications of customer dissatisfaction. The purpose of this practice is to identify and manage indicators of customer satisfaction and dissatisfaction. Thereby, this practice prescribes three activities:

- Measure Customer Satisfaction
- Conduct Customer Relationship Programs
- Implement Customercentric Improvements

Customer Satisfaction Management activities are accomplished throughout the project, but they are prominent during the Perform Phase and the Post Phase. Notwithstanding, an awareness of the customer's perception of project and project team performance should be maintained onward from the earliest stages of project activity involving the customer.

Measure Customer Satisfaction

The only way to know the level of customer satisfaction achieved is to measure it—on each and every project. Most customer satisfaction measurement actions can be performed by the project manager as prescribed by guidance in the project management methodology.

However, other organizational entities such as the project management office (PMO) and senior managers can also perform customer satisfaction measurements, sometimes independent of project performance. The following are a few examples of customer satisfaction measurements that can be conducted by the project manager and others in the organization:

- *Business Manager Follow-Up*—The individual responsible for the customer account and associated customer business generation can maintain contact with the customer to ascertain how well the customer is responding to project performance and progression.

- *PMO and Executive Follow-Up*—The business importance of the customer relationship will determine if PMO and executive involvement with the customer is warranted. If so, an executive-level relationship (i.e., contact and conversation) could be pursued with the customer at the executive level to obtain a senior management perspective on the progress of the project effort. The PMO can perform a similar role, as representative of senior management within the relevant organization, in collaborating with customer senior managers to ensure that project performance is meeting customer expectations.
- *Informal Customer Contact*—The project manager will likely be in continuous contact with a customer who is receptive to ongoing interactions with the project manager. This presents the project manager with recurring opportunities to discuss project progress and performance with customer representatives on an informal basis and to obtain personal insight into customer perspectives and satisfaction with the project effort. These insights should be documented for subsequent examination, with the recognition that they are obtained informally.
- *Formal Customer Satisfaction Surveys*—The project manager can collaborate with the PMO to determine the appropriate points in the project for conducting formal surveys of customer satisfaction. Surveys can be administered by the PMO or the project manager, depending on the nature of the business relationship with the customer. The following customer surveys can be considered at various junctures in the project:
  - Postcontract Survey—An evaluation of customer satisfaction relative to the business development and contracting processes encountered to initiate the project
  - Interim Surveys—An evaluation of customer satisfaction at specific junctures in the project management life cycle when a determination of customer satisfaction is deemed critical; for example, transition to the next project or technical phase, introduction of a new concept or practice, subcontractor performance, etc.
  - Test and Acceptance Evaluation—An evaluation of customer satisfaction in association with the customer's inspection and acceptance of project deliverables
  - End User's Evaluation—An evaluation, which could be pursued on a formal or informal basis, that considers the responses and reactions of end users in the customer's environment to the technical solution delivered by the project
  - Postproject Review—An evaluation of customer satisfaction with both project performance and the associated business relationship

  Any of these can be construed as customer satisfaction surveys, although some tend to be more technical in nature than others.
- *Project Status Meetings*—The project manager should include customer representatives as participants in a recurring meeting to review project status and progress. This provides the opportunity to solicit and obtain direct customer feedback, which should be documented in meeting minutes and separately as part of customer satisfaction results.
- *Customer Feedback Report*—The project manager can collaborate with the PMO to jointly determine customer satisfaction using a formal customer satisfaction feedback report, perhaps even an electronic survey instrument. This would be valuable when an extremely large project effort is conducted in a customer environment that spans a number of geographical locations, possibly distributed globally. This report allows customer managers and end users throughout the customer's organization to provide feedback regarding all aspects of project performance, but likely focusing on satisfaction with project deliverables. This type of survey may be created for a specific project and specific customer effort.

The PMO should be a recipient of all customer satisfaction measurement and feedback results. It can then examine these results against individual performance of project managers, group performance of project teams, and overall performance of all projects in the relevant organization. This will enable the PMO to prescribe corrective actions for individuals and teams where needed, but particularly to devise and implement actions for use across the project management environment to improve overall customer satisfaction indicators.

Conduct Customer Relationship Programs

Customer satisfaction is distinctly associated with projects that produce the desired deliverables and achieve the prescribed customer business objectives. Therefore, customer satisfaction can be determined in direct alignment with project success. The following highlights some additional examples of customer relationship programs that can be used to gain insight into customer satisfaction and to build stronger business relationships with each customer:

- *Customer Interest Surveys*—These are surveys of all or a portion of current and past customers to obtain their perspectives on business and technology, particularly as they pertain to the nature of project work conducted by the performing organization. Customer comments and opinions can be used to evaluate new project management practices or to examine new technology or technical solutions. They can also be used to ascertain any emerging opportunities within the customer's industry.

- *Customer Technical and Business Forums*—The organization can arrange and present single- or multiday programs for attendance by selected current and past customers. These forums can be used to facilitate collaboration and communication among customers using the products or services delivered by the relevant organization through project efforts and to obtain feedback on the current use of deliverables.
- *Customer Postproject Correspondence*—The organization, PMO, and project managers can keep in touch with customers through the use of general and specific correspondence. Such correspondence could be more informal and personal or represent an official follow-up at some time after project completion to inquire about project deliverable performance, business results achieved, and the state of customer satisfaction with the passage of time.
- *Customer Postproject Contact*—Similar to correspondence, this program represents personal contact by phone or in person. It demonstrates continued interest in the customer by the project manager and the performing organization, and uncommon business interest and commitment to the customer by the performing organization.
- *Customer Newsletters*—The organization (usually the PMO) can collaborate with leaders in the technical disciplines to design and publish relevant newsletters that are provided to current and past customers. They can highlight technical trends and innovations, particularly those introduced by professionals within the project management environment.

These follow-on customer programs help to build customer relationship over time and hopefully contribute to extending each business customer relationship beyond a single project effort. However, as these programs are considered, the organization must also be prepared and have the capability to respond to any adverse or otherwise negative customer feedback. Of course, the key is to ensure excellence in the delivery of project management and the technical solution for which the customer will have no lingering doubts of success or loss of satisfaction over time.

The organization's interest in these customer relationship programs is directly tied to its capability for project and business management integration. As the project management environment achieves greater capability, and the relevant organization becomes more mature in concepts and practices of modern project management, the organization will inherently be positioned to address business practices such as customer relationship management programs relative to the customer base it has created.

Implement Customercentric Improvements

Managing customer satisfaction includes addressing improvement actions the organization can take to increase the likelihood of customer satisfaction. Some improvement actions will be a result of natural business sense, and others will be more subtle—a result of discovery and analysis regarding how customers perceive the efficiency and effectiveness of the organization's project management environment.

The performing organization, usually through the PMO (when it exists), should compile and analyze customer satisfaction information to identify indicators for improvement of general and specific customer satisfaction issues and results. Analyses results should identify what improvements can be implemented in the integration of project management, technical management, and business management practices to increase overall customer satisfaction. This means examining the project management environment from a customer's perspective and determining what influence can be applied to engender a mutually rewarding customer business relationship. The specific examination of project performance from the customer's perspective makes this a customercentric activity.

The following prescribes a few areas to consider when examining ways to improve customer perceptions of the organization and overall customer satisfaction:

- Customer perceptions of project manager performance
  - Project management skill and qualifications
  - Leadership capability and experience
  - Technical capability and experience
  - Customer relationship skills
- Customer perceptions of project management practices
  - Communication of plans and documentation
  - Inclusion of the customer in key project decisions
  - Timeliness of project reporting
  - Collaboration and resolution of issues and problems
  - Scope and change management effectiveness
  - Project stakeholder management effectiveness
  - Contract administration (including invoice management)
- Customer perceptions of technical performance
  - Technical skill and qualifications of the project team
  - Inclusion of the customer in key technical decisions
  - Achievement of technical specifications
  - Timeliness of project deliverables
  - Quality of project deliverables
  - Configuration management effectiveness
  - Ability to effectively manage cohesive project teams

- Customer perceptions of business performance
  - Skill and qualification of the business manager
  - Business skill of the project manager
  - Attention given to the customer by executives and senior managers
  - Recognition of the customer's ongoing business relationship
  - Competitive pricing in the marketplace
  - Value of products and services obtained

The organization can examine these points and incorporate additional improvement indicators in its evaluations of customer satisfaction. It can then develop and implement improvements to its processes and practices according to the results of its examination of customer satisfaction.

Chapter 14

Project Business Management

Project Business Management highlights the influence that projects have on business interests and objectives. This methodology has promoted the concept that project management, in many regards, is business management. To that end, the project should always be conducted in a businesslike manner, with business interests and objectives in mind.

This statement also prompts two further considerations. First, each project manager has some degree of business performance responsibility, and thereby he or she requires the skill and capability to manage business elements of the project. Second, the organization's management, particularly senior operational managers and strategic managers, needs to be aware of project management concepts and how they are applied to project performance.

Ideally, a project management office (PMO) is established to monitor and manage the common interface between the interests of the business environment and the interests of the project management environment. However, with or without a PMO, practices are needed to guide project manager and stakeholder activities for appropriate integration of business and project management.

There are four practices associated with Project Business Management:

- Project Charter Development
- Project Governance and Oversight
- Project Audit Management
- Portfolio Management

It should become readily apparent that business aspects of project management will be more effectively introduced and managed across all projects with a PMO, rather than putting the burden on each project manager. The practices presented in this section will demonstrate centralized project management oversight and control as would be provided by a PMO, and will readily contribute to achieving business interests in the project management environment.

14.1 PROJECT CHARTER DEVELOPMENT

The concepts of modern project management have prompted expansion of traditional project management responsibilities. In particular, project managers have been given a broader range of project and business authority that enables them to accomplish their job responsibilities. The project charter represents the assignment of that authority to the project manager.

It is important that responsibility is identified in association with the authority given. Conversely, organizations need to use caution to ensure that such responsibility is not given without adequate authority. The project charter is a document that is conveyed by management to indicate the level of authority given to a project manager for a specific project.

Concept of This Practice

This practice represents management's completed review and acceptance of the project business case and the selection of a qualified individual who will be assigned to manage the associated project (and its business interests) through fulfillment of project objectives. The purpose of this practice is to provide the project manager with a written indication of project management and business management authority; the document also inherently represents management's endorsement and support for the project manager's assignment to the specified project.

Project Charter Development should always be performed during the Profile Phase. However, it should be updated at any time during the project as authority, funding, or responsibility elements are changed. It should be noted by methodology users that different industries and organizations provide for various connotations regarding what a project charter is and what purpose it is intended to serve. It would not be unusual to find a project charter in some organizations to be what we have defined herein as the project definition, the business case, or even the project plan. In contrast, this methodology prescribes the project charter as the fundamental "authority tool" of the project manager and distinguishes it from other related project documentation.

Identify Project Manager Authority

The PMO's role in this governance-based practice will be decided by its own level of authority as indicated in the broader PMO charter. If sufficiently vested, the PMO can serve to both specify levels of project manager authority and be the project charter issuing authority. Otherwise, the PMO's primary objective in this function is to prepare recommendations for project manager authority levels for review and approval within the organization.

The following are examples of project manager authority that should be considered for inclusion in the project charter:

- *Contractual Authority*—Determine if project managers have any signature authority relative to customer contracts. Often, the organization's sales management team and specific senior business managers will sign any master contract with the customer. Conversely, the organization may want project managers to have certain levels of authority to deal with such matters as contract modifications and statements of work issued subsequent to the signing of a master contract. Similarly, the organization will need to determine the project managers' authority relative to vendor and contractor contracts and subcontracts. The organization may also need to specify variations on project manager authority for matters dealing with "internal contracts."
- *Financial Authority*—The nature of the business should be applied to guide the organization in determining the extent of financial responsibility given to the project manager. This includes authorization to incur and manage expenses, oversee customer invoice management, oversee vendor and contractor invoice management, and, in some cases, allow special or additional employee compensation such as bonuses or rewards.
- *Resource Management*—Most project managers operate in an environment in which project team members are introduced to projects in a matrix format. This usually necessitates broad collaboration on resource utilization within the organization. Project resources working in a matrix format are assigned to resource managers; they are "borrowed" by project managers to work on specific project efforts and then returned to the purview of the resource manager. The organization should develop procedures and guidance regarding how resource management authority can be shared between the resource manager and the project manager.
- *Customer Relationships*—The organization will recognize that there are many business elements that influence each customer relationship. It needs to determine what role project managers will play as a part of the total business effort. Authority issues here deal with such matters as customer contact protocols, customer satisfaction responsibility, and customer issue resolution and elevation. This type of authority is particularly important when the project manager and project team perform work on-site at client facilities where they are the primary representatives of the organization.
- *Vendor and Contractor Relationships*—Determine the responsibility for project manager involvement in any prequalification of vendors and contractors, or specify this activity as a responsibility of the PMO. However, once vendors have been validated (prequalified), the organization may find it beneficial to give project managers vendor and contractor selection authority (i.e., vendor hiring) for specific work on most projects.

The organization can examine this list of project manager authority and modify it based on its business needs and interests. Then, in conjunction with issuing a project charter, the PMO or other senior management entity confirms the authority given to individuals.

The organization (or the PMO) may want to consider varying levels of authority. That is, project manager authority can increase as an individual advances to higher management roles or positions of responsibility. Also, the same authority can be given to all individuals who have project performance responsibility, where every project manager has the same authority level based on standard practices rather than on position in the organizational hierarchy.

Prepare the Project Charter

The project charter identifies the assignment of the project manager and specifies the range of project manager authority and responsibility. It may also identify other managers who will have oversight responsibility for the project, and other persons to whom the project manager can turn when issues of authority and responsibility need to be resolved or otherwise elevated.

A standard form can be used when issuing a project charter, such as the tool prescribed within the accompanying methodology toolkit. The project charter is normally signed by the senior executive holding responsibility for project success. This could be a business manager or a member of the executive control board, the project executive or sponsor, or the PMO manager when the PMO is so involved. An issued project charter indicates that a project has been selected and is essentially under way.

As project manager authority is specified across several areas, the project charter should particularly address the approved and pending project funding, which inherently specifies limits of financial authority. The "Business Recommendation" tool is used to review and approve project funding. Relevant project funding information can be transferred to the project charter, or the "Business Recommendation" tool can simply be appended to become part of the project charter document.

14.2 PROJECT GOVERNANCE AND OVERSIGHT

Project governance and oversight will be unique for each performing organization as it determines who will be involved in project management oversight and the extent of their involvement. Needless to say, there should be some visible management oversight of projects. While project managers are becoming more accountable for business interests across industries, it is still the executive echelon that has ultimate responsibility for business success and thereby warrants a distinct involvement in overseeing the project efforts that help determine business success.

It is suggested that project governance and oversight can be facilitated by having a PMO that is positioned to serve as the prime interface between project and business management. This reduces the impact of frequent involvement of senior managers and executives while providing the project manager with a reliable next level of support.

Concept of This Practice

This practice provides the project manager with the means and capability to coordinate and collaborate with executives and decision makers in the organization. It ensures that each project is following a path consistent with business needs and objectives.

While presented as a practice because it specifies executive and senior management involvement at junctures in the project management life cycle process, actual project governance and oversight procedures are usually defined by organizational managers and the established business culture, which is often separate from methodology implementation. Therefore, as project governance and oversight activities are prescribed by this methodology process, several prerequisites should be examined and fulfilled to align existing business procedures with prescribed methodology procedures.

Project Governance and Oversight is performed throughout all phases of the project management life cycle. The project governance and oversight practice will address the following three considerations:

- Determine executive oversight requirements.
- Align business and technical committees (organizations).
- Conduct project management oversight.

Once again, if a PMO exists, it should play a significant role in formulating and implementing these activities. If a PMO does not yet exist in the organization, then this practice might be used to prompt consideration for establishing a PMO.

Determine Executive Oversight Requirements

This effort is ideally initiated and led by the PMO, but any other established group of senior project and business managers could also perform this activity in the absence of a PMO. It begins with an examination of the project, business, and technical oversight requirements used or otherwise needed in the project management environment. In conjunction with this examination, the PMO also collaborates with any relevant executives or control board members to gain an understanding of the depth and extent of oversight that they would prefer to have within the organization's normal mode of project management operations.

For purposes of discussion, we will refer to an "executive control board" as the authority and decision maker in matters of determining project management oversight requirements. This board normally comprises one or more senior executives and may have either a business or technical orientation. The board's executive-level authority enables requirements to be implemented across all projects served by this methodology and presumably across the relevant organization.

The PMO should examine the following prominent functional areas to prepare an initial list of oversight recommendations for review and approval by the executive-level authority:

- *Methodology Development*—It should be determined if review and approval are needed to authorize and fund project management methodology development, customization, and implementation. Executive control board endorsement will certainly be desired, but it may defer methodology development and implementation decisions and responsibility to an appropriate technical board or committee, to an individual executive or senior manager, or to the PMO.
- *Knowledge Management*—This area of examination provides for the exchange of project management and project performance information in the form of status

reports, project work plans, and technical papers. This function also deals with implementing an "executive dashboard" that summarizes all project management information online for at-a-glance viewing. The executive control board will need to determine the type, frequency, and receipt methods for project information; it needs to stay informed and make timely business decisions. This may involve additional collaboration with other executives in the organization to identify their project information needs.

- *Project Governance*—The executive control board or executive sponsor will be the issuer of project management policies. The board must determine the scope of policies it will consider as a group, and which will be deferred to the executive sponsor or to the PMO. There are four prominent areas in which the PMO will want to recommend or otherwise develop policy guidance, as summarized here:
  - Business Interest—This type of policy guidance conveys and promotes the use of project management for purposes of achieving business objectives. Policies created in this area specify that project management and business processes and practices must be aligned and integrated. Such policies usually mandate the use of a preferred process (i.e., methodology) and indicate if it is primarily a business process introduced into the project management environment or a project management process introduced for use by business units.
  - Project Management as a Core Competency—This is a specific policy that transcends all business units in the relevant organization. It establishes that business will be pursued with a high degree of reliance on individual capabilities in project management. It is a business decision that can only come from the most senior executive in the organization.
  - Enterprise Continuous Improvement—This is a policy area that enables expansion of project management practices both within the project environment and throughout the relevant organization. It also represents expansion of PMO responsibilities, possibly across business units. Policies in this area specify or mandate the use of practices that provide more comprehensive oversight and support of project management activities, as is often aligned with pursuits of increased organizational maturity in project management as well as capability in portfolio management.
  - Project Management Practices—This policy area indicates the required use of the established project management methodology in the project management environment and possibly across the relevant organization or enterprise. It also specifies the preferred business practices, tools, and techniques that are applied in project management, and it presents requirements for use of project classification guidance. Also, it can specify requirements for project audits and reviews.

  It should be noted that policy development is a different context from guidance offered by standards, operating procedures, or regulatory requirements. Standards and procedures can be prepared and implemented by the PMO often on its own authority and perhaps with some level of senior management sponsorship and approval. However, the preparation of project management policy guidance is one of developing an "executive directive." This means that an executive or the executive control board within the relevant organization is establishing a formal business direction.
- *Organization and Structure*—The executive control board should influence deliberation and decisions regarding how project managers are functionally aligned and assigned to project management efforts. This examination could be particularly important if the PMO is recommending a change to the current organizational structure and practices. This also may be only a one-time consideration, but it warrants senior-level involvement.
- *Resource Training and Education*—The executive control board may want to be included among those initially trained in project management practices and principles. It, too, needs sufficient understanding of project management to effectively use the project management environment as a means to achieve business objectives, although not the intensive training given to project managers and team members. The executive control board will have to decide on the training it will receive and, through PMO recommendations, the training other project management participants will be given.
- *Project Auditing*—The executive control board may want to influence and possibly control project management audit efforts. It must determine if it will be involved in constructing the criteria or it should simply approve the PMO's recommended criteria for conducting project audits. It also should examine and determine the ideal junctures for routine audits and any "triggers" for special audits.
- *Program Management*—The executive control board may delegate the brunt of this oversight responsibility to the PMO, retaining options for involvement as the particular nature of each project dictates. This effort is examined to determine what oversight activities will be conducted for each project. To a large extent, program management oversight activities are already incorporated in this methodology (as per all the tools associated with the *Management* series of activities). This is

done with the PMO being the implied representative of the executive control board or some other organizational management authority.

- *Portfolio Management*—This function may be the most critical requirement for participation by the executive control board. Unless otherwise delegated, the executive control board, as a high-level executive group in the organization, inherently has responsibility for project portfolio management within the organization. The board should be involved in establishing both the process and the criteria that will be used to assist it in making project selection, continuation, and termination decisions, which inherently affect business outcomes.
- *Business Performance*—The executive control board will likely want to influence how the PMO supports its business initiatives and strategic business plan. Considerations in this functional area enable the executive control board to direct the PMO in specific business integration activities within the project management environment. This also includes the establishment of a PMO within the relevant organization, or even multiple PMOs within the enterprise—each having specific business-related responsibilities.

These are only a few samples of the functional considerations the PMO can formulate in preparing oversight recommendations for the executive control board. It is suggested that a new PMO start with just a few of the requirements and then add additional items for executive control board consideration over time. It can also be noted that the size, culture, and business objectives of the organization may influence delegation of some of these requirements to other technical or business committees that may be better positioned to deal with them.

Align Business and Technical Committees

The PMO's responsibility for some, if not all, operations in the project management environment will warrant interaction with existing business and technical committees within the organization. This is similar to its role within the executive control board, but here the PMO deals with soliciting collaboration and guidance from specific business activities and technical leadership groups. In larger organizations, there may be several such groups. In smaller organizations, the executive control board, as defined earlier, could be the sole group that also manages business and technical issues and guidance.

The primary objective of this activity is to ensure that project managers have the necessary input from guiding committees so as to effectively incorporate their interests, and sometimes their mandates, into the project management practices. The PMO can facilitate this by using the following three simple steps to conduct initial alignment with relevant business and technical groups: (1) Identify business and technical groups, (2) set up business collaboration and relationships, and (3) manage those relationships.

Realistically, the committees, groups, and forums suggested for examination may already be well entrenched in the project management environment. One of them may have even evolved to become the PMO. The PMO should then proceed to participate in the business and technical group relationships that are established and their associated activities.

Conduct Project Management Oversight

The primary activities associated with project governance and oversight can be conducted by the project executive/sponsor, or by the PMO. In some situations, certain oversight and control responsibilities may be extended or delegated to a technical or business committee within the organization.

It is important for each project manager in the organization to know and have access (at least indirectly, through the PMO) to the source of project governance and oversight guidance. There will undoubtedly be need for confirmation of use or clarification of intent for such policies and guidance over the course of project management.

As per assigned responsibility, the following are areas of project governance and oversight that should be considered for development and implementation in association with each phase of project management.

Profile Phase

This project management initiation phase calls for management involvement relative to project opportunity evaluation and selection activities and the introduction of a new project as a business effort. It includes project governance and oversight related to

- Customer pursuit decisions—new versus established business relationships
- Project opportunity pursuit decisions—capacity/capability to perform
- Project classification decisions—project definition and scope coverage
- Staffing decisions—availability, qualification, and commitment of resources
- Vendor decisions—qualification
- Business case reviews
  - Project business/financial analysis reviews
  - Project risk examinations
  - Project performance outlook/forecast reviews
- Business interest decisions
- Project selection and funding actions

- Project manager selection and project charter actions
- Project portfolio management—new project integration

Plan Phase

This project management planning phase calls for management involvement in ensuring that the project is adequately prepared to achieve specified needs, requirements, and objectives while attending to the formal business proposal contract that will be offered to the customer. It includes project governance and oversight related to

- Customer requirements reviews—assurance of understanding and stability
- Technical proposal reviews—collaboration on technical approach and deliverables
- Project plan reviews—plan selection and completeness
- Staffing decisions—resource acquisition progress and fulfillment of staffing needs
- Vendor decisions—selection and contract implementation
- Business proposal reviews
  - Contract elements
  - Terms and conditions
  - Pricing offer
- Management role decisions—gateway reviews, oversight activities, and PMO activities

Perform Phase

This project management implementation phase warrants management involvement in monitoring the status and progress of projects—individually and collectively—and for assuring the achievement of desired customer satisfaction and associated project performance success. It includes project governance and oversight related to

- Customer performance reviews—participation and expectations fulfillment
- Project performance reviews—cost, schedule, and resource utilization variance
- Staff performance reviews—allotment and assignment fulfillment
- Vendor performance reviews—deliverable quality and contract fulfillment
- Business performance reviews
  - Customer contract fulfillment
  - Cost and financial management fulfillment (invoice status)
  - Customer contract administration (change management)
- Management meetings and reviews
  - Project portfolio reviews
  - Project ready-to-execute and gateway reviews
  - Project audit reviews
  - Problem identification, elevation, and resolution

Post Phase

This project management closeout phase contains several areas for management involvement in the formal closing of each project. This may be a particularly important area of involvement if a formal project portfolio management process has been implemented in the organization. It includes project governance and oversight related to

- Lessons learned reviews
- Evaluation reviews
  - Customer evaluations
  - Project performance evaluations
  - Staff performance evaluations
  - Business performance evaluations
  - Management performance evaluations
- Project closeout activity reviews
- Project portfolio closeout

All in all, this practice area provides for some level of executive involvement in project management as appropriate to the needs of the relevant organization and the size of the project management environment.

14.3 PROJECT AUDIT MANAGEMENT

Project Audit Management is an activity that has a unique connotation and context across various industries and within different professional disciplines. A common aspect of auditing across multiple venues appears to be the concept of examination: observing, identifying, evaluating, or otherwise determining conditions. Some similarity can be found in that most auditing efforts examine overall efficiency, quality, and value of outcomes resulting from use or nonuse of a process, practice, policy, or capability. To that end, prescribed auditing activities will seek to identify the efficiencies, qualities, and values associated with projects and project management. Of course, this will naturally extend to an examination of business and technical aspects of project work as well.

The PMO will normally lead the development and implementation of auditing activities prescribed for use in the project management environment. The organization may specify the extent to which the PMO is actually involved in conducting audits and reviews, but it should be a participant in reviewing and deliberating results as a basis for ascertaining the overall health and effectiveness of project management in the organization.

Concept of This Practice

This practice provides the project manager and the organization with a means to examine critical elements of project and business performance. Most audits can be performed internally and will provide an adequate indication of performance. Sometimes, a distinct unbiased opinion of performance is sought, and that warrants use of external, third-party auditors.

Project Audit Management is planned in conjunction with other project management activities during the Plan Phase. In turn, they are executed as prescribed or as needed during the Perform Phase of the project management effort. The *Project Audit Management* practice will be examined in the following five areas:

- Identify auditing resources.
- Establish project audit performance points.
- Conduct primary project management audits.
- Conduct other project management audits.
- Conduct technical audits.

Once again, if a PMO exists, it should play a significant role in formulating and implementing project audit activities.

Identify Auditing Resources

The PMO may have responsibility for project auditing in the organization, but it will likely not have the staff depth or broad skill to conduct all required audits in the project management environment. To that end, it will have to evaluate project auditing requirements and designate preferred auditors and auditing teams.

An inherent issue in identifying project auditing resources is the need to qualify auditors. Audit training and experience are prominent factors in qualifying auditors. Also, requisite technical or project management competency is a primary factor for consideration of auditor qualification by the PMO. Qualified auditors can then use the PMO's prescribed approach to conduct audits. In addition to the PMO, there are four types of resources that can be used to conduct audits in the project management environment.

Project Managers and Project Team Members

Project managers have responsibility for continuous monitoring and management of project status and progress. They inherently conduct informal audits as part of their ongoing practice of project management. They can similarly be given responsibility for performing specific types of project audits specified by the PMO as project conditions warrant or project audit points are encountered. The key here is that they will distinctly use auditing guidance and processes prescribed by the PMO to ensure that planned audits are consistent across all projects.

Individuals serving as senior project managers have demonstrated their understanding of project management concepts and principles; they are more or less well versed in the nuances of project management within the relevant organization, and they presumably have the experience required to use and comprehend primary project condition indicators. This qualifies the more senior project managers to conduct audits on projects other than their own. The key here is for these resources to demonstrate an ability to achieve an impartial, business-oriented review of people, performance, and practices according to the procedures of the particular types of audits to which they are assigned.

Also, project team members who demonstrate technical or project management competency can also be used to conduct formal and informal project audits. They can assist the project manager in performing audits on their current project. Since they usually bring particular technical expertise, they can even lead certain technical audits and reviews. In some cases, individual expertise may warrant they be assigned to auditing teams that are convened to examine projects other than their own in the project management environment.

To the extent that the PMO relies on project managers and project team members to conduct project management and technical audits, consideration for training them in effective and efficient auditing practices is warranted. Particular consideration should be given to training of individuals designated as leaders of primary audits in the relevant organization.

Internal Auditors

The PMO can canvas the resources available within the organization to identify and qualify individuals from business units who can participate as auditors in the project management environment. In some cases, organizational policies and procedures, or inherent responsibilities of individuals in certain business positions, will designate auditor status.

The following is a sample listing of a few roles in the relevant organization that can be considered for participation as technical and project management auditors:

- Senior managers in any position (ideally, ones that interface with project management)
- Quality assurance managers
- Quality control managers
- Finance managers and specialists
- Business analysts
- Senior engineers and scientists
- Senior technical specialists

Auditing team assignments for these internal resources should have some alignment between their primary specialty or professional credentials, the type of audit being conducted, and their responsibilities for that audit. The qualifications of internal resources considered, there must be at least one influential individual on the auditing team who can demonstrate advanced competency in applying the concepts and content of modern project management practices.

Again, if the same internal resources are assigned to auditing duties on a recurring basis, some training in auditing practices as well as project management practices is recommended.

External Collaborative Auditors

The PMO can preclude an internal search to identify and qualify auditor candidates through use of external collaborating resources—project management auditing consultants. This approach is particularly cost effective when the frequency or type of primary audits conducted in the project management environment does not warrant an effort to fully qualify and train internal personnel in project management auditing practices and procedures. However, it can also be beneficial in organizations that desire to take advantage of third-party expertise and impartiality in conducting audits in the project management environment.

In taking this approach, the organization (i.e., the PMO) will have to manage external auditor qualification and selection. The PMO should anticipate project auditing needs and, with consideration for the process and acceptance for introducing external resources into the relevant organization, conduct necessary internal coordination and accomplish external auditing consultant evaluations to make the selection and assignment of auditors in a timely manner.

External Regulatory Auditors

The second type of external resource the organization might encounter is the regulatory auditor. This auditor may or may not have expertise in the full range of project management knowledge and practices but has a bona fide need and appropriate authorization to conduct an examination within the project management environment. Generally, such an auditor is introduced in association with government regulatory requirements or through government customer contract provisions. However, in some cases, the organization may be obligated to accept an auditor into the project management environment as a result of contractual provisions in a nongovernmental customer's contract or agreement. This auditing possibility makes it essential to review and understand the provisions of every customer contract or agreement.

The regulatory auditor should provide an agenda and identify the scope of the audit to be conducted. PMO assistance may be needed to schedule and arrange the participation of project managers and team members in auditor fact-finding meetings, document reviews, and other presentations, and to facilitate auditor administrative activities in the relevant organization. Otherwise, there is normally no formal PMO or relevant organizational responsibility for performing audit steps prescribed by the regulatory auditor's process.

The project manager (or PMO) is responsible for ensuring that relevant executives and senior managers are aware of any scheduled audit by an external regulatory auditor. Also, advance notification of upcoming external regulatory audits should be conveyed to project managers and project team members.

Establish Project Audit Performance Points

The organization can establish audit performance points to specify when or under what conditions an audit will be conducted in the project management environment. There are two types of audit performance points that will be identified—the routine project audit point and the triggered project audit point.

The *routine project audit point* is a designated point in the project management life cycle or in a technical process at which a specified type of project or technical audit or review is conducted. This type of audit is normally identified in the project work breakdown structure (WBS) and work plan, and its performance is anticipated as a routine part of the project management effort. Routine project audits include virtually all of the primary project management audits defined later in this section and many of the technical audits and reviews associated with the nature of the project deliverables. The PMO should define and incorporate any routine project audit points into the project management methodology and technical processes.

The *triggered project audit point* is an unscheduled audit or review conducted in response to a project performance indicator, or "trigger," which suggests that a more detailed examination of some aspect of project or technical performance is warranted. While a triggered project audit point is not necessarily anticipated at any specific point in the project, it should not present any major surprises to the project manager or project team. In a sense, it is a normal response to a highlighted condition in project performance. In fact, triggered project audit points can be identified in appropriate project plans, and they include the particular conditions under which such audits will be pursued.

The PMO may also seek and obtain the authority to conduct audits at its own discretion, in which a project audit performance point is not specified. Presumably, the PMO will apply superb judgment to guide decisions that initiate such unanticipated audits in the project management environment. Also, unannounced project audits should not always have a negative connotation. There may be circumstances under which the PMO, in collaboration with project managers, wants to examine project team performance and participation under project audit conditions. The PMO may need to conduct a minor audit across all currently active projects as a matter of collecting specific information for analysis. Also, the PMO may want to test the performance of a newly formed audit team in conducting an auditing process.

Conduct Primary Project Management Audits

Primary project management audits represent a few essential and fundamental audits that can be considered for use in the project management environment.

Project Management Audit

This audit is a broad-scope but fairly comprehensive examination of project management performance. The project manager or project team can perform this audit; however, it is highly recommended that this audit be conducted by the PMO or another third party to accomplish an impartial and objective appraisal from an unbiased perspective. This is a formal audit that may take one or more qualified auditors a full day or more to complete, depending on project size, and with additional time needed for any associated analysis of findings and report preparation.

This audit is accomplished through discussions and interviews with the project manager, technical leaders, and at least a sampling of project team members, in conjunction with a hands-on review of pertinent project documents. It normally includes examination of

- *Project work plan and support plans created to guide the project management effort*
  - Completion of required planning documents (per project classification)
  - Adequate inclusion of prescribed plan content
  - Appropriate inclusion of preferred practices and industry standards
- *Project work plan and support plan implementation effectiveness*
  - Accomplishment of project work efforts according to applicable plans
  - Demonstrated tracking of actual project results against work plan elements
  - Timely identification and response to work plan element variations
  - Use of approved change management procedures for modifying plan content
- *Project resource management and task performance oversight*
  - Identification of assigned project resources and their contributing competencies
  - Management of resource task assignments and task completion status
  - Accessibility and use of the project work plan and applicable support plans by project resources
- *Project vendor/contractor management and task performance oversight*
  - Identification of vendor/contractor project team role and responsibilities
  - Management of vendor/contractor assignment and deliverable status
  - Accomplishment of vendor/contractor deliverable approval and acceptance
  - Performance of vendor/contractor contract administration activities
- *Fulfillment of customer contractual obligations*
  - Accomplishment of adequate deliverable quality assurance activities
  - Achievement of timely presentation of deliverables and customer acceptance
  - Performance of customer contract administration activities

The general project audit is applicable to larger and longer-duration projects that are already under way beyond the Profile and Plan phases. It is an audit that can be performed as often as quarterly until the project reaches the closeout stage.

Project Performance Audit (aka Project Health Check)

This audit represents a detailed examination of the financial and business aspects of the project. In particular, earned value analysis or another preferred method of financial examination is applied, business case elements are reviewed, and the project risk management plan and activities are evaluated. This is a formal audit that will generally take one or more fully qualified auditors three to five days to identify conditions, analyze findings, and prepare a fundamental project performance audit report, depending on the size of the project and the scope of the audit. Validity of the audit is significantly enhanced when conducted by the PMO or another external, third-party auditor.

This audit can be conducted independently or in conjunction with a project management audit to review and validate the financial and business conditions of the project, with emphasis on evaluating and confirming the ability of the project to achieve specified objectives. This audit normally includes examination of

- *The business case used to manage selection and continuation of the project*
  - Relevance of business purpose and alignment with business interests

  - Achievement of staffing aligned with the resource allocation plan
  - Confirmation of trends toward achieving cost–benefit analysis results
  - Achievement and acceptance of project deliverables
  - Identification of customer relationship status and pertinent issues
- *Cost specified in the project work plan*
  - Review of cost tracking and reporting methods and accuracy
  - Identification and evaluation of cost performance (i.e., planned versus actual)
  - Identification and evaluation of cost variance
- *Schedule specified in the project work plan*
  - Review of schedule tracking and reporting methods and accuracy
  - Identification and evaluation of schedule performance (i.e., planned versus actual)
  - Identification and evaluation of schedule variance
- *Resource utilization specified in the project work plan*
  - Review of resource utilization tracking and reporting methods and accuracy
  - Identification and evaluation of resource utilization performance (i.e., planned versus actual)
  - Identification and utilization of resource utilization variance
- *The project risk management plan*
  - Achievement of project risk identification, analysis, and prioritization
  - Documented review and update of project risks at appropriate intervals
  - Specification of risk response strategies for high-priority risks
  - Inclusion of proactive risk response strategies in the project WBS
  - Preparation of contingency plans and acquisition of funding for reactive risk response strategies

The project performance audit is applicable to virtually all projects of discernable value and duration that are already under way beyond the Plan Phase. It is an audit that can be performed as often as quarterly until the project reaches the Post Phase. The PMO also can use this audit in conjunction with project portfolio management reviews.

Preproject (Plan Phase) Audit

This audit validates project readiness for execution. It is usually performed by the project manager and project team, but it can be accomplished by the PMO or another external auditing team or a third-party auditor. This audit presumes requisite project selection activities have been accomplished, and normally includes examination of

- *Initial project management documents and activities*
  - Finalization of the project definition
  - Validation of the project budget and resource allocation plan
  - Preparation of the project charter (project manager authority specification)
  - Authorization of project funding (if not in project charter)
  - Executive (sponsor) approval to proceed with project implementation
- *Initial technical documents and activities*
  - Review of customer requirements documents
  - Review of technical specifications documents
  - Review of technical survey documents
  - Preparation of project quality management plan
  - Identification of technical plans needed for the project
  - Preparation of initial technical plans required by methodology or policy
- *Initial project management planning documents and activities*
  - Preparation of the project work plan
  - Preparation of the project risk management plan
  - Preparation of the quality management plan
  - Preparation of the project communication plan
  - Preparation of the project change management plan
  - Preparation of the staff management plan (resource responsibility matrix)
  - Preparation of the vendor/contractor management plan
  - Identification of project management support plans needed for the project
- *Initial project team documents and activities*
  - Appropriate staff participation in project kickoff and planning meetings
  - Specification of project team member reporting requirements
  - Determination of project team readiness to begin project execution
- *Initial vendor and contractor documents and activities*
  - Coordination and acceptance of vendor/contractor technical approach
  - Specification of vendor/contractor reporting requirements
  - Execution of vendor/contractor contract or agreement
  - Determination of vendor and contractor readiness to begin project execution

- *Initial customer documents and activities*
  - Acceptance of technical solution by customer
  - Specification of customer reporting requirements
  - Execution of customer contract or agreement
  - Confirmation of customer readiness to begin project execution

  The preproject audit is applicable to virtually all projects of discernable value and duration. It is an audit that is performed as people and plans become ready for project execution. In a sense, it is a "gateway" audit that facilitates transition from the Plan Phase to the Perform Phase. Here, a review of planning emphasizes development of initial project management and technical plans necessary to describe the project's game plan. Additional project plans can be prepared in conjunction with project execution.

Postproject (Post Phase) Audit

This audit confirms project readiness for closure. It is usually performed by the project manager and project team, but it can also be accomplished by the PMO or another external auditing team or a third-party auditor. This audit normally includes examination of

- *Customer acceptance of project deliverables*
  - Receipt of interim and final customer acceptance statements
  - Completion of customer's evaluation of project performance
  - Preparation and submittal of invoices to customer
  - Receipt of customer invoice payments
- *Project lessons learned*
  - Review of project financial and business performance
  - Review of project management plan content and effectiveness
  - Review of technical plan content and effectiveness
  - Review of project team performance
  - Review of customer feedback and evaluations
- *Vendor/contractor closeout activities*
  - Evaluation of vendor/contractor performance
  - Receipt of vendor/contractor invoices
  - Payment of vendor/contractor invoices

  The postproject audit is applicable to virtually all projects of discernable value and duration. It is an audit that is performed when all project activities have been completed, deliverables have been accepted, and the project is ready for closure. This audit is the gateway audit that facilitates and essentially validates project closure.

Project Management Methodology Review

This audit examines use and validates the content effectiveness of the established project management methodology. The PMO or a qualified external third-party auditor normally accomplishes this audit. It is a review that transcends individual projects and project managers to gain a perspective of project management process and technique application across all projects in the relevant organization. This audit normally includes examination of

- *Project management methodology general content*
  - Contains adequate descriptions of process (what to do) and practice (how to do it) for project management life cycle phases, activities, and tasks
  - Designates project team member and other stakeholder role responsibility for participation in the accomplishment and oversight of methodology activity elements
  - Provides adequate tools to facilitate the accomplishment of methodology process elements; for example, automated tools or paper-based forms, checklists, templates, etc.
- *Project management methodology process content*
  - Presents a discernable process relationship and flow that advances the project through phases of initiation, planning, implementation/execution, and closeout
  - Specifies all essential project management activities and tasks within each phase (per project management standards and practices used)
  - Incorporates essential technical planning and performance activities in each phase (per technical standards and practices used)
- *Project manager and project team methodology utilization*
  - Examines project management methodology phase, activity, and task use on a representative sample of projects in a specified time period
  - Determines causes for nonuse of certain methodology elements
  - Reviews and evaluates user feedback regarding methodology use
  - Identifies achievement of project management benefits or detriments that can be associated with project management methodology use
  - Identifies achievement of business benefits or detriments that can be associated with project management methodology use

  The project management methodology review can normally be accomplished annually to ascertain completeness, effectiveness, and use.

Conduct Other Project Management Audits

Additional project management audits provide a wide array of activities that can be considered by the organization to achieve more detailed examination of project performance elements or to ascertain conditions in the project management environment.

The PMO or some other business entity can construct and perform audits to meet a variety of needs. The following list presents a few suggestions for additional project management audits that may be of value in the relevant organization:

- *Customer Satisfaction Audit*—An examination of the customer business relationship that identifies how well the customer perceives the project to be progressing toward the achievement of desired objectives.
- *Project Recovery Audit*—An audit similar to the combined content of the project management audit and the project performance audit, but with focus on the indicators of unsatisfactory project performance.
- *Project Support Plan Review*—A review of the guidance prescribed by any of the individual project support plans. The PMO or a third-party auditor usually conducts this audit to provide an unbiased perspective on plan content, comprehensiveness, and usability.
- *Project Resource Utilization Audit*—An examination of fulfillment of resource allocations and the timely assignment of resources for the accomplishment of specific tasks. This audit does not examine resource performance. The PMO or a third-party auditor usually conducts this audit to provide an unbiased perspective on issues and activities surrounding executive resource support and the effectiveness of project manager resource assignment management.
- *Project Team Performance Audit*—A review of project work assignments and their alignment with individual technical and professional competencies of project team resources. The PMO or a third-party auditor usually conducts this audit to provide an unbiased perspective on individual capability issues, appropriateness of individual assignments, and the effectiveness of project manager and technical leader supervision.
- *Vendor/Contractor Audits*—An audit or review using any of the described project or project management audits but one that is conducted in the vendor's project management environment. This type of audit is normally authorized and conducted in one of two ways. First, the vendor/contractor can request assistance from the performing organization in conducting an examination of its project management position and contribution to the overall project, and sometimes the PMO or project manager will encourage this. Second, the provisions of the applicable vendor/contractor services contract or agreement allow the performing organization to independently initiate and conduct project management audits in the vendor's project management environment.

These and other unique audits can be prescribed and performed as project performance conditions present requirements for such examinations in the project management environment. The PMO should maintain the documented process for any new audit for future use and refinement.

Conduct Technical Audits

Technical audits are an inherent part of project management responsibilities. However, they are distinctly aligned with the nature of product or service delivered to the customer and the particular technical skills and competencies found in the project management environment. Individual PMOs will need to define technical audits that are appropriate to and associated with the business operations of the relevant organization.

The following list presents a few generic types of technical audits that are applicable across different project management environments for consideration:

- *Technical Approach Review*—A thorough review of the technical solution prepared to produce required project deliverables and to achieve overall project objectives within the specified scope of work. It is normally accomplished early in the project planning effort, and sometimes in conjunction with the preproject audit.
- *Quality Assurance Audit*—An examination of the project quality management plan, associated test and acceptance plans, and quality control procedures, scheduled activities, and accomplishments. This type of audit is often aligned with responsibilities of quality management business units within the performing organization. A general review of the project quality management plan also may be performed during the preproject audit.
- *Project Gateway Review*—One of a series of reviews conducted at technical transition points or phases in the project, for example, design, build, produce, test, etc. The gateway review examines the readiness to proceed with the next major technical activity, including
  - Verification that all requisite technical activities have been properly accomplished
  - Determination that technical leaders and project team resources needed to conduct the technical work prescribed in the next technical phase are available and ready to begin the assignment
  - Confirmation that the executive (sponsor) and customer agree to proceed to the next technical activity

  - Receipt of required funding for the next technical activity
- *Structured Walk-Throughs*—A technical review usually conducted by a group of technical experts, including project team members, customer representatives, and external technical advisors, to validate a technical process or procedure, a technical design or approach, or a technical performance outcome normally associated with a project deliverable.
- *Technical Reviews*—An examination of technical content usually conducted by project team members to adjudge satisfactory completion of technical tasks that contribute to preparation of project deliverables. The PMO, in collaboration with technical leaders in the relevant organization, can construct procedures for required technical reviews in the project management environment.

The organization should prescribe routine technical audits for inclusion in the project work plan.

14.4 PORTFOLIO MANAGEMENT

Project Portfolio Management provides oversight for the collection of all projects under the purview of senior managers within the relevant organization. The project portfolio identifies all of the organization's current and pending projects, and allows each project to be viewed and examined individually, relative to all other projects in the portfolio collection.

Portfolio Management is the work performed to manage projects toward the achievement of business interests and strategic objectives. This is inherently a responsibility of executive and senior managers, and can be achieved either by individual executives, such as department heads, or by a group of senior managers composing a project portfolio review board (or the executive control board). However, the PMO can play an important role in establishing and managing the portfolio management capability and facilitating the participation of executive and senior managers, including

- Alignment of projects to business strategy
- Approval of the project business plan and funding
- Allocation of organizational resources for project work
- Prioritization of projects in the portfolio collection
- Review of ongoing project and portfolio performance
- Removal of completed or discontinued projects from the portfolio collection

The PMO can develop and implement processes and procedures for each of these project portfolio management activities, consistent with its level of responsibility and maturity. The nature of portfolio management suggests that any portfolio management capability pursued by the PMO will be accomplished in close collaboration with the relevant executive or senior management team.

This practice will provide only an overview of project portfolio management, which can have its own set of processes and procedures. Of course, it should interface directly with the practices of the methodology used.

Concept of This Practice

This practice provides the organization with insight into managing a portfolio of projects that are undertaken to achieve specific business purposes. It also provides insight and awareness for the project manager and project team relative to their contributions to the project portfolio management effort.

Portfolio Management is conducted throughout the project management life cycle. In the Profile Phase, a new project is examined for placement and priority among other projects in the portfolio as it is integrated into the portfolio. In the Plan and Perform phases, project performance is reviewed by the portfolio manager (executive or senior management team) on its own merits and in relation to its contribution to the portfolio of projects, and decisions are made regarding project retention or termination. In the Post Phase, project performance is evaluated and the project is removed from the portfolio.

A foundation for *Portfolio Management* must be established within the organization and its project management environment. This setup is not directly a part of day-to-day project management, and it will not be examined in detail in this section. See the Project Selection practice area for additional information related to portfolio management. However, there are several important portfolio management setup activities that need to be performed by the organization (usually by a PMO), and they are summarized here as a frame of reference.

- *Validate business strategy and interests.* Executives are responsible for establishing the strategic direction of the organization. That strategy provides the purpose, expectations, goals, and action steps necessary to guide business pursuits. Routine application of the business strategy narrows the range of possible business opportunities (i.e., projects) to only those distinctly aligned with business objectives. It also ensures that valuable organization resources (staff) are assigned only to those efforts that advance the business objectives set forth in the strategic business plan. It is essential that a well-conceived and well-articulated strategic context is available in order to align portfolio management activities with top-level business direction.
- *Identify project selection criteria.* The process of Project Selection is that of choosing which projects will be pursued and which will not. The alignment of a project

opportunity with the organization's business strategy usually makes it a candidate for selection but does not guarantee its selection. Conversely, a project opportunity that is not aligned with the organization's business strategy should never be selected. Project selection criteria should be identified to support project selection decisions.

- *Determine project selection mechanisms.* Once selection criteria are established, the organization can construct or use established mechanisms by which the criteria can be applied to evaluate candidate projects. Some mechanism examples include
  - New Project Classification Mechanism
  - Financial Calculations Mechanism
  - Balanced Scorecard Mechanism
  - Rank Order Matrix Mechanism
  - Poor Man's Hierarchy Mechanism
  - Peer/Oversight Committee Review Mechanism
- *Identify project portfolio management roles and responsibilities.* Project portfolio management is a business alignment function often associated with the PMO, and is one that requires coordination and collaboration across the relevant organization. The activities of project portfolio management will naturally transcend the boundaries of the PMO, and the PMO must ensure that all participants in project portfolio management know and understand the range of their responsibilities, including
  - Executive Control Board (a common portfolio owner group)
  - Project Executive/Sponsor (an individual who owns the portfolio or represents the portfolio owner group)
  - Portfolio Manager (the PMO manager or other designated individual responsible for day-to-day portfolio oversight)
  - Portfolio Management Team (a team designated to assist in portfolio management)
- *Establish a supportive project management environment.* The following activities should be considered for their benefit to the portfolio management capability:
  - Project Management Methodology Deployment
  - Project Information Collection and Reporting
  - Standards and Metrics Implementation
  - Information System Implementation

The *Portfolio Management* practice will be examined in the following four areas:

- Perform project selection.
- Integrate projects in the portfolio.
- Conduct project and portfolio reviews.
- Manage portfolio attrition.

Most of these activities will have some relevance in relation to the project management effort, but various aspects of project portfolio management could be outside the project manager's normal span of influence and control.

Perform Project Selection

The organization's project selection process ensures that all projects are bona fide business efforts and that every project is selected and conducted to implement a business strategy or to support a business objective. There are four fundamental activities of project selection:

- *Conduct project screening.* This activity is conducted to provide an indication of whether or not initial project planning (business plan development) should be pursued.
- *Develop project business plan.* This activity is used to identify and examine the project opportunity and customer needs and interests. It collects and compiles the information used in the subsequent project screening activity and includes preparation of the project definition, which specifies the scope and work effort to be undertaken.
- *Develop resource allocation plan.* This activity is used to identify resource requirements for the candidate project and to specify the financial and resource allocations that will be needed to fulfill project requirements.
- *Conduct project selection.* This activity applies established criteria and prescreening results to the information compiled in the business plan and project resource allocation plan to analyze and examine the candidate project for final selection.

Each of these action steps may be performed as a matter of process contained in the organization's project management methodology, or they can be a separate activity performed only by the portfolio management team. More details about these activities are presented in the Project Selection practice area; they are mentioned here because of their direct association with the portfolio management process.

Integrate Projects in the Portfolio

The practice of effective project portfolio management requires the participation of the executive portfolio owner. If that individual has not yet been involved in the initial selection activities, it is essential that executive participation begin at this juncture in the project portfolio management process.

There are three activities performed to achieve project integration:

- *Validate project selection.* A final executive-level reviewer signs off on the business plan as the approved approach for conducting the project. The executive reviewer also signs off on the resource allocation plan, if presented as a separate document, as the approved approach for staffing the project.

- *Determine project priority.* The executive portfolio owner (individual or team) assigns a project ranking to the selected project within the portfolio of projects.
- *Approve initial project funding.* The relevant executive signs off on project funding to enable the project to be "booked" and to authorize the expenditure of money for the specified initial project planning effort.

It should be noted that this activity may be performed as a part of the project selection effort conducted by members of the executive control board or as a separate activity performed by the portfolio management team (or portfolio manager), with participation and sign-off by the relevant executive owner.

Conduct Project and Portfolio Reviews

The essence of project portfolio management is reflected in the ongoing participation of executives and senior managers in reviewing individual projects and the overall portfolio on a recurring basis. These reviews are essential to keeping projects and related activities on course toward the achievement of strategic business objectives. Review activities must demonstrate sufficient rigor to enable serious business decisions to be made. In particular, project-level reviews must achieve adequate examination to make project retention or project termination decisions. Portfolio-level reviews must provide necessary information to judge business results from the collection of projects in the portfolio.

There are three primary activities involved in accomplishing project and portfolio reviews:

- *Compile project performance information.* A process linked to the project communication function and project status reporting capability is implemented to ensure that appropriate information is collected, compiled, and reported (by the project manager and the project team) for use in project and portfolio reviews.
- *Conduct project gateway reviews.* The specification of procedures for when and how to evaluate active projects is established. These are the reviews conducted at specified intervals or review points in the project management life cycle, and each review is conducted to address a specific project.
- *Conduct portfolio reviews.* The specification of procedures for when and how to examine the total collection of projects in the relevant organization's portfolio is established. These are the reviews conducted, perhaps at specified intervals, but usually at specified times in the annual "business cycle," such as monthly, quarterly, or annually. Each portfolio review is used to examine overall portfolio performance and the individual project's contribution to the portfolio.

Project and portfolio reviews can sometimes be included in the project WBS as a reminder of each event.

Manage Portfolio Attrition

The projects that come to make up the portfolio are first selected and then managed through a series of project gateway review points that facilitate examination and either approval for retention or termination. The project attrition funnel depicts how projects generally progress in a standard life cycle from initial selection, through various gateway review points, and then to final disposition. This means that it is expected, as a natural course of business, that only the most favorable projects will survive to completion. The remaining projects will be eliminated, ideally as early as possible, through attrition. One depiction of a project attrition funnel is illustrated in Figure II.14.1.

In general, the rate of project attrition through the project management life cycle, can be expected to occur as depicted in this diagram. It shows that the rate of attrition early in the project life cycle beginning with the project selection screening, can be as much as 75% of the original project opportunities identified during the Profile Phase.

Additional attrition occurs because of the rigorous evaluation and selection criteria applied at each decision point to all projects. During project planning (Plan Phase), the diagram indicates that as many as 30% of the in-progress projects can be terminated; as more information is known about the effort, resource utilization is weighed, and the examination of strategic alignment increases. This rate then decreases dramatically as "accepted" projects progress into the Perform Phase. The actual rate of project attrition is determined by the criteria established by the executives responsible for project portfolio management, as facilitated by the PMO.

When a project is either selected for termination or comes to an end through natural completion and fulfillment of its objectives, there are three primary activities that should be performed to manage the associated project attrition.

Perform Project Closeout

The prominent action from the perspective of the portfolio management team is to examine the decisions made to prematurely close out a project as an attrition action. In these cases, the closeout purpose should be specified with accompanying information concerning

- Evaluation of the initial selection decision (based on the established business case)

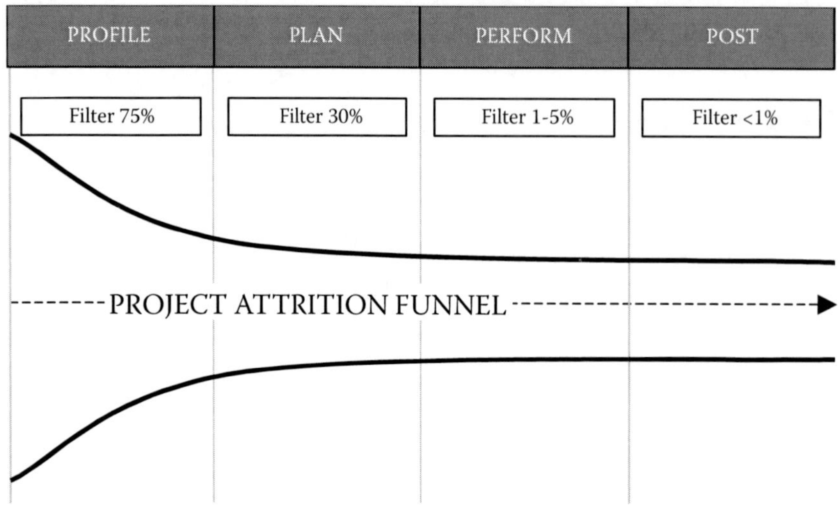

Figure II.14.1 Project attrition.

- Determination of what has changed since the initial project selection decision
- Identification of the influences that warranted a project discontinuation decision as internal or external
- Determination of whether the discontinuation influences were quick deliberation actions or anticipated over time
- Determination of what, if anything, could have been done at an earlier gateway review point to enable the project to continue

This specification of closeout purpose and associated influences or causes can be conveyed to the project selection process for application during the next new project selection activity. In addition, any early project termination decision must be conveyed to the appropriate project manager for immediate action.

In the event of a routine completion of the project, practices prescribed for project closeout (in the Post Phase) are accomplished and the project is removed from the portfolio according to established procedures. This includes completing actions specified in the following subsections of this practice.

Assess Strategic Advantage

Projects being removed from the portfolio collection should be examined for their impact on the organization's business strategy—beneficial or otherwise. This means looking at the project relative to the following considerations:

- Did the project complete its full life cycle, and were all of the project's objectives achieved?
- Did the project scope change or stay the same; what influenced any change?
- Did the project stay within the established criteria for which it was selected, thereby maintaining its alignment with business purpose and objectives?
- What business needs or interests were affected by project performance?
  - Profitability and return on investment (ROI)
  - Achievement of strategic goals
  - Expansion of organizational visibility in the industry
  - Expansion of organization visibility in the marketplace
  - Attainment of client satisfaction
- If the project terminated early, how does the cause of early project termination affect the organization's strategic position?
- If the project terminated early, how does the cause of early project termination affect other similar projects that are still being conducted?

Again, the results of this examination can be conveyed for incorporation into the selection process for use in the next new project selection activity as well as in project gateway review points by incorporating lessons learned. The organization can consider these evaluation points or add its own according to its business needs and interests.

Determine Level of Customer Satisfaction

This final activity step of project portfolio management is essentially an extension of the previous activity step. It addresses an examination of the customer aspects of strategic advantage resulting from this project. It focuses on gaining an understanding about the customer's level of satisfaction through compilation of various forms of feedback regarding the customer's perspective on the benefits gained from project performance.

It is important for the organization to examine how well the different types of projects placed in the portfolio are responding to customer needs. To that end, the PMO should conduct or otherwise facilitate the creation of processes that enable customer feedback and evaluation of customer satisfaction to be accomplished.

In general, the following information can be compiled, deliberated, and communicated to enhance future business decisions about project selection and project continuation, and to enhance the overall project portfolio management capability.

- Executive-level examination
  - General comments from executives on direct or indirect awareness of customer satisfaction at project closeout
  - Executive guidance addressing the desired course of any follow-on business relationship with the customer
  - Executive guidance addressing the desired course of business relationships with other customers based on results and reactions of this customer
- Customer survey and feedback
  - Completion of a customer end-of-project service/project satisfaction survey
  - Completion of a customer interim service/project satisfaction survey
  - Compilation of customer feedback based on discussions at closeout meetings
  - Review of customer feedback as presented by comments in quality and deliverable acceptance/sign-off documents
  - Review of customer issue and problem resolution actions during the project
- Project manager/PMO evaluation
  - Evaluation of customer satisfaction
  - Examination of customer's participation in the project
  - Identification and review of customer issues and problems encountered

Again, the organization will need to determine the specific points of evaluation that are desired in association with business needs and interests.

Chapter 15

Project Closeout

A project, by definition, has a finite duration. There are certain things individuals and organizations do when a project is active, and there are things they stop doing when a project is no longer active. Therefore, it is important to know when a project has been successfully completed, placed on hold, or otherwise stopped or terminated.

The process of closing a project and performing the practices of the Post Phase can be as demanding as any one of the practices encountered in earlier phases of the project management life cycle. The project is not completed, at least by business standards, until the final prescribed project management actions are completed.

There are three prominent practices associated with Project Closeout:

- Project Lessons Learned Preparation
- Project Termination Management
- Project Evaluation Administration

Project Closeout will provide the necessary communication to ensure that all project stakeholders become aware of pending or completed project closure activities.

15.1 PROJECT LESSONS LEARNED PREPARATION

It has become a common practice in business and industry to review and examine the work completed. This need holds true for the discipline of project management as well. It is valuable to recognize what works and what does not work through a review of personal or organizational experience. There are benefits to be achieved when corrections can be made prior to executing poor actions rather than responding to a project that is affected by poor actions already executed.

Concept of This Practice

This practice provides the project manager, the project team, and the organization with relevant information about project and project management performance that can be applied as a benefit to future, similar project efforts.

The purpose of this practice is to compile and analyze project and project management performance indicators identified through the discussion, input, and examination by individuals and groups that had various levels of involvement in the project under consideration. In turn, the lessons learned information for each project is stored for future access by project managers and others in the project management environment.

Project Lessons Learned is almost always done during project closeout. However, there are junctures in the project—when actions have been completed, when people depart the project, or when routine audits uncover particular findings—when lessons learned information collection and analysis is appropriate prior to actual project termination.

Conduct Project Lessons Learned Sessions

Lessons learned can be compiled from individual input, but it is generally accepted that such examinations produce better results when relevant topics are considered as a team or group. The project team is a prominent group used for collecting lessons learned. However, a variety of stakeholders should be tapped for participation in processing project lessons learned:

- Customer feedback
- Project manager feedback
- Project team feedback
- Vendor/contractor feedback
- Management feedback and guidance (e.g., project management office [PMO], project executive/sponsor)

One or more lessons learned meetings should be conducted to include most or all of these stakeholder groups as participants. At a minimum, the project manager and project team should meet to deliberate and identify lessons learned at the completion of each project.

It may be good to use a facilitator to lead the lessons learned deliberation session. This approach is particularly valuable when diverse stakeholder groups participate in the same session or when there is an unusually large number of participants (e.g., > 15). The facilitator should be skilled in eliciting feedback from within groups and generally not previously associated with the project as a means to ensure an unbiased approach to the effort.

Lessons learned are not evaluations, and project evaluation is covered as a subsequent subtopic later in this section on project closeout. However, it can sometimes become an effort to distinguish lessons that have been learned from the project in contrast to the ratings of project or people performance. Perhaps one way to approach a performance issue that is raised during a lessons learned session is to consider how that item could have been done better, rather than examining and rating the outcome it produced.

It remains that not all stakeholders (or individual project team members, for that matter) will always be available to attend group lessons learned feedback sessions. To that end, the project manager should solicit independent input from those individuals. Forms available in the toolkit can be used for that purpose. Such feedback can be incorporated into regular session feedback (when received in advance) and examined for potential areas of improvement.

Project Lessons Learned Examination Areas

The various stakeholder groups will have particular areas of interest that will prompt their identification of lessons learned. The organization should specify the particular areas of interest it wants to pursue when conducting lessons learned examinations.

The following are several areas of examination that can be considered when preparing lessons learned at the conclusion of the project:

- Review of project financial and business outcomes
- Review of project management plan content and effectiveness
- Review of technical plan content and effectiveness
- Review of technical and technology results
- Review of project team participation and performance
- Review of vendor participation and performance
- Review of customer participation
- Review of project estimating results

The project manager or the organization may adjust these examination areas to better address project management or business needs. The resulting compilation of lessons learned should be placed in the project management archives for future use. They should be placed in a manner that facilitates easy access and identified according the project type and classification.

Using Project Lessons Learned

The purpose of compiling lessons learned from each project conducted in the organization is to make project and project management performance better in the future. Information and recommendations from previously completed projects that can be applied to current project planning efforts should be made available to all project managers.

Project initiation activities include a review of lessons learned in conjunction with the preparation of the project definition. This is the time when project managers should first access the lessons learned archives. It is good practice to ensure that you do not repeat mistakes that could have been avoided by a brief review of lessons learned at the onset of a project.

Another point in time for a lessons learned review is when solution development and detailed project planning begins. The project manager and project team will both benefit from an examination of conditions faced on similar previous projects, with adjustments made during planning rather than in response to a problem that is subsequently encountered.

The value of the lessons learned practice is based in the availability of "findings" for future use. Lessons learned from past projects help you to understand conditions and situations before they have adverse impacts on your current project.

15.2 PROJECT TERMINATION MANAGEMENT

A project is completed when the specified objectives have been achieved. Sometimes, a project is completed prematurely when it is determined that specified objectives cannot or will not be achieved within the allotted time or financial constraints. These are conditions for project termination. As well, at times, there may be a need to place a project or project management activities on "hold" status. This is not quite a formal termination, but because of the extended period of project inactivity, it is often treated in much the same way as project termination.

Concept of This Practice

This practice provides the project manager, the project team, and the organization with a means to formally terminate project activity and to communicate that status to project stakeholders in the business and project management environments.

The purpose of this practice is to guide the performance of all required actions that are needed to terminate the project. Its use will eliminate carrying completed or inactive projects on lists and accounting ledgers long after they are done. It will help in the transition or inactivation of resources assigned to the project as a planned effort rather than as an afterthought. It will be a statement to involved stakeholders that, for better or worse, the project is terminated.

Project Termination Management is primarily done during project closeout. However, there are junctures in the project (e.g., when certain actions have been completed, when people depart the project, or when contracts are closed) that certain project termination activities may be performed.

Types of Project Termination

When a project is terminated, all project work is discontinued, and project and business management is concluded. There are three general types of project termination to consider.

- *Scheduled Termination*—This type of project termination can occur when the project has run its complete course, generally according to plans, and ideally with the fundamental achievement of cost, schedule, and resource utilization objectives. The project has been completed to the reasonable satisfaction of the customer and management.
- *Early Termination*—This type of project termination can occur when the project is halted before completing all of its specified objectives. This is sometimes referred to as "premature termination." There are various conditions that could prompt an early project termination, including the following examples:
  - The customer makes a business decision to discontinue the project early (within boundaries of contractual obligations).
  - The performing organization makes a business decision to discontinue project pursuits and withdraw from the effort (within boundaries of contractual obligations).
  - The significance of anticipated project scope changes warrants a new project (in lieu of current project replanning).
  - Project failure (with project recovery efforts being unsuccessful or not pursued).

  Early termination could occur anytime before the last prescribed project deliverable is accepted by the customer. Presumably, this would be a rare event for a long-term project with multiple deliverables. However, it can occur on any type of project during planning, during midproject solution implementation, or even approaching the scheduled project completion date.
- *Partial Termination (for Projects on Hold)*—This type of project termination occurs when project management efforts need to be reduced or halted for a period of time in which the project is placed on "hold" status. The project is reasonably expected to resume again and will pick up at that stopping point at some future time. The extent to which termination activities are performed for projects on hold depends on the progress of the project when halted and the anticipated hold period, which ideally is known when termination activities are performed. For this type of termination, project work ceases and project resources are reassigned (pending recall), but business aspects of the project (e.g., financial accounting ledgers and contracts) may still require minimal project management oversight.

Project Termination Activities

Project termination can take just a few days for smaller, shorter-duration projects but may take several weeks or more for larger, longer-duration projects. This variable must be considered before the entire project team is released and the project manager is assigned new duties. Closing a project is still an important part of the project manager's responsibility and should be given adequate attention. Such attention is specifically addressed as a part of the prescribed project termination activities.

Project termination activities are conducted to ensure that proper closure of each project is accomplished. The termination activities will be more rigorous for some projects than others. The organization should determine which of the following types of activities need to be performed for project termination.

- *Designation of Project Closeout Responsibility*—The assignment of responsibility to project team members for project closeout actions. On smaller, shorter-duration projects, one person may be able to handle project closeout actions with minimal assistance. However, on other projects, it may be necessary to designate a team of individuals who will share the closeout workload across the various activities. Aligned with this is the need to recognize the condition of reduced team effort and motivation that normally occurs toward the end of each project. Actions to compensate for this condition should be pursued, particularly with any residual staff involved in closeout.
- *Preparation of Lessons Learned*—This involves the compilation of information, as can be provided by all primary project participants, that will be used to adjust or adapt actions on similar future projects. The compiled lessons learned are prepared and then transferred to

the project management archives. This archive storage should make lessons learned accessible and available for review on subsequent project management efforts. See the previous section *Project Lessons Learned Preparation*, for more information on the practice.

- *Preparation of Performance Evaluations*—This deals with the rating of performance areas associated with project progress and participation, including evaluations for customer performance, project manager performance, overall project team and individual team member performance, vendor/contractor performance, and management and PMO performance. Performance evaluations can be retained in the project management archives or another designated location. Such disposition should make archived performance evaluations accessible and available for review on subsequent project management efforts. See the next section *Project Evaluation Administration*, for more information on the practice.
- *Staff Resources Disposition Management*—This involves the actions and oversight needed to transition project team members to a new project assignment, to facilitate their return to the control of their designated resource manager, or to otherwise discontinue their services.
- *Supplies and Equipment Disposition Management*—This deals with the actions and oversight needed to transition project supplies and equipment to a new project assignment, to facilitate their return to the control of their designated resource or storage manager, or to otherwise arrange for their disposal.
- *Facility Disposition Management*—This involves the actions and oversight needed to transition project facilities to a new project or to otherwise return them to the control of the facility owner or designated facility manager within the organization. The activity could include facility lease closeout and submittal of final lease payments.
- *Document Disposition Management*—This deals with the actions and oversight needed to collect and transfer project working materials and documentation to the project management archives or to the designated project documentation manager. It could include a review of materials (e.g., project plans, design documents, etc.) to determine their effectiveness and value to the project. Disposition should make project documents accessible and available for review on subsequent project management efforts.
- *Customer Contract Closeout*—This involves the actions needed to show the fulfillment of obligations and formally close the customer contract. Prescribed actions include
  - Acquiring written customer acceptance of deliverables
  - Returning any customer-owned materials, supplies, equipment, and facilities
  - Requesting the customer to complete a customer satisfaction survey
  - Conducting a customer contract closeout review meeting
  - Submitting a final invoice for products and services delivered to the customer
  - Receiving the final customer payment for products and services
- *Vendor Contract Closeout*—The actions needed to discontinue vendor participation on the project and to formally close the vendor contract. Prescribed activities include
  - Providing written acceptance of vendor deliverables
  - Receiving any organization materials, supplies, equipment, and facilities used by the vendor during the vendor contract period
  - Preparing any vendor-requested satisfaction survey or otherwise providing a vendor performance feedback
  - Conducting a vendor contract closeout review meeting
  - Receiving a final invoice for products and services delivered by the vendor
  - Making the final payment for vendor products and services
- *Project Stakeholder Closeout*—The effort conducted to inform all project stakeholders of project completion (or termination) and to obtain acknowledgement of closure from primary participants. It also addresses actions needed to plan and provide recognition or to express appreciation for the work accomplished by the project team and other key project participants, individually and collectively. This includes such matters as celebrations, merit awards, promotions, and financial rewards.

  This closeout activity is particularly important in that it provides the means to notify project team members and other relevant stakeholders that costs and expenses can no longer be charged to the account of the project being closed.
- *Project Account Closeout*—The internal business actions taken to show project completion (termination), including
  - Removing the project from the active business ledger
  - Closing new cost/expense access to the project's financial accounts
  - Storing the closed customer and vendor contracts
  - Reviewing project team disposition with HR and resource managers
  - Conducting a business performance review relative to the project

- *Project Management Closeout*—The internal management actions conducted by the relevant executive, senior management, PMO, and project manager to achieve project closure (termination), including
  - Conducting a business performance review relative to the project performance and the project outcome
  - Conducting project executive (sponsor) and executive control board closeout
  - Conducting portfolio closeout (see the practice on *Portfolio Management*)

15.3 PROJECT EVALUATION ADMINISTRATION

Management has an obligation to assess conditions of business performance as a basis for making decisions that affect the business. As projects are more and more becoming an integral part of business operations, they necessarily have to be evaluated for their contribution to business success. Also, the fundamental premise that projects in their own right need to be successful warrants the need to evaluate the various project components that determine the level of project success. The project executive/sponsor or executive control board, normally supported by the PMO, should establish the depth and extent of evaluation activities that each project manager will accomplish on projects.

Concept of This Practice

This practice provides the project manager, the project team, and the organization with relevant information about how well components of the project performed for a specific project effort. Although evaluation is generally a one-time event for each project, this practice also enables data to be collected across projects over time to help formulate an overall perspective on performance in the project management environment. In turn, project managers will be able to make better project management decisions, and the organization will be able to make better business management decisions.

The purpose of this practice is to guide the project manager or designee in performing all of the prescribed project evaluations, as is normally conducted at the end of each project. Evaluation results can then be applied directly or indirectly to staff and stakeholder performance reviews, as is determined by the organization.

Project Evaluation Administration is primarily done during project closeout. However, there are junctures in the project (e.g., when certain actions have been completed, when people depart the project, or when contracts are closed) when selective evaluation activities may be performed. It should be noted that project evaluations are distinguished from project audits, which are discussed separately in the *Project Audit Management* practice.

Evaluate Customer Performance

This performance evaluation is conducted to document the involvement of the customer and the nature of customer interactions on the project. The following are the default indicators used in this methodology to formulate a perspective on customer performance:

- *Customer Project Participation*—Consider the extent to which the customer was an active participant in the project; contrast the amount of customer involvement needed or required versus the amount actually given.
- *Customer Cohesiveness (One Voice)*—Consider how unified the customer representatives were in presenting thoughts, ideas, concerns, and problems; measure the customer's effectiveness relative to the level of cohesiveness demonstrated.
- *Commitment to Project Objectives*—Consider how well the customer organization and its representatives understood the objectives established for the project, and how well they maintained dedication to and focus on the achievement of those objectives.
- *Commitment to Project Budget*—Consider the means by which project funding activities were accomplished within the customer's organization; examine customer executive funding decisions, timeliness of executive funding authorizations, and the customer's internal procedures for making funds available to the project in progress; identify any lapses in customer funding availability and the conditions that caused them.
- *Commitment to Project Schedule*—Consider how well the customer organization and its representatives understood the schedule established for the project, and how well they maintained dedication to and focus on the achievement of that schedule.
- *Contribution to Project Scope Change Control*—Consider the customer's position and approach relative to project scope change control; assess how well the customer maintained and managed project scope in the customer's organization; assess how well the customer used the established and agreed-to project change control procedures when adjustments to the project scope were required.
- *Timeliness of Decisions and Responses*—Consider the executives, project team, and others in the customer's business environment relative to their timeliness of business decisions, technical decisions, accomplishment of project deliverable reviews, and other important responses needed to keep the project on budget and on schedule.

- *Timeliness of Deliverables Acceptance*—Consider the attention given and procedures used by the customer's representatives who held the responsibility for approving project deliverables; review any major delays in returning approvals and any particular issues related to instances of deliverable nonacceptance.
- *Timeliness of Invoice Payment*—Consider how timely the customer paid the invoices submitted for project work accomplishment; recall any situations or circumstances that required attention to invoice or payment issues and how well they were resolved.

The results of this customer evaluation can be applied to gain a better understanding of related project issues and events, to refine future agreements and contracts with the customer, or even to determine if the customer should be pursued in the future.

Evaluate Project Performance

This performance evaluation is conducted to document project results relative to the specified purpose and objectives. The following are the default indicators used in this methodology to formulate a perspective on project performance.

- *Project Planning Effort*—Consider how well project planning was accomplished and the effectiveness of resulting plans; also consider the extent and frequency of project planning document use during the project.
- *Project Scope Management and Change Control*—Consider how well project scope was maintained and the effectiveness of the change control process.
- *Project Variance Management (Track and Control)*—Consider the extent of project variance in terms of cost, schedule, and resource utilization, and the effectiveness of corrective actions taken to reduce project variance.
- *Commitment to Project Objectives*—Consider the extent to which the project manager, project team, and organization stakeholders demonstrated commitment to achieving the specified project objectives.
- *Commitment to Project Budget*—Consider the extent to which the project manager, project team, and organization stakeholders demonstrated commitment to achieving the specified project budget.
- *Commitment to Project Schedule*—Consider the extent to which the project manager, project team, and organization stakeholders demonstrated commitment to achieving the specified project schedule.
- *Commitment to Project Resource Utilization*—Consider the extent to which the project manager, project team, and organization stakeholders demonstrated commitment to achieving the specified project resource utilization.
- *Timeliness of Project Communication*—Consider how well the project communication plan served project needs; examine the effectiveness of communication relative to its influence on project performance.
- *Timeliness of Project Deliverables*—Consider the efficiency of providing project deliverables to the customer; consider how well the planned project delivery schedule was achieved.

The results of this project evaluation can be applied to gain a better understanding of project planning effectiveness and the need for specific project plans and supporting plans.

Evaluate Staff Performance

This staff evaluation is conducted to document how well project team members worked collectively as a cohesive unit to complete project technical assignments. The following are the default indicators used in this methodology to formulate a perspective on staff performance.

- *Awareness of Project Objectives and Business Purpose*—Consider how well project team members demonstrated awareness of the project objectives and business purpose, including how tasks were prioritized and collateral (prerequisite) work was performed.
- *Technical Performance Capability*—Consider how well project team members demonstrated collective capability (based on contributions of various individual skill levels) to achieve the project's technical objectives.
- *Technical Performance Quality*—Consider how well project team members applied collective capability (based on individual contributions) to achieve the project's technical objectives and meet technical specifications.
- *Technical Performance Timeliness*—Consider how well project team members managed individual and group efforts to stay within acceptable timelines for achieving assigned tasks and the project's technical objectives.

The results of this staff evaluation can be applied to gain a better understanding of project team effectiveness, with possible identification of preferred project team skill and capability combinations, as well as possible identification of preferred project team members for specific types of work and cohesive team compositions.

Evaluate Vendor Performance

This vendor evaluation is conducted to document how well assigned vendors worked to complete the project's technical assignments, including how well they integrated their work with larger-scale project objectives. The following are the default indicators used in this methodology to formulate a perspective on vendor performance:

- *Fulfillment of Deliverables*—Consider how well vendors completed assigned deliverables as contributions to the primary project effort, including how well tasks were managed and integrated with other project work.
- *Technical Performance Capability*—Consider how well vendors demonstrated capability to achieve the project's technical objectives.
- *Technical Performance Quality*—Consider how well vendors applied capability to achieve the project's technical objectives and meet technical specifications.
- *Technical Performance Timeliness*—Consider how well vendors managed their work efforts to stay within acceptable timelines for achieving assigned tasks and the project's technical objectives.

The results of this customer evaluation can be applied to gain a better understanding of vendor effectiveness, to refine future agreements and contracts with the vendors, or even to determine if the vendor is one that will be considered in the future for additional project work.

Evaluate Business Performance

This performance evaluation is conducted to document the involvement of the organization's business managers, in combination with project manager and project team responsibilities, to produce effective business results and management interactions on the project. The following are the default indicators used in this methodology to formulate a perspective on business performance:

- *Business Planning Effort*—Consider how well business planners worked together and the effectiveness of the project selection process, including timeliness of deliberation and determinations by project selection participants.
- *Project Classification*—Consider how well the assigned classification represented the project and how effective it was in influencing stakeholder participation, involvement, and interactions.
- *Project Portfolio Management*—Consider how well the project performed or otherwise contributed to achieving objectives of the project portfolio to which it was assigned.
- *Return on Investment (Customer Loyalty)*—Consider how well the project served or otherwise contributed to build or elicit ongoing customer loyalty.
- *Return on Investment (Financial)*—Consider how well the project served or otherwise contributed to produce the anticipated or an acceptable return on the financial investment.
- *Return on Investment (Market Position)*—Consider how well the project served or otherwise contributed to produce the desired market position or an indication of progress toward the desired market position.
- *Commitment to Project Resource Allocations*—Consider how well the specified project resource allocations were fulfilled or otherwise supported by management during the project.
- *Consistency of Business Case*—Consider how well the project's business case remained viable and continued to accurately reflect the business aspects of the project effort.

The results of this business evaluation can be applied to gain a better understanding of project selection effectiveness (selecting the right projects) and portfolio management needs, including refinement of processes and practices in those areas.

Evaluate Management Performance

This performance evaluation is conducted to document the involvement of management and the nature of management interactions on the project. The following are the default indicators used in this methodology to formulate a perspective on management performance:

- *PMO/Management Project Participation*—Consider how well the PMO, project executive, and executive control board contributed to the fulfillment of project objectives in terms of project management oversight, support, and control activities applied to the project.
- *PMO/Management Cohesiveness (One Voice)*—Consider how unified and receptive the PMO, project executive, and executive control board were in receiving thoughts, ideas, concerns, and problems, and in conveying decisions and guidance that minimized adverse impact on established project plans.
- *Commitment to Project Technical Approach*—Consider how well the PMO, project executive, and executive control board demonstrated ongoing acceptance and support of the "approved" technical approach used on the project.
- *Commitment to Project Budget*—Consider how well the PMO, project executive, and executive control board demonstrated ongoing acceptance and support of the "approved" project budget.
- *Commitment to Project Schedule*—Consider how well the PMO, project executive, and executive control board demonstrated ongoing acceptance and support of the "approved" project schedule.
- *Commitment to Project Resource Allocations*—Consider how well the PMO, project executive, and executive

control board demonstrated ongoing acceptance and support of the "approved" project resource allocations.

- *Timeliness of Decisions and Responses*—Consider how timely PMO, project executive, and executive control board decisions, reviews, and approvals were accomplished and conveyed to minimize impacts on the project budget, schedule, and resource availability.
- *Timeliness of Guidance and Feedback*—Consider how timely PMO, project executive, and executive control board guidance and feedback (e.g., business, portfolio, and project oversight matters) were accomplished and conveyed to minimize impacts on the project budget, schedule, and resource availability.
- *Timeliness of Project Funding*—Consider how timely PMO, project executive, and executive control board initial and subsequent funding approval decisions were accomplished and conveyed to minimize impacts on the project budget, schedule, and resource availability.

The results of this management evaluation can be applied to gain a better understanding of PMO and management team effectiveness in areas of support and guidance that affect project performance, and they provide a basis for review and refinement of associated processes and practices instituted for use by senior managers in the organization.

The Methodology Toolkit

III

This publication includes an accompanying disk that contains the complete set of 96 tools (templates) used by the *ProjectPRISM™ Project Management Methodology*. While it is recommended that these tools be used with the *ProjectPRISM™ Process Guide* and the *ProjectPRISM™ Practice Guide*, they can also be used independently to accomplish essential project management activities with or without reference to structured guidance.

UNDERLYING CONCEPTS OF TOOL USE

The tools contained on the accompanying disk, when properly applied, will provide sufficient rigor and prompt user attention toward completing essential activities for effective project management.

As a full set of 96 templates, these tools provide complete coverage for project management activities across a standard, four-phase project management life cycle. Users should develop at least a fundamental understanding of that life cycle and its prescribed processes. This can be done by reviewing information presented in Section I and Section II of this publication. In particular, users should review the primary methodology processes for each of the six performance areas and across each of the methodology phases. Also read the section, *The Four Phases of the Project Management Methodology*, which provides some additional insight into the activities of each phase.

All projects may not require the rigor or coverage offered by the full set of templates provided in this toolkit. Therefore, users can compare prescribed methodology processes (and associated tools) with their current processes and practices, and select just those tools that are needed for use on different projects.

USER PREPARATION FOR TOOL USE

Most professionals in the project management environment are likely to agree that competency in project management comes from a combination of learning and experience. The use of this project management methodology toolkit relies on users having some basic level of competency in project management. In itself, this toolkit does not teach project management; but it does prompt the performance of effective practices that can be learned in conjunction with using this toolkit.

Users should have some fundamental understanding of modern project management concepts in order to properly apply the accompanying tools to their project management efforts. This understanding can be obtained through formal education programs, concentrated seminars and workshops, independent studies and reading, and, of course, personal experience on the job. As well, users can refer to the *Methodology Practice Guide* in Section II. Users should find this toolset to be consistent with widely accepted project management standards.

USING THE METHODOLOGY TOOLS

This toolkit is based upon processes developed for cross-industry use. Because of this feature, most users should find tools that are applicable to many of their needs and activities. However, some users may find that preferred information elements are missing or reduced to limited data collection space on a particular tool. In such instances, users should use available data collection spaces (i.e., "fields") to fill-in and reference the information they need, to include supporting material or documents in other locations. For example, when limited data collection space is encountered on a particular tool, the user can simply enter "See XYZ Plan for more detail" in the data collection space that is available. Each tool also has an "attachments" table at the bottom of the page, and this can be used to enter file names and file locations, and even include electronic file or web-based hyperlinks as a means to associate supporting documents and data for use with each tool.

Tools on the accompanying disk can be printed and filled-in manually, or filled-in on the computer screen (on-line) and then printed for use.

THE METHODOLOGY TOOLS

The following pages illustrate the 96 primary methodology tools that are contained on the disk that accompanies this publication.

Chapter 1

Profile Phase Tools

These are the tools used in the Profile Phase:

- 1.1 Customer Profile
  - 1.1.1 Customer Directory
  - 1.1.2 Customer Business
  - 1.1.3 Customer Opportunity
  - 1.1.4 Customer Record
- 1.2 Project Profile
  - 1.2.1 Project Definition
  - 1.2.2 Project Estimates
  - 1.2.3 Project Classification
  - 1.2.4 Project Record
- 1.3 Staff Profile
  - 1.3.1 Staff Directory
  - 1.3.2 Staff Structure
  - 1.3.3 Staff Qualification
  - 1.3.4 Staff Record
- 1.4 Vendor Profile
  - 1.4.1 Vendor Directory
  - 1.4.2 Vendor Business
  - 1.4.3 Vendor Qualification
  - 1.4.4 Vendor Record
- 1.5 Business Profile
  - 1.5.1 Business Case
  - 1.5.2 Business Risk Examination
  - 1.5.3 Business Financial Analysis
  - 1.5.4 Business Recommendation
- 1.6 Management Profile
  - 1.6.1 Management Directory
  - 1.6.2 Management Portfolio
  - 1.6.3 Management Charter
  - 1.6.4 Management Record

1.1.1 CUSTOMER PROFILE—Customer Directory

PROCESS OVERVIEW
Identify the customer's organization as well as the key business and technical contacts in the customer's organization who will convey needs and requirements, establish the contract or agreement, collaborate on the project planning effort, and manage the performance and payment of project services and deliverables.

TOOL PREPARATION	
PREPARED BY	DATE
CHECK IF REPLICATED (SPECIFY FILE LOCATION) ☐	

PROJECT	CUSTOMER

▷ CUSTOMER DIRECTORY—ORGANIZATION				
CUSTOMER NAME (DEPARTMENT OR AGENCY)			WEB SITE ADDRESS	
POINT OF CONTACT	OFFICE TELEPHONE	MOBILE TELEPHONE	FAX	EMAIL

CUSTOMER DIRECTORY—BUSINESS MANAGER				
NAME				
DEPARTMENT			WEB SITE	
TITLE	OFFICE TELEPHONE	MOBILE TELEPHONE	FAX	EMAIL
ADDRESS	CITY/STATE-PROVINCE/ZIP (POSTAL CODE)		CONTACT NOTES	

CUSTOMER DIRECTORY—TECHNICAL MANAGER				
NAME				
DEPARTMENT			WEB SITE	
TITLE	OFFICE TELEPHONE	MOBILE TELEPHONE	FAX	EMAIL
ADDRESS	CITY/STATE-PROVINCE/ZIP (POSTAL CODE)		CONTACT NOTES	

CUSTOMER DIRECTORY—OTHER KEY CONTACTS				
NAME	TITLE	ADDRESS/LOCATION	TELEPHONE	EMAIL

ACTION/ACTIVITY/REVIEW – RESPONSIBILITY	START	FINISH	ACTIVITY STATUS

ATTACHMENTS	PREPARER	DATE	FILE OR DOCUMENT LOCATION

1.1.2 CUSTOMER PROFILE—Customer Business

PROCESS OVERVIEW
Compile and review the customer's business information to gain reasonable insight into the customer's business operations. This information can be used to facilitate subsequent business activities, project solution planning, and future business opportunities through demonstrated awareness of the customer's business.

TOOL PREPARATION	
PREPARED BY	DATE

PROJECT	CUSTOMER

▷ CUSTOMER BUSINESS—OVERVIEW		
BUSINESS TYPE) ☐ *PUBLIC* ☐ *PRIVATE* ☐ *GOVERNMENT* ☐ *NON-PROFIT*	ANNUAL REVENUE	NATURE OF BUSINESS—PRODUCT/SERVICE DESCRIPTION
BUSINESS SCOPE ☐ *GLOBAL* ☐ *NATIONAL* ☐ *REGIONAL* ☐ *LOCAL*	TOTAL CUSTOMER BUSINESS LOCATIONS	
YEAR CUSTOMER ORGANIZATION ESTABLISHED	TOTAL CUSTOMER STAFFING (RESOURCES)	
INDUSTRY	PARENT ORGANIZATION	

CUSTOMER BUSINESS—EXECUTIVE MANAGEMENT		
CHAIR)	COO	OTHER RELEVANT EXECUTIVES AND SENIOR MANAGERS
CEO	CIO	
CFO	CTO	

CUSTOMER BUSINESS—MARKET				
STRATEGIC BUSINESS OBJECTIVES—GOALS—INTERESTS	KEY CUSTOMERS	STOCK EXCHANGE/LISTING CODE		
		STOCK PRICE—1 MONTH	6 MONTHS	1 YEAR
		BUSINESS TREND/OUTLOOK		

CUSTOMER BUSINESS—ALIGNMENT		
CUSTOMER KEY DIVISIONS (DEPARTMENTS)	CUSTOMER BUSINESS PARTNERS	CUSTOMER INDUSTRY COMPETITORS

ACTION/ACTIVITY/REVIEW – RESPONSIBILITY	START	FINISH	ACTIVITY STATUS

ATTACHMENTS	PREPARER	DATE	FILE OR DOCUMENT LOCATION

1.1.3 CUSTOMER PROFILE—Customer Opportunity

PROCESS OVERVIEW
Obtain and examine relevant information to gain a reasonable understanding of the customer's business needs and interests as a basis for describing the customer opportunity. Use this information when preparing the project definition and in planning and collaborating the business and technical solutions with the customer.

TOOL PREPARATION	
PREPARED BY	DATE

PROJECT	CUSTOMER

▷ CUSTOMER OPPORTUNITY—DESCRIPTION		
POTENTIAL CONTRACT VALUE	OPPORTUNITY SOURCE	DATE

CUSTOMER OPPORTUNITY—CUSTOMER READINESS ASSESSMENT				
AWARENESS OF PREVIOUS WORK	VALUE OF PREVIOUS WORK	CUSTOMER INTEREST	INTENT TO PURSUE OPPORTUNITY	SELECTION OUTLOOK
☐ *INVOLVED IN PREVIOUS WORK*	☐ *HIGH*	☐ *INITIATED CONTACT*	☐ *HIGH – DECISION MADE*	☐ *STRONG*
☐ *AWARE OF PREVIOUS WORK*	☐ *MEDIUM*	☐ *RECEPTIVE TO CONTACT*	☐ *MEDIUM – DECISION NEEDED*	☐ *FAVORABLE*
☐ *NOT AWARE OF PREVIOUS WORK*	☐ *LOW*	☐ *ACCEPTED CONTACT*	☐ *LOW – EXPLORATORY*	☐ *WEEK*
☐ *NEW—NO PREVIOUS WORK*	☐ *NO AWARENESS*	☐ *RESISTED CONTACT*	☐ *UNCERTAIN*	☐ *UNCERTAIN*
SOURCE OF ASSESSMENT INFORMATION				DATE

CUSTOMER OPPORTUNITY—ANALYSIS				
CUSTOMER OPPORTUNITY TYPE		CUSTOMER NEEDS ANALYSIS		
☐ *ROUTINE*	☐ *STATISTIC*			
☐ *RECOVERY*	☐ *NEW PRODUCT*			
☐ *EXPANSION*	☐ *INNOVATION*			
☐ *IMPROVEMENT*	☐ *MANDATE*			
CUSTOMER-ESTIMATED ACTIVITY START DATE		CUSTOMER-SPECIFIED WORK LOCATION(S)	ANTICIPATED SELECTION ACTIVITIES ☐ *NON-COMPETITIVE PURCHASE* ☐ *RFP/RFQ/RFI* ☐ *PROPOSAL* ☐ *BEST AND FINAL OFFER (BAFO)* ☐ *SOUL SOURCE* ☐ *OTHER*	DUE DATE
CUSTOMER-ESTIMATED ACTIVITY DURATION				
CUSTOMER-ESTIMATED COMPLETION DATE				
CUSTOMER-ESTIMATED SOLUTION COST				
CUSTOMER-ESTIMATED INITIAL FUNDING AMOUNT		CUSTOMER-ESTIMATED RESOURCE REQUIREMENTS	CUSTOMER-IDENTIFIED COMPETITION FOR AWARD	
CUSTOMER-ESTIMATED INITIAL FUNDING DATE				

ACTION/ACTIVITY/REVIEW – RESPONSIBILITY	START	FINISH	ACTIVITY STATUS

ATTACHMENTS	PREPARER	DATE	FILE OR DOCUMENT LOCATION

1.1.4 CUSTOMER PROFILE—Customer Record

PROCESS OVERVIEW
Compile any current or previous work performed for this customer to review the customer's business history. Use this to examine business risk, reasonableness of the customer's pursuit of the opportunity, and probability of selection by the customer. Monitor and manage issues associated with the customer.

TOOL PREPARATION	
PREPARED BY	DATE

PROJECT	CUSTOMER

▷ CUSTOMER RECORD—CURRENT PROJECT			
CUSTOMER ID	AUTHORIZATION TO ANNOUNCE PROJECT/CONTRACT	AUTHORIZED BY	DATE
CUSTOMER ACCOUNT NUMBER	AUTHORIZATION TO USE IN MARKETING MATERIALS	AUTHORIZED BY	DATE
CUSTOMER CONTRACT/PO ID	AUTHORIZATION TO USE FOR CUSTOMER REFERRAL	AUTHORIZED BY	DATE

CUSTOMER RECORD—PROJECT WORK HISTORY						
PROJECT	CONTRACT/PO ID	PROJECT MANAGER	STATUS	DATE	REFERRAL/RATING	VALUE ($)
					TOTAL VALUE OF PREVIOUS WORK	
CUSTOMER WORK HISTORY NOTES						

CUSTOMER RECORD—ISSUES MANAGEMENT LOG ▷					
ISSUE DATE	ISSUE DESCRIPTION	SOURCE	REFERRED TO	RESOLUTION	CLOSE DATE

ACTION/ACTIVITY/REVIEW — RESPONSIBILITY	START	FINISH	ACTIVITY STATUS

ATTACHMENTS	PREPARER	DATE	FILE OR DOCUMENT LOCATION

1.2.1 PROJECT PROFILE—Project Definition

PROCESS OVERVIEW
Compile relevant information to develop a complete and comprehensive description of the project work effort. Specify project objectives and scope. Prepare initial project estimates (use tool 1.2.2 for more detailed planning estimates). Identify and associate project deliverables. Examine project assumptions and constraints.

TOOL PREPARATION	
PREPARED BY	DATE

PROJECT	CUSTOMER

▷ PROJECT DEFINITION—OBJECTIVES

ID	PROJECT OBJECTIVES	SOURCE	S-M-A-R-T CHECK

▷ PROJECT DEFINITION—SCOPE STATEMENT

ACTIVITIES AND METHODS IN SCOPE	ACTIVITIES AND METHODS OUT-OF-SCOPE

▷ PROJECT DEFINITION—INITIAL ESTIMATES

PROJECT START DATE	PROJECT FINISH DATE	DURATION ESTIMATE	RESOURCE ESTIMATE	COST ESTIMTE

PROJECT DEFINITION—KEY DELIVERABLES BY PHASE/ACTIVITY

ID	DELIVERABLE	PHASE/ACTIVITY	START DATE	FINISH DATE

PROJECT DEFINITION—ASSUMPTIONS AND CONSTRAINTS

PROJECT ASSUMPTIONS	PROJECT CONSTRAINTS

ACTION/ACTIVITY/REVIEW — RESPONSIBILITY	START	FINISH	ACTIVITY STATUS

ATTACHMENTS	PREPARER	DATE	FILE OR DOCUMENT LOCATION

1.2.2 PROJECT PROFILE—Project Estimates

PROCESS OVERVIEW
REPLICATE FOR EACH ESTIMATING EFFORT. Initial project estimates are usually order-of-magnitude estimates associated with the Project Definition. Budget, and definitive estimates are more detailed and aligned with the project work plan and WBS. Use lessons learned reviews to help prepare project estimates.

TOOL PREPARATION	
PREPARED BY	DATE
CHECK IF REPLICATED (SPECIFY FILE LOCATION) ☐	

PROJECT	CUSTOMER

▷ PROJECT ESTIMATES—OVERVIEW			
PURPOSE OF ESTIMATE ☐ INITIAL ESTIMATE ☐ PLANNING ESTIMATE ☐ SUBSEQUENT ESTIMATE (RE-ESTIMATE)		WBS FILE LOCATION (IF CONSTRUCTED)	DURATION ESTIMATE
TYPE OF ESTIMATE (ESTIMATE ACCURACY) ☐ Order-of-Magnitude (–25/+50 percent) ☐ Budget Estimate (–10/+25 percent) ☐ Definitive Estimate (–5/+10 percent)	ESTIMATING METHODS	DEPENDENCIES WITH OTHER PROJECTS	RESOURCE ESTIMATE COST ESTIMATE

PROJECT ESTIMATES—BRIEF DESCRIPTION OF THE TECHNICAL SOLUTION	ESTIMATING CHECKLIST
	☐ *PROJECT DEFINITION REVIEWED* ☐ *WBS OR TECHNICAL SOLUTION REVIEWED* ☐ *ESTIMATING STANDARDS APPLIED* ☐ *CUSTOMER EXPECTATIONS REVIEWED* ☐ *LESSONS LEARNED REVIEWED*

PROJECT ESTIMATES—DURATION ESTIMATE (SCHEDULE)						
PROJECT PHASES	PHASE-1	PHASE-2	PHASE-3	PHASE-4	PHASE-5	PHASE-6
PROJECT PHASE NAME						
PROJECT PHASE START						
PROJECT PHASE FINISH						
PROJECT DURATION	days	days	days	days	days	days

PROJECT ESTIMATES—RESOURCE UTILIZATION ESTIMATE (STAFFING)						
KEY AND LEAD STAFF						
OTHER STAFF						
VENDOR STAFF						
PROJECT RESOURCES	#	#	#		#	#

PROJECT ESTIMATES—INITIAL COST ESTIMATE (BUDGET)						
LABOR COSTS-$						
DIRECT COSTS-$						
INDIRECT COSTS-$						
CONTINGENCY FUND-$						
PROJECT COSTS	$	$	$	$	$	$

ACTION/ACTIVITY/REVIEW — RESPONSIBILITY	START	FINISH	ACTIVITY STATUS

ATTACHMENTS	PREPARER	DATE	FILE OR DOCUMENT LOCATION

1.2.3 PROJECT PROFILE—Project Classification

PROCESS OVERVIEW
Determine project classification based on an examination of criteria that describes and evaluates project business interests, project performance characteristics, and project complexity. The initial determination of project classification may be adjusted following subsequent business and opportunity analyses.

TOOL PREPARATION	
PREPARED BY	DATE

PROJECT	CUSTOMER

▷ PROJECT CLASSIFICATION—OVERVIEW				
PART 1—BUSINESS INTEREST AREA (Adjudged from the Nature of Work)				
☐ OPERATIONAL	☐ INNOVATION	☐ MANDATE	☐ CUSTOMER	☐ STRATEGIC
Work is conducted to fulfill operational needs—usually to develop or maintain internal operating capability	Work is conducted to design or develop new products, services or technology for subsequent internal use or external sale	Work is conducted to satisfy the requirements of an internal (business) or external (industry or government) mandate	Work is conducted to provide product or service deliverables and to fulfill objectives specified by internal/external customers	Work is conducted to achieve a marketplace position, or to achieve business expansion or other strategic objective
PART 2—PROJECT MANAGEMENT LEVEL (Assigned by Judgment or Calculated from Performance and Complexity Indicators)				
☐ Level-1	☐ Level-2	☐ Level-3	☐ Level-4	☐ Level-5
Simple (routine) technical specialty requirements; and/or no business complexity	Advanced technical specialty requirements; and/or minimal to no business complexity	Multiple technical specialty requirements; and/or low business complexity	Unique or advanced technical specialty requirements; and/or moderate business complexity	Multiple advanced technical specialty requirements; and/or high business complexity

PROJECT CLASSIFICATION—PROJECT PERFORMANCE INDICATORS

INDICATOR	VERY LOW	WT	LOW	WT	MODERATE	WT	HIGH	WT	VERY HIGH	WT	VALUE = WT × 5
Project Duration	< 6 weeks	0.2	< 6 months	0.4	< 12 months	0.6	< 24 months	0.8	< 24 months	1.0	
Project Team Size	≤ 3 Resources	0.2	≤ 5 Resources	0.4	≤ 10 Resources	0.6	≤ 25 Resources	0.8	≤ 25 Resources	1.0	
Project Value (Cost)	≤ $10,000	0.2	≤ $100,000	0.4	≤ $1 Million	0.6	≤ $5 Million	0.8	≤ $5 Million	1.0	

PROJECT CLASSIFICATION—PROJECT COMPLEXITITY INDICATORS

INDICATOR	VERY LOW	WT	LOW	WT	MODERATE	WT	HIGH	WT	VERY HIGH	WT	VALUE = WT × 5
Strategic Value	*Minimal*—prime focus is internal operations	0.2	*Limited*—reflects business-related objectives to be achieved	0.4	*Visible*—influence or cost/revenue, customer loyalty, or key operations	0.6	*Distinct*—has key and visible impact on industry and market position	0.8	*Critical*—has major impact and visibility on business outlook	1.0	
Business Risk	No Appreciable Business Risk	0.2	Some General Business Risk	0.4	Some Key Business Risk	0.6	Increased Key Business Risk	0.8	Extensive Critical Business Risk	1.0	
Technology	Standard	0.2	Leading Edge	0.4	Advanced	0.6	Industry New	0.8	In-Development	1.0	
Organization Scope	Single Internal Business Unit	0.2	Multiple Internal Business Units	0.4	Multiple Internal Business Units and One or More Vendors	0.6	Multiple Internal Business Units at Multi-Locations; One or More Vendors	0.8	Multiple Internal Business Units or Vendors at International Locations	1.0	
Technical Scope	Routine Requirements	0.2	Some Specialty Requirements	0.4	Multiple Specialty Requirements	0.6	Unique/ Advanced Specialty Requirements	0.8	Multiple Unique/ Advanced Specialty Requirements	1.0	

PROJECT CLASSIFICATION—PROJECT MANAGEMENT LEVEL	
TOTAL VALUE OF PERFORMANCE & COMPLEXITY INDICATORS (SUM OF VALUES ÷ 8)	

ACTION/ACTIVITY/REVIEW — RESPONSIBILITY	START	FINISH	ACTIVITY STATUS

ATTACHMENTS	PREPARER	DATE	FILE OR DOCUMENT LOCATION

1.2.4 PROJECT PROFILE—Project Record

PROCESS OVERVIEW
Identify the key project stakeholders involved in project performance, deliverable acceptance, and resource assignments. Review and identify lessons learned from previous projects of similar nature to this project — to guide project definition development. Monitor and manage issues associated with project performance.

TOOL PREPARATION	
PREPARED BY	DATE

PROJECT	CUSTOMER

▷ PROJECT RECORD—CURRENT PROJECT	
PROJECT ID	KEY STAKEHOLDERS
PROJECT ACCOUNT NUMBER	KEY LESSONS LEARNED APPLIED

PROJECT RECORD—STAKEHOLDER ANALYSIS

NAME	TITLE/ROLE	STAKEHOLDER INTERESTS	PROJECT IMPACTS (INFLUENCE)	EMAIL

PROJECT RECORD—LESSONS LEARNED REVIEW

PROJECT REVIEWED	LESSON CATEGORY	LESSON LEARNED	HOW LESSON WILL BE APPLIED TO THIS PROJECT

LESSONS LEARNED REVIEW NOTES

PROJECT RECORD—ISSUES MANAGEMENT LOG ▷

ISSUE DATE	ISSUE DESCRIPTION	SOURCE	REFERRED TO	RESOLUTION	CLOSED DATE

ACTION/ACTIVITY/REVIEW — RESPONSIBILITY	START	FINISH	ACTIVITY STATUS

ATTACHMENTS	PREPARER	DATE	FILE OR DOCUMENT LOCATION

1.3.1 STAFF PROFILE—Staff Directory

PROCESS OVERVIEW
Identify the staff organizations from which project staff can be acquired. Specify any notable technical leaders assigned to this project team. List the individual staff members of the project team who will be assigned for purposes of performing project work.

TOOL PREPARATION	
PREPARED BY	DATE

PROJECT	CUSTOMER

▷ STAFF DIRECTORY—PROJECT ORGANIZATION(S)			
PMO—CONTACT	ADDRESS/LOCATION	TELEPHONE	EMAIL
HUMAN RESOURCES—CONTACT	ADDRESS/LOCATION	TELEPHONE	EMAIL
DEPARTMENT OFFICE—CONTACT	ADDRESS/LOCATION	TELEPHONE	EMAIL
RECRUITER ORGANIZATION—CONTACT	ADDRESS/LOCATION	TELEPHONE	EMAIL

STAFF DIRECTORY—TECHNICAL LEADERS				
NAME	TITLE	ADDRESS/LOCATION	TELEPHONE	EMAIL

STAFF DIRECTORY—TEAM MEMBERS				
NAME	TITLE	ADDRESS/LOCATION	TELEPHONE	EMAIL

ACTION/ACTIVITY/REVIEW — RESPONSIBILITY	START	FINISH	ACTIVITY STATUS

ATTACHMENTS	PREPARER	DATE	FILE OR DOCUMENT LOCATION

1.3.2 STAFF PROFILE—Staff Structure

PROCESS OVERVIEW
Identify and describe the staff organization that will be created to support the project effort. List relevant resource managers that will be a staff resource. Develop a formal or informal depiction of the project organization chart

TOOL PREPARATION	
PREPARED BY	DATE

PROJECT	CUSTOMER

▷ STAFF STRUCTURE—OVERVIEW			
PROJECT MANAGER	PROJECT TEAM MEMBERS	STAFF-RFESOURCE MANAGERS	EXECUTIVES/CONTROL BOARD
☐ *FUNCTIONAL ALIGNMENT*	☐ *FUNCTIONAL ALIGNMENT*	☐ *FUNCTIONAL ALIGNMENT*	☐ *FUNCTIONAL ALIGNMENT*
☐ *GENERAL MATRIX ALIGNMENT*	☐ *GENERAL MATRIX ALIGNMENT*	☐ *ORGANIZATION AFFILIATION*	☐ *ORGANIZATION AFFILIATION*
☐ *INTEGRATED MATRIX ALIGNMENT*	☐ *INTEGRATED MATRIX ALIGNMENT*	☐ *PROJECT-INTEGRATED AFFILIATION*	☐ *PROJECT-INTEGRATED AFFILIATION*
☐ *PRO ALIGNMENT*	☐ *ALIGNMENT*	☐ *PMO AFFILIATION*	☐ *PMO AFFILIATION*

PROJECT MANAGEMENT OFFICE (PMO) LOCATION	PROJECT MANAGEMENT OFFICE (PMO) MANAGER	DEPARTMENT AFFILIATION		
ADDRESS	CITY/STATE-PROVINCE/ZIP (POSTAL)	TELEPHONE	FAX	PRO WEB SITE

STAFF STRUCTURE—RESOURCE MANAGERS				
NAME	TITLE	DEPARTMENT/LOCATION	TELEPHONE	EMAIL

STAFF STRUCTURE—PROJECT ORGANIZATION CHART

ACTION/ACTIVITY/REVIEW – RESPONSIBILITY	START	FINISH	ACTIVITY STATUS

ATTACHMENTS	PREPARER	DATE	FILE OR DOCUMENT LOCATION

1.3.3 STAFF PROFILE—Staff Qualification

PROCESS OVERVIEW
Review and specify project staff qualification requirements—things that have to be accomplished for individuals to work on the project. This includes certifications and licenses, specification and management of security, and access clearances and general training. (See Tool 2.3.2 for a detailed training and development log.)

TOOL PREPARATION	
PREPARED BY	DATE

PROJECT	CUSTOMER

▷ STAFF QUALIFICATION—GENERAL REQUIREMENTS (QUALIFICATION-CERTIFICATION-LICENSING)				
QUALIFICATION ITEM	REQUIRED BY	IDENTIFIED DATE	DUE DATE	STAFF REQUIREMENTS NOTES

STAFF QUALIFICATION—GENERAL TRAINING (AND ORIENTATION) REQUIREMENTS				
QUALIFICATION ITEM	REQUIRED BY	IDENTIFIED DATE	DUE DATE	STAFF REQUIREMENTS NOTES

STAFF QUALIFICATION—SECURITY AND ACCESS REQUIREMENTS				
QUALIFICATION ITEM	REQUIRED BY	IDENTIFIED DATE	DUE DATE	STAFF REQUIREMENTS NOTES

STAFF QUALIFICATION—RESOURCES AND PROVIDERS				
RESOURCE OR TRAINING PROVIDER	TELEPHONE	TYPE OF ACTIVITY	RESOURCE DATE	RESOURCE ACCESS METHOD

ACTION/ACTIVITY/REVIEW — RESPONSIBILITY	START	FINISH	ACTIVITY STATUS

ATTACHMENTS	PREPARER	DATE	FILE OR DOCUMENT LOCATION

1.3.4 STAFF PROFILE—Staff Record

PROCESS OVERVIEW
Manage staff resources information relative to project team assignment requirements, individual qualifications, experience and project history, and manage results of staff work performance and postproject activities.

TOOL PREPARATION	
PREPARED BY	DATE

PROJECT	CUSTOMER

▷ STAFF RECORD—STAFF RESOURCES OVERVIEW		
RESOURCES ALLOCATED	RESOURCE ALLOCATION NOTES	DATE
RESOURCES REQUESTED	RESOURCE REQUEST NOTES	DATE
RESOURCES ACQUIRED	RESOURCE ACQUISITION NOTES	DATE

STAFF RECORD—ASSIGNMENT SUMMARY LOG ▷

PROJECT TEAM MEMBER	CREDENTIALS	TRAINING	KICKOFF	AVAILABILITY COMMITTED (%)	AVAILABILITY PROVIDED (%)	PERFORMANCE RATING	STATUS/COMMENTS

STAFF RECORD—ISSUES MANAGEMENT LOG ▷

ISSUE ID DATE	ISSUE DESCRIPTION	SOURCE	REFERRED TO	RESOLUTION	CLOSE DATE

ACTION/ACTIVITY/REVIEW — RESPONSIBILITY	START	FINISH	ACTIVITY STATUS

ATTACHMENTS	PREPARER	DATE	FILE OR DOCUMENT LOCATION

1.4.1 VENDOR PROFILE—Vendor Directory

PROCESS OVERVIEW
REPLICATE FOR EACH VENDOR—Identify the vendor organization and vendor contacts that will establish and manage the vendor contract and agreement, collaborate on the vendor's work planning effort, and perform and manage the vendor's project work as well as invoicing of vendor products and services.

TOOL PREPARATION	
PREPARED BY	DATE
CHECK IF REPLICATED (SPECIFY FILE LOCATION) ☐	

PROJECT	CUSTOMER

▷ VENDOR DIRECTORY—ORGANIZATION				
VENDOR NAME			WEB SITE ADDRESS	
POINT OF CONTACT	OFFICE TELEPHONE	MOBILE TELEPHONE	FAX	EMAIL

VENDOR DIRECTORY—BUSINESS MANAGER				
NAME				
DEPARTMENT			WEB SITE ADDRESS	
TITLE	OFFICE TELEPHONE	MOBILE TELEPHONE	FAX	EMAIL
ADDRESS	CITY/STATE-PROVINCE/ZIP (POSTAL CODE)		CONTACT NOTES	

VENDOR DIRECTORY—TECHNICAL MANAGER				
NAME				
DEPARTMENT			WEB SITE ADDRESS	
TITLE	OFFICE TELEPHONE	MOBILE TELEPHONE	FAX	EMAIL
ADDRESS	CITY/STATE-PROVINCE/ZIP (POSTAL CODE)		CONTACT NOTES	

VENDOR DIRECTORY—OTHER KEY CONTACTS				
NAME	TITLE	ADDRESS/LOCATION	TELEPHONE	EMAIL

ACTION/ACTIVITY/REVIEW — RESPONSIBILITY	START	FINISH	ACTIVITY STATUS

ATTACHMENTS	PREPARER	DATE	FILE OR DOCUMENT LOCATION

1.4.2 VENDOR PROFILE—Vendor Business

PROCESS OVERVIEW
REPLICATE FOR EACH VENDOR—Obtain and examine relevant information about the vendor's business organization as a basis for vendor selection, vendor retention and assignment, vendor management, and for gaining insight into the vendor's business capability and business approach.

TOOL PREPARATION	
PREPARED BY	DATE
CHECK IF REPLICATED (SPECIFY FILE LOCATION) ☐	

PROJECT	CUSTOMER

VENDOR ORGANIZATION

⊳ VENDOR BUSINESS—OVERVIEW		
BUSINESS TYPE) ☐ *PUBLIC* ☐ *PRIVATE* ☐ *GOVERNMENT* ☐ *NON-PROFIT*	ANNUAL REVENUE	NATURE OF BUSINESS—PRODUCT/SERVICE DESCRIPTION
BUSINESS SCOPE ☐ *GLOBAL* ☐ *NATIONAL* ☐ *REGIONAL* ☐ *LOCAL*	TOTAL ENTERPRISE BUSINESS LOCATIONS	
YEAR ENTERPRISE ESTABLISHED	TOTAL ENTERPRISE STAFFING (RESOURCES)	
INDUSTRY	PARENT ORGANIZATION	

VENDOR BUSINESS—EXECUTIVE MANAGEMENT		
CHAIR)	COO	OTHER EXECUTIVES AND SENIOR MANAGERS
CEO	CIO	
CFO	CTO	

VENDOR BUSINESS—MARKET				
STRATEGIC BUSINESS OBJECTIVES—GOALS—INTERESTS	KEY CUSTOMERS	STOCK EXCHANGE/LISTING CODE		
		STOCK PRICE—1 MONTH	6 MONTHS	1 YEAR
		BUSINESS TREND/OUTLOOK		

VENDOR BUSINESS—ALIGNMENT		
VENDOR KEY DIVISIONS/DEPARTMENTS	CUSTOMER BUSINESS PARTNERS	CUSTOMER INDUSTRY COMPETITORS

ACTION/ACTIVITY/REVIEW — RESPONSIBILITY	START	FINISH	ACTIVITY STATUS

ATTACHMENTS	PREPARER	DATE	FILE OR DOCUMENT LOCATION

1.4.3 VENDOR PROFILE—Vendor Qualification

PROCESS OVERVIEW
Track and manage the list of vendors qualified by the organization and eligible to perform work assignments on this project. If desired, maintain two lists: one for vendors who will serve primarily as staff members to provide products and services, one for vendors who will serve primarily to provide goods and supplies.

TOOL PREPARATION	
PREPARED BY	DATE

PROJECT	CUSTOMER

VENDOR QUALIFICATION—QUALIFIED VENDORS AS SUBCONTRACTORS					
VENDOR (☒ ON THIS PROJECT)	CONTACT	NATURE OF BUSINESS	PHONE	CONTRACT START	CONTRACT FINISH
☐					
☐					
☐					
☐					
☐					
☐					
☐					
☐					
☐					
VENDORS AS SUBCONTRACTORS NOTES					

VENDOR QUALIFICATION—QUALIFIED VENDORS AS SUPPLIERS					
VENDOR (✓ ON THIS PROJECT)	CONTACT	NATURE OF BUSINESS	PHONE	CONTRACT START	CONTRACT FINISH
☐					
☐					
☐					
☐					
☐					
☐					
☐					
☐					
☐					
VENDORS AS SUPPLIERS NOTES					

ACTION/ACTIVITY/REVIEW — RESPONSIBILITY	START	FINISH	ACTIVITY STATUS

ATTACHMENTS	PREPARER	DATE	FILE OR DOCUMENT LOCATION

1.4.4 VENDOR PROFILE—Vendor Record

PROCESS OVERVIEW
REPLICATE FOR EACH VENDOR—Compile and review any previous project or services work conducted by each vendor (for the organization or for the customer) as a basis for vendor fit with this project. Use this when examining vendor business risk and vendor selection. Monitor and manage issues for this vendor.

TOOL PREPARATION	
PREPARED BY	DATE
CHECK IF REPLICATED (SPECIFY FILE LOCATION) ☐	

PROJECT	CUSTOMER

VENDOR ORGANIZATION

▷ VENDOR RECORD—CURRENT PROJECT			
VENDOR ID	PERMISSION TO ANNOUNCE PROJECT/CONTRACT	AUTHORIZED BY	DATE
VENDOR ACCOUNT NUMBER	PERMISSION TO USE IN MARKETING MATERIALS	AUTHORIZED BY	DATE
CURRENT CONTRACT/PO ID	PERMISSION TO USE FOR CUSTOMER REFERRAL	AUTHORIZED BY	DATE

VENDOR RECORD—WORK HISTORY						
PROJECT	CONTRACT/PO ID	PROJECT MANAGER	STATUS	DATE	REFERRAL/RATING	VALUE ($)
					TOTAL VALUE OF PREVIOUS WORK	
CUSTOMER WORK HISTORY NOTES						

VENDOR RECORD—ISSUES MANAGEMENT LOG ▷					
ISSUE DATE	ISSUE DESCRIPTION	SOURCE	REFERRED TO	RESOLUTION	CLOSE DATE

ACTION/ACTIVITY/REVIEW — RESPONSIBILITY	START	FINISH	ACTIVITY STATUS

ATTACHMENTS	PREPARER	DATE	FILE OR DOCUMENT LOCATION

1.5.1 BUSINESS PROFILE—Business Case

PROCESS OVERVIEW
REPLICATE FOR ADDITIONAL BUSINESS CASE REVIEWS—Obtain and examine relevant business information as a basis for making a project selection decision. Use this information in combination with other profile sheets to answer the fundamental question, "why should this project be selected?"

TOOL PREPARATION	
PREPARED BY	DATE
CHECK IF REPLICATED (SPECIFY FILE LOCATION) ☐	

PROJECT	CUSTOMER

⊳ BUSINESS CASE—PROJECT SCREENING (PERFORMANCE PERSPECTIVE EVALUATION)				
STRATEGIC INTEREST	NATURE OF PROJECT WORK	RESOURCE CAPACITY	COMPETITION	CUSTOMER READINESS
☐ *DIRECT ALIGNMENT*	☐ *CORE COMPETENCY*	☐ *STAFF IS AVAILABLE*	☐ *NONE EXPECTED*	☐ *COMMITTED*
☐ *INDIRECT ALIGNMENT*	☐ *EXPANDED COMPETENCY*	☐ *MINOR RESCHEDULING*	☐ *FEW SIGNIFICANT PLAYERS*	☐ *DECIDED*
☐ *UNCERTAIN ALIGNMENT*	☐ *NEW COMPETENCY*	☐ *CRITICAL RESCHEDULING*	☐ *MODERATE COMPETITION*	☐ *DELIBERATING*
☐ *NO ALIGNMENT*	☐ *NO INSIDE COMPETENCY*	☐ *NO INSIDE AVAILABLE*	☐ *STRONG COMPETITION*	☐ *UNCERTAIN*
PROJECT SCREENING NOTES				

BUSINESS CASE—BUSINESS PERSPECTIVE EVALUATION		
BUSINESS FACTORS	FACTOR BENEFITS—CRITERIA	CRITERIA ACHIEVED
☐ Project Cost/Savings—achieves project cost savings objectives		☐ Yes ☐ No
☐ Project Cost/Savings—achieves project cost savings objectives		☐ Yes ☐ No
☐ Customer Satisfaction—achieves retention/expansion objectives		☐ Yes ☐ No
☐ Business Advantage—achieves business and market objectives		☐ Yes ☐ No
☐ New Products—achieves new product introduction objectives		☐ Yes ☐ No
	OVERALL BUSINESS PERSPECTIVE RATING	

BUSINESS CASE—FINANCIAL PERSPECTIVE EVALUATION		
BUSINESS FACTORS	FACTOR BENEFITS—CRITERIA	CRITERIA ACHIEVED
☐ Investment Commitment—achieves investment amount goals		☐ Yes ☐ No
☐ Investment Returns—achieves ROI goals		☐ Yes ☐ No
☐ Investment Period—achieves project timeframe goals		☐ Yes ☐ No
☐ Investment Allocation—achieves project diversity funding goals		☐ Yes ☐ No
	OVERALL FINANCIAL PERSPECTIVE RATING	

BUSINESS CASE—NON-NUMERIC PERSPECTIVE EVALUATION		
BUSINESS FACTORS	FACTOR BENEFITS—CRITERIA	CRITERIA ACHIEVED
☐ Operating Need—achieves efficiency/effectiveness objectives		☐ Yes ☐ No
☐ Competitive Necessity—achieves business advantage positions		☐ Yes ☐ No
☐ Business Mandates—fulfills internal/external mandates		☐ Yes ☐ No
	OVERALL NON-NUMERIC PERSPECTIVE RATING	

ACTION/ACTIVITY/REVIEW — RESPONSIBILITY	START	FINISH	ACTIVITY STATUS

ATTACHMENTS	PREPARER	DATE	FILE OR DOCUMENT LOCATION

1.5.2 BUSINESS PROFILE—Business Risk Examination

PROCESS OVERVIEW
REPLICATE FOR ADDITIONAL BUSINESS CASE REVIEWS—Compile and review previous project work and associated business results for business risks that could be encountered with the selection and performance of this project. A general review of risk areas should be followed by a detailed analysis of business risks.

TOOL PREPARATION	
PREPARED BY	DATE
CHECK IF REPLICATED (SPECIFY FILE LOCATION) ☐	

PROJECT	CUSTOMER

▷ BUSINESS RISK—RISK AREA REVIEW				
MARKETPLACE RISK	FINANCIAL RISK	LEGAL RISK	TECHNOLOGY-BASED RISK	CUSTOMER-BASED RISK
☐ *INDUSTRY STANDARDS*	☐ *INFLATION/TAXATION*	☐ *LICENSE REQUIREMENTS*	☐ *QUALIFIED TECHNICIANS*	☐ *SATISFACTION FACTORS*
☐ *GOVERNMENT MANDATES*	☐ *CURRENCY VALUES*	☐ *CONTRACT AMBIGUITY*	☐ *USER QUALIFICATION*	☐ *CHANGE REQUESTS*
☐ *CONSUMER INTERESTS*	☐ *STOCK MARKET CHANGES*	☐ *BANKRUPTCIES*	☐ *NEW TECHNOLOGY*	☐ *DECISIONS & INDECISION*
☐ *SOCIAL CONDITIONS*	☐ *CASH FLOW*	☐ *LAWSUITS*	☐ *OLD TECHNOLOGY*	☐ *FUNDING COMMITMENT*
☐ *ENVIRONMENT IMPACTS*	☐ *PROJECT ESTIMATES*	☐ *COPYRIGHTS*		☐ *STRATEGY ADJUSTMENTS*
☐ *ACTS OF NATURE*	☐ *FUNDING COMMITMENT*	☐ *PARTNERSHIP IMPACTS*		☐ *MANAGEMENT CHANGES*
☐ *COMPETITION MOVES*		☐ *UNION AGREEMENTS*		
BUSINESS RISK AREA OVERVIEW NOTES				

BUSINESS RISK—ASSESSMENT LOG ▷				
BUSINESS RISK AREA	RISK EVENT AND DESCRIPTION	PROBABILITY (P)	IMPACT (I)	OVERALL (P X I)
		High Med Low	High Med Low	High Med Low
		High Med Low	High Med Low	High Med Low
		High Med Low	High Med Low	High Med Low
		High Med Low	High Med Low	High Med Low
		High Med Low	High Med Low	High Med Low
		High Med Low	High Med Low	High Med Low
		High Med Low	High Med Low	High Med Low

BUSINESS RISK—RESPONSE LOG ▷					
RISK EVENT	RISK RESPONSE ACTION	PRIORITY	ASSIGN TO	ASSIGN DATE	CLOSE DATE

ACTION/ACTIVITY/REVIEW – RESPONSIBILITY	START	FINISH	ACTIVITY STATUS

ATTACHMENTS	PREPARER	DATE	FILE OR DOCUMENT LOCATION

1.5.3 BUSINESS PROFILE—Business Financial Analysis

PROCESS OVERVIEW
REPLICATE FOR ADDITIONAL BUSINESS CASE REVIEWS—Compile and review any previous project work and associated business results to ascertain the cost/benefits of performing this project. Select the financial analyses to be performed, conduct the analysis, and enter the results of each analysis.

TOOL PREPARATION	
PREPARED BY	DATE
CHECK IF REPLICATED (SPECIFY FILE LOCATION) ☐	

PROJECT	CUSTOMER

▷ BUSINESS FINANCIAL ANALYSIS—INITIAL ESTIMATE				
FIRST QUARTER PROJECT COSTS	FIRST QUARTER REVENUE	FIRST QUARTER MARGIN	EFFECT DATE	PRE-CONTRACT/PRE-PROJECT COSTS
FIRST YEAR PROJECT COSTS	FIRST YEAR REVENUE	FIRST YEAR MARGIN	EFFECT DATE	
TOTAL PROJECT COSTS	TOTAL REVENUE	TOTAL MARGIN	EFFECT DATE	

BUSINESS FINANCIAL ANALYSIS—FUNDAMENTAL COSTS				
MAJOR PROJECT COST AREAS	COST	COST RECOVERY OPTIONS	MARKUP	FUNDAMENTAL COSTS NOTES
Pre-contract/Pre-project				
Internal Staff Resources				
Vendor Participation				
Equipment				
Facilities				
Fees and Licenses				
Travel				
Administrative				
Other				
Other				
TOTAL				

BUSINESS FINANCIAL ANALYSIS—SUPPORTING STUDIES AND ANALYSIS			
FINANCIAL CALCULATION	PURPOSE/FOCUS—CRITERIA	DATE	STUDY OR ANALYSIS RESULTS
Benefit-Cost			
Economic Analysis			
Feasibility Study			
Financing Analysis			
Prospectus Review			
Investment Analysis			
Inflation Analysis			
Cash Flow Analysis			
Other			

ACTION/ACTIVITY/REVIEW – RESPONSIBILITY	START	FINISH	ACTIVITY STATUS

ATTACHMENTS	PREPARER	DATE	FILE OR DOCUMENT LOCATION

1.5.4 BUSINESS PROFILE—Business Recommendation

PROCESS OVERVIEW
REPLICATE FOR ADDITIONAL BUSINESS CASE REVIEWS—Review the business case, along with other profile information and Project Definition to develop a recommendation for project selection. Also, identify the prominent selection criteria used and summarize the prepared "pro and con" arguments.

TOOL PREPARATION	
PREPARED BY	DATE
CHECK IF REPLICATED (SPECIFY FILE LOCATION) ☐	

PROJECT	CUSTOMER

▷ BUSINESS RECOMMENDATION—SUMMARY POSITION				
PROJECT-TYPE BUCKET				
☐ *OPERATIONAL*	☐ *INNOVATION*	☐ *MANDATE*	☐ *CUSTOMER*	☐ *STRATEGIC*
PERFORMANCE EVALUATION	BUSINESS PERSPECTIVE	FINANCIAL PERSPECTIVE	NON-NUMERICAL PERSPECTIVE	RECOMMENDATION
☐ *STRONG SUPPORT*	☐ *EXCEEDS CRITERIA*	☐ *EXCEEDS CRITERIA*	☐ *EXCEEDS CRITERIA*	☐ *SELECT*
☐ *MODERATE SUPPORT*	☐ *ACHIEVES CRITERIA*	☐ *ACHIEVES CRITERIA*	☐ *ACHIEVES CRITERIA*	☐ *SELECT ON CONTINGENCY*
☐ *WEAK SUPPORT*	☐ *DOESN'T MEET CRITERIA*	☐ *DOESN'T MEET CRITERIA*	☐ *DOESN'T MEET CRITERIA*	☐ *DEFER SELECTION—HOLD*
☐ *NOT EVALUATED*	☐ *NOT EVALUATED*	☐ *NOT EVALUATED*	☐ *NOT EVALUATED*	☐ *NON-SELECTION*
BUSINESS RECOMMENDATION NOTES				

BUSINESS RECOMMENDATION—BUSINESS CASE REVIEW				
NAME	DISTRIBUTION DATE	REVIEW COMMENTS	REVIEW DATE	CONCURRENCE/COMMENTS
BUSINESS CASE REVIEW NOTES				

BUSINESS RECOMMENDATION—PROJECT SELECTION (RETENTION) AND AUTHORIZATION			
SELECTION DECISION ☐ *SELECT* ☐ *SELECT ON CONTINGENCY* ☐ *DEFER SELECTION—HOLD* ☐ *NON-SELECTION*			PROJECT SELECTION NOTES
RESOURCE ALLOCATION ACCOUNT	INITIAL RESOURCE ALLOCATION	DATE	
FUNDING ACCOUNT	INITIAL FUNDING AMOUNT	DATE	
DECISION AUTHORIZATION BY:	SIGNATURE	DATE	

ACTION/ACTIVITY/REVIEW — RESPONSIBILITY	START	FINISH	ACTIVITY STATUS

ATTACHMENTS	PREPARER	DATE	FILE OR DOCUMENT LOCATION

1.6.1 MANAGEMENT PROFILE—Management Directory

PROCESS OVERVIEW
Identify and record the internal management contacts that will oversee or otherwise influence project performance, establishing the contract or agreement, collaborating on work planning, allocating staff, facilitating customer and vendor relationships, and managing deliverables and associated invoicing and payments.

TOOL PREPARATION	
PREPARED BY	DATE

PROJECT	CUSTOMER

▷ MANAGEMENT DIRECTORY—MANAGEMENT TEAM			
PROJECT MANAGER	ADDRESS/LOCATION	TELEPHONE	EMAIL
PROJECT MANAGEMENT OFFICE (PMO)	ADDRESS/LOCATION	TELEPHONE	EMAIL
BUSINESS UNIT MANAGER	ADDRESS/LOCATION	TELEPHONE	EMAIL
PROJECT EXECUTIVE-SPONSOR	ADDRESS/LOCATION	TELEPHONE	EMAIL
PROJECT CONTROL BOARD (CHAIR)	ADDRESS/LOCATION	TELEPHONE	EMAIL
OTHER KEY CONTACT	ADDRESS/LOCATION	TELEPHONE	EMAIL

MANAGEMENT DIRECTORY—PROJECT CONTROL BOARD MEMBERS				
NAME	TITLE/ROLE	ADDRESS/LOCATION	TELEPHONE	EMAIL

MANAGEMENT DIRECTORY—TECHNICAL REVIEW BOARD MEMBERS AND KEY TECHNICAL LEADERS				
NAME	TITLE/ROLE	ADDRESS/LOCATION	TELEPHONE	EMAIL

ACTION/ACTIVITY/REVIEW — RESPONSIBILITY	START	FINISH	ACTIVITY STATUS

ATTACHMENTS	PREPARER	DATE	FILE OR DOCUMENT LOCATION

1.6.2 MANAGEMENT PROFILE—Management Portfolio

PROCESS OVERVIEW
Examine the project for integration in the applicable portfolio in the organization; and establish the project priority and schedule for project and portfolio reviews. Identify the executive (sponsor), executive team or control board responsible for portfolio management, and for subsequent project and portfolio reviews.

TOOL PREPARATION	
PREPARED BY	DATE

PROJECT	CUSTOMER

▷ MANAGEMENT PORTFOLIO—OVERVIEW			
PORTFOLIO OWNER—NAME	DEPARTMENT	PORTFOLIO ACCOUNT	PORTFOLIO PERSON
MANAGEMENT PORTFOLIO NOTES			

MANAGEMENT PORTFOLIO—PORTFOLIO INTEGRATION MATRIX		
PORTFOLIO	PORTFOLIO VALUES	PROJECT PORTFOLIO INTEGRATION NOTES
Portfolio Bucket Name		
Number of Projects		
Total Value		
THIS PROJECT		
Project Value		
Project Position		

MANAGEMENT PORTFOLIO—PORTFOLIO REVIEW SCHEDULE				
REVIEW	REVIEW PERIOD DATE(S)	REVIEW MEETING DATE(S)	REVIEW FINDINGS/ADJUSTMENT DECISIONS	PROJECT STATUS
Period-1				
Period-2				
Period-3				
Period-4				
Period-5				

MANAGEMENT PORTFOLIO—PROJECT REVIEW SCHEDULE				
REVIEW	REVIEW PERIOD DATE(S)	REVIEW MEETING DATE(S)	REVIEW FINDINGS/ADJUSTMENT DECISIONS	PROJECT STATUS
Selection Review				
Contract Review				
Planning Review				
Performance Review				
Closeout Review				
Additional Review				
Additional Review				

ACTION/ACTIVITY/REVIEW – RESPONSIBILITY	START	FINISH	ACTIVITY STATUS

ATTACHMENTS	PREPARER	DATE	FILE OR DOCUMENT LOCATION

1.6.3 MANAGEMENT PROFILE—Management Charter

PROCESS OVERVIEW
Identify the project manager and specify the range of project manager authority and responsibility. Identify the managers having various types of oversight responsibility for the project, and the persons to whom the project manager can turn when issues of authority need to be resolved or otherwise elevated..

TOOL PREPARATION	
PREPARED BY	DATE

PROJECT	CUSTOMER

▷ MANAGEMENT CHARTER—STATEMENT			
PROJECT MANAGER	DEPARMENT	AUTHORITY LEVEL	DELEGATION LEVEL
PROJECT CHARTER STATEMENT			
PROJECT EXECUTIVE-SPONSOR	DEPARTMENT	TELEPHONE	DATE

MANAGEMENT CHARTER—PROJECT MANAGER AUTHORITY			
AUTHORITY AREA FOR THIS PROJECT	RESPONSIBILITY LEVEL	AUTHORITY LEVEL	AUTHORITY LIMITS/DESCRIPTION
Financial Authoriy			
Contractual Authority			
Resource Management Authority			
Customer Management Authority			
Vendor Management Authority			
Other Authority			
PROJECT MANAGER AUTHORITY NOTES			

MANAGEMENT CHARTER—PROJECT OVERSIGHT RESPONSIBILITY					
AUTHORITY AREA FOR THIS PROJECT	PROJECT MANAGER	PMO	BUSINESS UNIT	EXECUTIVE-SPONSOR	CONTROL BOARD
Financial Responsibility					
Contractual Responsibility					
Resource Management Responsibility					
Customer Management Responsibility					
Vendor Management Responsibility					
Other Responsibility					
PROJECT OVERSIGHT RESPONSIBILITY NOTES					

ACTION/ACTIVITY/REVIEW — RESPONSIBILITY	START	FINISH	ACTIVITY STATUS

ATTACHMENTS	PREPARER	DATE	FILE OR DOCUMENT LOCATION

1.6.4 MANAGEMENT PROFILE—Management Record

PROCESS OVERVIEW
Manage information relative to management team requirements and preparations for and conduct of portfolio and project performance reviews. Monitor and record other management activities and involvement in project management oversight and in pre- and post-project activities.

TOOL PREPARATION	
PREPARED BY	DATE

PROJECT	CUSTOMER

▷ MANAGEMENT RECORD—CURRENT PROJECT		
MANAGEMENT TEAM—INITIAL PROJECT ORIENTATION	EXECUTIVE-SPONSOR TEAM MEETINGS	MANAGEMENT RECORD NOTES
SPECIAL MANAGEMENT REPORT REQUIREMENTS	EXECUTIVE-SPONSOR CUSTOMER MEETINGS	

MANAGEMENT RECORD—MANAGEMENT TEAM LOG			
MANAGEMENT TEAM MEMBER	PROJECT-RELATED ACTIVITY/EVENT	COMMENTS—DECISIONS/RESULTS/OUTCOMES	DATE

MANAGEMENT RECORD—ISSUES MANAGEMENT LOG					▷
ISSUE ID DATE	ISSUE DESCRIPTION	SOURCE	REFERRED TO	RESOLUTION	CLOSE DATE

ACTION/ACTIVITY/REVIEW — RESPONSIBILITY	START	FINISH	ACTIVITY STATUS

ATTACHMENTS	PREPARER	DATE	FILE OR DOCUMENT LOCATION

Chapter 2

Plan-Phase Tools

The following are the tools used in the Plan Phase:

- 2.1 Customer Plan
  - 2.1.1 Customer Requirements
  - 2.1.2 Customer Technical Solution
  - 2.1.3 Customer Change Control Plan
  - 2.1.4 Customer Quality Management Plan
- 2.2 Project Plan
  - 2.2.1 Project Work Plan
  - 2.2.2 Project Risk Management Plan
  - 2.2.3 Project Communication Plan
  - 2.2.4 Project Support Plans
- 2.3 Staff Plan
  - 2.3.1 Staff Requirements
  - 2.3.2 Staff Management Plan
  - 2.3.3 Staff Acquisition (Request)
  - 2.3.4 Staff Assignments
- 2.4 Vendor Plan
  - 2.4.1 Vendor Solicitation
  - 2.4.2 Vendor Management Plan
  - 2.4.3 Vendor Proposal Evaluation
  - 2.4.4 Vendor Contract
- 2.5 Business Plan
  - 2.5.1 Business Requirements
  - 2.5.2 Business Solution
  - 2.5.3 Business Proposal
  - 2.5.4 Business Contract
- 2.6 Management Plan
  - 2.6.1 Management Oversight Plan
  - 2.6.2 Management Audit and Review Plan
  - 2.6.3 Management Facility Plan
  - 2.6.4 Management Supply and Equipment Plan

These tools are described in this chapter.

2.1.1 CUSTOMER PLAN—Customer Requirements

PROCESS OVERVIEW
Identify and compile information pertaining to the business, technical, and functional requirements of the project. Review source materials and examine sources to ensure consistent translation of needs and specifications to project requirements. List the requirements and then validate them to create a baseline.

TOOL PREPARATION	
PREPARED BY	DATE

PROJECT	CUSTOMER

▷ CUSTOMER REQUIREMENTS—OVERVIEW			
REQUIREMENTS IDENTIFICATION ACTIVITY	START	COMPLETE	REQUIREMENTS IDENTIFICATION NOTES
Requirements Gathering			
Requirements Documentation & Analysis			
Requirements Validation			
Requirements Baseline Set			

CUSTOMER REQUIREMENTS—GATHERING (BY TYPE OF REQUIREMENT)						
REQUIREMENTS SOURCE	COMPLETION DATE	BUSINESS	TECHNICAL	FUNCTIONAL	OTHER TYPE	REQUIREMENTS GATHERING COMMENTS
Statement of Work						
RFP/RFI/RFQ						
Technical Specifications						
Business Specifications						
Surveys and Analyses						
Workshops						
Interviews						

CUSTOMER REQUIREMENTS—DOCUMENTATION MANAGEMENT LOG ▷					
REQ ID	TYPE	REQUIREMENT	SOURCE	SPECIFICATION	WBS ELEMENT

CUSTOMER REQUIREMENTS—VALIDATION & BASELINE					
VALIDATION METHOD	RESULTS	PERFORMED BY	DATE	CUSTOMER BASELINE SIGNOFF	DATE
				PROJECT MANAGER BASELINE SIGNOFF	DATE
				PMO–MANAGEMENT BASELINE SIGNOFF	DATE

ACTION/ACTIVITY/REVIEW — RESPONSIBILITY	START	FINISH	ACTIVITY STATUS

ATTACHMENTS	PREPARER	DATE	FILE OR DOCUMENT LOCATION

2.1.2 CUSTOMER PLAN—Customer Technical Solution

PROCESS OVERVIEW
Identify the technical solution (technical approach) to be used to fulfill customer requirements, noting the type of technical effort to be performed and examining associated technical requirements. Specify the deliverables and milestones to be monitored and achieved; this supersedes the initial list in the *Project Definition*.

TOOL PREPARATION	
PREPARED BY	DATE

PROJECT	CUSTOMER

▷ CUSTOMER TECHNICAL SOLUTION—OVERVIEW		
TYPE OF TECHNICAL SOLUTION	TECHNICAL CAPABILITY REQUIREMENTS (NATURE OF WORK)	AWARD POTENTIAL
☐ Routine Capability ☐ Adapted Routine Capabiliity ☐ Advanced Capability ☐ Innovative Capability ☐ New Product/Service Capability	TECHNICAL PRECISION REQUIREMENTS (QUALITY MANAGEMENT) TECHNICAL MANAAGEMENT REQUIREMENTS (OVERSIGHT AND CONTROL)	☐ *CERTAIN* ☐ *STRONG* ☐ *AVERAGE* ☐ *WEAK* ☐ *UNCERTAIN*

CUSTOMER TECHNICAL SOLUTION—TECHNICAL APPROACH	
FACTORS AFFECTING THE TECHNICAL APPROACH	TECHNICAL APPROACH—DESCRIBE THE TECHNICAL SOLUTION TO BE DELIVERED

CUSTOMER TECHNICAL SOLUTION—DELIVERABLES LOG ▷

DELIVERABLE	RESPONSIBILITY	DUE DATE	ACTUAL DATE	REQ ID	WBS ELEMENT	% COMPLETE	STATUS DATE

CUSTOMER TECHNICAL SOLUTION—MILESTONES LOG ▷

DELIVERABLE	RESPONSIBILITY	DUE DATE	ACTUAL DATE	REQ ID	WBS ELEMENT	% COMPLETE	STATUS DATE

ACTION/ACTIVITY/REVIEW – RESPONSIBILITY	START	FINISH	ACTIVITY STATUS

ATTACHMENTS	PREPARER	DATE	FILE OR DOCUMENT LOCATION

2.1.3 CUSTOMER PLAN—Customer Change Control Plan

PROCESS OVERVIEW
Identify the means by which changes to project scope and customer requirements will be requested, reviewed, approved, and implemented. Maintain a central log of change requests, and monitor and manage their approval and implementation; monitor cost (value) associated with implementing approved changes.

TOOL PREPARATION	
PREPARED BY	DATE

PROJECT	CUSTOMER

▷ CUSTOMER CHANGE CONTROL PLAN—OVERVIEW				
CHANGE CONTROL PLAN PURPOSE AND GENERAL GUIDIANCE		PLAN DISTRIBUTION—PRIMARY USERS ☐ Executive/Sponsor ☐ PMO ☐ Project Team ☐ Customer ☐ Control Board	Other Stakeholders ☐ ☐ ☐ ☐	PLAN BASELINE DATE LAST PLAN REVISION DATE LAST DISTRIBUTION DATE
CHANGE CONTROL PLAN MANAGER	OFFICE TELEPHONE	MOBILE TELEPHONE	FAX	EMAIL

CUSTOMER CHANGE CONTROL PLAN—PLANNING DETAILS AND PROCEDURES		
APPLICABLE STANDARDS, POLICIES AND PRACTICES	CHANGE REQUEST PROCEDURES	KEY CHANGE MANAGEMENT ACTIVITIES ☒ COMPLETED ☐ Establish Change Management Procedures *MANAGE PROJECT CHANGE REQUESTS* ☐ Identify Requested Change (see Tool 3.1.3) ☐ Evaluate Change Impact and Cost ☐ Obtain Change Approval *MANAGE PROJECT CHANGE IMPLEMENTATION* ☐ Obtain Necessary Funding ☐ Update Relevant Contracts ☐ Update Relevant Documents and Plans ☐ Notify Customer and Relevant Users
CHANGE CONTROL PLAN REVIEW POINT(S)	CHANGE IMPLEMENTATION PROCEDURES	
CHANAGE CONTROL MANAGEMENT TOOL(S)		

CUSTOMER CHANGE CONTROL PLAN—CHANGE REQUEST AND APPROVAL LOG ▷

REQ #	CHANGE DESCRIPTION	SUBMITTAL DATE	FINAL REVIEW DATE	APPROVAL STATUS	IMPLEMENT DATE	VALUE ($)
					TOTAL VALUE OF ADJUSTED WORK	

ACTION/ACTIVITY/REVIEW — RESPONSIBILITY	START	FINISH	ACTIVITY STATUS

ATTACHMENTS	PREPARER	DATE	FILE OR DOCUMENT LOCATION

2.1.4 CUSTOMER PLAN—Customer Quality Management Plan

PROCESS OVERVIEW
Identify the standards to be used and the means by which quality assurance and quality control activities will be performed. Specify quality testing requirements, procedures, and customer acceptance criteria for associated project deliverables. Identify, schedule, and conduct quality testing and project quality technical reviews.

TOOL PREPARATION	
PREPARED BY	DATE

PROJECT	CUSTOMER

▷ CUSTOMER QUALITY MANAGEMENT PLAN—OVERVIEW				
QUALITY MANAGEMENT PLAN PURPOSE AND GENERAL GUIDANCE		PLAN DISTRIBUTION—PRIMARY USERS ☐ Executive/Sponsor ☐ PMO ☐ Project Team ☐ Customer ☐ Control Board	Other Stakeholders ☐ ☐ ☐ ☐	PLAN BASELINE DATE LAST PLAN REVISION DATE LAST DISTRIBUTION DATE
QUALITY MANGEMENT PLAN MANAGER	OFFICE TELEPHONE	MOBILE TELEPHONE	FAX	EMAIL

CUSTOMER QUALITY MANAGEMENT PLAN—PLANNING DETAILS AND PROCEDURES		
APPLICABLE STANDARDS, POLICIES AND PRACTICES	QUALITY ASSURANCE APPROACH	KEY QUALITY MANAGEMENT ACTIVITIES ☒ COMPLETED ☐ Review Technical Specifications *MANAGE QUALITY ASSURANCE* ☐ Plan & Conduct Quality Assurance Activities ☐ Plan & Conduct Quality Technical Reviews *MANAGE QUALITY CONTROL* ☐ Specify Quality Control Methods ☐ Identify Design & Development Reviews *PLAN QUALITY TEST & ACCEPTANCE* ☐ Plan Quality and Product/System Testing ☐ Manage Customer Acceptance
QUALITY MANAGEMENT PLAN REVIEW POINT(S)	QUALITY CONTROL APPROACH	
QUALITY MANAGEMENT TOOL(S)		

CUSTOMER QUALITY MANAGEMENT PLAN—QUALITY TESTING AND ACCEPTANCE LOG ▷					
QUALITY TESTING AND ACCEPTANCE PROCEDURES	TEST	SCHEDULED	ACCEPTANCE STATUS—RESULTS	TEST LEADER	TEST DATE

CUSTOMER QUALITY MANAGEMENT PLAN—QUALITY TECHNICAL REVIEWS LOG ▷					
QUALITY TECHNICAL REVIEW PROCEDURES	REVIEW	SCHEDULED	REVIEW STATUS—RESULTS	REVIEW LEADER	TEST DATE

ACTION/ACTIVITY/REVIEW — RESPONSIBILITY	START	FINISH	ACTIVITY STATUS

ATTACHMENTS	PREPARER	DATE	FILE OR DOCUMENT LOCATION

2.2.1 PROJECT PLAN—Project Work Plan

PROCESS OVERVIEW	TOOL PREPARATION	
Apply prescribed procedures and prepare a work breakdown structure (WBS) with cost, schedule, and resource estimates to guide project work. List the summary-level results of WBS construction, and identify variance thresholds to be monitored. Use automated tools or extension sheets to show further task decomposition.	PREPARED BY	DATE

PROJECT	CUSTOMER

▷ PROJECT WORK PLAN—OVERVIEW

WORK PLAN PURPOSE AND GENERAL GUIDANCE	PLAN DISTRIBUTION—PRIMARY USERS		PLAN BASELINE DATE
	☐ Executive/Sponsor	Other Stakeholders	
	☐ PMO	☐	LAST PLAN REVISION DATE
	☐ Project Team	☐	
	☐ Customer	☐	LAST DISTRIBUTION DATE
	☐ Control Board	☐	

WORK PLAN MANAGER	OFFICE TELEPHONE	MOBILE TELEPHONE	FAX	EMAIL

PROJECT WORK PLAN—PLANNING DETAILS AND PROCEDURES

APPLICABLE STANDARDS, POLICIES AND PRACTICES	WORK PLAN DEVELOPMENT—TASK DECOMPOSITION	KEY WORK PLANNING ACTIVITIES ☒ COMPLETED
		☐ Review the Project Definition (Tool 1.2.1)
		☐ Review Customer Requirements (Tool 2.1.1)
		☐ Perform Initial WBS Task Decomposition
		ADD ESTIMATES AT THE WBS WORK PACKAGE LEVEL
WORK PLAN REVIEW POINT(S)		☐ Refine the WBS—Schedule Development
		☐ Refine the WBS—Resource Intgeration
		☐ Refine the WBS—Cost Alignment
WORK PLAN MANAGEMENT TOOL(S)		☐ Obtain WBS Review and Approval
		☐ Specify Project Variance Thresholds

PROJECT WORK PLAN—WORK BREAKDOWN STRUCTURE (WBS) SUMMARY ▷

PROJECT PHASES	1	2	3	4	5	6
Project Phase Name						
Phase Start Date						
WORK PLAN ESTIMATES	*ESTIMATES BELOW RESULT FROM DETAILED WORK PLANNING AND WBS DEVELOPMENT, AND USE OF THE PROJECT ESTIMATES TOOL 1.2.2*					
Phase DURATION						
Phsse RESOURCES						
Phse COSTS						

PROJECT WORK PLAN—PROJECT VARIANCE THRESHOLDS (VALUES TO BE MONITORED

MONITORING LEVEL	COST VAR (CV)	SCHEDULE VAR (SV)	RESOURCE VAR (*/–)	BCWS	BCWP	ACWP	BAC	% COMPLETE
Normal Variance								
Elevated Variance								
Critical Variance								

ACTION/ACTIVITY/REVIEW – RESPONSIBILITY	START	FINISH	ACTIVITY STATUS

ATTACHMENTS	PREPARER	DATE	FILE OR DOCUMENT LOCATION

2.2.2 PROJECT PLAN—Project Risk Management Plan

PROCESS OVERVIEW
Develop procedures to identify, analyze, and prioritize project risks that have a high probability of occurrence or a high impact on the project. Prepare and maintain a project risk management log to summarize and monitor major project risks. Specify procedures for performing ongoing project risk management activities.

TOOL PREPARATION	
PREPARED BY	DATE

PROJECT	CUSTOMER

▷ RISK MANAGEMENT PLAN—OVERVIEW				
RISK MANAGEMENT PLAN PURPOSE AND GENERAL GUIDANCE		PLAN DISTRIBUTION—PRIMARY USERS ☐ Executive/Sponsor ☐ PMO ☐ Project Team ☐ Customer ☐ Control Board	Other Stakeholders ☐ ☐ ☐ ☐	PLAN BASELINE DATE LAST PLAN REVISION DATE LAST DISTRIBUTION DATE
PROJECT RISK MANAGEMENT PLAN MANAGER	OFFICE TELEPHONE	MOBILE TELEPHONE	FAX	EMAIL

PROJECT RISK MANAGEMENT PLAN—PLANNING DETAILS AND PROCEDURES		
APPLICABLE STANDARDS, POLICIES AND PRACTICES	RISK MANAGEMENT APPROACH	KEY RISK MANAGEMENT ACTIVITIES ☒ COMPLETED ☐ Review the Project WBS and Work Plan *CONDUCT INITIAL PROJECT RISK ASSESSMENT* ☐ Identify Project Risks ☐ Analyze Project Risks ☐ Prioritize Project Risks ☐ Develop Project Risk Response Strategy ☐ Determine Contingency Funding Needs *PERFORM FOLLOW-ON RISK MANAGEMENT* ☐ Incorporate the Risk Strategy in the WBS ☐ Monitor and Manage Identified Risks ☐ Conduct Subsequent Risk Assessments
RISK MANAGEMENT PLAN REVIEW POINT(S)		
RISK MANAGEMENT TOOL(S)		

PROJECT RISK MANAGEMENT PLAN—RISK MANAGEMENT LOG ▷

RISK ID	RISK ID DATE	PRIORITY	TYPE	RISK EVENT	PROB	IMPACT	OVERALL	STATUS	CLOSE DATE

ACTION/ACTIVITY/REVIEW — RESPONSIBILITY	START	FINISH	ACTIVITY STATUS

ATTACHMENTS	PREPARER	DATE	FILE OR DOCUMENT LOCATION

2.2.3 PROJECT PLAN—Project Communication Plan

PROCESS OVERVIEW
Develop the approach for managing project communication. Identify requirements and protocols for project information exchange and collaboration with various project stakeholders. Specify issue and problem escalation procedures. Prepare project report and document management procedures and a distribution matrix.

TOOL PREPARATION	
PREPARED BY	DATE

PROJECT	CUSTOMER

▷ COMMUNICATION MANAGEMENT PLAN—OVERVIEW

COMMUNICATION MANAGEMENT PLAN PURPOSE AND GENERAL GUIDANCE		PLAN DISTRIBUTION—PRIMARY USERS		PLAN BASELINE DATE
		☐ Executive/Sponsor	Other Stakeholders	
		☐ PMO	☐	LAST PLAN REVISION DATE
		☐ Project Team	☐	
		☐ Customer	☐	LAST DISTRIBUTION DATE
		☐ Control Board	☐	
COMMUNICATION MANAGEMENT PLAN MANAGER	OFFICE TELEPHONE	MOBILE TELEPHONE	FAX	EMAIL

COMMUNICATION MANAGEMENT PLAN—PLANNING DETAILS AND PROCEDURES

APPLICABLE STANDARDS, POLICIES AND PRACTICES	STAKEHOLDER COMMUNICATION PROTOCOL	KEY COMMUNICATION ACTIVITIES ☒ COMPLETED
		☐ Review the Knowledge Base (Tool 1.2.4)
		PLAN/MANAGE COMMUNICATION AND INFORMATION
COMMUNICATION PLAN REVIEW POINT(S)	ESCALATION MANAGEMENT PROCEDURES	☐ Identify Key Project Stakeholders
		☐ Specify Communication Protocols
		☐ Provide Issue/Problem Escalation Guidance
COMMUNICATION MANAGEMENT TOOL(S)	REPORT AND DOCUMENT MANGEMENT PROCEDURES	*PLAN/MANAGE REPORT & DOCUMENT DISTRIBUTION*
		☐ List Report Management Procedures
		☐ List Document Management Procedures

COMMUNICATION MANAGEMENT PLAN—REPORT AND DOCUMENT DISTRIBUTION MATRIX ▷

STAKEHOLDERS	EXECUTIVE-SPONSOR		PMO		PROJECT TEAM		CUSTOMER		CONTROL BOARD		OTHER	
Key Contact(s)												
DISTRIBUTION	☒	METHOD	☒	METHOD	☒	METHOD	☒	METHOD	☒	METHOD	☒	METHOD
Status Reports	☐		☐		☐		☐		☐		☐	
Management Reports	☐		☐		☐		☐		☐		☐	
Customer Reports	☐		☐		☐		☐		☐		☐	
Primary Plans	☐		☐		☐		☐		☐		☐	
Supporting Plans	☐		☐		☐		☐		☐		☐	
	☐		☐		☐		☐		☐		☐	
	☐		☐		☐		☐		☐		☐	
	☐		☐		☐		☐		☐		☐	
	☐		☐		☐		☐		☐		☐	

ACTION/ACTIVITY/REVIEW — RESPONSIBILITY	START	FINISH	ACTIVITY STATUS

ATTACHMENTS	PREPARER	DATE	FILE OR DOCUMENT LOCATION

2.2.4 PROJECT PLAN—Project Support Plans

PROCESS OVERVIEW
Review project management and technical and business planning requirements, and identify the individual project support plans that will be used in the project effort. Manage plan preparation activities.

TOOL PREPARATION	
PREPARED BY	DATE

PROJECT	CUSTOMER

▷ PROJECT SUPPORT PLANS—OVERVIEW					
PROJECT MANAGEMENT SUPPORT PLAN REQUIREMENTS	BUSINESS SUPPORT PLAN REQUIREMENTS		TECHNICAL SUPPORT PLAN REQUIREMENTS		
PROJECT SUPPORT PLAN MANAGER	OFFICE TELEPHONE	MOBILE TELEPHONE	FAX	EMAIL	

PROJECT SUPPORT PLANS—PLAN DEVELOPMENT					
PROJECT SUPPORT PLAN LIST	REQ	DUE DATE	ASSIGNED TO	SUPPORT PLAN STAUS	SUPPORT PLAN DESCRIPTION-CONTENT
Management Oversight Plan	☐				
Management Review Plan	☐				
Management Supply Plan	☐				
Management Logisics Plan	☐				
	☐				
	☐				
	☐				
	☐				
	☐				
	☐				
	☐				
	☐				
	☐				
	☐				
	☐				
	☐				
	☐				
	☐				
	☐				
	☐				
	☐				
	☐				

ACTION/ACTIVITY/REVIEW – RESPONSIBILITY	START	FINISH	ACTIVITY STATUS

ATTACHMENTS	PREPARER	DATE	FILE OR DOCUMENT LOCATION

2.3.1 STAFF PLAN—Staff Requirements

PROCESS OVERVIEW
Review customer requirements and the technical solution to determine the project staff positions needed to perform this project. Specify the category and number of resources needed in the manpower matrix. List the staff roles (and codes) by name or position title/technical discipline (e.g., engineer II) in the responsibility matrix.

TOOL PREPARATION	
PREPARED BY	DATE

PROJECT	CUSTOMER

▷ STAFF REQUIREMENTS—MANPOWER MATRIX						
PROJECT PHASES	1	2	3	4	5	6
Project Phase Name						
Phase Start Date						
Phase Finish Date						
STAFF CATEGORIES						
Management						
Technical						
Labor						
Administrative						
TOTAL STAFF						

STAFF REQUIREMENTS—RESPONSIBILITY MATRIX												
PROJECT PHASES	1		2		3		4		5		6	
Project Phase Name												
SPECIFIC STAFF ROLES	CODE	ACTIVITY	CODE	ACTIVITY	CODE	ACTIVITY	CODE	ACTIVITY	CODE	ACTIVITY	CODE	ACTIVITY

STAFF REQUIREMENTS MATRIX NOTES

CODE: P = PLAN; W = WORK; R = REVIEW; A = APPROVE

ACTION/ACTIVITY/REVIEW – RESPONSIBILITY	START	FINISH	ACTIVITY STATUS

ATTACHMENTS	PREPARER	DATE	FILE OR DOCUMENT LOCATION

2.3.2 STAFF PLAN—Staff Management Plan

PROCESS OVERVIEW
Review project resource staffing requirements to prepare guidance for project team formation and management during the project. Include a sourcing analysis to identify how staff requirements will be filled. Maintain a log of group and individual training .

TOOL PREPARATION	
PREPARED BY	DATE

PROJECT	CUSTOMER

▷ STAFF MANAGEMENT PLAN—OVERVIEW				
STAFF MANAGEMENT PLAN PURPOSE AND GENERAL GUIDANCE		PLAN DISTRIBUTION—PRIMARY USERS ☐ Executive/Sponsor ☐ PMO ☐ Project Team ☐ Customer ☐ Control Board	Other Stakeholders ☐ ☐ ☐ ☐	PLAN BASELINE DATE LAST PLAN REVISION DATE LAST DISTRIBUTION DATE
STAFF MANGEMENT PLAN MANAGER	OFFICE TELEPHONE	MOBILE TELEPHONE	FAX	EMAIL

STAFF MANAGEMENT PLAN—PLANNING DETAILS AND PROCEDURES		
APPLICABLE STANDARDS, POLICIES AND PRACTICES	TEAM FORMATION AND DISPERSAL PROCEDURES	KEY STAFF MANAGEMENT ACTIVITIES ☒ COMPLETED ☐ Review Resource Requirements *PLAN/MANAGE PROJECT RESOURCE ACQUISITION* ☐ Identify and Analyze Sourcing ☐ Request Resources ☐ Manage Team Formation *PLAN/MANAGE PROJECT TEAM PERFORMANCE* ☐ Manage Team Training and Development ☐ Manage Team Performance (and Reviews) ☐ Manage Team Dispersal
STAFF MANAGEMENT PLAN REVIEW POINT(S)	STAFF PERFORMANCE MANAGEMENT ACTIVITIES	
STAFF MANAGEMENT PLAN TOOL(S)		

STAFF MANAGEMENT—SOURCING ANALYSIS					
STAFF POSITION TYPE	DIRECT ASSIGNMENT	INTERNAL TRANSFER	NEW HIRE	OUTSOURCING	SOURCING ANALYSIS NOTES
Management					
Technical					
Labor					
Administrative					

STAFF MANAGEMENT—TRAINING AND DEVELOPMENT ACTIVITY LOG ▷					
ACTIVITY PARTICIPANT (OR GROUP)	ACTIVITY	SCHEDULED	STATUS—RESULTS	SOURCE	FINISH DATE

ACTION/ACTIVITY/REVIEW — RESPONSIBILITY	START	FINISH	ACTIVITY STATUS

ATTACHMENTS	PREPARER	DATE	FILE OR DOCUMENT LOCATION

2.3.3 STAFF PLAN—Staff Acquisition (Request)

PROCESS OVERVIEW
REPLICATE FOR EACH STAFF ACQUISITION REQUEST—Compile, monitor, and manage information that is used to request project staff members and to oversee the staff acquisition and team formation process. Identify project staffing needs, prepare the acquisition request, and track acquisition of staff resources.

TOOL PREPARATION	
PREPARED BY	DATE
CHECK IF REPLICATED (SPECIFY FILE LOCATION) ☐	

PROJECT	CUSTOMER

▷ STAFF ACQUISITION—RESOURCE REQUEST OVERVIEW					
PROJECT ROLE/POSITION – TO BE FILLED		PROJECT WORK LOCATION		PROJECT REPORTING OFFICIAL (IF KNOWN)	
PROJECT CLASSIFICATION	STRATEGIC INTEREST	NATURE OF THE PROJECT		PROJECT MANAGER	EXECUTIVE-SPONSOR
REQUESTER		OFFICE TELEPHONE	MOBILE TELEPHONE	FAX	EMAIL

STAFF ACQUISITION—RESOURCE MANAGER DISTRIBUTION				
TO THE RESOURCE MANAGER: This form is an INTERNAL REQUEST for you to provide a qualified staff resource to fill a required position on the identified project. Fundamental project and contact information is provided to help you make a resource decision and commitment to this work effort.				
RESOURCE MANAGER – NAME/TITLE	OFFICE TELEPHONE	MOBILE TELEPHONE	FAX	EMAIL
RESOURCE MANAGER – DEPARTMENT	ADDRESS		CITY/STATE–PROVINCE/ZIP (POSTAL CODE)	

STAFF ACQUISITION—RESOURCE REQUIREMENTS				
TECHNICAL SPECIALTY/POSITION TITLE		INDIVIDUAL – REQUESTED BY NAME (IF KNOWN)		PROJECT POSITION DESCRIPTION
EXPERIENCE	SALARY/GRADE	RESUME REQUESTED ☐ *YES* ☐ *NO*	RESPONSE REQUESTED BY	
START DATE	FINISH DATE	SPECIAL CREDENTIALS		
STAFF ACQUISITION DISCUSSION/NEGOTIATION NOTES				

STAFF ACQUISITION—RESOURCE COMMITMENT							
PROJECT ROLE/POSITION – TO BE FILLED		OFFICE TELEPHONE	MOBILE TELEPHONE	FAX		EMAIL	
DEPARTMENT		ADDRESS		CITY/STATE/ZIP			
RESOURCE MANAGER COMMITMENT	DATE	STAFF MEMBER COMMITMENT	DATE	PROJECT MANAGER ACCEPTANCE		DATE	

ACTION/ACTIVITY/REVIEW — RESPONSIBILITY	START	FINISH	ACTIVITY STATUS

ATTACHMENTS	PREPARER	DATE	FILE OR DOCUMENT LOCATION

2.3.4 STAFF PLAN—Staff Assignments

PROCESS OVERVIEW
REPLICATE FOR EACH STAFF MEMBER ASSIGNED—Compile, monitor, and manage information that is relevant to assigned project team members. Track individual project task assignments and associated work performance. Annotate leadership or task specialty assignments. A copy can be provided to the named staff member.

TOOL PREPARATION	
PREPARED BY	DATE
CHECK IF REPLICATED (SPECIFY FILE LOCATION) ☐	

PROJECT	CUSTOMER

▷ STAFF ASSIGNMENT—STAFF MEMBER OVERVIEW				
STAFF MEMBER NAME	OFFICE TELEPHONE	MOBILE TELEPHONE	FAX	EMAIL
STAFF MEMBER POSITION/TITLE	ADDRESS		CITY/STATE–PROVINCE/ZIP (POSTAL CODE)	
STAFF MEMBER PROJECT ROLE	SALARY/GRADE	COMMITMENT (% TIME)	TEAM ASSIGNMENT DATE	ESTIMATED FINISH DATE
SUPERVISION–ASSIGNED TEAM MEMBERS	OTHER PROJECTS (% TIME)	SPECIAL TEAMS & RESPONSIBILITIES		ASSIGNED MATERIALS AND EQUIPMENT

STAFF ASSIGNMENT—STAFF MEMBER INDUCTION				
REPORTING OFFICIAL/SUPERVISOR (THIS PROJECT)	OFFICE TELEPHONE	MOBILE TELEPHONE	FAX	EMAIL

INITIAL PROJECT MANAGER MEETING	DATE	TRAINING-DEVELOPMENT-CREDENTIAL REQUIREMENTS	TEAM MEMBER INDUCTION CHECKLIST ☒ COMPLETED ☐ Project Overview ☐ Customer Overview ☐ Project Scope/Change Management ☐ Project Assignments/Task Management ☐ Project Collaboration (Reports & Meetings ☐ Project Issue Resolution/Elevation ☐ Team Member Performance Review
INITIAL SUPERVISOR MEETING	DATE		
INITIAL TEAM/KICKOFF MEETING	DATE		
INITIAL CUSTOMER/KICKOFF MEETING	DATE	MOBILIZATION/TRAVEL REQUIREMENTS	

STAFF ASSIGNMENT—INDIVIDUAL TASK ASSIGNMENT & ACTIVITY TRACKING LOG ▷							
NAMES/STAFF ID	TASK/WBS ITEM	ASSIGN DATE	DUE DATE	START DATE	FINISH DATE	STATUS/COMPLETE (%)	PERFORMANCE RATING

ACTION/ACTIVITY/REVIEW — RESPONSIBILITY	START	FINISH	ACTIVITY STATUS

ATTACHMENTS	PREPARER	DATE	FILE OR DOCUMENT LOCATION

2.4.1 VENDOR PLAN—Vendor Solicitation

PROCESS OVERVIEW
REPLICATE FOR EACH UNIQUE SOLICITATION PREPARED—Identify the need for subcontracting or outsourcing, and describe the solutions needed in a statement of work. Indicate the WBS elements to which vendors will be assigned, and specify the vendor's deliverables. VENDORS—Please note submittal requirements.

TOOL PREPARATION	
PREPARED BY	DATE
CHECK IF REPLICATED (SPECIFY FILE LOCATION) ☐	

PROJECT	CUSTOMER

▷ VENDOR SOLICITATION–REQUIREMENTS OVERVIEW				
VENDOR REQUIREMENT	WBS ELEMENT	DESCRIPTION OF VENDOR PRODUCTS & SERVICES REQUIRED	START DATE	FINISH DATE
VENDOR PRODUCT & SERVICES NOTES				

VENDOR SOLICITATION–STATEMENT OF WORK		
SOLICITATION	TITLE	DATE
STATEMENT OF WORK		

VENDOR SOLICITATION–DELIVERABLES			
DELIVERABLE	DELIVERABLE SPECIFICATIONS	START DATE	FINISH DATE

VENDOR SOLICITATION–SUBMITTAL REQUIREMENTS				
ITEMS TO BE INCLUDED IN THE TECHNICAL PROPOSAL		ITEMS TO BE INCLCUDED IN THE BUSINESS PROPOSAL	SPECIAL SOLICITATION RESPONSE REQUIREMENTS	
☐ Technical Capability Statement ☐ Technical Approach ☐ Technical Work Plan (WBS) ☐ Staffing Plan ☐ Technical Experience and References		☐ Management Plan ☐ Quality Assurance Plan ☐ Deliverable(s) Schedule ☐ Deliverable(s) Pricing ☐ Other		
PROPOSAL SUBMITTAL TO	TELEPHONE	ADDRESS	CITY/STATE–PROVINCE/ZIP (POSTAL CODE)	DATE DUE

ACTION/ACTIVITY/REVIEW — RESPONSIBILITY	START	FINISH	ACTIVITY STATUS

ATTACHMENTS	PREPARER	DATE	FILE OR DOCUMENT LOCATION

2.4.2 VENDOR PLAN—Vendor Management Plan

PROCESS OVERVIEW
Review vendor subcontracting or outsourcing requirements that have bearing on the vendor's work effort. Prepare the plan that will guide vendor participation in the project, with focus on vendor integration and work performance.

TOOL PREPARATION	
PREPARED BY	DATE

PROJECT	CUSTOMER

▷ VENDOR MANAGEMENT PLAN—OVERVIEW

VENDOR MANAGEMENT PLAN PURPOSE AND GENERAL GUIDANCE	PLAN DISTRIBUTION—PRIMARY USERS	Other Stakeholders	PLAN BASELINE DATE
	☐ Executive/Sponsor		LAST PLAN REVISION DATE
	☐ PMO	☐	
	☐ Project Team	☐	LAST DISTRIBUTION DATE
	☐ Customer	☐	
	☐ Control Board	☐	

VENDOR MANGEMENT PLAN MANAGER	OFFICE TELEPHONE	MOBILE TELEPHONE	FAX	EMAIL

VENDOR MANAGEMENT PLAN—PLANNING DETAILS AND PROCEDURES

APPLICABLE STANDARDS, POLICIES AND PRACTICES	VENDOR INTEGRATION AND DISPERSAL PROCEDURES	KEY STAFF MANAGEMENT ACTIVITIES ☒ COMPLETED
		☐ Review Vendor Requirements
		PLAN/MANAGE VENDOR ACQUISITION
		☐ Perform Make/Buy (Sourcing) Analysis
		☐ Acquire Vendor Products and Services
VENDOR MANAGEMENT PLAN REVIEW POINT(S)	VENDOR PERFORMANCE MANAGEMENT ACTIVITIES	☐ Manage Vendor Integration
		PLAN/MANAGE VENDOR PERFORMANCE
		☐ Manage Vendor Integration
VENDOR MANAGEMENT PLAN TOOL(S)		☐ Manage Vendor Performance
		☐ Manage Vendor Contracts

VENDOR MANAGEMENT—MAKE/BUY (SOURCING) ANALYSIS

VENDOR REQUIREMENT	WBS ELEMENT	MAKE CAPABILITY	COST TO MAKE	COST TO BUY	TIME TO MAKE	TIME TO BUY	ADVANTAGE—MAKE OR BUY

VENDOR MANAGEMENT—TRAINING AND DEVELOPMENT ACTIVITY LOG ▷

ACTIVITY PARTICIPANT (OR GROUP)	ACTIVITY	SCHEDULED	STATUS—RESULTS	SOURCE	FINISH DATE

ACTION/ACTIVITY/REVIEW – RESPONSIBILITY	START	FINISH	ACTIVITY STATUS

ATTACHMENTS	PREPARER	DATE	FILE OR DOCUMENT LOCATION

2.4.3 VENDOR PLAN—Vendor Proposal (Evaluation)

PROCESS OVERVIEW
REPLICATE FOR EACH VENDOR—Monitor and manage information that is relevant to the vendor acquisition and selection process. Review vendor screening indicators, examine vendor interests and intent, and evaluate the vendor's proposal per the weighted factors specified in the associated solicitation.

TOOL PREPARATION	
PREPARED BY	DATE
CHECK IF REPLICATED (SPECIFY FILE LOCATION) ☐	

PROJECT	CUSTOMER

▷ VENDOR PROPOSAL—SUBMITTAL OVERVIEW			
VENDOR ORGANIZATION		SOLICITATION	RECEIPT DATE
VENDOR POINT OF CONTACT	ADDRESS/LOCATION	TELEPHONE	EMAIL

VENDOR PROPOSAL—QUALIFICATION SCREENING MATRIX				
PREVIOUS WORK BY VENDOR	VENDOR WORK CAPACITY	VENDOR INTEREST	VENDOR PRICING	VENDOR PROPOSAL (CHECKLIST)
☐ *PREVIOUS INTERNAL EXPERIENCE* ☐ *PREVIOUS RELATED EXPERIENCE* ☐ *NO PREVIOUS RELATED WORK*	☐ *WIDE RESOURCE SELECTION* ☐ *SUFFICIENT RESOURCES* ☐ *LIMITED STAFF STRENGTH*	☐ *ACTIVE RESPONSE* ☐ *DELAYED CONTACT* ☐ *DECLINED OPPORTUNITY*	☐ *HIGH* ☐ *AVERAGE* ☐ *LOW*	☐ *ADMINISTRATIVE COMPLIANCE* ☐ *UNDERSTANDS REQUIREMENTS* ☐ *TECHNICALLY COMPETENT*
QUALIFICATION SCREENING RECOMMENDATION		RECOMMENDATION REASON		

VENDOR PROPOSAL—EVALUATION								
SOLICITATION VENDOR-PROPOSED START DATE VENDOR-PROPOSED DURATION	VENDOR BUSINESS SOLUTION Price Management Approach Capability & Experience Staffing Approach Standards Compliancce	RATING	WT	SCORE	ADMINISTRATIVE RESPONSE Timely Proposal Submittal Completeness of Proposal Terms & Conditions (T&C) Special Requirements	RATING	WT	SCORE
VENDOR-PROPOSED FINISH DATE VENDOR-PROPOSED SOLUTION COST VENDOR-PROPOSED STAFFING	VENDOR TECHNICAL SOLUTION Technical Approach Planning and Collaboration Schedule Quality Assurance Deliverables	RATING	WT	SCORE	SCORING Business Solution Technical Solution Administrative Response TOTAL	RATING	WT	SCORE
VENDOR PROPOSAL EVALUATOR(S)	VENDOR PROPOSAL EVALUATION NOTES							

VENDOR PROPOSAL—SELECTION NOTIFICATION					
SELECTION DATE	VENDOR RESULT	REASON FOR RESULT	NOTIFICATION BY	NOTIFICATION METHOD	NOTIFICATION DATE

ACTION/ACTIVITY/REVIEW — RESPONSIBILITY	START	FINISH	ACTIVITY STATUS

ATTACHMENTS	PREPARER	DATE	FILE OR DOCUMENT LOCATION

2.4.4 VENDOR PLAN—Vendor Contract

PROCESS OVERVIEW
REPLICATE FOR EACH VENDOR—Compile the elements of the vendor contract (and modifications) for each vendor contract, and execute the contract when a vendor agreement has been reached. Use this to guide and manage vendor work performance and project participation and to track contract compliance matters.

TOOL PREPARATION	
PREPARED BY	DATE
CHECK IF REPLICATED (SPECIFY FILE LOCATION) ☐	

PROJECT	CUSTOMER

VENDOR ORGANIZATION

▷ VENDOR CONTRACT—OVERVIEW		
VENDOR ORGANIZATION	CONTRACT TITLE	CONTRACT DATE
VENDOR ID	CONTRACT BOOKING ☐ BOOKED	BOOKING DATE
CONTRACT INITIAL VALUE ($)	CONTRACT TYPE ☐ T&M ☐ FIXED ☐ CPFF ☐ CPIF ☐ OTHER	CONTRACT START
CONTRACT CURRENT VALUE ($)	INVOICE MANAGEMENT PROCESS	CONTRACT FINISH

VENDOR CONTRACT—TECHNICAL (WORK) PROVISIONS

VENDOR CONTRACT—TERMS AND CONDITIONS

VENDOR CONTRACT—MODIFICATION LOG ▷

MODIFICATION	DATE	REASON FOR MODIFICATION	ACCEPTANCE BY	VALUE ($)
000 (ORIGINAL)				

VENDOR CONTRACT—CONTRACT AND NEGOTIATION ACTIVITY LOG ▷

ACTIVITY/ACTION/EVENT	ISSUE/FOCUS (IF ANY)	SCHEDULED	STATUS–RESULTS	ISSUE LEAD	FINISH DATE

ACTION/ACTIVITY/REVIEW – RESPONSIBILITY	START	FINISH	ACTIVITY STATUS

ATTACHMENTS	PREPARER	DATE	FILE OR DOCUMENT LOCATION

2.5.1 BUSINESS PLAN—Business Requirements

PROCESS OVERVIEW
Obtain and review relevant internal and external business information as a basis for preparing the business solution and the business elements of the proposal for submittal to the customer. Ensure that customer-specified business factors and proposal evaluation factors are identified and addressed in the proposal.

TOOL PREPARATION	
PREPARED BY	DATE

PROJECT	CUSTOMER

▷ BUSINESS REQUIREMENTS—REVIEW				
KEY DOCUMENTS	PROJECT WORK PLAN	BUSINESS RISK	MANAGEMENT GUIDANCE	BUSINESS COMPETITION
☐ Customer Requirements ☐ Deliverable Specifications ☐ Project Definition ☐ Project Business Case ☐ Customer Solicitation	☐ WBS ☐ Cost ☐ Schedule ☐ Resource Utilization	☐ Marketplace ☐ Financial ☐ Legal ☐ Technology-based ☐ Customer-based	☐ Revenue Objectives ☐ Financial Return ☐ Portfolio Goals ☐ Pricing Guidelines ☐ Oversight Needs	☐ Competitors ☐ Market Position ☐ Product Value ☐ Staff Readiness ☐ Technical Innovation
Understand the business purpose	Understand the project effort	Examine business obstacles	Apply management guidance	Examine competition & market
BUSINESS REQUIREMENTS—REVIEW NOTES				

BUSINESS REQUIREMENTS—MANAGEMENT OVERSIGHT	
CUSTOMER–MANAGEMENT OVERSIGHT REQUIREMENTS	INTERNAL–MANAGEMENT OVERSIGHT REQUIREMENTS

BUSINESS REQUIREMENTS—BUSINESS FACTORS PRESCRIBED BY CUSTOMER				
BUSINESS FACTOR	SOURCE	TYPE	CRITERIA	ACHIEVED

BUSINESS REQUIREMENTS—PROPOSAL EVALUATION FACTORS PRESCRIBED BY CUSTOMER				
PROPOSAL EVALUATION FACTOR	SOURCE	TYPE	CRITERIA	ACHIEVED

ACTION/ACTIVITY/REVIEW — RESPONSIBILITY	START	FINISH	ACTIVITY STATUS

ATTACHMENTS	PREPARER	DATE	FILE OR DOCUMENT LOCATION

2.5.2 BUSINESS PLAN—Business Solution

PROCESS OVERVIEW
Identify the business solution (cost and pricing) that will be offered to fulfill customer requirements. Be sure to describe the type of management effort to be performed. Specify the pricing requirements and the desired contracting approach. Identify the preferred terms and conditions for the contract.

TOOL PREPARATION	
PREPARED BY	DATE

PROJECT	CUSTOMER

BUSINESS SOLUTION—REVIEW		
OVERALL PROJECT COSTS ($)	COST MANAGEMENT REQUIREMENTS	AWARD POTENTIAL ☐ *CERTAIN* ☐ *STRONG* ☐ *AVERAGE* ☐ *WEAK* ☐ *UNCERTAIN*
OVERALL PROPOSED PRICE ($)	PRICING CONDITIONS	
ANTICIPATED REVENUE ($)	PRICE REDUCTION AREAS (FOR SUBSEQUENT USE IN NEGOTIATIONS)	

BUSINESS SOLUTION—SOLICITATION FULFILLMENT STRATEGY	
FACTORS AFFECTING SOLICITATION FULFILLMENT	SOLICITATION FULFILLMENT STRATEGY

BUSINESS SOLUTION—PRICING STRATEGY	
FACTORS AFFECTING THE PRICING STRATEGY	PRICING STRATEGY

BUSINESS SOLUTION—CONTRACTING STRATEGY	
FACTORS AFFECTING THE CONTRACTING STRATEGY	CONTRACTING STRATEGY

BUSINESS SOLUTION—TERMS AND CONDITIONS

ACTION/ACTIVITY/REVIEW – RESPONSIBILITY	START	FINISH	ACTIVITY STATUS

ATTACHMENTS	PREPARER	DATE	FILE OR DOCUMENT LOCATION

2.5.3 BUSINESS PLAN—Business Proposal

PROCESS OVERVIEW
Identify proposal team members, and assign and track actions to develop and submit the combined technical and business proposal to the customer in a timely manner. Manage proposal preparation and submittal to the customer, and monitor customer proposal review and selection activities.

TOOL PREPARATION	
PREPARED BY	DATE

PROJECT	CUSTOMER

▷ BUSINESS PROPOSAL—OVERVIEW			
CUSTOMER SOLICITATION ID	CUSTOMER SOLICITATION TITLE		PROPOSAL DUE DATE
CUSTOMER SOLICITATION—CONTACT	CONTACT ADDRESS/LOCATION	TELEPHONE	EMAIL
PROPOSAL MANAGER	PROPOSAL MANAGER ADDRESS/LOCATION	TELEPHONE	EMAIL

BUSINESS PROPOSAL—PROPOSAL TEAM LEADERS				
NAME	POSITION	ADDRESS/LOCATION	TELEPHONE	EMAIL

BUSINESS PROPOSAL—DEVELOPMENT STEPS				
DEVELOPMENT ACTIVITY	ASSIGNED STATUS	DUE	START	FINISH
☐ Acquire resources to form the proposal team				
☐ Review business requirements (see review checklist in 2.5.1)				
☐ Prepare (write) the business solution				
☐ Incorporate (write or rewrite) the Technical Solution				
☐ Compile (combine, edit, publish) the proposal document				
☐ Review the proposal document				
☐ Develop the business negotiation strategy and approach (plan)				

BUSINESS PROPOSAL—SUBMITTAL					
PROPOSAL ID	SOLICITATION DATE	TECHNICAL REVIEW	DATE	FINAL REVIEW	DATE
PROPOSAL TITLE		BUSINESS REVIEW	DATE	PROPOSAL SUBMITTAL METHOD	DATE

BUSINESS PROPOSAL—SELECTION NOTIFICATION					
SELECTION DATE	SELECTION RESULT	REASON FOR RESULT	NOTIFICATION BY	NOTIFICATION METHOD	DATE

ACTION/ACTIVITY/REVIEW – RESPONSIBILITY	START	FINISH	ACTIVITY STATUS

ATTACHMENTS	PREPARER	DATE	FILE OR DOCUMENT LOCATION

2.5.4 VENDOR PLAN—Business Contract

PROCESS OVERVIEW
Compile and review the elements of the customer contract or contract modification. Execute the contract when an agreement has been reached with the customer. Use this contract document to guide and manage project team work performance and to manage business aspects of the project.

TOOL PREPARATION	
PREPARED BY	DATE

PROJECT	CUSTOMER

▷ BUSINESS CONTRACT—OVERVIEW		
CUSTOMER CONTRACT ID	CONTRACT TITLE	CONTRACT DATE
INTERNAL CONTRACT ID	CONTRACT BOOKING ☐ BOOKED	BOOKING DATE
CONTRACT INITIAL VALUE ($)	CONTRACT TYPE ☐ T&M ☐ FIXED ☐ CPFF ☐ CPIF ☐ OTHER	CONTRACT START
CONTRACT CURRENT VALUE ($)	INVOICE MANAGEMENT PROCESS	CONTRACT FINISH

BUSINESS CONTRACT—TECHNICAL (WORK) PROVISIONS

BUSINESS CONTRACT—TERMS AND CONDITIONS

BUSINESS CONTRACT—MODIFICATION LOG ▷

MODIFICATION	DATE	REASON FOR MODIFICATION	ACCEPTANCE BY	VALUE ($)
000 (ORIGINAL)				

BUSINESS CONTRACT—CONTRACT AND NEGOTIATION ACTIVITY LOG ▷

ACTIVITY/ACTION/EVENT	ISSUE/FOCUS (IF ANY)	SCHEDULED	STATUS–RESULTS	ISSUE LEAD	FINISH DATE

ACTION/ACTIVITY/REVIEW – RESPONSIBILITY	START	FINISH	ACTIVITY STATUS

ATTACHMENTS	PREPARER	DATE	FILE OR DOCUMENT LOCATION

2.6.1 MANAGEMENT PLAN—Management Oversight Plan

PROCESS OVERVIEW
Review management requirements and prepare guidance for PMO and senior manager involvement during the project. Specify PMO and Executive Control Board responsibilities and support requirements, and maintain a log of management oversight activities.

TOOL PREPARATION	
PREPARED BY	DATE

PROJECT	CUSTOMER

▷ MANAGEMENT OVERSIGHT PLAN—OVERVIEW					
MANAGEMENT OVERSIGHT PLAN PURPOSE AND GENERAL GUIDANCE		PLAN DISTRIBUTION—PRIMARY USERS ☐ Executive/Sponsor — Other Stakeholders ☐ PMO ☐ ☐ Project Team ☐ ☐ Customer ☐ ☐ Control Board ☐		PLAN BASELINE DATE LAST PLAN REVISION DATE LAST DISTRIBUTION DATE
MANAGEMENT OVERSIGHT PLAN MANAGER	OFFICE TELEPHONE	MOBILE TELEPHONE	FAX	EMAIL

MANAGEMENT OVERSIGHT PLAN—PMO ALIGNMENT WITH THE PROJECT			
PROJECT MANAGEMENT OFFICE POINT-OF-CONTACT	LOCATION	TELEPHONE	KEY PMO RESPONSBILITIES ☒ PLANNED ☐ *BUSINESS & PROJECT MANAGEMENT ANALYSES* ☐ *RESOURCE TRAINING AND DEVELOPMENT* ☐ *PLANNING FACILITATION AND REVIEW* ☐ *PROJECT AUDITS AND REVIEWS* ☐ *MENTORING SUPPORT* ☐ *KNOWLDGE MANAGEMENT* ☐ *FACILIIES AND EQUIPMENT*
PMO GUIDANCE & MANDATES	PMO PARTICIPATION & PROTOCOLS		

MANAGEMENT OVERSIGHT PLAN—EXECUTIVE AND CONTROL BOARD ALIGNMENT WITH THE PROJECT			
CONTROL BOARD POINT-OF-CONTACT	LOCATION	TELEPHONE	KEY EXECUTIVE AND BOARD RESPONSBILITIES ☒ PLANNED ☐ *PROJECT SELECTION REVIEW* ☐ *PROJECT MANAGEMENT CHARTER ISSUANCE* ☐ *PROJECT PROGRESS REVIEWS* ☐ *PROJECT MANAGEMENT PHASE GATEWAY REVIEWS* ☐ *PORTFOLIO REVIEWS AT PROGRAM GATEWAYS* ☐ *PROJECT AUDITS AND REVIEWS* ☐ *PROJECT CLOSEOUT REVIEW*
CONTROL BOARD POINT-OF-CONTACT	LOCATION	TELEPHONE	
CONTROL BOARD GUIDANCE & MANDATES	CONTROL BOARD PARTICIPATION & PROTOCOLS		

MANAGEMENT OVERSIGHT PLAN—OVERSIGHT ACTIVITY LOG ▷					
EXECUTIVE–CONTROL BOARD–PMO PARTICIPANT	OVERSIGHT ACTIVITY	SCHEDULED	STATUS—RESULTS	PROJECT LEAD	FINISH DATE

ACTION/ACTIVITY/REVIEW — RESPONSIBILITY	START	FINISH	ACTIVITY STATUS

ATTACHMENTS	PREPARER	DATE	FILE OR DOCUMENT LOCATION

2.6.2 MANAGEMENT PLAN—Management Audit and Review Plan

PROCESS OVERVIEW
Identify requirements and specify procedures for conducting project, business, and technical performance audits and reviews. Examine and specify the types of audits and reviews to be conducted. Maintain a project audit and review log.

TOOL PREPARATION	
PREPARED BY	DATE

PROJECT	CUSTOMER

▷ MANAGEMENT AUDIT AND REVIEW PLAN—OVERVIEW				
MANAGEMENT AUDIT AND REVIEW PLAN PURPOSE AND GENERAL GUIDANCE		PLAN DISTRIBUTION—PRIMARY USERS ☐ Executive/Sponsor ☐ PMO ☐ Project Team ☐ Customer ☐ Control Board	Other Stakeholders ☐ ☐ ☐ ☐	PLAN BASELINE DATE LAST PLAN REVISION DATE LAST DISTRIBUTION DATE
MANAGEMENT AUDIT AND REVIEW PLAN MANAGER	OFFICE TELEPHONE	MOBILE TELEPHONE	FAX	EMAIL

MANAGEMENT AUDIT AND REVIEW PLAN—PLANNING DETAILS AND PROCEDURES		
APPLICABLE STANDARDS, POLICIES AND PRACTICES	PROJECT AUDIT TRIGGERS, SCHDULE & PROCEDURES	KEY AUDIT & REVIEW ACTIVITIES ☒ PLANNED TECHNICAL AUDITS (SEE MANAGEMENT AUDIT PLANS) ☐ *PROJECT MANAGEMENT AUDIT – HEALTH CHECK* ☐ *PROJECT BUSINESS AUDIT* ☐ *PROJECT PERFORMANCE AUDIT* ☐ *PROJECT PORTFOLIO MANAGEMENT REVIEW* ☐ *PROJECT READY-TO-EXECUTE REVIEW*
MANAGEMENT AUDIT AND REVIEW PLAN REVIEW POINT(S)	PROJECT REVIEW TRIGGERS, SCHEDULE & PROCEDURES	☐ *PROJECT GATEWAY REVIEW* TECHNICAL REVIEWS (SEE QUALITY REVIEW PLANS) ☐ *STAFF TECHNICAL REVIEW* ☐ *PROJECT MANAGER TECHNICAL REVIEW*
MANAGEMENT AUDIT AND REVIEW PLAN TOOL(S)	PROJECT PORTFOLIO REVIEW SCHEDULE & PROCEDURES	☐ *MANAGEMENT TECHNICAL REVIEW*

MANAGEMENT AUDIT AND REVIEW PLAN—AUDIT AND REVIEW LOG ▷

AUDIT OR REVIEW ACTIVITY	REQUESTOR	SCHEDULED	STATUS—RESULTS	AUDIT LEADER	FINISH DATE

ACTION/ACTIVITY/REVIEW – RESPONSIBILITY	START	FINISH	ACTIVITY STATUS

ATTACHMENTS	PREPARER	DATE	FILE OR DOCUMENT LOCATION

2.6.3 MANAGEMENT PLAN—Management Facility Plan

PROCESS OVERVIEW
REPLICATE FOR EACH FACILITY—Identify and manage the requirements, acquisition, assignment, use, and disposition of one or more facilities (or work locations) required for the project. Maintain a facility management activity log.

TOOL PREPARATION	
PREPARED BY	DATE
CHECK IF REPLICATED (SPECIFY FILE LOCATION) ☐	

PROJECT	CUSTOMER

▷ MANAGEMENT FACILITY PLAN—OVERVIEW				
MANAGEMENT LOGISITICS PLAN PURPOSE AND GENERAL GUIDANCE		PLAN DISTRIBUTION—PRIMARY USERS ☐ Executive/Sponsor ☐ PMO ☐ Project Team ☐ Customer ☐ Control Board	Other Stakeholders ☐ ☐ ☐ ☐	PLAN BASELINE DATE LAST PLAN REVISION DATE LAST DISTRIBUTION DATE
MANAGEMENT AUDIT AND REVIEW PLAN MANAGER	OFFICE TELEPHONE	MOBILE TELEPHONE	FAX	EMAIL

MANAGEMENT FACILITY PLAN—PROJECT FACILITIES		
APPLICABLE STANDARDS, POLICIES AND PRACTICES	FACILITY ACQUISITION PROCEDURES	KEY LOGISTICS ACTIVITIES ☒ COMPLETED ☐ Identify Project Facility Requirements *PLAN/MANAGE PROJECT LOGISTICS* ☐ Manage Facility Acquisition ☐ Manage and Maintain Facility ☐ Manage Facility Disposition
MANAGEMENT FACILITY PLAN REVIEW POINT(S)	FACILITY MANAGEMENT PROCEDURES	
MANAGEMENT FACILITY PLAN TOOL(S)	FACILITY DISPOSITION PROCEDURES	

MANAGEMENT FACILITY PLAN—PROJECT FACILITIES				
FACILITY MANAGER	OFFICE TELEPHONE	MOBILE TELEPHONE	FAX	EMAIL
FACILITY ADDRESS	FACILITY NAME	FACILITY OWNER	ACQUISITION DATE	ACQUISITION METHOD
FACILITY CITY–STATE–ZIP	ACQUISITION COST	MAINTENANCE COST	PLANNED DISPOSAL DATE	ACTUAL DISPOSAL DATE

MANAGEMENT FACILITY PLAN—FACILITY MANAGEMENT ACTIVITY LOG ▷

FACILITY MANAGEMENT ACTIVITY	FACILITY	SCHEDULED	STATUS—RESULTS	PROJECT LEAD	FINISH DATE

ACTION/ACTIVITY/REVIEW — RESPONSIBILITY	START	FINISH	ACTIVITY STATUS

ATTACHMENTS	PREPARER	DATE	FILE OR DOCUMENT LOCATION

2.6.4 MANAGEMENT PLAN—Management Supply and Equipment Plan

PROCESS OVERVIEW
Identify the internal requisition and external (vendor) sources for project supplies, materials, and equipment; and monitor and manage project supply requests, acquisition, and utilization. Maintain a supply and equipment log.

TOOL PREPARATION	
PREPARED BY	DATE

PROJECT	CUSTOMER

▷ MANAGEMENT SUPPLY AND EQUIPMENT PLAN—OVERVIEW				
MANAGEMENT SUPPLY AND EQUIPMENT PLAN PURPOSE AND GENERAL GUIDANCE		PLAN DISTRIBUTION—PRIMARY USERS ☐ Executive/Sponsor — Other Stakeholders ☐ PMO ☐ ☐ Project Team ☐ ☐ Customer ☐ ☐ Control Board ☐		PLAN BASELINE DATE LAST PLAN REVISION DATE LAST DISTRIBUTION DATE
MANAGEMENT SUPPLY AND EQUIPMENT PLAN MANAGER	OFFICE TELEPHONE	MOBILE TELEPHONE	FAX	EMAIL

MANAGEMENT SUPPLY AND EQUIPMENT PLAN—PLANNING DETAILS AND PROCEDURES		
APPLICABLE STANDARDS, POLICIES AND PRACTICES	SUPPLY ACQUISITION & MANAGEMENT PROCEDURES	KEY SUPPLY ACTIVITIES ☒ COMPLETED ☐ Review Approved Supply Sources (Vendors) *PLAN/MANAGE SUPPLY & EQUIPMENT ACQUISITION* ☐ Identify Authorized Project Purchase Agents
SUPPLY AND EQUIPMENT PLAN REVIEW POINT(S)	EQUIPMENT ACQUISITION & MANAGEMENT PROCEDURES	☐ Select Source (Internal or Vendor) ☐ Establish Vendor Acquisition Method(s)
SUPPLY AND EQUIPMENT PLAN TOOL(S)	EQUIPMENT UTILIZATION MANAGEMENT PROCEDURES	☐ Manage Supply & Equipment Acquisition

MANAGEMENT SUPPLY AND EQUIPMENT PLAN—SUPPLY AND EQUIPMENT LOG ▷

SUPPLY/EQUIPMENT ITEM	REQUESTED BY	REQUEST DATE	ACQUIRE DATE	ASSIGNED TO	SOURCE/VENDOR	COMMENTS

ACTION/ACTIVITY/REVIEW — RESPONSIBILITY	START	FINISH	ACTIVITY STATUS

ATTACHMENTS	PREPARER	DATE	FILE OR DOCUMENT LOCATION

Chapter 3

Perform-Phase Tools

The following are the tools used in the Perform Phase:

- 3.1 Customer Performance
  - 3.1.1 Customer Meeting
  - 3.1.2 Customer Status Report
  - 3.1.3 Customer Change Management
  - 3.1.4 Customer Acceptance Management
- 3.2 Project Performance
  - 3.2.1 Project Tracking and Control Report
  - 3.2.2 Project Risk Management
  - 3.2.3 Project Communication Management
  - 3.2.4 Project Plan Management
- 3.3 Staff Performance
  - 3.3.1 Staff Meeting
  - 3.3.2 Staff Status Report
  - 3.3.3 Staff Performance Review
  - 3.3.4 Staff Management Report
- 3.4 Vendor Performance
  - 3.4.1 Vendor Meeting
  - 3.4.2 Vendor Status Report
  - 3.4.3 Vendor Performance Review
  - 3.4.4 Vendor Contract Administration
- 3.5 Business Performance
  - 3.5.1 Business Meeting
  - 3.5.2 Business Status Report
  - 3.5.3 Business Performance Review
  - 3.5.4 Business Contract Administration
- 3.6 Management Performance
  - 3.6.1 Management Meeting
  - 3.6.2 Management Status Report
  - 3.6.3 Management Performance Review
  - 3.6.4 Management Audit and Review Report

These tools are described in this chapter.

3.1.1 CUSTOMER PERFORMANCE—Customer Meeting

PROCESS OVERVIEW
REPLICATE FOR EACH CUSTOMER MEETING—Specify the location and planned arrangements for the customer meeting to be conducted. Identify and notify the meeting participants. Prepare and include the meeting agenda for premeeting review and preparation by customer meeting participants.

TOOL PREPARATION	
PREPARED BY	DATE
CHECK IF REPLICATED (SPECIFY FILE LOCATION) ☐	

PROJECT	CUSTOMER

▷ CUSTOMER MEETING—OVERVIEW					
MEETING (NAME)		ESTIMATED DURATION	START TIME	START DATE	
MEETING LOCATION–ADDRESS	MEETING LOCATION–DIRECTIONS		MEETING ARRANGEMENTS AND NOTES		
MEETING COORDINATOR	OFFICE TELEPHONE	MOBILE TELEPHONE	FAX	EMAIL	

CUSTOMER MEETING—PARTICIPANTS LIST ▷				
NAME	OFFICE/LOCATION	REQUIRED	ATTENDANCE	ATTENDANCE NOTES
PRE-MEETING PARTICIPANT PREPARATION REQUESTED				

CUSTOMER MEETING—AGENDA ▷				
DISCUSSION ITEM	SCHEDULE/PRIORITY	DISCUSSION LEADER	FOLLOW-ON ACTIONS	DUE DATE
CUSTOMER MEETING DISCUSSIONDATES				

ACTION/ACTIVITY/REVIEW — RESPONSIBILITY	START	FINISH	ACTIVITY STATUS

ATTACHMENTS	PREPARER	DATE	FILE OR DOCUMENT LOCATION

3.1.2 CUSTOMER PERFORMANCE—Customer Status Report

PROCESS OVERVIEW
REPLICATE FOR EACH CUSTOMER REPORT—Identify the general state of the project along with any pertinent problem areas for customer awareness. Specify general variance and project deliverable status for the period. Prepare a brief discussion of key project activities, and request customer assistance, as needed.

TOOL PREPARATION	
PREPARED BY	DATE
CHECK IF REPLICATED (SPECIFY FILE LOCATION) ☐	

PROJECT	CUSTOMER

▷ CUSTOMER REPORT—OVERVIEW					
REPORT TYPE			PROJECT PROGRESS	START PERIOD	END PERIOD
COST ☐ *ON TRACK* ☐ *MINOR VARIANCE* ☐ *MAJOR VARIANCE* *CV*	SCHEDULE ☐ *ON TRACK* ☐ *MINOR VARIANCE* ☐ *MAJOR VARIANCE* SV	RESOURCE UTILIZATION ☐ *ON TRACK* ☐ *MINOR VARIANCE* ☐ *MAJOR VARIANCE* RV	CHANGES APPROVED/IMPLEMENTED	PLANS/DOCUMENTS ISSUED/REVISED	

CUSTOMER REPORT—PROJECT ISSUES/PROBLEM MANAGEMENT				
ISSUE/PROBLEM DESCRIPTION	IDENTIFIED DATE	ACTION/RESOLUTION	STATUS	CLOSE DATE

CUSTOMER REPORT—PROJECT DELIVERABLES STATUS THIS REPORT PERIOD							
DELIVERABLE	RESPONSIBILITY	DUE DATE	ACTUAL DATE	REQ ID	WBS ELEMENT	% COMPLETE	ACCEPTANCE

CUSTOMER REPORT—PROJECT PROGRESS DISCUSSION		
ACTIVITY THIS PERIOD	ACTIVITY NEXT PERIOD	CUSTOMER ASSISTANCE/ATTENTION REQUESTED

ACTION/ACTIVITY/REVIEW – RESPONSIBILITY	START	FINISH	ACTIVITY STATUS

ATTACHMENTS	PREPARER	DATE	FILE OR DOCUMENT LOCATION

3.1.3 CUSTOMER PERFORMANCE—Customer Change Management

PROCESS OVERVIEW	TOOL PREPARATION	
REPLICATE FOR EACH CHANGE REQUEST—Identify the change requested, and include a brief description of pre- and postchange conditions. Evaluate and recommend change request disposition; describe the implementation effort and project impacts. Obtain approvals, and implement the approved project change.	PREPARED BY	DATE
	CHECK IF REPLICATED (SPECIFY FILE LOCATION) ☐	

PROJECT	CUSTOMER

▷ CUSTOMER CHANGE MANAGEMENT—CHANGE REQUEST OVERVIEW				
CHANGE TITLE/IDENTIFIER			REQUEST TYPE	REQUEST NUMBER
CAUSE – CURRENT CONDITION/SITUATION/STATUS	REQUESTED CHANGE		RESULT – NEW CONDITION/SITUATION/STATUS	
REQUESTOR–ORGANIZATION–DEPARTMENT	OFFICE TELEPHONE	MOBILE TELEPHONE	FAX	EMAIL

CUSTOMER CHANGE MANAGEMENT—CHANGE REQUEST EVALUATION				
BRIEF DESCRIPTION OF THE EFFORT NEEDED TO FULFILL THE CHANGE REQUEST (FOR USE BY IMPLEMENTATION)			AFFECTED AREAS ☐ *REQUIREMENTS* ☐ *WORK PLAN* ☐ *SPECIFICATIONS* ☐ *PROJECT PLAN(S)* ☐ *TECH SOLUTION* ☐ *PROJECT DOCUMENT* ☐ *BUS SOLUTION* ☐ *VENDOR/SUPPLIER* ☐ *CONTRACT* ☐ *OTHER*	
EVALUATION–IMPACTS ON COST			QUALITY IMPACTS	
EVALUATION–IMPACTS ON SCHEDULE			RISK IMPACTS	
EVALUATION–IMPACTS ON RESOURCE UTILIZATION (STAFFING)			PROJECT MANAGEMENT IMPACTS	
EVALUATOR	RECOMMENDATION	PROPOSAL REQUIRED	CONTRACT MOD REQUIRED	EVALUATION DATE

CUSTOMER CHANGE MANAGEMENT—CHANGE REQUEST APPROVAL AND IMPLEMENTATION				
CUSTOMER APPROVAL (AS REQUIRED)	APPROVAL COMMENTS	APPROVAL DATE	IMPLEMENTOR	REVISED PROPOSAL DATE
PROJECT MANAGER APPROVAL	APPROVAL COMMENTS	APPROVAL DATE	PROPOSAL DATE	REVISED CONTRACT DATE
PMO–MANAGEMENT APPROVAL (AS REQUIRED)	APPROVAL COMMENTS	APPROVAL DATE	REVISED FUNDING DATE	CHANGE COMPLETED DATE

ACTION/ACTIVITY/REVIEW — RESPONSIBILITY	START	FINISH	ACTIVITY STATUS

ATTACHMENTS	PREPARER	DATE	FILE OR DOCUMENT LOCATION

3.1.4 CUSTOMER PERFORMANCE—Customer Acceptance Management

PROCESS OVERVIEW
REPLICATE FOR EACH PROJECT DELIVERABLE—Specify the project deliverables and the associated acceptance criteria under consideration. Monitor internal and external deliverables testing, and manage the customer's response to each interim and final test. Obtain formal customer review and acceptance for each deliverable.

TOOL PREPARATION	
PREPARED BY	DATE
CHECK IF REPLICATED (SPECIFY FILE LOCATION) ☐	

PROJECT	CUSTOMER

▷ CUSTOMER ACCEPTANCE MANAGEMENT—DELIVERABLE OVERVIEW				
PROJECT DELIVERAB LE			REQUIRED ID	WBS ELEMENT ID
PROJECT DELIVERABLE DESCRIPTION			DELIVERABLE SPECIFICATION (OR REFERENCE)	
PROJECT DELIVERABLE MANAGER	OFFICE TELEPHONE	MOBILE TELEPHONE	FAX	EMAIL

CUSTOMER ACCEPTANCE MANAGEMENT—DELIVERABLE EVALUATION				
STANDARDS AND METRICS APPLIED	DOCUMENTATION CONVEYED WITH DELIVERY		DELIVERABLE VARIANCE OR OPTIONS APPLIED	
INTERIM REVIEW TESTING CONDUCTED			OUTCOME	
FINAL REVIEW/TESTING CONDUCTED			OUTCOME	
FOLLOW-ON ACTION/REVIEW/TESTING CONDUCTED			OUTCOME	
PROJECT MANAGEMENT REVIEW	SIGNATURE	DATE	DELIVERABLE DUE DATE	DELIVERED DATE
MANAGEMENT REVIEWER	SIGNATURE	DATE	REVIEW COMMENTS	
CUSTOMER REVIEWER	SIGNATURE	DATE	REVIEW COMMENTS	

CUSTOMER ACCEPTANCE MANAGEMENT—CUSTOMER REVIEW AND ACCEPTANCE			
CUSTOMER ACCEPTANCE OFFICIAL	SIGNATURE	DATE	ACCEPTANCE

ACTION/ACTIVITY/REVIEW – RESPONSIBILITY	START	FINISH	ACTIVITY STATUS

ATTACHMENTS	PREPARER	DATE	FILE OR DOCUMENT LOCATION

3.2.1 PROJECT PERFORMANCE—Project Tracking & Control Report

PROCESS OVERVIEW
REPLICATE FOR EACH PROJECT MANAGEMENT REVIEW—Review pertinent project management indicators on a routine, recurring basis. Examine and report project variance (cost, schedule, and resource utilization) and earned value, and apply project management controls or corrective actions, as needed.

TOOL PREPARATION	
PREPARED BY	DATE
CHECK IF REPLICATED (SPECIFY FILE LOCATION) ☐	

PROJECT	CUSTOMER

▷ PROJECT TRACKING AND CONTROL—OVERVIEW			
PROJECT STATUS/CONDITION ☐ *GREEN* ☐ *YELLOW* ☐ *RED*	PROJECT MANAGEMENT PHASE PROGRESS (STARTED) ☐ *PROFILE* ☐ *PLAN* ☐ *PERFORM* ☐ *POST*	TRACKING PERIOD START	TRACKING PERIOD END
PROJECT STATUS/CONDITION SUMMARY	TECHNICAL PHASE PROGRESS (STARTED) ☐ *DESIGN* ☐ *BUILD* ☐ *TEST* ☐ *INSTALL* ☐ *TRANSFER* MILESTONES THIS PERIOD / MILESTONES ACHIEVED	PMO OVERSIGHT/CONTROL/SUPPORT ACTIONS	

PROJECT TRACKING AND CONTROL—MANAGEMENT INDICATORS CHECKLIST		
RISK MANAGEMENT CHECKLIST ☐ *OUTSTANDING PROJECT RISKS:* ☐ *NEW PROJECT RISK IDENTIFIED:* ☐ *PROJECT RISKS REMAINING:*	CHANGE MANAGEMENT CHECKLIST ☐ *CHANGE REQUESTS RECEIVED:* ☐ *CHANGE REQUESTS APPROVED:* ☐ *CHANGES IMPLEMENTED:*	QUALITY MANAGEMENT CHECKLIST ☐ *QUALITY TESTING DUE:* ☐ *QUALITY TESTING DONE-ON-TIME:* ☐ *QUALITY TESTING REJECTS:*
PROJECT PLAN MANAGEMENT CHECKLIST ☐ *PROJECT PLAN NON-COMPLIANCE:* ☐ *PROJECT OUT-OF-SCOPE EVENTS:* ☐ *PROJECT PLAN RFVISIONS (PERIOD):*	GENERAL MANAGEMENT CHECKLIST ☐ *DELIVERABLES DUE:* ☐ *DELIVERABLES MADE ON-TIME:* ☐ *DELIVERABLE REWORKS/REJECTS:*	CONTRACT MANAGEMENT CHECKLIST ☐ *CONTRACT/NON-COMPLIANCE:* ☐ *CONTRACT ISSUE EVENTS:* ☐ *CONTRACT ISSUE ELEVATIONS:*
MANAGEMENT INDICATORS CONTROL ACTION		

PROJECT TRACKING AND CONTROL—EARNED VALUE AND PROJECT VARIANCE				
BCWS	BCWP	ACWP	BAC	PERCENT COMPLETE
COST VARIANCE (CV = BCWP – ACWP)		COST CONTROL ACTION		
SCHEDULE VARIANCE (SV = BCWP – BCWS)		SCHEDULE CONTROL ACTION		
RESOURCE VARIANCE (RV = +/– PLANNED STAFFING)		RESOURCE CONTROL PLAN		

ACTION/ACTIVITY/REVIEW – RESPONSIBILITY	START	FINISH	ACTIVITY STATUS

ATTACHMENTS	PREPARER	DATE	FILE OR DOCUMENT LOCATION

3.2.2 PROJECT PERFORMANCE—Project Risk Management

PROCESS OVERVIEW
REPLICATE FOR EACH PROJECT RISK REVIEW—Examine current project risks for control and abatement. Evaluate new risks identified; analyze and prioritize those that have a high probability of occurrence or a high impact on the project. Implement the risk response strategy for each priority project risk, as needed.

TOOL PREPARATION	
PREPARED BY	DATE
CHECK IF REPLICATED (SPECIFY FILE LOCATION) ☐	

PROJECT	CUSTOMER

▷ PROJECT RISK MANAGEMENT—EXAMINATION OVERVIEW				
CURRENT RISK SUMMARY	RISK RESPONSES APPLIED	PURPOSE FOR THIS RISK EXAMINATION		CONTINGENCY FUND AMOUNT AVAILABLE
☐ *TOTAL RISKS*	☐ *CONTINGENCY FUND*	☐ *INITIAL RISK REVIEW*	☐ *PHASE ADVANCEMENT*	$
☐ *PRIORITY RISKS*	☐ *MITIGATION*	☐ *ROUTINE RISK REVIEW*	☐ *PLAN REVISION*	DISCUSSION OF RISK EXAMINATION PURPOSE
☐ *RISKS RESOLVED*	☐ *ACCEPTANCE*	☐ *NOTEWORTHY EVENT*	☐ *PROPOSAL SUBMITTAL*	
☐ *RISKS OCCURRED*	☐ *TRANSFER*	☐ *CHANGE EVALUATION*	☐ *CONTRACT REVISION*	
☐ *NEW RISKS*	☐ *INSURANCE*	☐ *NEW TECHNOLOGY*	☐ *OTHER:*	

PROJECT RISK MANAGEMENT—RISK AREA OVERVIEW					
CUSTOMER	PROJECT TEAM	PROJECT MANAGEMENT	VENDOR MANAGEMENT	INTERNAL INFLUENCES	EXTERNAL INFLUENCES
☐ *EXPECTATIONS*	☐ *STAFF AVAILABILITY*	☐ *PLAN ADEQUACY*	☐ *CONTRACT*	☐ *CORPORATE CULTURE*	☐ *REGULARITY ISSUES*
☐ *RESPONSIVENESS*	☐ *TECHNICAL EXPERTISE*	☐ *PLAN ESTIMATES*	☐ *TECHNICAL EXPERTISE*	☐ *MANAGER DECISIONS*	☐ *LEGAL ISSUES*
☐ *DECISION-MAKING*	☐ *WORK PERFORMANCE*	☐ *SCHEDULE*	☐ *WORK FULFILLMENT*	☐ *LEADERSHIP CHANGES*	☐ *NATURAL HAZARDS*
☐ *SCOPE MANAGEMENT*	☐ *WORK QUALITY*	☐ *NEW TECHNOLOGY*	☐ *WORK QUALITY*	☐ *PORTFOLIO PRIORITY*	☐ *PUBLIC INTEREST*
☐ *FUNDING*	☐ *LEADERSHIP*	☐ *COMMUNICATION*	☐ *LEADERSHIP*	☐ *NATURE OF BUSINESS*	☐ *MARKET VARIATIONS*
PROJECT RISK AREA OVERVIEW NOTES					

PROJECT RISK MANAGEMENT—ASSESSMENT LOG ▷				
PROJECT RISK ID	RISK EVENT AND DESCRIPTION	PROBABILITY (P)	IMPACT (I)	OVERALL (P X I)
		High Med Low	High Med Low	High Med Low
		High Med Low	High Med Low	High Med Low
		High Med Low	High Med Low	High Med Low
		High Med Low	High Med Low	High Med Low
		High Med Low	High Med Low	High Med Low

PROJECT RISK MANAGEMENT—RESPONSE LOG ▷					
PROJECT RISK ID	RISK RESPONSE ACTION	PRIORITY	ASSIGNED TO	ASSIGN DATE	CLOSE DATE

ACTION/ACTIVITY/REVIEW — RESPONSIBILITY	START	FINISH	ACTIVITY STATUS

ATTACHMENTS	PREPARER	DATE	FILE OR DOCUMENT LOCATION

3.2.3 PROJECT PERFORMANCE—Project Communication Management

PROCESS OVERVIEW
Compile and maintain logs and information related to project management and oversight. Establish the Document Management Log, the Correspondence Management Log, and the Consolidated Project Issue Management Log as needed.

TOOL PREPARATION	
PREPARED BY	DATE

PROJECT	CUSTOMER

▷ COMMUNICATION MANAGEMENT—ADMINISTRATION OVERVIEW				
DOCUMENT HANDLING PROCEDURES	CORRESPONDENCE HANDLING PROCEDURES		ISSUES HANDLING PROCEDURES	
PROJECT ADMINISTRATOR	OFFICE TELEPHONE	MOBILE TELEPHONE	FAX	EMAIL

PROJECT ADMINISTRATION MANAGEMENT—DOCUMENT MANAGEMENT LOG ▷				
DOCUMENT	DATE	SOURCE	PURPOSE/ACTION	DEPOSITION

PROJECT ADMINISTRATION MANAGEMENT—CONTACT AND CORRESPONDENCE MANAGEMENT LOG ▷				
CONTACT–CORRESPONDENCE ITEM	DATE	FROM/TO	PURPOSE/ACTION	DEPOSITION

PROJECT ADMINISTRATION MANAGEMENT—ISSUE MANAGEMENT LOG ▷					
ISSUE ID DATE	ISSUE DESCRIPTION	SOURCE	REFERRED TO	RESOLUTION	CLOSE DATE

ACTION/ACTIVITY/REVIEW — RESPONSIBILITY	START	FINISH	ACTIVITY STATUS

ATTACHMENTS	PREPARER	DATE	FILE OR DOCUMENT LOCATION

3.2.4 PROJECT PERFORMANCE—Project Plan Management

PROCESS OVERVIEW
Compile and maintain a log and information related to project plan management and oversight. Perform and list all relevant actions related to project plan creation, review, update, distribution, and implementation.

TOOL PREPARATION	
PREPARED BY	DATE

PROJECT	CUSTOMER

▷ PROJECT PLAN MANAGEMENT—OVERVIEW					
GROUP ID–PLAN DISTRIBUTION GROUPS		PRIMARY PROJECT PLAN ELEMENTS REQUIRED		PLANS REQUIRING CUSTOMER: ☒ REVIEW ☒ APPROVAL	
		☐ *PROJECT WORK PLAN*	☐ *VENDOR MANAGEMENT*	☐ Rev ☐ App	
		☐ *RISK MANAGEMENT*	☐ *MANAGEMENT OVERSIGHT*	☐ Rev ☐ App	
		☐ *QUALITY & ACCEPTANCE*	☐ *MANAGEMENT REVIEW*	☐ Rev ☐ App	
		☐ *COMMUNICATION*	☐ *SUPPLY AND EQUIPMENT*	☐ Rev ☐ App	
		☐ *CHANGE CONTROL*	☐ *FACILITY MANAGEMENT*	☐ Rev ☐ App	
		☐ *STAFF MANAGEMENT*		☐ Rev ☐ App	
PROJECT ADMINISTRATOR	CREATED-TO-DATE	SUPPORT PLANS REQUIRED	CREATED-TO-DATE	PLAN DEVELOPMENT STATUS (%)	STATUS DATE

PROJECT PLAN MANAGEMENT—PLAN MANAGEMENT LOG ▷						
PLAN DATE	PLANNING DOCUMENT	CODE	PREPARED BY	DIST/GROUP ID	PLAN MANAGEMENT ACTION	ACTION DATE

ACTION/ACTIVITY/REVIEW – RESPONSIBILITY	START	FINISH	ACTIVITY STATUS

ATTACHMENTS	PREPARER	DATE	FILE OR DOCUMENT LOCATION

3.3.1 STAFF PERFORMANCE—Staff Meeting

PROCESS OVERVIEW
REPLICATE FOR EACH STAFF MEETING—Specify the location and planned arrangements for the staff meeting to be conducted. Identify and notify the meeting participants. Prepare and include the meeting agenda for premeeting review and preparation by staff meeting participants.

TOOL PREPARATION	
PREPARED BY	DATE
CHECK IF REPLICATED (SPECIFY FILE LOCATION) ☐	

PROJECT	CUSTOMER

▷ STAFF MEETING—OVERVIEW				
MEETING (NAME)		ESTIMATED DURATION	START TIME	START DATE
MEETING LOCATION–ADDRESS	MEETING LOCATION–DIRECTIONS		MEETING ARRANGEMENTS AND NOTES	
MEETING COORDINATOR	OFFICE TELEPHONE	MOBILE TELEPHONE	FAX	EMAIL

STAFF MEETING—PARTICIPANTS LIST ▷				
NAME	OFFICE/LOCATION	REQUIRED	ATTENDANCE	ATTENDANCE NOTES
PRE-MEETING PARTICIPANT PREPARATION REQUESTED				

STAFF MEETING—AGENDA ▷				
DISCUSSION ITEM	SCHEDULE/PRIORITY	DISCUSSION LEADER	FOLLOW-ON ACTIONS	DUE DATE
STAFF MEETING DISCUSSION DATES				

ACTION/ACTIVITY/REVIEW – RESPONSIBILITY	START	FINISH	ACTIVITY STATUS

ATTACHMENTS	PREPARER	DATE	FILE OR DOCUMENT LOCATION

3.3.2 STAFF PERFORMANCE—Staff Status Report

PROCESS OVERVIEW
REPLICATE FOR EACH STAFF STATUS REPORT—Identify the staff member and the general progress of project task assignments, along with any pertinent issues or problems requiring project manager attention. Prepare a brief discussion of key project activities, and request project manager/supervisor assistance, as needed.

TOOL PREPARATION	
PREPARED BY	DATE
CHECK IF REPLICATED (SPECIFY FILE LOCATION) ☐	

PROJECT	CUSTOMER

▷ STAFF REPORT—STAFF MEMBER OVERVIEW				
STAFF MEMBER	OFFICE TELEPHONE	MOBILE TELEPHONE	FAX	EMAIL
STAFF MEMBER ORGANIZATION	PROJECT POSITION/ROLE	COMMITMENT (% TIME)	ASSIGNMENT START DATE	ASSIGNMENT FINISH DATE
SUPERVISION–ASSIGNED TEAM MEMBERS	OTHER PROJECTS (% TIME)	SPECIAL TEAMS & RESPONSIBILITIES		ASSIGNED EQUIPMENT/MATERIALS

STAFF REPORT—STAFF MEMBER EXPENSE SUMMARY LOG ▷

EXPENSE ITEM	SOURCE	PURPOSE	CHARGE CODE	EXPENSE DATE	EXPENSE AMOUNT	COMMENTS
				TOTAL THIS REPORTING PERIOD		

STAFF REPORT—STAFF MEMBER ASSIGNMENT PROGRESS LOG ▷

TASK/WBS ELEMENT	NAME/STAFF ID	ASSIGN DATE	DUE DATE	START DATE	FINISH DATE	STATUS/COMPLETE (%)	COMMENTS

STAFF REPORT—STAFF MEMBER TASK ASSIGNMENT DISCUSSION		
ACTIVITY THIS PERIOD	ACTIVITY NEXT PERIOD	PROPERTY MANAGER/SUPERVISOR ATTENTION REQUESTED

ACTION/ACTIVITY/REVIEW – RESPONSIBILITY	START	FINISH	ACTIVITY STATUS

ATTACHMENTS	PREPARER	DATE	FILE OR DOCUMENT LOCATION

3.3.3 STAFF PERFORMANCE—Staff Performance Review

PROCESS OVERVIEW
REPLICATE FOR EACH STAFF PERFORMANCE REVIEW—Identify the staff member and relevant information pertaining to the member's project assignment. Specify general ratings for each performance category as well as for overall performance. List staff member performance comments for discussion, and conduct a performance review meeting.

TOOL PREPARATION	
PREPARED BY	DATE
CHECK IF REPLICATED (SPECIFY FILE LOCATION) ☐	

PROJECT	CUSTOMER

▷ STAFF PERFORMANCE REVIEW—OVERVIEW				
STAFF MEMBER	OFFICE TELEPHONE	MOBIL TELEPHONE	FAX	EMAIL
STAFF MEMBER PROJECT ROLE/POSITION	PROJECT LEAD/SUPERVISOR	COMMITMENT TIME (%)	ASSIGNMENT START DATE	ASSIGNMENT FINISH DATE
RATER	REASON FOR REVIEW		REVIEW PERIOD START	REVIEW PERIOD END

STAFF PERFORMANCE REVIEW—STAFF MEMBER GENERAL RATING					
TECHNICAL CAPABILITY	WORK QUALITY	TIME FULFILLMENT	TEAM LEADERSHIP	INTERPERSONAL SKILL	OVERALL RATING
☐ *MERITORIOUS*	☐ *MERITORIOUS*	☐ *MERITORIOUS*	☐ *MERITORIOUS*	☐ *MERITORIOUS*	☐ *MERITORIOUS*
☐ *SATISFACTORY*	☐ *SATISFACTORY*	☐ *SATISFACTORY*	☐ *SATISFACTORY*	☐ *SATISFACTORY*	☐ *SATISFACTORY*
☐ *UNSATISFACTORY*	☐ *UNSATISFACTORY*	☐ *UNSATISFACTORY*	☐ *UNSATISFACTORY*	☐ *UNSATISFACTORY*	☐ *UNSATISFACTORY*
☐ *NOT RATED*	☐ *NOT RATED*	☐ *NOT RATED*	☐ *NOT RATED*	☐ *NOT RATED*	☐ *NOT RATED*
MERIT VALIDATION	MERIT VALIDATION	MERIT VALIDATION	MERIT VALIDATION	MERIT VALIDATION	MERIT VALIDATION
NOTE: The MERITORIOUS level rating cannot be given for any performance category if an UNSATISFACTORY level rating appears in any other performance category.					

STAFF PERFORMANCE REVIEW—STAFF MEMBER PERFORMANCE DISCUSSION		
STAFF MEMBER PERFORMANCE CONTRIBUTION(S)	STAFF MEMBER PERFORMANCE IMPROVEMENT AREA(S)	STAFF MEMBER PERFORMANCE RECOMMENDATIONS

STAFF PERFORMANCE REVIEW—STAFF MEMBER REVIEW MEETING		
STAFF MEMBER REVIEW MEETING COMMENTS		RATER COMMENTS
STAFF MEMBER SIGNATURE/DATE	RATER SIGNATURE/DATE	PROJECT MANAGER SIGNATURE/DATE

ACTION/ACTIVITY/REVIEW — RESPONSIBILITY	START	FINISH	ACTIVITY STATUS

ATTACHMENTS	PREPARER	DATE	FILE OR DOCUMENT LOCATION

3.3.4 STAFF PERFORMANCE—Staff Management Report

PROCESS OVERVIEW
REPLICATE FOR EACH STAFF MANAGEMENT REPORT—Identify the current status of project staff strength. Specify staff strength forecasts, and identify status of critical positions to be filled. Prepare a brief discussion of pertinent project staff management actions, and request PMO/management assistance, as needed.

TOOL PREPARATION	
PREPARED BY	DATE
CHECK IF REPLICATED (SPECIFY FILE LOCATION) ☐	

PROJECT	CUSTOMER

▷ STAFF MANAGEMENT REPORT—OVERVIEW

PROJECT PERIOD	STAFF AUTHORIZATIONS	STAFF MEMBER ACQUISITION STATUS	STAFF STRENGTH NOTES
Current			
1-Month			
3-Month			
6-Month			
1-Year			
Maximum Staff Level			

STAFF MANAGEMENT REPORT—STAFF STRENGTH FORECAST

PROJECT PERIOD	CURRENT PLAN	CURRENT STRENGTH	1-MONTH FORECAST	3-MONTH FORECAST	6-MONTH FORECAST	1-YEAR FORECAST
Date						
STAFF REQUIREMENTS						
Management						
Technical						
Labor						
Administrative						
TOTAL STAFF						
CRITICAL STAFF POSITIONS						

STAFF STRENGTH FORECAST NOTES

STAFF MANAGEMENT REPORT—STAFF MANAGEMENT ACTIONS STATUS

PROJECT TEAM PERFORMANCE STATUS	PROJECT TEAM DEVELOPMENT/INTEGRATION STATUS	PMO/MANAGEMENT ASSISTANCE/ATTENTION REQUESTED

ACTION/ACTIVITY/REVIEW – RESPONSIBILITY	START	FINISH	ACTIVITY STATUS

ATTACHMENTS	PREPARER	DATE	FILE OR DOCUMENT LOCATION

3.4.1 VENDOR PERFORMANCE—Vendor Meeting

PROCESS OVERVIEW
REPLICATE FOR EACH VENDOR MEETING—Specify the location and planned arrangements for the vendor meeting to be conducted. Identify and notify the meeting participants. Prepare and include the meeting agenda for premeeting review and preparation by vendor meeting participants.

TOOL PREPARATION	
PREPARED BY	DATE
CHECK IF REPLICATED (SPECIFY FILE LOCATION) ☐	

PROJECT	CUSTOMER

▷ VENDOR MEETING—OVERVIEW					
MEETING (NAME)		ESTIMATED DURATION	START TIME	START DATE	
MEETING LOCATION–ADDRESS	MEETING LOCATION–DIRECTIONS		MEETING ARRANGEMENTS AND NOTES		
MEETING COORDINATOR	OFFICE TELEPHONE	MOBILE TELEPHONE	FAX	EMAIL	

VENDOR MEETING—PARTICIPANTS LIST ▷				
NAME	OFFICE/LOCATION	REQUIRED	ATTENDANCE	ATTENDANCE NOTES
PRE-MEETING PARTICIPANT PREPARATION REQUESTED				

VENDOR MEETING—AGENDA ▷				
DISCUSSION ITEM	SCHEDULE/PRIORITY	DISCUSSION LEADER	FOLLOW-ON ACTIONS	DATE DUE
STAFF MEETING DISCUSSION NOTES				

ACTION/ACTIVITY/REVIEW – RESPONSIBILITY	START	FINISH	ACTIVITY STATUS

ATTACHMENTS	PREPARER	DATE	FILE OR DOCUMENT LOCATION

3.4.2 VENDOR PERFORMANCE—Vendor Status Report

PROCESS OVERVIEW	TOOL PREPARATION	
REPLICATE FOR EACH VENDOR STATUS REPORT—Identify the vendor's task leader and pertinent vendor information. List the general progress of vendor task assignments. Prepare a brief discussion of key vendor project activities, and request project manager assistance, as needed.	PREPARED BY	DATE
	CHECK IF REPLICATED (SPECIFY FILE LOCATION) ☐	

PROJECT	CUSTOMER

▷ VENDOR REPORT—VENDOR OVERVIEW				
VENDOR TASK LEADER	OFFICE TELEPHONE	MOBILE TELEPHONE	FAX	EMAIL
VENDOR ORGANIZATION	VENDOR CONTRACT REFERENCE		CONTRACT START DATE	CONTRACT FINISH DATE
VENDOR TEAM MEMBERS	VENDOR DELIVERABLE(S)	SPECIAL TEAMS & RESPONSIBILITIES		ASSIGNED EQUIPMENT/MATERIALS

VENDOR REPORT—VENDOR EXPENSE SUMMARY LOG ▷

EXPENSE ITEM (LIST INVOICES)	SOURCE	PURPOSE	CHARGE CODE	EXPENSE DATE	EXPENSE AMOUNT	COMMENTS
				TOTAL THIS REPORTING PERIOD		

VENDOR REPORT—VENDOR ASSIGNMENT PROGRESS LOG ▷

TASK/WBS ELEMENT	NAME/STAFF ID	ASSIGN DATE	DUE DATE	START DATE	FINISH DATE	STATUS/COMPLETE (%)	COMMENTS

VENDOR REPORT—VENDOR TASK ASSIGNMENT DISCUSSION		
ACTIVITY THIS PERIOD	ACTIVITY NEXT PERIOD	PROPERTY MANAGER ASSISTANCE/ATTENTION REQUESTED

ACTION/ACTIVITY/REVIEW – RESPONSIBILITY	START	FINISH	ACTIVITY STATUS

ATTACHMENTS	PREPARER	DATE	FILE OR DOCUMENT LOCATION

3.4.3 VENDOR PERFORMANCE—Vendor Performance Review

PROCESS OVERVIEW
REPLICATE FOR EACH VENDOR PERFORMANCE REVIEW—Identify the vendor and relevant information pertaining to the vendor's project assignment. Specify general vendor ratings for each performance category as well as for overall performance. List vendor performance comments for discussion and conduct a performance review meeting.

TOOL PREPARATION	
PREPARED BY	DATE
CHECK IF REPLICATED (SPECIFY FILE LOCATION) ☐	

PROJECT	CUSTOMER

▷ VENDOR PERFORMANCE REVIEW—OVERVIEW				
VENDOR TASK LEADER	OFFICE TELEPHONE	MOBIL TELEPHONE	FAX	EMAIL
VENDOR ORGANIZATION	VENDOR CONTRACT REFERENCE		CONTRACT START DATE	CONTRACT FINISH DATE
RATER	REASON FOR REVIEW		REVIEW PERIOD START	REVIEW PERIOD END

VENDOR PERFORMANCE REVIEW—VENDOR GENERAL RATING					
TECHNICAL CAPABILITY	DELIVERABLE QUALITY	TIMELINESS OF WORK	TEAM INTEGRATION	CONTRACT FULFILLMENT	OVERALL RATING
☐ *OUTSTANDING*	☐ *OUTSTANDING*	☐ *OUTSTANDING*	☐ *OUTSTANDING*	☐ *OUTSTANDING*	☐ *OUTSTANDING*
☐ *SATISFACTORY*	☐ *SATISFACTORY*	☐ *SATISFACTORY*	☐ *SATISFACTORY*	☐ *SATISFACTORY*	☐ *SATISFACTORY*
☐ *UNSATISFACTORY*	☐ *UNSATISFACTORY*	☐ *UNSATISFACTORY*	☐ *UNSATISFACTORY*	☐ *UNSATISFACTORY*	☐ *UNSATISFACTORY*
☐ *NOT RATED*	☐ *NOT RATED*	☐ *NOT RATED*	☐ *NOT RATED*	☐ *NOT RATED*	☐ *NOT RATED*
VENDOR GENERAL RATING NOTES					

VENDOR PERFORMANCE REVIEW—VENDOR PERFORMANCE DISCUSSION		
VENDOR PERFORMANCE CONTRIBUTION(S)	VENDOR CONTRACT FULFILLMENT	VENDOR PERFORMANCE RECOMMENDATIONS

VENDOR PERFORMANCE REVIEW—VENDOR REVIEW MEETING		
VENDOR REVIEW MEETING COMMENTS		RATER COMMENTS
VENDOR REVIEW SIGNATURE/DATE	RATER SIGNATURE/DATE	NEXT VENDOR REVIEW ON THIS CONTRACT

ACTION/ACTIVITY/REVIEW – RESPONSIBILITY	START	FINISH	ACTIVITY STATUS

ATTACHMENTS	PREPARER	DATE	FILE OR DOCUMENT LOCATION

3.4.4 VENDOR PERFORMANCE—Vendor Contract Administration

PROCESS OVERVIEW
Identify each vendor and associated vendor contract information. Conduct vendor contract reviews, as needed. Summarize vendor contract performance status. Identify any administrative or legal activity associated with a listed vendor's contract.

TOOL PREPARATION	
PREPARED BY	DATE
CHECK IF REPLICATED (SPECIFY FILE LOCATION) ☐	

PROJECT	CUSTOMER

▷ VENDOR CONTRACT ADMINISTRATION—VENDOR CONTRACT OVERVIEW						
VENDOR ID	VENDOR ORGANIZATION	TYPE CONTRACT	CONTRACT REFERENCE	VALUE	START	FINISH
			VENDOR CONTRACT VALUE TOTALS TO DATE			

VENDOR CONTRACT ADMINISTRATION—VENDOR CONTRACT REVIEWS				
VENDOR ID	VENDOR ORGANIZATION	REVIEW DATE	REVIEW PURPOSE	COMMENTS

VENDOR CONTRACT ADMINISTRATION—VENDOR MANAGEMENT STATUS		
VENDOR DELIVERABLESFULFILLMENT	VENDOR TERMS AND CONDITIONS FULFILLMENT	VENDOR CONTRACT ISSUES

VENDOR CONTRACT ADMINISTRATION—VENDOR CONTRACT ADMINISTRATION ACTIVITY LOG ▷				
ACTIVITY/ACTION/EVENT	START	FINISH	PARTICIPANT(S)	OUTCOME/COMMENTS

ACTION/ACTIVITY/REVIEW — RESPONSIBILITY	START	FINISH	ACTIVITY STATUS

ATTACHMENTS	PREPARER	DATE	FILE OR DOCUMENT LOCATION

3.5.1 BUSINESS PERFORMANCE—Business Meeting

PROCESS OVERVIEW
REPLICATE FOR EACH BUSINESS MEETING—Specify the location and planned arrangements for the business meeting to be conducted. Identify and notify the meeting participants. Prepare and include the meeting agenda for premeeting review and preparation by business meeting participants.

TOOL PREPARATION	
PREPARED BY	DATE
CHECK IF REPLICATED (SPECIFY FILE LOCATION) ☐	

PROJECT	CUSTOMER

▷ BUSINESS MEETING—OVERVIEW					
MEETING (NAME)		ESTIMATED DURATION	START TIME	START DATE	
MEETING LOCATION–ADDRESS	MEETING LOCATION–DIRECTIONS		MEETING ARRANGEMENTS AND NOTES		
MEETING COORDINATOR	OFFICE TELEPHONE	MOBILE TELEPHONE	FAX	EMAIL	

BUSINESS MEETING—PARTICIPANTS LIST ▷				
NAME	OFFICE/LOCATION	REQUIRED	ATTENDANCE	ATTENDANCE NOTES
PRE-MEETING PARTICIPANT PREPARATION REQUESTED				

BUSINESS MEETING—AGENDA ▷				
DISCUSSION ITEM	SCHEDULE/PRIORITY	DISCUSSION LEADER	FOLLOW-ON ACTIONS	DATE DUE
STAFF MEETING DISCUSSION NOTES				

ACTION/ACTIVITY/REVIEW — RESPONSIBILITY	START	FINISH	ACTIVITY STATUS

ATTACHMENTS	PREPARER	DATE	FILE OR DOCUMENT LOCATION

3.5.2 BUSINESS PERFORMANCE—Business Status Report

PROCESS OVERVIEW	TOOL PREPARATION	
REPLICATE FOR EACH BUSINESS STATUS REPORT—Identify key business information, and review preferred business indicators related to the project. Compile the expense (costs) summary for the report period, and incorporate revenue numbers to complete the financial analysis portion of the report.	PREPARED BY	DATE
	CHECK IF REPLICATED (SPECIFY FILE LOCATION) ☐	

PROJECT	CUSTOMER

▷ BUSINESS STATUS REPORT—BUSINESS OVERVIEW					
BUSINESS CONTRACT REFERENCE		CONTRACT TOTAL CURRENT VALUE		CONTRACT START DATE	CONTRACT FINISH DATE
COST—% COMPLETE	COSTS—EXPENDED	COSTS—REMAINING (EST)	TIME—% COMPLETE	TIME—EXPENDED	TIME—REMAINING (EST)

GENERAL BUSINESS INDICATORS	BUSINESS INDICATOR RATING	BUSINESS INDICATOR COMMENTS
☐ Project Cost Management (Savings)	☐ *HIGH* ☐ *GOOD* ☐ *FAIR* ☐ *POOR*	
☐ Customer Satisfaction Level	☐ *HIGH* ☐ *GOOD* ☐ *FAIR* ☐ *POOR*	
☐ Contract Retention/Expansion Opportunity	☐ *HIGH* ☐ *GOOD* ☐ *FAIR* ☐ *POOR*	
☐ Public Perception of Technical Work/Value	☐ *HIGH* ☐ *GOOD* ☐ *FAIR* ☐ *POOR*	

BUSINESS STATUS REPORT—PROJECT EXPENSE SUMMARY LOG ▷

EXPENSE ITEM (LIST INVOICES PAID)	SOURCE	PURPOSE	CHARGE CODE	EXPENSE DATE	EXPENSE AMOUNT	COMMENTS
				TOTAL EXPENSES THIS REPORTING PERIOD		

BUSINESS STATUS REPORT—PROJECT FINANCIAL ANALYSIS			
ANALYSIS PREPARED FOR THE PERIOD:		ANALYSIS DATE	FINANCIAL ANALYSIS NOTES
PROJECT COSTS FOR PERIOD	PROJECT REVENUE FOR PERIOD	PROJECT MARGIN FOR PERIOD	
QUARTER-TO-DATE PROJECT COSTS	QUARTER-TO-DATE REVENUE	QUARTER-TO-DATE MARGIN	
YEAR-TO-DATE PROJECT COSTS	YEAR-TO-DATE REVENUE	YEAR-TO-DATE MARGIN	
PROJECT-TO-DATE COSTS	PROJECT-TO-DATE REVENUE	PROJECT-TO-DATE MARGIN	

ACTION/ACTIVITY/REVIEW – RESPONSIBILITY	START	FINISH	ACTIVITY STATUS

ATTACHMENTS	PREPARER	DATE	FILE OR DOCUMENT LOCATION

3.5.3 BUSINESS PERFORMANCE—Business Performance Review

PROCESS OVERVIEW
REPLICATE FOR EACH BUSINESS PERFORMANCE REVIEW—Identify the project portfolio owner/manager and relevant portfolio information. Specify general ratings for each performance category as well as for overall performance. List comments for discussion, and provide recommendations for managing business aspects of the project.

TOOL PREPARATION	
PREPARED BY	DATE
CHECK IF REPLICATED (SPECIFY FILE LOCATION) ☐	

PROJECT	CUSTOMER

▷ BUSINESS PERFORMANCE REVIEW—PROJECT PORTFOLIO OVERVIEW				
PORTFOLIO OWNER/MANAGER	OFFICE TELEPHONE	MOBIL TELEPHONE	FAX	EMAIL
PORTFOLIO ORGANIZATION	PORTFOLIO REFERENCE		PORTFOLIO START DATE	START PRIORITY
PROJECT PORTFOLIO BUCKET	REASON FOR REVIEW		PORTFOLIO REVIEW DATE	CURRENT PRIORITY

BUSINESS PERFORMANCE REVIEW—GENERAL BUSINESS RATING					
STRATEGIC MANAGEMENT	BUSINESS MANAGEMENT	TECHNICAL MANAGEMENT	CUSTOMER MANAGEMENT	PROJECT MANAGEMENT	OVERALL RATING
☐ *OUTSTANDING*	☐ *OUTSTANDING*	☐ *OUTSTANDING*	☐ *OUTSTANDING*	☐ *OUTSTANDING*	☐ *OUTSTANDING*
☐ *SATISFACTORY*	☐ *SATISFACTORY*	☐ *SATISFACTORY*	☐ *SATISFACTORY*	☐ *SATISFACTORY*	☐ *SATISFACTORY*
☐ *UNSATISFACTORY*	☐ *UNSATISFACTORY*	☐ *UNSATISFACTORY*	☐ *UNSATISFACTORY*	☐ *UNSATISFACTORY*	☐ *UNSATISFACTORY*
☐ *NOT RATED*	☐ *NOT RATED*	☐ *NOT RATED*	☐ *NOT RATED*	☐ *NOT RATED*	☐ *NOT RATED*
GENERAL BUSINESS RATING NOTES					

BUSINESS PERFORMANCE REVIEW—PERFORMANCE DISCUSSION		
STRATEGIC OBJECTIVES/PURPOSE/INTERESTS	PROJECT CONTRIBUTIONS TO OBJECTIVES/PURPOSE	BUSINESS PERFORMANCE RECOMMENDATIONS

BUSINESS PERFORMANCE REVIEW—PORTFOLIO ANALYSIS							
THIS PROJECT	PROJECT MANAGER	PRIORITY	PRIORITY DATE	CONTRACT VALUE	PERFORMANCE RATING	NEW PRIORITY	NEW DATE
PROJECTS IN PORTFOLIO	PROJECT MANAGER	PRIORITY	PRIORITY DATE	CONTRACT VALUE	PERFORMANCE RATING	NEW PRIORITY	NEW DATE

ACTION/ACTIVITY/REVIEW – RESPONSIBILITY	START	FINISH	ACTIVITY STATUS

ATTACHMENTS	PREPARER	DATE	FILE OR DOCUMENT LOCATION

3.5.4 BUSINESS PERFORMANCE—Business Contract Administration

PROCESS OVERVIEW
Identify business contract information. Conduct customer contract reviews, as needed. Summarize business contract performance status. Identify any administrative or legal activity associated with the customer's business contract.

TOOL PREPARATION	
PREPARED BY	DATE

PROJECT	CUSTOMER

▷ BUSINESS CONTRACT ADMINISTRATION—CONTRACT OVERVIEW						
CONTRACT MANAGER		OFFICE TELEPHONE	MOBIL TELEPHONE	FAX	EMAIL
BUSINESS CONTRACT DATE	BOOKED DATE	LAST MODIFICATION DATE	MODIFICATION NUMBER	CONTRACT INITIAL VALUE	CONTRACT CURRENT VALUE
BUSINESS CONTRACT TYPE		BUSINESS CONTRACT REFERENCE		CONTRACT START DATE	CONTRACT FINISH DATE

BUSINESS CONTRACT ADMINISTRATION—CONTRACT REVIEWS				
MOD NUMBER	CONTRACT AREA	REVIEW DATE	REVIEW PURPOSE	COMMENTS

BUSINESS CONTRACT ADMINISTRATION—MANAGEMENT STATUS		
DELIVERABLES FULFILLMENT	TERMS AND CONDITIONS FULFILLMENT	CONTRACT ISSUES

BUSINESS CONTRACT ADMINISTRATION—CONTRACT ADMINISTRATION ACTIVITY LOG				
ACTIVITY/ACTION/EVENT	START	FINISH	PARTICIPANT(S)	OUTCOME/COMMENT

ACTION/ACTIVITY/REVIEW — RESPONSIBILITY	START	FINISH	ACTIVITY STATUS

ATTACHMENTS	PREPARER	DATE	FILE OR DOCUMENT LOCATION

3.6.1 MANAGEMENT PERFORMANCE—Management Meeting

PROCESS OVERVIEW
REPLICATE FOR EACH MANAGEMENT MEETING—Specify the location and planned arrangements for the management meeting to be conducted. Identify and notify the meeting participants. Prepare and include the meeting agenda for premeeting review and preparation by management meeting participants.

TOOL PREPARATION	
PREPARED BY	DATE
CHECK IF REPLICATED (SPECIFY FILE LOCATION) ☐	

PROJECT	CUSTOMER

⊳ MANAGEMENT MEETING—OVERVIEW				
MEETING (NAME)		BUSINESS DURATION	START TIME	START DATE
MEETING LOCATION—ADDRESS	MEETING LOCATION—DIRECTIONS		MEETING ARRANGEMENTS AND NOTES	
MEETING COORDINATOR	OFFICE TELEPHONE	MOBILE TELEPHONE	FAX	EMAIL

MANAGEMENT MEETING—PARTICIPANTS LIST				⊳
NAME	OFFICE/LOCATION	REQUIRED	ATTENDANCE	ATTENDANCE NOTES
PRE-MEETING PARTICIPANT PREPARATION REQUESTED				

MANAGEMENT MEETING—AGENDA				⊳
DISCUSSION ITEM	SCHEDULE/PRIORITY	DISCUSSION LEADER	FOLLOW-ON ACTIONS	DATE DUE
MANAGEMENT MEETING DISCUSSION NOTES				

ACTION/ACTIVITY/REVIEW — RESPONSIBILITY	START	FINISH	ACTIVITY STATUS

ATTACHMENTS	PREPARER	DATE	FILE OR DOCUMENT LOCATION

3.6.2 MANAGEMENT PERFORMANCE—Management Status Report

PROCESS OVERVIEW
REPLICATE FOR EACH MANAGEMENT REPORT—Identify the general state of the project along with any pertinent problem areas for management awareness. Specify project variance and deliverable status for the period. Prepare a discussion of key project activities, and request management assistance, as needed.

TOOL PREPARATION	
PREPARED BY	DATE
CHECK IF REPLICATED (SPECIFY FILE LOCATION) ☐	

PROJECT	CUSTOMER

▷ MANAGEMENT REPORT—OVERVIEW					
REPORT TYPE			PROJECT PROGRESS	START PERIOD	END PERIOD
COST ☐ *ON TRACK* ☐ *MINOR VARIANCE* ☐ *MAJOR VARIANCE* *CV*	SCHEDULE ☐ *ON TRACK* ☐ *MINOR VARIANCE* ☐ *MAJOR VARIANCE* SV	RESOURCE UTILIZATION ☐ *ON TRACK* ☐ *MINOR VARIANCE* ☐ *MAJOR VARIANCE* RV	PROJECT MANAGEMENT CORRECTIVE ACTIONS TAKEN		

MANAGEMENT REPORT—PROJECT ISSUES/PROBLEM MANAGEMENT

ISSUE/PROBLEM DESCRIPTION	IDENTIFIED DATE	ACTION/RESOLUTION	STATUS	CLOSE DATE

MANAGEMENT REPORT—PROJECT DELIVERABLES STATUS THIS REPORT PERIOD

DELIVERABLE	RESPONSIBILITY	DUE DATE	ACTUAL DATE	REQ ID	WBS ELEMENT	% COMPLETE	ACCEPTANCE

MANAGEMENT REPORT—PROJECT PROGRESS DISCUSSION

ACTIVITY THIS PERIOD	ACTIVITY NEXT PERIOD	MANAGEMENT ASSISTANCE/ATTENTION REQUESTED

ACTION/ACTIVITY/REVIEW – RESPONSIBILITY	START	FINISH	ACTIVITY STATUS

ATTACHMENTS	PREPARER	DATE	FILE OR DOCUMENT LOCATION

3.6.3 MANAGEMENT PERFORMANCE—Management Performance Review

PROCESS OVERVIEW
REPLICATE FOR EACH MANAGEMENT PERFORMANCE REVIEW—Identify the project portfolio owner/manager and relevant portfolio information. Specify review results relative to checklist items. List comments for discussion, and provide recommendations for managing performance aspects of the project.

TOOL PREPARATION	
PREPARED BY	DATE
CHECK IF REPLICATED (SPECIFY FILE LOCATION) ☐	

PROJECT	CUSTOMER

▷ MANAGEMENT PERFORMANCE REVIEW—OVERVIEW				
PERFORMANCE REVIEW ELEMENTS ☐ *READY-TO-EXECUTE* ☐ *PROJECT STATUS* ☐ *PORTFOLIO STATUS*		REVIEW MEETING DATE	REVIEW PERIOD START	REVIEW PERIOD END
REPORTS EXAMINED ☐ *CUSTOMER STATUS REPORT* ☐ *TRACKING AND CONTROL REPORT* ☐ *STAFF STATUS REPORT* ☐ *STAFF MANAGEMENT REPORT* ☐ *BUSINESS STATUS REPORT*	OTHER MATERIALS EXAMINED	PREPARATION DATE	REVIEWER	
		DISCUSSION POINTS		

MANAGEMENT PERFORMANCE REVIEW—READY-TO-EXECUTE CHECKLIST				
CHECKLIST ☐ *PROJECT PLANS READINESS* ☐ *CUSTOMER CONTRACT READINESS* ☐ *VENDOR CONTRACT READINESS* ☐ *PROJECT RESOURCE READINESS* ☐ *PROJECT LOGISTICS READINESS*	REVIEW COMMENTS	DISCUSSION SUMMARY/ACTIONS		
READY-TO-EXECUTE AUTHORITY		AUTHORIZATION DATE	START PERIOD	END PERIOD

MANAGEMENT PERFORMANCE REVIEW—PROJECT STATUS REVIEW CHECKLIST		
CHECKLIST ☐ *PROJECT VARIANCE (COST-SCHEDULE-RESOURCES)* ☐ *PROJECT MANAGEMENT–ISSUES & PROBLEMS* ☐ *PROJECT TECHNICAL PERFORMANCE* ☐ *RESOURCE AVAILABILITY/UTILIZATION* ☐ *VENDOR WORK PERFORMANCE*	REVIEW COMMENTS	DISCUSSION SUMMARY/ACTIONS

MANAGEMENT PERFORMANCE REVIEW—PORTFOLIO STATUS CHECKLIST		
CHECKLIST ☐ *BUSINESS CASE ALIGNMENT* ☐ *RESOURCE ALLOCATION ALIGNMENT* ☐ *CUSTOMER SATISFACTION* ☐ *PROJECT BUSINESS PERFORMANCE* ☐ *PROJECT PORTFOLIO PRIORITIZATION*	REVIEW COMMENTS	DISCUSSION SUMMARY/ACTIONS

ACTION/ACTIVITY/REVIEW — RESPONSIBILITY	START	FINISH	ACTIVITY STATUS

ATTACHMENTS	PREPARER	DATE	FILE OR DOCUMENT LOCATION

3.6.4 MANAGEMENT PERFORMANCE—Management Audit and Review Report

PROCESS OVERVIEW
REPLICATE FOR EACH MANAGEMENT AUDIT (REVIEW) CONDUCTED—Outline key planning elements, identify documents reviewed and interviews conducted, specify pertinent audit/review findings, and determine corrective and follow-on actions that need to be performed, including the identification of responsible individuals.

TOOL PREPARATION	
PREPARED BY	DATE
CHECK IF REPLICATED (SPECIFY FILE LOCATION) ☐	

PROJECT	CUSTOMER

▷ MANAGEMENT AUDIT & REVIEW REPORT—OVERVIEW			
AUDIT INITIATION ☐ *SCHEDULED* ☐ *TRIGGERED* ☐ *REQUESTED* ☐ *DISCRETIONARY*	AUDIT INITIATOR	AUDIT START DATE	AUDIT END DATE
AUDIT LOCATION / AUDIT TEAM MEMBERS	AUDIT PURPOSE		
LEAD AUDITOR / OFFICE TELEPHONE	MOBILE TELEPHONE	FAX	EMAIL

MANAGEMENT AUDIT & REVIEW REPORT—PROJECT STATUS EXAMINATION		
PRIMARY DOCUMENT REVIEWS (* REQUIRED)	PRIMARY INTERVIEWS (* REQUIRED)	OTHER EXAMINATION AREAS OR AUDIT CONTACTS
☐ *PROJECT DEFINITION (SCOPE-OBJECTIVES)**	☐ *PROJECT MANAGER**	
☐ *PROJECT WORK PLAN (BUDGET-SCHEDULE-STAFF)**	☐ *PROJECT TEAM MEMBERS*	
☐ *RISK MANAGEMENT PLAN (PROJECT RISK)**	☐ *TECHNICAL LEADERS*	
☐ *QUALITY PLAN (PROJECT DELIVERABLES)*	☐ *PROJECT PLANNERS*	
☐ *COMMUNICATION PLAN (REPORTING)*	☐ *MANAGEMENT)*	
☐ *OTHER:*	☐ *OTHER:*	
GENERAL PROJECT STATUS EXAMINATION NOTES		

MANAGEMENT AUDIT & REVIEW REPORT—PERFORMANCE EXAMINATION					
EXAMINATION AREA	TOTAL	PLANNED-TO-DATE	ACTUAL-TO-DATE	PERFORMANCE EVALUATION RATING	DATE
☐ *COST*				☐ *EXCELLENT* ☐ *GOOD* ☐ *MARGINAL* ☐ *POOR*	
☐ *SCHEDULE*				☐ *EXCELLENT* ☐ *GOOD* ☐ *MARGINAL* ☐ *POOR*	
☐ *RESOURCE UTILIZATION*				☐ *EXCELLENT* ☐ *GOOD* ☐ *MARGINAL* ☐ *POOR*	

MANAGEMENT AUDIT & REVIEW REPORT—PERFORMANCE EXAMINATION						
ID	CONDITION FOUND	BASIS OF FINDING	CAUSE OF FINDING	RECOMMENDATION	RESPONSIBLE	STATUS

ACTION/ACTIVITY/REVIEW – RESPONSIBILITY	START	FINISH	ACTIVITY STATUS

ATTACHMENTS	PREPARER	DATE	FILE OR DOCUMENT LOCATION

Chapter 4

Post-Phase Tools

These are the tools used in the Post Phase:

- 4.1 Customer Posting
  - 4.1.1 Customer Lessons Learned
  - 4.1.2 Customer Evaluation
  - 4.1.3 Customer Satisfaction Survey
  - 4.1.4 Customer Transition and Closeout
- 4.2 Project Posting
  - 4.2.1 Project Lessons Learned
  - 4.2.2 Project Performance Evaluation
  - 4.2.3 Project Administration Closeout
  - 4.2.4 Project Plan Closeout
- 4.3 Staff Posting
  - 4.3.1 Staff Lessons Learned
  - 4.3.2 Staff Performance Evaluation
  - 4.3.3 Staff Performance Recognition
  - 4.3.4 Staff Reassignment and Closeout
- 4.4 Vendor Posting
  - 4.4.1 Vendor Lessons Learned
  - 4.4.2 Vendor Performance Evaluation
  - 4.4.3 Vendor Invoice Management
  - 4.4.4 Vendor Contract Closeout
- 4.5 Business Posting
  - 4.5.1 Business Lessons Learned
  - 4.5.2 Business Performance Evaluation
  - 4.5.3 Business Invoice Management
  - 4.5.4 Business Contract Closeout
- 4.6 Management Posting
  - 4.6.1 Management Lessons Learned
  - 4.6.2 Management Evaluation
  - 4.6.3 Management Satisfaction Survey
  - 4.6.4 Management Closeout

These tools appear in the following pages.

4.1.1 CUSTOMER POSTING—Customer Lessons Learned

PROCESS OVERVIEW
Review the project from the perspective of customer activity and interactions, with a focus on what went well and what didn't. Reference the short checklist, and attempt an unbiased review. Identify conditions (lessons), but don't evaluate yet, as that's done in a separate activity. A facilitated group session is recommended.

TOOL PREPARATION	
PREPARED BY	DATE

PROJECT	CUSTOMER

▷ CUSTOMER LESSONS LEARNED—OVERVIEW			
WHAT WENT WELL	WHAT WENT NOT SO WELL	WHAT MAJOR ISSUES WERE UNEXPECTED	CUSTOMER LESSONS CHECKLIST ☐ *CUSTOMER ACTIVITIES BY PHASE* ☐ *CUSTOMER PARTICIPATION* ☐ *CUSTOMER COMMUNICATION* ☐ *CUSTOMER SCOPE MANAGEMENT* ☐ *CUSTOMER PROJECT COMMITMENT*
SUMMARY OF LESSONS LEARNED HIGHLIGHTS (FROM FINDINGS BELOW)		SUMMARY OF MAJOR RECOMMENDATIONS (FROM FINDINGS BELOW)	

CUSTOMER LESSONS LEARNED—FINDINGS LOG		▷
LESSON—EVENT OR CONDITION	LESSON—IMPACT ON PROJECT OR BUSINESS	LESSON—RECOMMENDED IMPROVEMENT OR CHANGE

ACTION/ACTIVITY/REVIEW — RESPONSIBILITY	START	FINISH	ACTIVITY STATUS

ATTACHMENTS	PREPARER	DATE	FILE OR DOCUMENT LOCATION

4.1.2 CUSTOMER POSTING—Customer Evaluation

PROCESS OVERVIEW
REPLICATE FOR EACH EVALUATION PREPARED—Conduct an internal evaluation of the project experience with the customer to rate indicators of customer performance. Identify key and notable customer contacts, and provide comments about working with this customer.

TOOL PREPARATION	
PREPARED BY	DATE
CHECK IF REPLICATED (SPECIFY FILE LOCATION) ☐	

PROJECT	CUSTOMER

▷ CUSTOMER EVALUATION—OVERVIEW			
REASON FOR EVALUATION	PROJECT START DATE	PROJECT MANAGER SIGNOFF—SIGNATURE	DATE
TYPE OF EVALUATION ☐ *INDIVIDUAL* ☐ *GROUP* ☐ *CONSOLIDATED*	PROJECT END DATE	PMO/MANAGEMENT SIGNOFF—SIGNATURE	DATE
EVALUATION TEAM MEMBERS		EXECUTIVE-SPONSOR SIGNOFF—SIGNATURE	DATE

CUSTOMER EVALUATION—CUSTOMER PERFORMANCE INDICATORS		
GENERAL CUSTOMER EVALUATION INDICATORS	1-WEAK-----STRONG-5	EVALUATION COMMENTS
Customer project participation	☐ ☐ ☐ ☐ ☐ ☐	
Customer cohesiveness–one voice	☐ ☐ ☐ ☐ ☐ ☐	
Commitment to project objectives	☐ ☐ ☐ ☐ ☐ ☐	
Commitment to project budget	☐ ☐ ☐ ☐ ☐ ☐	
Commitment to project schedule	☐ ☐ ☐ ☐ ☐ ☐	
Contribution to project scope change control	☐ ☐ ☐ ☐ ☐ ☐	
Timeliness of decisions and responses	☐ ☐ ☐ ☐ ☐ ☐	
Timeliness of deliverable(s) acceptance	☐ ☐ ☐ ☐ ☐ ☐	
Timeliness of invoice payment	☐ ☐ ☐ ☐ ☐ ☐	

CUSTOMER EVALUATION—KEY AND NOTABLE CONTACTS		
CUSTOMER CONTACT	POSITION/TITLE/ROLE	COMMENTS—PROJECT INFLUENCE

CUSTOMER EVALUATION—GENERAL COMMENTS AND DISCUSSION
GENERAL CUSTOMER RATING COMMENTS RELATIVE TO THE PROJECT EXPERIENCE

ACTION/ACTIVITY/REVIEW – RESPONSIBILITY	START	FINISH	ACTIVITY STATUS

ATTACHMENTS	PREPARER	DATE	FILE OR DOCUMENT LOCATION

4.1.3 CUSTOMER POSTING—Customer Satisfaction Survey

PROCESS OVERVIEW
REPLICATE FOR EACH SURVEY TO BE DISTRIBUTED AND COMPLETED—This customer satisfaction survey is to be completed by the customer at the end of the project (or other designated interim evaluation period). The overview section can be filled in prior to distribution.

TOOL PREPARATION	
PREPARED BY	DATE
CHECK IF REPLICATED (SPECIFY FILE LOCATION) ☐	

PROJECT	CUSTOMER

▷ CUSTOMER SATISFACTION SURVEY—OVERVIEW		
EVALUATION REQUEST TO CUSTOMER *Your comments are very important to us, and we appreciate the time you take to complete this survey form. Please rate our performance in each of the evaluation areas listed below.*	PROJECT MANAGER	PROJECT START DATE
	NATURE OF PRODUCTS AND SERVICES DELIVERED	PROJECT END DATE

CUSTOMER SATISFACTION SURVEY—EVALUATION		
EVALUATION AREAS (CIRCLE RATING-OR INSERT AT BEGINNING OF COMMENTS	EVALUATION AREA COMMENTS	GENERAL INQUIRY
1—What is your evaluation of the achievement of engagement objectives? (SATISFACTION WITH ENGAGEMENT RESULTS) 1 2 3 4 5 6 7 8 9 10 Poor---------------------------Satisfactory--------------------Excellent		IS THIS OUR FIRST PROJECT OR ENGAGEMENT WITH YOUR ORGANIZATION? ☐ *YES* ☐ *NO* ☐ *UNSURE*
2—What is your evaluation of the project team's technical performance? (SATISFACTION WITH PROJECT TEAM CAPABILITY) 1 2 3 4 5 6 7 8 9 10 Poor---------------------------Satisfactory--------------------Excellent		WERE YOU INVOLVED IN ANY OF OUR PREVIOUS WORK? ☐ *YES* ☐ *NO* ☐ *UNSURE*
3—What is your evaluation of the project manager? (SATISFACTION WITH PROJECT MANAGER CAPABILITY) 1 2 3 4 5 6 7 8 9 10 Poor---------------------------Satisfactory--------------------Excellent		COULD YOU WORK WITH US AGAIN ON ANOTHER PROJECT/ ENGAGEMENT? ☐ *YES* ☐ *NO* ☐ *UNSURE*
4—What is your evaluation of the technical approach used for product and service delivery? (SATISFACTION WITH THE DELIVERY PROCESS) 1 2 3 4 5 6 7 8 9 10 Poor---------------------------Satisfactory--------------------Excellent		WOULD YOU RECOMMEND US FOR USE BY OTHERS ON A PROJECT/ENGAGEMENT? ☐ *YES* ☐ *NO* ☐ *UNSURE*
5—What is your evaluation of the achievement of business objectives? (SATISFACTION WITH BUSINESS RESULTS) 1 2 3 4 5 6 7 8 9 10 Poor---------------------------Satisfactory--------------------Excellent		MAY WE USE YOU AS A REFERENCE FOR OUR PROJECT PERFORMANCE? ☐ *YES* ☐ *NO* ☐ *UNSURE*

CUSTOMER SATISFACTION SURVEY—REVIEWERS			
CUSTOMER—NAME/TITLE	SIGNATURE	DATE	COMMENTS
PROJECT MANAGER—NAME/TITLE	SIGNATURE	DATE	COMMENTS
PMO/MANAGEMENT—NAME/TITLE	SIGNATURE	DATE	COMMENTS

ACTION/ACTIVITY/REVIEW — RESPONSIBILITY	START	FINISH	ACTIVITY STATUS

ATTACHMENTS	PREPARER	DATE	FILE OR DOCUMENT LOCATION

4.1.4 CUSTOMER POSTING—Customer Transition and Closeout

PROCESS OVERVIEW
Review customer transition and closeout activities with the customer, and track their status toward completion. When completed, obtain the customer's sign-off for final deliverable acceptance and termination of the project. This generally concludes the customer business relationship portion of the project.

TOOL PREPARATION	
PREPARED BY	DATE

PROJECT	CUSTOMER

▷ CUSTOMER TRANSITION AND CLOSEOUT—OVERVIEW		
PROJECT TERMINATION REASON ☐ *ROUTINE* ☐ *NON-ROUTINE*	SCHEDULED END DATE	ACTUAL END DATE
SUMMARY OF CUSTOMER TRANSITION AND CLOSEOUT ACTIONS		

CUSTOMER TRANSITION AND CLOSEOUT—TRANSITION CHECKLIST			
CUSTOMER TRANSITION CHECKLIST	STATUS	ASSIGNED TO	CLOSE DATE
☐ *FINAL IMPLEMENTATION/INSTALLATION/TESTING* ☐ *PROCESS-SYSTEM-PRODUCT CUTOVER* ☐ *PROCESS-SYSTEM-PRODUCT TRAINING* ☐ *PROCESS-SYSTEM-PRODUCT CERTIFICATION* ☐ *OWNERSHIP HANDOVER* ☐ *PROCESS-SYSTEM-PRODUCT MAINTENANCE*			

CUSTOMER TRANSITION AND CLOSEOUT—PROJECT CLOSEOUT CHECKLIST			
CUSTOMER PROJECT CLOSEOUT CHECKLIST	STATUS	ASSIGNED TO	CLOSE DATE
☐ *PROJECT SCOPE REVIEW AND LESSONS LEARNED* ☐ *AGREEMENT ON ACCEPTANCE OF DELIVERABLES* ☐ *WORK ASSIGNMENT/WORK ORDER CLOSURE* ☐ *CUSTOMER SATISFACTION SURVEY* ☐ *ON SITE STAFF DEPARTURES (IF ANY)* ☐ *ON SITE FACILITY USE TERMINATION (IF ANY)* ☐ *FINAL INVOICE TO CUSTOMER* ☐ *CUSTOMER CONTRACT CLOSURE* ☐ *OTHER*			

CUSTOMER TRANSITION AND CLOSEOUT—ACKNOWLEDGMENT OF CLOSEOUT			
CUSTOMER REPRESENTATIVE	SIGNATURE	DATE	COMMENTS
PROJECT MANAGER	SIGNATURE	DATE	COMMENTS

ACTION/ACTIVITY/REVIEW – RESPONSIBILITY	START	FINISH	ACTIVITY STATUS

ATTACHMENTS	PREPARER	DATE	FILE OR DOCUMENT LOCATION

4.2.1 PROJECT POSTING—Project Lessons Learned

PROCESS OVERVIEW
Review the project from the perspective of planned and actual work performance, with a focus on what went well and what didn't. Reference the short checklist, and attempt an unbiased review. Identify conditions (lessons), but don't evaluate yet, as that's done in a separate activity. A facilitated group session is recommended.

TOOL PREPARATION	
PREPARED BY	DATE

PROJECT	CUSTOMER

▷ PROJECT LESSONS LEARNED—OVERVIEW			
WHAT WENT WELL	WHAT WENT NOT SO WELL	WHAT MAJOR ISSUES WERE UNEXPECTED	PROJECT LESSONS CHECKLIST ☐ *PROJECT MANAGEMENT BY PHASE* ☐ *PROJECT PLANNING* ☐ *PROJECT COMMUNICATION* ☐ *PROJECT SCOPE MANAGEMENT* ☐ *PROJECT TRACKING AND CONTROL*
SUMMARY OF LESSONS LEARNED (FROM FINDINGS BELOW)		SUMMARY OF PROMINENT RECOMMENDATIONS (FROM FINDINGS BELOW)	

PROJECT LESSONS LEARNED—FINDINGS LOG ▷		
LESSON—EVENT OR CONDITION	LESSON—IMPACT ON PROJECT OR BUSINESS	LESSON—RECOMMENDED IMPROVEMENT OR CHANGE

ACTION/ACTIVITY/REVIEW — RESPONSIBILITY	START	FINISH	ACTIVITY STATUS

ATTACHMENTS	PREPARER	DATE	FILE OR DOCUMENT LOCATION

4.2.2 PROJECT POSTING—Project Performance Evaluation

PROCESS OVERVIEW
REPLICATE FOR EACH EVALUATION PREPARED—Conduct an internal examination of project planning and management activities to rate indicators of project performance. Identify key and notable project contacts. Provide comments on managing this project's performance. Obtain management-level review.

TOOL PREPARATION	
PREPARED BY	DATE
CHECK IF REPLICATED (SPECIFY FILE LOCATION) ☐	

PROJECT	CUSTOMER

▷ PROJECT PERFORMANCE EVALUATION—OVERVIEW			
REASON FOR EVALUATION	PROJECT START DATE	PROJECT MANAGER—SIGNATURE	DATE
TYPE OF EVALUATION ☐ *INDIVIDUAL* ☐ *GROUP* ☐ *CONSOLIDATED*	PROJECT END DATE	PMO-MANAGEMENT—SIGNATURE	DATE
EVALUATION TEAM MEMBERS		EXECUTIVE-SPONSOR—SIGNATURE	DATE

PROJECT PERFORMANCE EVALUATION—PROJECT PERFORMANCE INDICATORS		
GENERAL PROJECT EVALUATION INDICATORS	1-WEAK- - - - -STRONG-5	EVALUATION COMMENTS
Project planning effort	☐ ☐ ☐ ☐ ☐ ☐	
Project scope management and change control	☐ ☐ ☐ ☐ ☐ ☐	
Project variance management (track & control)	☐ ☐ ☐ ☐ ☐ ☐	
Commitment to project objectives	☐ ☐ ☐ ☐ ☐ ☐	
Commitment to project budget	☐ ☐ ☐ ☐ ☐ ☐	
Commitment to project schedule	☐ ☐ ☐ ☐ ☐ ☐	
Commitment to project resource utilization	☐ ☐ ☐ ☐ ☐ ☐	
Timeliness of project communication	☐ ☐ ☐ ☐ ☐ ☐	
Timeliness of project deliverables	☐ ☐ ☐ ☐ ☐ ☐	

PROJECT PERFORMANCE EVALUATION—KEY AND NOTABLE INDIVIDUALS		
CUSTOMER CONTACT	POSITION/TITLE/ROLE	COMMENTS—PROJECT INFLUENCE

PROJECT PERFORMANCE EVALUATION—GENERAL COMMENTS AND DISCUSSION
GENERAL PROJECT RATING COMMENTS RELATIVE TO PROJECT PERFORMANCE

ACTION/ACTIVITY/REVIEW — RESPONSIBILITY	START	FINISH	ACTIVITY STATUS

ATTACHMENTS	PREPARER	DATE	FILE OR DOCUMENT LOCATION

4.2.3 PROJECT POSTING—Project Administration Closeout

PROCESS OVERVIEW
Compile project materials, work products and documents as a reference list and prepare them for archiving. When completed, obtain archive manager and project manager signoff for this aspect of the project. This is normally the last closeout performed, and it concludes the communication and correspondence of the project.

TOOL PREPARATION	
PREPARED BY	DATE

PROJECT	CUSTOMER

⊳ PROJECT ADMINISTRATION CLOSEOUT—OVERVIEW		
PROJECT TERMINATION REASON ☐ *ROUTINE* ☐ *NON-ROUTINE*	SCHEDULED END DATE	ACTUAL END DATE
SUMMARY OF PROJECT ADMINISTRATION CLOSEOUT ACTIONS		

PROJECT ADMINISTRATION CLOSEOUT—PROJECT TECHNICAL CLOSEOUT CHECKLIST			
PROJECT ADMINISTRATION CHECKLIST—TECHNICAL	STATUS	ARCHIVE LOCATION	CLOSE DATE
☐ *PROJECT DELIVERABLES (COPIES)* ☐ *PROJECT TECHNICAL WORKING PAPERS* ☐ *PROJECT DESIGN AND REFERENCE DOCUMENTS* ☐ *PROJECT TEST AND ACCEPTANCE DOCUMENTS* ☐ *PROJECT SOFTWARE MATERIALS*			

PROJECT ADMINISTRATION CLOSEOUT—PROJECT MANAGEMENT CLOSEOUT CHECKLIST			
PROJECT ADMINISTRATION CHECKLIST—PM	STATUS	ARCHIVE LOCATION	CLOSE DATE
☐ *PROJECT BUSINESS CASE* ☐ *PROJECT REQUIREMENTS* ☐ *PROJECT PLANS (SEPARATE CLOSEOUT TOOL)* ☐ *PROJECT AUDITS* ☐ *PROJECT CONTRACT (SEPARATE CLOSEOUT TOOL)* ☐ *PROJECT CORRESPONDENCE* ☐ *PROJECT MANAGEMENT TOOLKIT* ☐ *PROJECT MEETING DOCUMENTS* ☐ *PROJECT AND PROJECT MANAGEMENT REPORTS* ☐ *PROJECT LESSONS LEARNED AND EVALUATIONS*			

PROJECT ADMINISTRATION CLOSEOUT—ACKNOWLEDGMENT OF CLOSEOUT			
PROJECT ARCHIVE MANAGER	SIGNATURE	DATE	COMMENTS
PROJECT MANAGER	SIGNATURE	DATE	COMMENTS

ACTION/ACTIVITY/REVIEW — RESPONSIBILITY	START	FINISH	ACTIVITY STATUS

ATTACHMENTS	PREPARER	DATE	FILE OR DOCUMENT LOCATION

4.2.4 PROJECT POSTING—Project Plan Closeout

PROCESS OVERVIEW
Compile project planning documents, including materials used for project estimating and any proposal documentation. List and prepare them for archiving. When completed, obtain plan manager and project manager signoff. This concludes the plan documentation and change control portions of the project.

TOOL PREPARATION	
PREPARED BY	DATE

PROJECT	CUSTOMER

▷ PROJECT PLAN CLOSEOUT—OVERVIEW		
PROJECT TERMINATION REASON ☐ *ROUTINE* ☐ *NON-ROUTINE*	SCHEDULED END DATE	ACTUAL END DATE
SUMMARY OF PROJECT PLAN CLOSEOUT ACTIONS		

PROJECT PLAN CLOSEOUT—PLANNING MATERIALS CLOSEOUT CHECKLIST			
PROJECT PLAN CLOSEOUT CHECKLIST—MATERIALS	STATUS	POST-USE EVALUATION	CLOSE DATE
☐ *PROJECT ESTIMATING WORKSHEETS*		☐ *POOR* ☐ *FAIR* ☐ *GOOD*	
☐ *PROJECT PROPOSAL DOCUMENTS & WORKSHEETS*		☐ *POOR* ☐ *FAIR* ☐ *GOOD*	
☐ *VENDOR SOLICITATION(S) AND RESPONSES*		☐ *POOR* ☐ *FAIR* ☐ *GOOD*	
☐ *PROJECT SUPPORT PLANS*		☐ *POOR* ☐ *FAIR* ☐ *GOOD*	

PROJECT PLAN CLOSEOUT—PRIMARY PLAN CLOSEOUT CHECKLIST			
PROJECT PLAN CLOSEOUT CHECKLIST—PRIMARY PLANS	STATUS	POST-USE EVALUATION	CLOSE DATE
☐ *PROJECT WORK PLAN*		☐ *POOR* ☐ *FAIR* ☐ *GOOD*	
☐ *PROJECT RISK MANAGEMENT PLAN*		☐ *POOR* ☐ *FAIR* ☐ *GOOD*	
☐ *PROJECT QUALITY MANAGEMENT PLAN*		☐ *POOR* ☐ *FAIR* ☐ *GOOD*	
☐ *PROJECT COMMUNICATION PLAN*		☐ *POOR* ☐ *FAIR* ☐ *GOOD*	
☐ *PROJECT CHANGE CONTROL PLAN*		☐ *POOR* ☐ *FAIR* ☐ *GOOD*	
☐ *PROJECT STAFF MANAGEMENT PLAN*		☐ *POOR* ☐ *FAIR* ☐ *GOOD*	
☐ *PROJECT VENDOR MANAGEMENT PLAN*		☐ *POOR* ☐ *FAIR* ☐ *GOOD*	
☐ *PROJECT MANAGEMENT OVERSIGHT PLAN*		☐ *POOR* ☐ *FAIR* ☐ *GOOD*	
☐ *PROJECT MANAGEMENT AUDIT AND REVIEW PLAN*		☐ *POOR* ☐ *FAIR* ☐ *GOOD*	
☐ *PROJECT SUPPLY AND EQUIPMENT PLAN*		☐ *POOR* ☐ *FAIR* ☐ *GOOD*	
☐ *PROJECT FACILIT MANAGEMENT PLAN*		☐ *POOR* ☐ *FAIR* ☐ *GOOD*	

PROJECT PLAN CLOSEOUT—ACKNOWLEDGMENT OF CLOSEOUT			
PROJECT PLAN MANAGER	SIGNATURE	DATE	COMMENTS
PROJECT MANAGER	SIGNATURE	DATE	COMMENTS

ACTION/ACTIVITY/REVIEW — RESPONSIBILITY	START	FINISH	ACTIVITY STATUS

ATTACHMENTS	PREPARER	DATE	FILE OR DOCUMENT LOCATION

4.3.1 STAFF POSTING—Staff Lessons Learned

PROCESS OVERVIEW
Review the project from the perspective of planned and actual project staffing, with a focus on what went well and what didn't. Reference the short checklist, and attempt an unbiased review. Identify conditions (lessons), but don't evaluate yet, as that's done in a separate activity. A facilitated group session is recommended.

TOOL PREPARATION	
PREPARED BY	DATE

PROJECT	CUSTOMER

▷ STAFF LESSONS LEARNED—OVERVIEW			
WHAT WENT WELL	WHAT WENT NOT SO WELL	WHAT MAJOR ISSUES WERE UNEXPECTED	STAFF LESSONS CHECKLIST ☐ *STAFF ACTIVIIES BY PHASE* ☐ *STAFF QUALIFICATION* ☐ *STAFF REPORTING/COMMUNICATION* ☐ *STAFF SCOPE MANAGEMENT* ☐ *STAFF PROJECT COMMITMENT*
SUMMARY OF LESSONS LEARNED (FROM FINDINGS BELOW)		SUMMARY OF PROMINENT RECOMMENDATIONS (FROM FINDINGS BELOW)	

STAFF LESSONS LEARNED—FINDINGS LOG ▷		
LESSON—EVENT OR CONDITION	LESSON—IMPACT ON PROJECT OR BUSINESS	LESSON—RECOMMENDED IMPROVEMENT OR CHANGE

ACTION/ACTIVITY/REVIEW — RESPONSIBILITY	START	FINISH	ACTIVITY STATUS

ATTACHMENTS	PREPARER	DATE	FILE OR DOCUMENT LOCATION

4.3.2 STAFF POSTING—Staff Performance Evaluation

PROCESS OVERVIEW
REPLICATE FOR EACH EVALUATION PREPARED—This internal evaluation is prepared by the project manager or any supervisor of a distinct group within the project team to evaluate collective team performance. Identify key and notable project contacts. Obtain management-level review.

TOOL PREPARATION	
PREPARED BY	DATE
CHECK IF REPLICATED (SPECIFY FILE LOCATION) ☐	

PROJECT	CUSTOMER

▷ STAFF PERFORMANCE EVALUATION—OVERVIEW			
REASON FOR EVALUATION	PROJECT START DATE	PROJECT MANAGER—SIGNATURE	DATE
TYPE OF EVALUATION ☐ *INDIVIDUAL* ☐ *GROUP* ☐ *CONSOLIDATED*	PROJECT END DATE	PMO-MANAGEMENT—SIGNATURE	DATE
GROUP OR SUBTEAM SUPERVISOR	SUPERVISOR ROLE	EXECUTIVE-SPONSOR—SIGNATURE	DATE

STAFF PERFORMANCE EVALUATION—TEAM EVALUATION (COLLECTIVE PERFORMANCE)	
TEAM EVALUATION AREAS (CIRCLE RATING OR INSERT IN COMMENTS) 1—Work aligned with project objectives and business purpose 1 2 3 4 5 6 7 8 9 10 Poor---------------------------Satisfactory--------------------Excellent 2—Technical performance capability 1 2 3 4 5 6 7 8 9 10 Poor---------------------------Satisfactory--------------------Excellent 3—Technical performance quality 1 2 3 4 5 6 7 8 9 10 Poor---------------------------Satisfactory--------------------Excellent 4—Technical performance timeliness (including time commitment) 1 2 3 4 5 6 7 8 9 10 Poor---------------------------Satisfactory--------------------Excellent	TEAM EVALUATION AREA COMMENTS

STAFF PERFORMANCE EVALUATION—KEY AND NOTABLE INDIVIDUALS		
STAFF MEMBER	POSITION/TITLE/ROLE	COMMENTS—PROJECT INFLUENCE

STAFF PERFORMANCE EVALUATION—GENERAL COMMENTS AND DISCUSSION
GENERAL STAFF RATING COMMENTS RELATIVE TO COLLECTIVE PROJECT TEAM PERFORMANCE

ACTION/ACTIVITY/REVIEW – RESPONSIBILITY	START	FINISH	ACTIVITY STATUS

ATTACHMENTS	PREPARER	DATE	FILE OR DOCUMENT LOCATION

4.3.3 STAFF POSTING—Staff Performance Recognition

PROCESS OVERVIEW
REPLICATE FOR EACH RECOGNITION EVENT—Specify the location and planned activities for the event. Prepare citations for staff members who have excelled in project work performance. Be sure to include staff members who left the project team prior to its official closure. Identify and notify the event participants.

TOOL PREPARATION	
PREPARED BY	DATE
CHECK IF REPLICATED (SPECIFY FILE LOCATION) ☐	

PROJECT	CUSTOMER

⊳ STAFF PERFORMANCE RECOGNITION—EVENT OVERVIEW				
RECOGNITION EVENT TYPE ☐ *FORMAL EVENT* ☐ *INFORMAL EVENT* ☐ *NO EVENT—JUST RECOGNITION*		ESTIMATED DURATION	START TIME	START DATE
EVENT LOCATION—ADDRESS	EVENT LOCATION		EVENT ARRANGEMENTS AND NOTES	
RECOGNITION AND EVENT COORDINATOR	OFFICE TELEPHONE	MOBIL TELEPHONE	FAX	EMAIL

STAFF PERFORMANCE RECOGNITION—EVENT AGENDA			
EVENT ACTIVITY	ESTIMATED START	ACTIVITY LEADER	COMMENTS

STAFF PERFORMANCE RECOGNITION—MANAGEMENT AND GUEST PARTICIPANTS				
NAME	RECOGNITION ROLE	CONTACTED	CONFIRMED	MANAGEMENT AND GUEST PARTICIPATION NOTES

STAFF PERFORMANCE RECOGNITION—RECOGNIZED STAFF LIST				
NAME	TYPE OF RECOGNITION	CONTACTED	CONFIRMED	STAFF RECOGNITION NOTES

ACTION/ACTIVITY/REVIEW — RESPONSIBILITY	START	FINISH	ACTIVITY STATUS

ATTACHMENTS	PREPARER	DATE	FILE OR DOCUMENT LOCATION

4.3.4 STAFF POSTING—Staff Reassignment and Closeout

PROCESS OVERVIEW
Monitor staff departures from the project upon completion of assignments and time commitments. Use the departure checklist for individual disposition, and fill in the checklist for en mass team departures at the end of the project. List actual staff departures from the project team.

TOOL PREPARATION	
PREPARED BY	DATE

PROJECT	CUSTOMER

▷ STAFF REASSIGNMENT AND CLOSEOUT—OVERVIEW				
PROJECT MANAGER		PROJECT DURATION	PROJECT START DATE	PROJECT FINISH DATE
STAFF ASSSIGNED BY PHASE (RUNNING TOTAL)	STAFF CURRENTLY ASSIGNED BY PHASE		STAFF DEPARTURES BY PHASE	
1–PROFILE 2–PLAN 3–PERFORM 4–POST	1–PROFILE 2–PLAN 3–PERFORM 4–POST		1–PROFILE 2–PLAN 3–PERFORM 4–POST	
STAFF MANAGEMENT COODINATOR	OFFICE TELEPHONE	MOBIL TELEPHONE	FAX	EMAIL

STAFF REASSIGNMENT AND CLOSEOUT—DEPARTURE CHECKLIST			
STAFF DEPARTURE CHECKLIST	STATUS	ASSIGNED TO	CLOSE DATE
☐ *PROJECT DOCUMENTS RETURNED*			
☐ *PROJECT COMPUTERS RETURNED*			
☐ *PROJECT EQUIPMENT/TOOLKITS RETURNED*			
☐ *WORKING PAPERS TRANSFERRED/ARCHIVED*			
☐ *WORK-IN-PROCESS HANDOVER*			
☐ *STAFF MEMBER PERFORMANCE EVALUATION*			
☐ *STAFF MEMBER ASSIGNMENT/DISPOSITION*			

STAFF REASSIGNMENT AND CLOSEOUT—DEPARTURE TRACKING LIST				

ACTION/ACTIVITY/REVIEW – RESPONSIBILITY	START	FINISH	ACTIVITY STATUS

ATTACHMENTS	PREPARER	DATE	FILE OR DOCUMENT LOCATION

4.4.1 VENDOR POSTING—Vendor Lessons Learned

PROCESS OVERVIEW
Review the project from the perspective of vendor activity and interactions, with a focus on what went well and what didn't. Reference the short checklist, and attempt an unbiased review. Identify conditions (lessons), but don't evaluate yet, as that's done in a separate activity. A facilitated group session is recommended.

TOOL PREPARATION	
PREPARED BY	DATE

PROJECT	CUSTOMER

⊳ VENDOR LESSONS LEARNED—OVERVIEW			
WHAT WENT WELL	WHAT WENT NOT SO WELL	WHAT MAJOR ISSUES WERE UNEXPECTED	VENDOR LESSONS CHECKLIST ☐ *VENDOR ACTIVIIES BY PHASE* ☐ *VENDOR QUALIFICATION* ☐ *VENDOR COMMUNICATION* ☐ *VENDODR CONTRACT MANAGEMENT* ☐ *VENDOR PROJECT COMMITMENT*
SUMMARY OF LESSONS LEARNED (FROM FINDINGS BELOW)		SUMMARY OF PROMINENT RECOMMENDATIONS (FROM FINDINGS BELOW)	

VENDOR LESSONS LEARNED—FINDINGS LOG ⊳		
LESSON—EVENT OR CONDITION	LESSON—IMPACT ON PROJECT OR BUSINESS	LESSON—RECOMMENDED IMPROVEMENT OR CHANGE

ACTION/ACTIVITY/REVIEW – RESPONSIBILITY	START	FINISH	ACTIVITY STATUS

ATTACHMENTS	PREPARER	DATE	FILE OR DOCUMENT LOCATION

4.4.2 VENDOR POSTING—Vendor Performance Evaluation

PROCESS OVERVIEW
REPLICATE FOR EACH VENDOR EVALUATION PREPARED—Conduct an internal evaluation of the project experience with the selected vendor(s) to rate indicators of vendor performance. Identify key and notable vendor contacts, and provide comments on working with each vendor.

TOOL PREPARATION	
PREPARED BY	DATE
CHECK IF REPLICATED (SPECIFY FILE LOCATION) ☐	

PROJECT	CUSTOMER

▷ VENDOR PERFORMANCE EVALUATION—OVERVIEW			
REASON FOR EVALUATION	PROJECT START DATE	PROJECT MANAGER—SIGNATURE	DATE
VENDOR	PROJECT END DATE	PMO-MANAGEMENT—SIGNATURE	DATE
VENDOR PROJECT MANAGER	VENDOR ROLE	EXECUTIVE-SPONSOR—SIGNATURE	DATE

VENDOR PERFORMANCE EVALUATION—VENDOR EVALUATION	
VENDOR EVALUATION AREAS (CIRCLE RATING) 1—Fulfillment of deliverables 1 2 3 4 5 6 7 8 9 10 Poor---------------------------Satisfactory--------------------Excellent 2—Technical performance capability 1 2 3 4 5 6 7 8 9 10 Poor---------------------------Satisfactory--------------------Excellent 3—Technical performance quality 1 2 3 4 5 6 7 8 9 10 Poor---------------------------Satisfactory--------------------Excellent 4—Technical performance timeliness (including time commitment) 1 2 3 4 5 6 7 8 9 10 Poor---------------------------Satisfactory--------------------Excellent	VENDOR EVALUATION AREA COMMENTS

VENDOR PERFORMANCE EVALUATION—KEY AND NOTABLE INDIVIDUALS		
VENDOR CONTACT	POSITION/TITLE/ROLE	COMMENTS—PROJECT INFLUENCE

VENDOR PERFORMANCE EVALUATION—GENERAL COMMENTS AND DISCUSSION
GENERAL VENDOR RATING COMMENTS RELATIVE TO VENDOR PERFORMANCE

ACTION/ACTIVITY/REVIEW — RESPONSIBILITY	START	FINISH	ACTIVITY STATUS

ATTACHMENTS	PREPARER	DATE	FILE OR DOCUMENT LOCATION

4.4.3 VENDOR POSTING—Vendor Invoice Management

PROCESS OVERVIEW
Post and manage vendor invoices for accuracy and timely submittal, as received throughout the project. Track vendor invoice receipts and payments, and perform invoice actions as necessary. Perform closeout of vendor invoices in association with the final payment to each vendor.

TOOL PREPARATION	
PREPARED BY	DATE

PROJECT	CUSTOMER

⊳ VENDOR INVOICE MANAGEMENT—OVERVIEW				
PROCEDURES FOR VENDOR INVOICE SUBMITTAL		SUBMITTAL TERMS—WHEN VENDOR SUBMITTAL IS DUE		
		PAYMENT TERMS—WHEN VENDOR PAYMENT IS DUE		
		TERMS FOR FINAL VENDOR INVOICE PAYMENT		
PROJECT INVOICE MANAGER	OFFICE TELEPHONE	MOBIL TELEPHONE	FAX	EMAIL

VENDOR INVOICE MANAGEMENT—VENDOR INVOICE TRACKING LOG ⊳						
VENDOR ID	VENDOR ORGANIZATION	INVOICE DATE	INVOICE DESCRIPTION	INVOICE AMOUNT	PAID AMOUNT	PAID DATE
			VENDOR TOTALS TO DATE			

VENDOR INVOICE MANAGEMENT—VENDOR INVOICE MANAGEMENT ACTIONS				
VENDOR ID	VENDOR ORGANIZATION	ACTION DATE	ACTION DESCRIPTION	COMMENTS

VENDOR INVOICE MANAGEMENT—VENDOR INVOICE CLOSEOUT						
VENDOR ID	VENDOR ORGANIZATION	TOTAL INVOICES	CONTRACT REFERENCE	TOTAL BILLED	TOTAL AMOUNT	LAST PAY DATE

ACTION/ACTIVITY/REVIEW — RESPONSIBILITY	START	FINISH	ACTIVITY STATUS

ATTACHMENTS	PREPARER	DATE	FILE OR DOCUMENT LOCATION

4.4.4 VENDOR POSTING—Vendor Contract Closeout

PROCESS OVERVIEW
REPLICATE FOR EACH VENDORS DEPARTURE—Review vendor closeout activities with the vendor, and track their status toward completion. When completed, obtain the vendor's sign-off for termination of vendor participation in the project. This generally concludes the vendor's business relationship portion of the project.

TOOL PREPARATION	
PREPARED BY	DATE
CHECK IF REPLICATED (SPECIFY FILE LOCATION) ☐	

PROJECT	CUSTOMER

▷ VENDOR CONTRACT CLOSEOUT—OVERVIEW		
VENDOR CLOSEOUT REASON ☐ *ROUTINE* ☐ *NON-ROUTINE*	SCHEDULED END DATE	ACTUAL END DATE
SUMMARY OF VENDOR CLOSEOUT ACTIONS		

VENDOR CONTRACT CLOSEOUT—VENDOR WORK TRANSITION CHECKLIST			
VENDOR WORK TRANSITION CHECKLIST	STATUS	ASSIGNED TO	CLOSE DATE
☐ *FINAL IMPLEMENTATION/INSTALLATION/TESTING* ☐ *PROCESS-SYSTEM-PRODUCT CUTOVER* ☐ *PROCESS-SYSTEM-PRODUCT TRAINING* ☐ *PROCESS-SYSTEM-PRODUCT CERTIFICATION* ☐ *OTHER*			

VENDOR CONTRACT CLOSEOUT—VENDOR CLOSEOUT CHECKLIST			
VENDOR CLOSEOUT CHECKLIST	STATUS	ASSIGNED TO	CLOSE DATE
☐ *PROJECT SCOPE REVIEW ANDF LESSONS LEARNED* ☐ *AGREEMENT ON ACCEPTANCE OF DELIVERABLES* ☐ *VENDOR ASSIGNMENT WORK ORDER CLOSURE* ☐ *DATA AND RECORDS CONVEYANCE FROM VENDOR* ☐ *VENDOR EQUIPMENT/TOOLKIT RETURN* ☐ *ON THE SITE VENDOR STAFF DEPARTURES (IF ANY)* ☐ *ON SITE FACILITY USE TERMINATION (IF ANY)* ☐ *FINAL INVOICE FROM VENDOR* ☐ *VENDOR CONTRACT CLOSURE*			

VENDOR CONTRACT CLOSEOUT—ACKNOWLEDGMENT OF CLOSEOUT			
VENDOR REPRESENTATIVE	SIGNATURE	DATE	COMMENTS
PROJECT MANAGER	SIGNATURE	DATE	COMMENTS

ACTION/ACTIVITY/REVIEW – RESPONSIBILITY	START	FINISH	ACTIVITY STATUS

ATTACHMENTS	PREPARER	DATE	FILE OR DOCUMENT LOCATION

4.5.1 BUSINESS POSTING—Business Lessons Learned

PROCESS OVERVIEW
Review the project from the perspective of business activity and interactions, with a focus on what went well and what didn't. Reference the short checklist, and attempt an unbiased review. Identify conditions (lessons), but don't evaluate yet, as that's done in a separate activity. A facilitated group session is recommended.

TOOL PREPARATION	
PREPARED BY	DATE

PROJECT	CUSTOMER

▷ BUSINESS LESSONS LEARNED—OVERVIEW			
WHAT WENT WELL	WHAT WENT NOT SO WELL	WHAT MAJOR ISSUES WERE UNEXPECTED	BUSINESS LESSONS CHECKLIST ☐ *BUSINESS ACTIVIIES BY PHASE* ☐ *BUSINESS PORTFOLIO MANAGEMENT* ☐ *BUSINESS COMMUNICATION* ☐ *BUSINESS CONTRACT MANAGEMENT* ☐ *BUSINESS COMMITMENT TO PROJECT*
SUMMARY OF LESSONS LEARNED (FROM FINDINGS BELOW)		SUMMARY OF PROMINENT RECOMMENDATIONS (FROM FINDINGS BELOW)	

BUSINESS LESSONS LEARNED—FINDINGS LOG ▷		
LESSON—EVENT OR CONDITION	LESSON—IMPACT ON PROJECT OR BUSINESS	LESSON—RECOMMENDED IMPROVEMENT OR CHANGE

ACTION/ACTIVITY/REVIEW — RESPONSIBILITY	START	FINISH	ACTIVITY STATUS

ATTACHMENTS	PREPARER	DATE	FILE OR DOCUMENT LOCATION

4.5.2 BUSINESS POSTING—Business Performance Evaluation

PROCESS OVERVIEW
REPLICATE FOR EACH EVALUATION PREPARED—Conduct an internal examination of project business activities to rate indicators of business performance. Identify key and notable business contacts. Provide comments on managing this project's business performance. Obtain management-level review.

TOOL PREPARATION	
PREPARED BY	DATE
CHECK IF REPLICATED (SPECIFY FILE LOCATION) ☐	

PROJECT	CUSTOMER

▷ BUSINESS PERFORMANCE EVALUATION—OVERVIEW			
REASON FOR EVALUATION	PROJECT START DATE	PROJECT MANAGER—SIGNATURE	DATE
TYPE OF EVALUATION ☐ *INDIVIDUAL* ☐ *GROUP* ☐ *CONSOLIDATED*	PROJECT END DATE	PMO-MANAGEMENT—SIGNATURE	DATE
EVALUATION TEAM MEMBERS		EXECUTIVE-SPONSOR—SIGNATURE	DATE

BUSINESS PERFORMANCE EVALUATION—BUSINESS PERFORMANCE INDICATORS		
GENERAL PROJECT EVALUATION INDICATORS	1-WEAK- - - - -STRONG-5	EVALUATION COMMENTS
Business planning effort	☐ ☐ ☐ ☐ ☐ ☐	
Project classification	☐ ☐ ☐ ☐ ☐ ☐	
Project portfolio management	☐ ☐ ☐ ☐ ☐ ☐	
Return on investment—customer loyalty	☐ ☐ ☐ ☐ ☐ ☐	
Return on investment—financial	☐ ☐ ☐ ☐ ☐ ☐	
Return on investment—market position	☐ ☐ ☐ ☐ ☐ ☐	
Commitment to project resource allocations	☐ ☐ ☐ ☐ ☐ ☐	
Consistency of business case	☐ ☐ ☐ ☐ ☐ ☐	
Use of new concepts/technology	☐ ☐ ☐ ☐ ☐ ☐	

BUSINESS PERFORMANCE EVALUATION—KEY AND NOTABLE INDIVIDUALS		
CUSTOMER CONTACT	POSITION/TITLE/ROLE	COMMENTS—PROJECT INFLUENCE

BUSINESS PERFORMANCE EVALUATION—GENERAL COMMENTS AND DISCUSSION
GENERAL CUSTOMER RATING COMMENTS RELATIVE TO BUSINESS PERFORMANCE

ACTION/ACTIVITY/REVIEW – RESPONSIBILITY	START	FINISH	ACTIVITY STATUS

ATTACHMENTS	PREPARER	DATE	FILE OR DOCUMENT LOCATION

4.5.3 BUSINESS POSTING—Business Invoice Management

PROCESS OVERVIEW
Post and manage business invoices for accuracy and timely submittal, as submitted throughout the project. Track customer invoice submittals and payments, and perform invoice actions as necessary. Perform closeout of business invoices in association with the final payment from the customer.

TOOL PREPARATION	
PREPARED BY	DATE

PROJECT	CUSTOMER

▷ BUSINESS INVOICE MANAGEMENT—OVERVIEW				
PROCEDURES FOR CUSTOMER INVOICE SUBMITTAL		SUBMITTAL TERMS—WHEN INVOICE SUBMITTAL IS DUE		
		PAYMENT TERMS—WHEN CUSOMER PAYMENT IS DUE		
		TERMS FOR FINAL CUSTOMER INVOICE PAYMENT		
PROJECT INVOICE MANAGER	OFFICE TELEPHONE	MOBIL TELEPHONE	FAX	EMAIL

BUSINESS INVOICE MANAGEMENT—CUSTOMER INVOICE TRACKING LOG ▷						
VENDOR ID	SUBMITTAL ORGANIZATION	INVOICE DATE	INVOICE DESCRIPTION	INVOICE AMOUNT	PAID AMOUNT	PAID DATE
			CUSTOMER INVOICE TOTALS TO DATE			

BUSINESS INVOICE MANAGEMENT—CUSTOMER INVOICE ACTIONS				
VENDOR ID	SUBMITTAL ORGANIZATION	ACTION DATE	ACTION DESCRIPTION	COMMENTS

BUSINESS INVOICE MANAGEMENT—CUSTOMER INVOICE CLOSEOUT						
VENDOR ID	SUBMITTAL ORGANIZATION	TOTAL INVOICES	CONTRACT REFERENCE	TOTAL BILLED	TOTAL PAID	LAST PAY DATE

ACTION/ACTIVITY/REVIEW — RESPONSIBILITY	START	FINISH	ACTIVITY STATUS	

ATTACHMENTS	PREPARER	DATE	FILE OR DOCUMENT LOCATION	

4.5.4 BUSINESS POSTING—Business Contract Closeout

PROCESS OVERVIEW
Review business closeout activities, and track their status toward completion. When completed, obtain the PMO or portfolio manager's sign-off for termination of project business activities. This generally concludes the formal activities of the project.

TOOL PREPARATION	
PREPARED BY	DATE

PROJECT	CUSTOMER

⊳ BUSINESS CONTRACT CLOSEOUT—OVERVIEW		
PROJECT CLOSEOUT REASON ☐ *ROUTINE* ☐ *NON-ROUTINE*	SCHEDULED END DATE	ACTUAL END DATE
SUMMARY OF BUSINESS CLOSEOUT ACTIONS		

BUSINESS CONTRACT CLOSEOUT—BUSINESS ADMINISTRATION CLOSEOUT CHECKLIST			
BUSINESS ADMINISTRATION CLOSEOUT CHECKLIST	STATUS	ASSIGNED TO	CLOSE DATE
☐ *CONTRACT DOCUMENT CONSOLIDATION* ☐ *POST-PROJECT FINANCIAL ANALYSIS/AUDIT* ☐ *POST-PROJECT MANAGEMENT REVIEW* ☐ *PROJECT PORTFOLIO MANAGEMENT CLOSEOUT* ☐ *PMO OVERSIGHT AND SUPPORT REVIEW* ☐ *OTHER*			

BUSINESS CONTRACT CLOSEOUT—BUSINESS CONTRACT CLOSEOUT CHECKLIST			
BUSINESS CONTRACT CLOSEOUT CHECKLIST	STATUS	ASSIGNED TO	CLOSE DATE
☐ *PROJECT COST & REVENUE GENERATION REVIEW* ☐ *PROJECT CUSTOMER SATISFACTION REVIEW* ☐ *PROJECT MANAGEMENT EFFICIENCY REVIEW* ☐ *CONTRACT TERMS AND CONDITIONS FULFILLMENT* ☐ *CONTRACT DELIVERABLES FULFILLMENT* ☐ *FINAL INVOICE TO CUSTOMER* ☐ *FINAL PAYMENT FROM CUSTOMER* ☐ *BUSINESS CONTRACT CLOSURE* ☐ *OTHER*			

BUSINESS CONTRACT CLOSEOUT—ACKNOWLEDGMENT OF CLOSEOUT			
PMO/PORTFOLIO MANAAGER	SIGNATURE	DATE	COMMENTS
PROJECT MANAGER	SIGNATURE	DATE	COMMENTS

ACTION/ACTIVITY/REVIEW — RESPONSIBILITY	START	FINISH	ACTIVITY STATUS

ATTACHMENTS	PREPARER	DATE	FILE OR DOCUMENT LOCATION

4.6.1 MANAGEMENT POSTING—Management Lessons Learned

PROCESS OVERVIEW
Review the project from the perspective of management activity and interactions, with a focus on what went well and what didn't. Reference the short checklist, and attempt an unbiased review. Identify conditions (lessons), but don't evaluate yet, as that's done in a separate activity. A facilitated group session is recommended.

TOOL PREPARATION	
PREPARED BY	DATE

PROJECT	CUSTOMER

▷ MANAGEMENT LESSONS LEARNED—OVERVIEW			
WHAT WENT WELL	WHAT WENT NOT SO WELL	WHAT MAJOR ISSUES WERE UNEXPECTED	MANAGEMENT LESSONS CHECKLIST ☐ *MANAGEMENT ACTIVIIES BY PHASE* ☐ *MANAGEMENT AND PMO SUPPORT* ☐ *MANAGEMENT COMMUNICATION* ☐ *MANAGEMENT GUIDANCE* ☐ *MANAGEMENT COMMITMENT*
SUMMARY OF LESSONS LEARNED (FROM FINDINGS BELOW)		SUMMARY OF PROMINENT RECOMMENDATIONS (FROM FINDINGS BELOW)	

MANAGEMENT LESSONS LEARNED—FINDINGS LOG ▷		
LESSON—EVENT OR CONDITION	LESSON—IMPACT ON PROJECT OR BUSINESS	LESSON—RECOMMENDED IMPROVEMENT OR CHANGE

ACTION/ACTIVITY/REVIEW — RESPONSIBILITY	START	FINISH	ACTIVITY STATUS

ATTACHMENTS	PREPARER	DATE	FILE OR DOCUMENT LOCATION

4.6.2 MANAGEMENT POSTING—Management Evaluation

PROCESS OVERVIEW
REPLICATE FOR EACH EVALUATION PREPARED—Conduct an internal examination of PMO/senior manger activities to rate indicators of management performance. Identify key and notable management contacts. Provide comments on managing this project's management performance. Obtain management-level review.

TOOL PREPARATION	
PREPARED BY	DATE
CHECK IF REPLICATED (SPECIFY FILE LOCATION) ☐	

PROJECT	CUSTOMER

▷ MANAGEMENT EVALUATION—OVERVIEW			
REASON FOR EVALUATION	PROJECT START DATE	PROJECT MANAGER—SIGNATURE	DATE
TYPE OF EVALUATION ☐ *INDIVIDUAL* ☐ *GROUP* ☐ *CONSOLIDATED*	PROJECT END DATE	PMO-MANAGEMENT—SIGNATURE	DATE
EVALUATION TEAM MEMBERS		EXECUTIVE-SPONSOR—SIGNATURE	DATE

MANAGEMENT EVALUATION—CUSTOMER PERFORMANCE INDICATORS		
GENERAL CUSTOMER EVALUATION INDICATORS	1-WEAK-----STRONG-5	EVALUATION COMMENTS
PMO/management project participation	☐ ☐ ☐ ☐ ☐ ☐	
PMO/management cohesiveness—one voice	☐ ☐ ☐ ☐ ☐ ☐	
Commitment to project technical approach	☐ ☐ ☐ ☐ ☐ ☐	
Commitment to project budget	☐ ☐ ☐ ☐ ☐ ☐	
Commitment to project schedule	☐ ☐ ☐ ☐ ☐ ☐	
Commitment to project resource allocations	☐ ☐ ☐ ☐ ☐ ☐	
Timeliness of decisions and responses	☐ ☐ ☐ ☐ ☐ ☐	
Timeliness of guidance and feedback	☐ ☐ ☐ ☐ ☐ ☐	
Timeliness of project funding	☐ ☐ ☐ ☐ ☐ ☐	

MANAGEMENT EVALUATION—KEY AND NOTABLE INDIVIDUALS		
CUSTOMER CONTACT	POSITION/TITLE/ROLE	COMMENTS—PROJECT INFLUENCE

MANAGEMENT EVALUATION—GENERAL COMMENTS AND DISCUSSION
GENERAL CUSTOMER RATING COMMENTS RELATIVE TO BUSINESS PERFORMANCE

ACTION/ACTIVITY/REVIEW – RESPONSIBILITY	START	FINISH	ACTIVITY STATUS

ATTACHMENTS	PREPARER	DATE	FILE OR DOCUMENT LOCATION

4.6.3 MANAGEMENT POSTING—Management Satisfaction Survey

PROCESS OVERVIEW
REPLICATE FOR EACH SURVEY TO BE DISTRIBUTED AND COMPLETED—This management satisfaction survey is to be completed by senior managers in the PMO and business units at the end of the project (or other designated interim evaluation period). The overview section can be filled in prior to distribution.

TOOL PREPARATION	
PREPARED BY	DATE
CHECK IF REPLICATED (SPECIFY FILE LOCATION) ☐	

PROJECT	CUSTOMER

▷ MANAGEMENT SATISFACTION SURVEY—OVERVIEW		
PLEASE RETURN SURVEY TO	PROJECT MANAGER	PROJECT START DATE
RETURN SURVEY BY (DATE)	NATURE OF PRODUCTS AND SERVICES DELIVERED	PROJECT END DATE

MANAGEMENT SATISFACTION SURVEY—EVALUATION	
EVALUATION AREAS	EVALUATION AREA COMMENTS
1—What is your evaluation of the achievement of engagement objectives? (SATISFACTION WITH ENGAGEMENT RESULTS) 1 2 3 4 5 6 7 8 9 10 Poor---------------------------Satisfactory--------------------Excellent	
2—What is your evaluation of the project team's technical performance? (SATISFACTION WITH PROJECT TEAM CAPABILITY) 1 2 3 4 5 6 7 8 9 10 Poor---------------------------Satisfactory--------------------Excellent	
3—What is your evaluation of the project manager's performance? (SATISFACTION WITH PROJECT MANAGER CAPABILITY) 1 2 3 4 5 6 7 8 9 10 Poor---------------------------Satisfactory--------------------Excellent	
4—What is your evaluation of the technical approach used for product and service delivery? (SATISFACTION WITH THE DELIVERY PROCESS) 1 2 3 4 5 6 7 8 9 10 Poor---------------------------Satisfactory--------------------Excellent	
5—What is your evaluation of the achievement of business objectives? (SATISFACTION WITH BUSINESS RESULTS) 1 2 3 4 5 6 7 8 9 10 Poor---------------------------Satisfactory--------------------Excellent	

MANAGEMENT SATISFACTION SURVEY—REVIEWERS			
PROJECT MANAGER—NAME/TITLE	SIGNATURE	DATE	COMMENTS
PMO/MANAGEMENT—NAME/TITLE	SIGNATURE	DATE	COMMENTS
EXECUTIVE-SPONSOR—NAME/TITLE	SIGNATURE	DATE	COMMENTS

ACTION/ACTIVITY/REVIEW — RESPONSIBILITY	START	FINISH	ACTIVITY STATUS

ATTACHMENTS	PREPARER	DATE	FILE OR DOCUMENT LOCATION

4.6.4 MANAGEMENT POSTING—Management Closeout

PROCESS OVERVIEW
Review management closeout activities, and track their status toward completion. When completed, obtain the PMO or project executive's sign-off for termination of project management oversight activities. This concludes any involvement of the PMO, business unit managers, and control boards, and represents project closure.

TOOL PREPARATION	
PREPARED BY	DATE

PROJECT	CUSTOMER

▷ MANAGEMENT CLOSEOUT—OVERVIEW		
PROJECT CLOSEOUT REASON ☐ *ROUTINE* ☐ *NON-ROUTINE*	SCHEDULED END DATE	ACTUAL END DATE
SUMMARY OF BUSINESS CLOSEOUT ACTIONS		

MANAGEMENT CLOSEOUT—PROJECT MANAGEMENT CLOSEOUT CHECKLIST			
PROJECT MANAGEMENT CLOSEOUT CHECKLIST	STATUS	ASSIGNED TO	CLOSE DATE
☐ *LESSONS LEARNED PREPARATION* ☐ *PROJECT VENDOR DISPERSAL* ☐ *PROJECT FACILITY DISPOSITION* ☐ *PROJECT SUPPLIES AND EQUIPMENT DISPOSITION* ☐ *PROJECT MATERIALS ARCHIVAL* ☐ *PROJECT STAFF DISPERSAL* ☐ *CUSTOMER CLOSEOUT*			

MANAGEMENT CLOSEOUT—OVERSIGHT CLOSEOUT CHECKLIST			
OVERSIGHT CLOSEOUT CHECKLIST	STATUS	ASSIGNED TO	CLOSE DATE
☐ *VENDOR AND SUPPLIER INVOICES PAID-IN-FULL* ☐ *CONTRACTS AND SUBCONTRACTS CLOSED* ☐ *ACCOUNTING CHARGE CODE DEACTIVATED* ☐ *PROJECT CLOSURE COMMUNICATED* ☐ *CUSTOMER FINAL PAYMENT RECEIVED* ☐ *PROJECT MANAGER REASSIGNED*			

MANAGEMENT CLOSEOUT—ACKNOWLEDGMENT OF CLOSEOUT			
PROJECT MANAAGER	SIGNATURE	DATE	COMMENTS
PMO-MANAGEMENT	SIGNATURE	DATE	COMMENTS
PROJECT EXECUTIVE-SPONSOR	SIGNATURE	DATE	COMMENTS

ACTION/ACTIVITY/REVIEW — RESPONSIBILITY	START	FINISH	ACTIVITY STATUS

ATTACHMENTS	PREPARER	DATE	FILE OR DOCUMENT LOCATION

Appendix—Extended Tool Logs

As mentioned at the beginning of Section III, sometimes space available for data collection is limited. In particular, information logs are presented within some tools, and their position within the template limits the number of entries that can be made. The series of toolkit logs in this Appendix overcomes this limitation. These are "extended tools" that allow the user to maintain extensive log information beyond the capacity of the basic toolkit. The extended tools are contained in a separate electronic file that was included with the disk that accompanies this book.

It was mentioned that these tool logs can also be used independently to assist users in managing the project. In doing so, the users miss several important activities, including foregoing most project initiation activities (particularly, preparation of the project definition), much of the primary project planning effort, and many of the project closure activities.

Therefore, we discourage most users from following this practice. However, in certain cases of less complex and extremely simple projects, the "extended tool" logs can be used as the project manager's minimal toolkit.

TOOLKIT EXTENSION—Issue Management Log

TOOLKIT EXTENSION NOTES

TOOL PREPARATION	
PREPARED BY	DATE

PROJECT	CUSTOMER

ISSUES MANAGEMENT LOG ▷

ISSUE ID DATE	ISSUE DESCRIPTION	SOURCE	REFERRED TO	RESOLUTION	CLOSE DATE

ACTION/ACTIVITY/REVIEW – RESPONSIBILITY	START	FINISH	ACTIVITY STATUS

ATTACHMENTS	PREPARER	DATE	FILE OR DOCUMENT LOCATION

TOOLKIT EXTENSION—Risk Assessment Log

TOOLKIT EXTENSION NOTES

TOOL PREPARATION	
PREPARED BY	DATE

PROJECT	CUSTOMER

RISK ASSESSMENT LOG ▷				
BUSINESS RISK AREA	RISK EVENT AND DESCRIPTION	PROBABILITY (P)	IMPACT (I)	OVERALL (P X I)
		High Med Low	High Med Low	High Med Low
		High Med Low	High Med Low	High Med Low
		High Med Low	High Med Low	High Med Low
		High Med Low	High Med Low	High Med Low
		High Med Low	High Med Low	High Med Low
		High Med Low	High Med Low	High Med Low
		High Med Low	High Med Low	High Med Low
		High Med Low	High Med Low	High Med Low
		High Med Low	High Med Low	High Med Low
		High Med Low	High Med Low	High Med Low
		High Med Low	High Med Low	High Med Low
		High Med Low	High Med Low	High Med Low
		High Med Low	High Med Low	High Med Low
		High Med Low	High Med Low	High Med Low
		High Med Low	High Med Low	High Med Low
		High Med Low	High Med Low	High Med Low
		High Med Low	High Med Low	High Med Low
		High Med Low	High Med Low	High Med Low
		High Med Low	High Med Low	High Med Low
		High Med Low	High Med Low	High Med Low
		High Med Low	High Med Low	High Med Low
		High Med Low	High Med Low	High Med Low
		High Med Low	High Med Low	High Med Low
		High Med Low	High Med Low	High Med Low
		High Med Low	High Med Low	High Med Low
		High Med Low	High Med Low	High Med Low
		High Med Low	High Med Low	High Med Low
		High Med Low	High Med Low	High Med Low

ACTION/ACTIVITY/REVIEW — RESPONSIBILITY	START	FINISH	ACTIVITY STATUS

ATTACHMENTS	PREPARER	DATE	FILE OR DOCUMENT LOCATION

TOOLKIT EXTENSION—Risk Response Log

TOOLKIT EXTENSION NOTES

TOOL PREPARATION	
PREPARED BY	DATE

PROJECT	CUSTOMER

RISK RESPONSE LOG ▷

RISK EVENT	RISK RESPONSE ACTION	PRIORITY	ASSIGNED TO	ASSIGN DATE	CLOSE DATE

ACTION/ACTIVITY/REVIEW — RESPONSIBILITY	START	FINISH	ACTIVITY STATUS

ATTACHMENTS	PREPARER	DATE	FILE OR DOCUMENT LOCATION

TOOLKIT EXTENSION—Document Management Log

TOOLKIT EXTENSION NOTES

TOOL PREPARATION	
PREPARED BY	DATE

PROJECT	CUSTOMER

DOCUMENTATION MANAGEMENT LOG ▷

REQ ID	TYPE	REQUIREMENT	SOURCE	SPECIFICATION	WEB ELEMENT

ACTION/ACTIVITY/REVIEW — RESPONSIBILITY	START	FINISH	ACTIVITY STATUS

ATTACHMENTS	PREPARER	DATE	FILE OR DOCUMENT LOCATION

TOOLKIT EXTENSION—Deliverables Log

TOOLKIT EXTENSION NOTES

TOOL PREPARATION	
PREPARED BY	DATE

PROJECT	CUSTOMER

DELIVERABLES LOG ▷

DELIVERABLE	RESPONSIBILITY	DUE DATE	ACTUAL DATE	REQ ID	WBS ELEMENT	% COMPLETE	STATUS DATE

ACTION/ACTIVITY/REVIEW — RESPONSIBILITY	START	FINISH	ACTIVITY STATUS

ATTACHMENTS	PREPARER	DATE	FILE OR DOCUMENT LOCATION

TOOLKIT EXTENSION—Milestones Log

TOOLKIT EXTENSION NOTES

TOOL PREPARATION	
PREPARED BY	DATE

PROJECT	CUSTOMER

MILESTONES LOG ▷

MILESTONE	PURPOSE	DUE DATE	ACTUAL DATE	REQ ID	WBS ELEMENT	STATUS	STATUS DATE

ACTION/ACTIVITY/REVIEW – RESPONSIBILITY	START	FINISH	ACTIVITY STATUS

ATTACHMENTS	PREPARER	DATE	FILE OR DOCUMENT LOCATION

TOOLKIT EXTENSION—Change Request and Approval Log

TOOLKIT EXTENSION NOTES

TOOL PREPARATION	
PREPARED BY	DATE

PROJECT	CUSTOMER

CUSTOMER CHANGE CONTROL PLAN—CHANGE REQUEST AND APPROVAL LOG ▷

REQ #	CHANGE DESCRIPTION	SUBMITTAL DATE	FINAL REVIEW DATE	APPROVAL STATUS	IMPLEMENT DATE	VALUE ($)
					TOTAL VALUE OF ADJUSTED WORK	

ACTION/ACTIVITY/REVIEW – RESPONSIBILITY	START	FINISH	ACTIVITY STATUS

ATTACHMENTS	PREPARER	DATE	FILE OR DOCUMENT LOCATION

TOOLKIT EXTENSION—Quality Test and Acceptance Log

TOOLKIT EXTENSION NOTES

TOOL PREPARATION	
PREPARED BY	DATE

PROJECT	CUSTOMER

QUALITY TESTING AND ACCEPTANCE LOG ▷

QUALITY TESTING AND ACCEPTANCE PROCEDURES	TEST	SCHEDULED	ACCEPTANCE STATUS—RESULTS	TEST LEADER	TEST DATE

ACTION/ACTIVITY/REVIEW – RESPONSIBILITY	START	FINISH	ACTIVITY STATUS

ATTACHMENTS	PREPARER	DATE	FILE OR DOCUMENT LOCATION

TOOLKIT EXTENSION—Quality Technical Reviews Log

TOOLKIT EXTENSION NOTES

TOOL PREPARATION	
PREPARED BY	DATE

PROJECT	CUSTOMER

QUALITY TECHNICAL REVIEWS LOG ▷					
QUALITY TECHNICAL REVIEW PROCEDURES	REVIEW	SCHEDULED	REVIEW STATUS—RESULTS	REVIEW LEADER	REVIEW DATE

ACTION/ACTIVITY/REVIEW – RESPONSIBILITY	START	FINISH	ACTIVITY STATUS

ATTACHMENTS	PREPARER	DATE	FILE OR DOCUMENT LOCATION

TOOLKIT EXTENSION—Work Breakdown Structure (WBS) Summary

TOOLKIT EXTENSION NOTES

TOOL PREPARATION	
PREPARED BY	DATE

PROJECT	CUSTOMER

WORK BREAKDOWN STRUCTURE (WBS) SUMMARY ▷						
PROJECT PHASES	1	2	3	4	5	6
Projest Phase Name						
Phase Start Date						
WORK PLAN ESTIMATES	*ESTIMATES BELOW RESULT FROM DETAILED WORK PLANNING, AND WBS DEVELOPMENT, AND USE OF THE PROJECT ESTIMATES TOOL 1.2.2*					
ACTIVITY NAME						
Activity DURATION						
Activity RESOURCES						
Activity COSTS						
ACTIVITY NAME						
Activity DURATION						
Activity RESOURCES						
Activity COSTS						
ACTIVITY NAME						
Activity DURATION						
Activity RESOURCES						
Activity COSTS						
ACTIVITY NAME						
Activity DURATION						
Activity RESOURCES						
Activity COSTS						
ACTIVITY NAME						
Activity DURATION						
Activity RESOURCES						
Activity COSTS						
Phase DURATION						
Phase RESOURCES						
Phase COSTS						

ACTION/ACTIVITY/REVIEW — RESPONSIBILITY	START	FINISH	ACTIVITY STATUS

ATTACHMENTS	PREPARER	DATE	FILE OR DOCUMENT LOCATION

TOOLKIT EXTENSION—Risk Management Log

TOOLKIT EXTENSION NOTES

TOOL PREPARATION	
PREPARED BY	DATE

PROJECT	CUSTOMER

PROJECT RISK MANAGEMENT PLAN—RISK MANAGEMENT LOG ▷

RISK ID	RISK ID DATE	PRIORITY	TYPE	RISK EVENT	PROB	IMPACT	OVERALL	STATUS	CLOSE DATE

ACTION/ACTIVITY/REVIEW — RESPONSIBILITY	START	FINISH	ACTIVITY STATUS

ATTACHMENTS	PREPARER	DATE	FILE OR DOCUMENT LOCATION

TOOLKIT EXTENSION—Report and Document Distribution Matrix

TOOLKIT EXTENSION NOTES

TOOL PREPARATION	
PREPARED BY	DATE

PROJECT	CUSTOMER

REPORT AND DOCUMENT DISTRIBUTION MATRIX ▷

STAKEHOLDERS	EXECUTIVE-SPONSOR		PMO		PROJECT TEAM		CUSTOMER		CONTROL BOARD		OTHER	
Key Contact(s)												
DISTRIBUTION	☒	METHOD	☒	METHOD	☒	METHOD	☒	METHOD	☒	METHOD	☒	METHOD
Status Reports	☐		☐		☐		☐		☐		☐	
Management Reports	☐		☐		☐		☐		☐		☐	
Customer Reports	☐		☐		☐		☐		☐		☐	
Primary Plans	☐		☐		☐		☐		☐		☐	
Supporting Plans	☐		☐		☐		☐		☐		☐	
	☐		☐		☐		☐		☐		☐	
	☐		☐		☐		☐		☐		☐	
	☐		☐		☐		☐		☐		☐	
	☐		☐		☐		☐		☐		☐	
	☐		☐		☐		☐		☐		☐	
	☐		☐		☐		☐		☐		☐	
	☐		☐		☐		☐		☐		☐	
	☐		☐		☐		☐		☐		☐	
	☐		☐		☐		☐		☐		☐	
	☐		☐		☐		☐		☐		☐	
	☐		☐		☐		☐		☐		☐	
	☐		☐		☐		☐		☐		☐	
	☐		☐		☐		☐		☐		☐	
	☐		☐		☐		☐		☐		☐	
	☐		☐		☐		☐		☐		☐	
	☐		☐		☐		☐		☐		☐	
	☐		☐		☐		☐		☐		☐	
	☐		☐		☐		☐		☐		☐	
	☐		☐		☐		☐		☐		☐	
	☐		☐		☐		☐		☐		☐	
	☐		☐		☐		☐		☐		☐	
	☐		☐		☐		☐		☐		☐	
	☐		☐		☐		☐		☐		☐	
	☐		☐		☐		☐		☐		☐	
	☐		☐		☐		☐		☐		☐	
	☐		☐		☐		☐		☐		☐	

ACTION/ACTIVITY/REVIEW — RESPONSIBILITY	START	FINISH	ACTIVITY STATUS

ATTACHMENTS	PREPARER	DATE	FILE OR DOCUMENT LOCATION

TOOLKIT EXTENSION—Training and Development Activity Log

TOOLKIT EXTENSION NOTES

TOOL PREPARATION	
PREPARED BY	DATE

PROJECT	CUSTOMER

TRAINING AND DEVELOPMENT ACTIVITY LOG ▷

ACTIVITY PARTICIPANT (OR GROUP)	ACTIVITY	SCHEDULED	STATUS–RESULTS	SOURCE	FINISH DATE

ACTION/ACTIVITY/REVIEW — RESPONSIBILITY	START	FINISH	ACTIVITY STATUS

ATTACHMENTS	PREPARER	DATE	FILE OR DOCUMENT LOCATION

TOOLKIT EXTENSION—Task Assignment Activity Tracking Log

TOOLKIT EXTENSION NOTES

TOOL PREPARATION	
PREPARED BY	DATE

PROJECT	CUSTOMER

STAFF ASSIGNMENT—INDIVIDUAL TASK ASSIGNMENT & ACTIVITY TRACKING LOG ▷

NAMES/STAFF ID	TASK/WBS ITEM	ASSSIGN DATE	DUE DATE	START DATE	FINISH DATE	STATUS/COMPLETE (%)	PERFORMANCE RATING

ACTION/ACTIVITY/REVIEW – RESPONSIBILITY	START	FINISH	ACTIVITY STATUS

ATTACHMENTS	PREPARER	DATE	FILE OR DOCUMENT LOCATION

TOOLKIT EXTENSION—Contract Modification Log

TOOLKIT EXTENSION NOTES

TOOL PREPARATION	
PREPARED BY	DATE

PROJECT	CUSTOMER

CONTRACT	ISSUED BY

CONTRACT MODIFICATION LOG ▷

MODIFICATION	DATE	REASON FOR MODIFICATION	ACCEPTANCE BY	VALUE ($)
000 (ORIGINAL)				

ACTION/ACTIVITY/REVIEW – RESPONSIBILITY	START	FINISH	ACTIVITY STATUS

ATTACHMENTS	PREPARER	DATE	FILE OR DOCUMENT LOCATION

TOOLKIT EXTENSION—Contract and Negotiation Activity Log

TOOLKIT EXTENSION NOTES

TOOL PREPARATION	
PREPARED BY	DATE

PROJECT	CUSTOMER

CONTRACT	ISSUED BY

CONTRACT AND NEGOTIATION ACTIVITY LOG ▷

ACTIVITY/ACTION/EVENT	ISSUE/FOCUS (IF ANY)	SCHEDULED	STATUS–RESULTS	ISSUE LEAD	FINISH DATE

ACTION/ACTIVITY/REVIEW – RESPONSIBILITY	START	FINISH	ACTIVITY STATUS

ATTACHMENTS	PREPARER	DATE	FILE OR DOCUMENT LOCATION

TOOLKIT EXTENSION—Management Oversight Activity Log

TOOLKIT EXTENSION NOTES

TOOL PREPARATION	
PREPARED BY	DATE

PROJECT	CUSTOMER

MANAGEMENT OVERSIGHT ACTIVITY LOG ▷

EXECUTIVE–CONTROL BOARD–PMO PARTICIPANT	OVERSIGHT ACTIIVITY	SCHEDULED	STATUS–RESULTS	PROJECT LEAD	FINISH DATE

ACTION/ACTIVITY/REVIEW — RESPONSIBILITY	START	FINISH	ACTIVITY STATUS

ATTACHMENTS	PREPARER	DATE	FILE OR DOCUMENT LOCATION

TOOLKIT EXTENSION—Audit and Review Log

TOOLKIT EXTENSION NOTES

TOOL PREPARATION	
PREPARED BY	DATE

PROJECT	CUSTOMER

AUDIT AND REVIEW LOG ▷

AUDIT OR REVIEW ACTIVITY	REQUESTOR	SCHEDULED	STATUS–RESULTS	AUDIT LEADER	FINISH DATE

ACTION/ACTIVITY/REVIEW – RESPONSIBILITY	START	FINISH	ACTIVITY STATUS

ATTACHMENTS	PREPARER	DATE	FILE OR DOCUMENT LOCATION

TOOLKIT EXTENSION—Facility Management Activity Log

TOOLKIT EXTENSION NOTES

TOOL PREPARATION	
PREPARED BY	DATE

PROJECT	CUSTOMER

FACILITY MANAGEMENT ACTIVITY LOG ▷

FACILITY MANAGEMENT ACTIVITY	FACILITY	SCHEDULED	STATUS–RESULTS	PROJECT LEAD	FINISH DATE

ACTION/ACTIVITY/REVIEW – RESPONSIBILITY	START	FINISH	ACTIVITY STATUS

ATTACHMENTS	PREPARER	DATE	FILE OR DOCUMENT LOCATION

TOOLKIT EXTENSION—Supply and Equipment Log

TOOLKIT EXTENSION NOTES

TOOL PREPARATION	
PREPARED BY	DATE

PROJECT	CUSTOMER

SUPPLY AND EQUIPMENT LOG ▷

SUPPLY/EQUIPMENT ITEM	REQUESTED BY	REQUEST DATE	ACQUIRE DATE	ASSISGNED TO	SOURCE/VENDOR	COMMENTS

ACTION/ACTIVITY/REVIEW — RESPONSIBILITY	START	FINISH	ACTIVITY STATUS

ATTACHMENTS	PREPARER	DATE	FILE OR DOCUMENT LOCATION

TOOLKIT EXTENSION—Meeting Participants List

TOOLKIT EXTENSION NOTES

TOOL PREPARATION	
PREPARED BY	DATE

PROJECT	CUSTOMER

MEETING PARTICIPANTS LIST ▷

NAME	OFFICE LOCATION	REQUIRED	ATTENDANCE	ATTENDANCE NOTES

ACTION/ACTIVITY/REVIEW – RESPONSIBILITY	START	FINISH	ACTIVITY STATUS

ATTACHMENTS	PREPARER	DATE	FILE OR DOCUMENT LOCATION

TOOLKIT EXTENSION—Meeting Agenda

PROCESS OVERVIEW

TOOL PREPARATION	
PREPARED BY	DATE

PROJECT	CUSTOMER

MEETING AGENDA ▷

DISCUSSION ITEM	SCHEDULE/PRIORITY	DISCUSSION LEADER	FOLLOW-ON ACTIONS	DUE DATE

ACTION/ACTIVITY/REVIEW — RESPONSIBILITY	START	FINISH	ACTIVITY STATUS

ATTACHMENTS	PREPARER	DATE	FILE OR DOCUMENT LOCATION

TOOLKIT EXTENSION—Contact and Correspondence Management Log

TOOLKIT EXTENSION NOTES

TOOL PREPARATION	
PREPARED BY	DATE

PROJECT	CUSTOMER

CONTACT AND CORRESPONDENCE MANAGEMENT LOG ▷

CONTACT-CORRESPONDENCE ITEM	DATE	FROM/TO	PURPOSE/ACTION	DISPOSISTION

ACTION/ACTIVITY/REVIEW – RESPONSIBILITY	START	FINISH	ACTIVITY STATUS

ATTACHMENTS	PREPARER	DATE	FILE OR DOCUMENT LOCATION

TOOLKIT EXTENSION—Plan Management Log

PROCESS OVERVIEW

TOOL PREPARATION	
PREPARED BY	DATE

PROJECT	CUSTOMER

PLAN MANAGEMENT LOG ▷

PLAN DATE	PLANNING DOCUMENT	CODE	PREPARED BY	DIST/GROUP ID	PLAN MANAGEMENT ACTION	ACTION DATE

ACTION/ACTIVITY/REVIEW – RESPONSIBILITY	START	FINISH	ACTIVITY STATUS

ATTACHMENTS	PREPARER	DATE	FILE OR DOCUMENT LOCATION

TOOLKIT EXTENSION—Expense Summary Log

PROCESS OVERVIEW

TOOL PREPARATION	
PREPARED BY	DATE

PROJECT	CUSTOMER

EXPENSE SUMMARY LOG ▷

EXPENSE ITEM	SOURCE	PURPOSE	CHARGE CODE	EXPENSE DATE	EXPENSE AMOUNT	COMMENTS
				TOTAL THIS REPORTING PERIOD		

ACTION/ACTIVITY/REVIEW — RESPONSIBILITY	START	FINISH	ACTIVITY STATUS

ATTACHMENTS	PREPARER	DATE	FILE OR DOCUMENT LOCATION

TOOLKIT EXTENSION—Assignment Progress Log

PROCESS OVERVIEW

TOOL PREPARATION	
PREPARED BY	DATE

PROJECT	CUSTOMER

ASSIGNMENT PROGRESS LOG ▷

TASK/WBS ELEMENT	NAME/STAFF ID	ASSIGN DATE	DUE DATE	START DATE	FINISH DATE	STATUS/COMPLETE (%)	COMMENTS

ACTION/ACTIVITY/REVIEW — RESPONSIBILITY	START	FINISH	ACTIVITY STATUS

ATTACHMENTS	PREPARER	DATE	FILE OR DOCUMENT LOCATION

TOOLKIT EXTENSION—Contract Administration Activity Log

PROCESS OVERVIEW

TOOL PREPARATION	
PREPARED BY	DATE

PROJECT	CUSTOMER

CONTRACT ADMINISTRATION ACTIVITY LOG ▷

ACTIVITY/ACTION/EVENT	START	FINISH	PARTICIPANT(S)	OUTCOME/COMMENTS

ACTION/ACTIVITY/REVIEW – RESPONSIBILITY	START	FINISH	ACTIVITY STATUS

ATTACHMENTS	PREPARER	DATE	FILE OR DOCUMENT LOCATION

TOOLKIT EXTENSION—Lessons Learned Findings Log

PROCESS OVERVIEW

TOOL PREPARATION	
PREPARED BY	DATE

PROJECT	CUSTOMER

LESSONS LEARNED FINDINGS LOG ▷		
LESSON—EVENT OR CONDITION	LESSON—IMPACT ON PROJECT OR BUSINESS	LESSON—RECOMMENDED IMPROVEMENT OR CHANGE

ACTION/ACTIVITY/REVIEW — RESPONSIBILITY	START	FINISH	ACTIVITY STATUS

ATTACHMENTS	PREPARER	DATE	FILE OR DOCUMENT LOCATION

TOOLKIT EXTENSION—Invoice Tracking Log

PROCESS OVERVIEW

TOOL PREPARATION	
PREPARED BY	DATE

PROJECT	CUSTOMER

VENDOR INVOICE TRACKING LOG—INCOMING ▷

VENDOR ID	VENDOR ORGANIZATION	INVOICE DATE	INVOICE DESCRIPTION	INVOICE AMOUNT	PAID AMOUNT	PAID DATE
			VENDOR INVOICE TOTALS TO DATE			

CUSTOMER INVOICE TRACKING LOG—OUTGOING ▷

VENDOR ID	SUBMITTAL ORGANIZATION	INVOICE DATE	INVOICE DESCRIPTION	INVOICE AMOUNT	PAID AMOUNT	PAID DATE
			CUSTOMER INVOICE TOTALS TO DATE			

ACTION/ACTIVITY/REVIEW — RESPONSIBILITY	START	FINISH	ACTIVITY STATUS

ATTACHMENTS	PREPARER	DATE	FILE OR DOCUMENT LOCATION

TOOLKIT EXTENSION—General Continuation Sheet 1

PROCESS OVERVIEW

TOOL PREPARATION	
PREPARED BY	DATE

PROJECT	CUSTOMER

TOOLKIT GENERAL EXTENSTION SHEET		
NAME	PURPOSE	TOOL REFERENCE

CONTENT

ACTION/ACTIVITY/REVIEW – RESPONSIBILITY	START	FINISH	ACTIVITY STATUS

ATTACHMENTS	PREPARER	DATE	FILE OR DOCUMENT LOCATION

TOOLKIT EXTENSION—General Continuation Sheet 2

PROCESS OVERVIEW

TOOL PREPARATION	
PREPARED BY	DATE

PROJECT	CUSTOMER

TOOLKIT GENERAL EXTENSTION SHEET		
NAME	PURPOSE	TOOL REFERENCE

CONTENT

ACTION/ACTIVITY/REVIEW – RESPONSIBILITY	START	FINISH	ACTIVITY STATUS

ATTACHMENTS	PREPARER	DATE	FILE OR DOCUMENT LOCATION

Index

C

D

S

T

U

V

W